RESEARCH IN ASIAN ECONOMIC STUDIES

Volume 6 • 1995

ASIA-PACIFIC ECONOMIC COMMUNITY?

CONSULTING EDITORS

RESEARCH IN ASIAN ECONOMIC STUDIES

ASIA-PACIFIC ECONOMIC COMMUNITY?

Editors: M. DUTTA
Rutgers University

DAVID JAY GREEN
Asian Development Bank

SUTHIPHAND CHIRATHIVAT
Chulalongkorn University

PAITOON WIBOONCHUTIKULA
Chulalongkorn University

VOLUME 6 • 1995

Emerald

United Kingdom – North America – Japan –
India – Malaysia – China

Emerald Group Publishing Limited
Howard House, Wagon Lane, Bingley BD16 1WA, UK

First edition 1995

Published by Emerald Group Publishing Limited in 2008

First published by Elsevier in 1995

Reprints and permission service
Contact: books@emeraldinsight.com

British Library Cataloguing in Publication Data
A catalogue record for this book is available from the British Library

Printed and bound in Great Britain by
CPI Antony Rowe, Chippenham and Eastbourne

ISBN: 978-1-5593-8918-1

CONTENTS

LIST OF CONTRIBUTORS

Meena Acharya	Institute for Integrated Development Studies Kathmandu, Nepal
K.K. Bhargava	Indian Council for Research on International Economic Relations New Delhi, India
Suthiphand Chirathivat	Faculty of Economics Chulalongkorn University Bangkok, Thailand
Dean DeRosa	International Food Policy Research Institute Washington, DC
M. Dutta	Economics Faculty Rutgers University New Brunswick, NJ
David Jay Green	Asian Development Bank Manila, Philippines
Richard Hooley	University of Pittsburgh Pittsburgh, PA
Michiko Ikeda	School of Economics & Political Science Tokai University Kanagawa, Japan
ADV de S. Indraratna	University Grants Commission University of Colombo Colombo, Sri Lanka

Masumi Kishi
Faculty of Commerce
Chuo University
Tokyo, Japan

Chee Peng Lim
Development and Social
Commission for Asia and the
Pacific
Bangkok, Thailand

Xiaoxuan Liu
Institute of Economics
Chinese Academy of Social Sciences
Beijing, China

Gilberto M. Llanto
Philippine Institute for
Development
Studies, Manila Philippines

Detlef Lorenz
Free University of Berlin
Berlin, Germany

Linda Low
Department of Business Policy
National University of Singapore
Singapore

Anwar Naustion
Department of Economics
University of Indonesia
Jakarta, Indonesia

Paitoon Wiboonchutikula
Faculty of Economics
Chulalongkorn University
Bangkok, Thailand

S.A.L. Reza
Bangladesh Institute of
Development Studies
Dhaka, Bangladesh

George Rosen
Department of Economics
University of Illinois, Chicago

Yoko Sazanami
Department of Economics
Kieo University
Tokyo, Japan

Edita Tan
School of Economics
University of the Philippines
Manila, Philippines

Hajjah Rosni Haji Tungkat
Unit Pengarah
Government of Brunei
Brunei Darussalam

Yao Tinggang
Institute of World Economics
Shanghai Academy of Social Sciences
Shanghai, China

PREFACE

In 1989, Asia-Pacific Economic Cooperation (APEC) became institutionalized with a membership of thirteen sovereign nations—the United States, Canada, Japan, South Korea, Australia, New Zealand, Pacific Islands, Brunei Darusssalam, Indonesia, Malaysia, Philippines, Singapore and Thailand. In 1992, Taiwan, Hong Kong and the Mainland China became APEC members. Mexico joined the group in 1993, and Chile became the eighteenth member of APEC in 1994.

Economic regionalization in the Asia-Pacific became all too manifest. It happened soon after 1985 when the European Economic Community (EEC), founded January 1, 1958, adopted the Single European Act. It was a few years sooner than 1992, when the EEC voted for the Maastricht Treaty and became the European Union (EU) with a well-specified agenda for a "deep integration". Will APEC evolve into an Asia-Pacific Economic Community? then to an Economic Union? Dynamics of events must remain unpredictable. The question, however, warrants an articulate dialogue.

In Part I, seven contributions discuss the subject from different perspectives. In the opening chapter, I have asked the question if economic regionalization of sovereign member-economies can ensure optimization of economic gains for micro-units—households and business firms—in all member countries in the absence of an intra-regional coordination of macroeconomic policies. Detlef Lorenz presents his thesis on "differences and consequences" of experiments in economic regionalization in Western Europe and East Asia.

George Rosen adds to the debate by an evaluation of the comparative roles of China and India in the context of Asia-Pacific regionalization. David Jay Green reports his instructive findings on "convergence and cohesion" within the four economies in Southeast Asia, a subregional group within APEC. Dean A. DeRosa presents a treatise on the ASEAN Free Trade Area (AFTA) and intra-regional trade in developing Asia. Chee Peng Lim examines "trends, challenges and prospects" in economic regionalism in the Asia-Pacific. Yao Tinggang reviews the emerging profile of economic integration of Mainland China, Taiwan and Macao.

In Part II, microeconomic issues in its many and varied facets are examined. Gilberto M. Llanto examines the case of "micro impacts" from the perspective of the Philippines. Masumi Kishi presents "a case study of capital flow between Japan and Thailand." Linda Low studies "investment-led regionalism and trade liberalization" from the ASEAN perspective. Yoko Sazanami presents her study with a focus on "Japanese Service enterprises" in the context of Asian interdependence. Michiko Ikeda examines "technology and trade friction" with "cases of Japanese industries". Richard Hooley outlines "sources, rate and contribution to growth" of savings in Southeast Asia. Xiaoxuan Liu studies the "lesson for China" from the Korean experience of foreign trade liberalization. Hajjah Rosni Haji Tungkat presents an economic profile of Brunei Darassalam. Suthiphand Chirathivat presents a study on "Thailand's trade in services" in the Asia-Pacific region. Paitoon Wiboonchutikula examines intra-regional "trade in manufactured goods" from the perspective of Thailand.

In Part III, issues of economic regionalization in the Asia-Pacific are examined from the perspective of South Asia. ADV de S. Indraratna examines "the prospect of a trading block in South Asia." Sardel A. L. Reza discusses "the issues in trade cooperation in South Asia" from the perspective of Bangladesh. Meena Acharya presents a discourse on "the case of Nepal". K. K. Bhargava examines "The SAARC Experience" in the context of economic regionalism.

This volume draws upon the contributions of the authors and we owe them a vote of thanks and sincerest appreciation.

Our very special thanks are due to:

- President Charas Suwanwela, Chulalongkorn University, Bangkok, Thailand;
- Dean Thienchay Kiranandana, Faculty of Economics, Chulalongkorn University;
- Sumalee Pitayanon, Paisal Lekuthai, Salinee Vorabuntoon, Sriwongse Sumitra, Kitti Limsakul, Teerna Bhongmakapat, Kwanjai Arunsmit, Jittapatr Kruavan, Somchai Ratanakomut, Attacharn Pattanajidvilai,

Charuma Ashakul, Chaiwoot Chaiphan, Waranya Patarasook, - Faculty of Economics, Chulalongkorn University;

- Narongchai Akrasanee, Chairman and CEO, General Finance and Security Company, Bangkok; and Ammar Siamwala, President, Thailand Development Research Institute, Bangkok;
- H. W. Arndt, The Australian National University, Canberra, Australia; Edna E. Ehrlich, Ehrlich International Consulting, New York; Alan Heston, University of Pennsylvania, Philadelphia, PA; T. B. Lin, The Chinese University of Hong Kong, Hong Kong; Anwar Nasution, The University of Indonesia, Jakarta, Indonesia; Peter A. Petri, Brandeis University, Waltham, MA; Mark Sidel, The Ford Foundation, Bangkok; Somsak Tambunlertchai, The Asian Pacific Development Center, Kuala Lumpur, Malaysia; Ton Si Kinh, Institute for Economic Research, Ho Chi Minh City, Vietnam;
  Chyau Tuan, The Chinese University of Hong Kong, Hong Kong;
- Rutgers—The State University of New Jersey, New Brunswick, NJ, (USA); and Chulalongkorn University, Bangkok, Thailand;
- The Ford Foundation, New York, NY;
- Toyotane Sohma, Director, Off-Campus Activities, Japan;
- Manich Seosakul, Chulalongkorn University, Bangkok;
- Tasadej Arunsmit, Chairman and CEO, Richmonde (Thailand) Ltd.;
- International Economics Forum, Chulalongkorn University;
- Academic Development Endowment Fund, Chulalongkorn University.

Tammy Todaro of JAI PRESS INC., has offered her generous help and cooperation which alone made the publication of this volume successful and she has earned our sincerest thanks.

M. Dutta

PART I.

ASIA-PACIFIC ECONOMIC REGIONALIZATION

ECONOMIC REGIONALIZATION IN THE ASIA-PACIFIC: MACROECONOMIC CORE AND MICROECONOMIC OPTIMIZATION

M. Dutta

Given technology and the production function and taste and consumer preference-map, the Theory of Comparative Advantage taught us how trade in wine and clothes across the borders of two sovereign nation-states would optimize gains for both England and Portugal. At successive stages, Heckscher-Ohlin Theory of Factor Endowment, Kravis proposition of Factor Availability, Ruttan's Product Cycle theorem enriched our education in international economics.

The soveriegn nation-states remained the micro units. The monetary-fiscal policies adopted by each such state became the macroeconomic core for the optimization of economic welfare/profit, however defined, of microeconomic units—households and business organizations—belonging to each member sovereign nation-state engaged in international economic transactions. Income- and price elasticities of traded goods were extensively, often laboriously,

Research in Asian Economic Studies, Volume 6, pages 3-30.

ISBN: 1-55938-918-4

estimated and ideally each sovereign micro nation-state was free to do its share of competitive buying and selling in the free and competitive world market.

The idealized textbook paradigm often met with real world challenges, allowing international economic relations—trade/investment of any sovereign nation-state—to become the "hand-maiden" of its government's foreign policy. Off-the-market negotiations and security and strategic considerations became a part of the game the governments played.

In addition, the historical progression of the Industrial Revolution, broadening the production frontiers of economies, posed a serious challenge to the structural stability of the sovereign nation-state based economic units. Scholars tell us that the world is at the threshold of the Fourth Industrial Revolution as robotics, bio-techs and superconductivity come to redefine the production maps of individual economies.

As and when international economics was limited to trade in final products—goods and services—the theory was relatively simple. Soon, free flow of capital—financial as well as physical—became a part of the tradables. In recent decades, free flow of human capital has become routine in international economics. Perhaps, it began with the importation of "cheap", indentured or slave labor. It was then followed by liberalization of immigration laws as demand for skilled/professional manpower became a point of consideration.

I have argued elsewhere that yet another facet of human capital flow across the borders of sovereign nation-state based economies warrant further attention (Dutta 1990; Dutta & Tantum 1988). International transmission of research results and frontier knowledge in science and technology have become a part of academic freedom. Movement is fast, if not instantaneous by global computer linkages. Availability of scientists and engineers is no longer limited to specific economies. Transmitted scientific/technological findings, which are essentially in the public domain, are tested, replicated, refined and further developed for "*adaptation with innovation*" to any particular economic structure with comparative ease. They can then be put into the production process, with no act of "copying" and no violation of copyright in its strict traditional sense. This international free flow of disembodied human capital provides the base for the new paradigm of "adaptive" innovation.

The world market has progressed to a level of unification wherein the concept of stability of traditional sovereign nation-state based micro economic units seem to have become outdated. A move toward one integrated world market is still far out in the agenda of human civilization, but a new regional supranational macroeconomic core is in order. It is difficult to accept the changes and no one has said it better than Monnet (1978, p. 109),

> "....people only accept change when they are faced with necessity, and only recognize necessity when a crisis is upon them."

I. HISTORICAL PERSPECTIVE OF ECONOMIC REGIONALIZATION

The concept of economic regionalism has been known earlier in one or another form. In its pre-World War II manifestation, it centered on currency regions—a given region anchored to a given currency—the British Sterling, the French Franc, the Dutch Guilder, the U.S. Dollar, the Japanese Yen. In this "colonial" mold of economic regionalization, monetary-fiscal policies of the "HOME" governments provided a macroeconomic core for microeconomic welfare optimization of individual trading economies. Indeed, the common macroeconomic core was the economic factor contributing to the growth of intra-regional trade in a specific currency region. The system liquidated itself as its "tilt" in favor of optimizing the welfare function of the specific "Home" economy at the expense of the satellite nation-state based micro units within the imperial currency region came to be challenged.

In the post-World War II era came a new economic order, and its macroeconomic core was based on the U.S. Dollar—for US$ 35 an ounce of pure gold. The progress to a uni-polar macroeconomic core soon was challenged by the hostilities of the Cold War. The response was the formation of "strategic" regionalization among groups of allied nation-states in specific regions of the world.

Kindleberger (1986) has forcefully argued that the delivery of the international public goods in the form of free world monetary-fiscal stability plus the military security component became too costly for the United States. The U.S. dollar-based international monetary system eventually broke down on August 15, 1971. There was a de-linking of the U.S. dollar from its per gold value and a free float of world's currencies became the order of the day. Some economists hailed it as the dawn of a new era of a return to one hundred percent pure gold standard. That was not what happened and in September 1985, the free market was summarily replaced by a managed exchange rate regime, first by the G-5 (Group of Five), then by the G-7. Some economists believe the system in effect reduced itself to the G-3 regime anchored to U.S. dollar, Japanese yen and German mark.

The free market was observed to have failed. The monetary-fiscal policies of the major trading countries failed to be coordinated. The resulting chaos in the global monetary-fiscal stability showed the absence of an institutional mechanism. The point was straightforwardly made that in the absence of a macroeconomic core, closely and *intelligently* coordinating monetary-fiscal policies of the major trading/investing economies, the system could not optimize economic gains (welfare) of micro units of the trading sovereign nation-state based economies. Blame for the failure to adopt generally cohesive and coordinated monetary-fiscal policies could, of course, be widely shared.

The basic argument is that pure market forces in the absence of idealized perfect competition have been found to provide an ineffective and unrealistic paradigm. Efforts to make perfectly competitive market work by the politically powerful collaborative efforts of the G-7, or for that matter of any other international economic grouping of 150-plus sovereign nation-state members, such as the General Agreement of Trade and Tariff (GATT), have produced only limited results. An alternative paradigm is the one of economic regionalism—a supra-national macroeconomic core of sovereign nation states in a naturally well-defined geographical region. Still, others continue to argue that in *the long run* the market will prevail.

A. Customs Union/Free Trade Area

Earlier efforts to resolve the conflict by way of bypassing the macroeconomic core issues resulted in the argument for a Customs Union (Viner 1950). The debate was joined as to whether a customs union's contribution is to trade-creation or trade-diversion (Park & Yoo 1989). Indeed, a modification of Viner's thesis on customs union has recently found its articulate expression in the Free Trade Areas (FTA) (Schott 1989). The United States has signed two FTA Treaties, one with Canada (1988, effective 1989) and another with Israel (1985).

The adoption of the North American Free Trade Area (NAFTA) of Canada-United States-Mexico in 1994 following its "fast" track initialization in October 1992 adds yet another chapter. Indeed, many Latin American sovereign states, no longer concerned for high-handed economic domination by the United States, appear to welcome an FTA of the Americas (FTAA).

However, to the extent, sovereign nation-state based member economies in an FTA fail to straightforwardly address a common monetary-fiscal economic policy agenda, they remain less than economic regionalization.

II. EUROPEAN COMMUNITY-ECONOMIC REGIONALIZATION IN WESTERN EUROPE

The European Community (EC) of twelve members, fifteen, in 1995 in Western Europe offers a unique paradigm of economic regionalization. EC is much more than a traditional customs union and its scope is far beyond a free trade area. It offers a paradigm for a supra-national macroeconomic core for the optimization of economic gains (welfare) of microeconomic units—households as well as business firms—belonging to all sovereign nation-state based member economies (Dutta 1992 b).

The Treaty of Rome was signed in 1957, and in 1958 the grouping of five Western European economies became functional. Later, seven other European economies joined the Community's membership. The Single European Act of 1985 and the Maastricht Treaty of 1992 are the next two important dates in the progressive development of European regionalization. Another important date for EC is 1993, when, following a tortuous process of adoption of the Maastricht Treaty by all 12 member-states, the European Monetary Institute (EMI) in Frankfurt was established—the first step towards the European Central Bank with one common currency.

The *three* necessary conditions for EC's monetary union are: (i) total and irreversible convertibility of member currencies; (ii) complete liberalization of capital transaction and full integration of banking and financial markets; and (iii) elimination of margins of fluctuations and locking of exchange rate parities (European Commission 1989, 1990).

The goal for a common European System of Central Banks (ESCB) has been clearly stated. The European Monetary System was set up in 1979 with ECU (the European Currency Unit) as the unit of accounting, though *not* as the medium of exchange. Hesse (1992) points out that in the first eight years of the EMS, only 12 realignments were necessary, while between January 1987 and September 1992, over a period of about six years, no major ENS realignment took place. The European Monetary System has been sufficiently robust to arrange accommodations for the exchange rate crisis for specific member currencies in 1992.

The EC has certainly experienced many difficulties. However, the paradigm of a supra-national macroeconomic core has prevailed and it continues to move progressively towards its stated goal: creation of a zone of monetary-fiscal stability with provisions for multilateral surveillance of the member nations within the EC.

All twelve sovereign nation-state based members of EC have approved of the Maastricht Treaty. Interestingly enough, Denmark, which has as high as 90 percent score on its overall performance on the community's integration laws (see Table 1), at first voted it down in a referendum on the Treaty in 1992 only to reverse itself in a subsequent referendum in 1993.

Commenting on the difficulties of establishing one European Central Bank, as envisaged in the EC agenda and also in the Maastricht Treaty, one U.S. central banker has observed that the debate over the process of establishment of the U.S. Federal Reserve System bringing together its twelve regional federal reserve banks was no less difficult (Forrestal 1992).

In addition, the *four* elements of the EC's macroeconomic core are: (i) the single market with free mobility of goods, services, capital and labor; (ii) free and perfectly competitive common market of member-economies; (iii) common intra-regional policies aimed at structural and regional development; and (iv) coordination of intra-regional budgetary policies.

The Treaty of Maastricht in 1992 sets *four* major conditions to ensure an intra-regional macroeconomic core with well-defined bands for variations in:

(1) national consumer price increases (the rate of inflation), (2) government deficit as a ratio of gross domestic product, (3) national currency ratē relative to the normal band of the EMS exchange rate fluctuation, and (4) national interest rate on long-term government bonds (Hesse 1992).

The emphasis on *intra-regional structural development* deserves special mention. Indeed, it makes EC's paradigm of economic regionalization different from other Cold War economic groupings of nations, the North and the South or any other form of "strategic" groupings. The EC paradigm seeks to define itself in term of a contiguous *continental* geographical region.

One must hasten to add that the process of integration in the EC, albeit in progress, is far from achieving its targeted goal of "deep" economic union. However, the system has immense flexibility and its ultimate success may very much depend upon its in-built principles of accommodation. Provision for the safety net is essential for the success of any given system.

A. On the Road to a Single Market

On the road to a Single Market, each member government must enact about 170 legislative measures that bring individual national laws into accord with other members' laws and European Community policies. A progress report as of mid-August, 1992 has recently been reported. Of course, these are crude indices, but they do shed some light on the situation.

B. EC Intra-and Inter-Regional Trade

The EC intra-regional trade has grown phenomenally (see Table 2.A - 2.B). Provision for a common macroeconomic core explains much of this. Table 2.A presents annual data on total trade volume—export + import—while Table 2.B gives that on total trade shares for 1960-1991.

Disaggregation of total trade volume by regions—United States, Canada, Japan, ANZ (Australia-New Zealand) and the OPTAD (Organization for Pacific Trade and Development—U.S., Canada, Japan and ANZ) total, ASEAN-6 (Association of Southeast Asian Nations—Brunei, the Philippines,

Table 1. Percentage of Measures enacted:

Belgium	64.3	Spain	67.3
Luxemburg	69.9	Italy	70.6
Ireland	72.5	Britain	73.1
Netherlands	75.0	Greece	75.3
Portugal	78.4	Germany	78.6
France	83.4	Denmark	89.8

Source: European Commission (The New York Times, November 16, 1992).

Indonesia, Malaysia, Singapore and Thailand), NIE-3 (Newly Industrialized Economies—South Korea, Taiwan, Hong Kong), China, PACISL (Pacific Islands) and non-OPTAD (APEC-OPTAD) total, APEC (Asia-Pacific Economic Cooperation)—(OPTAD + non-OPTAD), SAARC-7 (South Asian Association for Regional Cooperation—India, Pakistan, Bangladesh, Sri Lanka, Nepal, Bhutan, Maldives), EC, LAFTA (Latin America FTA), ROW (Rest of the World) point to the fact that EC trade, both intra-regional and inter-regional, has grown. There has been a shift from OPTAD to non-OPTAD subgroup within the APEC group.

Table 2.B on trade shares points out that in 1960 the APEC share of total EC trade was 19.8 percent, while in 1991 the share is 16.8 percent. The EC intra-regional share in 1960 was 39.8 percent and the figure rose to 63.9 percent in 1991.

Further disaggregation of total EC trade by export and import shares, intra-regional vis-à-vis inter-regional APEC share, presents the following results: For EC's total export trade, the intra-regional shares are 41.2 and 66.1 percentages in 1960 and 1991, respectively. Corresponding figures for inter-regional APEC shares are 17.1 and 14.3. For EC's total import trade, the intra-regional shares are 38.5 and 61.8 percentages in 1960 and 1991, respectively. The corresponding figures for inter-regional APEC shares are 22.3 and 19.2, respectively.

The intra-regional EC trade—of total trade, and also of exports and imports, has grown. EC's inter-regional APEC trade shares, total trade, export, import—have marginally declined. The EC's intra-regional performance can be viewed comparable to the world trade growth and its share distributions.

One can then argue that if with the relative stability of intra-regional macroeconomic core, EC intra-regional trade, both by volume and share, has risen, a Pareto Optimality condition in the general sense that the EC region has made economic gains (welfare) for itself—its member sovereign states, at least by the trade index—without making any other sovereign-state based national economy or a group of economies *poorer*, is approached (Dutta 1992.a).

Tables 3.1 - 3.2 present annual growth rates of intra-regional and inter-regional trade—(i) total trade - export + import, (ii) export and (iii) import of selected regions—(a) APEC, (b) EC, (c) NONOPTAD sub-group members of APEC, (d) OPTAD sub-group members of APEC and two major trading countries—(e) U.S.A. and (f) Japan for the three successive decades—1960-1969, 1970-1979 and 1980-1989. Evidently, a pattern for an inter-regional trade profile is emerging, except for Japan. There is no evidence that a specific region is increasing its intra-regional trade share at the expense of its inter-regional trade shares.

It is important to appreciate that the concept of "Fortress Europe" is no part of EC economic regionalization paradigm. It is indeed a supra-national macroeconomic core for the region's sovereign state-based member economies

Table 2.A. Total Trade of the European Community at 1980 Prices (in millions of SUS)

YEAR	TOTAL	USA	CANADA	JAPAN	ANZ	OPTAD	ASEAN6	NIE3	CHINA	PAC.ISL.	NONOPT	APEC	SAARC6	EC	LAFTA	ROW
60	375,101	40,439	10,405	2,924	12,948	66,716	3,951	1,783	2,331	408	8,473	75,189	8,499	150,448	18,576	122,391
61	392,751	39,737	10,582	3,514	11,605	65,436	4,262	1,787	1,350	438	7,817	73,253	8,378	164,994	18,934	127,193
62	421,910	43,097	10,034	3,842	12,396	69,368	3,834	2,019	1,170	414	7,437	76,805	7,823	186,014	20,327	130,941
63	447,364	44,306	9,798	4,251	12,499	70,854	3,793	2,375	1,278	509	7,955	78,809	7,834	204,849	18,609	137,263
64	506,863	50,554	11,299	5,050	14,070	80,973	3,550	2,818	1,482	556	8,406	89,378	8,023	238,173	20,019	151,269
65	549,633	55,430	12,247	5,219	13,815	86,712	3,846	3,157	2,319	701	10,024	96,736	8,155	262,044	20,940	161,759
66	586,035	60,877	12,303	5,941	13,324	92,445	6,985	3,565	2,964	583	14,096	106,541	7,737	280,171	22,391	169.196
67	611,417	62,460	12,667	6,974	12,183	94,283	6,923	3,687	3,200	639	14,448	108,731	7,451	294,236	23,255	177,744
68	692,504	74,647	13,779	8,003	12,882	109,312	7,110	4,396	2,941	746	15,193	124,505	7,133	338,338	24,250	198,277
69	800,318	79,122	14,519	9,793	14,010	117,445	7,933	5,380	3,091	865	17,268	134,713	6,828	407,821	27,463	223,493
70	888,974	86,644	17,229	12,978	14,074	130,924	8,712	6,018	2,953	1,144	18,828	149,752	6,290	461,640	29,007	242,285
71	960,501	87,287	17,301	13,958	14,040	132,586	8,948	7,006	2,717	1,015	19,686	152,271	6,645	512,879	28,996	259,710
72	1,031,049	88,319	16,372	16,460	14,104	135,255	8,759	7,606	2,852	1,285	20,502	155,757	6,587	564,244	29,498	274,962
73	1,128,402	93,733	16,083	19,587	14,707	144,110	11,404	8,850	3,694	1,282	25,230	169,339	7,010	614,901	31,473	305,678
74	1,167,637	91,212	16,122	17,870	14,223	139,427	12,379	8,967	3,548	1,301	26,195	165,622	6,627	600,677	32,180	362,532
75	1,091,245	79,372	13,923	16,858	11,982	122,136	10,821	8,646	3,893	1,466	24,826	146,962	6,936	559,813	28,962	348,572
76	1,192,425	82,689	14,675	19,205	12,895	129,464	12,975	11,787	3,920	1,212	29,894	159,358	7,616	630,246	27,358	367,846
77	1,272,546	89,191	14,271	22,466	12,545	138,474	14,631	12,459	3,111	1,401	31,602	170,076	8,597	665,020	33,255	395,597
78	1,338,702	95,780	13,462	24,946	12,095	146,284	15,275	14,996	4,492	1,254	36,016	182,300	9,402	718,124	32,912	395,964
79	1,435,861	101,360	14,504	25,581	12,124	153,569	16,595	16,491	5,813	1,451	40,350	193,919	9,821	782,195	36,066	413,861
80	1,449,727	103,439	13,916	26,046	10,565	153,967	16,930	16,315	5,226	1,368	39,838	193,805	9,206	759,601	37,300	449,816
81	1,437,288	110,479	14,042	27,992	10,700	163,213	17,553	17,970	5,366	1,203	42,092	205,305	9,692	728,618	40,036	453,637
82	1,457,201	113,126	13,119	29,467	11,777	167,490	18,587	17,452	5,257	1,121	42,417	209,906	10,917	758,766	37,327	440,284
83	1,503,671	118,758	13,580	32,720	11,415	176,473	19,780	18,736	6,233	1,144	45,893	222,366	10,422	798,661	36,270	435,952
84	1,592,497	139,935	15,642	36,161	13,376	205,115	20,829	20,953	7,151	1,455	50,388	255,502	11,821	837,822	38,600	448,751
85	1,663,976	149,478	16,923	38,956	14,772	220,129	20,069	21,827	10,832	1,463	54,191	274,320	12,590	891,552	38,999	446,514
86	1,755,011	145,380	17,243	51,226	13,915	227,764	19,893	27,837	11,559	1,539	60,827	288,591	13,292	999,259	33,681	420,188
87	1,779,446	138,244	17,483	54,417	13,674	223,818	21,349	34,134	11,251	1,250	67,985	291,803	13,754	1,038,232	29,733	405,924
88	1,719,262	135,888	18,596	59,469	13,856	227,809	23,827	38,045	12,317	1,528	75,717	303,526	12,194	978,610	29,736	395,196
89	1,449,754	120,650	16,044	51,993	12,921	201,608	23,160	31,972	10,432	824	66,388	267,996	10,988	811,582	25,301	333,887

Table 2.B. Share Distribution of Total EC Trade

TOTAL TRADE SHARES OF THE EUROPEAN COMMUNITY (EC)
(in percentage)

YEAR	USA	CAN	JAPAN	ANZ	OPTAD	ASEAN6	NIE3	CHINA	PAC.ISL	NONOPT	APEC	EC	SAA/LAF	ROW
60	10.6	2.8	0.8	3.4	17.6	1.0	0.5	0.6	0.1	2.2	19.8	39.8	7.2	33.2
61	10.0	2.6	0.9	2.8	16.3	1.1	0.4	0.3	0.1	2.0	18.3	42.2	6.9	32.6
62	10.1	2.3	0.9	2.8	16.1	0.9	0.5	0.3	0.1	1.7	17..9	44.3	6.6	31.3
63	9.9	2.1	0.9	2.7	15.6	0.8	0.5	0.3	0.1	1.7	17.4	45.9	5.9	30.8
64	9.9	2.2	1.0	2.7	15.8	0.7	0.5	0.3	0.1	1.6	17.4	46.9	5.5	30.2
65	10.0	2.2	0.9	2.5	15.6	0.7	0.6	0.4	0.1	1.8	17.4	47.6	5.2	29.8
66	10.2	2.1	1.0	2.2	15.5	1.2	0.6	0.5	0.1	2.4	17.9	48.0	5.0	29.1
67	10.1	2.0	1.1	1.9	15.2	1.1	0.6	0.5	0.1	2.3	17.5	48.3	4.9	29.3
68	10.6	1.9	1.1	1.8	15.5	1.0	0.6	0.4	0.1	2.2	17.7	49.2	4.4	28.7
69	9.7	1.8	1.2	1.7	14.4	1.0	0.7	0.4	0.1	2.1	16.6	51.2	4.2	28.0
70	9.6	1.9	1.5	1.6	14.5	1.0	0.7	0.3	0.1	2.1	16.7	51.9	3.9	27.5
71	9.1	1.8	1.5	1.5	13.8	0.9	0.7	0.3	0.1	2.1	15.8	53.0	3.7	27.4
72	8.5	1.6	1.6	1.3	13.0	0.8	0.7	0.3	0.1	2.0	15.0	54.7	3.5	26.9
73	8.2	1.4	1.7	1.2	12.5	1.0	0.8	0.3	0.1	2.2	14.7	54.8	3.4	27.2
74	7.8	1.4	1.5	1.2	11.8	1.0	0.8	0.3	0.1	2.2	14.0	51.4	3.3	31.2
75	7.2	1.2	1.5	1.0	11.0	1.0	0.8	0.4	0.1	2.2	13.3	51.4	3.3	32.1
76	7.1	1.2	1.7	1.0	10.9	1.1	0.9	0.3	0.1	2.4	13.4	52.5	3.0	31.1
77	6.9	1.1	1.8	0.9	10.7	1.1	1.0	0.2	0.1	2.4	13.2	52.5	3.3	31.1
78	7.1	1.0	1.8	0.9	10.9	1.1	1.1	0.3	0.1	2.7	13.5	53.8	3.1	29.6
79	7.0	1.0	1.8	0.8	10.6	1.1	1.1	0.4	0.1	2.8	13.4	54.6	3.2	28.8
80	7.2	1.0	1.8	0.7	10.6	1.2	1.1	0.4	0.1	2.7	13.4	52.4	3.2	31.0
81	7.8	1.0	2.0	0.7	11.5	1.2	1.2	0.4	0.1	2.9	14.4	50.5	3.5	31.6
82	7.8	0.9	2.0	0.8	11.6	1.3	1.2	0.4	0.1	2.9	14.4	51.9	3.3	30.3
83	8.0	0.9	2.2	0.8	11.8	1.3	1.2	0.4	0.1	3.0	14.8	52.9	3.1	29.1
84	8.8	1.0	2.3	0.8	12.9	1.3	1.3	0.4	0.1	3.1	16.0	52.5	3.2	28.2
85	9.0	1.0	2.3	0.9	13.3	1.2	1.3	0.6	0.1	3.2	16.5	53.5	3.1	26.9
86	8.3	1.0	2.9	0.8	12.9	1.1	1.6	0.7	0.1	3.4	16.4	56.8	2.7	24.1
87	7.8	1.0	3.0	0.8	12.6	1.2	1.9	0.6	0.1	3.8	16.3	58.2	2.6	22.9
88	7.6	1.0	3.3	0.8	12.7	1.3	2.1	0.7	0.1	4.1	16.8	58.6	2.5	22.1
89	7.7	1.0	3.3	0.8	12.7	1.4	2.0	0.7	0.1	4.2	16.9	58.4	2.5	22.2
90	7.9	0.9	3.5	0.7	13.1	1.7	2.0	0.7	0.1	4.5	17.6	64.7	2.6	15.0
91	7.5	0.9	3.5	0.6	12.6	1.8	1.5	0.9	0.1	4.2	16.8	63.9	2.6	16.7

Table 3.1 Annual Growth Rates*

REGION	*SUBJECT*	*PERIOD*	*TOTAL*	*EC*	*APEC*
APEC	Exports	1960-69	8.7%	5.2%	11.9%
APEC	Exports	1970-79	7.0%	5.3%	6.8%
APEC	Exports	1980-89	5.3%	5.5%	7.3%
APEC	Imports	1960-69	10.5%	9.4%	12.7%
APEC	Imports	1970-79	5.5%	9.9%	4.6%
APEC	Imports	1980-89	6.7%	9.7%	8.3%
APEC	Trade	1960-69	9.9%	7.6%	12.5%
APEC	Trade	1970-79	6.2%	3.0%	5.6%
APEC	Trade	1980-89	5.8%	7.3%	7.6%
EC	Exports	1960-69	7.7%	9.9%	7.9%
EC	Exports	1970-79	5.5%	5.6%	2.0%
EC	Exports	1980-89	1.6%	2.5%	6.5%
EC	Imports	1960-69	8.6%	11.0%	6.5%
EC	Imports	1970-79	4.0%	4.0%	2.5%
EC	Imports	1980-89	1.6%	3.4%	3.7%
EC	Trade	1960-69	8.2%	10.5%	7.1%
EC	Trade	1970-79	4.7%	4.8%	2.3%
EC	Trade	1980-89	1.7%	3.0%	4.9%

*regression estimates of log of real values with time

resulting in the gains of microeconomic units—households and business corporations—of all 12 member countries. The EC market is "open" to the rest of the world, and the world market is "open" to EC, as it must be in a free global market—a marriage between "regionalism" and "globalism"—a paradigm of an "open" economic regionalism. The EC agenda eliminates all intra-regional trade barriers within the Community. The trade barriers between EC and the rest of the world, as exist, warrant continued inter-regional negotiations at the global forum of GATT.

III. ASIA-PACIFIC ECONOMIC REGION

The important dates toward economic regionalization in Western Europe (EC) are on record. Although no comparable economic movement can be discerned in the Asia-Pacific region, an effort to respond to the growing movement in Western Europe can be noted there. There has been a response—a passive one at best—to the unfolding of economic regionalization in Western Europe.

The first response came in 1968 when the Organization for Pacific Trade and Development (OPTAD) consisting of Australia, New Zealand, the United States, Japan and Canada became a conceptual reality (Drysdale 1968; Kojima 1968).

Table 3.2 Annual Growth Rates*

REGION	SUBJECT	PERIOD	TOTAL	EC	APEC
NONOPTAD	Exports	1960-69	12.9%	9.9%	14.0%
NONOPTAD	Exports	1970-79	9.0%	8.0%	9.0%
NONOPTAD	Exports	1980-89	7.9%	9.0%	8.9%
NONOPTAD	Imports	1960-69	16.1%	15.3%	16.3%
NONOPTAD	Imports	1970-79	8.0%	5.0%	7.4%
NONOPTAD	Imports	1980-89	7.7%	9.8%	8.7%
NONOPTAD	Trade	1960-69	15.6%	14.2%	16.0%
NONOPTAD	Trade	1970-79	8.5%	6.5%	8.3%
NONOPTAD	Trade	1980-89	6.9%	8.3%	7.9%
OPTAD	Exports	1960-69	7.8%	4.5%	11.2%
OPTAD	Exports	1970-79	6.4%	4.7%	5.9%
OPTAD	Exports	1980-89	4.2%	4.4%	6.5%
OPTAD	Imports	1960-69	9.6%	8.6%	12.0%
OPTAD	Imports	1970-79	5.0%	0.1%	3.9%
OPTAD	Imports	1980-89	6.4%	9.7%	8.2%
OPTAD	Trade	1960-69	8.9%	6.7%	11.7%
OPTAD	Trade	1970-79	5.6%	2.3%	4.7%
OPTAD	Trade	1980-89	5.4%	7.0%	7.4%
USA	Exports	1960-69	5.4%	4.6%	8.1%
USA	Exports	1970-79	6.5%	5.1%	5.9%
USA	Exports	1980-89	3.8%	3.3%	6.6%
USA	Imports	1960-69	9.3%	10.4%	13.2%
USA	Imports	1970-79	5.3%	-0.0%	3.2%
USA	Imports	1980-89	6.7%	8.3%	9.4%
USA	Trade	1960-69	7.6%	7.6%	11.2%
USA	Trade	1970-79	5.7%	2.4%	4.2%
USA	Trade	1980-89	5.5%	5.8%	8.3%
JAPAN	Exports	1960-69	17.2%	17.5%	19.1%
JAPAN	Exports	1970-79	8.9%	9.8%	7.6%
JAPAN	Exports	1980-89	3.9%	7.7%	6.0%
JAPAN	Imports	1960-69	12.6%	11.9%	11.7%
JAPAN	Imports	1970-79	4.9%	2.2%	3.8%
JAPAN	Imports	1980-89	6.3%	16.7%	8.3%
JAPAN	Trade	1960-69	14.1%	14.1%	14.2%
JAPAN	Trade	1970-79	6.6%	6.3%	5.4%
JAPAN	Trade	1980-89	5.1%	11.3%	7.1%

*regression estimates of log of real values with time

In September 1980 came the next important step at the Canberra seminar on the Pacific Economic Cooperation Conference (PECC). In 1989, a further progression toward Asia-Pacific economic integration came when the Asia-Pacific Economic Cooperation (APEC) was institutionalized with provisions for periodic meetings at the "ministerial level". The APEC original membership included five OPTAD countries, six ASEAN countries, South Korea, and the Pacific Islands. Soon, following the Korean initiative, in 1992, China, Hong Kong and Taiwan became its members, bringing the total membership of APEC to sixteen, eighteen in 1995.

APEC offers no parallel mechanism for an intra-regional macroeconomic core. It is more informal, and it seems to be waiting to learn from EC experiences. Should the EC integration movement succeed, APEC may be ready to make an appropriate follow-up move.

One must take note of the fact that the APEC meeting in 1993 in the United States for the first time witnessed participation by Heads of member sovereign states—Presidents/Prime Ministers—rather than being limited to the ministerial level of participation, as before.

An alternative scheme may result in two separate intra-regional macroeconomic cores—one rooted in the Americas—Free Trade Area (FTAA) a progressive extension of NAFTA, with U.S. dollar as the anchor currency, and another in the Asia-Pacific with the Japanese yen as its reference currency. However, any speculation on this at present stage would be idle.

A. APEC: An Emerging Economic Profile

In what follows we present an emerging Asia-Pacific Economic Cooperation (APEC) profile based on trade flows. A subset of APEC countries—the United States, Japan, Korea, Taiwan, Thailand and Malaysia—has been selected for this presentation.

We analyze total trade (export + import), as well as export and import of each of these countries. Graphic presentations (Graphs 1.1, 1.2 and 1.3) point to the fact that APEC intra-regional trade, especially with non-OPTAD APEC countries, has been growing. The pattern is somewhat general and the pre-1975 and post-1975 profiles are to be carefully noted. The OPTAD subgroup of APEC are far richer economies, while non-OPTAD APEC countries are newly industrialized.

The shift in the pattern indicates a movement toward intra-regional economic cooperation. While the APEC intra-regional shift is evident for the United States and Japan, it is more pronounced for Korea and Taiwan, and much more so for Malaysia and Thailand.

We further analyze the APEC intra-regional vis-à-vis inter-regional profile based on total trade for the United States, Japan, Korea, Taiwan, China, ASEAN-6, and Australia-New Zealand (ANZ), with a set of bar graphs (Graphs 2.1, 2.2, 2.3, 2.4, 2.5, 2.6, and 2.7, respectively). We disaggregate our analyses by two sub-groups of APEC economies—OPTAD (industrialized, richer and affluent) and non-OPTAD (industrializing, relatively less affluent). The pattern of dominance of intra-regional trade flow is evident.

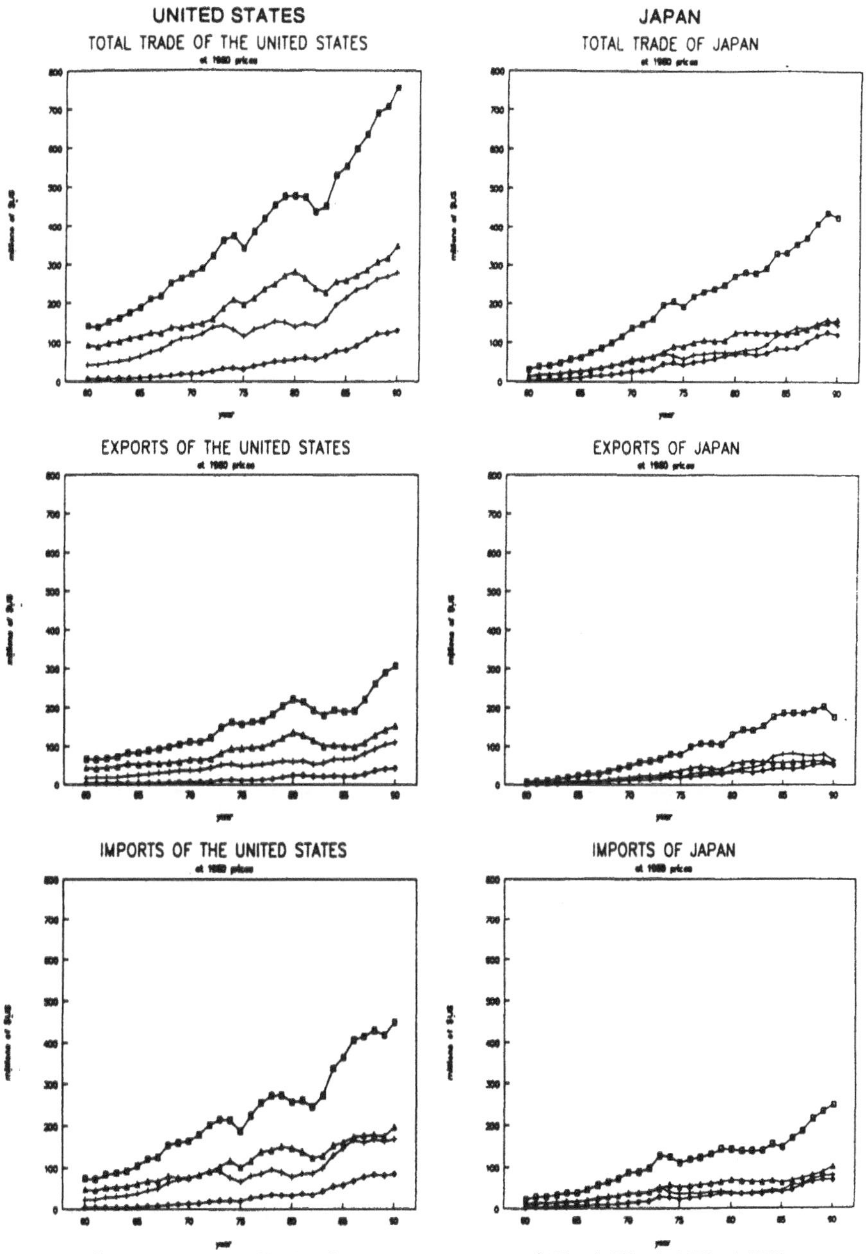
UNITED STATES
TOTAL TRADE OF THE UNITED STATES
JAPAN
TOTAL TRADE OF JAPAN
EXPORTS OF THE UNITED STATES
EXPORTS OF JAPAN
IMPORTS OF THE UNITED STATES
IMPORTS OF JAPAN

Graph 1.1

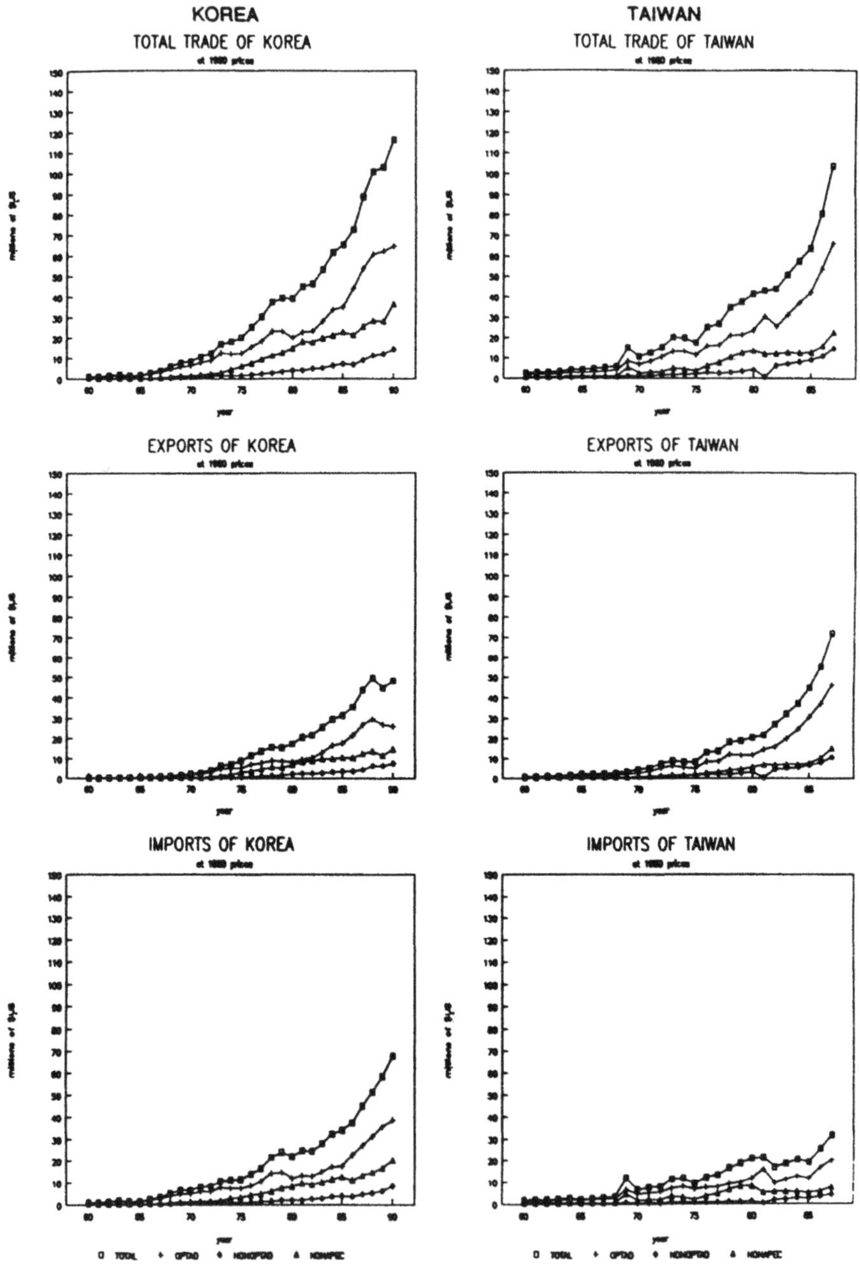
KOREA
TAIWAN
TOTAL TRADE OF KOREA
TOTAL TRADE OF TAIWAN
EXPORTS OF KOREA
EXPORTS OF TAIWAN
IMPORTS OF KOREA
IMPORTS OF TAIWAN

Graph 1.2

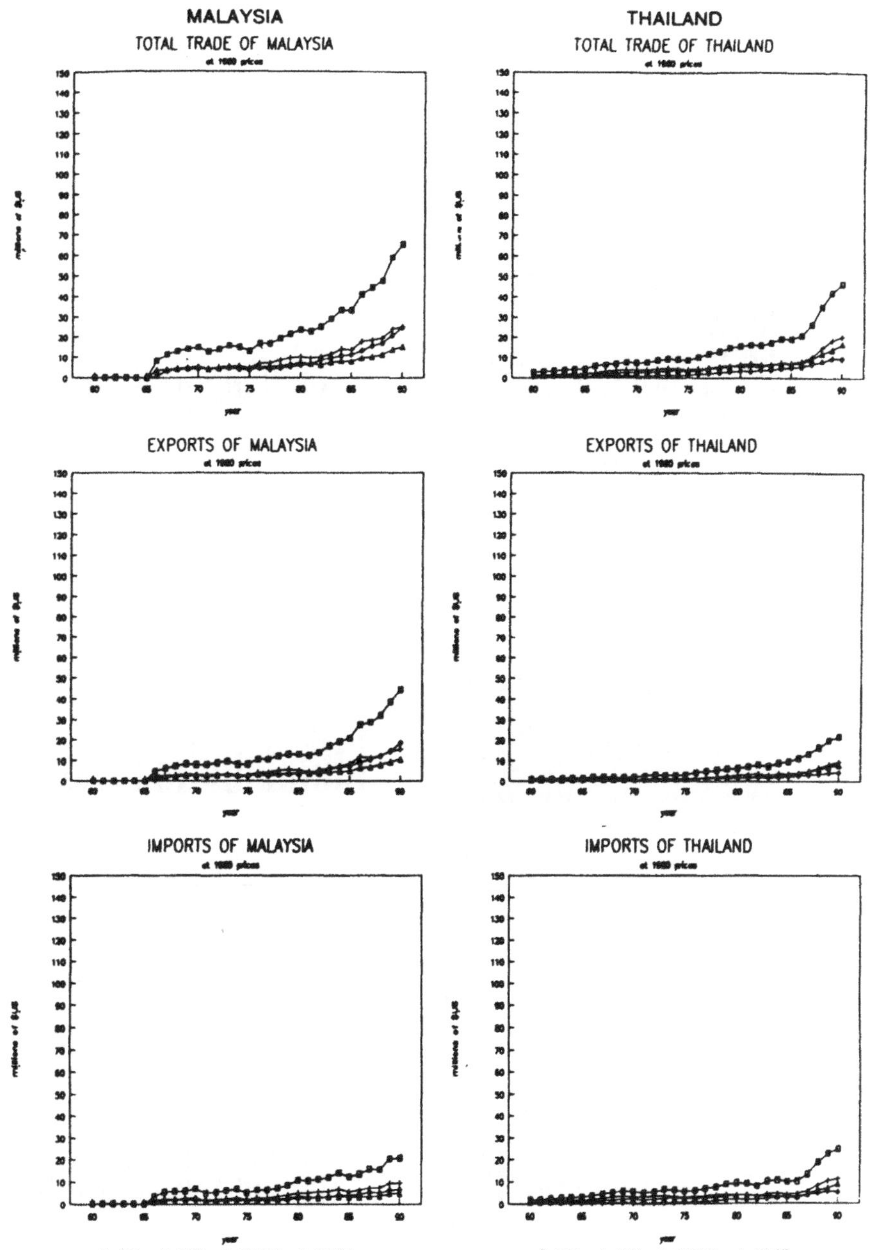
MALAYSIA
TOTAL TRADE OF MALAYSIA
THAILAND
TOTAL TRADE OF THAILAND
EXPORTS OF MALAYSIA
EXPORTS OF THAILAND
IMPORTS OF MALAYSIA
IMPORTS OF THAILAND

Graph 1.3

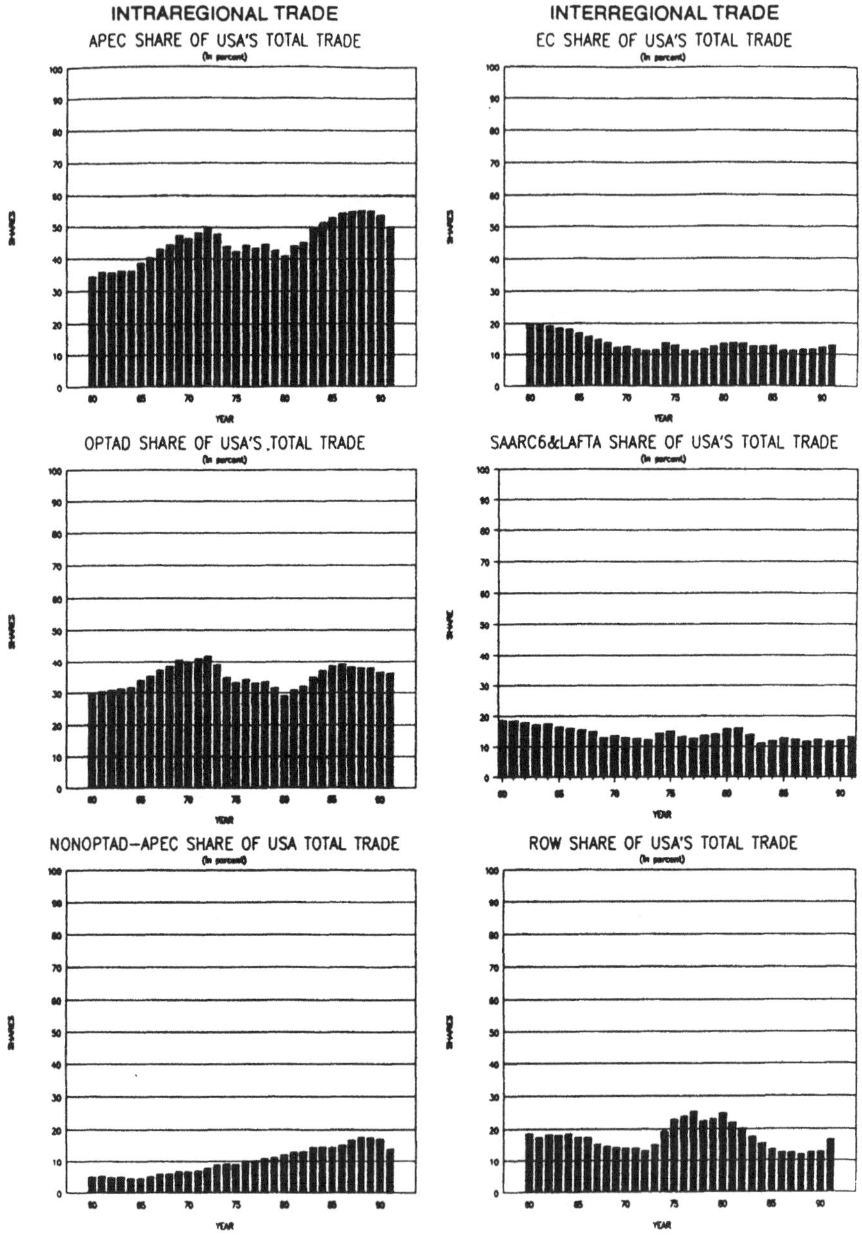
INTRAREGIONAL TRADE
APEC SHARE OF USA'S TOTAL TRADE
(in percent)
INTERREGIONAL TRADE
EC SHARE OF USA'S TOTAL TRADE
(in percent)
OPTAD SHARE OF USA'S TOTAL TRADE
(in percent)
SAARC6&LAFTA SHARE OF USA'S TOTAL TRADE
(in percent)
NONOPTAD–APEC SHARE OF USA TOTAL TRADE
(in percent)
ROW SHARE OF USA'S TOTAL TRADE
(in percent)
SHARES
YEAR

Graph 2.1

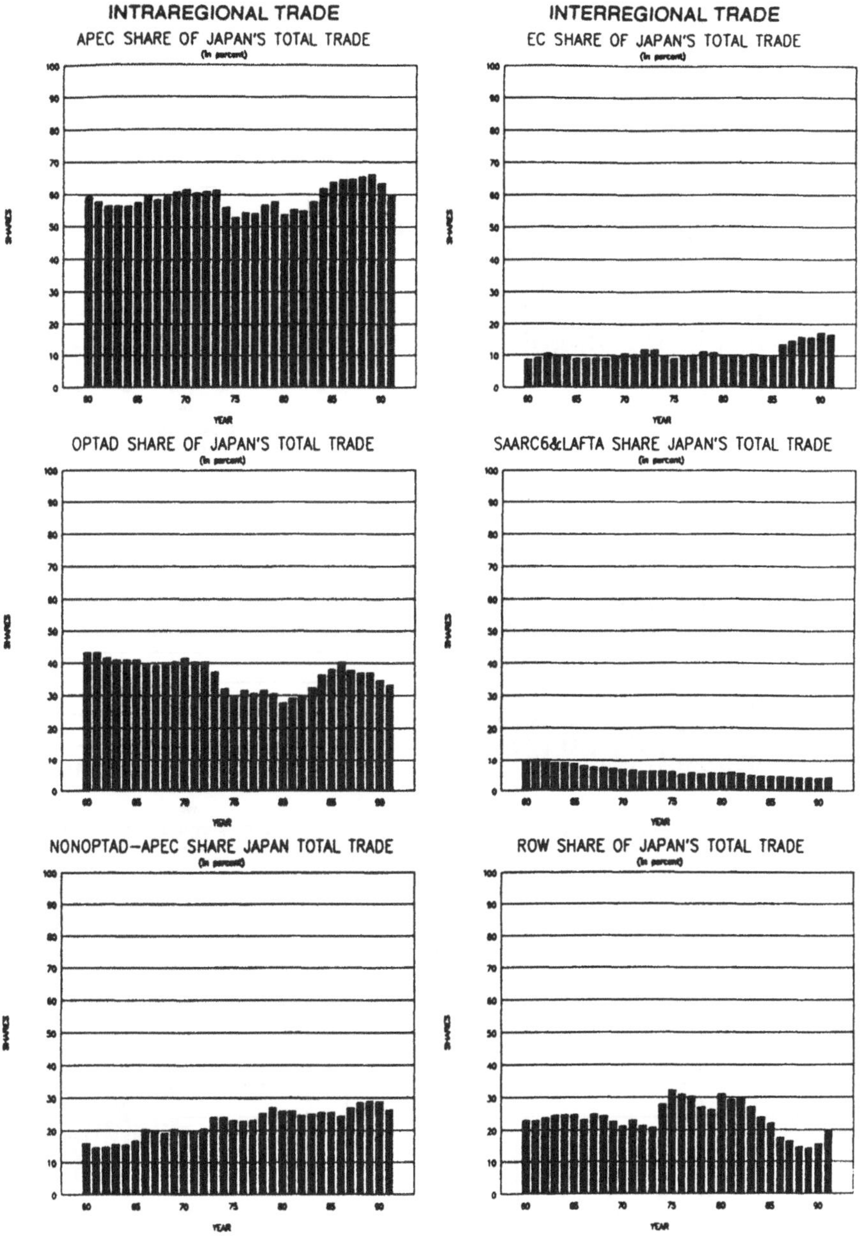
INTRAREGIONAL TRADE
APEC SHARE OF JAPAN'S TOTAL TRADE
INTERREGIONAL TRADE
EC SHARE OF JAPAN'S TOTAL TRADE
OPTAD SHARE OF JAPAN'S TOTAL TRADE
SAARC6&LAFTA SHARE JAPAN'S TOTAL TRADE
NONOPTAD-APEC SHARE JAPAN TOTAL TRADE
ROW SHARE OF JAPAN'S TOTAL TRADE

Graph 2.2

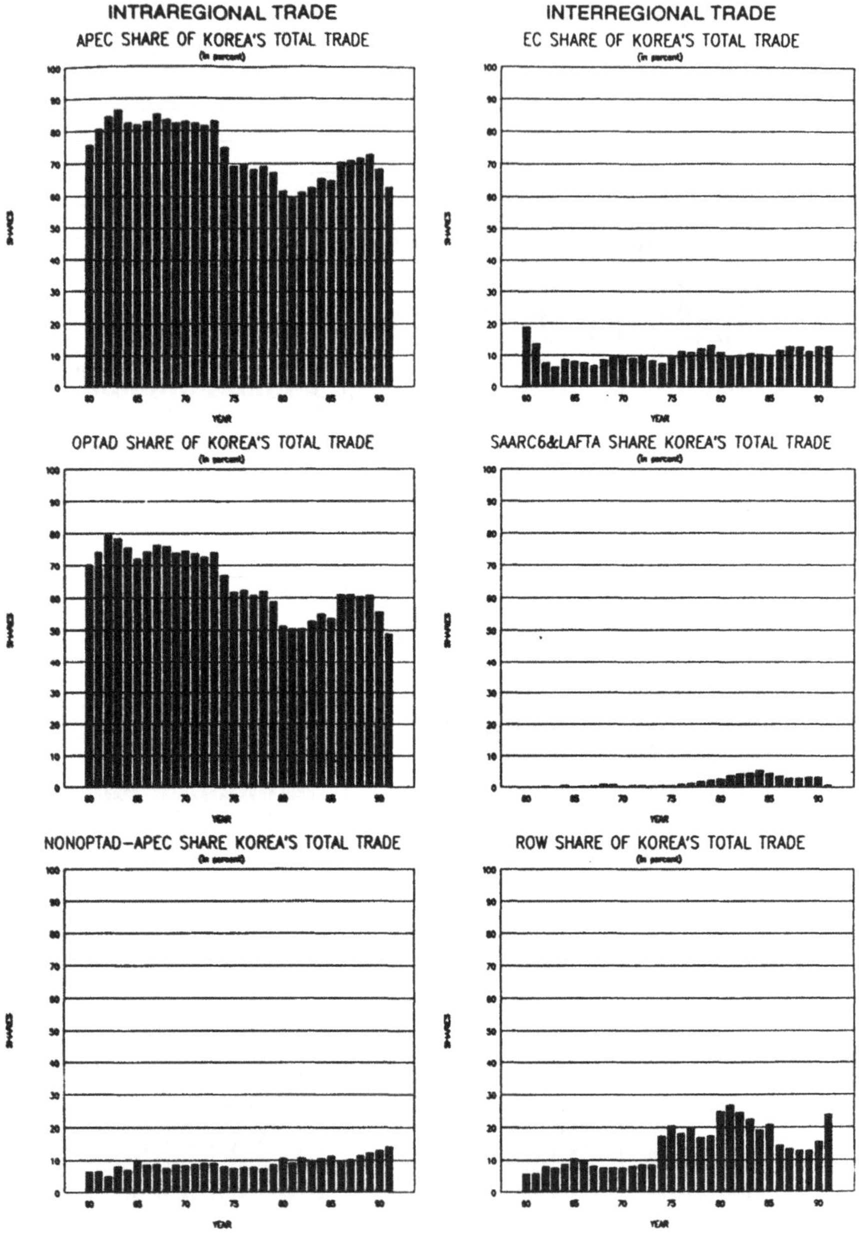
INTRAREGIONAL TRADE
APEC SHARE OF KOREA'S TOTAL TRADE
INTERREGIONAL TRADE
EC SHARE OF KOREA'S TOTAL TRADE
OPTAD SHARE OF KOREA'S TOTAL TRADE
SAARC6&LAFTA SHARE KOREA'S TOTAL TRADE
NONOPTAD-APEC SHARE KOREA'S TOTAL TRADE
ROW SHARE OF KOREA'S TOTAL TRADE

Graph 2.3

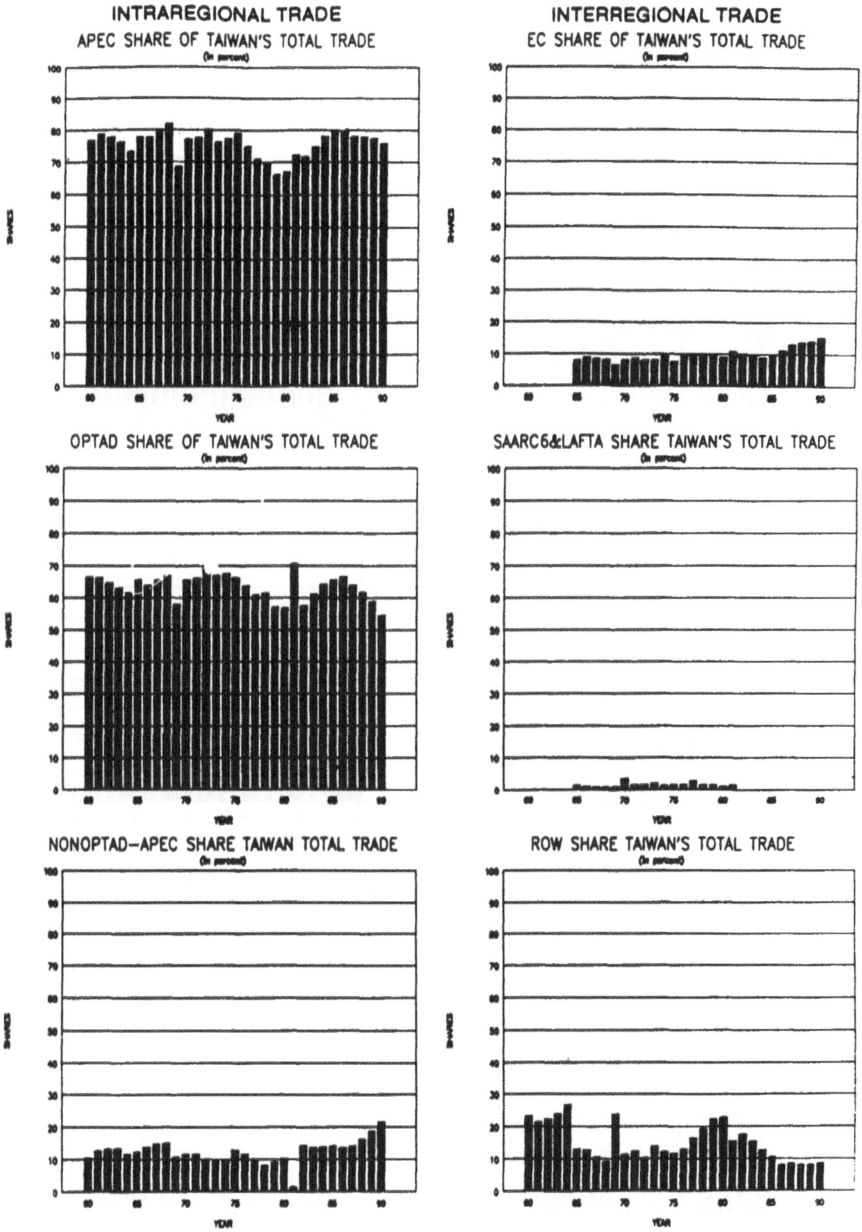

• 1960–64 figures for EC are included in ROW

Graph 2.4

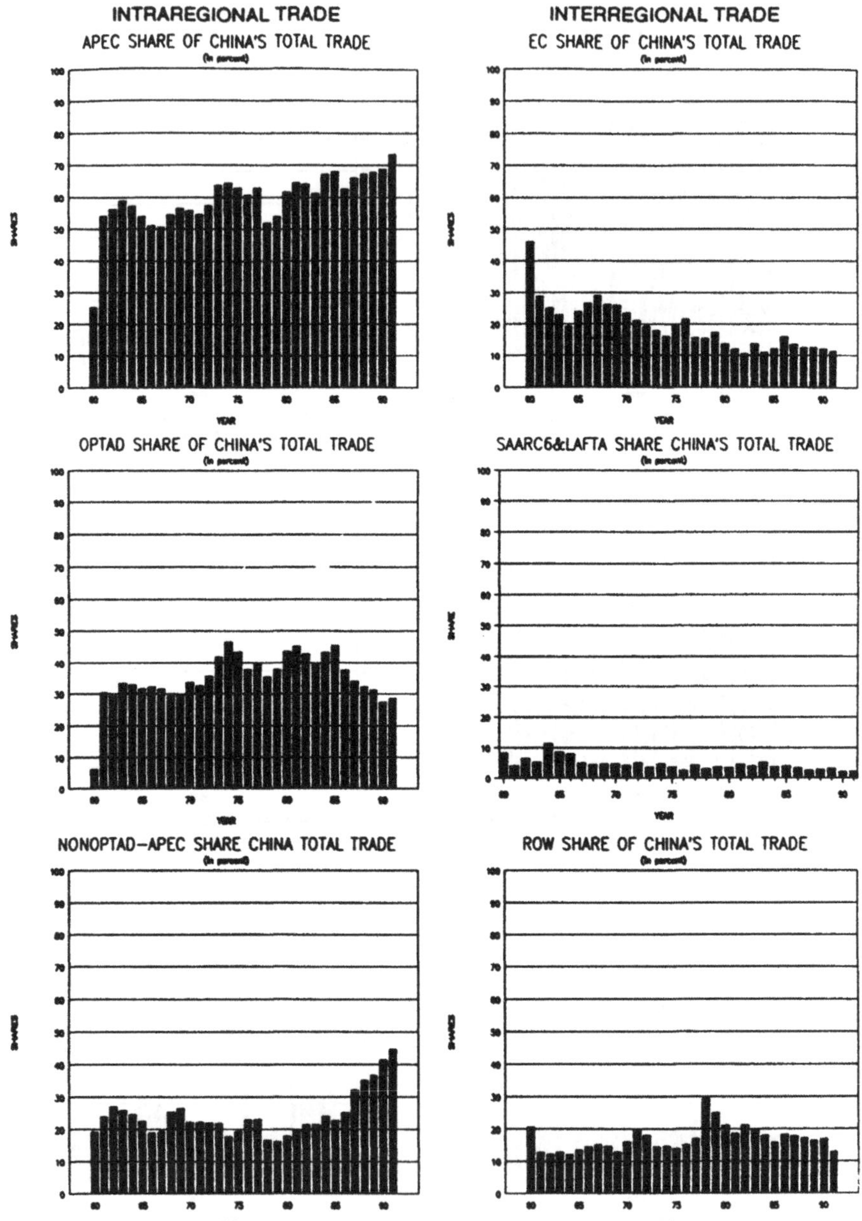
INTRAREGIONAL TRADE
APEC SHARE OF CHINA'S TOTAL TRADE
INTERREGIONAL TRADE
EC SHARE OF CHINA'S TOTAL TRADE
OPTAD SHARE OF CHINA'S TOTAL TRADE
SAARC6&LAFTA SHARE CHINA'S TOTAL TRADE
NONOPTAD-APEC SHARE CHINA TOTAL TRADE
ROW SHARE OF CHINA'S TOTAL TRADE

Graph 2.5

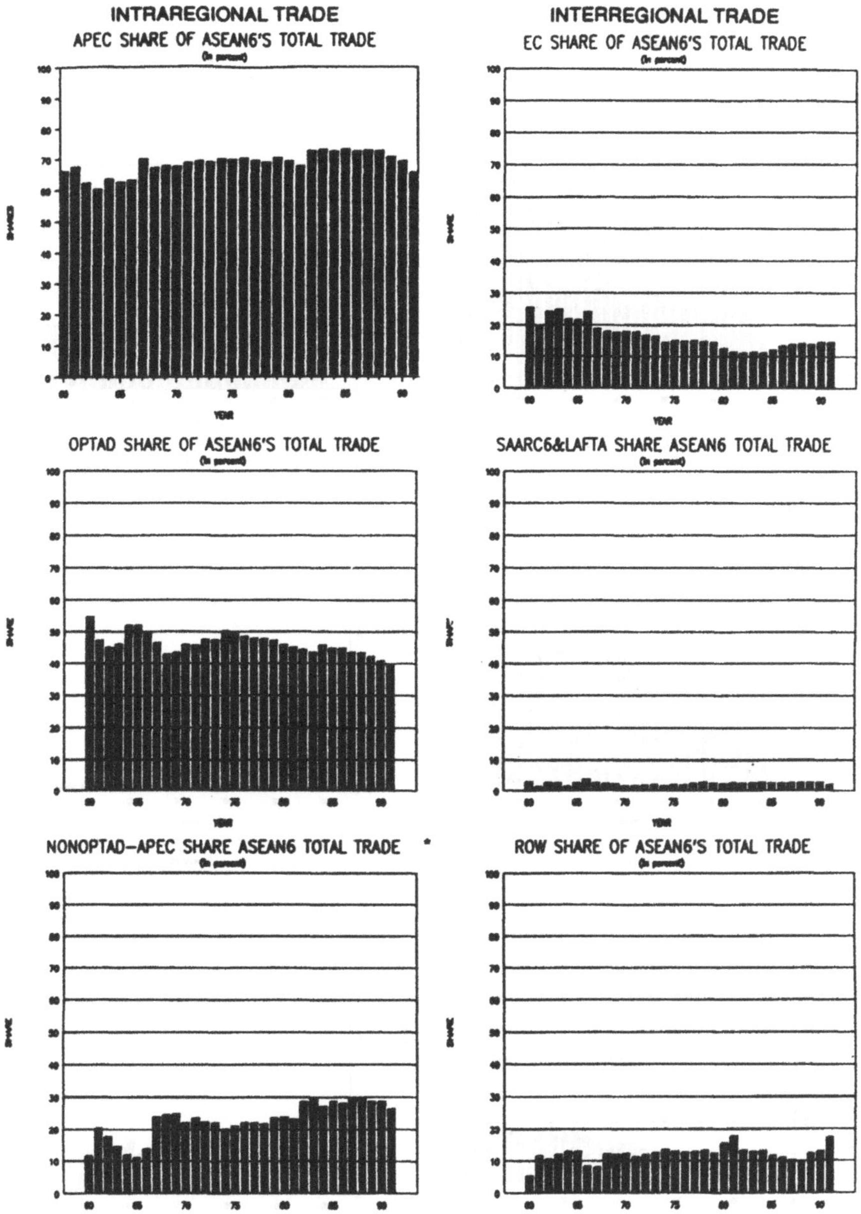

* includes intra-ASEAN6 trade

Graph 2.6

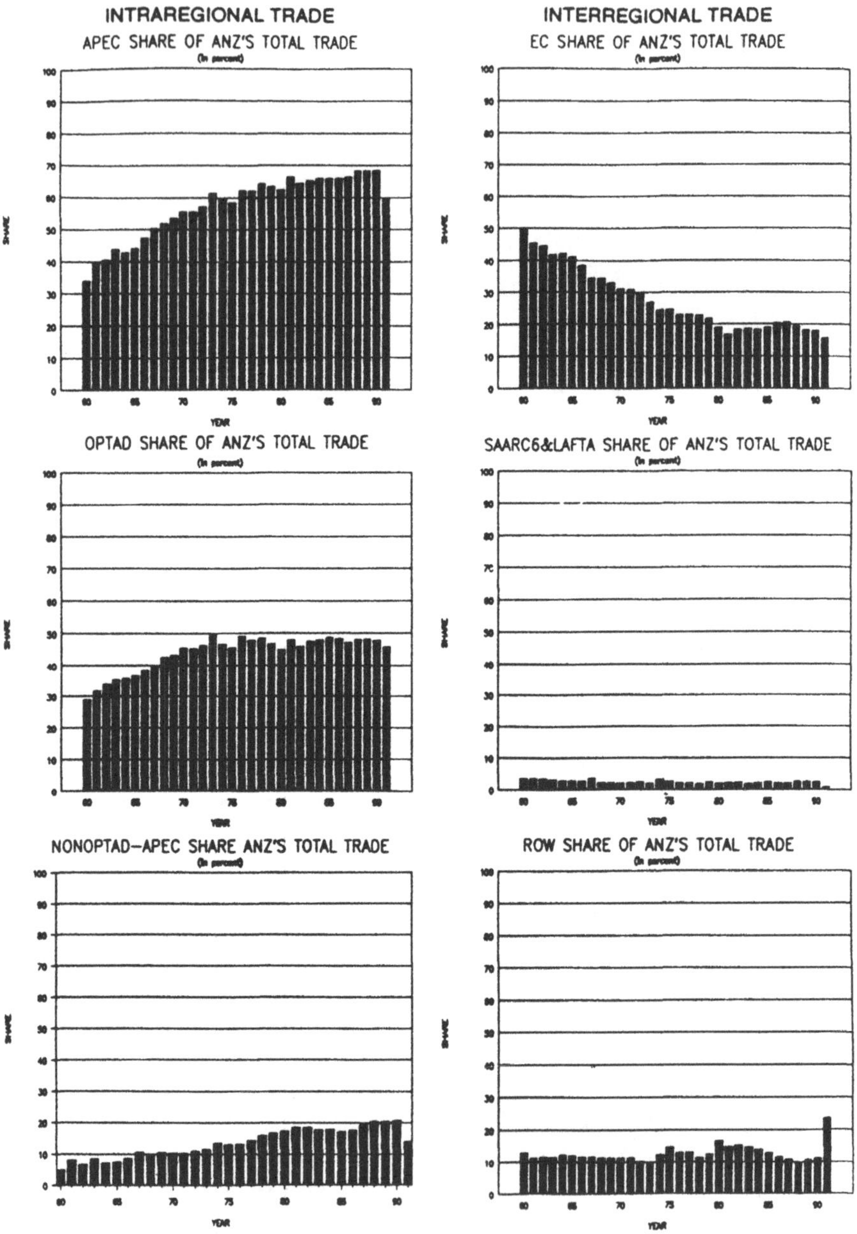

* includes trade between Australia and New Zealand

Graph 2.7

APEC share of U.S. total trade is noticeably increasing, while shares of EC, SAARC7-LAFTA have declined. The pattern is in general the same for Japan, however, EC share of Japan's total trade is growing. In both cases, within APEC, a shift in favor of non-OPTAD countries is observed. For Korea and Taiwan, the APEC intra-regional share is far too dominant in their respective total trades. In each case, there is an over-reliance on OPTAD vis-à-vis non—OPTAD markets within APEC. True, since mid-1970s, both Korea and Taiwan have moved to explore trade in non-OPTAD countries within APEC.

Some focus on the trade profiles of China, ASEAN-6 and ANZ should be instructive. For China, more than 70 percent of its total trade is intra-regional within APEC, and its shift towards intra-APEC markets in the 1990s is evident, with approximately 40 percent of trade being with non-OPTAD and 30 percent with OPTAD groups. China's exploration of non-OPTAD markets in the APEC region should be emphasized.

For the total trade of ASEAN-6, the intra-regional APEC share is generally a little over 40 percent, with distribution of 40 and 20 percentages between OPTAD and non-OPTAD markets. For ANZ total trade, APEC share between 1972-1991 has been 60 percent or over, with splits of 50 and 20 between OPTAD and non-OPTAD markets in the region.

It is interesting to note that EC shares of total trade of U.S., Korea, Taiwan, China, and ASEAN-6 have stabilized around 10 percent. However, EC shares of total trade of Japan recently approaches 18-19 percent. More interestingly EC share of ANZ's total trade has been steadily declining from a high of 50 percent in 1960 to less than 20 percent in late 1980s and early 1990s.

B. An Economic Performance

Research findings to identify convergence paths of regional economies has been reported on. Others have reported convergence paths for the North and the South, that is, the rich economies in the North and the poor ones in the South. Our preliminary findings, based on the two specific indices: (i) total trade, export plus import as a percentage of gross domestic product, $(X + M)/(GDP)$ and (ii) trade balance as a percentage of income $(X - M)/(GDP)$ provide mixed results. For the ASEAN-4—Indonesia, Philippines, Thailand and Malaysia—the first index points to a convergence path, while the second index points to a trade dependence for Thailand and the Philippines. For India and China, evidences hardly point to a systematic convergence pattern. For India, trade-dependence is far more spectacular. Korea, Hong Kong, Singapore point to convergence paths by both indices. Based on the two specific indices, Japan is seen to perform better than the United States by both the indices.

C. Investment Flow Analysis

The trade analysis is supplemented by a brief investigation of flow of investment. Pending further scrutiny, investment flows do lend support to an emerging intra-regional pattern, excepting the United States. Japan has become a dominant investor in the Asia-Pacific region, perhaps replacing the United States (also see Drysdale 1988). In addition to Japan, other savings-surplus Asian countries, especially Korea, Taiwan, Hong Kong have increased their shares of investment in neighboring regional economies.

IV. APEC INTRA-REGIONAL MACROECONOMIC CORE

There exists no institutionalized APEC macroeconomic core. The level and intensity of APEC intra-regional economic cooperation is at its preliminary stage. One can, of course, suggest that there is an out-effect of EC integration movement as the APEC begins to prepare to face full EC competition.

We need to answer two sets of questions. Are there basic economic forces—productivity, factor endowment, comparative advantages, factor availability—which will explain the APEC intra-regional economic integration and explain it wholly and fully? These issues must remain open to further research.

We have restrained ourselves from joining many others in estimating parameters of price and income elasticities. The price data which is very much subject to exchange rate management can hardly be accepted as "market" determined. For the present, exchange rates are managed by the G-7 (or the G-3) in a global managed exchange rate regime.

The second set of questions relate to the basic need for a macroeconomic core. The monetary-fiscal policy coordination of a regional set of sovereign nation-state based economies may progressively facilitate intra-regional trade/investment flows. EC experiences may be cited in support of the argument. Absence of a supra-national regional macroeconomic core is more likely to hurt progression of economic growth. However, monetary-fiscal policy coordination at the global level has been found to be difficult.

EC paradigm points to the fact that regional coordination of such core macroeconomic policies is a more achievable target, albeit not an easy one. It can be argued that an institutional arrangement for immediate communication among member nations of a regional economic compact is likely to be far more effective. Exchange rate fluctuations and currency wars, or threats thereof, are known to affect adversely international trade and investment flows. An intra-regional macro-economic core can be a shield.

The creation of a zone of *increasing economic stability* with institutional provisions for *multilateral surveillance* by the region's member countries, based on sovereign nation-state based economies, is a rational economic goal. Certain key issues must be addressed to this end.

1. *Regionalism and Globalism:* It has been forcefully argued that regionalism without globalism is bound to be counter-productive, and will minimize global economic gains (welfare) (Okita 1989). In a global competitive market, free inter-regional trade-and investment flows alone can maximize total welfare.

2. *The Principle of Inclusion:* EC offers a model for initiating the process. It is based on the principle of inclusion, not exclusion. In 1958, it was a group of five, and it then grew to be a group of twelve. Should Sweden, Finland, Austria and Switzerland become members, EC membership will increase to sixteen. If and when Norway, Liechtenstein and Iceland join the club, EC will have an economic region of Europe with some 280 million people from "the Arctic to the Mediterranean."

The EC institutional mechanism also provides flexibility for leave of absence for a member in duress. The core principle for an intra-regional supra-national macroeconomic core must be *one* that is based on voluntary coordination of monetary-fiscal policies by sovereign nation-state based member economies.

The APEC membership, initially limited to 5 OPTAD sovereign economies, soon became a group of 16, and its membership may continue to grow. Economic regionalization, following EC, should limit itself to a naturally defined contiguous geographical region. Sovereign member nations of the region should have an open invitation to join the group. In this respect, it is instructive to note that the EC paradigm, as outlined in the Maastricht Treaty of 1992, places a specific focus on structural development of member economies of the region which are relatively less developed/underdeveloped.

3. *Toward an APEC Macroeconomic Core:* Much debate is in progress as to whether an APEC macroeconomic core, a la the EC paradigm, is necessary or practical.

The APEC trade profile is based on natural market forces. The paradigm of export-led growth of specific economies with access to the U.S. open market under some form of "strategic regionalization", industrialization of Japan and of selected Asian countries, are natural factors. There is some merit, therefore, to the argument that there is no necessity to institute APEC regionalization with a formal macroeconomic core.

It is however crucial to appreciate that much of the Asia-Pacific growth zone emerged under the strict condition of *free* delivery of international public goods in terms of both monetary-fiscal stability, and military and strategic security by the United States. The arrangement did contribute to the mutual economic gains of the United States and its Asian economic partners in the post-World War II decades. However, early in 1970s, there came new challenges.

Kindleberger (1986) raised the question of the U.S. ability to indefinitely bear the cost of providing macroeconomic stability to its allies. Klein (1990) has asked if export-led growth can continue indefinitely. Issues relative to sustained trade imbalances for the U.S., the pressure on the international value of US dollar (exchange rate), plus the U.S. government fiscal policy resulting in budget deficits of 1980s adding US$ 3 Trillion to U.S. national debt in a decade are familiar factors for all international economic partners of the United States. The Asia-Pacific partners have a very immediate burden to share. Evidently, the post-World War II paradigm has outlived its usefulness.

A new economic paradigm to build further upon the successful U.S.-Asia economic cooperation is very much in order. To coordinate monetary-fiscal policies of regional trading partners is an obvious need. Each sovereign APEC member must directly participate in the process of coordination of intra-regional monetary-fiscal policies. The process thus calls for an intra-regional supra-national macroeconomic core for sovereign nation-state based economies. Otherwise, an inflationary policy or a self-serving fiscal policy by an individual sovereign nation can cause a great deal of economic distress to its trading partners. An APEC macroeconomic core can address these core issues with direct and cooperative participation of all the participating sovereign nation-state based member-economies.

4. *The Regional Reference Currency and its Domination:* There is concern that in a given scheme of economic regionalization, one member currency becomes the anchor for monetary stability of the region and the sovereign nation of the anchor currency will become a super-power. However, although in the EC, the Deutsche Mark has become the anchor currency for the Ecu (European Currency Unit), it has not resulted in the German domination of EC.

In APEC, there are two reference currencies, the US dollar and the Japanese yen. They may soon be joined by the Korean won and the new Taiwan dollar. The US dollar was the lone anchor currency for the world for many years. So were the British Sterling, the French Franc, the Dutch Guilder in the past. The anchor currency status is earned by the basic economic strength of the economy of a given currency. Indeed, this historical lesson should further support the argument for intra-regional coordination of monetary-fiscal policies of sovereign national economies.

A. Economies of Asia-Pacific Region and Their Divergences

For APEC economies, EC economic regionalization paradigm is a non sequitur, argue some scholars. After the two world wars, France, Germany England and their European neighbors have known better. Inter-racial, inter-religious, inter-cultural, inter-culinary art divergences among the multi-lingual sovereign member nations of Europe is a unique model of diversity. The EC is an experiment of unity in diversity well-defined in terms of stable macroeconomic core policies. Asia-Pacific sovereign economies on the two shores of the Pacific also have diversity, no more or no less.

It has been argued that intra-regional comparison based on economic/technological developments gave EC member nations at a much greater advantage. Asia-Pacific economies are far more divergent at their respective levels of economic/technological development. However, this argument at best evades the issue. It is irrelevant to argue whether the economic gap between Ireland-Greece-Portugal-and Spain and their eight richer EC sister-economies was any less. The critical issue of coordination of monetary-and fiscal policies under an umbrella supra-national macroeconomic core is to facilitate sustained and stable intra-regional economic growth. One can argue that such coordination is even more important for less industrialized and newly industrialized/industrializing sovereign economies.

V. CONCLUSION

The present study by its nature must remain inconclusive. However, it is safe to say that should the EC paradigm of economic regionalization, with or without modifications of the Maastricht Treaty, succeed, the rest of the world will make similar experiments in their respective regional contexts. The NAFTA Treaty may then take on a new economic meaning. Should the NAFTA evolve into an Economic Community of the American hemisphere (FTAA), embracing North and South Americas? Should the APEC follow a new direction? Should the APEC be an Economic Community of Americas and Asia, facing EC? Should EC be able to absorb European continental integration from "the Atlantic to the Urals" under one macroeconomic core? What will be the form of economic regionalization in the continent of Africa and the rest of the world?

ACKNOWLEDGMENT

An earlier version of this paper was presented at the First Conference on APEC: ASEAN/SAARC, sponsored by American Committee on Asian Economic Studies in cooperation with Chulalongkorn University, at its campus, Bangkok, Thailand, December 16-18, 1992 and published in the *Journal of Asian Economics, 51*, Spring, 1994. For their comments and critiques, I remain indebted to Robert J. Alexander, Mohamed Ariff, H. W. Arndt, Lawrence B. Krause, Detlef Lorenz, George Rosen, Kazuo Sato, Anthony M. Tang and participants at the Bangkok Conference. My special thanks are due to Edwin Milan and Amiya Sharma for their help over the past several years. Errors are mine.

REFERENCES

Drysdale, Peter. (1968). "Pacific Economic Integration: An Australian View" in Kojima (ed.), *Pacific Trade and Development* Tokyo, Japan, Economic Research Center.

———. (1988). *International Economic Pluralism: Economic Policy in East Asia and the Pacific.* New York, Columbia University Press, 294 pp.

Dutta, M. (1990). "The United States an Asian Economy: New Dimensions in U.S.-Asia Economic Relations" an invited lecture at the 14th International Symposium of Hose University at Tama Campus, Tokyo, Japan, September 26-28, to be published in Japanese *Sekai-Keizai no Seicho Senta-Azia Paiheiyou Chiiki* (*Asia-Pacific Region as a Center for Growth in the World Economy*) edited by, Yoshihiko Hirata. Taga Publishing Company, Tokyo, Japan, 1992.

———. (1992a). "Asia-Pacific Economic Cooperation: Structure of a Common Economic Region." *Journal of Asian Economics,* 3.1, Spring, pp. 1-28.

———. (1992b). "Economic Regionalization in Western Europe: Asia-Pacific Economies—Macroeconomic Core and Microeconomic Optimization." *American Economic Review, Papers and Proceedings,* 82.2, May, pp. 67-73.

Dutta, M., & Tantum, D. (1988). "Industrialization of Japan and Selected East Asian Countries: The Structural Divergence Hypothesis." in *Asian Industrialization: Changing Economic Structures.* Greenwich, CT: JAI Press, Part A, pp. 17-46.

European Commission. (1989). *Committee for the Study of Economic and Monetary Union in the European Community* Brussels, EC.

———. (1990). *Report on Economic and Monetary Union in the European Community* (Delors Commission Report), Luxemburg, EC.

Forrestal, Robert P. (1993). "The Role of Central Banks in a Global Marketplace: Exchange Rates and Policy Coordination". *Journal of Asian Economics,* 4.1, pp. 131-137.

Hesse, Helmut. (1993). "ECU—Now and Later: Some Considerations After Maastricht." *Journal of Asian Economics,* 4.1, pp. 139-152.

Kindleberger, Charles F. (1986). "International Public Goods without International Government." *American Economic Review,* March, pp. 1-13.

Klein, Lawrence R. (1990). "Can Export-led Growth Continue Indefinitely? An Asia-Pacific Perspective." *Journal of Asian Economics,* 1.1, pp. 1-12.

Kojima, Kiyoshi. (1968). (ed.), *Pacific Trade and Development.* Tokyo, Japan, Economic Research Center.

Monnet, Jean. (1978). *Memoirs,* Garden City, NY: Doubleday, 544 pp.

Okita, Saburo. (1989). "Policy Approaches to the Problem" in Emmerij, L. (ed.), *One World or Several.* Paris: OECD Development Center, p. 41-50.

Park, Yung Chul, & Jang H. Yoo. (1989). "More Free Trade Areas: A Korean Perspective", in Jeffrey J. Schott (ed.), *Free Trade Areas and U.S. Trade Policy.* Washington, DC: Institute for International Economics, pp. 141-158.

Schott, Jeffrey J. (ed.) (1989). *Free Trade Areas and U.S. Trade Policy.* Washington, DC: Institute for International Economics, pp. 141-158.

Viner, Jacob. (1950). *The Customs Union Issue.* New York: Carnegie Endowment for International Peace.

REGIONALIZATION IN EUROPE AND EAST ASIA:

DIFFERENCES AND CONSEQUENCES

Detlef Lorenz

Since the middle of the 1980s three very different events fortuitously became the background for re-visiting regionalism:

1. the revitalization of the European process of integration (EC 1992) initiated by the Single European Act,
2. the free trade agreement (FTA) among Canada and the United States to be finally folowed by the North American Free Trade Agreement (NAFTA) and, last but not least,
3. the appreciation of the yen which successfully pushed ahead the process of regional interdependence in East Asia that already had begun earlier.

Finally and very remarkably, in 1986 the Uruquay Round of the General Agreement on Tariffs and Trade (GATT) was installed, too. The new regionalism and the old multilateralism appear to be progressing in head to head "competition", as it were. At least since the conference on "More Free

Research in Asian Economic Studies, Volume 6, pages 31-44.

ISBN: 1-55938-918-4

Trade Areas?" (Schott 1989; Lorenz 1989a) academic discourses on the subject abound, culminating in a World Bank conference of April and a GATT conference of September 1992. Indeed, the international establishment of the profession became deeply involved in this issue.

Nevertheless, much of the "inflationary" discussions remained more or less polarized and speculative, mainly variations of the old Vinerian dichotomy of trade creation and trade diversion- until today. Regionalism was understood differently as stumbling *or* building *blocs*. Of course, the debate over time also was accompanied by a good deal of positive interpretation; regionalism being considered different in a different world economy of the 1990s, as opposed to the one of the 1930s; eventually, "open regionalism" fulfilled more and more a complementary rather than a substitutive function within the GATT-System. One even could defend the thesis: Without a successful Uruquay Round the world trading system certainly will lose- without regionalization possibly too!

However, instead of making any effort to distinguish between a negative and a positive regional*ism*, it may be more adequate to use just a "neutral" term, that is, *regionalization*. The term places emphasis on an essential element of the *development* and *pattern* of the world economy (Lorenz 1991). Regionalization then is focused on the rising intra-regional interdependence (clusters) of trade and other economic activities such as direct investments etc. as the *natural* outcome of the regional development processes. The world economy as a network of natural regions should help us not "to confuse regionalization with the intention of creating a bloc" (Pomfret, 1992) and also to see that process more principally as a helpful *reference model* compared to the traditional one (Lorenz 1992).

Before we further elaborate on this subject, a few remarks on the well-known centers of "bloc-building" and the empirical evidence of regionalization might be in order (sections I and II). These are followed by a discussion of the three developmental issues of regionalization, generally sidestepped by main-stream critics. *First*, approaches to "natural" and "optimal" regions are emphasized, (Section III). *Second*, analysis of transaction costs as the basic empirical and theoretical basis of research is discussed at some length (Section IV). *Finally*, two different perspectives of integration of principal importance, that is, extra- and intra-regional strategies, are examined in order to broaden the conventional approach by some *developmental* consequences of regionalization.

I. DIFFERENT EMPIRICAL ASPECTS AND PATTERNS OF REGIONALIZATION

Though in these days, Europe (EC) and America (NAFTA) have taken the front-line-East Asia (Japan) presumably being satisfied with speculations about an opaque East-Asian bloc-the focus in this paper nevertheless is concentrated on Europe and East Asia. Four reasons are of particular importance:

First of all these two regions are widely taken as prototypes of two very different strategies of integration: institutional versus functional integration, or "discriminatory" versus marketdriven integration (Drysdale and Garnaut 1993); the latter distinction being very much in favor in the Pacific area.
Second, both regions appear far more convergent with regard to *integration* processes-although with quite a discernible lag in the degree of integration, and apart from political goals (Yamazawa 1992). The United States (a continental economy!) on the other hand has been already integrated and is naturally far less integration-minded à la European Community (EC) or East Asian style integration, following a more modest *trade* policy strategy of "hub and spoke".
Third, though trade and macroeconomic disequilibria are far more conspicuous on the strong than on the weak side of the famous "bloc-triangle"-USA, Japan, EC-an essential point of distinction should be underlined for the relatively weak connection (EC-Japan), that is, inward versus outward looking preferences/strategies. This is particularly so if defensive attitudes of Western Europe are seen as a reaction to extra-regional export-led strategies of East Asia (Young 1993 pp. 122-123).
Finally, as Petri (1992b) rightly emphasizes, for some years there seem to be developments, which have worked to limit the post WWII supreme extra-regional reach of the US vis-à vis Japan and Europe. This may shed some light on a possible delicate arbitrator-function of the United States regarding regionalism versus multilateralism. The case of regionalization for the huge, vastly heterogeneous Asia-Pacific region (East Asia plus America), as envisaged in the Asia Pacific Economic Cooperation (APEC) grouping, seems rather inappropriate for seveal reasons not to be discussed in this paper.

Regionalization as an empirical phenomenon still needs much clarification. On the whole, recent studies seem to follow earlier investigations (Sautter 1983), suggesting that there is in fact no dicernible rising trend toward regionalization. They are very cautious to follow simple calculations of intra-regional trade. However, there are indicators for the interpretations of regionalization which should be considered seriously.

1. Though Lawrence (1991) in general sees no "strong long-run trends toward increased reliance on intra-regional trade," he nevertheless underlines an important point, regarding the special significance of *manufactured goods*. It apparently is not very useful to put all trade flows in one basket. Primary goods, in particular, have different determinants and are of no value for intra-industry trade which, however, is much relevant for regional development of

trade interdependence and industrialization. Hence, if "there is some evidence of an increased regional concentration in intra-regional trade in *manufactured* goods in Western Europe and Asia" (p. 29) that certainly warrants attention.

2. Though Lloyd (1992) in his OECD investigation finds no evidence either for regionalization in the *narrow* sense, that is, within Regional Free Trade Agreements (FTAs), trade within more *broadly* defined regions such as OECD Europe and Pacific Asia shows up differently! "Thus, one may conclude from the evidence that there is a tendency for world trade to become more regionalized in terms of broadly defined regions" (p.21), apparently, independent of the economic framework.

3. Lloyd also recognized, as did others (Anderson and Nordheim 1993; Drysdale and Garnaut 1993) that we have to evaluate rising intra-regional relations in the context of overall and parallel trade expansion as a consequence of (1) the liberalization of world trade and the growing share of GDP that is traded in general and (2) the rapid and successful developments in the new (Pacific) gravity center of the world economy, the East Asia region in particular (as previously in the EC!). The same result follows if viewed from the opposite perspective: intra-regional integration arrangements may have caused some trade diversion, nevertheless the world has been opening up sufficiently rapidly for inter-regional integration to continue. Although this outcome may limit the *relative* regionalization thesis (measuring the *share* of trade) it doesn't devalue the *absolute* importance of *natural* regions in the meaning of clusters of high intra-regional developmental interdependence.

4. Perhaps most remarkably, investigations by Anderson and Nordheim (1993) revealed a specific counter-effect of the North-South "Ottawa" perferences: "Much of Europe's intra-regional economic integration ... since the mid-1940s has resulted from the dismantling of imperial trade preferences, the global welfare effects of which need not have been negative" (p.45). On the other hand, regarding Japan and East Asia, the fall of Japanese imperial policies (co-prosperity strategy of the 1930s!) after the war contrarily did lead to an upsurge of *inter*-regional trade very much underlined by the export-led strategy which was extra-regionally directed for plausible reasons. So, abolition of imperial preferences in case of Europe considerably increased *intra*-regional trade in Western Europe (trade diversion from South-North-colonial trade to North-North-industrial trade) whereas in case of East Asia *at first* it favored the contrary, namely, *inter*-regional trade. Only later, especially in the 1980s, the success of the East Asian NIEs changed the picture.

II. NATURAL AND OPTIMAL REGIONS

Closely related with the issue of empirical regionalization is the theoretical phenomenon of *natural regions*. Recently, Krugman and Summers

("Economist" 1991, p. 55) have argued that if the share of intra-regional trade exeeds roughly one half of the region's total trade it can be regarded as a "natural" bloc. Kreinin and Plummer (1994) found an alternative, more sophisticated, formulation together with an interesting East Asian consequence:

> "In terms of economic efficiency it is beneficial for a country to join a regional bloc if such a step would not greatly distort its comparative advantage .... If such preservation occurs in all members of a proposed FTA, than the grouping can be labeled a "natural" bloc. On that definition a bloc consisting of ASEAN and the Asian NIEs and certainly one consisting of the above countries plus Japan, is a "natural" economic grouping." (p. 204).

If the term natural is equalized with proximity than an old geographical criterion joins the economic considerations: close neighbors are natural geographical trading partners. If they eliminate tariff and non-tariff barriers on substantially all trade (GATT, Article 24) or create "single markets" they are well prepared to become natural integration areas: "The EC fits perfectly well the description of "natural integration" at least as far as manufactured goods are concerned" (Jaquemin and Sapir 1991 p. 169).

These might all be important aspects of regionalization in order to rationalize deviations from the rules of the global world trade system (GATT). If, however, theoretical considerations get priority then the issue of *natural* regions has to be qualified by the further question of *optimal* regions which are smaller than the world as a whole.

Micro-economic theory in general and trade theory in particular never raised the question of optimal regions. Contrary to location and space theory, borders of a region are not to be explained. They are given by exogenous, non-economic that is, political factors. Of course, the idealized world of free trade makes borders rather meaningles: the optimum free trade area is the world economy. Nevertheless, apart from "optimal currency areas" to be tackled on a different level, three approaches to optimal economic areas can be distiguished.

First, the responsibility of governments, (international organizations) for the provision of public goods should be mentioned. Cooper (1976) at an early stage proposed the interesting idea of "optimal areas of jurisdiction", which derived from economies of scale, externalities and stabilization policies. The recognition of two further public goods of more recent origin, namely, deregulation and co-ordination of the management of a highly interdependent (and unstable) international economy, might make those regions even more important. Because cooperation of deregulated economies and markets at the global level has become more and more complex and cumbersome, many of the responses to globalization have had to take place at a sub-global level (see Lawrence 1991, p. 13; Lorenz 1989a).[1]

Second, optimal areas/regions could also be put in close neighborhood to what Tinbergen (1965) once called "positive" integration policies in contrast to only reducing "negative" measures of cross-border barriers. This overlaps with the distinction between "deep" and "shallow" integration by Lawrence (1991). Areas of positive and deeper integration, of course, share the common criterion of *institutional integration.* Furthermore, they come only into existence efficiently if they also share the common character of a *natural geographic* or *geo-political region.* Close common political and economic preferences are one of the essential premises of a natural integration region. Economic growth and efficiency should be enhanced by the success of neighborly cooperation and by economic and social affinities (Lorenz 1990 p. 19).

Third, analyzing "optimal" regions, moreover, could be cast into a far more principal focus. As I have argued in a recent paper on Western Europe (1992), it appears analytically more convincing to have satisfying and adequate reference models at hand. Perspectives and methods of international relations do indeed depend essentially on whether nations are reduced to dimensionless points, or seen as regions of economic and political cooperation.

Following Viner's well-known customs-union dualism, regional integration is a second-best or worse case. The world economy of neoclassical free trade and universalism is founded on the notion of an aggregate of atomistic small countries held together by a legalistic GATT and the principle of non-discrimination. Each country has one vote but no economic space, politics or history. Customs union theory was based at least implicitly, on small coalitions unlike Western Europe-quite apart from other centers of gravity like the Pacific Rim. Intra-regional relations in the sense of *natural integration* by the way are as alien to the GATT as neoclassical reasoning is to intra-industry trade.

Rather than reallocating given national stocks of factor endowments, locational and regional theory aims at explaining the *development* of international patterns and distribution of production and trade flows. Economies of scale and savings in transportation costs have always been central to location and space theory. If dynamic growth pole analysis of different origins, gravity models and transaction costs analysis are viewed in synthetic compact, regionalization of the world economy becomes more self-evident.

Apart from the general analysis there is a further specific point: The old core areas have reasserted their importance and have become, as well and most interestingly, centers of gravity for peripheral areas such as the newly industrializing economies (NIEs): U.S.-Canada-Mexico/Latin American countries; EC-second enlargement/Mediterranean countries/Eastern Europe; Japan-East Asia/ASEAN. With respect to these special and newly emerging developments, geographic concentration of production no longer requires resources based on primary products as was the case in earlier times and studies. Their place has been taken by industrial technology complexes and so-called networks (benefiting from what modern students of multinational corporations call "psychic proximity") which offer essential advantages of agglomeration (including scale economies).[2]

III. TRANSACTION COST ANALYSIS

Whereas the approach by gravity models may be too technical and whereas the approach a la new theories of location needs far more sophisticated analysis, the third alternative-*transaction cost analysis*-appears more rewarding and highly relevant for East Asia if,for instance, arguments presented by Petri (1992b) and Drysdale and Garnaut (1993) are taken into account. Fortunately, both these studies are also relevant vis-à-vis Western Europe (EC).

In general, if regional groupings of countries (regions) are not to be explained merely by preferential free trade agreements (FTAs) or if there shall be a more convincing explanation of a natural region, the successful overcoming or abolition of obstacles to trade other than transportation cost is highly relevant. Apparently, international trade bears higher transaction costs than domestic trade and, consequently, "differences in transaction costs across countries ... affect the direction of trade and the degree of regionalization ... " (Amelung 1990 p. 2). Empirical investigations concentrating on three factors determining transaction costs in international trade-lack of enforceable property rights, the spatial distance between trading partners and the lack of information goods-leads Amelung to conclude:

> "The case of the Asia Pacific areas clearly shows that regional entities are likely to evolve even without any progress in institutional integration schemes especially when transaction costs are low because of a common cultural tradition and geographical proximity between the countries. Especially the latter determinant seems to suggest, that economic regions can be delimited within geographic areas, even though technical progress has reduced costs of freight and communication substantially." (p. 26).

Looking more specifically into a long period of historical events and developments in East Asia, Petri (1992b) based his "simple model of bloc formation" both on comparatively lower intra-bloc transactions costs *and* on increasing investment-flow based intra-bloc linkages. The latter factor is of particular interest as a dynamic accelerator with respect to the fast growing NIE region in East Asia. The key point of Petri's dynamic transaction costs model are "positive feedback effects" on the grounds of "the endogeneity of trade facilitating investments", which create a strong intraregional low-cost interdependence. The argument is valid presently in East Asia but, by the way, it was so previously in Europe. "This story is consistent with Europe's integration process in the 1950s and 1960s".

Last but not least, Drysdale and Garnaut (1993) elaborated an "unusual model of regional trade" to explain the rapid expansion of intra-regional trade within East Asia by reducing resistances to trade, that is, lowering various kinds of transaction costs. In addition, they wanted to demonstrate that this regionalization avoids institutional discriminatory policies so prominent in Europe (EC). "East Asian and Asia Pacific regional trade expansion is very different in nature from that which is currently emerging in North America and from what has been established and continuing to develop in Europe. There has been no economically important trade-expanding discrimination in East Asia" (p. 186).

This "new" model of regional and international trade expansion is said to be not only consistent with the spirit of the GATT but goes beyond GATT. The distinguishing features are (pp. 187/188):

1. Unilateral liberalization along the standard trade theory which is not a concession but a gain ("prisoner's delight"!);
2. Official barriers have not been lower for intra-regional than for extra-regional trade expansion (nondiscrimination); and
3. Reduction of non-official barriers to trade (transaction costs) is of overriding importance for trade expansion and economic development.

The importance of lowering transaction costs, that is, reductions of objective and subjective resistances to trade in the terminology of Drysdale and Garnaut, is underscored without reservation. This very much parallels the studies by Amelung and Petri in this regard.

The different welfare effects of reducing resistances (trade creation) on the one hand and building institutional integration frameworks a la Europe and America (trade diversion) on the other hand, are far less clear-quite apart from the rather unique process of economic *and* political integration in Western Europe (EC).

The essence of the Drysdale and Garnaut argument regarding the all important subjective resistances to trade is the avoidance of trade diversion. The overcoming of resistances creates superior gains from trade with a new partner. The switch will "direct" trade from a less profitable to a more profitable partner: from extra- to intra-regional trade and it is therefore more likely to be associated with a preponderance of classical trade creation over trade diversion. Consequently, "the general theory of economic integration brings out the crucial distinction between the reductions in resistances in some trading relationships through a process of official discrimination [EC] and reductions in the resistances through a process of market and nondiscriminatory integration [East Asia] (pp. 193/194).

This theory of building dynamic natural regions of integration without institutional discrimination seems plausible per se. But an adverse criticism of regional integration as in the case of the EC, which *logically* implies discrimination because of the provision for 100 percent intra-regional liberalization (tariffs and non-tariff barriers) for EC-member nations, appears less plausible.[3]

The following points therefore deserve attention:

1. Let us begin with the remark: that all FTAs "are discriminatory by definition. Indeed, that is their distinguishing feature." (Lloyd 1992, p. 15). But we have also to realize that at least the EC qua *institutional* integration did not and does not deliberately aim at discriminating non-members. The building of the customs union of the Rome Treaty as well as the new Single Market project prefer the regional liberalization simply as a more adequate strategy of *natural* regional integration instead of strategic fortress building. It is also very important to note that the process of EC integration was equally "a catalyst in the reduction of Europe's external protection" (Sapir 1992, p. 1500). Finally, and more generally, *formal* trade agreements as such are hardly decisive with respect to the degree of tariff and non-tariff protection regarding actual trade policy. Discrimination and openness of the trading system indeed depend little on the *formal regime*. Both Western Europe and East Asia are proof enough in many cases,and the GATT, too. Even in the Drysdale and Garnaut approach subjective resistances to trade are considered far more relevant than official, objective resistances!

2. The *politically* oriented, institutionalized EC approach of regionalization in Europe can as well be explained by transaction cost analysis, as argued earlier, and in the context of location theory or economic geography in Krugman's (1991) terminology. This is also very much in accordance with the Drysdale and Garnaut approach for a "*general* theory of economic integration" (pp. 189). Preferences for regionalization determined by transaction cost analysis appear to have priority in Europe and East Asia (in the 1990s)—or for that matter generally!

3. Revitalizing the Common Market into a Single Market equally shifts profitabilities to new activities in accordance with the new integration model. "... the EC has also demonstrated that free trade in goods leaves plenty of scope for further steps to reduce transaction costs in order to create a genuinely unified EC market" (Elek 1992, p.12).[4] If the stagnant European markets, once characterized by "eurosclerosis", really are revitalized to a forcefully and competitive single market accompanied by large income-increasing effects of trade creation, European markets may *again* become profitable. Temporary disadvantages vis-á-vis third countries (non-members) should be overcome by way of strengthening natural integration.

4. Finally, looking at regionalization as part of (unequal) *development* of the world economy, the following argument needs to be recognized. Trade expansion in East Asia as a process of export-led growth *at first* followed an extra-regional (worldwide) integration strategy-made possible by reducing

objective and subjective trade resistances in America and Europe (Lorenz, 1989b). *Later on* with a more and more successful and rapid development of the intra-regional East Asian market potential ("Binnenmarkt!"), *intra*-regional integration more and more gained importance. In that context it consequently has to be taken into account that *at first* the old countries outside East Asia figured as "locomotives" producing the demand (purchasing power) for the rapidly growing East Asian supply (Lorenz 1990, p. 25).[5]

IV EXTRA- AND INTRA-REGIONAL TRADE AND DEVELOPMENTAL INTEGRATION

Regional economic integration strategies of the present day will have to achieve a great deal in order to avoid non-cooperative, neo-mercantilistic games falling back into the troubled waters of the thirties.

In order to set a different stage we must keep in mind two premises:

1. Regionalization is to be understood as a process of dynamic development of the *pattern* of the world economy by way of building gravity centers. Gravity centers in Europe and Asia, however, are at different stages of development facing different constellations of forces of integration which explains their respective institutional and market integration patterns.[6]
2. In order to characterize European and East Asian models of regionalization very briefly we deliberately make use of two very common *cliches* regarding the EC and Japan. The EC is seen as the center of protectionism and "discriminatory integration" and Japan on the other hand is interpreted as a center of mercantilistic disequilibria. Translated into regional perspectives we could say: *extra*-regional displacement trade is a trade-mark for Japan and East Asia whereas intra-regional trade is a trade-mark for the EC or Western Europe. As already mentioned, this is not independent of each center's position within the development process of the world economy. Interestingly this furthermore can be illustrated by taking into consideration the enlarged North-South gravity centers in Europe and East Asia (industrialized centers and NIEs) with respect to their "triangular trade".

Apparently, this constellation conceals a very high potential of conflict when non-cooperative games are played (Sapir 1992, p.1505). If, for example, we observe worldwide structural adjustment in the context of a simple model of leaders and followers as well as a part of a very rapid and specialized process of catching -up or strong substitutive displacement competition, the international division of labor as an adjustment process and as a problem of socio-economic international "management" will be put to the test.

Enhancement of domestic (internal) competition by liberalization of external trade (Jaquemin and Sapir 1991) is not quite the same as the export-led trade growth stategy of East Asia.

The GATT and the World Bank never earnestly addressed these development problems. The well-known extra-regional trade surpluses of East Asia—far more important vis-à-vis the APEC-partner USA than vis-à-vis Europe—were not interpreted as part of the formidable "fallacy of composition" debate. Rather, as in accordance with the postulate that extra-regional trade is "unlimited" it was never considered a threat to the functioning of the North-South as well as the GATT trading system. Consequently, regionalization encompassing adjustment of both extra- and intra-regional trade shares and pressures (Lorenz, 1989b) was not seen as useful. Of course, a lot depends on whether a cooperative or noncooperative game is chosen but regionalization meanwhile (1993/94) is not any longer simply reduced to regionalism.

Nevertheless, economic reality in Europe and East Asia with regard to regionalization still seems to be at a limbo. The extraordinary internal adjustment problems in the context of the EC 1992 Single Market-project and the enlargement of the European Economic Area are yet to be overcome. Whether they will go hand in hand with a process of "open regionalism" is a problem that in the end remains to be answered in the future. Moreover, not only the EC has to increase her competitiveness hand in hand with "open" trade policies, Japan, too, has to adapt its economy for staying competitive vis-à-vis the fast growing NIEs of East/Southeast Asia. That partly has already been done "naturally" by closer functional market integration (Yamazawa 1992, p. 1523).

However, the hypothesis could also be evaluated that the famous "flying geese model" might be transformed into a "Japan-Plus-model" dominating the East Asia region as a whole. Particularly, if increasing interdependence is only a side-effect and becomes an efficient means for improving the *inter*-regional (international) competitiveness à la Japan, the strengthening of the flying geese model in the end might show up as a powerful *extra*-regional strategy (Siems 1992; Young 1993a, pp. 122-123). Then instead of developing the regional (= internal) market and balancing the (extra/intra-)regional shares and absolute levels of international activities (trade plus direct investment), a fragmentation scenario of the world trading system looms at the corner.

This pessimistic perspective may be substituted by an optimistic one following what is in progress in Europe. The European Economic Area has been altered from a North-North (EC of Six and Nine) to a North-South region adding Southern and even Eastern Europe. Then, the more general and principal argument should be: the rise of an "internal North-South Market" in East Asia between the late industrializing NIEs and Japan could be an adequate revision of an *overdrawn* strategy of North-North competition.

However, a well-known economic argument still appears to be a counter-argument. Given the strong extra-regional dependencies and strategies, and given "the fact that Japan, the largest economy in the region, is unlikely to become the major absorber of the region's manufactured exports in the near future, the scope of any intra-regional integration scheme will likely be quite limited" (Han 1992, p.33). Though this statement is of recent origin, quite a lot of other investigations give more than anecdotal evidence that the East/Southeast Asia region becomes more and more integrated creating not only new growth poles (compare Lee 1991; Yamazawa 1992, pp. 1525), but also building a region with mutual absorption capacities beyond the Japanese economy. In the same vein we may read the statement by Soogil Young (1993a, p. 128):

> While trade liberalization will help, the East Asian economies should also make independent efforts to complement it in order to reduce reliance on the extra-regional markets for the growth of their exports and economies. They need to promote intra-regional, intra-industry trade by promoting functional integration through intra-regional infrastructural investment and subregion-building. With their continued growth, the East Asian economies should create new markets not only for themselves but for everybody, easing the burden of adjustment for other, thus addressing the ultimate source of global trade tensions.

Though the particular *inter*-regional relationships of the gravity centers in the future remain an open-ended question, warranting much further research, open regional North-South integration in Europe and East Asia instead of destabilizing North-North competition appears to be a positive contribution of regionalization to the development of the world economy and a revitalized world trading system.

NOTES

1. Compare in this context also the distinction between "Economic Regionalism, Macroeconomic Core and Microeconomic Optimization" by Dutta (1992).

2. Compare the interpretation Fukasaku (1992) has given to the decisive role of intra-industry trade (IIT) in the North-South context: "To the extent that the catching-up of the South through outward-oriented industrialization is associated with the North's globalization of corporated activities, the emergence of IIT can be regarded as a sign of closer integration in manufacturing production between the two ... Thus the emergence of IIT in the North-South context may be regarded as the emregence of a new form of interdependence between developed and developing countries. It goes beyond the conventional view of the North-South relationship based on the traditional factor proportion theory" (p.26).

3. The distinction should not be overlooked between discrimination for political reasons as for example CAP and ACP-preferences on the one hand and economic preferences vis-à-vis Community members giving large potential for "trade creation" on the other hand.

4. The general statement by Yamazawa (1992) equally fits the EC approach perfectly well: "It is worth noting that trade is only a part of the liberalization agenda. Nowadays, investment, services and other forms of transactions across national borders are also important. The

harmonization of rules and the process of making national regulations transparent will encourage other member country enterprises to do business across borders while not necessarily discriminating against outsiders. Free trade agreements currently being negotiated all include harmonization of rules and deregulation—this is much wider than the classic perception of the free trade area" (p.1528).

5. Compare also the following statement by Young (1993b, p. 129): "East Asia as a whole continues to penetrate the markets for manufactures in North America and Western Europe without (until recently) much reciprocal import of those goods. Consequently, East Asia has been a major source of adjustment pressure for the rest of the world during the past two decades, at both the industry and macroeconomic levels. This pressure has contributed to a rapid surge of trade frictions and the consequent weakening of the multilateral trading system."

6. "East Asia has not been enthusiastic about formal economic integration of the EC type. there has neither been a Rome Treaty nor a region-wide free trade agreement. *East Asia has not reached that stage of integration yet.* The coordination of macro-economic politicies has never been attempted among the APEC member governments. However, member economies are interdependent through trade, investment and services flows in this region and no member economy is fully insulated from the impact of others' policy. It is necessary to have a regular policy dialogue to try and affect each other's policy making in a *subtle* way." (Yamazawa 1992, p. 1527, emphasis added).

REFERENCES

Amelung, T. (1990). "Explaining Regionalization of Trade in Asia Pacific: A Transaction Cost Approach," *Kiel Working Paper* 423, June.

Anderson, K. and Nordheim, H. (1993). "History, Geography and Regional Economic Integration" in Kym Anderson and Richard Blackhurst (eds.), *Regional Integration and the Global Trading System*, pp. 19-51.

Cooper, Richard N. (1976). "Worldwide versus Regional Integration: Is there an Optimum Size of the Integration Area?" Pp. 40-53 in Fritz Machlup (ed.), *Economic Integration Worldwide, Regional, Sectoral,* (pp. 40-53). London: McMillan.

Drysdale, P. and Garnaut, R. (1993). "The Pacific: An Application of a General Theory of Economic Integration." In C. Fred Bergsten and Marcus Noland (eds.), Pacific Dynamism and the International Economic System. Washington DC: Institute for International Economics.

Dutta, M. (1992). "Economic Regionalization in Western Europe: Asia-Pacific Economies—Macroeconomic Core and Microeconomic Optimization," *American Economic Review,* 82 (2): 67-73.

The Economist: "Shoot-out at Jackson Hole," August 31, 1991, p. 55.

Elek, A. (1992). "Pacific Economic Co-operation: Policy Choices for the 1990s." Asia-Pacific Economic Literature, 6 (1): pp. 1-15.

Fukasaku, K. (1992). "Economic Regionalization and Intra-Industry Trade: Pacific Asian Perspectives." Mimeo, OECD Development Center, Paris, February.

GATT Secretariat. (1992). Workshop on Regionalism and the Global Trading System. Geneva, September 3-5.

Han, Sun-Taik. (1992). European Integration: The Impact on Asian Newly Industrializing Economies. OECD Development Center, Paris, April.

Jacquemin, Alexis and Sapir, André. (1991). "Europe Post 1992: Internal and External Liberalization", *American Economic Review, 81* (May) pp. 166-170.

Kreinin, M.E. and Plummer, M.G. (1994). "Natural Economic Blocs: An Alternative Formulation", *The International Trade Journal, VIII* (2): 113-205.

Krugman, Paul R. (1991). *Geography and Trade*: Leuven University Press.

Lawrence, Robert Z. (1991). "Scenarios for the World Trading System and their Implications for Developing Countries", *Technical paper* 47, OECD Development Center, Paris.

Lee, T.Y. (ed.). (1991). "Growth Triangle" *The Johor-Singapor-Riau Experience*. Singapore Institute of Southeast Asian Studies.

Lloyd, Peter. (1992). "Regionalization and World Trade", OECD *Economic Studies* 18, Paris.

Lorenz, Detlef. (1989a). "Trends Toward Regionalism in the World Economy. A Contribution to a New International Economic Order?" *Intereconomics, Review of International Trade and Development,* 24 pp. 64-70.

________ . (1989b). "Intra-Regional Trade and Pacific Cooperation: Problems and Prospects", in *Trends of Economic Development in East Asia: Essays in Honor of Willy Kraus*, edited by Wolfgang Klenner. Berlin: Springer-Verlag, pp. 65-74.

________ . (1990). "Regionale Entwicklungslinien in der Weltwirtschaft Tendenzen zur Bildung von Wachstumspolen?" in Erhard Kantzenbach and Otto G. Mayer (eds.), *Perspektiven der weltwirtschaftlichen Entwicklung und ihre Konsequenzen für die Bundesrepublik Deutschland, Hamburg Verlag Weltarchiv, pp. 11-31.*

________ . (1991). "Regionalization versus Regionalism—Problems of Change in the World Economy." *Intereconomics, Review of International Trade and Development*, 26, pp. 3-10.

________ . (1992). "Economic Geography and the Political Economy of Regionalization: The Example of Western Europe." *American Economic Review* 82 (May 2), pp. 88-91.

Petri, Peter A. (1992a). "One Bloc, Two Blocs or None? Political- Economic Factors in Pacific Trade Policy." In Kaoru Okuizumi, Kent E. Calder and Gerrit W. Gong, (eds.), *The U.S.-Japan Economic Relationships in East and Southeast Asia: A Policy Framework for Asia-Pacific Economic Cooperation Significant Issues and Answers,* Vol. 14, No. 1. pp. 39-70. Washington: Center for Strategic and International Studies.

________ . (1992b.) "The East Asian Trading Bloc: An Analytic History" Discussion paper No. 315. Brandeis University, Department of Economics, Waltham, MA.

Pomfret, R. (1992). "Are Regional Trading Arrangements Hurting Australia?" Unpublished paper, University of Adelaide, June.

Sapir, A. (1992). "Regional Integration in Europe." *Economic Journal, 102* (November), pp. 1491-1506.

Sautter, H. (1983). *Regionalisierung und komparative Vorteile im internationalen Handel.* Tübingen: C.B. Mohr.

Schott, J.J. (ed.) (1989). *Free Trade Areas and U.S. Trade Policy*. Washington, D.C. Institute for International Economics.

Siems, D. (1992). "Japans außenwirtschafts- und entwicklungspolitische Strategien gegenüber China und ASEAN. Ein Beitrag zu den Regionalisierungstendenzen im pazifisch-asiatischen Raum. Europäische Hochschulschriften." *Reihe* V, No. 1334

Tinbergen, Jan. (1965). *International Economic Integration.* Amsterdam, North Holland.

World Bank and CEPR. (1992). Conference on New Dimensions in Regional Integration. Washington, April 2-3.

Yamazawa, I. (1992). "On Pacific Economic Integration." *Economic Journal, 102.* (November), pp. 1519-1529.

Young, S. (1993a). "Globalism and Regionalism: Complements or Competitors?" C. Fred Bergsten and Marcus Noland (eds.), *Pacific Dynamism and the International Economic System.* Washington DC: Institute for International Economics, pp. 111-135.

________ . (1993b). "East Asia as a Regional Force for Globalism" in Kym Anderson and Richard Blackhurst (eds.), *Regional Integration and the Global Trading System.* London: McMillan, pp. 126-143.

CHINA AND INDIA IN AN ASIAN-PACIFIC ECONOMIC COMMUNITY

George Rosen

A regionalization of the world economy seems to be taking place and possibly even accelerating. In a period such as the present, such regionalization may be a politically acceptable intermediate step between the extremes of greater national closure with higher trade barriers to protect domestic industries, and world trade markets. M.J. Dutta, in several articles, has examined the economic arguments for this regionalization. He has presented various possible scenarios for an Asian-Pacific common market, and discussed current sub-regional arrangements. Those articles[1] formulated the theme of this conference.

The broadest ongoing Asian economic grouping, currently a discussion group rather than a common market, is the Asian-Pacific Economic Cooperation (APEC) group. This includes Japan, China, the "4 little tigers" (NIEs), the six members of the Association of Southeast Asian Nations (ASEAN), the two ANZAC countries and United States and Canada. Within APEC the ASEAN countries have established modest preferential trade arrangements among themselves; Australia and New Zealand have established

Research in Asian Economic Studies, Volume 6, pages 45-59.

ISBN: 1-55938-918-4

one common market, while the United States and Canada have established another; and there have been proposals for various other groupings of the Pacific Basin countries. An even broader Asian grouping would add to APEC the South Asian countries which have set up their own regional grouping-SAARC-for discussions among their leaders. Today SAARC has little, if any, regional economic function, nor has it any connection with any East Asian or Pacific Basin grouping.

Among the South Asian countries India is by far the most important in gross economic terms; with China it is one of the two largest countries in the world in terms of population. If the South Asian countries were added to the Asian-Pacific Economic Cooperation grouping but exclusive of the United States and Canada, and this new group did establish an effective regional economic community, it would be one of the world's largest common markets-one of multicontinental size. This would establish one of Dutta's "three regional economic power centers based on the DM, US$ and [Japanese]...[Uniting] 'sovereign nation-states in a regional economic nation with one 'key' currency for the region will be the new international economic order."

He goes on to add that "each member economy must fulfill its responsibility to keep its vigil in an institutional form over the intra-regional monetary management of its region. The issue is one of rational management of the region's economy and its monetary system by a duly structured regional authority." But for the maximizing of global welfare, member states in the regional group must be free "to engage in a two-track competition-intra-region and inter-region."[2]

Arndt, in the paper he has written for this conference[3], identifies three different kinds of "supra-national regionalism," with varying degrees of government initiative and economic integration distinguishing each kind. Dutta's concept combines elements of two of those types. This paper discusses Chinese and Indian reactions to Dutta's broad concept of regionalism. The reactions of those two countries to the other types of regionalism identified by Arndt might well be quite different, as is obvious in China's participation in a Growth Triangle, which is one of Arndt's types. I am not discussing China's and India's reactions to those other types of regionalism. Neither will I be examining in any detail the reactions of other Asian countries, many of major economic importance, either in APEC or SAARC, to regionalism as defined in the paper. This reflects both my assignment and my ignorance of those countries.

What are the possibilities that this widest Asian-Pacific economic group, including both the APEC and SAARC countries, will be established? That is the question I have been asked to examine, with emphasis upon the Chinese and Indian roles and attitudes. I will first look at present trade and investment patterns within Asia,[4] with stress on China and India. As part of this I will examine the results of the past economic reforms in those two countries upon their trade and investment patterns, and the implications of such developments for their possible membership in a formal Asian-Pacific economic grouping. I will then look at the possible political constraints in those two countries, as well as more generally, toward their eventual membership in such a regional grouping. In concluding I will pull together the above analyses to draw some tentative implications as to the willingness of the two countries to join such an Asian economic grouping over the coming decade.

I. CHINA AND INDIA IN INTRA-REGIONAL TRADE

M.J. Dutta and James Riedel have recently carried out statistical analyses of Asian-Pacific and intra-Asian patterns in the late 1980s. In addition the Asian Development Bank's (ADB) Key Indicators of Developing Asian and Pacific Countries for 1991 provides most recent data by countries.[5] I will rely on those statistical sources, citing the precise source of the data I use when appropriate.

In the early 1980s the share of the exports of those Asian developing countries that were members of the ADB in the total value of world merchandise exports was only about 8-9 percent. By 1988 and 1989 that share had risen to 13-14 percent, or by more than 50 percent.[6] A major contributing factor to this increase was that "in the 1980s incomes in Asia grew more than twice as fast as in the rest of the world... [The] exports of the Asian countries also expanded at about double the rate in North America and Europe..." Accompanying this increase in total exports was an increasing importance of other Asian countries as markets for those exports. Beginning in 1986, a profound shift occurred in the geographic pattern of Asian exports, with Asia becoming its own important and most rapidly expanding market. By 1988, 38 percent of the total exports of Asian countries were sold within Asia.

A. China

Within that overall growth pattern the growth of exports and intra-Asian trade by the Peoples Republic of China is especially striking. In 1977 Chinese exports were on the order of $7 billion dollars; by 1989 the export figure had reach $52 billion. This increase in trade was a result of a deliberate "open door" policy with respect to trade and investment after the death of Mao. In the 1970s China's exports had been less than 6 percent of its total output; by 1989 they had increased to over 13 percent of its significantly larger Domestic National Product (DNP).[8] Of those 1989 exports, over 60 percent of the total value went to other Asian countries, with 40 percent of that total (or two-thirds of its intra-Asian exports) going to Hong Kong. Riedel estimates that China is responsible for over 15 percent of the total intra-Asian export value.[9]

Hong Kong is the single most important direct market for China's exports and sources of China's imports. A large proportion of the China-Hong Kong trade is entrepot trade; i.e. imports from China are purchased by Hong Kong merchants for re-export to third countries, and imports from third countries to Hong Kong are re-exported from Hong Kong to China. In 1988 Riedel estimates that a very large proportion of China's exports to non-Asian countries went through Hong Kong. A smaller but significant share of China's imports followed the same path. Some of Hong Kong's major role is explained by the massive investments of Hong Kong business men in processing and assembly plants in South China. But in Riedel's opinion much of it arises from the far greater heterogeneity and diversification of Chinese export of manufactured products today than in the past. This has led to higher transaction costs for trade with China and a greater need for intermediation between Chinese producers and especially non-Asian buyers. (The degree of intermediation through Hong Kong for China's trade with Japan and Singapore, although not for Indonesia, is far less than for non-Asian countries).[10]

If Hong Kong is excluded, Japan was China's major Asian trading partner in 1989, taking $8 billion, equal to 15 percent, of China's exports, and selling $10 billion of its own exports to China (about 20 percent of China's total imports). Outside of Asia the United States is China's largest trading partner. The ADB data show China exporting $4.4 billion worth of products to the United States in 1989 and importing $7.9 billion from the United States. However, these figure are far less than the American trade statistics "which includes as imports from China those commodities transshipped to the United States through Hong Kong." The American 1989 figures show U.S. imports of $12 billion from China and exports to China of $5.8 billion. If one uses ADB figures in 1989 about 12 percent of China's trade was with the United States; the American figures place the United States share of China's trade at 16 percent.[11]

Paralleling the massive increase in the role of foreign trade in the Chinese economy there has been a surge of direct foreign investment into China. It is estimated that from 1979-1989 direct foreign investment into China totalled approximately $18.5 billion dollars; of this Japan's share was $1.8 billion. Hong Kong is estimated to be the source of over two-thirds of the total direct foreign investment into China during that decade but part of Hong Kong's total arises from its role as an intermediary for investment from third world countries, especially Taiwan. (For the three years 1987 to 1989, Harding estimates total Taiwanese investment into China at over $1.0 billion, in 1990 alone he estimates such investment at another $1.4 billion). Riedel believes that a major reason for foreign investment in China has been the "relocating [of] labor-intensive manufacturing from higher wage to lower wage economies in Asia...[especially] among the People's Republic of China; Hong Kong and Taipei, China...[The] number of workers employed by Hong Kong firms in the PRC now substantially exceeds the number employed in manufacturing in Hong Kong."[12] Such foreign investment would be a major factor behind the massive increase in China's exports during the 1980s. The businessmen in the investing countries shifted from plants producing more, to those producing less, labor-intensive manufactured exports in their own countries as wages rose in their countries; they moved their more labor intensive production facilities to China.

B. India

India's foreign trade experience over the past decade is very different from that of China. While there were important economic reforms in India during that period there was no comparable "open door" policy. In 1977 India's exports were about $6 billion in value, by 1989 they had risen to $16 billion, or by about 2-1/2 times, compared to China's seven-fold increase. In 1989 India's exports were approximately 6 percent of its GNP in that year. Of its total exports, about 20 percent went to other Asian countries, but the total share of all the South Asian countries, India included, was less than 2 percent of the entire Asian market for exports in 1987; it may have risen some by 1989. (There was no equivalent to Hong Kong as an entrepot country for India's exports within Asia.)[13]

Japan was India's largest market for its exports to Asia in 1989, taking somewhat more than 10 percent of those exports. Within the entire world the United States was India's largest national market absorbing somewhat less than 20 percent of all Indian exports, but Western Europe as a whole was the largest regional market taking almost 30 percent. India's market for exports is not only far smaller than China's but also much more dispersed, with Asian countries other than Japan of minor importance in the total. With respect to the sources of Indian imports Japan was the largest supplier, followed by Germany, the United States and the United Kingdom, with Japan supplying somewhat above 10 percent of the total and each of the others somewhat below.[14]

As far as foreign investment into India the figures are very low compared to China. While the annual level grew from $14 million in 1981 to $50 million in 1983 to over $100 million per year after 1984 the total from 1981-1987 was still only about $500 million. During this same period total direct foreign investment in each of Singapore, Taiwan and Thailand was about $4 billion and in China $9 billion. Japan's direct investment in India totalled $148 million before 1988, far smaller than in any Asian country outside South Asia.[15]

The above figures reflect India's deliberate policy of inward looking industrialization. Trade was discouraged not only by one of the highest average tariff rates in all of Asia at over 65 percent in the early 1980s, but by a complex set of regulations; the same was true for direct foreign investment. While such a policy had positive effects for India's industrialization, by the 1980s there were significant negative effects in terms of technology and the pattern of growth. This contributed to the economic reforms of the 1980s but these reforms were primarily directed towards easing controls on *internal* production and trade rather than on *foreign* trade and foreign investment in industry. In the 1990s a renewed reform program has sought to deal more vigorously with constraints on foreign trade and investment. What is clear is that in the recent past India's involvement in the economy of the wider region of Asia has been marginal, significantly less than that of China, and significantly below the opportunities that might arise from its potential comparative advantage in activities using a relatively low-wage but skilled and educated labor force.

II. FUTURE REFORM ISSUES IN CHINA AND INDIA, AND THEIR IMPLICATIONS FOR TRADE

It is obviously difficult, if not impossible, for an outsider to predict future internal economic policy changes in these two countries. It is possible however to indicate issues that may arise in the future, and that would effect the intra-regional trade patterns of the two countries. Looking at China first it is clear that its massive increase in foreign trade and investment is a direct result of the policy changes with respect to both of those following the death of Mao. Furthermore in that expansion Hong Kong, as a separate free trading state on China's border, has played a key intermediary role for trade with, and investment by, other Asian states, some not recognized by the People's Republic, and non-Asian countries. It is improbable that China's open-door policy will be reversed after the present generation of leaders passes from the scene. However, there are economic management issues that have not been resolved over the past decade and these may overhang China's foreign economic relationships both in the region and in the world.

One of these issues arises from the high degree of decentralization-political and economic-within the country. This decentralization, with its devolution of control over economic issues and of resources and revenues to provinces and some cities, has been a major factor behind the economic growth and trade expansion of the 1980s. But that decentralization has not been accompanied by establishment of effective central macro-economic control institutions. The close relationship between local political power, local control over economic resources, and high central government deficits without effective institutions for macro-economic monitoring at the center, contributes to sharp economic swings with periods of boom followed by sharp contractions. The booms have been characterized by inflationary price rises and deteriorating balance of payments; the sharp contractions result from the strict controls imposed by the center to deal with the booms. This political-economic situation has not changed in the 1990s, which would indicate that such sharp economic fluctuations will continue.

In addition, for political and ideological reasons, the micro-mechanisms to control the industrial sectors of the economy are unlikely to change greatly. Harding anticipates that "[for] the foreseeable future, some prices will be set administratively, financial credit and investment capital will be allocated bureaucratically, exports and imports will be subject to government regulation, and foreign investment projects will receive official scrutiny...Peking is also...using favorable exchange rates and government subsidies to promote exports... while employing various devices to protect its economy from foreign competition...Evidence is mounting that some Chinese exports are arriving in the United States through illegal channels." Some exports have apparently been produced in factories associated with penal institutions; some have been given false labels of origin and trans-shipped through non-quota countries. On the investment side there is criticism of China's copyright and patent laws for not protecting foreign intellectual and property rights, and of the loose, often informal procedures and regulations which frequently make investment and trade a matter of bargaining and connections, resulting in delays and misunderstandings.[16]

Another complication may arise after the incorporation of Hong Kong into China in 1997. While Hong Kong, under the agreement of incorporation, is to retain its present economic institutions, there may be an informal extension of China's economic and administrative rules and procedures to Hong Kong. This could have a discouraging effect upon the intermediary role played by Hong Kong with respect to China's trade and investment, and thus on the volume of both China's total trade and foreign investment.

Under present trading arrangements these issues need not be faced explicitly. If however a formal regional trading arrangement- an Asian or Asian-Pacific Economic Community-were set up they would have to be faced if procedures governing trade and currency relations are to be formalized within the regional community.

The Indian and South Asian role in world, intra-Asian or Asian-Pacific trade today is very small, far smaller than that of China. This reflects past ideology and policies. The current economic reform program in India seeks to change those policies drastically to both greatly expand exports and attract far more direct foreign investment than in the past. One direction of economic reform aims to gradually lower the average rate of tariff protection over the next three or four years from the present 65 percent to 25 percent. It is also hoped to make the rupee a freely convertible currency for trading purposes within the same period of time. Steps have been taken to ease control procedures on foreign trade and foreign investment within India, although the agencies that administer such controls on the national and state levels continue to function.[17]

Indian officials *and* private businessmen have begun to visit other countries which trade with, and invest in India; and significantly for the first time to Taiwan and South Korea. This is in part an effort to find new markets to make up for the loss of the former Soviet Union countries as markets, as the trade arrangements with the old Soviet Union have ended. But even more it is a recognition of the fast growing East Asian and ASEAN countries which have been more or less ignored by India in the past.[18]

India's potential comparative advantage in the industrial areas lies in those fields where its large supply of skilled, relatively low-wage labor can be utilized. These fields range from low level technology industries such as the production of tennis raquets, textiles and leather products, through intermediate technology industries such as motor vehicle production, to the high tech electronic and computer industries. The rising labor costs in the Newly Industrializing Economies of East Asia, and the high costs in Japan, would make India an attractive country for investment from those countries in the same fashion as China, Thailand and Malaysia have already become. In turn Indian manufacturers of such products hope that foreign investors would provide the technical and marketing skills to make Indian exports competitive in world markets. Foreign investors however are also interested in sales to India's potentially large internal market, and they contrast the relative closure of that market compared to China.

Entry into the growing Asian market on a far greater scale than in the past would benefit India economically in terms of exports and foreign exchange earnings. But in the short run there is some doubt as to whether Indian firms could compete effectively within India against foreign imports of high and medium tech products from other Asian countries. In the longer run this would probably change as India's technology is improved and costs are reduced as a result of the response of both India's own industrialists to the changing environment and the direct foreign investment in ongoing or new Indian firms, but this transition might be difficult. The expectation too of growing export markets for Indian products assumes of course that world trade continues to grow as the world economy grows and; with such growth demands for protection against those exports could be expected to diminish.

III. THE POLITICS OF A REGIONAL COMMON MARKET

What are some of the political issues within China and India which would influence the willingness of those two countries to join as Asian economic community eventually centered around Japan and the yen, as Dutta envisions? For both of those countries membership in such a regional community would call for significant policy and institutional changes which I propose to briefly examine. Such changes would require political decisions which would certainly reflect costs and benefits of those changes to influential groups within the two countries, and would in turn influence the intentions of their political leaders with respect to participation in the Asian common market. Elek has identified four policy areas where changes might be necessary in the individual countries to establish a minimal degree of regional commonality.[19] These are (a) the removal of restrictive market barriers of a non-physical nature; (b) the improvement of physical infrastructure to ease the flow of intra-regional trade and investment; (c) placing the laws and regulations that deal with international transactions on a common basis among member countries; (d) devising an agreed-upon mechanism to handle disputes among the countries with respect to trade and investment. If such a regional arrangement goes further to center around a "key" currency for the area, such as the Yen, as Dutta envisions, then there would be a fifth area of possible policy change. Each member country would have to establish an institutional capacity to control the functioning of its own monetary and fiscal system so that it yields a macro-economic performance harmonious with other member countries, especially with Japan since the Yen would be the central currency of the regional market. The New York Times, in a November 1992 article[20], pointed out that to establish the European regional market framework, "the European Commission, the executive branch of the community," proposed 276 legal and regulatory directives. It was expected that 95 percent of these would be in place by the end of 1992. That achievement would call for "each member government... [to] enact about 170 legislative measures that bring national laws into accord with other members' laws and European Community policies." By mid-August 1992 each of the 12 member countries had passed from 64 to 90 percent of those measures (varying from Belgium with the lowest percentage and Denmark the highest).

A. China

What are the political constraints within China and India that could influence their willingness to move toward such policy changes to achieve a regional common market, and would the economic benefits of being a member of such a market compensate for the potential costs? If we look at China first it is obvious that China already plays a very significant role in intra-Asian trade and investment within the present system. As noted earlier over 60 percent of China's exports go to other Asian countries, and those are on the order of 15 percent of total intra-Asian export trade. There is already a *de facto* triangular trade and investment arrangement among China, Hong Kong and Taiwan that contributes to this result, with Hong Kong playing a major intermediary role for Chinese trade, and for investment into China. China also has close economic ties with Japan and the United States, and it is likely that ties with South Korea will be strengthened. This has had major consequences for the development of China's manufacturing industry in the area around Hong Kong, and employment in manufacturing in that region is well above that in Hong Kong. That expansion has occurred despite a complex administrative and regulatory system, characterized by its *ad hoc* and localized decision-making, and the absence of an effective central macro-economic control system. In fact the existence of a separate Hong Kong with a very efficient trading and financial system functioning on internationally acceptable institutional lines has freed China from the need of making its own institutional changes.

If a regional common market were set up the gains to China would not be large, *if* it could remain outside of that market while trading freely with it. This might be possible so long as Hong Kong remains independent but trades freely with China while itself becoming a member of the Asian market. But when Hong Kong becomes part of China in 1997 such an intermediary role would probably not be acceptable if China were not part of the common market. In that case if China found its trade within Asia, and possibly elsewhere, sharply reduced, the economic cost to it would be substantial.

There would however be costs of moving ahead in the indicated policy areas to various groups within the Chinese system. Removing trade protection quickly would eliminate a large number of jobs in the large government-owned industrial sector which is currently supported by massive fiscal subsidies. It would be politically very difficult if those enterprises closed- and in fact it has not been possible to pass an effective bankruptcy law. This would have to occur gradually; other Asian member countries might well consider assisting China toward the establishment of a fund to provide incomes and job-retraining for workers forced out of their jobs as a result of readjustments caused by ending protection and entering a common market.

Apart from the political costs of reducing protection there would also be political costs from establishing a uniform administrative and regulatory system for trade and investment. That would reduce "back-door" income gained by local party leaders and others, arising from their ability to control investment and trading decisions. Similarly the establishment of an effective central macro-economic control mechanism over the country's financial and fiscal systems would reduce the powers of provincial and local leaders within their regional economies. This might have a limiting effect upon local economic growth and incomes in general, quite apart from any reduction of the incomes of local leaders themselves.

There could also be broader political objections to further opening up the economy by joining an Asian market. As China's socialist system came under the greater influence of capitalist market forces this could create ideological objections. Objections might also arise on nationalist grounds if it were felt that China would become economically subordinate to Japan, whose Yen became the central currency. There is still a strong memory of Japan's effort to dominate China in the 1930s and 1940s, as well as a belief that China's own position as a great power would be threatened by such subordination. Finally there may be an underlying fear among China's present Communist Party leaders that further opening of the economy and the country to foreign influence through entry into a common market could stimulate demand for greater democracy within China as well, and thus to a repeat of the events of 1989.

It is difficult, if not impossible for an outsider to predict the consequences of these various costs and benefits in terms of China's willingness to enter a common market. But since China currently has many of the economic benefits of such a market without politically costly policy changes, I would not expect rapid action on China's part to accelerate or join in such movement. That might change after 1997 when Hong Kong becomes part of China, which could lead to its reduced intermediary role. Over the same period of time many of the present generation of leaders who go back to the Revolution will have left, which could bring in a new structure of power as well as other attitudes and ideas. Finally if a common Asian market were established, or is threatened to be established without China, this could significantly reduce China's access to Asian markets and direct investment. The economic costs of that might well force China to become a member; in turn other Asian members, by providing economic aid, might reduce some of the economic costs of membership to China, and thereby encourage it.

B. India

What about the political constraints within India to membership in such a regional economic community? I believe that India would benefit very significantly in economic terms from joining an Asian common market. Today India's volume of foreign trade in the world as a whole, and within Asia in particular, is far below that of China. With a reduction in its protective policies, and an upgrading of its industrial technology and greater access to foreign markets through imports and direct foreign investment, India would have a more efficient industrial base, to go with its already able entrepreneurs and its relatively less expensive but educated and skilled labor force. It would have a capability to produce world-competitive goods over a wide technological range from textiles and leather products at the lower extreme through medium-tech motor vehicles to high-tech electronic and computer products. It has also a middle and upper income population, in absolute numbers exceeding 100 million people, that offers a potentially large internal market for such products. Producing for such a market would yield scale economies that would further reduce production costs and enhance expert competitiveness. But to take advantage of such potentialities the Indian government would have to further extend the reforms currently underway to reduce protection and permit direct foreign investment, both of which would also be necessary for its entry into an Asian common market.

In the mid-1980s, under Rajiv Gandhi, India embarked upon a major series of reforms to reduce controls within the country. These had the effect of increasing competition within industry significantly. But the reform process bogged down in political conflicts, as well as in fiscal problems that contributed to serious foreign exchange difficulties. The past reforms did not continue over a sufficiently long period to do away with the complex administrative and regulatory mechanism, nor did they deal other than marginally with foreign trade and foreign investment. The current set of reforms seem to be far broader in their coverage, and more thorough in their efforts to reduce complexity, than those of the past.

Apart from ideological issues the political difficulties in decontrolling industry reflect the fact that some Indian industrialists in the past have benefitted substantially from the monopoly rents gained by using the controls to prevent competition. Political figures at local and national levels, as well as bureaucrats who administer the controls, have also gained either by contributions to their parties for elections, or by personal income-raising corruption. India, like China, has a large number of industrial firms, many government owned, which are unprofitable at present, and which would be further threatened if the country were freely open to foreign products. Large public subsidies maintain these firms today. Such marginal enterprises employ a large number of the workers in industry, and if they were forced to close industrial unemployment would rise by a large amount. Clearly any reform program to reduce protection would have to be gradual to permit those workers to be supported while they sought new jobs, and to be retrained for such work. As in the case of China, foreign aid might help in carrying through such a transition.

One indication of the number of excess workers in India in the past, and of the limited employment effects of the reforms of the 1980s, is the fact that while the index of manufacturing production rose by 80 percent from 1981-88, there was little or no increase in the number of employed workers in the manufacturing sector.[21] If India were able to double its 1989 export volume in the relatively short-run by joining an Asian common market this would have a profoundly stimulating effect upon industrial production, and future employment in manufacturing. (That export volume would still be well below that of China in 1989). If the direct increase in employment were accompanied by a widespread extension of subcontracting from larger to smaller enterprises the income and employment multiplier effects to the rural areas could be major, as they were in China over the past decade.

While there would be political costs associated with the reforms that would be necessary to join an Asian common market those costs have apparently diminished today compared to five years ago. This is indicated by the greater willingness of the Indian government today to adopt and implement such reforms. There is a wider public recognition and demand that economic growth should be speeded up and that the benefits of that growth should be more widely dispersed than in the past. India's political leaders recognize that their political future in a democracy may well depend upon their ability to achieve those economic results, and this achievement too might ease India's serious ethnic and religious conflicts. Ideological opposition to the reforms has also decreased. It is recognized that controls and corruption are not a necessary part of socialism and that greater reliance upon the market may be preferable to direct controls. There is also of course general knowledge of the Soviet economic collapse, which may contribute to wider acceptance of the reforms among intellectuals.

One difference between India and China in making the institutional changes for entry into a common market is that India already has a working macroeconomic control system that would permit its economic policy-makers to adjust Indian macro-performance to maintain a stable rupee/yen currency relationship. There would also not be as intense a degree of nationalist antagonism to Japan in India to establishing the Yen as the key regional currency as there might be in China.

There would be substantial gains for India from joining an Asian regional market with the probable increase in its foreign trade and direct foreign investment resulting from membership. It would call for a strong political leadership within India willing to extend the policy changes required for this, and to persuade both the important demand groups within the political system and the voting public that such steps are necessary and broadly beneficial. This in turn is heavily dependent on a continuously expanding Asian and world market for industrial exports. Without that expansion India's entry into a static Asian common market would only create fear of Indian competition in the Asian countries and strengthen reluctance to accept India as a member. The result then would be the worst of both worlds for both India itself, which would lose the possible benefits of entry, and for the other Asian countries, the peoples of which would not gain the lower prices arising from India's potential comparative advantage in the production of a large variety of manufactured products.

III. SUMMARY CONCLUSIONS

Thus to conclude, today China has many of the benefits of the possible Asian common market achieved through its "open door" reforms of the 1980s, and its close economic relationships with Hong Kong and Japan, as well as its growing contacts with Taiwan and Korea. If those benefits can be maintained without the changes that might be required to join an Asian market-changes which could be politically costly-there would be little incentive for China to join an Asian market in the short run. This could however change sharply if such a market became in fact established by 1997 and China including Hong Kong, was not a member. That would be economically very costly for China, possibly forcing it to reconsider and to adopt the policies to become a member.

As far as India is concerned the potential economic gains of membership in a common regional market would be very significant in the short run, but would call for an intensification of the current reform program to open the country to foreign trade and investment. There are political and immediate economic costs of such an intensified reform program but an effective political leadership might well be able to overcome opposition by stressing the greater potential economic benefits in the medium and longer run from the reforms. An economic reform-minded leadership is in place today. The willingness of other Asian countries to accept India in an extended regional market depends in turn upon the continued growth of the Asian market. Indian membership would contribute to such growth by opening the potentially large Indian market to exports and investment from the other Asian countries, as occurred in the case of China after 1980.

NOTES

1. M.J. Dutta, "Asia-Pacific Economic Cooperation: Structure of a Common Economic Region," *Journal of Asian Economics*, vol. 3, no. 1 (1992), pp. 1-27; "Economic Regionalization in Western Europe: Asia-Pacific Economies (Macroeconomic Core: Microeconomic Optimization)," *American Economic Review*, vol. 82, no.2 (1992), pp. 67-73; and his 1990 paper, "The United States a Pacific Economy: New Dimensions in U.S.-Asia Economic Cooperation" (typed).
2. Dutta, "Asia-Pacific Economic Cooperation," p. 3.
3. H.W. Arndt, "Anatomy of Regionalism" (typed), 1992.
4. For this purpose Asia is defined to consist of the countries east of Afghanistan and south of Russia on the mainland, plus the eastern island countries in the Pacific and Southeast Asia, and Sri Lanka.
5. Dutta, "Asia-Pacific Economic Cooperation," pt. V and the Appendices of "The United States a Pacific Economy"; J. Riedel, "Intra-Asian Trade and Foreign Direct Investment," *Asian Development Review*, vol. 9, no. 1 (1991), pp. 111-146; Asian Development Bank (ADB), *Key indicators of Developing Asian and Pacific Countries*, vol. 22 (July, 1991), esp. Tables 4, 26-30 and the Country Tables in Part 3. I am using those statistics as given, not making any attempt to reconcile them.
6. ADB, *op cit.*, Table 26 on p. 35.
7. Riedel, *op cit.*, pp. 126-127.
8. For the 1970s see G. Rosen, *Contrasting Styles of Industrial Reform* (Chicago, 1992), p. 92; for 1989 see ADB, *op. cit.*, Table 26 (p.35) for 1989 exports and Table II (p. 20) for GNP.
9. ADB, *op. cit.*, pp. 116-117 and Riedel, *op. cit.*, Table 7, p. 132.
10. See Riedel, *op. cit.*, pp. 136-139 on this.

11. ADB, *op. cit.*, p. 117; H. Harding, *A Fragile Relationship: The United States and China since 1972* (Washington, DC, 1992). Quote on p. 190; U.S. figures in Table A-2, p. 364.
12. Riedel, *op.cit.*, p. 143 for quote and pp. 139-143 for data; Harding, *op.cit.*, Table A-9, p. 369.
13. ADB, *op. cit.*, pp. 154-155 and Table II, p. 20; Riedel, *op. cit.*, Table 7, P.132.
14. ADB, *op. cit.*, p. 155 and 157.
15. Rosen, *op. cit.*, pp. 106-107; Harding, *op. cit.*, Table A-7, p. 368; Riedel, *op.cit.*, p.140.
16. For quotation see Harding, *op. cit.*, pp. 337-338; also see p. 339.
17. See "Aid Consortium Goal is Proposed" in *India Abroad*, June 19, 1992, p. 24; and "India: The Awakening Giant," Interview with D.R. Pendse in *Economic Reform Today*, Winter, 1992, p. 26.
18. See "Long Shunned, Taiwan is Wooed," *India Abroad*, July 10, 1992, p. 24 and the two articles "Becoming More Competitive" and "Computer Giant Widening Base" in *India Abroad*, July 17, 1992, p.
19. One of the most perceptive broader analyses of such issues in the Asian context is A. Elek's "Pacific Economic Cooperation: policy choices for the 1990s," *Asian-Pacific Economic Literature*, vol. 6, no. 1 (May, 1992), pp. 1-15.
20. R.W. Stevenson, "A Unifying Europe Tries to Dot Its 'I's'," *The New York Times* (Chicago ed.), November 16, 1992, p. C1.
21. ADB, *op. cit.*, Manufacturing Production Index in Table 24, p. 33; Manufacturing Employment, pp. 150-151.

REFERENCES

Arndt, H.W. (1992). "Anatomy of Regionalism," (typed).

Asian Development Bank. (1991). *Key Indicators of Developing Asian and Pacific Countries, 22* (July). Manila.

Dutta, M.J. (1992). "Asia-Pacific Economic Cooperation," *Journal of Asian Economics, 3*(1), pp. 1-27.

———. (1992). "Economic Regionalization in Western Europe: Asia-Pacific Economies (Macroeconomic Core: Microeconomic Optimization)," *American Economic Review, 82*(2), pp. 67-73.

———. (1990). "The United States a Pacific Economy: New Dimensions in U.S.-Asia Economic Cooperation" (typed).

Elek, A. (1992). "Pacific Economic Cooperation: policy choices for the 1990s." *Asian-Pacific Economic Literature, 6*(1), pp. 1-15.

Harding, H. (1992). *A Fragile Relationship: The United States and China since 1972*. Washington DC: Brookings.

Pendse, D.R. (1992). "India: The Awakening Giant." Interview in *Economic Reform Today*, Winter.

Riedel, J. (1991). "Intra-Asian Trade and Foreign Direct Investment," *Asian Development Bank Review, 9*(1), pp. 111-146.

Rosen, G. (1992). *Contrasting Styles of Industrial Reform*, Chicago: University of Chicago Press.

Stevenson, R.W. (1992). "A Unifying Europe Tries to Dot Its 'I's'" *The New York Times* (Chicago ed.), November 16. *India Abroad* (Chicago ed.), issues of June 19, 1992, p. 24; July 10, 1992, p. 24 and July 17, 1992, p. 24.

For Further Reading:

Garnaut, R. and Liu Guoguang (Eds.), (1992). *Economic Reform and Internationalization:* China and the Pacific Region, St. Leonards, NSW, Australia 1992. (This was read after my paper was written; it has many articles dealing with related themes with respect to China).

CONVERGENCE AND COHESION WITHIN THE ASEAN-4

David Jay Green

I. INTRODUCTION

The Association of Southeast Asian Nations (ASEAN, initiated in 1967 by Indonesia, Malaysia, Philippines, Singapore, and Thailand, and joined by Brunei in 1984) has been an important forum for discussions concerning regional economic cooperation. One recent study prepared for the ASEAN Standing Committee put the matter very simply: "There is a growing convergence of views within ASEAN as to the viability of enhanced ASEAN economic integration."[1] The most concrete plans came in a 1992 meeting in Singapore which called for the establishment of an ASEAN Free Trade Area (AFTA), which would focus on a common tariff system providing for uniform tariff rates on trade by members with other, non-member states. AFTA builds on previous plans for enhanced cooperation which have been primarily directed towards encouraging regional trade through a set of common tariff and trade policies.[2]

Research in Asian Economic Studies, Volume 6, pages 61-92

ISBN: 1-55938-918-4

Much of the impetus for regional economic cooperation in the Asia-Pacific area has been stimulated by similar discussion in Europe: the European Community (EC) is an archetypal association for the rest of the world. M. Dutta (1992a and 1992b), for one, has noted the influence of the evolution of European regional institutions on planning in the Asia-Pacific region. This was also a theme in Sahathavan Meyanathan and Ismail Haron (1987). Under the recent Maastricht treaty, the EC agreed to move further by finalizing plans for a rather complete economic integration. The treaty has not been accorded uniform acceptance in all countries and, more importantly, it appears to have been derailed as a result of incompatible monetary and exchange rate policies and performance. However, given the commitments by the member countries, any discussion of the future of the European Community must take the Maastricht Treaty as a starting point.

Although there is currently little support for any far-reaching political integration in the ASEAN region, the European experience still provides a powerful lesson for policy-makers; even those with relatively modest goals for regional cooperation. This is true even for the ASEAN countries which have hitherto focused rather narrowly on trade matters. We argue that, in terms of the ability to implement even simple trade-pacts, in the future, a purely tariff-oriented framework will prove too slender a foundation to survive. Our thesis is that trade pacts rest on implicit pictures of how trade will develop, and sharp, divergent movements in exchange rates could easily disrupt the expected patterns and the agreement could prove politically difficult to maintain. Trade compacts call for at least some minimal relative stability in exchange rates. Moreover, capital flows, including foreign direct investment activity, are as important to a developing economy as exports. With the development of national and regional capital markets, it is not inconceivable to think that relative interest rates could become the staple of conversation and concern fully as much as exchange rates currently are. In this event too, smooth economic relations may depend on maintaining some common stability for financial and monetary variables. This need has not been unrecognized. For example, referring again to the ASEAN Secretariat study noted above, we find: "Increasing intra-ASEAN economic linkages underline the need for greater macroeconomic consultation, cooperation, and harmonization, including macroeconomic and fiscal policies ... ." (Philippine Institute for Development Studies (1992, p. 3)).

Reflecting this concern, this paper asks whether or not the ASEAN economies appear to be moving in a direction that will support greater cooperation. The answer would seem to that there has indeed been considerable commonality in both performance and policy. Economic cohesion in the ASEAN region appears significant even when compared to the European experience where formal agreements linked government policy in an attempt to further economic coordination.

In support of this conclusion, the analysis below examines the extent to which the ASEAN-4 economies; Indonesia, Malaysia, Philippines, and Thailand, are following similar lines with respect to specific measures of either economic policy or performance. Singapore and Brunei were not included in the ASEAN grouping in this preliminary analysis: both countries are rather atypical in the region as high per capita incomes and small populations provide very different development patterns and policy questions. To establish a reference standard a group of EC countries were selected; the EC-4 comprising France, Germany, Italy, and the United Kingdom. The European countries were chosen to represent the core group of the larger economies present in the association.

As suggested above, in this paper we take the simple position that it is far more likely that any moves towards deeper economic integration will succeed if the economies are moving along similar growth and development pathways.[3]This is the explicit premise underlying the current plans in Europe as noted in the Maastricht Treaty, signed 7 February 1992, which was to set the stage for a proposed economic and monetary union (EMU): "Resolved to achieve the strengthening and the convergence of their economies and to establish an economic and monetary union including, in accordance with the provisions of this Treaty, a single and stable currency."[4] In this plan, four criteria were chosen to signify for individual countries the readiness for tighter economic integration. These included; price stability, sustainable fiscal policy, stable foreign exchange rates and common patterns for long-term interest rates.[5] Specific measures of these "convergence criteria" were also adopted:[6]

i. With respect to price stability, the inflation rate for each country is to be compared to the average of the lowest three inflation rates among all the countries in the EC. Performance would be considered satisfactory if a country's inflation was within 1.5 percentage points of this average.
ii. With respect to fiscal policy, two measures were noted: the deficit of the national government would have to be less than 3 percent of GDP, and the public debt ratio would have to be less than 60 percent of GDP.
iii. Exchange rates, set under the previous existing exchange rate mechanism, must have been stable enough over the last 2 years not to have suffered a devaluation. This means that the exchange rates should not have changed more than 2-1/4 percent off their central values.
iv. Long-term interest rates would be measured against the average of the three countries with the most price stability, and success determined by whether or not a country was within 2 percentage points of this target.

The Maastricht treaty emphasizes the attainment of a set of standards at one point in time. With the exception of requiring a two year track record for exchange rates, the remaining criteria specify targets for a given year. While this provides for an administratively simple judgement, otherwise it does not appear to be defensible. What is likely to be important from the standpoint of establishing a sustainable framework for cooperation is not the momentary achievement of some goal, but the ability to maintain a common and mutually compatible set of results over a period of time, in spite of changing external and internal conditions. The very example of the European monetary system being derailed, at least temporarily, by incompatible interest rates and exchange rates would seem to prove the case. No less an authority than Helmut Schlesinger(1992, pp. 116), President of the Deutsche Bundesbank has stated that "A meaningful test requires that the test is passed not only in 'periods of fine weather,' but also at stormy times." Reflecting those considerations, in this paper, we will presume that there is a need for a group of countries to show common trends over a decade to be considered convergent economies.

The analysis in this paper proceeds by examining a series of measures including exchange rates and monetary and fiscal policy variables such as interest rates and money supply growth rates. The principal focus will be on exchange rates as being the variable most important to inter-country economic relations. Other variables will receive attention roughly in relationship to their expected influence on exchange rates. Thus, working from somewhat of a monetarist framework, a good deal of attention will be paid to interest rates but significantly less to fiscal policy variables.The basic data were taken from the International Monetary Fund's *International Financial Statistics*. Specific details concerning the data set are available from the author. Identical series or measures could not be found for each country, but typically consistent data were available over the period 1970 to 1990.

The principal statistical tool used to indicate convergence was a reliability index, the standardized coefficient $\propto$ (Cronbach's standardized coefficient alpha).[7] This statistic, commonly used in psychometrics and in educational testing, arises from looking at the collection of national measures for each variable as separate and distinct measures of some underlying "true" variable. Thus Thai inflation and Philippine inflation will be seen as separate measures of some underlying ASEAN-4 inflation rate. The question then is how reliable are the individual national measures as indicators of the underlying variable. If we use X_i to stand for the ith country's reading on the unobservable variable X, then the $\propto$ statistic is calculated as:

$$\alpha = \frac{k}{k\text{-}1} \left(1 - \frac{\sum_{i=1}^{k} Var(X_i)}{Var \sum_{i=1}^{k} X_i}\right),$$

where *Var* refers to the sample variance and for both groups of countries, $k = 4$. The $\propto$ coefficient is bounded from above at a value of 1.0 but can have large negative values when the individual measures diverge from one another. If there is any suggestion that the individual country measures differ by a scale factor, the $\propto$ coefficient will only be a lower bound for the maximum likelihood reliability index. (An addendum to this paper presents a more detailed analytical presentation on this subject.) As a result, it is common in this form of analysis to use standardized variables—variables deflated by the sample standard deviations.[8] In this case, the coefficient becomes a relatively simple transformation of the average bilateral correlation coefficient.

$$\alpha = \frac{kr}{1 + (k\text{-}1)\, r},$$

where r is the average value of the correlation coefficients, ρ_{ij}, across the different pairs of countries (X_i and X_j):

$$r = \frac{2}{k\,(k\text{-}1)} \sum_{all\ i,j:}^{k} \sum_{i<j}^{k} \rho_{ij}\,.$$

To examine critically the issue of cohesion, using annual data, we measure the $\propto$ coefficient over 10 year periods, and look at the rolling change in the 10-year measure. The 1979 coefficient $\propto$ then uses data from the years 1970 through 1979; the 1980 measure from the years 1971 through 1980. The use of decades as a base is somewhat arbitrary, however, it allows the latest data point to include the period of time after the second oil shock. The second oil shock resulted in severe disruption to international trade and capital flows and was often accompanied by considerable confusion of policy. The last data point varies from series to series depending on the availability of data, but in all cases the last data point in the generated series of $\propto$ coefficients only utilizes data after 1979.

The computer program used provides not only the $\propto$ coefficients for the group but also for the group after removing one member at a time. The latter set of statistics provides an efficient manner for checking if any one country is most obviously out of step with the others.

II. EXCHANGE RATES

We start our analysis by looking at exchange rate movements. As Martin Feldstein noted "Exchange rate targeting has become a central focus of all discussions of international economic cooperation" (1988, p. 5).

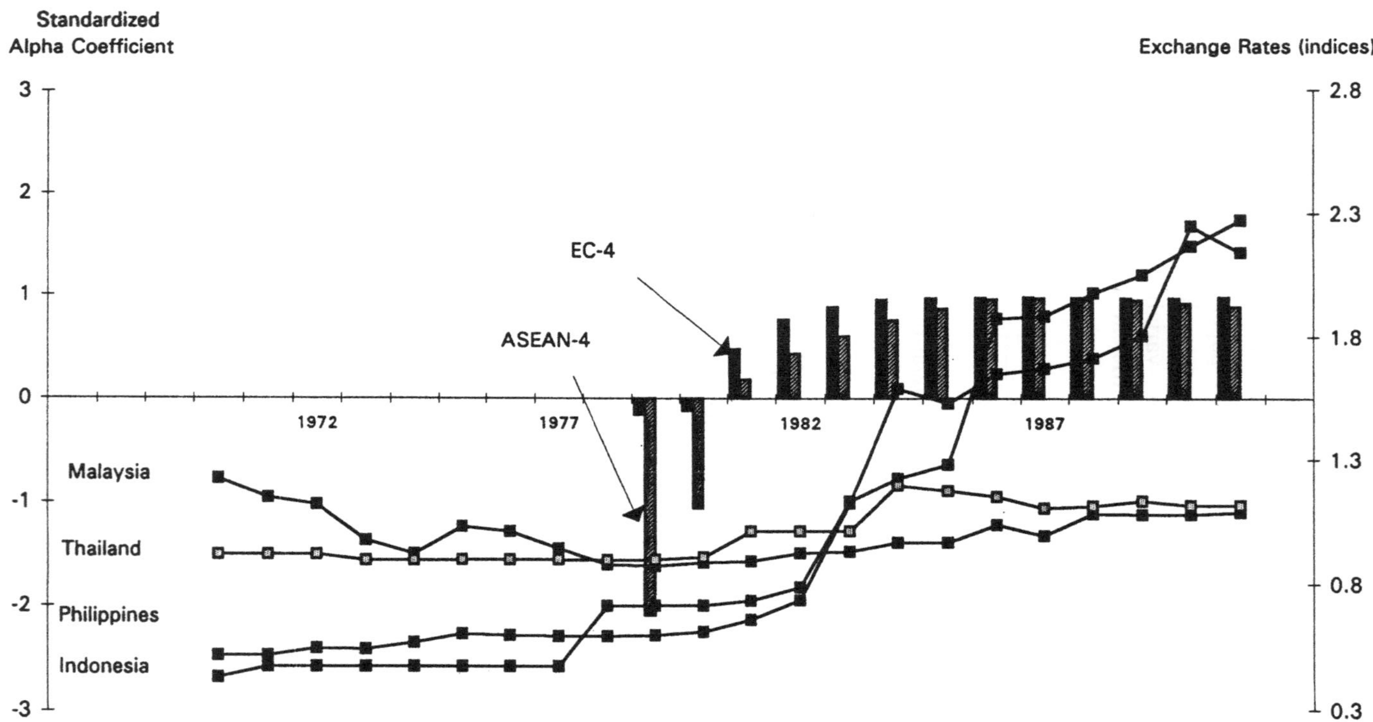

Figure 1. Nominal Exchange Rates

The exchange rate, after all, is the means by which domestic economic signals are translated to the rest of the world. The Maastricht Treaty recognized the importance of stable exchange rates as a foundation for European integration and set definite stability targets. Figure 1 contains the exchange rate indices (with mean values set to 1.0) for the ASEAN-4 countries as well as the $\propto$ coefficients for both the ASEAN-4 and EC-4 groupings. In all cases, the national currency that can be exchanged for one US dollar is the basic measure so that increases in the exchange rate imply depreciation and decreases in the exchange rate imply appreciation of the home currency. The results are striking: both the EC-4 and the ASEAN-4 groupings show strong convergence with $\propto$ coefficients moving from negative values to values greater than .90 for most of the later part of the 1980s and early 1990s.

The data in Table 1 provide more details on the numerical relationships underlying the $\propto$ coefficient calculations. The average correlation coefficient, between different national exchange rate movements, over the period 1981 to 1990, for the ASEAN-4, is 0.75 and the $\propto$ coefficient is 0.92. In this period of time, in general, the exchange rates for Thailand appear to have moved with the least sympathy with those of the other countries: the $\propto$ coefficient for the three other countries, Philippines, Indonesia, and Malaysia is 0.98. In part this reflects the post-1984 trend for the Thai baht to appreciate during a period in which other currencies are depreciating, particularly those for the Philippines and Indonesia.

The degree of convergence for exchange rates in the ASEAN-4 is striking given the complete lack of formal cooperation and the rather different exchange rate regimes. The European countries achieved average bilateral correlation coefficients of just under .90 during the decade 1981 through 1990, however, much of this was due to a formal system linking currencies. In accounting for this cohesion of exchange rates in the ASEAN-4, we should note that, although all the ASEAN-4 countries have flexible exchange rates, they are subject to varying amounts of Government influence through intervention activities. The

Table 1. Exchange Rate Convergence

Pearson Correlation Coefficients (ρ) for Standardized Variables
observations = 10, decade: 1981-1990

	Philippines	*Indonesia*	*Malaysia*	*Thailand*
Philippines	1.00	0.917	0.875	0.714
Indonesia	0.917	1.00	0.952	0.520
Malaysia	0.875	0.952	1.00	0.531
Thailand	0.714	0.520	0.531	1.00

Average $\rho = 0.752$
Standardized α Coefficient = .924.

Indonesian Government is most explicit (and probably the most consistent) in attempting to manage the currency. In particular, in recent years the rupiah has been set under a general policy of supporting a diversification of exports away from oil (World Bank, 1992a, p. 30). There has been an explicit attempt to maintain, and perhaps even enhance international competitiveness through aggressive foreign exchange rate adjustments. Primary consideration for the Indonesian Government in affecting changes in the rupiah has been developments that could result in shifts in exports and imports.

The Central Bank of the Philippines also heavily intervenes in foreign exchange markets, but currently does not attempt to closely manage the currency, taking the position that the market for foreign exchange must determine the overall movements in the exchange rate. However, the Central Bank has concluded that the foreign exchange market has tended to reflect current account developments. For example, sharp changes in the terms of trade, leading perhaps to increasing trade deficits, could be expected to increase the potential for a foreign exchange market reaction leading to an eventual depreciation in the peso. In support of this, the Central Bank has argued that the single most important signal of impending sharp changes in the peso has been the level of official gross international reserves, which responds to changes in the trade, or more broadly, the current account (Zialcita, 1991).

In Thailand, where the baht has generally been 'fixed' by the Government, trade considerations have also been important. This was very clear in 1984 when, in response to U.S. dollar appreciation, the baht was depreciated 15 percent against the dollar and tied more closely to other major currencies. In this action, an important consideration was "to increase the competitiveness of Thai exports … ." (Wibuslwasdi and Tanvanich, 1993 p. 9). The subsequent growth of exports was considered a sign of the success of the actions.[9]

If it is true that exchange rate movements have strongly reflected external sector developments, then the issue of exchange rate stability must be examined further by looking at the movements of real exchange rates; nominal exchange rates adjusted for relative movements in price levels. That is, it is real exchange rates that affect current account balances, and any attempt by the market or by official intervention to equilibrate imbalances in the current account must be taken with respect to the real exchange rate.

Figure 2 illustrates the recent experience by using real effective exchange rates for the ASEAN-4, calculated using a trade weighted basket of currencies. The comparable series for the European countries were only available from the mid-1970s so that the rolling decade measure for the $\propto$ coefficient could only be started in the mid-1980s. The figure shows that, even throughout the turbulent decade of the 1970s, ASEAN-4 real effective exchange rates exhibited some commonality in movements. Measured in 1979, the $\propto$ coefficient was slightly over 0.73 (indicating an average bilateral correlation coefficient of 0.41).

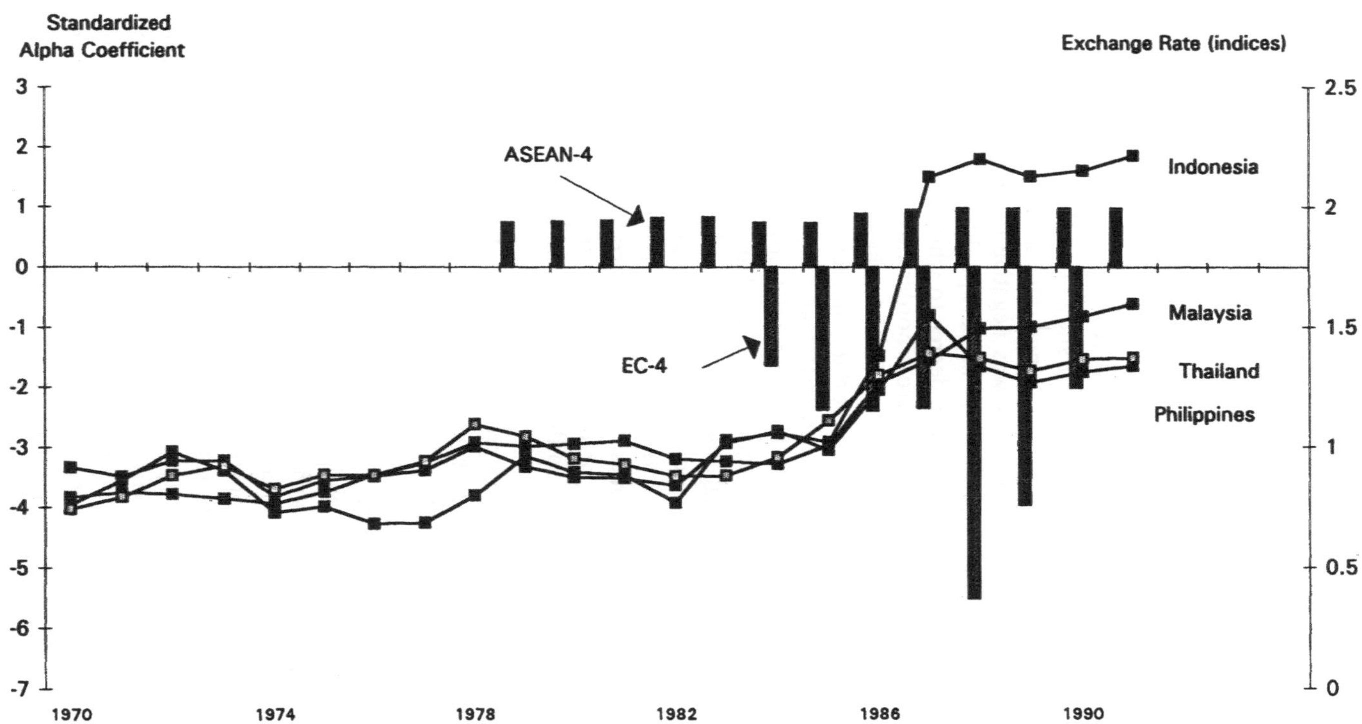

Figure 2. Real Exchange Rates

By 1991, real exchange rates appeared to converge significantly for the $\propto$ coefficient increased to 0.98 reflecting an average bilateral correlation coefficient of 0.92.[10]

The importance of maintaining competitive trading positions in international markets in official policy and as an apparent focus of currency markets, helps explain the high degree of real exchange rate convergence during this period—real rates were the "target." Official policy and foreign exchange markets ensured, for example, that domestic inflation trends were reflected in real exchange rates.

In this there appears a clear distinction between the economic structure in Europe and in the ASEAN region. Figure 2 shows that there has simply been no significant cohesion between real exchange rates in the EC-4, indeed the average bilateral correlation coefficient was negative during the period for which data were available. The situation in Europe differs from that of the ASEAN region most importantly in the degree to which capital markets are both less regulated and more open to cross-border flows, particularly those of an intra-regional nature. Unlike the ASEAN-4, where we could argue that trade developments had a very important influence on exchange rate movements, capital flows have been extremely important in Europe in determining exchange rate fluctuations and capital flows tend to be sensitive to short-run financial market movements such as changes in interest rates.

The reliability index then suggests that for the ASEAN-4 there has been considerable commonality in the overall trends for nominal and, even more so, for real exchange rates. However, common trends are, of course, not the only manner in which to view cohesion or convergence. A common trend can be discerned in spite of shocks or differential movements that can create, maintain, or even enlarge absolute differences. As noted above, the Maastricht Treaty suggests alternative criteria, which, for exchange rates rests on simple stability defined as an absence of depreciation against the European Monetary System's reference value over the previous two years. Reinterpreting this slightly, in 1991 and 1990, both Malaysia and Thailand show considerable stability with less than a 2 percent change from their end-of-year values in 1989. Indonesia, however, shows, on average, somewhat greater than 5 percent nominal depreciation per year; and the Philippines suffered a substantial shock of a 24.8 percent devaluation in 1990 that was only partly reversed in 1991.

Thus, although there may be considerable cohesion in terms of long-term trends there is clearly no room for complacency concerning the future prospects of intra-regional exchange rate stability. Moreover, during the last decade considerable efforts have been made among all of the countries to deregulate financial markets and reduce barriers to international capital flows. To the extent that domestic markets become less subject to government control, to the extent that a regionally integrated capital market develops, exchange rates should become more sensitive to financial and monetary developments.

The liberalization in the 1990s of foreign exchange transactions in the Philippines provides an example of this process. Of the more significant changes, the Central Bank raised the retention level for exporters so that they may keep up to 100 percent of their foreign exchange earnings. In the past, exporters had been able to retain only a part of their foreign exchange earnings, as little as 2 percent in some periods, and the rest had to be remitted to the Central Bank. This and other steps taken to free foreign exchange markets, have clearly eased concerns that investors would not be able to repatriate funds once committed to the Philippines and have reduced the once substantial perception of sovereign risk concerning investing in the country. One immediate result of these policy changes was large inflows of capital chasing relatively high returns to peso-denominated investments such as Treasury bills. T-bill rates in the Philippines were considerably higher, in nominal terms, than could be found in other financial markets. For instance, during the first quarter of 1992, the average annualized rate of return for 91-day T-bills was 18.6 percent, sharply higher than the average 4.1 percent return from an investment in a certificate of deposit in the United States during the same period. The inflows of short-term, portfolio capital were widely regarded as contributing to an appreciation of the peso, an appreciation that occurred in spite of a large merchandise trade deficit. In this respect the Philippine peso appears to be responding more to short-term capital market conditions and less, as it did in the past, to trade conditions.

The situation in Malaysia is similar with respect to a growing importance of financial market variables in exchange rate movements. Malaysia has, in comparison to the other ASEAN members dealt with in this paper, always had more of the characteristics of a small open economy. Tariff structures in Malaysia, for example, generally have been considerably lower than in the other ASEAN-4 countries (Sahathavan Meyanathan and Ismail Haron, 1987, pp. 21-23). As such, in earlier periods the ringgit has been heavily influenced by world commodity price fluctuations and trade developments (Noland, 1990, p. 62). By the end of the 1980s, however, with the deepening of domestic capital markets, financial variables have become important. During 1992, for example, the ringgit appears clearly to have been appreciating as a result of inflows of short-term capital. The Government has noted not just high domestic interest rates, but that the considerable expansion of the stock market has also been a focus for foreign investors (Ministry of Finance, Malaysia, 1992, pp. 229 and 261-265).

Formally in Thailand cross-border capital movements have been controlled. However, even here, a World Bank (1990, p. 6) study has noted that there is strong evidence that these controls were not fully effective—that capital has been moving in response to international financial considerations. In a similar fashion, Wibulswasdi and Tanvanich (1993) suggest that the 1990 formal acceptance of Article VIII of the IMF's Articles of Agreement, calling for the liberalization of foreign exchange regulations, simply ratified pre-existing practices. They further note that as of 1993, "exchange control is quite minimal... " (p. 21).

III. INTEREST RATES: OFFICIAL AND OTHERWISE

The recent European experience suggests that when foreign exchange markets are heavily influenced by financial markets, any attempt to stabilize relative exchange rates will place an increased premium on broad economic coordination. Exchange rates will not simply be subject to government fiat—to being determined at a Ministerial meeting—rather, interest rates and other economic variables would need to be set in a fashion consistent with the targets for exchange rates. This section continues this theme by examining the ASEAN-4 experience with financial variables, using both official and money market interest rates.

In a number of respects the analysis in this section is less informative than that for exchange rates. In particular, official interest rates, discount rates, are not as important as a policy instrument in the ASEAN-4 as in countries such as the United States or some of the European countries. With the exception of Malaysia, discount rates are not used as a primary tool of monetary policy.[11] Furthermore, throughout the 1970s and within the region generally, the broader structure of interest rates has tended to be regulated and monetary (and development) policy conducted through the use of directed credit. This has been less the case with Malaysia than with the other countries, and a reliance upon directed credit and non-market based interest rates is becoming less a feature of overall policy in the 1990s in the other countries. But as indicated, for the period of observation, central bank discount or official rates were not commonly used as an integral policy instrument. Limiting the analysis, data on Thai Central Bank rates were not available for years previous to 1976. The analysis of the European countries was similarly constrained, as the French discount rate was unchanged at 9.5 percent from 1977 through 1991. Clearly, we cannot push the examination of this variable too far.

In spite of the problems, however, the trend analysis reveals some interesting aspects. For the European countries (excluding France) the α coefficient moved from a value of 0.51 in the decade ending in 1979 to 0.90 by 1986, maintaining a level consistently above 0.78 for the 1980s (see Figure 3). It fell to 0.73 in 1990, and then precipitously to 0.29 in 1991 with the sharp divergence of the British and German interest rates. The U.K. treasury bill rate (used in lieu of a discount rate variable) fell from 14.1 percent in 1990 to 11.0 percent in 1991 while the German discount rate rose from 6 percent to 8 percent. Clearly, just as the earlier convergent movements of interest rates helped explain the stability of the exchange rate regime, the divergent movements in 1991 were setting the

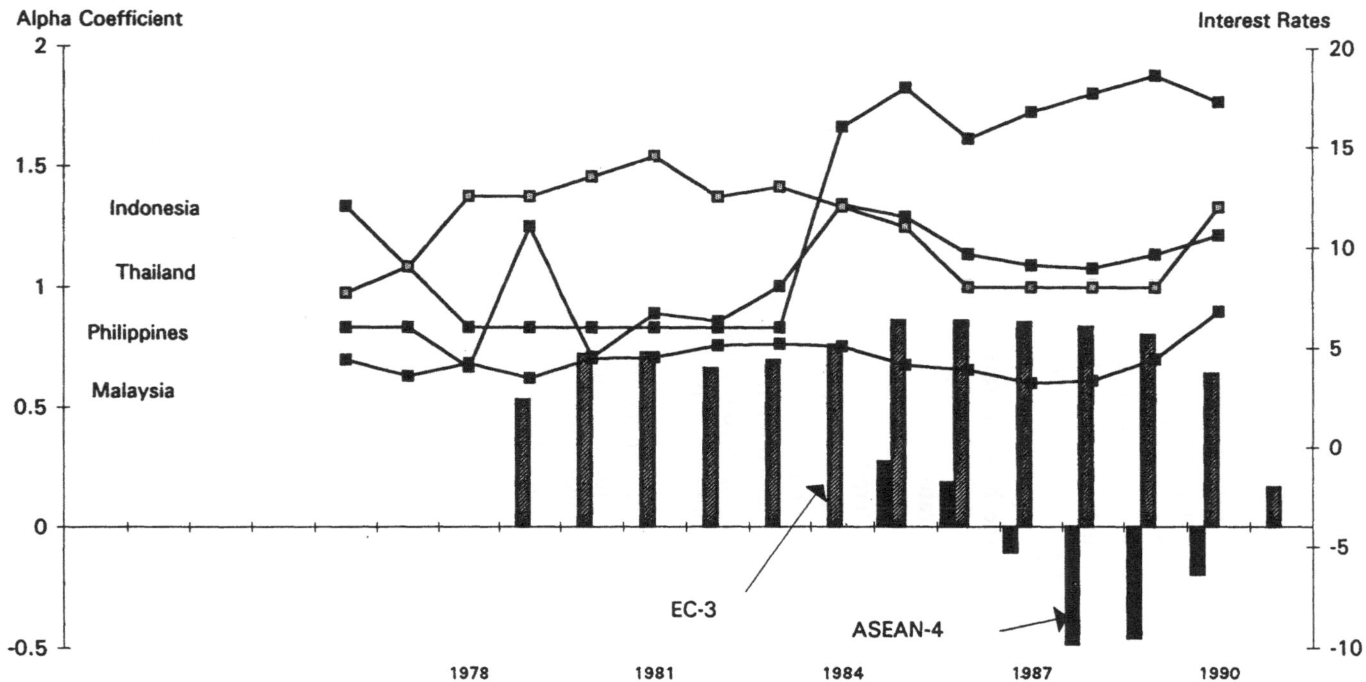

Figure 3. Official (Discount) Interest Rates

stage for the collapse of the exchange rate structure in 1992. However, the recent problems should not obscure the overall high level of cohesion in the 1980s observed for the three countries for which we have data.

For the ASEAN-3 countries (excluding Thailand) the movements of the interest rate variables show little or no real convergence. The α coefficients were often either negligible or negative. There is some significant bilateral correlation present considering just the Philippines and Indonesia. But much of the strength in the bilateral correlation comes in the mid-1980s with large changes in the interest rate measures for both countries. In 1983 a large, two-year increase in the discount rate in the Philippines led by one year a similar two-year increase in interest rates in Indonesia and set the stage for more parallel movements. Although fortuitously close in timing, the underlying causal factors for the large hikes in rates were quite different. Philippine discount rates doubled from 1982 through 1984 as a result of a financial crisis which included a brief moratorium on foreign commercial debt payments. (Juan Muñoz and Diwa Guinigundo, 1989).

The Indonesian hike in interest rates followed a decision announced in June 1983 to promote structural reform in the financial system. The actions included deregulation of bank interest rates and a movement away from directed credit policies to a more market oriented interest rate structure. Follow-up activities during the next several years included the broadening of the scope of financial instruments available to commercial banks and the start of Central Bank rediscounting activities.

The timing for the actions in both Indonesia and the Philippines were greatly influenced by factors specific to the country, but a broader perspective shows them to be part of a general world-wide movement, towards the deregulation of financial markets, leading to market determined interest rates:

> At the beginning of the 1980s, the development of financial sectors in most countries of Southeast Asia was hampered by numerous restrictions, an absence of competition and poor non-bank financial services. Progressive financial liberalization and deregulation started to take place in all countries.... In recent years, the pace of financial reforms has accelerated considerably (Asian Development Bank, 1992, p. 33).

Examples of financial market deregulation, in addition to the previously mentioned Indonesian actions, are easy to find in the ASEAN-4, throughout the latter half of the 1980s.

1. The importance of capital market developments in Malaysia has already been mentioned. Malaysia, although moving to restrict foreign controlled banking interests in the country (through the Banking and Financial Institutions Act of 1989), has seen an expansion of the industry supported by the underlying rapid economic growth, deregulation of

certain key interest rates, and a considerable expansion in the scope of complementary capital markets such as the stock market.

2. In the Philippines, deregulation of interest rates in the late 1980s was joined by nearly complete foreign exchange control deregulation in 1992.
3. Thailand, which saw perhaps the slowest pace of deregulation through the 1980s, witnessed however a burst of activity at the end of 1989 with the deregulation of interest rates and steps to encourage more cross-competition in both banking and non-banking financial industries (Wibulswasdi and Tanvanich, 1993, pp. 22-25). As in Malaysia, a deepening of the stock market has been an important feature.

In view of the general movement towards less regulated financial markets, money market instruments (short-term financial assets) were examined for indications of cross-country patterns in cohesion. Figure 4 provides the basic picture of ASEAN-4 data and ∝ coefficients for both regional groupings.

The European data on money market interest rates provides a picture similar to that discussed above for official interest rates: considerable cohesion was seen for money market interest rates during the mid-1980s, with ∝ coefficients above 0.90, but a divergence could be clearly noted in the late part of the decade. In particular, German money market interest rates more than doubled from 1987 to 1990, and continued to rise from 1990 to 1991 as interest rates in the other countries fell.

In the ASEAN region, money market interest rates showed a generally higher level of cohesion than was seen from the discount rate data: over the entire period 1977-1990 for which the ∝ coefficient could be assembled, a mean value of 0.68 (for six decade measures) was registered. While the cohesion is not extremely tight, convergence is noted with the ∝ coefficients generally increasing in value during the last few years.

Examining the issue from another standpoint, Andrew Sheng (1987), looked at interest rate differentials between 1984 and 1986, for a number of key rates, and found some shrinkage in what had been a "fairly wide disparity" between countries (including Singapore). Using our data on money market rates, there does appear to be some reduction in cross-country differentials from the high points reached in 1984. The average (absolute) cross-country interest rate differential for money market rates in 1984 was 10.0 percentage points. This dropped sharply by 1986 to 3.5 percentage points. After that, to 1990, the average differential widened, staying, however, in a fairly narrow range of 5.9 to 6.7 percentage points. In terms of maintaining stability for exchange rates and capital flow patterns, these interest rate differentials for money markets may be as important as the trends examined above. Within increasingly deregulated financial markets, money market rates—suggesting base rates for activity by commercial banks—could well become key signals in the regional capital market.

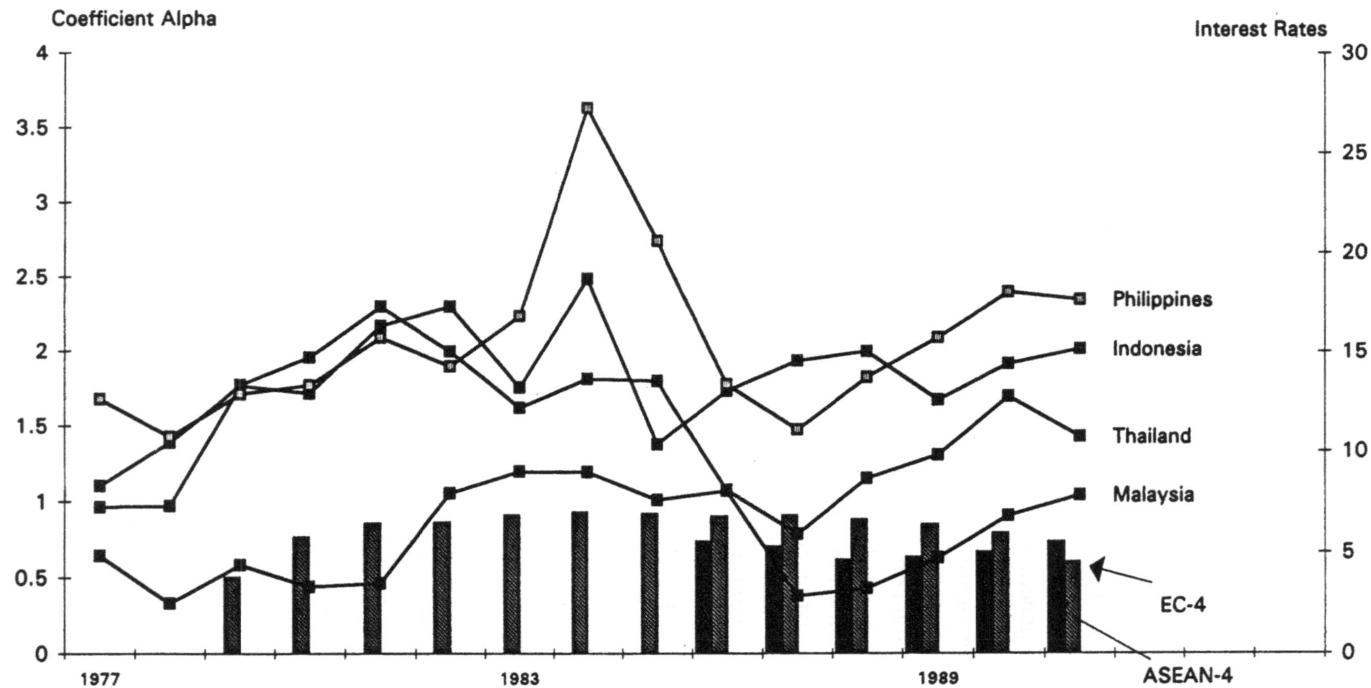

Figure 4. Money Market Interest Rates

IV. MONEY SUPPLY GROWTH

The analysis above has suggested that, in the ASEAN-4, in the course of continued deregulation, we can expect an increased presence of financial market related developments in the determination of exchange rates and interest rates. Government policy is likely to shift in emphasis from the active management of exchange and interest rates to a greater concern with targeting the money supply, both as a channel of influence for government policy to affect real variables and as a signal of future policy. The EC has recognized the importance of some degree of commonality in monetary policy as a prerequisite for closer economic integration. Schlesinger (1992, p. 115) was quite clear on this matter:

> The goal of stage one of the European Economic and Monetary Union, which started on July 1, 1990, is to gear member states' monetary policies more to the requirements of monetary stability—and thus of exchange rate stability—and to improve budgetary discipline wherever this is imperative for an Economic Union.

Figure 5 shows that there has been some degree of cohesion in money supply growth rates in the ASEAN-4.[12] This is especially true relative to the experience in the EC-4. The $\propto$ coefficient for the EC-4 fell precipitously in 1987 continuing through 1990 when the value dropped to -0.8. The 1987 bulge in the U.K. money supply and the 1990 German money supply jump were two obvious events contributing to divergent monetary tracking but the problems appeared to be more broadly based.

In contrast to the EC-4, the ASEAN-4 shows surprising cohesion. The 1983 Philippine experience when money supply growth touched 30 percent is the most noticeable outlier. This occurred when the money supply growth rates of the other countries, particularly Malaysia were shrinking. Overall, however, the ASEAN-4 show positive cross-correlation in most time periods.

The preceding discussion provides some answers as to why the experience in the EC-4 and the ASEAN-4 appear to have been so different. The discussion on interest rates and exchange rates suggests that, in the EC-4, money supply targets were secondary policy goals to the maintenance of stability for interest rates and exchange rates. Specified levels for interest rates and, more importantly, exchange rates were the primary targets for government policy and the money supply was one tool to meet these targets. This is clear from the sequencing of events: the overall European Community arrangement on exchange rates fell apart in 1992 and interest rates started diverging in 1991 but money supply growth rates showed divergent trends since the late 1980s and became obviously divergent in 1990. Problems in the EC over a lack of cohesion appear to have been building.

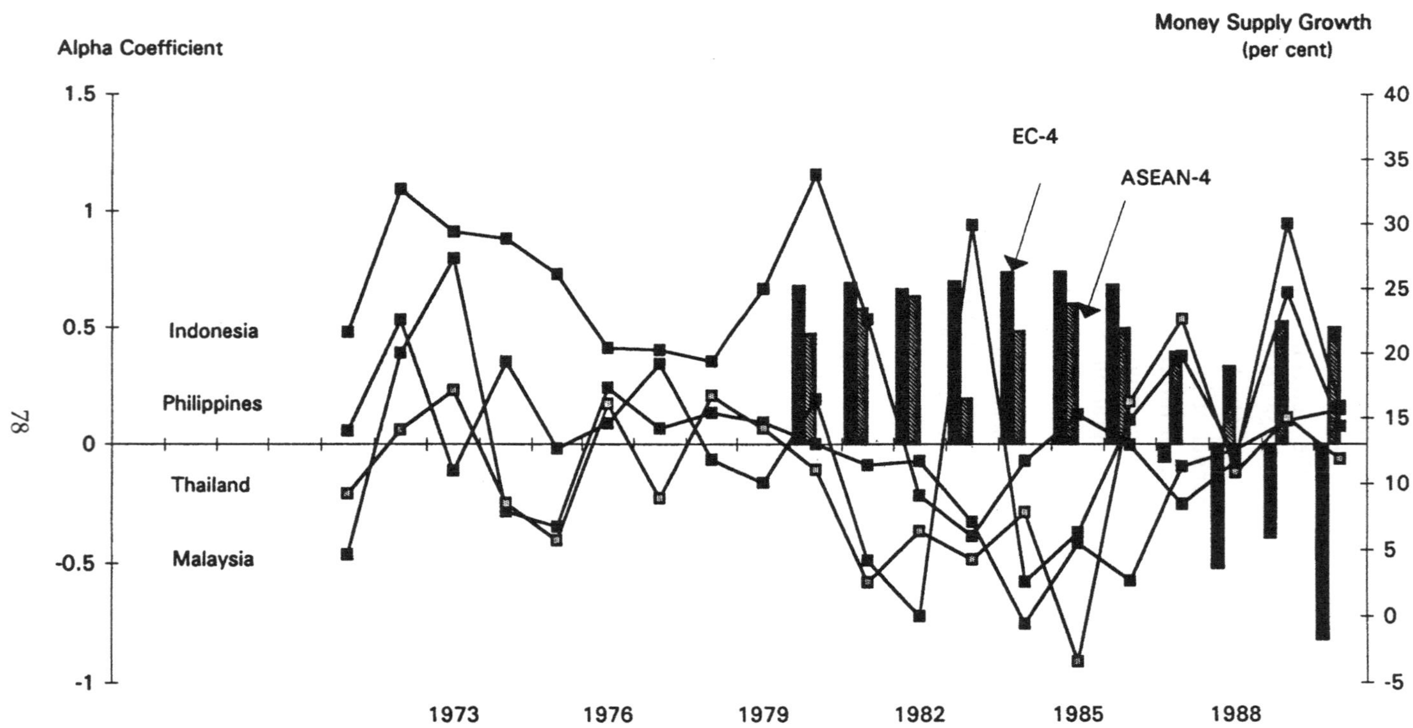

Figure 5. Money Supply Growth

During the same period of time, in the ASEAN-4, there was less of a reliance upon market based interest and exchange rates and more ability to attain targets for these variables by decree. This left the money supply for satisfying other concerns. Money supply growth could be used to provide an adequate liquidity base for aggregate demand management, to provide for growth, to deal with inflation, and for easing government financing problems. In the ASEAN-4, similar money supply paths reflect the considerable commonality in growth patterns for the economy and for government deficits. This is likely to change. Without repeating the earlier discussion, in looking into the future, continued deregulation and an increased openness of financial markets could have serious implication for the ability of governments to manage interest rates. This is likely to mean that financial market developments will have to be taken into consideration in determining money growth. There will be less freedom for the central bank money managers.

V. GOVERNMENT FISCAL BALANCE

A principal tool policy instrument in the ASEAN-4 has been the level of government spending and the size of the government budget deficit. Fiscal policy, macroeconomic management has been widely used as a stimulus for growth, to help control inflation, and to redress external imbalances. Of course, these conflicting concerns can be a hinderance to policy determination. Clear tradeoffs are often visible between tighter policy to limit inflation or trade deficits and easier policy to maintain real growth. Control of the government budget is, moreover, not a perfect policy tool: the traditional characterization of fiscal policy as having relatively long implementation lags is quite apparent in the ASEAN-4 arena. Moreover, vested interests, including government bureaucracies, make reductions in spending exceedingly difficult. As a result there is considerable momentum or inertia in patterns of government spending. In spite of these considerations, within the ASEAN region, with the exception of Malaysia, there appears to be considerable cohesion in government spending (see Figure 6). With the exception of Malaysia, over the 20 years of comparable data, for the three other countries, for 58.7 percent of the observations fiscal balances are smaller than 4 percent of GDP. With specific respect to the Maastricht Treaty, all but Malaysia would have passed the test of having a budget deficit of less than 3 percent of GDP in the final year of our sample period.

Malaysia appears to be quite different, with 9 of 20 observations showing a fiscal deficit of more than 9 percent of GDP. World Bank staff analysis of Malaysia suggests that the attempt to maintain real economic growth in the early 1980s, a period of growing trade deficits, resulted in a rise in public sector budget deficits to 19 percent of GNP by 1982. The restoration of smaller

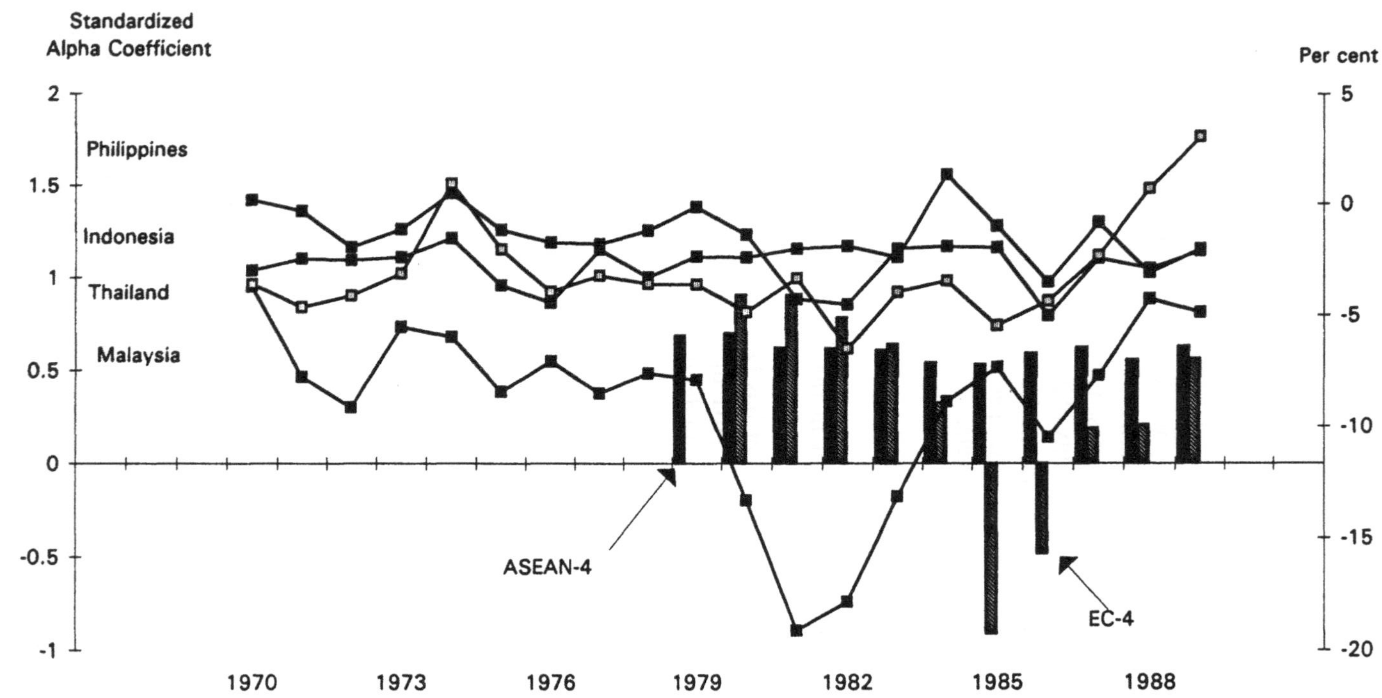

Figure 6. Government Fiscal Balance as Share of GDP

macroeconomic imbalances was only accomplished by sharp cutbacks in federal deficit spending through 1985 (World Bank, 1992b, pp. 2-3).

The last few data points show an interesting trend for Thailand: the fiscal deficit turned into a surplus. Indeed by mid-1993, Thailand had run 5 straight years of budgetary surpluses; a result of extremely high growth rates for the economy.

The emergence of budget surpluses raises an interesting issue. The Maastricht Treaty speaks only of a restriction on deficit spending, it does not speak of any problems associated with surpluses. However, stability in capital flows can be disrupted by sharp movements of government budgets into surpluses fully as much as by movements into deficits (or larger deficits). Of course, as mentioned, government budget surpluses are quite rare, especially during the 1980s. There may simply be an element of realism to the implied suggestion that government budgetary surpluses, to the extent that they pose a problem, can be ignored.

Returning to a discussion of trends, government budgets, deficits or surpluses, are important to successful economic cooperation or integration through their impact on the ability to stabilize or coordinate monetary and exchange rate policy. Schlesinger (1992, p. 118) is quite clear on this. Greater economic and financial integration, he argues, reduces the normal checks to unrestrained deficit spending. In particular, national interest rate reactions to sharp changes in government borrowing will be muted through the access to broader regional capital markets at fixed exchange rates. Thus greater economic coordination or integration which attempts to stabilize exchange rates may well demand intergovernmental agreements on the extent to which governments could practice deficit spending and on the means by which governments could finance these deficits. Dutta (1992a), for one has identified the "absence of a higher order of convergence of fiscal problems..." as a serious problem inhibiting coordinated monetary policy and exchange rate stability (p. 9).

Given the limited objectives of this paper, it would not do, however, to overemphasize this point. Coordinating deficit spending is not likely to be as immediate a concern as coordinating the use of other policy instruments. The data we are using to represent the European experience suggests, for example, that there has been little cohesion in government budget balances since 1984. Nonconvergence in this variable is not as serious a matter as it might be for nonconvergence in interest rates. More importantly, the ASEAN group has the *luxury* of seeing their economies as small economies from the standpoint of world capital markets, changes in government borrowing habits are not necessarily destabilizing to interest rates if there is open access to international markets and the perception of risk on the part of international lenders does not change. The EC-4, particularly Germany, cannot be so sanguine.

Even in the EC there is some suspicion that this variable is not considered important, in and of itself, especially not the value for any particular year. Rather it may have been included in the Maastricht Treaty as a generalized indicator for the overall *health* of an economy. *The Economist*'s tongue-in-cheek suggestion that, in reality, convergence in Europe means "a group of 12 closely-knit, high-growth, low-inflation, rich economies with scarcely a budget deficit in sight" supports this contention (December 14, 1991, p. 54). In a more formal sense Dutta (1992b, p. 68) suggests that economic regionalism, to be successful, may demand the provision of a "Macroeconomic Core" or common standards for economic policy. The Maastricht Treaty may have included in its slim list of criteria for membership in a closer economic union, a reference to fiscal budget deficits as a screening mechanism to keep out governments facing economic difficulties; to require that countries conform to the macroeconomic core of policy directions. This suspicion is reinforced by the inclusion in the Maastricht treaty of limits on public debt (as a function of GDP) as an additional requirement for a "passing grade." In a European context, changes in public debt may be simply, in Helmut Schlesinger's terms, a matter of "budgetary discipline."

For the ASEAN-4, a group of developing governments, the issue of public indebtedness should be seen in a different light. Unlike European countries, the ASEAN-4 have a large number of developmental responsibilities including the provision of infrastructure. "Budgetary discipline" must be weighed against the imperatives of providing for the infrastructure investment so crucial for high rates of sustainable growth. Notwithstanding this, it is interesting that, except for Malaysia the public debt to GDP ratio is less than the 60 percent European limit. Using the latest comparable data available (either 1989 or 1990), the public debt (both domestic and foreign) to GDP ratio was a low for Thailand at 19.6 percent; for Indonesia it was 39.7 percent; and for the Philippines, 51.4 percent. In Malaysia, as mentioned earlier, government spending represents a large part of the total economy and this is reflected in a debt to GDP ratio of 88.6 percent.

Concerning Malaysia, it is important to note that 73.1 percent of the total public debt in 1989 was denominated in ringgit, not foreign currency. This is an important distinction. Judging fiscal soundness or discipline in a small developing country demands different criteria than would be used in the European context. The normal measures used to evaluate the fiscal soundness of developing countries would be the total external or foreign exchange debt. For a developing country it is not so much who incurred the debt, public or private, but whether the debt is denominated in foreign exchange. In part this is simply a recognition that debt service burdens change uniformly with currency devaluations and currency devaluations are themselves often a function of changes in indebtedness. On these grounds, in the ASEAN context, there appears to be a general increase in creditworthiness. In all four cases, total external debt appears to be shrinking in importance: as a function of GNP, external debt has declined in the ASEAN-4 in the late 1980s. This appears to be true even for the Philippines where, in spite of the gradual decrease in the external debt burdens, external debt problems are clearly present.

The discussion in this section suggests that issues surrounding economic integration and public finance decisions should not be considered simply from the standpoint of convergent or divergent trends. Fiscal policy is not preeminently important from the standpoint of contributing to the stability of international cooperation agreements. Nor do the European-oriented considerations appear to be relevant in the context of ASEAN development needs. More so than in Europe, the developmental responsibilities of the ASEAN-4 countries argue that fiscal decisions, decisions concerning debt, should not be viewed in absolute terms, but rather against the general growth in the economy.

VI. INFLATION AND GDP GROWTH

In addition to the criteria discussed above, the remaining condition for economic integration contained in the Maastricht Treaty refers to inflation. As a measure of economic performance, it will be discussed along with an additional measure of performance, economic growth. With the exception of the Philippines, the ASEAN-4 have generated generally stronger economic growth than most economies—developing or otherwise. The average annual growth rate for GDP in the ASEAN-4 during the decade of 1971-1980 was 7.4 percent; and in 1981-1990, 5.2 percent (see Table 2). The Philippine experience was clearly atypical with growth falling from an average annual rate of 6.0 percent during the earlier decade to only 1.0 percent during the latter 10 year-period (Asian Development Bank, 1992, p. 288). The ASEAN-4 average compares quite favorably to growth in the industrialized world where real GDP grew on average 2.8 percent per year in the decade ending 1990. More importantly regional growth was quite a bit better than found in most of the developing world where growth rates often averaged less than 3.0 per year during 1980 to 1990. For example, during the decade of the 1980s, growth rates in sub-saharan Africa averaged 2.2 percent per year, while Latin American economies grew on average only 1.6 percent per year.[13] It is this record of growth within the ASEAN-4 region that prompts observers to label particularly Thailand and Malaysia as the next *Tiger Economies* or NIEs (Newly Industrializing Economies). The experience on inflation is somewhat less enviable, but still reasonable, especially given the growth records.

Table 2. ASEAN-4 GDP Growth and Inflation Performance

	GDP Growth Rates		*Inflation Rates*	
	1971-80	*1981-90*	*1971-80*	*1981-90*
ASEAN-4 Averages	7.4	5.2	13.6	7.5
Indonesia	7.7	5.5	17.5	8.6
Malaysia	7.8	5.2	6.0	3.2
Philippines	6.0	1.0	14.8	13.0
Thailand	7.9	7.8	10.0	4.4

Source: Asian Development Bank, *Asian Development Outlook*, 1992, Tables A9 and A1

Figure 7 provides the summary ∝ coefficients for both the ASEAN-4 and the EC-4 for these two measures of economic performance—GDP growth rates and inflation. The generally moderate levels of commonality given for both performance indicators for the ASEAN-4 appeared to take turns for the worse in the mid-1980s. This results from a combination of external and internal events. The Philippines produced negative growth rates at the end of the Marcos Administration when financial sector distress and a cessation of international commercial lending to the country contributed to considerable economic disruption. Falling oil prices, however, took a toll on the Indonesian and Malaysian economies at the same time. As a result the actual convergence in economic performance as dictated by some underlying common development process is overstated by the coincidence of the most important shocks of the decade.

More importantly, the recent convergence in performance for the ASEAN-4 does not provide a guide to how shocks might be transmitted between countries in the event of tighter economic cooperation. In comparing the ASEAN-4 with the EC-4, on GDP growth rates, it is clear that it is not just a matter of less convergence, there was also less stability overall on the ASEAN-4 side. Over the whole period, the standard deviation in the growth rates ranged from 2.7 to 4.7 percentage points for the ASEAN-4, but only 1.4 to 2.3 for the EC-4. In the ASEAN-4 case, the variability increased from the 1970s to the 1980s, in the EC-4 it appears to be diminishing. As might be expected, the variability is also greater for inflation with the ASEAN-4 varying between 3.4 and 7.3 percentage points, against the EC-4 with 2.0 to 4.3 over the period. In both country groupings, for inflation, there appears to be a general decline in variability in the second half of our sample. The smaller degree of cohesion in performance in the ASEAN-4 should not be a surprise: smaller economies are simply likely to be more subject to shocks than bigger ones. But, it is also probably true that the higher the variability

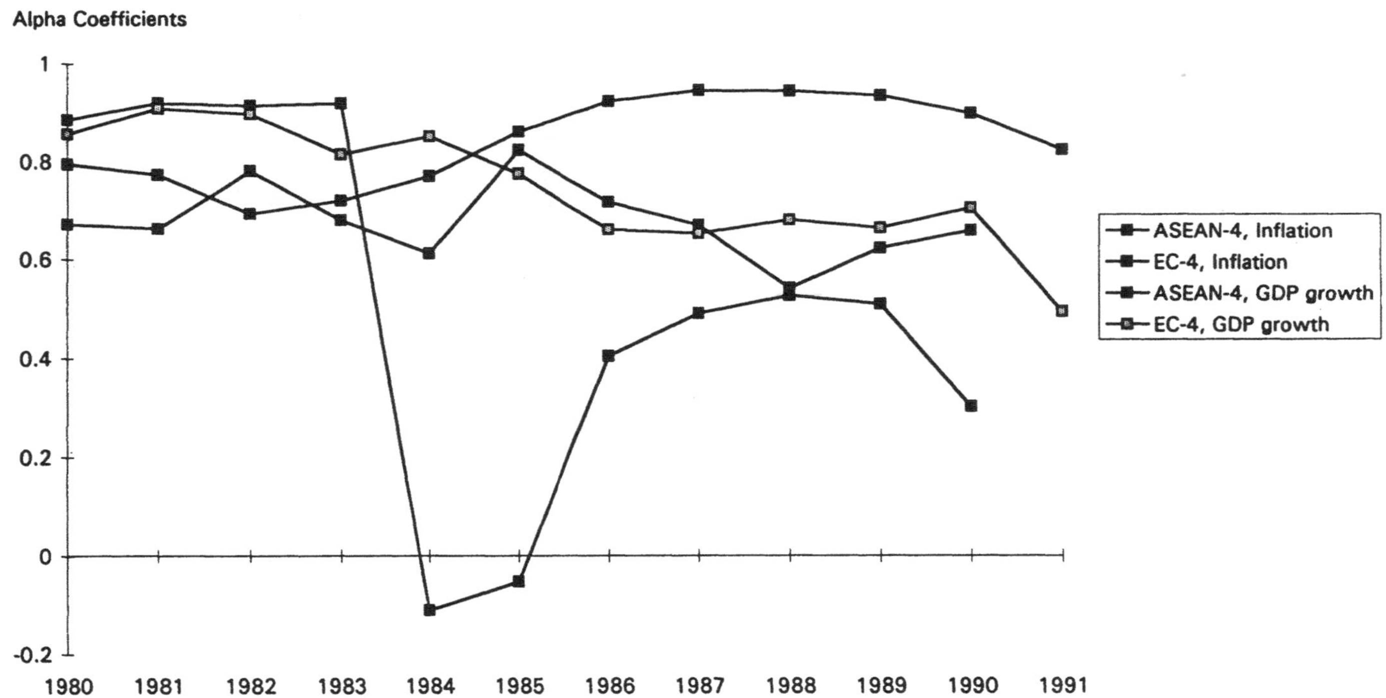

Figure 7. Inflation and GDP Growth Rates

of performance the more difficult it will be to establish tighter mechanisms for economic cooperation.

VII. SUMMARY AND CONCLUSIONS

There is a clear and continuing discussion concerning economic cooperation in the ASEAN region. What form, what institutional structure this enhanced cooperation may take is, as of yet, unknown. But the discussion regarding possible structures is likely to take its cues from the ongoing moves for closer economic integration in the EC. This paper examines a core group of four ASEAN countries: Indonesia, the Philippines, Malaysia, and Thailand. On the basis of a small set of policy and performance measures these ASEAN-4 were compared to a core group of EC countries: the EC-4 comprising France, Germany, Italy, and the United Kingdom.

The focal point of the discussion was the degree of cohesion, within each country grouping, for different measures of economic performance and policy including exchange rates, interest rates, and money supply growth rates. Analytically a reliability index, the $\propto$ coefficient, was used to indicate convergence or cohesion.

Exchange rate stability is the likely focal point for any future economic integration in the ASEAN region, as it has been in Europe. Here the data suggest that there was both considerable cohesion in *nominal* as well as for *real* exchange rates. However, increasingly deregulated and open financial markets imply that, in the future, exchange rates will have to be consistent with broader financial market variables. Thus continued stability of exchange rates will require concomitant stability in financial and monetary policies.

In looking at comparative monetary policy, strictly speaking little convergence in trends for interest rates can be seen. Somewhat more cohesion can be seen for money supply growth rates. However, in both cases, the underlying institutional structure is clearly changing and the past results may not be indicative of future tendencies.

Looking beyond variables that can have an immediate impact on exchange rate structures, fiscal policy variables exhibited considerable nonconvergence in the late 1980s. However, three of the ASEAN-4 have relatively limited Government fiscal imbalances, and would appear to pass the kind of tests for greater economic integration that the European countries have adopted. With respect to performance indicators, including real growth rates and inflation, in the late 1980s considerable cohesion was apparent. This is so even in comparison to the EC-4 countries which, having linked their fortunes, might be expected to show much greater measures of convergence and cohesion.

APPENDIX

Notes on the Construction of a Reliability Measure

A. *Model Structure*

1. Let C_i be an economic variable for some country (i) such as inflation or money supply growth, with an additional index (t) indicating the year (C_{it}). In the discussion in the paper, there are four countries i=1,2,3,4 and typically 10 years, t=1,..., 10.

2. Assume that for each possible observation, there is an underlying true measure (T_t), which is stochastic, but which does not depend on the country; and a stochastic error (e_{it}) which is country specific:

$$C_i = T + e_i, \qquad i=1,\ldots k\ (t=1,\ldots n)$$

3. In this expression, and in general, the subscript for the time period has been left off. It should be stressed that the underlying population, over which the observations are drawn is signified by the time subscript; that is, all expectations are taken with respect to time. Further notational conventions include the following:

a. E signifies the expectation across all possible time periods for a random variable;
b. ρ signifies the covariance of two random variables; and
c. σ^2 signifies the variance of a random variable.

4. The stochastic properties assumed are given below.

a.	$E(e_i) = 0$;	the error terms have mean zero.
b.	$\rho(e_i, e_{i'}) = 0$; for all $i \neq i'$	the error terms are uncorrelated across countries, for all time periods.
c.	$\rho(e_i, T) = 0$; or all i	the error terms and the driving variable are uncorrelated across countries and for each country for all time periods.
d.	$\sigma^2(e_i) = \sigma^2(e_{i'})$	the variance of the error terms are equal across countries for all time periods.

B. *The Parallel Model*

5. The assumptions that the expectation of T is not dependent upon the country and that the variances of e_i are equal across countries and over time are crucial parts of what is termed the *parallel* model in measurement theory. "In the context of the classical test theory model, which deal only with first- and second-order moments, parallel measurements are completely interchangeable." (Novick and Lewis, 1967, pp. 3-4).

C. *The Reliability of a Composite Measure*

6. The traditional discussion of reliability uses a composite measure (**C**) that is the *sum* of the individual country variables.

$$\mathbf{C} = \Sigma_i \, c_i$$

In this case, the composite measure can then be expressed in terms of the component aggregates:

$$\mathbf{C} = \mathbf{T} + \mathbf{e},$$

where

$$\mathbf{T} = \Sigma_i \, T = kT \text{ , and } \mathbf{e} = \Sigma_i \, e_i.$$

7. *Reliability* is defined as the ratio of the variance of an underlying true variable to the variance of the observed variable $\sigma^2 (\mathbf{T})/\sigma^2 (\mathbf{C})$

8. The test statistic can be generated by noting that:

$$\rho \, (C_i,C_i') = \rho(T+e_i, T+e_i') = \sigma^2 \, (T) + \rho \, (T,e_i) + \rho \, (T,e_i') + \rho(e_i,e_i'),$$

Since the last three terms on the left-hand-side of the equation are zero,

$$\rho \, (C_i,C_i') = \sigma^2(T).$$

9. Moreover, because the variance of the true-valued variables (T) are constant across countries (across all i=1,...k), the variance of the aggregate true valued-variable (**T**) can be simply expressed:

$$\sigma^2(\mathbf{T}) = k^2\sigma^2(\mathbf{T})$$

10. Given this, the variance of the composite measure **C** can be expressed as:

$$\sigma^2(\mathbf{C}) = \sigma^2(\Sigma_i \mathrm{C_i}) = \Sigma_i \sigma^2(\mathrm{C_i}) + \sum_{i \neq i'} \Sigma \rho (\mathrm{C_i}, \mathrm{C_{i'}}) = \Sigma_i \sigma^2(\mathrm{C_i}) + \mathrm{k(k\text{-}1)}\sigma^2(\mathrm{T}).$$

Thus the variance of the composite measure is composed of k^2 terms, which can be segregated into two separate summations, one over n and the other over $k(k\text{-}1)$ terms. Substituting in from the expression for $\sigma^2(\mathbf{T})$:

$$\sigma^2(\mathrm{C}) = \Sigma_i\sigma^2(\mathrm{C_i}) + [(\mathrm{k\text{-}1})/\mathrm{k}]\sigma^2(\mathbf{T})$$

11. This provides for a solution for the variance of the composite true measure (**T**) in terms of functions of the observed variables, $\mathrm{C_i}$ and **C**:

$$\sigma^2(\mathrm{T}) = [\mathrm{k}/(1\text{-}\mathrm{k})][\sigma^2(\mathrm{C}) - \Sigma_i\sigma^2(\mathrm{C_i})]$$

12. As a result, the reliability of the composite measure can be expressed in terms of the population variances for C_i and the aggregate **C**.

$$\sigma^2(\mathrm{T})/\sigma^2(\mathrm{C}) = \frac{\mathrm{k}(\sigma^2(\mathrm{C}) - \Sigma_i\sigma^2(\mathrm{C_i}))}{(\mathrm{k\text{-}1})\ \sigma^2(\mathrm{C})}$$

13. The right-hand expression is the coefficient alpha or Cronbach's coefficient $\alpha(\mathbf{C},\mathbf{T})$). Thus, under the assumptions of the parallel model given above, the reliability of the composite measure is equivalent to the coefficient alpha:

$$\sigma^2(\mathrm{T})/\sigma^2(\mathrm{C}) = \alpha(\mathbf{C},\mathbf{T}).$$

14. Because Ci and **C** represent observable variables, their population variances in the expression in para. can be replaced by the maximum likelihood estimates, the sample statistics, to construct a reliability measure.

D. The Reliability of the Average of a Group of Variables

15. The derivation given above for reliability is in terms of the composite measure **C**, which is the sum of the individual variables. In economics it is not common to sum individual measures together. It is, however, common to use a mean or an average of a group of different measures. It is trivial to show that the reliability for the composite **C** is equivalent to the reliability for an average, **C′**, of the individual variables ($\mathrm{C_i}$). Define **C′** such that:

$$\mathbf{C}' = \Sigma_i \mathrm{C_i}/\mathrm{k} = \mathbf{C}/\mathrm{k}$$

In which case,

$$\mathbf{C}' = \mathbf{T}' + \mathbf{e}',$$

where

$$T' = \sum_i T/k = T/k, \text{ and } e' = \sum_i e_i/k = e/k$$

Thus the reliability for the mean of the observed variables would be

$$\sigma^2(T')/\sigma^2(C') = \sigma^2(T/k)/\sigma^2(C/k) = (k^2/k^2)\,\sigma^2(T)/\sigma^2(C) = \sigma^2(T)/\sigma^2(C)$$

E. Robustness with Respect to Violations of the Parallel Model Assumptions

17. A crucial aspect of the above derivation is given in para. 5, that the different measures are considered strictly parallel, in particular, that the true variable determines the value of the observed up to an additive stochastic variable. A more general model, for example, might simply specify that the true values are related by a linear function. That is, we redefine the model so that

$$C_i = \mathbf{T}_i + e_i, \qquad i=1,\ldots k\ (t=1,\ldots n), \text{ and}$$

$$\mathbf{T}_i = a_i + b_i\mathbf{T} \qquad i=1,\ldots k\ (t=1,\ldots n).$$

Thus each T_i can be expressed as a linear transformation of any other T_i': $i \neq i'$.

18. Using a derivation only slightly more complicated than that given above, it can be shown that the coefficient alpha is a *lower* bound for the reliability test. (Novick and Lewis, 1967). Thus, a violation of the strict assumptions concerning the parallel model, results in the equality in para. 12 being replaced by an inequality:

$$\sigma^2(T)/\sigma^2(C) \geq \frac{k(\sigma^2(C) - \Sigma_i\,\sigma^2(C_i))}{(k-1)\,\sigma^2(C)}$$

or

$$\sigma^2(T)/\sigma^2(C) \geq \alpha(C,T).$$

19. Thus it can be said that the coefficient alpha is a conservative measure of reliability: the statistic is biased against providing for the acceptance of the hypothesis that the composite measure is a reliable measure of the true variables.

ACKNOWLEDGMENT

The views expressed are those of the author and do not represent the Asian Development Bank. The author is grateful to David Edwards, Richard W. A. Vokes, and Director P. McCawley of the Asian Development Bank and to participants at the ACAES conference on "Economic Regionalism: Macroeconomic Core and Microeconomic Optimization," at Chulalongkorn University, Bangkok (December 1992), for useful comments and criticism.

NOTES

1. Philippine Institute for Development Studies and the ASEAN Secretariat, Secretariat, *ASEAN Economic Cooperation for the 1990s*, Manila 1992.ASEAN Economic Cooperation for the 1990s, 1992, p. 1. This study refers to the possibility of expanding current arrangements in the region to encompass greater institutional economic integration as the "ASEAN Free Trade Area Plus" (p. 25).
2. Other cooperative activities by ASEAN members have included attempts at regionally oriented industrial investment projects. See the short discussion in Marcus Noland, 1990, pp. 140-141.
3. This simple presumption is present in many other studies. This simple presumption is present in many other studies. See, for example Tan (1992).
4. *Official Journal of the European Communities*, vol. 35, C series 191, July 29 1992, Treaty on European Union (p. 1). Referred to as the Maastricht Treaty.
5. Maastricht Treaty, article 109j, p.20.
6. Maastricht Treaty, Protocols on the excessive deficit procedure and on the convergence criteria, pp. 84-85. See also *The Economist,* 14 December 1991, p. 52.
7. The key papers on this statistic are Lee J. Cronbach (1951) and Melvin R. Novick and Charles Lewis (1967).
8. In general, with the data used, there appeared to be little practical difference as to whether one used standardized or unstandardized variables. When standardized variables were used, either because of scale-factor differences or for presentation purposes, it is so noted.
9. Increasingly in the 1980s, Thailand has encouraged the use of *forward* foreign exchange trading. The forward market appears to be useful in part for establishing policy consistency.
10. Preliminary results reported at the ACAES conference in Bangkok erroneously suggested that real effective exchange rates had diverged somewhat during the 1980s.
11. The comment by the World Bank (1992c, p. 30) concerning the Philippines is typical: "... the discount window as a monetary policy instrument is of minor importance... ."
12. See also Sheng (1987, pp. 152-154) who suggested that there have been decreasing "disparities" for mean rates of money supply growth in the ASEAN region between the later half of the 1970s and the first half of the 1980s.
13. Data on the industrialized world were for the G-7 nations. The source of this data and for Africa and Latin America were World Bank estimates.

REFERENCES

Asian Development Bank. (1991). *Asian Development Outlook 1992*, Manila.

Cronbach, Lee J. (1951). "Coefficient Alpha and the Internal Structure of Tests," *Psychometrika*, (16/#3), pp. 297-334, September.

Dutta, M. (1992a). "Asia-Pacific Economic Cooperation: Structure of a Common Economic Region," *Journal of Asian Economics*, (*3*/1) (Spring). pp. 1-27.

———. (1992b). "Economic Regionalization in Western Europe: Asia Pacific Economies (Macroeconomic Core: Microeconomic Optimization)", *American Economic Review Papers and Proceedings*, May, pp. 67-73.

European Communities. (1992). *Official Journal of the European Communities, 35*, C series, 191, July 29, Treaty on European Union.

Feldstein, Martin. (1988). "International Economic Cooperation: Introduction," in Martin Feldstein (ed.), *International Economic Cooperation*, Chicago: University of Chicago Press, pp. 1-10.

Meyanathan, Sahathavan and Ismail Haron. (1987). "Asean Trade Cooperation: A Survey of the Issues," in Noordin Sopiee, et al., (eds.), *ASEAN at the Crossroads*, Institute of Strategic and International Studies, Kuala Lumpur, Malaysia, pp. 13-53.

Ministry of Finance (Malaysia). (1992). *Economic Report 1992/93*. Kuala Lumpur.

Muñoz, Juan Antonio E. and Diwa C. Guinigundo. (1989). "Exchange Rate Policy in the Philippines," *CB Review*, XLI/#11, November, pp. 11-21.

Noland, Marcus. (1990). *Pacific Basin Developing Countries: Prospects for the Future*. Institute for International Economics, Washington.

Novick, Melvin R. and Charles Lewis. (1967). "Coefficient Alpha and the Reliability of Composite Measurements," *Psychometrika*, 32(1), March, pp. 1-13.

Philippine Institute for Development Studies and the ASEAN Secretariat. (1992). *ASEAN Economic Cooperation for the 1990s*, Manila.

Schlesinger, Helmut. (1992). "European Monetary Restructuring and its Implications for Interest Rate and Exchange Rate Policies." *Journal of Asian Economics, 3*(1) Spring, pp. 111-119.

Sheng, Andrew. (1987). "Asean Cooperation in Money and Banking," in Noordin Sopiee, et al. (eds.) *ASEAN at the Crossroads*. Institute of Strategic and International Studies, Kuala Lumpur, Malaysia, pp. 139-160.

Tan, Augustine. (1992). (main contributor) "Internal Policy Consultation," in Philippine Institute for Development Studies and ASEAN Secretariat, *ASEAN Economic Cooperation for the 1990s*. Manila, pp. 82-90.

The Economist, various issues.

Wibulswasdi, Chaiyawat and Orasa Tanvanich. (1993). *Liberalization of the Foreign Exchange Market in Thailand*. Paper presented at Conference on Liberalization of the Foreign Exchange Markets in Asian Countries. Central Bank of the Philippines, January 14-15.

World Bank. (1992a). *Indonesia: Growth, Infrastructure and Human Resources*. Report no. 10470-INO, May 26.

World Bank. (1992b). *Malaysia: Fiscal Reform for Stable Growth*. Report No. 10120-MA, April 24.

World Bank. (1992c). *Philippines: Capital Market Study*. Report no. 10053-PH, February 24, vols. I and II.

World Bank. (1990). *Thailand Financial Sector Study*. Report no. 8403-TH, May 25, vol. I.

Zialcita, Edgardo P. (1991). "The Antecedents and After Effects of Four Major Devaluations in the Philippines." Central Bank of the Philippines, mimeo, August 12.

THE ASEAN FREE TRADE AREA PLAN AND INTRA-REGIONAL TRADE IN DEVELOPING ASIA

Dean A. DeRosa

I. INTRODUCTION

A number of developing countries in Asia have been the focus of considerable attention because of their strong economic growth and especially their robust export performance. The newly industrialized countries (NICs) of East Asia—Hong Kong, Korea, Singapore, and Taiwan—have received the most attention, but in recent years some less-advanced countries in Southeast Asia, particularly Malaysia and Thailand, have been identified as a possible "second wave" of Asian NICs.

In attempting to explain the economic success of these countries, many economists have emphasized the importance of "open" economic policies (e.g., Hughes 1991; Drysdale and Garnaut 1993). According to their view, when appropriately supported by sustainable monetary and fiscal policies, outward-oriented economic policies provide an environment more conducive to the

Research in Asian Economic Studies, Volume 6, pages 93-123.

ISBN: 1-55938-918-4

adoption of internationally-competitive technologies and products following the underlying comparative advantage of countries and thereby contribute to the attainment of higher levels of economic growth and welfare. In recent years, more open and liberal economic policies have gained wider acceptance not only in Southeast Asia (e.g., Indonesia), but also in South Asia where important reforms to trade, industry, and investment policies have been instituted in several countries, including India, Pakistan, and Sri Lanka. And in China, Asia's potential economic giant, the spread of special economic zones and the persistent interest of foreign investors could portend the adoption of more liberal economic policies in the future.

Frequently, discussions of the developing Asian countries also focus on problems arising from the increasing integration of these countries in the global trading system. For example, "surges" of labor-intensive exports from these countries frequently trigger suits for administered protection in Europe and the United States. But closer economic ties among the Asian countries themselves is an important feature of the emergence of the developing Asian countries in the world economy (Riedel 1991). And, although this fact often goes unrecognized, it has implications for continued robust economic growth and development in the developing Asia region, which is formed by the low-income countries of Central and South Asia, the low- and middle-income countries of Southeast Asia, and the high-income countries of East Asia.

Trade cooperation has been a shared objective of many developing countries, mainly in connection with the formation of regional systems of preferential trading arrangements designed to promote greater trade in manufactures as a spur to industrialization (e.g., Linnemann 1992). But in East and Southeast Asia, unilateral adoption, and maintenance, of relatively low levels of protection during the past twenty-five years has contributed independently to increasing economic integration in the region. Indeed, Riedel (1991) contends that intra-regional economic relations in developing Asia are expanding along discernible lines of comparative advantage. In particular, trade and investment flows among the countries in the three sub-regions of developing Asia are expanding following perceptible differences in accumulated human capital, measured in terms of education, basic labor skills, and managerial experience.[1]

Ostensively, increasing regionalism in the world economy seeks to expand trade and investment on a preferential basis within narrowly-delineated blocs of countries. This represents a potential threat to the economic prosperity of the East Asian NICs and other "emerging" countries in developing Asia whose economies have relied heavily on exports, access to foreign markets, and inflows of foreign investment. In particular, the Europe 1992 Plan to form a common monetary and customs union among the European Community and European Free Trade Area countries and the North American Free Trade Agreement to forge closer trade and investment ties among Canada, Mexico, and the United States have caused considerable alarm in Asia.

Beginning in 1995, however, greater regionalism will also become a factor within Asia, with the formation of a free trade area among the Association of Southeast Asian Nations (ASEAN). The ASEAN Free Trade Area (AFTA) plan is generally regarded as a strategic response by the ASEAN countries—Brunei, Indonesia, Malaysia, Philippines, Singapore and Thailand—to the increasing polarization of trade relations in Europe and North America. But, the new ASEAN trading arrangements are also discriminatory in nature and represent a threat to the gains from expanding intra-regional trade in Asia. They also represent a possibly forgone source of economic welfare for the ASEAN countries themselves. That is, notwithstanding that domestic political economy factors pose an important obstacle, an alternative policy of continued liberalization of ASEAN trade relations on a nondiscriminatory, most-favored-nation (MFN) basis should be expected to lead to substantially larger economic gains than the AFTA plan.

The effects of the AFTA plan on ASEAN trade relations with other countries in developing Asia are explored in the remainder of this paper using a computable general equilibrium (CGE) model that describes the trade relations of the ASEAN countries with other developing countries in Asia as well as the largest trading partners of the Southeast Asian countries, the major industrial countries. In Part II, the main features of the new AFTA plan are described. Then in Part III, the ASEAN trade simulation model is introduced, and in Part IV the results of a simulation analysis to estimate the effects of the AFTA plan on ASEAN trade relations mainly with other developing Asian countries, but also with the major industrial countries, are presented. Finally, in the concluding part of the paper, the findings of the paper are summarized.

II. THE AFTA PLAN

The Association of Southeast Asian Nations was founded in 1967. Its initial goals were mainly political and were shaped predominantly by concerns for the security of the (then five) fledgling Southeast Asian countries, often from insurgent elements within their own boundaries. Although political dimensions remain important, economic arrangements among the ASEAN countries are arguably of greater importance today (Wong 1985).

The most visible aspect of ASEAN efforts to promote regional economic cooperation is the ASEAN preferential trading arrangements (PTA) system, which was adopted in 1977 to expand intra-ASEAN trade through the extension of reduced tariffs and lower nontariff barriers on manufactured goods wholly, or substantially, produced in member countries (ASEAN 1978). Despite several stages in the evolution of the PTA, little increase in intra-ASEAN trade was achieved by the mid-1980s (Wong 1985; Meyanathan and Haron 1987). In the late-1980s, new proposals for substantially increasing the coverage of ASEAN trade arrangements were put forward, the most prominent of which was the so-called Rieger proposal (Rieger 1985). These proposals called for the establishment of a customs union among the four natural resource-abundant ASEAN countries (Indonesia, Malaysia, Philippines, and Thailand) and a free trade area with Singapore. None of the proposals for a new ASEAN trading system was adopted because they posed adjustment costs that were higher than several ASEAN countries were willing to bear (Naya and Imada 1987).

Notwithstanding the disappointing results of the PTA, the objective of increasing economic integration through expanded intra-bloc trade remained strongly embedded in ASEAN. And, in recent years it received new impetus from the increasing bilateralism of the major industrial countries and the uncertainty of a successful outcome to the Uruguay Round of multilateral trade negotiations.

In January 1992, the ASEAN heads of state meeting in Singapore announced an agreement, the so-called Singapore Declaration, to establish the ASEAN Free Trade Area, beginning in 1993 and to be fully implemented by the year 2008 (ASEAN 1992a, 1992b, and 1992c). AFTA is a bold strategy to promote trade within ASEAN. But implementing the AFTA plan has been slower than originally envisioned, because of continued concerns for adjustment costs and the distribution of economic gains. In 1994, it was agreed that the plan would not commence before 1995, but would be fully implemented ahead of schedule, by 2003.

The basic elements of the new plan are straightforward. Under what is termed the common effective preferential tariff (CEPT) scheme, each ASEAN country will seek to reduce the level of its tariffs on imports on manufactures, including capital goods and processed agricultural products but not all food, agricultural, and other natural resource commodities, to a minimum range of 0-5 percent over an 8-year period. During an initial 5-year period, the objective will be to reduce the level of tariffs to about 20 percent. Then during the remaining 3 years of the agreement, each ASEAN country will seek to reduce its tariff levels to the 0-5 percent range. Although the new scheme makes provisions for safeguard measures in cases of "serious injury" to domestic producers, the new scheme explicitly calls for the simultaneous elimination of nontariff barriers, including foreign exchange restrictions, to intra-ASEAN trade in manufactures. The new scheme also reduces the ASEAN content requirement for goods received preferential treatment from the present level of 50 percent to 40 percent.

The reductions in tariff levels are to be accomplished following schedules to be announced by each ASEAN country annually. Whether the process will in fact prove to be entirely automatic is problematic. Indeed, this uncertainty seems to be recognized in the AFTA plan itself, because the plan singles out several categories of manufactures for accelerated tariff reductions (Table 1).

Table 1. Manufactures for Accelerated Trade Liberalization under the AFTA Plan

Selected Manufactures	*SITC*	*Average Rate of Tariffs plus Para-Tariffs (Frequency Ratio of Nontariff Barriers) (in percent)* Indonesia	Malaysia	Philippines	Singapore	Thailand
Vegetable oils	22+42	29.3	4.6	31.4	0.0	49.7
		(100.0)	(0.0)	(26.0)	(4.0)	(96.0)
Cement, ceramic & glass products, gems & jewelry	66	26.1	18.3	40.5	0.0	48.1
		(100.0)	(13.4)	(33.5)	(0.0)	(8.0)
Chemicals, plastics	5	11.0	9.4	23.4	0.0	35.5
		(95.6)	(3.0)	(47.7)	(49.0)	(6.0)
Pharmaceuticals	54	4.8	3.3	17.5	0.0	30.5
		(100.0)	(0.0)	(95.0)	(95.0)	(0.0)
Fertilizers	56	0.0	0.6	22.6	0.0	10.0
		(100.0)	(0.0)	(100.0)	(0.0)	(0.0)
Rubber Products	62	10.3	32.6	33.7	0.0	52.0
		(66.1)	(0.0)	(46.3)	(0.0)	(0.0)
Leather Products	61+83	28.2	27.5	38.9	0.2	64.1
		(100.0)	(0.0)	(29.4)	(0.0)	(0.0)
Pulp	64	29.4	16.4	40.5	0.0	40.7
		(84.5)	(0.0)	(57.9)	(0.0)	(21.5)
Textiles	65+84	32.7	28.9	48.2	1.7	61.5
		(87.5)	(0.5)	(12.8)	(8.5)	(0.9)
Electronics, copper cathodes	76+77	25.2	20.5	37.4	0.0	43.3
		(80.5)	(5.4)	(98.1)	(11.8)	(15.6)
Wooden Furniture	82	42.2	40.4	52.1	2.2	63.6
		(100.0)	(0.0)	(46.4)	(0.0)	(0.0)
Memorandum Items:						
Primary Commodities	(0-4)+68	14.7	8.7	31.9	0.1	38.0
		(98.9)	(4.5)	(40.5)	(15.3)	(24.4)
Manufactures	(5-8)	19.6	16.2	33.5	0.4	42.5
	less 68	(93.1)	(3.2)	(46.3)	(14.1)	(7.8)
Selected Manufactures	—	22.8	19.3	36.3	0.4	46.4
		(92.0)	(1.9)	54.5	(12.0)	(14.3)
All Goods	0-9	18.2	14.3	33.1	0.3	41.2
		(94.7)	(3.7)	(44.9)	(14.7)	(12.4)

Notes: SITC refers to Standard International Trade Classification. Levels of import restrictions are circa-1987.

Sources: *ASEAN (1992a) and Appendix.*

This group of products is an important admixture of goods of keen interest to ASEAN exporters and policymakers. Vegetable oils and wooden furniture, for instance, are of interest to manufacturers in several of the natural resource-abundant ASEAN countries, and producers interested in expanding their output of labor-intensive apparel, other textile products, and electronic components are to be found in all member countries. Products of higher capital-intensity, such as cement, chemicals, and pulp paper, which are more likely to be outside of the present comparative advantage of the ASEAN countries (except possibly Singapore), are also to be found in the list of products targeted for accelerated trade liberalization. As seen in Table 1, the levels of tariff and NTB protection associated with these products are similar, on average, to those covering all manufactured imports in each ASEAN country. Most important, the frequency ratios of nontariff barriers are substantial in magnitude in many instances, underlining the importance of liberalizing NTBs as well as tariff measures under the AFTA plan.

III. THE ASEAN TRADE SIMULATION MODEL

A. Overview

The ASEAN Free Trade Area plan is envisioned as contributing to expansion of the global trading system. This view however is highly subjective given the essentially discriminatory nature of the new ASEAN preferential trading arrangements. Indeed, the ASEAN countries have not addressed how the AFTA plan will achieve its objectives without some diversion of trade, predominantly with the major industrial countries but also with the developing countries in Asia. The quantitative and qualitative effects of the new ASEAN trading arrangements on trade flows and related economic variables are uncertain, however, without systematic empirical analysis of the sort presented in the remainder of this paper.

A simple computable general equilibrium model, termed the ASEAN trade simulation model, is employed here to estimate the medium- to long-term effects of the AFTA plan. The model shares a number of features with other CGE models applied widely in analyses of international trade and development policy issues.[2]

In the ASEAN trade simulation model, simultaneous linear equations depict the conditions for equilibrium in markets for 27 traded goods, a single nontraded good, and labor services for each ASEAN country (excluding Brunei). Based upon the assumption of utility- and profit-maximizing behavior by consumers and producers, respectively, goods satisfy both intermediate and final demands for consumption.[3] Primary factors of production are fixed in aggregate supply and are fully employed at their value marginal product. Labor is assumed mobile between producing sectors, but other primary factors of production, such as physical capital and natural resources, are assumed specific to individual sectors. Also, although labor and other primary factors (combined) are assumed to be substitutable for one another in the production of value-added, all intermediate inputs to production and the quantum index of value-added itself are combined only in fixed proportions.[4] Aggregate expenditures on final demand are assumed predominantly determined by macroeconomic policies and other predetermined (or exogenous) conditions. Changes in revenues from import duties, however, are redistributed to consumers and accordingly are reflected in demands for both traded and nontraded goods in the model. Finally, closure of the model takes the neo-classical form of an international payments constraint that, through adjustments in exchange rates as well as other variables, requires aggregate expenditures on domestic and foreign goods to equal the sum of revenues from production plus possible sources of external financing.[5]

Following Armington (1969), traded goods are assumed to be differentiated according to their place of production.[6] Thus, the model distinguishes similar goods produced by all countries, whereby the producers of each geographically-differentiated commodity or manufactured product, as a group, face identifiable demands for their output in their home country and each importing country. The result is a system of bilateral demands for traded goods that facilitates the analysis of discriminatory tariffs and nontariff barriers to imports from non-ASEAN countries.[7]

The representation of tariffs is straightforward in the model; with exchange rates, they translate world prices for foreign-produced traded goods into domestic prices for imports. A preferential reduction of tariff rates applied to goods imported from ASEAN countries lowers the domestic price of the goods, thereby increasing demand for imports from ASEAN countries and simultaneously reduced demand for competing imports from non-ASEAN countries. Following Deardorff and Stern (1986) and DeRosa (1992), nontariff barriers are also explicitly represented in the model, namely, as tariff-equivalent measures of protection that may be reduced on a preferential basis to increase the volume of imports governed by administered protection measures. In sum, changes in trade policies represented by combinations of changes in tariffs and NTBs, along with actual or assumed values for parameters describing fundamental behavioral and technical relationships in the model, provide the basis for simulating changes in trade, production, consumption, and related variables, including relative prices and exchange rates, for each ASEAN country.

B. Parameter Values

Underlying the ASEAN trade simulation model is an extensive set of trade and industry statistics, principally for the ASEAN countries but also for their major trading partners (Table 2). The model also incorporates information about the structure of nominal protection in the ASEAN countries and assumed values for key substitution elasticity parameters. The 27 categories

Table 2. The ASEAN Trade Simulation Model: Product Categories, Elasticity of Substitution Values, and Country Coverage

Products and Values of Substitution Elasticity Parameters				
		Elasticity of Substitution		
Product Category	*SITC*	*Consumption*	*Production*	*Countries*
Primary Commodities	(0-4)+68	—	—	
Foods	0+1+22+4	—	—	*ASEAN*
Cereals (1)	041-045	3.00	1.00	
Vegetable oils & oil seeds (2)	22+42	3.00	1.00	Indonesia (IN)
Other foods (3)	—[a]	3.00	1.00	
				Malaysia (MA)
Agricultural raw materials	2 less (22+27+28)	—	—	
Textile fibers (4)	26	3.00	1.00	Philippines (PH)
Other raw materials (5)	—[a]	3.00	1.00	
				Singapore (SI)
Crude fertilizers & mineral ores (6)	27+28	3.00	1.00	
Mineral fuels (7)	3	3.00	1.00	Thailand (TH)
Non-ferrous metals (8)	68	3.00	1.00	
Manufactures	(5-8) less 68	—	—	*Other Developing Asian Countries*
Chemicals	5	—	—	China (CH)
Pharmaceuticals (9)	54	3.00	1.00	
Toiletries & perfumes (10)	55	3.00	1.00	East Asia (EA—Hong Kong, Korea, Taiwan)
Manufactured fertilizers (11)	56	3.00	1.00	
Other chemicals (12)	—[a]	—	—	South Asia (SA—Bangladesh, Sri Lanka, India, and Pakistan)
Iron & steel (13)	67	3.00	1.00	

Machinery & equipment	7	—	—	*Industrial Countries*
Non-electrical machinery (14)	71-75	3.00	1.00	
Electrical machinery (15)	76+77	3.00	1.00	United States (US)
Transport equipment (16)	78+79	3.00	1.00	
Other machinery & equipment (17)	—[a]	3.00	1.00	Japan (JA)
Other manufactured products	(6+8) less (67+68)	—	—	Australia-New Zealand (AZ)
Leather & travel goods (18)	61+83	3.00	1.00	
Rubber products (19)	62	3.00	1.00	Canada (CA)
Wood products (20)	63	3.00	1.00	
Paper products (21)	64	3.00	1.00	Europe (EU—Belgium, France, Germany, Italy,
Textiles & clothing (22)	65+84	3.00	1.00	Netherlands, United Kingdom, and
Non-metal mineral products (23)	66	3.00	1.00	Switzerland)
Furniture (24)	82	3.00	1.00	
Footwear (25)	85	3.00	1.00	
Professional equipment (26)	87+88	3.00	1.00	*Other Countries*
Other manufactures (27)	—[a]	3.00	1.00	
				Rest of the World (RW)
Other				
Nontraded goods (28)	—	—	1.00	

Notes: SITC refers to Standard International Trade Classification. Consumption elasticities refer to the elasticity of substitution in demand of similar traded goods differentiated by country of origin. Production elsticities refer to the elasticity of substitution among primary factors of production in value-added.

[a] Residual product category.

of traded goods distinguished in the model are composed of 5 broad categories of agricultural goods, crude fertilizers and mineral ores, mineral fuels, nonferrous metals, and 19 categories of manufactured products. For each category of traded goods, statistics on the bilateral imports of the five major ASEAN countries and 20 other industrial and developing countries were gathered for 1988, the most recent year for which the requisite trade statistics were available for all countries.[8] Using these data, matrices of world trade for each commodity category were constructed, identifying the origin as well as the destination of trade flows by commodity for each ASEAN country, other individual countries, and the bloc of the rest of the world.[9]

Implementing the ASEAN trade simulation model requires estimates of domestic consumption of locally-produced traded goods, or so-called internal trade flows. These flows, along with values of the parameters indicating the inter-industry structure of production in the ASEAN economies, were estimated using information gathered from consistent 1975 input-output tables for the ASEAN countries, Japan, Korea, and the United States developed by the Institute of Developing Economies (IDE 1982). In brief, internal trade flows were estimated for each traded goods category by applying the ratio of domestic to foreign demand in the 1975 input-out tables for the eight countries to the level of 1988 exports for each country in the model.[10] Inter-industry parameters indicating the shares of goods in intermediate and final demand—required in the model only for the ASEAN countries—were assumed equal to values estimated directly from the input-output tables for the five countries.[11]

Uniform values across goods sectors are assumed for two important sets of behavioral and technical parameters in the model, elasticities of substitution in demand between the geographically-differentiated products and elasticities of substitution in production between labor and other primary factors (Table 2). The values, 3.0 for the demand elasticities of substitution and 1.0 for the supply elasticities of substitution, are mainly notional values but they are within the range of econometric estimates for U.S. trade and production (Deardorff and Stern 1986; de Melo and Tarr 1992). Moreover, they do not differ substantially from those specified in other applications of both the Armington demand system and systems of separable production functions (Stern, Francis, and Schumacher 1976; Whalley 1985).

Finally, the last set of parameters employed in the ASEAN trade simulation model describes the in incidence of tariffs and nontariff barriers in the ASEAN countries, circa 1987 (see Appendix). These data are compiled from the UNCTAD inventory of trade control measures in developing countries (UNCTAD 1987, 1989). Frequency ratios of nontariff barriers provide the basis for determining the incidence of NTBs in each category of goods imported by the ASEAN countries. Then, liberalization of tariffs is depicted in the model by reductions in ad valorem customs duties for those subsets of imported goods principally affected by tariffs, and similarly the liberalization of nontariff barriers is depicted by increases in the volume of imports affected principally by quantitative and other administered import control measures.

Notably, the model also includes representation of the extent of nontariff barriers enforced in each ASEAN partner country. Thus, simulations of the model are conditional on basic aspects of administered protection levels in each industrial and developing country in the model. The frequency ratios of nontariff barriers in developing countries are compiled from the same UNCTAD inventory as the corresponding ASEAN country values. Those for the industrial countries, on the other hand, are compiled from Nogues et al. (1986) and refer to trade control measures enforced by industrial countries during the early-1980s.

The UNCTAD trade control measures data are insufficient to distinguish reliability between the preferential and general import restrictions enforced by each of the ASEAN countries in the base period (i.e., 1988), especially in light of the reported large numbers of exemptions from the former ASEAN preferential trading system for safeguard or other reasons. Thus, the model assumes that imports from all sources, including other ASEAN countries, initially face the same import restrictions on a nondiscriminatory basis. Whereas the initial tariff (and para-tariff) levels are those reported in the UNCTAD inventory, the initial tariff-equivalent rates of protection provided by nontariff barriers are problematic. In the simulations of the model, the liberalization of nontariff barriers is represented by increases of administered imports by 20 percent, in quantity terms. This represents a medium between a priori "upper-bound" and "lower-bound" estimates, of 80 percent and 90 percent respectively, of the extent to which NTBs in the ASEAN countries restrict imports relative to their (unknown) free trade levels. Finally, again for lack of more comprehensive information about trade and related industrial policies in the ASEAN countries, no attempt is made to adjust the baseline data, or the empirical model itself, for possible exemptions to tariffs or nontariff barriers extended to favored industrialists or to special investment or development projects in the national economic plans of the ASEAN countries.

C. Limitations of the Model

The ASEAN trade simulation model possesses a number of attributes, but it has some noteworthy shortcomings as well. Most important, the model yields only "partial" estimates of the international effects of the AFTA plan. This follows because the model illuminates the trade relations of the ASEAN countries in an asymmetric way, namely, involving the simultaneous adjustment of the ASEAN economies, on the one hand, but only the partial adjustment—through the adjustment of bilateral trade flows—of non-ASEAN economies, on the other hand. To the extent, however, that the ASEAN countries are mainly "small" countries in the global trading system, economic developments originating in the ASEAN countries should be expected to have only minor impacts on the economies of the major industrial countries and developing countries outside of Southeast Asia, with few (if any) significant "feedback" effects on the ASEAN economies.

More generally, the ASEAN trade simulation model shares the shortcomings of most CGE models. Beyond its comparative static design, the model is limited by its rather rigid specification of technical and behavioral relations describing production, consumption, and trade. Though these relationships provide the basis for valuable insights to the process of adjustment in traded and nontraded goods sectors in each country, they still fall considerably short of the dynamic aspects of adjustment envisioned in the pure theory of international trade where international competitive forces are frequently viewed as guiding international investment and the adoption of common production technologies across countries until relative factor rewards and prices of traded goods tend to converge in countries trading freely with one another.[12]

IV. ESTIMATES OF INTRA-REGIONAL TRADE EFFECTS

A. AFTA Plan versus MFN Liberalization Scenarios

The simulation results refer to two basic scenarios that represent the basic variants of the AFTA plan, namely, complete removal of tariffs and nontariff barriers to intra-ASEAN trade in all manufactures (Scenario I) and to intra-ASEAN trade in only the selected manufactures identified previously (Scenario II). In addition, "shadow" scenarios involving nondiscriminatory liberalization of ASEAN trade relations are considered. These latter scenarios are intended to gauge the effects of adopting more liberal policies towards imports on an unconditional MFN-basis—that is, on a, nondiscriminatory basis.

B. Simulation Results

Table 3 provides an overview of the changes in wage rates, other economywide variables, and international trade for each ASEAN country. As expected, the results demonstrate that the wider is the scope of import liberalization in terms of traded goods and partner countries, the greater is the impact on domestic variables and especially international trade flows. Thus, liberalization of all manufactures under the AFTA plan has larger effects on variables than limiting the AFTA plan to only selected manufactures. Similarly, liberalization of ASEAN trade on an MFN, rather than a preferential, basis has larger effects than either variant of the AFTA plan.

Table 3. Changes in Economywide Variables and International Trade

Import Liberalization Scenario	AFTA Plan					MFN Liberalization				
			Exchange Rates		Trade			Exchange Rates		Trade
	Wage Rate (%)	Expenditures (%)	Nominal (%)	Real (%)	Exports/Imports (millions US$)[a]	Wage Rate (%)	Expenditures (%)	Nominal (%)	Real (%)	Exports/Imports (millions US$)[a]
I. All Manufactures										
Indonesia	-0.33	0.00	-0.41	0.34	176	-7.95	0.00	-12.44	7.18	1,899
Malaysia	0.03	0.00	-0.42	0.00	432	0.82	0.00	-6.19	0.03	1,652
Philippines	0.42	0.00	0.15	0.05	135	5.03	-0.01	-10.24	0.68	904
Singapore	0.18	0.00	0.68	0.00	847	-0.50	0.00	-1.60	0.01	437
Thailand	0.47	0.00	-1.01	0.06	319	4.04	-0.05	-15.47	0.83	2,701
ASEAN	—	—	—	—	1,908	—	—	—	—	7,591
II. Selected Manufactures										
Indonesia	0.01	0.00	-0.09	0.11	108	-0.79	0.00	-5.29	2.22	841
Malaysia	-0.07	0.00	-0.38	0.00	337	0.51	0.00	-4.29	0.03	1,183
Philippines	0.24	0.00	-0.23	0.04	77	3.78	0.00	-6.46	0.45	529
Singapore	0.08	0.00	0.35	0.00	513	-0.39	0.00	-1.13	0.01	290
Thailand	0.62	0.00	-0.35	0.01	170	3.46	-0.02	-7.71	0.29	1,360
ASEAN	—	—	—	—	1,206	—	—	—	—	4,203

Notes: Simulations of the ASEAN trade simulation model using 1988 trade flows and circa-1987 import control measures as baseline data and assuming ad valorem customs duties are reduced to zero and nontariff barriers are liberalized to increase the volume of administered imports by 20 percent, on a preferential basis (AFTA plan) and, alternatively, on a most-favored-nation (MFN) basis.

[a] Per annum, measured in 1988 U.S. dollars.

With regard to the economywide variables, some seeming anomolies are apparent in the simulation results, particularly for the changes in wage rates and expenditures. The results suggest that both preferential and nondiscriminatory liberalization of ASEAN imports might lower wage rates in some ASEAN countries (Indonesia, Malaysia, and Singapore). Although these countries are generally considered relatively labor-abundant countries, the simulation results suggest that under some import liberalization scenarios the adjustment of production would involve shifting (assumed) fully-employed labor resources from more labor-intensive activities such as production of apparel and other light manufactures, to less labor-intensive activities including production of primary commodities and capital-intensive manufactures, thereby requiring a reduction in the domestic wage rate.

Virtually no change in expenditures occurs because the simulation model assumes that total consumption expenditures are predominantly exogenously determined. Although changes in tariff revenues are permitted to affect the aggregate level of these expenditures, the estimation results indicate that the induced changes in customs duty collections are largely inconsequential to the level of total expenditures and hence to the outcome of the import liberalization scenarios.

In most instances, the nominal exchange rate (in terms of U.S. dollars) declines in order to accommodate import liberalization. Notably, however, under both variants of the AFTA plan the Singapore dollar appreciates in value because of the initial high degree of openness of the Singapore economy and the strong demand for Singapore's exports induced by the lowering of restrictions to intra-bloc trade in the other ASEAN countries. In all cases, the real exchange rate—defined as the aggregate price of exportables relative to nontraded goods—rises, reflecting the increased demand for domestic resources to be devoted to traded goods production.

As noted previously, the estimated changes in total trade are greater, the greater is the scope of the import liberalization. That both exports and imports increase by the same amount in each case follows from the balance of payments constraint, which requires that changes in the exchange rate and other economywide variables be sufficient to maintain external equilibrium and, more fundamentally, to maintain the national budget constraint that changes in total expenditures on intermediate and final goods must be matched exactly by changes in total revenues from production.

With regard to changes in trade, liberalization of all manufactures under the AFTA plan stimulates an expansion of ASEAN exports of about $1.9 billion, whereas liberalization of selected manufactures stimulates an expansion of about $1.2 billion. The shadow simulation results, on the other hand, indicate that expanding ASEAN trade through import liberalization on an MFN-basis would be expected to result in gains in total ASEAN trade that are more than three times larger than under the AFTA plan, between $7.6 billion and $4.2 billion.

While the expansion of ASEAN trade is generally greater when the liberalization of imports is accomplished on a nondiscriminatory basis, this generalization does not apply to Singapore. The expansion of Singapore's trade is greatest under the AFTA plan. Within ASEAN, Singapore is the largest "beneficiary" of the trade diversion effects of the AFTA arrangements because it is the one ASEAN country that competes most directly with the major industrial countries and East Asian NICs in providing exports of capital-intensive and other manufactures to the more natural resource-abundant, lower-income, ASEAN countries. When the preferences extended to exporters from Singapore under the AFTA plan are removed under the shadow MFN scenarios, the expansion of Singapore's trade is substantially lower. In fact, it is lower than that of any of the ASEAN countries (between $400 and $300 million). Finally, it should be noted that the Philippines is estimated to achieve appreciably smaller gains in trade than the other natural resource-abundant ASEAN countries under both the AFTA plan and the shadow MFN scenarios. This occurs because a substantial portion of Philippine exports (about one-third) is not classified by goods category and therefore is not covered by the simulation results.

The benefits of regional trading arrangements are generally examined in terms of their trade creation and trade diversion effects (e.g., Viner 1950). They may also be examined in welfare-theoretic terms, in particular, by examining Hicksian measures of equivalent variations in income (Just et al. 1982). The focus of the present analysis, however, is simply on the effects of the AFTA plan on ASEAN trade relations with other developing countries in Asia. These effects are examined mainly in terms of changes in *total* ASEAN trade—that is, exports plus imports—with other developing Asian countries. Thus, of particular interest here are changes in ASEAN trade with China, the South Asian countries (mainly Bangladesh, India, Pakistan, and Sri Lanka), and the East Asian NICs (Hong Kong, Korea, and Taiwan).

The simulated changes in ASEAN trade with different blocs of developing Asian countries and the major industrial countries (including Japan) are presented in Table 4. Under the AFTA plan, total intra-ASEAN trade is expanded substantially, by $4.1 billion in Scenario I and $2.5 billion in Scenario II. The changes in ASEAN trade relations with other blocs of developing countries in Asia and the industrial countries are negative in most instances, with the largest diversion of trade estimated for ASEAN trade with the industrial countries (between $176 million and $89 million). The diversion of ASEAN trade with other developing Asian countries is modest by comparison (between about $30 million and about $20 million). In proportion, however, to the baseline 1988 trade levels, the diversion of ASEAN trade with other developing Asian countries is comparable to that with the major industrial countries, about 0.2 percent. This percentage change is small, but it should be borne in mind that the estimated changes in trade are measured on a per

Table 4. Changes in ASEAN Trade with Developing Asian and Industrial Countries (in millions of US dollars)[a]

Import Liberalization Scenario	Exports (X)						Imports (M)						Total Trade (X+M)					
	World	ASEAN	South Asia	China	East Asia	Industrial Countries	World	ASEAN	South Asia	China	East Asia	Industrial Countries	World	ASEAN	South Asia	China	East Asia	Industrial Countries
I. All Manufactures—AFTA Plan																		
Indonesia	176	125	0	-2	7	45	176	186	-0	-0	-1	-8	352	311	0	-2	6	37
Malaysia	432	352	-1	-2	18	64	432	676	-2	-7	-28	-189	863	1,029	-3	-9	-10	-125
Philippines	135	158	0	0	-4	-19	135	137	0	0	-1	-3	269	294	0	0	-5	-22
Singapore	847	1,226	0	10	-61	-249	847	280	5	25	62	360	1,694	1,506	5	35	1	111
Thailand	319	165	-1	-5	20	125	319	747	-6	-14	-42	-302	638	912	-7	-19	-21	-177
ASEAN[b]	1,908	2,027	-2	1	-20	-35	1,908	2,027	-3	4	-9	-142	3,817	4,053	-5	5	-29	-176
	(1.8)	(13.5)	(0.1)	(0.0)	(0.2)	(0.1)	(1.9)	(13.5)	(0.3)	(0.1)	(0.1)	(0.2)	(1.9)	(13.5)	(0.2)	(0.1)	(0.1)	(0.2)
All Manufactures—MFN Liberalization																		
Indonesia	1,899	85	2	-76	263	1,561	1,899	128	5	55	202	1,355	3,797	213	7	-21	465	2,916
Malaysia	1,652	423	-22	-33	279	984	1,652	358	1	4	233	1,031	3,303	781	-21	-29	512	2,015
Philippines	904	135	-0	-12	97	683	904	66	-2	-1	335	508	1,808	201	-2	-14	432	1,191
Singapore	437	284	-2	-6	20	89	437	726	-5	-41	-7	-3487	1,010	-7	-47	12	55	
Thailand	2,701	373	-10	-81	311	1,885	2,701	22	50	61	443	2,311	5,401	395	39	-19	754	4,196
ASEAN[b]	7,591	1,300	-32	-208	969	5,202	7,591	1,300	49	77	1,206	5,171	15,182	2,600	17	-130	2,174	10,373
	(7.1)	(8.7)	(1.5)	(6.8)	(9.0)	(8,.8)	(7.7)	(8.7)	(5.1)	(2.2)	(13.3)	(9.1)	(7.4)	(8.7)	(0.5)	(2.0)	(10.9)	(8.9)
II. Selected Manufqactures—AFTA Plan																		
Indonesia	108	101	-0	-0	1	8	108	111	-0	-0	-0	-2	217	211	-0	-0	0	6
Malaysia	337	263	-1	-2	17	58	337	535	-2	-5	-21	-155	673	799	-3	-7	-4	-97
Philippines	77	70	0	-0	1	7	77	97	0	-1	-5	-11	155	167	-0	-1	-4	-4
Singapore	513	725	-0	8	-40	-126	513	205	3	13	34	196	1,027	929	2	22	-6	70
Thailand	170	116	-0	-2	8	43	170	326	-2	-5	-15	-107	340	442	-3	-7	-8	-64
ASEAN[b]	1,206	2,274	-2	4	-14	-10	1,206	1,274	-2	2	-7	-79	2,412	2,548	-3	6	-22	-89
	(1.1)	(8.5)	(0.1)	(0.1)	(0.1)	(0.0)	(1.2)	(8.5)	(0.2)	(0.1)	(0.1)	(0.1)	(1.2)	(8.5)	(0.1)	(0.1)	(0.1)	(0.1)
Selected Manufactures—MFN Liberalization																		
Indonesia	841	68	1	-32	113	661	841	79	3	40	100	525	1,682	146	4	8	214	1,186
Malaysia	1,183	333	-15	-22	195	681	1,183	278	4	5	184	681	2,366	610	-12	-17	379	1,361
Philippines	529	50	-0	-9	57	430	529	52	0	1	260	247	1,057	101	0	-8	317	677
Singapore	290	185	-1	-2	11	70	290	445	-1	-23	10	-6	580	630	-3	-26	21	64
Thailand	1,360	191	-6	-41	159	934	1,360	-928	83	96	331	884	2,720	164	77	55	490	1,818
ASEAN[b]	4,203	826	-21	-106	535	2,775	4,203	826	88	118	885	2,330	8,405	1,652	66	12	1,420	5,105
	(3.9)	(5.5)	(1.0)	(3.5)	(5.0)	(4.7)	(4.2)	(5.5)	(9.1)	(3.4)	(9.7)	(4.1)	(4.1)	(5.5)	(2.1)	(0.2)	(7.1)	(4.4)

Notes: Simulations of the ASEAN trade simulation model using 1988 trade flows and circa-1987 import control measures as basline data and assuming ad valorem customs duties are reduced to zero and nontariff barriers are liberalized to increase the volume of administered imports by 20 percent, on a preferential basis (AFTA plan) and, alternatively, on a most-favored-nation (MFN) basis.

[a] Per annum, measured in 1988 U.S. dollars.

[b] Numbers in parentheses are changes in trade as a percentage, measured in absolute value, of basline 1988 trade flows.

annum basis. Thus, the cumulative effect of such small changes could loom large, particularly at the margins of investment decisions and a final accounting of effects on the economic welfare of ASEAN consumers as well as producers.

In regard to intra-regional trade, ASEAN trade with the East Asian NICs is reduced by the largest amount (between $29 million and $22 million), followed by that with the block of South Asian countries (between $5 million and $3 million). Notably, under the AFTA plan, ASEAN trade relations with China are estimated to expand (between $6 million and $5 million). Also, while the trade relations of the ASEAN countries with other developing countries in Asia are estimated to contract, Singapore's trade relations with the other developing countries in Asia are most often estimated to expand. This result is related to the low initial levels of protection in Singapore and the estimated appreciation in value of the Singapore dollar, which induce an increase in the net exports of the city-state to the other ASEAN countries and an increase in its net imports from the rest of the world.

Changes in the commodity composition of the combined trade relations of the ASEAN countries with other developing Asian countries and the major industrial countries under the AFTA plan are presented in Table 5. The decline in ASEAN trade ties with the East Asian countries is concentrated predominantly in manufactures (chemicals, machinery, textile products, and unspecified other manufactures). The decline in ASEAN trade with the low-income Asian countries, on the other hand, is concentrated not only in manufactures (mainly textiles and clothing, wood products, and non-metal mineral manufactures), but also in food and other agricultural commodities. Broadly speaking, these categories of primary and manufactured goods are those in which ASEAN trade relations with other developing Asian countries have deepened as economic integration in Asia has gradually increased during the past few decades.

The shadow MFN simulation results present a much different set of changes in ASEAN trade relations (Table 4). Most discernibly, total ASEAN trade with the major industrial countries is stimulated by amounts much larger than found in the AFTA simulation results (between $10.4 billion and $5.1 billion), and the expansion of intra-ASEAN trade (between $2.6 million and $1.7 billion) is matched almost evenly in amount by the expansion of ASEAN trade with the East Asian NICs (between about $2.2 billion and $1.4 billion). Moreover, ASEAN trade relations with the low-income Asian countries are estimated to increase, except in the shadow scenario involving liberalization of all manufactures. In this important case, ASEAN trade with the South Asian countries increases by $17 million, but that with China declines by $130 million.[13]

In proportional terms, the estimated increases in intra-ASEAN trade under MFN liberalization (9 percent and 6 percent), are several percentage points smaller than those under the AFTA plan (14 percent and 9 percent). However,

Table 5. Changes in ASEAN Trade with Developing Asian and Industrial Countries by Sector—AFTA Plan (in millions of US dollars)[a]

Import Liberalization Scenario	Exports (X)						Imports (M)						Total Trade (X+M)					
	World	ASEAN	South Asia	China	East Asia	Industrial Countries	World	ASEAN	South Asia	China	East Asia	Industrial Countries	World	ASEAN	South Asia	China	East Asia	Industrial Countries
I. All Manufactures																		
Primary Products	155.17	61.64	-2.24	-2.26	13.70	89.39	109.74	61.55	-0.93	9.27	-0.19	-13.45	264.91	123.29	-3.17	6.99	13.51	75.94
Foods	107.30	62.36	-1.75	-1.25	4.51	41.26	49.23	62.39	-0.29	-1.09	-0.51	-9.86	156.53	124.75	-2.04	-2.34	4.00	31.40
Cereals	0.05	0.01	0.01	0.00	0.02	0.00	-0.72	0.01	0.00	0.01	0.00	-0.74	-0.67	0.02	0.01	0.01	0.02	-0.74
Vegetable Oils & Oil Seeds	53.83	49.02	-0.73	1.31	-0.04	3.40	49.65	49.05	0.02	-0.00	-0.04	0.06	103.48	98.07	-0.71	1.31	-0.08	3.46
Other Foods	53.42	13.33	-1.03	-2.56	4.53	37.86	0.30	13.33	-0.31	-1.10	-0.47	-9.18	53.72	26.66	-1.34	3.66	4.06	28.68
Agricultural Raw Material	43.91	9.59	-0.47	-2.97	11.83	28.84	-2.70	9.58	-0.90	-1.82	-0.47	-5.03	41.21	19.17	-1.37	-4.79	11.36	23.81
Textile Fibers	0.05	-0.04	0.00	-0.06	0.17	0.01	-6.02	-0.04	-0.90	-0.53	-0.23	-2.45	-5.97	-0.08	-0.90	-0.59	-0.06	-2.44
Other Agricultural Raw Materials	43.86	9.63	-0.47	-2.91	11.66	28.83	3.32	9.62	0.00	-1.29	-0.24	-2.58	47.18	19.25	-0.47	-4.20	11.42	26.25
Crude Fertilizers & Mineral Ores	2.77	0.03	0.04	-0.01	0.49	2.26	-9.11	0.03	-0.73	-0.82	-0.48	-4.93	-6.34	0.06	-0.69	-0.83	0.01	-2.65
Mineral Fuels	1.54	-11.24	-0.07	1.93	-2.48	16.31	67.79	-11.24	1.01	13.07	0.75	4.22	69.33	-22.48	0.94	15.00	-1.73	20.53
Non-Ferrous Metals	-0.35	0.90	0.01	0.02	-0.65	0.70	4.53	0.89	-0.02	-0.07	0.52	2.15	4.18	1.79	-0.01	-0.05	-0.13	2.85
Manufactures	1,753.09	1,964.88	0.57	3.58	-33.4	-123.96	1,798.55	1,964.95	-2.40	-5.37	-9.21	-128.12	3,551.64	3929.83	-1.83	-1.79	-42.61	-252.08
Chemicals	261.36	294.18	-0.69	3.72	-10.52	-11.82	233.89	294.19	-0.62	-1.60	-5.52	-39.91	495.25	588.37	-1.31	2.12	-16.04	-51.73
Pharmaceuticals	8.73	10.40	-0.08	-0.01	-0.02	-1.59	6.05	10.40	-0.06	-0.25	-0.15	-3.51	14.78	20.80	-0.14	-0.26	-0.17	-5.10
Toiletries, Perfumes	14.86	16.54	0.01	0.03	-0.24	-0.46	14.64	16.54	0.05	0.03	-0.24	-1.73	29.50	33.08	0.06	0.06	-0.48	-2.19
Manufactured Fertilizers	17.90	18.14	-0.01	0.17	-0.01	-0.20	8.87	18.15	-0.22	-0.02	-2.92	-2.66	26.77	36.29	-0.23	0.15	-2.93	-2.86
Other Chemicals	219.87	249.10	-0.61	3.53	-10.5	-9.57	204.33	249.10	-0.39	-1.36	-2.21	-32.01	424.20	298.20	-1.00	2.17	-12.46	-41.58
Iron & Steel	35.46	39.26	0.23	0.06	-0.68	-2.36	21.07	39.27	-0.02	-0.80	-1.67	-9.75	56.53	78.53	0.21	-0.74	-2.35	-12.11
Machinery & Equipments	953.01	1,148.96	0.99	1.56	-20.72	-141.07	1,083.28	1,148.98	0.49	-0.40	5.94	-70.44	2,036.29	2,297.84	1.48	1.16	-14.78	-211.51
Non-Electric Machinery	245.15	321.84	0.19	0.08	-5.79	-66.68	330.59	321.85	0.51	0.03	3.34	4.49	575.74	643.69	0.70	0.11	-2.45	-62.19
Electric Machinery	569.44	668.99	0.60	1.17	-13.07	-64.99	623.84	669.00	0.03	-0.06	5.03	-47.24	1,193.28	1,337.99	0.63	1.11	-8.04	-112.23
Transport Equipment	30.31	33.12	0.06	-0.23	-0.15	-0.23	19.39	33.12	0.03	0.11	1.78	-17.03	49.7	66.24	0.09	-0.12	1.63	-17.26
Other Machinery & Equipment	108.11	125.01	0.14	0.54	-1.71	-9.17	109.46	125.01	-0.08	-0.48	-4.21	-10.66	217.57	250.02	0.06	0.06	-5.92	-19.83
Other Manufactures	503.26	482.48	0.04	-1.76	-1.48	31.29	460.31	482.51	-2.25	-2.57	-7.96	-8.02	963.57	964.99	-2.21	-4.33	-9.44	23.27
Leather & Travel Goods	7.77	4.15	0.00	-0.01	0.43	3.03	4.15	4.15	0.10	-0.13	-0.55	0.47	11.92	8.30	0.10	-0.14	-0.12	3.50
Rubber Products	11.69	13.18	0.01	0.02	-0.18	-0.61	12.27	13.18	-0.01	0.06	-0.21	-0.74	23.96	26.36	0.00	0.08	-0.39	-1.35
Wood Products	15.68	6.22	-0.02	-1.59	1.57	9.70	6.71	6.22	0.01	0.04	0.24	0.24	22.39	12.44	-0.01	-1.55	1.81	9.94
Paper Products	43.78	47.02	-0.06	0.00	-1.40	-0.37	49.54	47.03	0.00	0.37	0.17	1.30	93.32	94.05	-0.06	0.37	-1.23	0.93
Textile & Clothing	175.61	159.41	0.06	-0.40	1.43	12.51	147.63	159.42	-0.29	-2.30	-4.85	-2.62	323.24	318.83	-0.23	-2.70	-3.42	9.89
Non-Metal Mineral Products	36.66	26.78	0.19	0.00	1.26	8.78	22.89	26.79	-2.03	0.15	-0.17	-2.16	59.55	53.57	-1.84	0.15	1.09	6.62
Furnitures	8.02	5.06	0.00	0.00	0.14	2.88	5.60	5.06	0.00	0.06	0.13	0.19	13.62	10.12	0.00	0.06	0.27	3.07
Footwear	6.26	2.09	0.00	0.00	0.11	3.35	2.85	2.09	0.01	0.014	0.32	0.34	9.11	4.18	0.01	0.04	0.43	3.69
Professional Equipment	25.83	30.67	-0.02	0.03	-0.65	-1.11	31.50	30.66	0.02	-0.04	0.05	0.95	57.33	61.33	0.00	-0.01	-0.60	-0.16
Other Manufactures	171.96	187.90	-0.12	0.19	-4.19	-6.87	177.17	187.91	-0.06	-0.82	-3.90	-5.99	349.13	357.81	-0.18	-0.63	-7.28	-12.86
All Traded Goods Sectors	1,908.26	2,026.52	-1.67	1.30	-19.70	-34.57	1,908.29	2,026.60	-3.33	3.90	-.940	-141.57	3,816.55	4,053.12	-5.00	5.20	-29.10	-176.14

II. Selected Manufactures																		
Primary Products	112.39	60.11	-1.49	-0.50	10.12	48.22	81.60	60.11	-0.63	4.22	-0.39	-10.14	193.99	120.22	-2.12	3.72	9.73	38.08
Foods	77.33	54.81	-1.04	0.08	1.65	21.34	44.53	54.82	-0.43	-1.13	-0.33	-7.31	121.86	109.63	-147	-1.05	1.32	14.03
Cereals	0.00	0.00	-0.01	0.00	001	0.00	-0.62	0.00	0.00	0.01	0.00	-0.58	-0.62	0.00	-0.01	0.01	0.01	-0.58
Vegetable Oils & Oil Seeds	52.79	48.03	-0.62	1.14	-0.04	3.57	48.13	48.04	0.01	-0.11	-0.06	-0.08	100.92	96.07	-0.61	1.03	-0.10	3.49
Other Foods	24.54	6.78	-0.41	-1.06	1.68	17.77	-2.98	6.78	-0.44	-1.03	-0.27	-6.65	21.56	13.56	-0.85	-2.09	1.41	11.12
Agricultural Raw Material	27.88	7.20	-0.39	-1.60	8.19	16.75	1.24	7.20	-0.42	-0.70	-0.37	-2.95	29.12	14.40	-0.81	-2.30	7.82	13.80
Textile Fibers	0.07	-0.03	0.00	-0.03	0.11	0.08	-3.18	-0.03	-0.42	-0.20	-0.22	-1.60	-3.11	-0.06	-0.42	-0.23	-0.11	-1.52
Other Agricultural Raw Materials	27.81	7.23	-0.39	-1.57	8.08	16.67	4.42	7.23	0.00	-0.50	-0.15	-1.35	32.23	14.46	-0.39	-2.07	7.93	15.32
Crude Fertilizers & Mineral Ores	1.60	-0.11	0.02	0.01	0.28	1.45	-5.05	-0.11	-0.30	-0.55	-0.17	-2.55	-3.45	-0.22	-0.28	-0.54	0.11	-1.10
Mineral Fuels	5.01	-2.26	-0.08	1.00	-0.31	8.18	39.14	-2.26	0.52	6.63	0.35	2.05	44.15	-4.52	0.44	7.63	0.04	10.23
Non-Ferrous Metals	0.57	0.47	0.00	0.01	0.31	0.50	1.74	0.46	0.00	-0.03	0.13	0.62	2.31	0.93	0.00	-0.02	0.44	1.12
Manufactures	1,093.41	1,213.89	-0.24	4.62	-24.29	-58.07	1,124.17	1,213.86	-1.03	-1.83	-7.05	-69.20	2,217.58	2,427.75	-1.27	2.79	-31.34	-127.27
Chemicals	258.17	295.27	-0.75	4.11	-12.01	-13.93	259.94	295.27	-0.37	-0.87	-3.97	-22.63	518.11	590.54	-1.12	3.24	-15.96	-36.56
Pharmaceuticals	8.14	10.44	-0.10	0.01	-0.02	-2.19	8.36	10.44	-0.03	-0.12	-0.07	-1.67	16.50	20.88	-0.13	-0.11	-0.09	-3.86
Toiletries, Perfumes	14.42	16.51	0.01	0.05	-0.40	-0.58	15.44	16.52	0.04	0.01	-0.20	-0.92	29.86	33.03	0.05	006	-0.60	-1.50
Manufactured Fertilizers	18.21	18.51	-0.01	0.21	-0.01	-0.23	11.11	18.50	-0.18	-0.02	-2.35	-2.10	29.32	37.01-	0.19	0.19	-2.36	-2.33
Other Chemicals	217.40	249.81	-0.65	3.84	-11.58	-10.93	225.03	249.81	-0.20	-0.74	-1.35	-17.94	442.43	499.62	-0.85	3.10	-12.93	-28.87
Iron & Steel	0.43	0.32	-0.03	0.00	0.03	0.28	-5.27	0.31	0.00	-0.20	-0.71	-2.95	-4.84	0.63	-0.03	-0.20	-0.68	-2.67
Machinery & Equipment	562.86	665.07	0.54	1.00	-12.18	-67.39	624.59	665.04	0.24	0.01	3.51	-42.86	1,187.45	1,330.12	0.78	1.01	-8.67	-110.25
Non-Electric Machinery	-8.67	1.14	0.03	0.01	-0.58	-8.59	15.39	1.13	0.21	0.04	2.26	11.23	6.72	2.27	0.24	0.05	1.68	2.64
Electric Machinery	572.04	661.54	0.46	1.04	-11.48	-57.82	609.79	661.52	0.02	0.01	1.36	-50.44	1,181.83	1,323.06	0.48	1.05	-10.12	-108.26
Transport Equipment	-0.33	0.32	0.02	-0.11	-0.05	0.06	-4.13	0.33	0.01	0.05	0.79	-5.87	-4.46	0.65	0.03	-0.06	0.74	-5.81
Other Machinery & Equipment	-0.18	2.07	0.03	0.06	-0.07	-1.04	3.54	2.07	0.00	-0.09	-0.90	2.22	3.36	4.14	0.03	-0.03	-0.97	1.18
Other Manufactures	271.95	253.23	0.00	-0.49	-0.13	22.97	244.91	253.23	-0.90	-0.77	-5.88	-0.76	516.86	506.46	-0.90	-1.26	-6.01	22.21
Leather & Travel Goods	5.27	3.87	0.00	0.00	0.15	1.26	3.97	3.87	0.02	-0.07	-0.22	0.32	9.24	7.74	0.02	-0.07	-0.07	1.58
Rubber Products	11.47	13.06	0.00	0.02	-0.20	-0.73	11.38	13.07	-0.01	0.04	-0.29	-1.35	22.85	26.13	-0.01	0.06	-0.49	-2.08
Wood Products	3.67	2.13	-0.02	-0.36	0.24	2.08	2.40	2.12	0.00	0.02	0.14	0.13	6.07	4.25	-0.02	-0.34	0.38	2.21
Paper Products	43.23	46.83	-0.05	0.04	-1.70	-0.47	49.73	46.83	0.00	0.31	0.18	1.40	92.96	93.66	-0.05	0.35	-1.52	0.93
Textile & Clothing	165.34	156.43	0.05	-0.20	0.70	8.68	145.53	156.43	-0.23	-1.21	-5.47	-2.38	310.87	1312.86	-0.18	-1.41	-4.77	6.30
Non-Metal Mineral Products	29.49	26.02	0.03	0.01	0.38	3.43	25.44	26.02	-0.69	0.13	-0.11	-0.43	54.93	52.04	-0.66	0.14	0.27	3.00
Furnitures	6.34	4.77	0.00	0.01	0.03	1.59	4.95	4.75	0.00	0.03	0.06	0.04	11.29	9.52	0.00	0.04	0.09	1.63
Footwear	2.49	0.36	0.00	0.00	0.06	1.78	0.65	0.36	0.00	0.01	0.11	0.14	3.14	0.72	0.00	0.01	0.17	1.92
Professional Equipment	0.44	0.03	0.00	0.00	0.16	0.65	1.49	0.04	0.01	0.00	0.10	1.33	1.93	0.07	0.01	0.00	0.26	1.98
Other Manufactures	4.21	-0.27	-0.01	-0.01	0.05	4.70	-0.63	-0.26	0.00	-0.03	-0.38	0.04	3.58	-0.53	-0.01	-0.04	-0.33	4.74
All Traded Goods Sectors	1,205.80	1,274.00	-1.73	4.12	-14.17	-9.85	1,205.77	1,273.97	-1.66	2.39	-7.44	-79.34	2,411.57	2,547.97	-3.39	6.51	-21.61	-89.19

Notes: Simulations on the ASEAN trade simulation model using 1988 trade flows and circa-1987 import control measures as baseline data and assuming ad valorem customs duties are reduced to zero and nontariff barriers are liberalized to increase the volume of administered imports by 20 percent, on a preferential basis (AFTA plan) and, alternatively, on a most-favored-nation (MFN) basis.

[a] Per annum, measured in 1988 U.S. dollars.

Table 6. Changes in ASEAN Trade with Developing Asian and Industrial Countries by Sector—MFN Liberalization (in millions of US dollars)[a]

Import Liberalization Scenario	Exports (X) World	ASEAN	South Asia	China	East Asia	Industrial Countries	Imports (M) World	ASEAN	South Asia	China	East Asia	Industrial Countries	Total Trade (X+M) World	ASEAN	South Asia	China	East Asia	Industrial Countries
I. All Manufactures																		
Primary Products	2,752.96	-243.17	-42.22	-113.01	539.18	2,498.29	-2,142.67	-243.18	-53.76	-167.32	-76.78	-749.74	610.29	-486.35	-95.98	-208.33	462.40	1,748.55
Foods	1,149.86	88.84	-32.04	-47.80	109.32	952.38	-437.70	88.585	-14.50	-47.13	-24.34	-341.95	712.16	177.69	-46.54	-94.93	84.98	610.43
Cereals	0.14	-0.04	-0.45	0.00	0.57	0.05	-21.39	-0.04	-0.01	-0.06	0.00	-18.54	-21.25	-0.08	-0.46	-0.06	0.57	-18.49
Vegetable Oils & Oil Seeds	170.35	46.93	-15.96	-6.69	6.16	124.14	87.21	46.93	0.09	20.87	5.16	14.42	257.56	93.86	-15.87	14.18	11.32	138.56
Other Foods	979.37	41.95	-15.63	-41.11	102.59	828.19	-503.52	41.96	-14.58	-67.94	-29.50	-337.83	475.85	83.91	-30.21	-109.05	73.09	490.36
Agricultural Raw Material	777.64	0.47	-7.71	-57.21	229.39	599.92	-294.71	0.47	-22.55	-36.25	-24.26	-126.79	-482.93	0.94	-30.26	-93.46	205.13	473.13
Textile Fibers	6.39	-1.07	0.10	-1.12	4.14	3.61	-140.11	-1.07	-21.52	-10.48	-11.48	-61.74	-133.72	-2.14	-21.42	-11.60	-7.34	-58.13
Other Agricultural Raw Materials	771.25	1.54	-7.81	-56.09	225.25	596.31	-154.60	1.54	-1.03	025.77	-12.78	-65.05	616.65	3.08	-8.84	-81.86	212.47	531.26
Crude Fertilizers & Mineral Ores	106.72	-7.29	-0.65	-0.82	18.46	96.73	-214.45	-7.30	-13.71	-23.13	-9.12	-100.59	-107.73	-14.59	-14.36	-23.95	9.34	-3.86
Mineral Fuels	624.28	-322.80	-1.43	-6.32	146.10	796.51	-1,014.01	-322.81	-2.39	-55.08	-5.12	-61.12	-389.73	-645.61	-3.82	-61.40	140.98	735.39
Non-Ferrous Metals	94.46	-2.39	-0.39	-0.86	35.91	52.75	-181.80	-2.39	-0.61	-5.73	-13.94	-119.29	-87.34	-4.78	-1.00	-6.59	21.97	-66.54
Manufactures	4,838.30	1,543.08	9.89	-94.47	429.52	2,703.50	9,733.90	1,543.05	103.23	244.72	1,282.51	5,920.51	14,572.20	3,086.13	113.12	150.25	1,712.03	8,624.01
Chemicals	269.28	165.36	0.19	-12.20	44.03	78.35	1,634.72	165.35	8.74	42.44	95.40	1,099.06	1,904.00	330.71	8.93	30.24	139.43	1,177.41
Pharmaceuticals	6.93	6.17	0.05	-0.38	0.10	0.23	101.85	6.17	0.75	7.62	4.39	73.95	108.78	12.34	0.80	7.24	4.498	74.18
Toiletries, Perfumes	25.44	13.18	-0.08	-0.53	6.08	7.16	117.52	13.17	0.88	2.32	9.47	88.23	142.96	26.35	0.80	1.79	15.55	95.39
Manufactured Fertilizers	6.35	9.95	0.28	-8.94	0.32	3.56	2.84	9.95	-1.28	-0.22	-6.69	-4.43	9.19	19.90	-1.00	-9.16	-6.37	-0.87
Other Chemicals	230.56	136.06	-0.06	-2.35	37.53	67.40	1,412.51	136.06	8.39	32.72	88.23	941.31	1,643.07	272.12	8.33	30.37	125.76	1,008.71
Iron & Steel	92.47	25.87	-0.80	-2.25	9.52	58.24	418.62	25.86	0.45	11.34	61.95	231.79	511.09	51.73	-0.35	9.9	71.47	290.03
Machinery & Equipment	2,128.32	913.98	2.48	-14.91	162.33	1,000.15	4,864.38	913.98	8.49	26.44	351.12	3,404.44	6,992.70	1,827.96	10.97	11.53	513.45	4,404.59
Non-Electric Machinery	434.59	229.71	-0.03	-0.04	17.27	185.92	529.87	229.71	-0.28	1.61	20.62	265.25	964.46	459.42	-0.31	1.57	37.89	451.17
Electric Machinery	1,412.80	551.83	1.99	-0.77	118.73	697.15	2,334.33	551.82	2.07	7.92	188.19	1,521.18	3,747.13	1,103.65	4.06	7.15	306.92	2,218.33
Transport Equipment	83.06	30.87	-0.09	-9.67	6.58	39.80	803.95	30.89	2.07	2.02	19.12	710.75	887.01	61.76	1.98	-7.65	25.70	750.55
Other Machinery & Equipment	197.87	101.57	0.61	-4.43	19.75	77.28	1,196.23	101.56	4.63	14.89	123.19	907.26	1,394.10	203.13	5.24	10.46	142.94	984.54
Other Manufactures	2,348.23	437.87	8.02	-65.11	213.64	1,566.76	2,816.18	437.86	85.55	164.50	774.04	1,185.22	5,164.41	875.73	93.57	99.39	987.68	2,751.98
Leather & Travel Goods	84.37	7.61	0.05	-0.16	10.16	58.90	63.27	7.61	0.54	3.55	36.88	14.99	147.64	15.22	0.59	339	47.04	73.89
Rubber Products	31.542	8.83	0.08	-0.08	3.13	15.11	65.18	8.82	0.37	0.36	7.50	44.80	96.70	17.65	0.45	0.28	10.63	59.91
Wood Products	396.00	7.75	0.24	-54.63	58.81	368.12	13.20	7.74	0.03	0.65	0.66	3.09	409.20	15.49	0.27	-53.98	59.47	371.21
Paper Products	71.88	42.27	0.27	-1.16	18.16	8.58	229.99	42.28	0.14	5.45	11.47	123.32	301.87	84.55	0.41	4.29	29.63	131.90
Textile & Clothing	719.71	172.06	0.58	-6.74	38.78	391.22	1,155.54	172.06	33.15	118.56	530.19	235.56	1,875.25	344.12	33.73	111.82	568.97	626.78
Non-Metal Mineral Products	244.95	31.21	6.57	-0.85	31.85	169.33	287.37	31.20	48.12	5.49	21.24	157.48	532.32	62.41	54.69	4.64	53.09	326.81
Furnitures	126.04	7.56	0.07	-0.28	5.33	113.17	30.57	7.56	0.08	0.25	2.46	19.01	156.61	15.12	0.15	-0.03	7.79	132.18
Footwear	85.51	4.76	0.07	0.00	2.79	65.09	12.21	4.76	-0.03	1.79	4.66	0.15	97.72	9.52	0.04	1.79	7.45	65.24
Professional Equipment	107.55	18.19	0.01	-0.03	26.11	61.90	189.06	18.19	0.29	1.73	11.93	149.52	296.61	36.38	0.30	1.70	38.04	211.42
Other Manufactures	480.70	137.63	0.08	-1.18	18.52	315.34	769.79	137.64	2.86	26.67	147.05	437.30	1250.49	275.27	2.94	25.49	165.57	752.64
All Traded Goods Sectors	7,591.26	1,299.91	-32.33	-207.48	968.70	5,201.79	7,591.23	1,299.87	49.47	77.40	1,205.73	5,170.77	15,182.49	2,599.78	17.14	-130.08	2,174.43	10,372.56

II. Selected Manufactures																		
Primary Products	1,470.40	-106.55	-25.90	-62.49	303.24	1,299.05	-1,185.10	-106.62	-30.58	-88.75	-40.72	-425.37	285.30	-213.17	-56.48	-151.24	262.52	873.68
Foods	619.46	59.38	-19.05	-25.85	57.20	505.27	-232.58	59.34	-9.83	-17.41	-11.36	-197.47	386.88	118.72	-28.88	-43.26	45.84	307.80
Cereals	-0.02	-0.01	-0.32	0.00	0.28	0.03	-13.71	-0.02	-0.01	-0.04	0.00	-11.81	-13.73	-0.03	-0.33	-0.04	0.28	-11.78
Vegetable Oils & Oil Seeds	115.35	43.30	-10.82	-4.24	3.89	73.05	94.34	43.29	0.15	24.354	5.70	17.31	209.69	86.59	-10.67	20.11	9.59	90.36
Other Foods	504.13	16.09	-7.91	-21.61	53.03	432.19	-313.21	16.07	-9.97	-41.72	-17.06	-202.97	190.92	32.16	-17.88	-63.33	35.97	229.22
Agricultural Raw Material	432.61	5.40	-5.20	-31.58	134.44	321.55	-151.92	5.37	-11.51	-18.87	-13.48	-69.07	280.69	10.77	-16.71	-50.45	120.96	252.48
Textile Fibers	3.62	-0.61	0.04	-0.61	2.26	2.19	-73.54	-0.63	-10.91	-5.16	-6.13	-33.83	-69.92	-1.24	-10.87	-5.77	-3.87	-31.64
Other Agricultural Raw Materials	428.99	6.01	-5.24	-30.97	132.18	319.36	-78.39	6.00	-0.60	-13.71	-7.35	-35.24	350.61	12.01	-5.84	-44.68	124.83	284.12
Crude Fertilizers & Mineral Ores	53.34	-5.09	-0.43	-0.38	9.84	49.20	-121.49	-5.09	-7.23	-13.74	-4.72	-56.16	-68.15	-10.18	-7.66	-14.12	5.12	-6.96
Mineral Fuels	324.88	-163.08	-0.99	-4.29	83.93	401.50	-576.54	-163.09	-1.69	-35.78	-3.27	-36.52	-251.66	-326.17	-2.68	-40.07	80.66	364.98
Non-Ferrous Metals	40.11	-3.16	-0.23	-0.39	17.83	21.53	-102.57	-3.15	-0.32	-2.95	-7.89	-66.15	-62.46	-6.31	-0.55	-3.34	9.94	-44.62
Manufactures	2,732.26	932.43	4.43	-43.71	231.55	1,476.08	5,387.73	932.43	118.37	207.13	925.84	2,755.55	8,119.99	1,864.86	122.80	163.42	1,157.39	4,231.63
Chemicals	266.14	198.27	-0.07	-8.17	28.70	55.93	2,106.59	198.29	12.68	54.31	126.81	1,413.28	2,372.73	396.56	12.61	46.14	155.51	1,469.21
Pharmaceuticals	7.00	7.26	0.01	-0.26	0.06	-0.59	132.64	7.27	1.16	9.43	5.55	97.83	139.64	14.53	1.17	9.17	5.61	97.24
Toiletries, Perfumes	21.77	14.03	-0.05	-0.42	4.15	4.66	142.97	14.03	1.04	2.69	11.77	019.22	164.74	28.06	0.99	2.27	15.92	113.88
Manufactured Fertilizers	9.68	12.73	0.18	-6.80	0.20	2.52	35.04	12.74	-0.51	-0.11	0.54	6.83	44.72	25.47	-0.33	-6.91	0.74	9.35
Other Chemicals	227.69	164.25	-0.21	-0.69	24.29	49.34	1,795.94	164.25	10.99	42.30	108.95	1,199.40	2,023.63	328.50	10.78	41.61	133.24	1,248.74
Iron & Steel	17.91	-2.38	-0.41	-0.64	2.96	17.49	-254.68	-2.40	-0.26	-7.82	-30.85	-150.69	-236.77	-4.78	-0.67	-8.46	-27.89	-133.20
Machinery & Equipment	1,141.53	491.38	1.16	-4.96	87.30	538.02	1,691.66	491.39	-1.12	3.23	162.32	996.62	2,833.19	982.77	0.04	-1.73	249.62	1,534.64
Non-Electric Machinery	74.99	-43.12	-0.09	-0.05	9.78	106.01	-310.85	-43.12	-1.01	-0.94	-25.48	-229.84	-235.86	-86.24	-1.10	-0.99	-15.70	-123.83
Electric Machinery	1,016.82	539.35	1.15	-0.21	68.16	391.14	2,858.99	539.35	2.768	10.94	243.45	1,979.27	3,875.81	1,078.70	3.93	10.73	311.61	2,370.41
Transport Equipment	17.08	-0.13	-0.04	-3.07	2.29	12.43	-357.50	-0.13	-0.90	-0.67	-8.49	-333.83	-340.42	-0.26	-0.94	-3.74	-6.20	-31.40
Other Machinery & Equipment	32.84	-4.72	0.14	-1.63	7.07	28.44	-498.98	-4.71	-1.99	-6.10	-47.16	-418.98	-466.34	-9.43	-1.85	-7.73	-40.09	-390.54
Other Manufactures	1,306.68	245.16	3.75	-29.94	112.59	864.64	1,844.16	245.15	107.07	157.41	667.56	496.34	3,150.84	490.31	110.82	127.47	780.15	1,360.98
Leather & Travel Goods	52.18	5.76	005	-0.12	6.54	35.51	78.05	5.76	1.00	4.50	45.92	21.00	130.23	11.52	1.05	4.38	52.46	56.51
Rubber Products	26.03	9.45	0.05	-0.05	2.38	11.11	78.44	9.44	0.46	0.50	8.96	54.89	104.47	18.89	0.51	0.45	11.34	66.00
Wood Products	174.63	2.98	0.12	-23.74	25.54	163.03	0.93	3.00	-0.02	-0.23	-0.59	-1.05	175.56	5.98	0.10	-23.97	24.95	161.98
Paper Products	58.05	42.44	0.10	-0.66	9.49	5.26	289.30	42.45	0.18	7.44	15.14	159.40	347.35	84.89	0.28	6.78	24.63	164.66
Textile & Clothing	534.20	165.50	0.45	-4.15	25.98	271.72	1,336.70	165.49	41.04	147.61	625.93	279.30	1,870.90	330.99	41.49	143.46	651.91	551.02
Non-Metal Mineral Products	146.60	27.95	2.82	-0.41	17.27	95.72	372.14	27.95	65.56	7.27	27.69	210.02	518.74	55.90	68.38	6.86	44.96	305.74
Furnitures	75.23	6.29	0.04	-0.15	2.97	65.96	33.16	6.28	0.09	0.31	2.85	22.16	108.39	12.57	0.13	0.16	5.82	88.12
Footwear	49.35	1.79	0.04	0.00	1.62	38.84	-3.61	1.79	-0.02	-0.66	-2.73	-1.53	45.74	3.58	0.02	-0.66	-1.11	37.31
Professional Equipment	38.04	-3.27	0.01	-0.03	10.45	29.07	-122.65	-3.29	-0.17	-0.75	-10.16	-103.89	-84.61	6.56	-0.16	-0.78	0.29	-74.82
Other Manufactures	152.37	-13.73	0.07	-0.63	10.35	148.42	-218.30	-13.27	-1.05	-8.58	-45.45	-143.96	-65.93	-27.45	-0.98	-9.21	-35.10	4.46
All Traded Goods Sectors	4,202.66	825.88	-21.47	-106.20	534.79	2,775.13	4,202.63	825.81	87.79	118.38	885.12	2,330.18	8,405.29	1,651.69	66.32	12.18	1,419.91	5,105.31

Notes: Simulations of the ASEAN trade simulation model using 1988 trade flows and circa-1987 import control measures as baseline data and assuming ad valorem customs duties are reduced to zero and nontariff barriers are liberalized to increase the volume of administered imports by 20 percent, on a preferential basis (AFTA plan) and, alternatively, on a most-favored-nation (MFN) basis.

[a] Per annum, measured in 1988 U.S. dollars.

the MFN scenarios imply increases in ASEAN trade with the East Asian NICs and, to a lesser extent, the major industrial countries that range between 11 percent when all manufactures are liberalized and 7 percent when only selected manufactures are liberalized. If weighted by the expected gains from trade based on comparative advantage considerations, the latter increases in trade could outweigh any "shortfall" in the expansion of intra-ASEAN trade under MFN liberalization.

Changes in the commodity composition of the combined trade relations of the ASEAN countries with partner countries under the shadow MFN liberalization scenarios are presented in Table 6. ASEAN trade ties expand strongly with all developing Asian countries and the major industrial countries in many of the same categories of manufactures identified previously in connection with the AFTA plan. That ASEAN trade relations decline with China in the case of MFN liberalization of all manufactures occurs because of sharp estimated declines in trade in foods and agricultural raw materials. ASEAN trade relations with the East Asian NICs, on the other hand, are estimated to expand in virtually all categories of primary goods as well as manufactures, indicating the particular potential for greater economic integration between the ASEAN and East Asian countries under a policy of nondiscriminatory trade liberalization.

V. CONCLUSION

The estimation results reported here indicate that in the medium- to long-term the ASEAN countries might increase their total intra-bloc trade by between $4.1 billion and $2.5 billion through the formation of the ASEAN Free Trade Area, depending upon the extent to which different manufactured products are covered by the new ASEAN trading arrangements. In the Vinerian sense, this expansion of trade is predominantly trade-creating. That is, the magnitude of the diversion of ASEAN trade with other countries, both within and outside of Asia, is substantially smaller than the magnitude of the total increase in intra-ASEAN trade.

Nonetheless, the empirical results presented here indicate that the trade relations of the ASEAN countries with other countries in the global trading system would be affected. The greatest diversion of ASEAN trade would occur, as expected, to ASEAN trade with the major industrial countries. But the simulation results also indicate that the growth of economic integration among countries in developing Asia would also be affected. ASEAN trade relations with the East Asian NICs would be adversely affected most, reflecting the strong ties between the East and Southeast Asian economies. But measured in proportional terms, the AFTA plan would also adversely affect ASEAN trade relations with the low-income countries of South Asia appreciably. In the simulation results reported here, only ASEAN trade relations with China would appear to be stimulated by the AFTA plan.

Though not fully developed in the analysis here, the implications for economic integration among the developing countries of Asia go beyond a simple accounting of trade creation and trade diversion effects. At issue is fundamentally the efficiency of resource use underlying different patterns of ASEAN trade, the incentives these patterns provide for greater domestic and foreign investment, and ultimately the implications for economic welfare of consumers as well as producers under different trade regimes. The "open regionalism" practiced by most East and Southeast Asian countries in the past has gradually led to opportunities for more productive use of labor, agricultural, natural resources in developing Asia, large inflows of foreign capital (and technology), and substantial economic benefits to consumers and producers in the region. At the margin, the AFTA plan represents a threat to this progression of economic opportunities.

Finally, although not easily pursued because of domestic political resistance, the alternative strategy of liberalization of ASEAN trade relations on a nondiscriminatory basis is seen in the empirical results to offer the greatest opportunity for broadly expanding ASEAN trade relations. Although intra-ASEAN trade would expand by a smaller total amount than under the AFTA plan, MFN liberalization would bestow on the ASEAN countries much greater gains in economic efficiency and welfare, through the exploitation of wide differences in international comparative advantage among particularly the ASEAN countries, the newly industrialized countries of East Asia, and the major industrial countries.

(Appendix follows)

APPENDIX

Import Restrictions in ASEAN Countries by Primary Product and Manufacturing Sectors, 1987[1] (in percent)

	Tariff and Para-Tariffs		Frequency of Nontariff Barriers[2]				
				Quantitative Restrictions			
	Mean Tariff	Total Charges[3]	All NTBs	License	Quota	Prohib.	Other[4]
Indonesia							
Primary products	14.7	14.7	98.9	61.7	13.8	21.8	1.6
Foods	24.5	24.5	99.8	21.5	29.4	45.6	3.3
Cereals	3.6	3.6	100.0	0.0	0.0	56.4	43.6
Vegetable oils & oil seeds	29.3	29.3	100.0	2.0	0.0	98.0	0.0
Agricultural raw materials	10.2	10.3	95.8	94.0	0.0	1.8	0.0
Textile fibers	8.8	9.1	89.0	89.0	0.0	0.0	0.0
Crude fertilizers & mineral ores	4.4	4.4	99.7	99.7	0.0	0.0	0.0
Mineral fuels	4.7	4.7	100.0	100.0	0.0	0.0	0.0
Non-ferrous metals	9.2	9.2	100.0	98.5	0.0	0.0	1.5
Manufactured products	19.4	19.6	93.1	87.0	1.5	0.5	4.1
Chemicals	11.0	11.0	95.6	88.2	6.7	0.7	0.0
Pharmaceuticals	4.8	4.8	100.0	100.0	0.0	0.0	0.0
Toiletries & perfumes	24.1	24.1	99.0	99.0	0.0	0.0	0.0
Manufactured fertilizers	0.0	0.0	100.0	100.0	0.0	0.0	0.0
Iron & Steel	8.2	8.2	99.3	58.4	0.0	0.0	40.9
Machinery & equipment	16.4	16.7	91.3	84.1	0.0	1.2	6.0
Non-electric machinery	12.6	13.1	96.6	87.2	0.0	0.0	9.4
Electric machinery	25.2	25.2	80.5	77.4	0.0	3.1	0.0
Transportation equipment	17.9	17.9	86.8	82.2	0.0	2.8	1.8
Other manufactured products	27.3	27.4	92.1	91.3	0.2	0.2	0.4
Leather & travel goods	28.2	28.2	100.0	100.0	0.0	0.0	0.0
Rubber products	10.3	10.3	66.1	66.1	0.0	0.0	0.0
Wood products	26.0	26.0	100.0	100.0	0.0	0.0	0.0
Paper products	29.1	29.4	84.5	84.5	0.0	0.0	0.0
Textiles and clothing	32.7	32.7	87.5	87.3	0.0	0.0	0.2
Non-metal mineral products	26.1	26.1	93.6	93.6	0.0	0.0	0.0
Furniture	42.2	42.2	100.0	100.0	0.0	0.0	0.0
Footwear	54.0	54.0	100.0	100.0	0.0	0.0	0.0
Professional equipment	12.7	12.7	98.4	98.4	0.0	0.0	0.0
All goods	18.1	18.2	94.7	80.1	4.9	6.4	3.3

Malaysia							
Primary products	8.6	8.7	4.5	4.3	0.0	0.2	0.0
Foods	12.3	12.5	5.6	5.4	0.0	0.2	0.0
Cereals	2.0	2.0	30.8	30.8	0.0	0.0	0.0
Vegetable oils & oil seeds	4.6	4.6	0.0	0.0	0.0	0.0	0.0
Agricultural raw materials	7.4	7.4	6.1	5.7	0.0	0.4	0.0
Textile fibers	2.3	2.3	0.0	0.0	0.0	0.0	0.0
Crude fertilizers & mineral ores	3.5	3.5	3.7	3.7	0.0	0.0	0.0
Mineral fuels	5.5	5.6	0.0	0.0	0.0	0.0	0.0
Non-ferrous metals	7.1	7.2	0.0	0.0	0.0	0.0	0.0
Manufactured products	15.4	16.2	3.2	3.2	0.0	0.1	0.0
Chemicals	8.9	9.4	3.0	3.0	0.0	0.1	0.0
Pharmaceuticals	3.3	3.3	0.0	0.0	0.0	0.0	0.0
Toiletries & perfumes	7.4	8.3	0.0	0.0	0.0	0.0	0.0
Manufactured fertilizers	0.0	0.6	0.0	0.0	0.0	0.0	0.0
Iron & Steel	6.1	6.1	8.3	8.3	0.0	0.0	0.0
Machinery & equipment	11.5	11.6	4.0	3.8	0.0	0.2	0.0
Non-electric machinery	7.1	7.1	1.9	1.6	0.0	0.3	0.0
Electric machinery	20.3	20.5	5.4	5.3	0.0	0.1	0.0
Transportation equipment	15.2	15.4	10.7	10.7	0.0	0.0	0.0
Other manufactured products	21.0	22.5	2.3	2.3	0.0	0.0	0.0
Leather & travel goods	27.5	27.5	0.0	0.0	0.0	0.0	0.0
Rubber products	31.7	32.6	0.0	0.0	0.0	0.0	0.0
Wood products	23.1	23.1	0.0	0.0	0.0	0.0	0.0
Paper products	15.4	16.4	0.0	0.0	0.0	0.0	0.0
Textiles and clothing	26.0	28.9	0.5	0.5	0.0	0.0	0.0
Non-metal mineral products	17.7	18.3	13.4	13.4	0.0	0.0	0.0
Furniture	40.4	40.4	0.0	0.0	0.0	0.0	0.0
Footwear	33.6	36.4	0.0	0.0	0.0	0.0	0.0
Professional equipment	6.8	6.9	0.0	0.0	0.0	0.0	0.0
All goods	13.6	14.3	3.7	3.6	0.0	0.1	0.0

(continued)

Appendix (Continued)

	Tariff and Para-Tariffs		Frequency of Nontariff Barriers[2]				
				Quantitative Restrictions			
	Mean Tariff	Total Charges[3]	All NTBs	License	Quota	Prohib.	Other[4]
Philippines							
Primary products	26.9	31.9	40.5	32.9	3.6	1.7	2.3
Foods	35.8	40.8	60.0	45.6	7.7	3.2	3.5
Cereals	36.9	41.9	100.0	57.7	38.5	0.0	3.8
Vegetable oils & oil seeds	26.4	31.4	26.0	26.0	0.0	0.0	0.0
Agricultural raw materials	22.7	27.7	24.2	20.2	0.0	0.9	3.1
Textile fibers	21.8	26.8	2.3	0.0	0.0	0.0	2.3
Crude fertilizers & mineral ores	12.6	17.6	12.7	12.7	0.0	0.0	0.0
Mineral fuels	16.0	21.0	75.0	75.0	0.0	0.0	0.0
Non-ferrous metals	21.4	26.4	0.0	0.0	0.0	0.0	0.0
Manufactured products	28.5	33.5	46.3	42.7	0.6	0.4	2.6
Chemicals	18.4	23.4	47.7	47.2	1.8	0.0	0.0
Pharmaceuticals	12.5	17.5	95.0	95.0	17.5	0.0	0.0
Toiletries & perfumes	32.5	37.5	16.78	16.7	0.0	0.0	0.0
Manufactured fertilizers	17.6	22.6	100.0	100.0	0.0	0.0	0.0
Iron & Steel	14.3	19.3	20.1	20.1	0.0	0.0	0.0
Machinery & equipment	23.7	28.7	87.6	87.3	0.2	0.0	0.1
Non-electric machinery	20.5	25.5	88.2	88.1	0.0	0.0	0.1
Electric machinery	32.4	37.4	98.1	97.5	0.6	0.0	0.0
Transportation equipment	21.7	26.7	65.1	65.1	0.0	0.0	0.0
Other manufactured products	37.1	42.1	28.0	20.9	0.5	0.8	5.8
Leather & travel goods	33.9	38.9	29.4	2.9	0.0	0.0	26.5
Rubber products	28.7	33.7	46.3	36.9	0.0	18.8	0.0
Wood products	38.5	43.5	17.3	14.9	0.0	0.0	2.4
Paper products	35.5	40.5	57.9	55.5	0.0	0.0	2.4
Textiles and clothing	43.2	48.2	12.8	9.0	0.0	0.0	3.8
Non-metal mineral products	35.5	40.5	33.5	24.1	0.0	0.0	9.4
Furniture	47.1	52.1	46.4	46.4	0.0	0.0	0.0
Footwear	47.0	52.0	25.0	25.0	0.0	0.0	0.0
Professional equipment	19.3	24.3	16.5	13.4	1.8	0.0	1.3
All goods	28.1	33.1	44.9	40.2	1.5	0.7	2.5

Singapore							
Primary products	0.1	0.1	15.3	15.3	0.0	0.0	0.0
Foods	0.1	0.1	21.8	21.8	0.0	0.0	0.0
Cereals	0.0	0.0	30.8	30.8	0.0	0.0	0.0
Vegetable oils & oil seeds	0.0	0.0	4.0	4.0	0.0	0.0	0.0
Agricultural raw materials	0.0	0.0	19.4	19.4	0.0	0.0	0.0
Textile fibers	0.0	0.0	15.9	15.9	0.0	0.0	0.0
Crude fertilizers & mineral ores	0.0	0.0	4.5	4.5	0.0	0.0	0.0
Mineral fuels	1.9	1.9	1.6	1.6	0.0	0.0	0.0
Non-ferrous metals	0.0	0.0	0.0	0.0	0.0	0.0	0.0
Manufactured products	0.4	0.4	14.1	13.8	0.0	0.4	0.0
Chemicals	0.0	0.0	49.0	48.6	0.0	0.4	0.0
Pharmaceuticals	0.0	0.0	95.0	95.0	0.0	0.0	0.0
Toiletries & perfumes	0.0	0.0	42.4	42.4	0.0	0.0	0.0
Manufactured fertilizers	0.0	0.0	0.0	0.0	0.0	0.0	0.0
Iron & Steel	0.0	0.0	0.0	0.0	0.0	0.0	0.0
Machinery & equipment	0.3	0.3	4.0	3.3	0.0	0.7	0.0
Non-electric machinery	0.0	0.0	1.0	1.0	0.0	0.0	0.0
Electric machinery	0.0	0.0	11.8	9.5	0.0	2.5	0.0
Transportation equipment	2.4	2.4	2.9	2.3	0.0	0.6	0.0
Other manufactured products	0.7	0.7	5.4	5.2	0.0	0.2	0.0
Leather & travel goods	0.2	0.2	0.0	0.0	0.0	0.0	0.0
Rubber products	0.0	0.0	0.0	0.0	0.0	0.0	0.0
Wood products	0.0	0.0	0.0	0.0	0.0	0.0	0.0
Paper products	0.0	0.0	0.0	0.0	0.0	0.0	0.0
Textiles and clothing	1.7	1.7	8.5	8.1	0.0	0.4	0.0
Non-metal mineral products	0.0	0.0	0.0	0.0	0.0	0.0	0.0
Furniture	2.2	2.2	0.0	0.0	0.0	0.0	0.0
Footwear	0.0	0.0	0.0	0.0	0.0	0.0	0.0
Professional equipment	0.0	0.0	0.0	0.0	0.0	0.0	0.0
All goods	0.3	0.3	14.7	14.4	0.0	0.3	0.0

(continued)

Appendix (Continued)

	Tariff and Para-Tariffs		*Frequency of Nontariff Barriers*[2]				
				Quantitative Restrictions			
	Mean Tariff	*Total Charges*[3]	*All NTBs*	*License*	*Quota*	*Prohib.*	*Other*[4]
Thailand							
Primary products	28.0	38.0	24.4	21.0	0.0	8.2	0.0
Foods	41.4	51.4	36.9	30.5	0.0	16.5	0.0
Cereals	50	15.0	61.5	30.8	0.0	30.8	0.0
Vegetable oils & oil seeds	39.7	49.7	96.0	96.0	0.0	48.0	0.0
Agricultural raw materials	23.7	33.7	14.9	14.9	0.0	0.0	0.0
Textile fibers	32.0	42.0	2.3	2.3	0.0	0.0	0.0
Crude fertilizers & mineral ores	9.2	19.2	17.9	17.9	0.0	0.0	0.0
Mineral fuels	10.7	20.7	11.1	11.1	0.0	0.0	0.0
Non-ferrous metals	15.2	25.2	5.7	1.9	0.0	4.7	0.0
Manufactured products	32.5	42.5	7.8	5.9	0.0	1.8	0.1
Chemicals	25.5	35.5	6.0	5.9	0.0	0.2	0.0
Pharmaceuticals	20.5	30.5	0.0	0.0	0.0	0.0	0.0
Toiletries & perfumes	45.3	55.3	0.0	0.0	0.0	0.0	0.0
Manufactured fertilizers	0.0	0.0	0.0	0.0	0.0	0.0	0.0
Iron & Steel	16.2	26.2	8.0	6.0	0.0	2.0	0.0
Machinery & equipment	23.4	33.4	9.4	8.1	0.0	1.3	0.0
Non-electric machinery	19.5	29.5	5.8	5.8	0.0	0.0	0.0
Electric machinery	33.3	43.3	15.6	13.8	0.0	1.9	0.0
Transportation equipment	22.8	32.8	14.0	8.1	0.0	5.8	0.1
Other manufactured products	41.2	51.2	7.7	4.9	0.0	2.8	0.0
Leather & travel goods	54.1	64.1	0.0	0.0	0.0	0.0	0.0
Rubber products	42.0	52.0	0.0	0.0	0.0	0.0	0.0
Wood products	26.7	36.7	83.3	83.3	0.0	0.0	0.0
Paper products	30.7	40.7	21.5	15.3	0.0	6.3	0.0
Textiles and clothing	51.5	61.5	09	0.5	0.0	0.4	0.0
Non-metal mineral products	31.8	48.1	8.0	1.8	0.0	6.3	0.0
Furniture	53.6	63.6	0.0	0.0	0.0	0.0	0.0
Footwear	54.0	64.0	0.0	0.0	0.0	0.0	0.0
Professional equipment	25.7	35.7	1.4	0.0	0.0	1.4	0.0
All goods	31.2	41.2	12.4	10.2	0.0	3.6	0.0

Notes: [1] Statistics by country are simple averages of rates of protection across trade categories.
[2] Percentage of tariff lines affected by NTBs.
[3] Customs duties plus customs surcharges and surtaxes, stamp taxes, certain other fiscal charges, and tax on foreign exchange transactions.
[4] Foreign exchange restrictions, decreed customs value, or state trading monopolies.

Source: UNCTAD (1987, 1989).

ACKNOWLEDGMENT

The author is a research fellow in the Trade and Macroeconomics Division of the International Food Policy Research Institute. This paper was prepared for the Conference on "Economic Regionalism: Macroeconomic Core and Microeconomic Optimization," organized by the American Committee on Asian Economic Studies and Chulalongkorn University, December 16-18, 1992, Bangkok, Thailand. The research assistance of Marcelle Thomas is gratefully acknowledged.

NOTES

1. For a broader perspective on the comparative advantage of the ASEAN countries in the global trading system, see DeRosa (1993).

2. The ASEAN trade simulation model is presented, with improvements in DeRosa (1995). On the application of similar CGE models to trade and development issues, see *inter alia* Dervis, de Melo and Robinson (1982), Deardorff and Stern (1986), and de Melo and Tarr (1992).

3. Among the simplifying assumptions underlying the analysis is that the elasticities of substitution in intermediate and final demand are the same in value in each traded goods category of the model.

4. Production in each sector of the model is assumed to be separable, such that inputs of primary factors may be considered a single aggregate that is combined in fixed proportions with similar aggregates of different intermediate goods. On the theory of separable production functions, see Solow (1955). For the derivation of the production functions employed in the ASEAN trade simulation model, see Deardorff and Stern (1986).

5. Nontraded goods are the numerative commodity in each country, with their prices in local currency terms assumed equal to unity. For non-ASEAN countries identified in the model, exchange rates and all sectoral prices and levels of production are assumed constant.

6. The Armington system of demands for traded goods may be derived formally from utility functions that are homogeneous and separable, following the utility-tree notion developed by Solow (1955), Strotz (1957), and others. Also, see Greene (1964) and Deaton and Muellbauer (1980). The upper-level utility functions governing preferences for *goods* are assumed to be Cobb-Douglas in form, while the lower-level ones governing preferences for geographically-differentiated *products* are assumed to be constant elasticity of substitution (CES) in form. The upper-level functions imply that income and uncompensated own-price elasticities of demand for goods are unitary in value and all cross-price elasticities of demand for goods are zero. While these assumptions are clearly restrictive, their "neutrality" serves to focus attention on assumptions concerning the extent of substitution among products in the lower-level CES utility functions and the implications of the assumptions for the resulting system of bilateral demands for traded goods.

7. Bilateral demands, as discussed further below, are inter-related by the elasticity substitution in demand for similar products in each importing market.

8. The import data for Bangladesh refer to the year 1987.

9. Similar matrices might have been constructed using statistics detailing exports by reporting country to partner countries. Import data, however, are relied upon because customs information about imports are frequently more accurate. Insurance and transportation charges are not explicitly considered.

10. U.S. ratios were applied to the export statistics for Canada, Australia-New Zealand, and European countries; Korean ratios to those for other East Asian countries; and Indonesian ratios for other Asian countries and the rest of the world.

11. The IDE inter-industry tables are so-called international input-output tables that identify inter-industry flows between, as well as within, countries. To be consistent with the specification of production relationships in the ASEAN trade simulation model, the IDE tables were first "compressed" to eliminate the differentiation of intermediate goods by country of origin. Finally, in applying 1975 values of inter-industry coefficients, the implicit assumption is that little change has occurred in the intervening years to basic production techniques or efficiencies.

12. For further discussion of this and related analytical problems of CGE models, see Shoven and Whalley (1984) and Winters (1986).

13. The simulation results for ASEAN trade with low-income Asian countries are particularly sensitive to the underlying assumptions about the product coverage of ASEAN trade liberalization. Notably, if ASEAN trade in both primary commodities and manufactures is liberalized on an MFN basis, ASEAN trade with the South Asian countries and China is estimated to increase by $77 million and $95 million, respectively.

REFERENCES

Armington, Paul A. (1969). A theory of demand for products distinguished by place of production. *IMF Staff Papers* 16: 159-178.

ASEAN (Association of Southeast Asian Nations). (1978). *10 Years ASEAN*. Jakarta, Indonesia: ASEAN Secretariat.

———. (1992a). *Singapore declaration of 1992*. Singapore: Fourth ASEAN Summit (January).

———. (1992b). *Framework agreement on enhancing ASEAN economic cooperation*. Singapore: Fourth ASEAN Summit (January).

———. (1992c). *Agreement on the common effective preferential tariff (CEPT) scheme for the ASEAN free trade area (AFTA)*. Singapore: Fourth ASEAN Summit (January).

Deaton, Angus, and John Muellbauer. (1980). *Economics and Consumer Behavior*. Cambridge: Cambridge University Press.

Deardorff, Alan V., and Robert M. Stern. (1986). *The Michigan Model of World Production and Trade: Theory and Applications*. Cambridge, MA: The MIT Press.

de Melo, Jamie, and David Tarr. (1992). *A General Equilibrium Analysis of U.S. Foreign Trade Policy*. Cambridge, MA: The MIT Press.

DeRosa, Dean A. (1992). Protection and export performance in Sub-Saharan Africa. *Weltwirtschaftliches Archiv* 128(1): 88-124.

———. (1993). Sources of comparative advantage in the international trade of the ASEAN countries. *The ASEAN Economic Bulletin 10* (1): 1-11.

———. (1995). *Regional Trading Arrangements among Developing Countries: The ASEAN Example*. Research Report 103. Washington, DC: International Food Policy Research Institute.

Dervis, Kemal, Jaime de Melo and Sherman Robinson. (1982). *General Equilibrium Models for Development Policy*. Cambridge: Cambridge University Press.

Drysdale, Peter and Ross Garnaut. (1993). The Pacific: An application of a general theory of economic integration. *In Pacific Dynamisms and the International Economic System*, eds., C. Fred Bergsten and Marcus Noland. Washington, DC: Institute for International Economics.

Green, H.A.J. (1964). *Aggregation in Economic Analysis*. Princeton, New Jersey: Princeton University Press.

Hughes, Helen. (1991). Does APEC make sense? *ASEAN Economic Bulletin 8*. (November): 125-137.

IDE (Institute of Developing Economies). (1982). *International input-output tables for ASEAN countries 1975*. Tokyo.

Just, Richard E., and Darrell L. Hueth, and Andrew Schmitz. (1982). *Applied Welfare Economics and Public Policy*. Englewood Cliffs, NJ: Prentice-Hall.

Linnemann, Hans, ed. (1992). *South-South Trade Preferences*. New Delhi: Sage Publications.

Mayanathan, Sahathavan, and Ismail Haron. (1987). ASEAN trade co-operation: a survey of the issues. In *ASEAN at the Crossroads*, ed., Noordin Sopiee, Chew Lay See, and Lim Siang Jin. Kuala Lumpur, Malaysia: Institute of Strategic and International Studies.

Naya, Seiji, and Pearl Imada. (1987). *Towards an ASEAN trade area*. Kuala Lumpur, Malaysia: Institute of Strategic and International Studies.

Nogues, J., and A. Olechowski, and L.A. Winters. (1986). The extent of non-tariff barriers to imports in industrial countries. World Bank staff working paper 789. Washington, D.C.

Riedel, James. (1991). Intra-Asian trade and foreign direct investment. *Asian Development Review* 9(1): 111-146.

Rieger, Hans Christoph. (1985). *ASEAN Co-operation and intra-ASEAN trade*. Research and discussion paper no. 57. ASEAN Economic Research Unit. Singapore: Institute of Southeast Asian Studies.

Shoven, John B., and John Whalley. (1984). Applied general-equilibrium models of taxation and international trade: an introduction and survey. *Journal of Economic Literature* 22(September): 1007-1051.

Solow, Robert. (1955-1956). The production function and the theory of capital. *The Review of Economic Studies* 23: 101-108.

Stern, Robert M., Jonathan Francis, and Bruce Schumacher. (1976). *Price Elasticities in International Trade: An Annotated Bibliography*. London: Macmillan for the Trade Policy Research Centre.

Strotz, R.H. (1957). The empirical implications of a utility tree. *Econometrica* 25 (April).

UNCTAD (United Nations Conference on Trade and Development). (1987). *Handbook of Trade Control Measures of Developing Countries 1987*. Geneva.

________. (1989). *Handbook of Trade Control Measures of Developing Countries 1987:* supplement. Geneva.

Viner, J. (1950). *The Customs Union Issue*. New York: Carnegie Endowment for International Peace.

Whalley, John. (1985). *Trade Liberalization Among Major World Trading Areas*. Cambridge, MA: The MIT Press.

Winters, L.A. (1986). Trade liberalization among major world trading areas. *Journal of Economic Literature* 24(1): 111-112.

Wong, John. (1985). ASEAN's experience in regional economic cooperation. *Asian Development Review* 3(1): 79-98.

ECONOMIC REGIONALISM IN THE ASIAN AND PACIFIC REGION:

TRENDS, CHALLENGES AND PROSPECTS

Chee Peng Lim

While economic regionalism developed rapidly in Latin America, Europe and Africa, it was more or less dormant in Asia and the Pacific[1] for several years after World War II. Several factors retarded the growth of economic regionalism in this region, not the least of which was the Cold War which had a divisive impact on the movement for regional cooperation. By 1960 however, the need for greater cooperation stimulated some countries to form sub-regional groups such as ASEAN and SAARC. More recently, growing economic interdependence and globalization as well as the intensification of economic regionalism in other regions, especially Europe, have prompted a resurgence of economic regionalism in Asia and the Pacific.

This paper focuses on the current wave of regionalism in Asia and the Pacific and explores the scope and prospects for enhancing regional cooperation in the region. Following the introduction, Section 1 analyses the functions and progress of the various subregional and regional groups concerned with economic cooperation in Asia and the Pacific while Section 2 highlights the

Research in Asian Economic Studies, Volume 6, pages 125-144.

ISBN: 1-55938-918-4

distinguishing features of cooperative arrangements in the region. Section 3 discusses the challenges and prospects for further regional economic cooperation. Finally, the concluding section offers some suggestions for fostering such cooperation within the context of accelerating overall development in the Asian and Pacific region.

I. REGIONAL ECONOMIC COOPERATION IN ASIA AND THE PACIFIC

The quest for regional economic cooperation among the peoples inhabiting the geographically dispersed and socio-economically diverse Asian and Pacific region began a decade ago with the establishment of the United Nations Economic and Social Commission for Asia and the Pacific (ESCAP), then known as the Economic Commission For Asia and the Far East (ECAFE). However, despite numerous efforts by ESCAP, the impulses for regional cooperation remained weak and few cooperative schemes of any significance were implemented in the first two decades of ESCAP's existence. Several countries in the region were too preoccupied either with their newly found independence or were pursuing political and economic policies so divergent that there was hardly any commonality of views. Nevertheless, ESCAP did make some tangible gains in fostering regional economic cooperation through the establishment of various cooperative schemes, such as the Asian Development Bank (1966), the Asian Clearing Union (1973) and the Bangkok Agreement on Trade Expansion (1976). However, except for the Asian Development Bank, participation in the other schemes such as the Bangkok Agreement was rather limited.

Economic regionalism appeared to have found a more receptive environment at the subregional level with the establishment of several subregional groups, beginning with the Economic Cooperation Organization (ECO) founded in 1964. (It was then called Regional Cooperation for Development). ECO is a tripartite arrangement aiming at closer economic, technical and cultural cooperation and tries to cooperate in certain industrial projects and standards, trade, tourism, transport (including the building of road and rail links), communications and cultural affairs. The introduction of a preferential trade system was announced in July 1987, and the establishment of a joint reinsurance company was announced in September, the same year. The members of ECO are the Islamic Republic of Iran, Pakistan and Turkey. ECO did not appear to have made much progress. However, its future has been enhanced with the participation of all the Central Asian republics (except Kazakhstan) of the former U.S.S.R. in February 1992.

Much more progress has been achieved with the Association of Southeast Asian Nations (ASEAN), which was established following the signing of the

Bangkok Declaration on 8 August, 1967 by the Foreign Minister of Indonesia, Malaysia, Philippines, Singapore and Thailand. Its major objectives were to: accelerate economic growth, social progress, and cultural development in the region through cooperative endeavours; promote regional peace and stability; promote active collaboration and mutual assistance in matters of common interest; provide assistance to each other in the form of training and research facilities; maintain close and beneficial cooperation with existing international and regional organizations with similar aims and purposes, and explore all avenues for even closer cooperation among themselves.

The Heads of State or Government of member countries are the highest authority in ASEAN while the Secretary-General, who is located in Jakarta, is the chief executive of the ASEAN Secretariat. Apart from summit meetings and ministerial meetings of foreign ministers, economic ministers or other ministers, there is an ASEAN Standing Committee and Committees on Trade and Tourism (COTT), on Industry, Minerals and Energy (COIME), on Food, Agriculture and Forestry (COFAF), on Transportation and Communications (COST), on Social Development (COSD), on Culture and Information (COCI) and on Budget. In each member country, day-to-day work is coordinated by the ASEAN National Coordinating Agency. At the governmental level, ASEAN has committees and subcommittees on various subjects. In the private sector, it works through chambers of commerce and industry with a number of working groups, industrial clubs and commodity clubs. ASEAN has established several subsidiaries to pursue specialized activities such as the ASEAN Insurance Council, ASEAN Centre on Trade and ASEAN Council on Petroleum. (For details, see Institute of Strategic and International Studies, 1987 and Alagappa, 1987. The ASEAN institutional framework has been restructured following the Fourth ASEAN Summit in Singapore in 1992.)

Although ASEAN has generated an extensive interactive network of governmental and private sector agencies, ASEAN regional economic cooperation is still viewed in many quarters as not rapid enough, especially in the crucial areas of trade liberalization and industrial cooperation. For example, in spite of the ASEAN Preferential Trading Arrangement and Complementation Scheme, intra-ASEAN trade has yet to reach 25 percent, which was the peak achieved before ASEAN was established. (For details, see H.C. Rieger 1985). Intra-ASEAN exports increased marginally from 16.7 percent in 1980 to 17.4 percent in 1989, which largely reflected Singapore-Malaysia and Singapore-Indonesia trade. In fact, the share of exports from the Philippines and Thailand to other ASEAN countries has declined. (By comparison with ASEAN, intra-EC trade in 1991 was around 60.8 percent of its total trade.)

Nevertheless, ASEAN is perhaps the most successful subregional cooperation group in Asia and the Pacific. The Association has been successful in speaking out with one voice on major international trade and economic issues. It presented a joint stand at the Uruguay Round of multilateral talks on improving world trade rules and it has jointly worked out trade benefits with the EEC, Japan and other major trading partners. ASEAN is now preparing to build on its success by setting up the ASEAN Free Trade Area (AFTA). Under the scheme proposed in 1991, ASEAN has decided on a 15-year time frame to reduce tariffs on manufactured products to 5 percent or less. (AFTA is expected to have a net trade-creation effect and accelerate the expansion of intra-ASEAN trade. For details, see Philippine Institute of Development Studies 1992 and Imada, Montes Naya, 1991.)

In the Pacific, the first meeting of the South Pacific Forum which represented the gathering of Heads of Government of the independent and self-governing States of the South Pacific was held in 1971. It meets annually and provides an opportunity for informal discussions on a wide range of common issues and problems. The Forum has no written constitution or international agreement covering its activities, nor any formal rules relating to its purpose, membership or the conduct of meetings. Decisions are always reached by consensus, it never having been found necessary or desirable to vote formally on issues.

The Forum is served by the South Pacific Forum Secretariat which was established in 1973 and located in Suva. The secretariat's executive board is a Committee which comprises representatives and senior officials from all member countries. It meets twice a year, immediately before the meetings of the Forum and at the end of the year, to discuss in detail the secretariat's work programe and annual budget. The secretariat is headed by a director with an executive staff of 25 drawn from member countries, and coordinates regional action on trade promotion and marketing; industrialization; transport; energy; law of the sea; and development planning. It assists in negotiating trade and commodity agreements and manages a disaster relief fund. The Secretariat also cooperates in the South Pacific Regional Environment Programme and has been instrumental in setting up a regional shipping company, the Pacific Forum Line, which is now commercially successful, after suffering initial losses. (For details, see United Nations, 1990a, 227).

The third initiative on subregional cooperation came with the formation of the South Asian Association for Regional Cooperation (SAARC) in 1985 by the leaders of seven South Asian nations (Bangladesh, Bhutan, India, Maldives, Nepal, Pakistan and Sri Lanka) to improve regional cooperation, particularly in economic development. SAARC holds a meeting of Heads of State or Government once a year while the Council of Ministers (foreign ministers of member States) meets at least twice a year. The meetings review progress, and take decisions on new areas or cooperation, on additional mechanisms and other matters of general interest. A standing committee, comprising foreign secretaries, meets as necessary, provides overall monitoring and coordination, approves projects and programs and their financing, determines priorities and mobilizes resources. The SAARC Secretariat comprises a Secretary-General, appointed by the Council of Ministers for a two-year term, which position rotates among member States, directors on a three-year tenure, and general service staff. Technical committees, comprising representatives of member States, implement, coordinate and monitor programmes in their respective areas. Action committees are concerned with implementation of projects involving some but not all member States.

The current areas of cooperation of SAARC relate to agriculture and forestry; health and population activities; meteorology; rural development; telecommunications; transport; science and technology; postal services; sports, arts and culture; women in development; and drug trafficking and abuse. Following the directive of the Bangalore Summit in 1986, SAARC implemented the South Asian Documentation Centre, promoted organized tourism among member countries, instituted SAARC chairs, fellowships and scholarships, and launched an organized volunteers' program. (For details, see R. Kumar 1988, 99-116) and S.H.N. Naqvi, 1989 pp. 163-186.)

Partly as a result of the increasing dynamism of the East and South-East Asian countries and partly as a response to the resurgence of regionalism in other parts of the world, several proposals emerged towards the end of the 1980s for more wide-ranging and effective forms of regional cooperation in the region. Some of these initiatives sought to establish links, primarily in the field of trade, among the economies around the Pacific Ocean rim.

One of the first efforts was the establishment of the Pacific Economic Cooperation Council (PECC), a non-governmental organization (NGOs), now known as the Pacific Economic Cooperation Council. PECC, was founded in September 1980 at the initiative of former prime ministers Malcolm Fraser of Australia and Masayoshi Ohira of Japan. Its members are drawn from the government, business and academic sectors of 20 countries and economies around the Pacific, each of which has established a national committee. A general meeting of the organization is held every 18 months. PECC also has a standing committee of 17 members, including members of ASEAN, Australia, Canada, China, Japan New Zealand, the Pacific island countries, the Republic of Korea, Taiwan Province of China and the United States of America. However, apart from conducting studies and holding discussions on economic issues of common concern to its members, PECC has not initiated any significant scheme for regional economic cooperation.

Asian Pacific Economic Cooperation (APEC), which shares many of the perceptions of PECC was established as an intergovernmental body in January 1989 at the initiative of the Australian Prime Minister Robert Hawke partially in response to the slow progress in the Uruguay Round of multilateral trade negotiations. Its inaugural meeting was attended by ministers from 12 countries around the Pacific. The proposal to establish APEC arose from a recognition of the need for effective consultations among their decision makers to:

a. Help strengthen the multilateral trading system and enhance the prospects for success in the Uruguay Round;
b. Provide an opportunity to assess prospects for and obstacles to increased trade and investment flows within the Asian and Pacific region;
c. Identify the range of practical common economic interests.

Membership of APEC currently consists of Australia, Brunei Darussalam, Canada, China, Hong Kong, Indonesia, Japan, Malaysia, New Zealand, the Philippines, the Republic of Korea, Singapore, Taiwan, Thailand, and the United States. On the basis of its current membership, APEC is more of an interregional than a regional economic grouping, although its membership includes most of the dynamic economies of the region. Following its inception, APEC identified and implemented various projects relating to economic studies, trade liberalization, investment, technology transfer, human resource development and sectoral cooperation. In 1992, APEC became an intergovernmental institution with a Ministerial Council and established a Secretariat in Singapore. (For details, see Elek, 1992).

The most recent proposal for cooperation in the Asia-Pacific region is the East Asian Economic Group (EAEG), proposed by the Malaysian Prime Minister Mahathir Mohammed in 1990 following the failure of the Uruguay Round to resolve differences over farm subsidies between the United States and Europe. According to the proposal, the objective of EAEG was to defend the multilateral trading system and it emphasized the need for close consultation and cooperation among the countries of the region for the common good. Many of the details of EAEG are not yet available, but public statements of the proponents emphasize the following.

First, EAEG was intended to be a consultative forum in which member countries would consult, on an ongoing basis, on trade and economic issues of mutual interest. Initially, it would cooperate to ensure the success of the Uruguay Round but, in time, the consultative process would be strengthened to enhance economic cooperation in trade and investment. Second, EAEG was not intended to become a trade bloc or play a confrontational role *vis-a-vis* any other region, country or bloc. Third, EAEG would be consistent with GATT (General Agreement on Tariffs and Trade) and contribute to the success of the Uruguay Round in its attempt to maintain and enhance the global trading system. Fourth, EAEG would be investment and trade generating and not aim at trade diversion or create unnecessary barriers to third country imports. Fifth, EAEG would not focus narrowly and concentrate on trade; instead it would explore all other areas of potentially productive cooperation across the whole spectrum of economic interrelationships. At the same time, EAEG would not indulge in unproductive duplication of efforts undertaken by other relevant organizations. Finally, it is proposed to include the ASEAN countries,

China, Hong Kong, Japan, Myanmar, the Republic of Korea, Taiwan Province of China and Viet Nam among the founding members.

When EAEG was first proposed it encountered such strong objections, particularly from the United States, that the proposal was diluted and the concept was renamed the East Asian Economic Caucus (EAEC), apparently to serve more as a discussion forum rather than the trade bloc which its opponents feared that it would turn out to be. Opposition to EAEC still remains, so the proposal is still without an organizational structure or even a schedule of meetings.

In addition to the above, mention should also be made of various other attempts at promoting economic regionalism. These include the "growth triangles," the Australia-New Zealand Closer Economic Relations and Trade Agreement, the Baht Economic Zone, the Greater China Economic Zone, the Yellow Sea Economic Zone, and the Northeast Asia Non-Governmental Economic Cooperation Association (NANECA). Most of these attempts are at the non-governmental level, and some of them, such as the "growth triangles" are largely confined to areas rather than countries. Other arrangements such as the various "zones" are still at the planning stage; however some of them may crystalize following recent developments.

For example, the establishment of diplomatic ties between China and the Republic of Korea in September 1992 has improved prospects for turning the Yellow Sea Economic Zone into a reality. The development will set the stage for increased regional cooperation among the complementary economies of Northern China, the Democratic People's Republic of Korea, the Republic of Korea, the eastern part of the Russian Federation and Japan, as these Northeast Asian economies complement each other. For example, China has an abundance of human resources, the Far East region of the Russian Federation is rich in natural resources while Japan and the Republic of Korea have the capital and the technology. A growth area encompassing these countries would, by some estimates, have a population of about 300 million people, roughly equal to that of the Single European Market; its combined GNP would be about $US 3 trillion and will account for almost one third of total global trade.

In short, it would appear that after a hiatus of nearly four decades, the Asian-Pacific region is riding on a wave of regionalism which will enhance regional economic cooperation.

II. DISTINGUISHING FEATURES OF ECONOMIC REGIONALISM IN ASIA AND THE PACIFIC

From the above survey of regionalism in Asia and the Pacific, some distinctive features may be highlighted. Firstly, regional economic cooperation arrangements in Asia and the Pacific are taking place at various levels, ranging from very geographically restricted schemes such as the "growth triangles" to interregional schemes with a bias towards "open regionalism" such as APEC. (Generally, the "growth traingles" do not incorporate the entire country but only a certain region. For example, the whole of Singapore is included in the "southern growth triangle," only Batam Island, Indonesia and Johore state in Malaysia are covered. For a discussion of the concept of "open regionalism," see Drysdale and Garnaut, 1992.) Unfortunately, most of these schemes are taking place independently of each other and there is hardly any linkage or even dialogue among the various subregional or regional groups with the exception of ASEAN and APEC. So far no formal mechanism or institution has been created to provide a forum to bring the subregional groups together to discuss or propose any scheme for inter-subregional cooperation. The lacuna renders it difficult to coordinate regional cooperation efforts or manage them more systematically in a way which will create wider economic spaces in the region.

Secondly, cooperation arrangements among countries in the region are not exclusive to developing or developed countries and even extend to countries outside the region, such as in the case of APEC. This may be desirable, since regional cooperation exclusively confined to developing countries have not been very successful. Although the inclusion of developed and developing countries may exacerbate conflicting interests, such a combination enhances complementarity. Similarly, the inclusion of countries outside the region may provide the critical mass for expanding intraregional trade and investment.

Thirdly, regional economic cooperation in Asia and the Pacific has generally focused on a relatively shallow level of cooperation in trade, industrial development, environment management and exchange of information. Cooperation has generally shied away from more substantive areas such as harmonisation of trade and investment policies, liberalisation of factor markets or macroeconomic policy coordination. Trade cooperation figures most prominently among the ASEAN countries following the adoption of the ASEAN Free Trade Area (AFTA). On the other hand, SAARC has deliberately avoided any discussion on trade cooperation. APEC is focussing its attention on promoting trade liberalisation. Given the growing volume of intraregional trade, cooperation in trade may be intensified, although the prospects for the establishment of an Asian Common Market are still a long way off. Similarly, industrial development offers potential scope for regional economic development, in view of the exhaustion of secondary import substitution in several countries in the region. Again ASEAN has gone furthest down the road in this direction with its ASEAN Industrial Complementation Scheme. Further cooperation may be expected in the promotion of medium and small scale enterprises where there is tremendous scope and economies to be exploited. (For details, see Chee, Peng Lim 1992, Part A.)

Fourthly, regional cooperation in Asia and the Pacific is not governed by any legislative binding force, in the form of a treaty, such as in the case of the European Economic Community (EEC). On the contrary, the arrangement is usually loose and flexible, and is generally based on a simple memorandum of understanding. In the case of the "growth triangles", the processes are generally market driven and initiated by the private sector rather than the government. Apparently, not many Asian and Pacific countries are prepared to move towards a more binding form of association. For example, at the ASEAN Economic Ministers meeting in Malaysia in 1991, the Association turned down a Philippines' proposal for an ASEAN Treaty of Economic Cooperation along the lines of the EEC. In addition, regional cooperation arrangements in Asia and the Pacific tend to avoid any highly complex institutional structure. For example, APEC, several years after its establishment did not have a permanent secretariat. When a decision was taken to create a secretariat in Singapore in 1992, APEC insisted on a small staff with only about 7-8 officials. Similarly, ASEAN operated through a small secretariat in Jakarta for more than two decades, before it decided to enlarge the staff. But even then, the total number of officials is not expected to exceed 20. In this respect, economic regionalism in Asia and the Pacific differs significantly from the EEC paradigm, which as Dutta (1992, p. 68) points out, "provides for a macroeconomic core of the community with respect to monetary and fiscal stability for microeconomic actors (Households and firms) in all EC member economies, concurrently ensuring a degree of economic pluralism for the member economies," (European Commission, 1989, 1990).

Fifthly, it is interesting to note that current attempts at regional cooperation, as exemplified by APEC and EAEC are situated around the Asian Pacific Rim, and tends to exclude South Asia. This has naturally caused some concern in South Asia which regards APEC and EAEC as disguised attempts to redefine the Asian and Pacific region which is generally accepted to stretch westward, beyond Thailand to the Islamic Republic of Iran. There is also a fear that such a development will exclude those countries, west of Thailand, from the benefits of the growth poles, emanating from Japan, the NIEs and China. Subsequently, countries which are not part of the new regional groupings may be at a disadvantage when they compete in the markets of the dynamic economies of Asia and the Pacific.

Sixthly, with few exceptions, such as the southern growth triangle and PECC, the private sector has minimal participation in regional cooperation efforts in Asia and the Pacific which have been largely initiated and implemented by government officials. Private sector participation in the southern growth triangle, enabled the scheme to take off within a period of three years while the lack of meaningful private sector participation slowed down ASEAN's progress for at least two decades.In ASEAN for example, the private sector has often complained of being asked to endorse rather than being consulted in the design of cooperation projects. For instance, guidelines for the ASEAN Industrial Complementation Scheme were drawn up without private sector participation and were subsequently described as inflexible and impractical by ASEAN businessmen. Even though there is an ASEAN-Chamber of Commerce and Industry (ASEAN-CCI), the Chamber has complained that in its years of existence, it has had little success in making its voice heard at meetings of ASEAN heads of state and economic ministers. A number of private sector representatives note that the pronouncements by ASEAN heads of state according recognition to the private sector's role in regional economic cooperation had not been translated into practice, because, "at the working level, government servants have not got the right kind of perception and understanding of their role." (Chee, Peng Lim 1987 pp. 106-107.)

Finally, compared to other developing regions in Africa and Latin America, economic regionalism in Asia and the Pacific emphasises cooperation and is more outward oriented. Although it does not generally rely on multilateralism in its approach to trade policy implementation, Asian and Pacific regionalism is less discriminatory towards non-members since it is generally accompanied by some unilateral trade liberalisation (World Bank, 1992 p. 12).

III. CHALLENGES AND POTENTIAL

Although the need for enhanced economic regionalism is being felt by Asian and Pacific countries, there is some hesitation in moving towards more comprehensive forms of regional cooperation for three main reasons. First, the region's growth dynamism owes its strength to expansion and liberalisation of global rather than regional trade, and regional economic cooperation is viewed mainly as an insurance against external political threats. Second, the hesitation arises from the emerging disparities among the economies of the region, which leads to a reluctance among the strong as much as the weak, based on the perception that the gains from cooperation might be inequitable and inequitably shared. Third, nationalism continues to prevail over regional interests. For example, when the United States offered ASEAN preferential trade benefits, similar to those extended to Mexico and the Caribbean, the ASEAN countries insisted that Washington sign six separate treaties with them. The U.S. offer was subsequently shelved ("Cooperation in a pipe-dream," *Bangkok Post*, 11 November, 1991, p.26).

Notwithstanding the caution, there is considerable scope for greater regional economic cooperation in Asia and the Pacific, which could prove mutually beneficial to a large number of economies in the region without conflicting with their national objectives and priorities. The externalities created by regional economic cooperation on a wider scale could more than offset some of the perceived disadvantages. In any case, there are compelling market forces, recently set in motion by significant changes in the global and regional economic environment which will induce countries in the region to seek closer accommodation with each other. These developments are relatively more evident in East and Southeast Asia where the momentum for regional economic cooperation is most promising. The emergence of an improved environment for cooperation has been strengthened by the reality of the increasing interdependence among the economies of the region. The process has been supported by the emerging complementarities in production and the convergence of macroeconomic policies in Asia and the Pacific.

Data on intra-regional trade and investments confirm the phenomenal increase in economic interdependence in Asia and the Pacific over the last decade or so. Between 1980 and 1988, for example, intraregional exports and imports among developing countries in the region increased by 3.7 and 3.3 fold respectively. (The Asia Society predicts that intra-Asian trade may reach 50 percent of the region's total trade by the Year 2,000. "Asian regional economy growth under spotlight," *Bangkok Post*, 17 March, 1992.) The increase in intra-regional trade may be largely explained by accelerated growth in Asia and the Pacific and has little to do with economic regionalism. (For details, see Riedel, 1991.)

The trends in intra-regional trade were reinforced by the emerging pattern of investment flows in the region. Foreign direct investment increased by 12 percent a year in real terms between 1970 and 1989 in Asia and the Pacific. In the last ten years, Japan has replaced the United States and Western Europe as the overall leading investor in the region, while during the last five years, investment from the Asian newly industrializing economies (NIEs) has, in turn, replaced Japan as the leading investor in several Asian developing countries. (For details, see Chee, Peng Lim, 1989).

In short, higher levels of intraregional trade and investment are gradually shaping a truly interdependent regional economy in the Asian and Pacific region. The basis of this growing interdependence is the linking of the production structures of several economies in the region through the development of a dynamically changing regional division of labor. This regional complementarity is most evident in the East and South-East Asian subregions and may be seen not only between developed and developing countries but also, more remarkably, among developing countries.

Traditionally, complementarity has been the key element of Japan's trade with Asia and the Pacific: Japan exported machinery and other manufactured goods and imported natural resources from the developing countries in the region. (For details, see A. Hirata and T. Nohara 1989.) In recent years, however, there has been a growing complementarity among developing countries in Asia and the Pacific, brought about in part by global interdependence, as is illustrated by developments in the textile industry. The textile industry originated in the United Kingdom from whence it spread to

Japan during the Meiji Restoration in 1868, but by the early 1960s, a third generation of textile manufacturers appeared in the NIEs. This pattern of development was repeated in the 1980s with another generation of economies moving up the textile ladder, namely, China and South-East Asia. More recently, the development has spread to South Asia, particularly Bangladesh and Sri Lanka. In the process, a clear division of labor has emerged among developing countries in the textile industry. While the newcomers engage in the lower end of the industry, using their abundant human resources, the NIEs have enhanced their value added and graduated to the more capital-intensive segments of the textile industry. The eventual integration of the Asian States of CIS into the Asian and Pacific economy should now introduce a further dimension in regional complementarity. Since some of the Asian Republics of the Commonwealth of Independent States (CIS) (together with India and Pakistan) are major cotton producers the resumption of trade between these States and South Asia may enhance backward linkages in the textile industry and lead to the development of an integrated industry in the Asian and Pacific region. This new development is beginning to be reflected in the growth of intra-industry trade in the region.

Finally, more and more countries in the Asian and Pacific region are realizing that liberalizing their economies and enhancing their market orientation may be a relatively effective strategy for accelerating economic development. Thus, although there may be some differences in development objectives, there has been a noticeable convergence in development strategies as well as in the choice of planning and policy instruments in the region, especially since the early 1980s. For example, in the past, the Asian newly industrializing economies adopted a development strategy of outward-orientation, market-based structural reforms and reliance on private enterprise (including transnational corporations from the developed and the developing countries), while the South Asian countries generally depended on the strategy of "inward-looking-import-substituting-development" based on low-return yielding public enterprises in core areas. Some years ago, however, Sri Lanka and Bangladesh switched to a relatively more open and private initiative-based development strategy. Pakistan made a radical departure from its earlier policy regime in the first half of 1991, while India took its first bold initiatives in restructuring its economy towards more open and market-oriented economy with bigger role for private enterprise in July 1991. All four major South Asian countries (Bangladesh, India, Pakistan, and Sri Lanka) have, moreover, initiated structural economic reforms under the impact of balance of payments support from the International Monetary Fund. Such economic reforms in South Asia, as well as those in the transition economies, have led to a gradual convergence of perceptions of development objectives. This, in turn, will facilitate the process of regional economic cooperation, since policy makers can operate on the basis of a shared view of the development process which is pragmatic rather than ideological in nature.

Briefly, recent developments and trends appear to favor economic regionalism in Asia and the Pacific and these have been reinforced by a rising tide of enthusiasm among countries in the region. Such enthusiasm was clearly manifested in the adoption of the 1992 Beijing Declaration on Enhancing Regional Economic Cooperation at the forty-eighth session of the Economic and Social Commission for Asia and the Pacific. The Declaration was sponsored by nearly 40 member countries of the Economic and Social Commission of Asia and the Pacific, including China, India, Japan and the United States and called upon all members to give full and active support to the principles and objectives of regional economic cooperation. It also strongly urged that promotion of intraregional trade and investment, and greater cooperation in science and technology and in the development of infrastructure, should receive high priority in economic cooperation in Asia and the Pacific.

As for the scope for regional cooperation, the potential is equally promising. However the experience of regional economic cooperation show that progress will be extremely difficult unless such cooperation is given time to mature. For example, the ASEAN Preferential Trading Arrangement had little impact on intraregional trade not only because it was restricted but also because of the absence of exploitable complementarities. (For details, see S. Meyananthan and I. Haron (1988) and also R. J. Langhammer, 1988). Similarly, it will be very difficult to agree on any practical scheme for investment harmonization among countries at very different levels of development and resource endowments. This need not imply that there are no substantial areas for cooperation among Asian and Pacific countries; on the contrary, the potential is significant.

Firstly, in view of its significance for promoting regional development cooperation in infrastructure should be given priority. Physical infrastructure comprises all those basic industries, such as transport, communications, power or multi-purpose water-resource development schemes, which must precede the more quick-yielding, directly productive investments. The scope for regional cooperation appears substantial in such areas as transport, communications, power and riverine systems. More specifically, within the context of recent developments, there is an urgent need to facilitate the movement of goods, people and vehicles at border crossings to enhance trading and tourism through the provision of land transport infrastructure at main border crossings. In the past, several countries in Asia and the Pacific were artificially separated from their neighbors because of ideological differences. Now that the cold war has ended and borders have reopened, it is imperative to establish links among countries sharing a common economic watershed. For example, the construction of an Eastern Highway linking Southern China, Viet Nam, the Lao People's Democratic Republic, Thailand and Myanmar will greatly complement the Asian Highway linking South-East Asia with South and Southwest Asia. (For details, see "East-West highway key to prosperity",

Bangkok Post, 6 September 1989, p.16). Similarly, ECO and SAARC could cooperate in facilitating the development of infrastructure between the Asian Republics of CIS and South Asia. Presently transport networks in the Asian Republics are aligned with those of the Russian Federation. Following the assumption of interdependence, it may be more rational for the Asian Republics of CIS to strengthen economic ties with neighboring countries particularly Islamic Republic of Iran, Turkey, China and Pakistan. Such a development would be facilitated by the development of joint infrastructure projects between ECO and SAARC. The need is particularly urgent in view of the fact that all the Asian Republics are land-locked. Thus an investment program for strengthening international links and regional transport network based on an analysis of present status and future projections should be of significance in enhancing regional cooperation.

Secondly, there is tremendous scope in regional coordination in science and technology which until now has taken a bilateral rather than a multilateral approach. Fortunately the dynamic economic growth and industrial and technological development in several countries in the region over the past decade or so have created better conditions for regional cooperation in science and technology. Such cooperation should be based on and foster science and technology endogenous capacity-building with prime focus on technological capability development.

Thirdly, regional cooperation should also focus on managing the environment more effectively. The recent sensitivity to global environmental concerns provides one of the most powerful rationales behind regional cooperation in the promotion of environmental management. Fruitful areas include the need for countries to harmonize their environmental regulations, particularly with respect to the disposal of hazardous wastes. The current efforts taken by ASEAN to strengthen its environmental impact evaluation procedures is a step worth emulating by other subregional and regional groups. In addition, since certain environmental assessment and management measures are fairly well developed in some countries, the transfer of such technologies can achieve successful results. There are a number of local or regional institutions which can be utilized for this purpose and serve as potential regional centers of excellence. Training and manpower development can also be promoted through these institutions; an example of such an institute in the field of desert control technology is the Central Arid Zone Research Institute in India. Environmental impact analysis guidelines for several types of development projects, with necessary modifications, can be easily adopted by other countries for the assessment of their development projects. In the field of legislation Japan, the Philippines and Thailand have enacted specific laws and set standards which can be used as guidelines for other countries for developing or introducing environmental management policies and standards. In particular, Japan and Singapore have had considerable success in solid waste management programs. Their experience in collection, transfer and disposal of waste could be useful for countries faced with the problem of having to institute similar programs. There are also other environmental technological capabilities in the region which may be used as the basis for regional cooperation. (For details, see United Nations 1990.)

Fourthly, an emerging problem in the Asian and Pacific region is the migration of labor from the surplus to the deficit countries. In the coming years, this problem is expected to intensify and reach a scale not since the 1940s. Up till now, the movement of workers in the region was directed to the Middle East, Europe and North America, fuelled by diminishing employment opportunities at home and increasing demand for labor abroad. While the migration to Europe has been reduced to a trickle, and that to the Middle East has not seen much buoyancy since the Persian Gulf War, the new wave of migration in and from the Pacific region is likely to be fuelled by differing rates of growth in per capita income and currency revaluations of successful export-led developing economies in the region. Already increasing pressure for such migration is emerging in the region, largely through illegal channels. One way of avoiding the problem is for the labor shortage and surplus economies in the region to coordinate policies and measures which will not only ameliorate the present system of largely illegal immigration but also improve the welfare of migrant workers.

While Hong Kong, Japan, Malaysia, the Republic of Korea, Singapore and Taiwan Province of China are short of labor, many others in the region, such as Indonesia, the Philippines and Sri Lanka have an abundance. In an increasingly interdependent world, workers will become more mobile, while employers will reach across borders to find the skills they need. At present, illegal immigration causes not only social problems in the host countries, but also the exploitation of migrant workers by unscrupulous middlemen. Another problem is that of the skill, brain and capital drains associated with the migration of those endowed with human and financial capital, who are preferred by labor-importing countries, especially, Australia, Canada and the United States. Thus a major challenge for regional cooperation will be not only to design a system which will ensure that migrant workers are given adequate protection and at the same time minimize the social problems which their presence may cause in the host countries, but also to compensate developing countries for their loss of skill and capital. In brief, there is a critical need to develop a regional mechanism to respond to the mass migration of workers, which no existing international agency is yet equipped to handle effectively.

Finally, economic cooperation in areas where significant externalities and public goods (education, research and development, infrastructure, environment) exist, is also a potentially important area for dynamic benefits. Cooperation in such areas can take many different forms, ranging from the simple exchange of information through the provision of joint training facilities to the mutual recognition and adoption of rules and regulations, to the implementation of joint policies.

IV. PROSPECTS

As the world enters the final decade of the twentieth century, more significant changes appear to have taken place in the last few years than in all of the last few decades put together. Given the accelerated rate of changes taking place, Asian and Pacific economies need to prepare themselves to face the new challenges which are beginning to emerge in the world economy. Regional economic cooperation is one way of meeting the challenges of a rapidly changing world economy. Such cooperation will become increasingly desirable for two major reasons.

One, regionalism appears to have gained the upper hand over multilateralism all over the world. There is a fear that the world is breaking into inward-looking regional blocs and entering an era of protectionism and carefully administered trade. The Uruguay Round of Multilateral Trade Negotiations was resolved long after its scheduled completion date. At the same time, new regional groups have appeared on the scene. Among these, NAFTA which will have the world's largest market, when Mexico is included, is scheduled to become effective in January 1994. NAFTA, to a greater extent than the Single European Market, has created more anxieties in Asia and the Pacific than any other regional groups, largely because the United States accounts for around 20 percent of the region's total exports. Moreover, Mexico, which has about the same per capita income as Malaysia, may divert significant trade and investment from the region. Several leaders in the region have responded to the perceived threat by calling for the formation of countervailing groups. For example, the former Indian prime minister, V.P. Singh, recently urged SAARC to form an economic community on the pattern of the EEC. ("Ex-PM wants S. Asian community," *Bangkok Post*, 11 September, 1992). Much earlier, the Malaysian Prime Minister Dr. M. Mahathir had suggested the formation of EAEG. Even though regional trade blocs may not be undesirable, if they are not inward-looking, there is a concern that trade wars may erupt if regionalism replaces multilateralism. (For arguments in support of regional trade blocs, see H. Preeg 1990, 4-9). Unfortunately, such a trend may appear inevitable, given the frustrations of trying to accommodate conflicting interests in such a large and disparate forum such as GATT. Negotiations are easier in smaller groups where interests of participating countries are congruous. Thus whether or not the Uruguay Round survives its present stalemate, regionalism will continue to gain strength.

Two, regional economic cooperation will facilitate the transition to a post-Cold War economy in Asia and the Pacific, particularly in view of the emerging pattern of comparative advantage. Regional cooperation creates new opportunities among the countries to discover mutual complementarities and competitiveness, allowing them to respond positively to the changing pattern of comparative advantage in the region. It thus provides a strong stimulus for market expansion and increased intraregional trade and investment. Intra-regional, no less than international trade itself, opens up avenues for overcoming the small size of the domestic market, permitting the developing countries to attain economies of scale in many economic and technological activities, and in the process enabling them to make fuller use of their underutilized human, technological and natural resources. In the long term it also provides the basis for sustained growth and structural change. Equally important, economic regionalism will facilitate the "catching up" process for the least developed countries in the region and thus reduce regional disparity.

In view of the above, regional cooperation enhances developing countries' capacity to meet the emerging challenges of the 1990s, especially the globalization of production and the application of newly emerging technologies. The market of the 1990s will be increasingly consolidated into a single global market. To a large extent this has already happened in financial services, especially the stock market. The fastest way Asia and the Pacific can compete in such a market is to attain "scale economies" through regional economic cooperation.

The benefits from regional economic cooperation may be enhanced if such cooperation is based on certain guiding principles, which could include the following:

a. cooperation should be based on the principles of equality, equity and mutual benefit, taking fully into account the economic, social and cultural diversity among the countries in the region;
b. cooperation should involve a commitment to open dialogue and consensus with equal respect for the views of all the participants, and should provide a forum for consultation and consultative discussions on economic issues; it should not be in the form of mandatory directives or regulations;
d. cooperation should be based on the modalities of economic openness and interdependence and should be consistent with the principles of GATT;
e. cooperation should encourage private sector participation. The private sector should be consulted at every stage in formulating and implementing any scheme for regional economic cooperation.

It is difficult to predict the future course of economic regionalism in Asia and the Pacific. But over the decade leading up to the next century, there is a possibility that ASEAN may be expanded to include the Indochinese countries while APEC may come to embody the kind of "open regionalism" which may pave the way for globalism. One thing however is certain. Given the predominance of its trade, foreign direct investment and official development assistance in Asia and the Pacific, Japan will play a significant role in shaping the future contours of economic regionalism in the region.

V. CONCLUSION

The current wave of economic regionalism in Asia and the Pacific evolved initially as a response to the movement in Europe and North America but it would appear that Asian and Pacific regionalism has acquired a form and momentum of its own. In contrast to EC's paradigm of "deep" integration, regionalism in Asia and the Pacific is not aimed at any form of union albeit customs, monetary or political. At the same time it should also be pointed out that unlike the EC, regionalism has yet to show any concern for the poorer states in Asia and the Pacific which has 8 out of the 10 poorest countries in the world. Compared to other developing regions, Asian and Pacific economic regionalism trends towards the North-South rather than the South-South variety. Also unlike the other developing regions, there is no pan-Asian Pacific organization representing all the countries in the region such as the Organization of American States and the Organization for African Unity in the Americas and Africa respectively. Instead various groups have evolved at the subregional level to serve the needs of different groups of countries in Northwest, South, Southeast Asia and the Pacific. (Countries in Northeast Asia are still not represented in any active subregional groups.)

But whatever its manifestations, critics decry that regionalism, result in a fragmented world trading system and threatens globalism. In this connection, there is a fear that economic regionalism in Asia and the Pacific is fuelling the emergence of three contending regional trade blocs. However, proponents of economic regionalism in Asia and the Pacific claim that this is far from obvious. On the contrary, they point out that vigorous efforts have been made to reinforce multilateralism, as exemplified by APEC. In addition, proponents also claim that regionalism is a second best solution in an imperfect world and may even be a desirable step towards globalism. The initial move towards expanded regional markets stimulated through regionalism provides a significant progression towards the creation of an interlocked and interrelated global marketplace which may eventually pave the way to globalism. In any case, regional arrangements involving a small group of countries pursuing compatible policies are easier to manage than huge cumbersome institutions like GATT which are ineffective given the complexity of trade issues and divergences in macroeconomic policies. Moreover, the proponents of Asian and Pacific economic regionalism maintain that what is emerging is not a regional trade bloc but attempts to take advantage of growing intra-regional trade and investment.

Whatever its critics and supporters may say, the current wave of economic regionalism, far from being a transitory phenomenon is unlikely to subside in Asia and the Pacific. Nevertheless, the movement may be more widely accepted if it is based on the principle of "openess", not only in terms of being consistent with GATT but also, gradually, in terms of membership access for all countries in Asia and the Pacific. Even then, economic regionalism should be regarded as a temporary expedient and the major tasks of policy-makers in the region should be to ensure the successful conclusion of the Uruguay Round of Multilateral Negotiations. Individually, most countries in Asia and the Pacific are relatively small players in the world's market, so they have the most to gain from promoting multilateralism.

With the end of the Cold War, there has been an ascendancy of economics over political considerations, especially in Asia and the Pacific. The basic dismantling of the Cold War architecture will provide the foundation for the countries in this region to build a new condominium based on cooperation instead of confrontation. The resurgence in economic regionalism in Asia and the Pacific may be stimulated by the wave from Europe and North America but it is being driven by the tide of a strong impulse and enthusiasm for greater economic cooperation among the countries in the region. More importantly, the form of economic regionalism which Asia and the Pacific is embracing is not the apostasy from free trade which has served the region extremely well but a different genre which may yet set the standard for other regions. Ultimately, policy-makers in Asia and the Pacific owe a responsibility to future generations to create a harmonious community of Asian and Pacific nations which will heal the rifts which have divided the region in the past through such forces as colonialism, wars and poverty. While the concept of an Asian Pacific community may be a distant dream, the first step may already have been taken with the establishment of APEC.

ACKNOWLEDGMENT

The views expressed by the author in this paper are solely his own and do not necessarily reflect those of the U.N.-ESCAP Secretariat where he is attached.

NOTE

1. The term "Asian and Pacific region" in this paper is the one used by the United Nations and refers to the group of countries beginning with the Islamic Republic of Iran in the west to the Pacific developing countries in the east. (For details, see United Nations, 1989).

REFERENCES

Alagappa, M. (1987). "ASEAN Institutional Framework and Modus Operandi: Recommendations For Change, in N. Sopiee and others, eds., op.cit.,pp.183-203.

Chee, Peng Lim. (1987). "ASEAN Cooperation In Industry: Looking Back and Looking Forward," in N. Sopiee, and others, eds., op.cit., pp. 91-138.

———. 1989). "Intra-regional Investment-patterns and Prospects for Cooperation Among Asian and Pacific Developing Countries," *Development & South-South Cooperation*, Vol.5, No.8, June, pp. 171-189.

———. (1992). "Nature, Potential, Problems and Assistance For Small and Medium Scale Industries," in S.J. Kim and J.W. Suh, eds., *Cooperation in Small and Medium Scale Industries in ASEAN*, K.L., Asian and Pacific Development Centre, Part A.

Drysdale, P. and R. Garnaut. (1992). "The Pacific: An Application of a General Theory of Economic Integration, Washington, D.C., Twentieth Pacific Trade and Development Conference, (mimeo), September.

Dutta, M., (19982). "Economic Pluralism: Asia-Pacific Economies," *The American Economic Review*, Vol.82, No.2, May, pp. 67-73.

Elek, A. (1982). "Pacific Economic Cooperation: Policy Choices for the 1990s", *Asian Pacific Economic Literature*, 6(1), May.

Hirata, Akira and T. Nohara. (1989). "Changing Patterns in International Division of Labour in Asia and the Pacific," in Shinohara, M. and F.C. Lo, eds., *Global Adjustment and the Future Asian Pacific Economy*, K.L., Asian and Pacific Development Centre, and Tokyo, Institute of Developing Economies, pp. 434-468.

Imada, Pearl, M.Montes and S. Naya. (1991). "A Free Trade Area: Implications For ASEAN," Paper presented at the ISEAS-IPS ASEAN Roundtable on Economic Cooperation for the 1990s, June 27-28.

Institute of Strategic and International Studies (ISIS) (1987). *An Anthology on ASEAN Economic Cooperation*, K.L., ISIS.

Kumar, R. (1988). "The Coordination Problem," in Asian Development Bank, *Towards Regional Cooperation in South Asia*, Manila, pp. 99-116.

Langhammer, R.J. (1987). "Facilities of Transposition: What ASEAN Should Learn From Other Integration Efforts," in N. Sopiee and others, eds. op.cit., pp. 535-552.

Meyananthan, S. and I. Haron (1987). "ASEAN Trade Cooperation: A Survey of Issues," in N. Sopiee and others, eds., op.cit., pp. 13-54.

Naqvi, S.H.N. (1989). "Possibilities of Economic Integration", in B. Prasad, ed., *Regional Cooperation in South Asia, Problems and Prospects,* New Delhi: Vikas Publishing House, pp. 163-186.

Philippines Institute of Development Studies. (1992). *ASEAN Economic Cooperation For the 1990s*, Manila.

Preeg, H. (1990). "The Growth of Regional Trading Blocs," *Economic Impact*, pp. 4-9, January.

Riedel, James. (1991). "Intra-Asian Trade and Foreign Investment," *Asian Development Review*, Vol.9, No.1, pp. 111-146.

Rieger, Hans Christoph (1985). "ASEAN Cooperation and Intra-ASEAN Trade," Research and discussion paper No.57, ASEAN Economic Research Unit, Singapore, Institute of Southeast Asian Studies.

Sopiee, Nordin and others, eds. (1987). *ASEAN At The Crossroad,* Institute of Strategic and International Studies, Kuala Lumpur.

United Nations, (1989). *ESCAP Today*, Bangkok.

——— (1990a). *Economic and Social Survey of Asia and the Pacific 1990*, Bangkok.

——— (1990b). *State of the Environment in Asia and the Pacific 1990*, Bangkok.

World Bank (1992). "Regional integration, Old and New," Washington, D.C., Policy Research Working Papers No. 985, October.

TOWARDS ECONOMIC INTEGRATION OF CHINA'S MAINLAND WITH TAIWAN, HONG KONG AND MACAO

Yao Tinggang

I. GLOBAL TENDENCY OF REGIONAL ECONOMIC GROUPING

After the Second World War, the development of international trade, investment and multinational corporations are enhancing the global economic integration. Since the 1980s, as a result of gradual deepening in the degree of global economic integration, there has been a remarkabl international tendency for various countries to organize themselves into regional economic blocs so as to increasee their overall competitiveness and put them into a better position to guard against protectionism. In some regions, where economic grouping is unfeasible at the moment, several sub-regional economic blocs may emerge in place of regional economic grouping.

Research in Asian Economic Studies, Volume 6, pages 145-159.

ISBN: 1-55938-918-4

By sub-regional economic bloc, we mean that due to the differences in historical, cultural, traditional, religious background and the disparities in economic development level, the major countries in a certain region are unable to organize themselves into a regional economic group in the near future, then several neighboring countries which have close links in history, culture and traditions, and the same interest in promoting their economic performance through eliminating tariff and non-tariff barriers among them and thus liberalizing the flow of goods, services and capital so as to form a sub-regional economic group in the form of a free trade zone or a unified market; eventually on the basis of these kind of sub-regional economic blocs, the formation of a regional economic group can be realized. The first major step in this direction was taken by the 12 European Community nations, when they decided to set up at the beginning of 1993 a single market allowing free movement of goods, services, capital and people among the 12 member nations. As things stand now, there is little doubt that this objective of theirs could be realized in the main, though the actual establishment of the single market might be postponed somewhat. In the meantime the 12 EC nation's have reached an agreement with the 7 member nations of the European Free Trade Association to form a more loosely organized European Economic Area. It would not be surprising that both the European Community and the European Economic Area might be further extended to include more new members. On the other side of the Atlantic, the United States and Canada, after concluding between themselves an agreement of free trade to eliminate all tariffs and investment restrictions before the end of 1998 at the latest, proceeded to sign with Mexico on October 7, 1992 and thereby set up a Free Trade Area of North America, with the further possibility of its extending southward into Central America and South America in years to come and growing into a free trade area of all Americas. Faced with these pressing developments, existing organizations of regional economic cooperation in Africa, Latin America and Asia have also begun to hold preliminary discussions or take some measures with a view to strengthening cooperation and moving towards some forms of regional economic blocs. Especially in the Asia-Pacific region, where economic growth rates are currently leading the world, men of insight have repeatedly been calling for the formation of an economic group large enough to match the Single Market of Europe and the North American Free Trade Area. For one reason or another, an economic bloc of this scale cannot be expected to come into being in the near future, and so in its stead quite a number of sub-regional economic blocs have been proposed such as the East Asian Trade Group, the Northeast Asian Economic Sphere, the Southeast Asian Economic Sphere, the Chinese Economic Zone or, alternatively, the South China Economic Zone, and so forth.

In the midst of this surging tide of regional economic integration, China naturally cannot afford to stand idle. In order not to be left outside and suffer from other countries' protectionism, and also for the sake of expediting its own economic development so as to be able to rank among medium-developed countries by the middle of the next century, it cannot *but* take an active part in various projects of sub-regional economic groups under contemplation, particularly the Chinese Economic Zone with China's mainland at its core.

II. FORMATION OF A CHINESE ECONOMIC ZONE

The idea of a Chinese economic zone was first pub forward by Prof. Z. L. Huang from Hong Kong. By the 1980s, with the development of the international trend towards regional economic integration, similar ideas have been suggested by scholars from various parts of the world including, among others, Hong Kong, Taiwan, the United States, Japan and Chinese mainland. That is to say, the idea of forming a Chinese economic zone so as to enhance the overall economic development of the Chinese nation as a whole and deal more effectively with the trade protectionism rising with the trend of regional economic integration has become a consensus shared by the Chinese people on both sides of the Taiwan Straits as well as compatriots in Hong Kong and Macao.

As to the precise meaning of a Chinese economic zone there are different interpretations. To some it stands for an organization for economic cooperation composed of all mainland provinces, Hong Kong, Macao, Taiwan as well as Chinese communities in various Southeast Asian countries like Singapore. To others it means a regional economic bloc consisting of Hong Kong, Macao, Taiwan and three mainland provinces: Guangdong, Fujian and Hainan, and is sometimes called South China Economic Zone. In this paper, however, we use the term Chinese Economic Zone to denote an economic cooperative group consisting primarily of Hong Kong, Macao, Taiwan and four southern mainland provinces Guangdong, Guangxi, Fujian and Hainan, but also encompassing the whole mainland, particularly Jiangsu, Zhejiang and Shanghai. It is true that Hong Kong and Macao have most of their close mainland business connections with Guangdong Province while Taiwan mostly with Fujian Province, but already to a considerable extent their trade and economic relations have been expanding northward to other coastal areas like Shanghai, Jiangsu and Zhejiang, and even to some interior cities and provinces. In my view, therefore, this economic zone should not be limited to Hong Kong, Macao, Taiwan and a few southern provinces; instead it should cover all parts of the mainland, of course with Guangdong, Guangxi, Fujian and Hainan playing a major role. For lack of pertinent data, Macao is skipped in most of this paper's discussions; generally speaking what is said of Hong Kong also applies to Macao, and the latter's proportion is relatively small.

There exists objectively a good foundation for the formation of the Chinese Economic Zone.

Potential members of the Chinese Economic Zone are all from the same ancestral origin, speaking the same language, having the same social customs and inheriting and cherishing the same culture; all of them share the common aspiration for developing the Chinese economy and enabling the Chinese nation to rank among the world's major powers. For many years Hong Kong, Macao and Taiwan had been colonies of England, Portugal and Japan respectively; Taiwan has remained under Kuomintang rule for several decades since its return to China after the victory of the Anti-Japanese War, and have been practicing political and economic systems very different from those of the mainland. Yet, in spite of all this, the residents of these regions have always been yearning for the motherland and have innumerable ties of all sorts with mainland people.

Of the present population of Hong Kong and Macao, most originated from Guangdong, but also a considerable proportion came from Shanghai, Zhejiang and Jiangsu around the liberation of the mainland, and quite a number of big businessmen are emigrants from Shanghai. All of them are constituent elements of the Chinese Nation, many of their relatives are living on the mainland, and their close ties with mainland people are inseparable. By 1997 and 1999 respectively, Hong Kong and Macao will become China's two special administrative areas upon their return to the People's Republic of China.

Taiwan's native inhabitants belong to the same grand family of the Chinese nations, and many of their ancestors came from Fujian. Besides, a sizable portion of Taiwan's present population consists of mainlanders who moved to this island on the eve of the mainland's liberation or their descendants; they, too, have many relatives in the mainland and local family connections remain strong. Though the present Taiwan authorities are still trying hard to hold on to their claim to be a separate political entity and refuse to be unified with the mainland, they cannot deny that there is only one China, of which Taiwan is a part. In the meantime, Taiwan residents have been visiting the mainland in ever increasing numbers (now no less then 1 million a year) to meet relatives and friends or to seek ancestral origins. Taiwan businessmen and investors have been rushing into the mainland, supplying capital and technology for mainland's economic development while at the same time seeking to get for themselves a part of the vast mainland market.

Thus, geographical propinquity, a common language, a common culture and a common aspiration for economic development of the Chinese nation, all combine to strengthen their economic cooperation and promote the progress towards economic integration.

Economic interdependence has been growing to a higher and higher degree. For regions or countries to realize their economic integration, an indispensable prerequisite of the most fundamental nature is the existence among them a high degree of economic interdependence. The trade and economic relations, both between the Chinese mainland and the three regions Hong Kong, Macao and Taiwan, and between Taiwan and the two other regions Hong Kong and Macao, have all been increasing steadily, raising their economic interdependence to a progressively higher degree, and thereby laying a solid foundation for economic integration.

Since the Chinese mainland began to carry out the reform and open policy at the end of the 1970s, there has been a rapid growth in its trade and economic intercourse with Hong Kong and Macao as well as with Taiwan. After Taiwan authorities formally lifted that ban on non-governmental contacts between the people in the two sides of the Taiwan Straits, the volume of trade and other economic activities between the two sides of the Straits and between either side of the Straits and Hong Kong and Macao haven been increasing even more rapidly. According to statistics, Taiwan's trade with the mainland via Hong Kong amounted to $1.038 billion in 1985, and by the end of 1989 the cumulative total volume of indirect trade between the mainland and Taiwan added up to $11.7 billion, representing an annual growth rate of 46.2 percent. Since then, such indirect trade continued to increase, reached $4.04 billion in 1990, jumped almost to $5.8 billion in 1991, up 44 percent over the previous year, and hit an all time high of $7.4 billion in 1992.[1] Together with $2 billion of Taiwan's trade with the mainland via other countries and direct trade across the Straits, the total volume of trade between the two sides of the Taiwan Straits, direct and indirect, could add up to around $10 billion.[2] The Taiwan Institute for Economic Research predicts the mainland's share of Taiwan's exports in 1992 will exceed 10 percent. As estimated in the American journal "Fortune", the Chinese mainland could supersede the United States as Taiwan's largest trade partner in 10 years, should the volume of trade between the two sides of the Taiwan Straits keep on growing at this rate. Taiwan's investment in the mainland has been rapidly increasing too. According to statistics published by the Three Star Institute of Economic Research (a South Korean institution), Taiwan's investment in the mainland amounted to $0.1 billion in 1987, $0.98 billion in 1990, $1.39 billion in 1991; by the end of 1991, the accumulative total of Taiwan's investment in the mainland added up to $3.2 billion, distributed over more than 3,000 projects, making Taiwan the third largest investor, after Hong Kong and the United States.[3] Latest statistics show that in 1992, Taiwan businessmen had invested in the mainland a contractual value of $4 billion. Of these investment funds, Fujian Province got the lion's share; by the end of January 1992, this province has approved 1,239 Taiwan-funded projects with $1.63 billion of contractual investment. Now Taiwan businessmen, in addition to continue to make investments in Fujian, have been expanding their investment activities into other coastal areas such as Guangdong, Hainan, Shanghai, Jiangsu, Zhejiang and so forth.

Hong Kong's trade and economic relations with the mainland have been much closer. Today Hong Kong and the mainland have become each other's largest trade partner and largest investor. According to IMF's *Direction of*

Trade Statistics, the trade volume between Hong Kong and the mainland increased from \$4.923 billion in 1980 to \$11.91 billion in 1985, more than doubled in five years, and reached \$49.561 billion in 1991 (see Table 1). Hong Kong government's publication *Hong Kong 1992* gives more detailed figures: in 1989 Hong Kong's volume of import-export trade and entrepot trade with the mainland accounted to HK\$343.44 billion, accounting for 30.3 percent of its total volume of import-export trade and entrepot trade (HK\$ 1,133.29 billion), ranking first on the list; its imports from the mainland accounted for 34.9 percent of its total volume of imports, also ranking first; its exports to the mainland accounted for 19.3 percent of its total volume of exports, ranking second after the United States (32.3%); its entrepot trade with the mainland accounted for 29.9 percent of its total entrepot trade, also ranking first. In 1991, Hong Kong's volume of import-export trade and entrepot trade with the mainland accounted for 32.4 percent of its total volume of import-export trade and entrepot trade (HK\$ 1,544.868 billion), up 2.1 percentage points over 1989, still ranking first; its imports from the mainland accounted for 37.7 percent of its total volume of imports, up 2.8 percentage points over 1989; its exports to the mainland accounted for 23.5 percent of its total volume of exports, up 4.2 percentage points over 1989; its entrepot trade with the mainland accounted for 28.7 percent of its total volume of entrepot trade, slightly lower by 1.2 percentage points as compared to 1989. Table 2 shows how highly dependent Hong Kong is on the Chinese mainland in the matter of trade.

On the other hand, the Chinese mainland is also dependent on Hong Kong to a quite considerable extent in the matter of external trade. According to IMF's *Direction of Trade Statistics,* in 1980 the Chinese mainland's trade with Hong Kong amounted to \$4.923 billion, accounting for 13.1 percent of its total volume of external trade of \$37.644 billion; in 1985 its trade with Hong Kong increased to \$11.910 billion, accounting for 17.1 percent of its total external trade of \$69.809 billion, up 4 percentage points over 1980; in 1991 its trade with Hong Kong expanded further to hit \$49.561 billion, accounting for 36.5 percent of its total external trade of \$135.943 billion, up 19.4 percentage points over 1985[4] (see Table 1).

With regard to investments, there has also been a very close relationship of two-way flow between the mainland on the one side and Hong Kong and Macao on the other. According to statistics, from 1979 through the end of

Table 1. China's Trade with Hong Kong (in billion U.S. dollars)

	1980	*1985*	*1986*	*1987*	*1988*	*1989*	*1990*	*1991*
China's external trade	37.644	69.809	74.614	82.686	103.015	112.054	118.949	135.943
Hong Kong	4.923	11.910	15.348	22.201	30.244	34.456	41.728	49.561

Source: IMF's *Direction of Trade Statistics Yearbook, 1992,* pp. 134-135.

Table 2. Kong Kong's Trade with Mainland China and Taiwan (in billion H.K. dollars)

	1989	*1990*	*1991*
Total	1,133.290	1,282.404	1,544.868
Import	562.781	642.530	778.982
Export	224.104	225.875	231.045
Entrepot	346.405	413.999	534.841
With mainland China	343.440	394.512	501.078
Import	196.676	236.134	293.356
Export	43.272	47.470	54.404
Entrepot	103.492	110.908	153.318
With Taiwan	72.525	85.052	105.422
Import	51.587	58.084	74.591
Export	4.460	5.720	6.066
Entrepot	16.478	21.248	24.765

Source: *Hong Kong 1992.* p. 380.

1991, the mainland approved altogether upwards of 44,000 overseas-funded projects, with $121.5 billion of contractual investment, of which $76.9 billion had been used; in the first half of 1992, 13,052 more firms wholly or partly funded with overseas capital were approved with $14.7 billion of contractual investment.[5] Of this overall total of overseas investment, Hong Kong was ranked at the top, both in amount of investment funds and in number of projects, estimated to account for two-thirds of the total.[6] These Hong Kong investments cover quite a wide area of the mainland, but most of them have been centered on the Pearl River Delta. By the end of 1991, in Guangdong Province alone there had already been upwards of 14,000 firms funded with Hong Kong investments, with their output value equivalent to 80 percent of the output value of the whole manufacturing industry in Hong Kong itself. In the Pearl River Delta more than 2 million workers are on the payroll of firms funded with Hong Kong businessmen's investments; together with others similarly employed in other provinces there are at present about 3 million people in the mainland working for firms funded with Hong Kong investments. As pointed out in *A Report on China's Economic Reform* recently issued by the Hong Kong Trade and Development Council, in the past 13 years, Hong Kong businessmen concentrated their investments mostly in export-oriented manufacturing industries, but recently have obviously been turning towards tertiary industries such as real estate, communication, tourist trade, finance and banking, and so forth.[7] On the other hand, the mainland, too, has very sizable investments in Hong Kong, estimated to have reached around $15 billion,[8] mostly invested in real estate, making the Chinese mainland the biggest proprietor in Hong Kong. As Mr. Rodger Chu (division manager for promotion of Chinese market, the Hong Kong Trade and Development

Council) put it: "our ties with China are getting closer and closer, ad we are going to be inseparable."

On account of Taiwan authorities' refusal to practice the three direct links between Chinese Mainland and Taiwan, Hong Kong has been serving as a bridge for Taiwan to effect its trade and investment activities with the mainland, and, as a result, the relationship of economic interdependence between Taiwan and Hong Kong is also getting increasingly closer. As is shown in Table 2, trade intercourses between Hong Kong and Taiwan have been rapidly increasing in recent years. In 1989 Hong Kong's import-export trade and entrepot trade with Taiwan amounted to HK$72.525 billion, accounting for 6.4 percent of Hong Kong's total volume of import-export and entrepot trade, and Taiwan ranked as Hong Kong's fourth largest trade partner; in 1991 Hong Kong's trade with Taiwan increased to HK$ 105.422 billion, the relative share rose to 6.8 percent, and Taiwan remained the fourth largest trade partner of Hong Kong. Taiwan's trade with Hong Kong also constitutes a considerable proportion of its total external trade, though not as high as Taiwan's proportion in Hong Kong's total external trade. There are also some cross investments between Hong Kong and Taiwan, but Taiwan's direct investment in Hong Kong constitutes a relatively small proportion of its total investment in various Asian countries. For example, in the 11 years from 1980 through 1990, Taiwan investment in Hong Kong added cumulatively to $57.343 million, accounting for 5.5 percent of the total amount $1,035.156 million of its direct investment in Asia, whereas its investment in Singapore, the Philippines, Indonesia, Thailand and Malaysia accounted for 6.4 percent, 22.1 percent, 8.1 percent, 22.1 percent and 34.4 percent respectively.[9]

In short, since the beginning of the 1980s, there has been a tremendous development in the tripartite trade and economic relations between the Chinese mainland, Hong Kong and Taiwan, and with the stepping-up and deepening of the mainland's opening to the outside world and economic restructuring, they are being commercially stitched together ever more tightly, thus laying a solid foundation for their economic integration. All along Hong Kong has been playing the important role of a bridge linking the mainland and Taiwan in their trade and economic intercourse, and at the same time benefits very considerably from so doing.

The intensification of international competition provided another additional motive force from the outside for the formation of a Chinese Economic Zone. Upon entering the post-cold-war era, all countries are faced with intense economic competition and contest of overall national strength. Of the "four little dragons" of East Asia, Hong Kong and Taiwan rank first and third in per capita GNP, and both of them are possessed with considerable amount of capital funds as well as technology, management expertise and marketing channels, all of which could well be of use to the mainland. On the other hand, they are having problems in marketing their products. The United States and

Western Europe, the two largest international markets, on which they had relied so much for the development of their economies, are stepping up practices of trade protectionism. The Japanese market, which was very closed to the outside world and has just begun to open a little bit, could hardly be expected to play any role significant enough to be a satisfactory substitute for the American market. Besides, both Hong Kong and Taiwan are short of natural resources and their domestic markets are limited in capacity; the accelerating rise in labor and land costs are gradually depriving them of the comparative advantages some of their industries used to enjoy; and as yet their scientific and technological strength has not been strong enough to develop new high-tech industries. Thus they are confronted with a rather grim situation in international competition. At present the Chinese mainland is just at the stage of economic take-off, but its staple export products are also faced with tough competition from a number of Southeast Asian countries like Thailand, Malaysia, Indonesia, the Philippines and even Vietnam. Nevertheless, it is rich in natural resources, is possessed of an abundant supply of cheap human resources as well as a rather strong force of scientific and technological personnel and some lines of new high technology capable of keeping pace with developed countries, and has a huge market of more than 1.1 billion people. That is to say, the mainland, Hong Kong and Taiwan have between them a very high degree of economic complementarity. If they can proceed in the right direction towards gradual realization of economic integration, using their respective strong points and to make up each other's deficiencies and carrying out between them some appropriate arrangement of division of labor and coordination, their overall competitiveness will be greatly raised so as to win for them an advantageous position in international competition both at present and in years to come. This will certainly go a long way in enabling the economic strength of the whole Chinese nation to make great strides forward, raising its people's livelihood to a much higher level and thereby ranking itself among the world community of developed countries. Academic circles in the mainland as well as in Hong Kong and Taiwan have all arrived at the same conclusion, and are doing their utmost for early achievement of this common goal. Thus, the objective necessity to win an invincible position in international competition has become a strong external driving force to promote the formation of the Chinese Economic Zone.

It must be stressed that the reform and open policy that is being carried out in the Chinese mainland is a prerequisite for making any progress towards the formation of the Chinese Economic Zone. Before the mainland launched its reform and open policy in 1979, there had indeed been some economic intercourse between the mainland and Hong Kong and Macao, but only on a very limited scale, while the mainland and Taiwan were completely closed to each other. Only after 1979, the trade and economic intercourse between the mainland and Hong Kong began to pick up at an accelerating pace, both import-export and entrepot trade growing with each passing day, accompanied by a steady increase in mutual investment activities. The trade and economic relations between the mainland and Taiwan also began their growth in the 1980s, especially since the mid-eighties. It is simply unimaginable that they could ever grow so rapidly without the mainland's reform and opening. The 14th National Congress of the Communist Party of China has made the historical decision to step up China's reforms, establish a socialist market economy, open wider to the outside world and make more and better use of foreign funds, resources, technology and management expertise. Opening wider to the outside world means, in the first place, more areas are to be opened so as to bring about a new pattern of opening in all directions. Not only opening will be widened along the coast and along the big rivers, but at the same time steps will be taken to open more areas along borders and step up opening in the interior provinces and autonomous regions, so that the pattern of opening will be pushed ahead from the East to the West and from the South to the North. Thus the development and opening up of Shanghai's Pudong area is to serve as a "dragon head" (playing a vanguard role), expediting the opening of more cities and ports along the Yangtze and thereby fusing a new leap forward in economic development in the Yangtze River Delta and the whole river basin including seven provinces and one municipality. Another aspect of opening wider is to open to foreign investment various tertiary industries, a new field considered to be a forbidden zone until very recently, and foreign investment are to be channeled in an appropriate way into banking, commerce, tourist trade, real estate, restaurant trade, transportation and storage, information and consultant service, and so forth. Tertiary industries have now become a hot spot for investment in the eyes of foreign investors in such areas as the Yangtze River Delta and the Pearl River Delta. There is every reason to expect that, as the mainland opens itself still wider to the outside world and steps up its reforms, there is bound to be in the 1990s an unprecedented development in its economic relations with Taiwan, Hong Kong and Macao as well as Taiwan's economic ties with Hong Kong and Macao, and the economic interdependence between the three regions will be raised to an even higher level, thus providing a more powerful motive force for their economic integration and the formation of the Chinese Economic Zone.

III. COMMENTS ON THE OPPOSITION OF FORMING A CHINESE ECONOMIC ZONE

As stated above, the high degree of economic complementarity between the Chinese mainland, Hong Kong, Macao and Taiwan, together with their ever growing economic and trade ties and the continuous progress of their economic interdependence has laid a solid foundation for their integration into a Chinese economic zone. Today, not only people from academic circles in the mainland, Hong Kong and Taiwan are repeatedly calling for close cooperation between the three regions, even personages in high political circles have begun to be interested in this prospect. For example, Mr. Qiu Chung Huan, one of Taiwan's senior political advisors to the "presidency', has shown his interest by writing an article to spread the idea of a "China-Hong Kong Economic Zone." It cannot be taken for granted, however, that the above-mentioned objective conditions for, and the necessity of establishing a Chinese economic zone could be readily transformed into reality. As matters stand now, there are still some economic restrictive factors and especially some political obstacles hampering the process toward economic integration.

Some scholars raised the following points on ground of economic considerations: firstly, with a wide gap in their levels of economic development, the mainland, Hong Kong and Taiwan naturally have different development aims, and so can hardly be expected to take well-coordinated steps towards the establishment of a Chinese economic zone; the considerable difference in the degree of trade liberalization between these three regions will prevent them from establishing even the lowest form of economic integration—a free trade zone; and thirdly, their different economic systems make it impossible for them to behave all in accordance with the principle of comparative advantages and set up between them a natural pattern of division of labor.[10] There are still others, who, besides repeating these restrictive conditions, put forward an additional argument that no close connection exists between the economies of the mainland and Taiwan, and so integration could not bring them much economic benefit.[11]

It is true that, generally speaking, the mainland's present level of economic development is much lower than that of either Hong Kong or Taiwan. Hong Kong's per capita GNP has exceeded $10,000, that of Taiwan is quite close to $10,000, whereas the mainland's per capita GNP is currently around $400. But disparities in development level need not prevent countries or regions from effecting economic integration. There are quite considerable differences in per capita GNP among various members of the European Community, and between the United States, Canada and Mexico, the three countries that have just concluded the North American Free Trade Agreement, the disparities in per capita GNP are even wide. But this has not prevented them from organizing themselves into a free trade area (integration of a low level) or a unified market (integration of a medium level) or even an organization of a high level of integration such as an economic union.

It is also true that at present there does exist some difference in the degree of trade liberalization between the mainland and Hong Kong and Taiwan. Hong Kong is a free port and naturally has the highest level of trade liberalization, Taiwan ranks next, while the mainland is just beginning its economic take-off and it is imperative to take some appropriate measures to protect its infant industries. We must not lose sight of the fact that right now the mainland is actively seeking to regain its contracting party status in GATT, and this question of its re-entry could very well come to a satisfactory solution in 1995, with Taiwan joining GATT at the same time as a separate customs territory. Of course, developing countries as members of GATT are to be given a period of transition during which they are allowed some leeway in meeting GATT requirements and permitted to relax trade control step by step before finally reaching the degree of trade liberalization as required by GATT. Thus for the moment there are still some restrictive factors hampering trade liberalization, but in a few years most of these restrictions will be removed so as to clear the way for the realization of a low form of economic integration.

The difference in economic systems is indeed a major factor standing in the way to economic integration. If the mainland continues to practice a system of central planning economy while Hong Kong and Taiwan practice a system of market economy, it would be hardly possible to realize even the lowest form of economic integration. But Deng Xiaoping has made it very clear, in his talks during his inspection tour of South China early in 1992, that the mainland is to develop a socialist market economy, and a decision to this effect has been made at the recently convened CPC's 14th National Congress. Of course, the socialist market economy will be different from a capitalist market economy, in that the former is to have an ownership pattern with public ownership as its core while allowing other forms of ownership to exist and develop side by side, is to practice a distribution system mainly on the principle of "to each according to his work", and is to have the state exercise some macro-economic regulation instead of adopting a policy of complete laissez-faire; but in spite of all this the system will be working around market prices as its center and the law of value is to guide all economic activities. A socialist market economy like this can readily work in harmony with Hong Kong's or Taiwan's capitalist economy, and would not constitute a restrictive factor hampering the gradual realization of economic integration of these three regions. Surely, the system of central planning economy which has been practiced for decades in the Chinese mainland could not be turned overnight into a socialist market economy, it takes a process and some time to do this. But the decision has been made, people's ways of thinking have already been changing, and the establishment of a socialist market economy is no longer a remote dream but a concrete program to be realized before the end of this century.

There are already very close economic ties between the mainland and Hong Kong and also a high degree of economic interdependence. As to the relationship between the mainland and Taiwan, their economic interdependence has not attained as high a level as could be desired, and that is not because the development of trade and economic intercourse could not bring much benefit to the two sides, but because there are still some man-made obstacles. Once these man-made obstacles are removed and undesirable bans and restrictions regarding direct air and shipping services, mail exchanges, trade and investment are lifted, the trade and economic intercourses between the two sides would grow at a much faster pace, their economic interdependence would soon be raised to a new higher level, and the economic benefits that these developments could bring to both sides would be very great indeed. In fact, even under present circumstances and in spite of existing restrictions, Taiwan businessmen have already rushed in considerable numbers to the mainland to invest and develop business connections. In 1992 only, about 1.3 million Taiwan businessmen and tourists visited the mainland. Nothing could show more clearly than this that cooperation between these two regions is profitable to both sides and is pregnant with huge potentialities.

In my opinion, today and in the near future the real obstacle hindering us from establishing a Chinese economic zone is political. To achieve economic integration, even of the lowest level, like the formation of a free trade area, it is necessary for the governments concerned to act to make organizational arrangements. Hong Kong will be a special administrative area after its return to China in 1997, as such can be coordinated on its behalf by the central government and should present no political difficulty. The problem lies in the relationship between the mainland and Taiwan. Before 1979 they were in a state of hostile separation from each other; after 1979, especially since the mid-eighties, there has been a gradual growth of indirect trade and economic intercourse, but so far it remains very unlikely that the authorities on the two sides of the Taiwan Straits could take coordinated actions necessary for the establishment of a Chinese economic zone. There still seem to be insurmountable obstacles. The authorities in Taiwan have been keeping a wary eye and resistant attitude towards the mainland's Taiwan policy and have been trying to adopt counter measures. They look upon the proposition of "one country, two systems" as a sort of "united front" tactic with the ultimate objective of swallowing up Taiwan, so that they refuse to accept and, instead, put forward counter slogans such as "one country, two governments", "one country, two regions", 'two political entities of equal status" and so forth, and demand that the mainland should "renounce invasion of Taiwan by force", should give Taiwan "space for international activities", and so on. They are even suspicious of the mainland's open policy, worrying that the development of Taiwan's trade and economic relations with the mainland might have political consequences, that it could create a commercial dependence on the mainland that one day might make Taiwan a hostage to Beijing, that Taiwan's economy might get "hollowed" and, as a result, the mainland might have its economy raised from a relatively weak position to a strong one while Taiwan's economy might fall from its originally strong position to a relatively weak one. On the other hand, such demands as "two political entities of equal status", "renouncing invasion of Taiwan by force", giving Taiwan "space for international activities" are unacceptable to the mainland government because of their incompatibility with national reunification. Thus, in the near future, it is hardly possible for the two sides to sit down at the same table to hold face-to-face talks, let alone take coordinative actions for economic integration. We must admit, therefore, that because of these political obstacles the immediate prospect for economic integration does seem a bit dim. Nevertheless, the basic thing is economic. With the trade and economic intercourse between the mainland, Taiwan, Hong Kong and Macao developing further and their economic interdependence growing to higher and higher levels, eventually economic considerations will exert a force strong enough to overcome political obstacles and the Chinese Economic Zone will be established some day not too distant in the future.

Thus we are faced with the dual fact that in the long run a Chinese Economic Zone will eventually be established as the inevitable result of economic developments while at the same time it cannot be expected to realize in a short period of time. Under these circumstances the proper course we should take is to actively create conditions so as to enable the mainland, Taiwan, Hong Kong and Macao all to move ahead gradually towards the ultimate objective of forming a Chinese Economic Zone, to be realized through a number of stages.

In the first stage, a coordinative organization of a loose type is to be set up to tighten still further economic cooperation between the three regions. At present there have already been two non-governmental coordinative bodies, one on each side of the Strait, the mainland's Association for Relations across the Taiwan Strait and Taiwan's Strait Exchange Foundation, on the basis of which a loose coordination organization could be set up to manage the flood of private and unofficial contacts across the Strait, to work for early realization of "the three direction links", to coordinate and promote economic cooperation between the two sides, and to develop further their trade and economic relations. In this stage Hong Kong is to keep on playing the role of a bridge for closer economic cooperation between the two sides of the Taiwan Strait, and should be invited to join the said organization so as to form a tripartite coordinative body.

In the second stage, a semi-official coordinative body is to be established to promote cooperation (or integration) between firms as well as between industries. As soon as coordination of a loose type practiced in the first stage has achieved considerable success in developing further economic cooperation between the three regions, a semi-official coordinative body could be established, to draft rules and regulations in the interests of, all three sides concerned regarding tariffs, trade, investment, legal matters, industrial division of labor, and so on, and to promote tripartite cooperation in matters regarding the development of high-tech industries, the formation of big enterprises on an international scale or multi-national corporations, the handling of financial or securities business, and so on.

In the third stage, an official coordinative organization is to be formally set up and a free trade agreement is to be signed, establishing a Chinese free trade area or a Chinese unified market.

Thus through common efforts of all three sides—the mainland, Taiwan, and Hong Kong and Macao—gradual progress is to be made stage by stage from purely non-official coordination to semi-official coordination and finally to official coordination. In the process political obstacles would be gradually removed and eventually, on the basis of more matured economic conditions, the concept of forming a Chinese Economic Zone would be turned from a mere possibility into reality.

NOTES

1. These estimates were made on the basis of Hong Kong's indirect trade with China, and so they were quite reliable.
2. Data were quoted from the *Fortune* (Oct. 5, 1992, p. 40, "A New China Without Border")
3. See the *South Korean Economic Weekly* (Aug. 26, 1992, "The Prospect of a Chinese Economic Zone").
4. Data compiled by IMF's *Direction of Trade Statistics.*
5. *China Daily* (Oct. 19, 1992, Autumn Trade Fair Supplement).
6. See the recent policy report by U.S. Policy Council on China.
7. English news report from *French News Union,* July 25, 1992.
8. Ibid 7.
9. See the *World Economy* (May, 1992, p. 71).
10. Quoted from Taiwan Professor Z. Guan's paper presented to the 1992 International Symposium on the Co-ordination of Chinese Economic System, held in Hong Kong.
11. See Dr. C. Gao's paper presented to the same symposium.

PART II.

MICRO IMPACTS/FINANCE/INVESTMENT/ SERVICE SECTOR/TECHNOLOGY

MICRO IMPACTS OF MACRO ADJUSTMENT POLICIES: THE PHILIPPINE CASE

Gilberto M. Llanto

I. INTRODUCTION

Structural adjustment policies are motivated by the desire to induce efficiency and growth in the economy through a set of policy measures that will correct distortions in the market economy and prepare it for greater competitiveness in the local and world markets. However, adjustment policies have differential impacts on households and firms. Adjustment policy measures implemented to correct serious economic imbalances and distortions may have unanticipated and differential welfare impact on households and firms. The recognition of the welfare effects of adjustment policies at the micro levels is extremely necessary for the crafting of appropriate adjustment policies.

The paper by Lamberte, Llanto, Lapar and Orbeta (1991) provides a general framework for analyzing the micro impacts of macroeconomic adjustment policies (Figure 1). In particular, three transmission channels of these macro

Research in Asian Economic Studies, Volume 6, pages 163-180.

ISBN: 1-55938-918-4

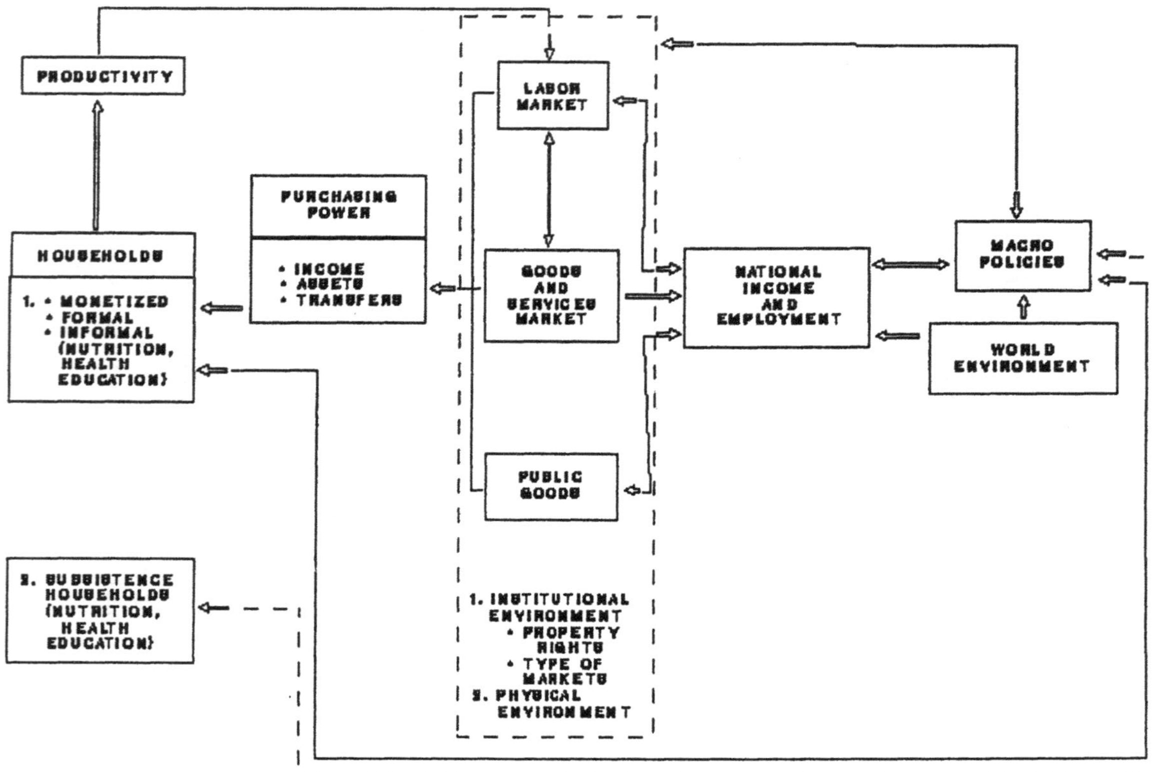

Source: Lamberte, Llanto, Lapas and Orbeta (1991).

Figure 1. Micro Impact of Macroeconomic Policies: General Framework

policies, namely, factor markets, product markets and government expenditures given the country's institutional structure were identified. Households and firms are both consumers and producers in varying capacities. They participate in the market economy through the factor and product markets and through their utilization of public goods and services. This participation is affected and determined by the parameters set by government policies, regulatory/institutional environment, external factors and initial endowments.

However, there is a vast knowledge void on how a particular policy works its way through the identified channels and eventually impacts on micro units; on the specific costs borne by different sectors; the coping mechanisms or survival strategies of vulnerable groups: information that will be crucial in formulating the appropriate policy handles and intervention.[1] Thus, current Philippine research on this area consists of specifying testable hypotheses on how adjustment policies affect the welfare of households, especially the vulnerable groups and quantifying the welfare impact of those hypotheses.[2] This paper presents an overview of the Philippine experience with structural adjustment programs and focuses on their implications on vulnerable groups.[3] It argues for more empirical research on these issues in view of suggestions to postpone or even abandon much-needed reforms because of the pain that arises from the correction of market distortions. Despite the painful adjustment costs faced by the vulnerable groups, it seems that viewed from the experience of newly industrializing Asian countries, the only way out for the economy is through growth-oriented policies that should be sensitive, however, to the social and political milieu and *not* by way of more unsustainable subsidies and reversal of market-oriented economic policies. There is a good case though for creating well-designed safety nets for the vulnerable groups who are adversely affected by the policy reforms. But there is certainly a stronger case for reorienting the economy towards more efficiency and competitiveness which in the long-run will bring a higher level of welfare than temporary subsidies.

II. MACROECONOMIC IMBALANCES AND ADJUSTMENT MEASURES

An economy experiencing macroeconomic imbalances must adopt economy-wide policy reforms to correct the fundamental disequilibrium situations in the external and internal accounts of the country. The Philippines suffered the worst balance of payments (BOP) crisis in 1983-1985 when GNP growth rate averaged −4.8 percent. The incoming Aquino administration undertook major policy reforms to address the structural weaknesses of the economy. The economy recovered during the first three years of the Aquino administration with real GNP growth rate averaging 5.5 percent. However, the momentum of growth was not sustained. In 1989 real GNP growth rate started to decline and became negative in 1991. The first quarter growth rate for 1992 was only 2.4 percent. Both external and internal factors arrested the growth of the economy. The recession in major trading partners adversely affected demand for Philippine exports. The Gulf crisis also raised tremendously the oil import bill of the country. In addition, a series of natural calamities and the instability created by several *coup* attempts inflicted severe costs as local and foreign investors lost confidence in the economy. Another major factor was the delay in the implementation of necessary structural reforms. For example, the restructuring of the tariff system was implemented only in 1991 and over a five-year period yet. Tax reforms, the liberalization of bank entry and branching and of the foreign exchange market were only undertaken in the 1990s.

As early as 1986 the BOP has shown worsening signs. The current account position which was US$996 million in 1986 declined to −US$2.7 billion in 1990. The merchandise trade deficit widened from US$202 to US$4 billion over the period 1986-1990. In sum, from a surplus of 3.4 percent of GNP in 1986, the current account deficit surged to 6.1 percent in 1990 (Table 1). By end-1990 the gross international reserves stood at US$2 billion, way below the target level of US$3 billion. At the fiscal point, despite efforts to increase the revenue effort, the consolidated public sector deficit rose from 2.2 percent of GNP in 1987 to 5.4 percent of GNP in 1990 (Table 2). This was due to the deficit of the national government, government corporations and the Central Bank of the Philippines. In particular the huge deficit of the Central Bank reduced its effectiveness in monetary policy formulation. The Aquino administration assumed the non-performing assets of ailing government financial institutions and undertook an expansionary fiscal program in an effort to revive the economy. Even as revenue effort was being improved to reduce the fiscal deficit, the rise in interest payments on domestic debt, the increase in salaries of government employees, the advances related to the debt reduction program and subsidies to the Oil Price Stabilization Fund (OPSF) resulted into the huge fiscal deficit of 1990. Money creation funded part of the public sector deficit. Base money growth accelerated between 1986-1990 and together with cost-push factors such as weather disturbances and natural calamities and the third oil shock, exerted pressure on domestic prices (Table 3). Inflation rate rose from 0.8 percent in 1986 to 17.7 percent in 1991.

A new economic stabilization program had to be implemented in 1991. Thus, the following measures were introduced: selective cut on expenditures; elimination of subsidies to the OPSF; increasing revenues through improved tax collection; increasing user charges of government corporations and imposing a 9 percent import levy because of the refusal by Congress to pass

Table 1. Balance of Payments Account[1] 1986-1991 (In Million US Dollars)

Item	1986	1987	1988	1989	1990	1991
I. CURRENT TRANSACTIONS						
Merchandise trade	-202	-1017	-1085	2598	-4020	-3212
Exports	4842	5720	7074	7821	8186	8839
Imports	5044	6737	8159	10419	12206	12051
Non-Merchandise Trade	757	0	-80	312	611	1351
Inflow	3791	3454	3592	4586	4842	5624
Outflow	3034	3454	3672	4274	4231	4273
Transfers	441	573	775	830	714	827
Inflow	445	575	778	832	717	828
Outflow	4	2	3	2	3	1
CURRENT ACCOUNT, TOTAL	996	-444	0390	-1456	-2695	-1034
% of GNP	3.4	-1.4	-1	-3.5	-6.1	-2.3
II. NON-MONETARY CAPITAL						
Long-Term Loans	815	159	-519	381	406	922
Inflow	2545	2598	2412	2797	4321	3613
Outflow	1730	2439	2931	2416	3915	2691
Foreign Investments	140	326	986	843	480	654
Inflow	186	439	1077	961	706	798
Outflow	46	113	91	118	226	144
Short-Term Capital	-814	80	-303	-89	19	369
Errors and Omissions	-102	0144	479	383	587	-150
NON-MONETARY CAPITAL, TOTAL	39	421	643	1518	1492	1795
Monetization of Gold	279	365	314	288	218	245
Allocatin of SDR	0	0	0	0	0	0
Revaluation Adjustments	-72	-78	83	101	800	399
III. UNREMITTABLE ARREARS/ ADJUSTMENTS	0	0	0	0	0	0
IV. OVERALL SURPLUS/ DEFICIT (-)	1242	264	650	451	-185	1405

Note: [1] After rescheduling and new money.
Source: Central Bank of the Philippines.

new tax measures. The stabilization program produced the following results: the current account deficit dropped to 2.3 percent of GNP in 1991; gross international reserves rose from US$2 billion in 1990 to US$4.5 billion at end-1991; the consolidated public sector deficit dropped to an estimated 2.5 percent of GNP at end-1991 from 5.4 percent in 1990 and the annualized monthly inflation rates in the last months of 1991 and the first half of 1992 decelerated to less than 10 percent.[4]

Table 2. Revenues, Disbursements, and Deficits, 1980-91 (in Billion Pescos)

Year	*Revenue*	*As % of GNP*	*Disbursements*	*As % of GNP*	*Deficit*	*As % of GNP*
1980	34.7	13.13	38.1	14.41	3.4	1.28
1981	35.9	11.82	48.1	15.84	12.2	4.02
1982	38.2	11.39	52.6	15.68	14.4	4.29
1983	45.6	12.04	53.0	13.99	7.4	1.95
1984	56.8	10.77	66.9	12.69	10.1	1.92
1985	69.0	11.54	80.1	13.40	11.1	1.86
1986	79.2	12.88	110.5	17.98	31.3	5.09
1987	103.2	14.67	119.9	17.05	16.7	2.37
1988	112.9	13.72	136.1	16.54	23.2	2.82
1989	152.4	15.84	172.0	17.88	19.6	2.04
1990	180.9	15.97	218.9	19.33	37.2	3.29
1991	219.9	17.30	246.3	19.38	26.4	2.09

Sources: Department of Budget and Management.
Bureau of the Treasury.

Table 3.

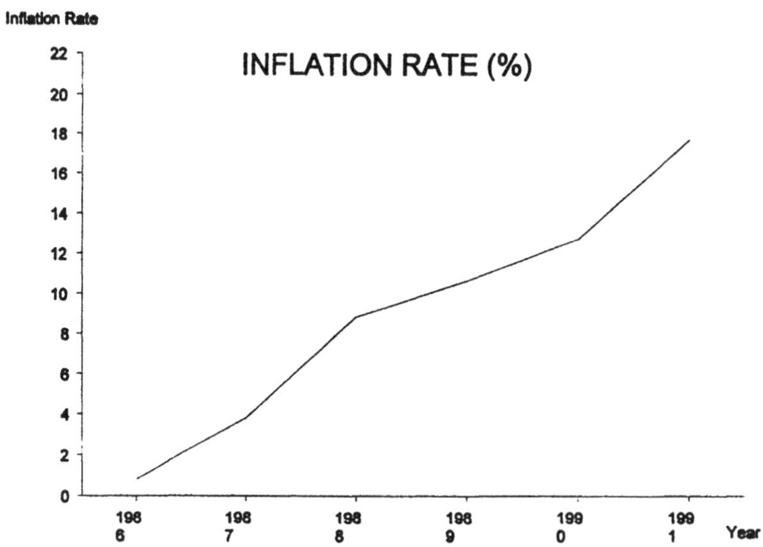

The macroeconomic indicators seem to portray a "successful" stabilization program. However, with a tight monetary and fiscal program the economy underwent a recession as output and employment shrank. The correction of the current account imbalance was done through a stiff import levy that dampened imports and stifled economic activity. Thus, instead of increasing the attractiveness of exports and thereby correcting the structure of trade, the government merely made imports prohibitive. Steep cuts in capital outlay reduced the fiscal deficit but given the poor state of infrastructure in the country, such cuts would adversely affect the productive capacity of the economy. The import levy was recently eliminated but it seems that Congress is in no mood to impose new taxes. The social costs inflicted on the economy are rather high. Between 1985 and 1988 when the economy achieved relatively good growth rates, poverty incidence only marginally decreased from 58.9 percent to 55.2 percent. In terms of actual levels the number of families falling below the poverty line increased from 5.8 million in 1985 to 5.817 million families in 1988. Considering the recent slowdown in the economy a worsening of the poverty levels can be expected.

The issue is not whether the country should pursue an adjustment program because clearly the need for it is obvious. The economy has to be restructured to have greater efficiency and competitiveness. Rather, the issue is whether there are alternative options that will put the economy into the growth path but extract lesser social costs during the adjustment process. This is not, however, the main concern of this paper but we note the recent work by Medalla (1992) and Intal (1992) which pointed out that certain policy measures could correct macroeconomic imbalances with perhaps lesser social costs. For instance, if the government had given exchange rate policy a greater role and reduced its reliance on fiscal and monetary tools, there would have been lower social costs of stabilization. The government instead pursued an exchange rate policy during the period 1986-1991 that weakened the country's competitiveness *vis-àvis* other ASEAN countries (see Lamberte, Llanto and Orbeta 1992). The point being made is that adjustment programs that were carried out by the Philippines in the past were mainly concerned with their impact on macro aggregates and with little attention, if any, on their impact at the micro level. The adjustment programs assumed that accelerating growth in the economy will eventually make up for the differential impact of adjustment policies on households and in particular, the vulnerable groups. While World Bank-supported adjustment programs expressed concern about the impact of adjustment policies on poverty and income distribution, those adjustment programs were implemented using the performance of macro aggregates as indicator of success.

III. THE SOCIAL SERVICES SECTOR: FRAMEWORK, TRANSMISSION MECHANISMS AND DIFFERENTIAL IMPACTS

A. Framework and Transmission Mechanisms

The impacts of adjustment policies on the welfare of households indicated by health, nutrition and education outcomes can be understood by considering the various transmission mechanisms of these policies. The literature identifies three transmission mechanisms, namely: (a) relative prices; (b) incomes or purchasing power and (c) access to public goods. Economic agents respond to relative prices by changing the structure of demand for and supplies of inputs and outputs. When adjustment policies tilt relative output prices of a given good, resources shift towards that sector that produces the particular good and the sector is benefitted by the adjustment policies. The reverse happens in the sector that produces the goods which face a weak demand. This sector loses resources. Households who possess the skills that have become redundant because of the shift in demand for skills induced by the increased production in the favored sector suffer a welfare loss. The second transmission mechanism determines the consumption bundle of households and household members who lose their jobs during the adjustment process and suffer the consequences of a reduction in well-being. By the same token, an adjustment program with a tight fiscal and monetary component will likely reduce the amount of public goods that the government "produces." Households who are dependent for their well-being on the continuous access to decent health, nutrition and education service, will be immediately affected by the budget cuts. Thus, the lack of access and the short availability of public goods will adversely affect the level of household welfare. This section looks at the recent information on the impact of declining incomes and reduced public goods on health, nutrition and education status of households.

Social sector outcomes are products of human capital decisions of households involving health inputs (e.g., health service utilization, sanitation), dietary/nutrient intake and school participation. These decisions are made in the context of prior and/or concurrent other household choices such as fertility and family size, work participation of family members and migration of household members. Out of these decisions emerge social sector outcomes which are seen in terms of health, nutrition and education status of households and their individual members. A distinct feature of relationships in the social order is that the link between prices, incomes and public goods on the one hand *and* social sector outcomes on the other hand, is rarely direct. These relationships go through an intricate web of intervening processes. Thus, the strength (weakness) of the intermediate relationships determines whether the impact is magnified (dissipated) as it goes through the series of mediation processes. However, it must be recognized that macroeconomic policies act together with a host of other change agents whose net effect must be discounted so that the specific impact of adjustment policies on human capital outcomes may be determined.

In terms of categorizing differential effects of macroeconomic adjustment policies on social sector outcomes at least two modalities are identifiable: *first,* the impact of changes in key macroeconomic variables will vary depending on the type of household (rich vs. poor; urban vs. rural), on the type of income (wages vs. return to land, capital), on the components of the total price (money price vs. time price), and by individual member(s) of households (husband vs. wife; children vs. adults; males vs. females); and *second,* the differential effects are dependent on the nature of the process involved and the extent of participation of households in these processes. In particular, the differential effects are manifested in terms of: (1) whose health is affected (children vs. adults; males vs. females) and the causes of morbidity or mortality (communicable vs. degenerative diseases); (2) whose nutritional status is affected (children vs. adult; males vs. females), and the type of nutritional deficiency involved (dietary insufficiency vs. micro-nutrient deficiency); and (3) whose schooling is affected (males vs. females; younger vs. older siblings) and the type of schooling affected (formal vs. informal; basic vs. higher education).

Impacts Through the Labor Market

Three major mechanisms can be identified through which adjustment programs affect social sector outcomes through the labor market. First, the wage rate is the opportunity cost of time. The cost of accessing social sector services, particularly, health services, includes the cost of waiting in the queue for the service. The higher the wage rate, the higher is the cost of waiting, therefore, the higher is the total cost of the service. Any adjustment program that will affect the wage rate will affect the utilization rates of health services and eventually health sector outcomes.

Second, social sector expenditures are human capital investments which feed back to the labor market in terms of increases in labor productivity. In turn, human capital investment decisions of households respond to relative rewards in the labor market. Adjustment programs that alter relative returns in the labor market will affect human capital investment decisions of households, and hence, will also affect social sector outcomes.

Third, wages and returns to other assets form part of household income and private expenditures on nutrition, health, and education are determined by income just like any other expenditure. Adjustment programs that alter wages (and returns of assets) will alter household income and therefore, will also affect choices of household over expenditures on human capital inputs.

Impacts Through the Goods Market

Social sectors and expenditures require material inputs, for example, paper and pencil for education, medicine for health, and food for nutrition. Adjustment programs that affect the prices (or the supply given the demand) of these goods will affect social sector outcomes. For instance, a devaluation will affect the price of medicine since either the compounds used in the manufacture of medicines or the whole formulation are imported. This can also trigger a series of substitution possibilities with varying impacts on health outcomes.

To the extent that relative prices mean varying incomes, social sector outcomes will be affected depending on the way the private spending on health, education and food respond as a result of declining (increasing) growth of incomes. In addition, changes in relative prices trigger substitution between related goods. For instance, studies reviewed by Behrman and Deolalikar (1988) provide evidence of positive income-compensated food price effects on nutrient intake, reflecting a strong substitution among foods with different nutrient contents. Thus, when the price of a particular food item increases, the household may shift demand for other relatively nutritious foods so that the decrease in nutrient intake from the food item whose price increased maybe more than offset by an increase in nutrient intake from the substituted foods.

Impacts Through the Provision of Public Goods

A considerable proportion of social sector services and goods is provided by the government. Adjustment programs that call for a reduction in budget deficit will then have profound impacts on social sector outcomes. To pursue this example, take note that this intermediate policy objective of reducing the budget deficit can be achieved either by reducing government expenditures or by increasing tax revenues or both. The increase in tax revenues could be achieved by increasing the tax rates and/or by improving tax compliance. Each of these policy instruments can have different impacts on the incomes of and prices facing different households. Suppose the means taken is to reduce government expenditures. The effect of this on households will depend on the nature of the expenditure cut, both on what is reduced and how it was reduced. Suppose further that the decision is to reduce expenditures for social services, in particular, health, more than the other components of government expenditures. The effect of this reduction would again depend on both the extent of the cut and the manner of the cut. If, for example, the expenditures for drugs and transportation allowances of field workers are reduced more than the other components of the health budgets, then the price (total costs) of health services facing poor households in rural areas is likely to increase more than the cost of health services facing rich households in urban areas.

Differential Impacts on Different Groups

Different income groups will likely have different spending propensities on human capital inputs. Therefore, in addition to the general response to increases (decreases) in income are the differential effects due to different behavior by income class.

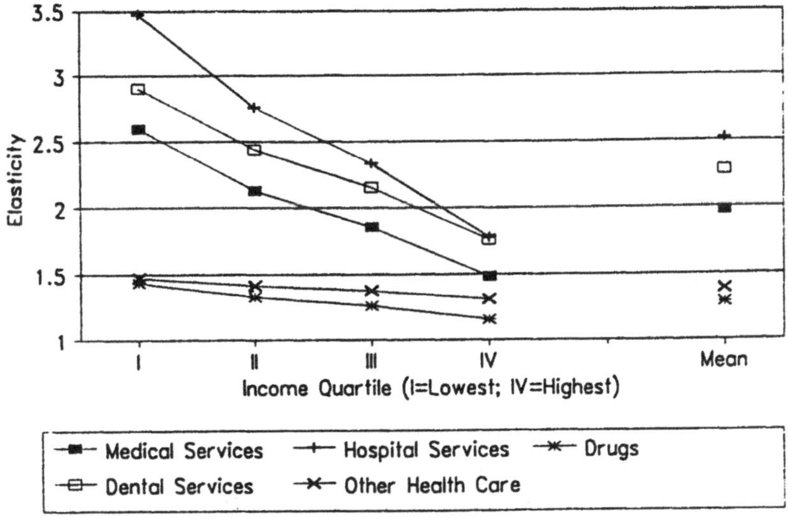

Source: Russo, G. and A.N. Herrin, (forthcoming): data from 1985 FIES

Figure 2. Estimated Income Elasticities of Health Care Expenditures; Philippines, 1985

Figure 2 shows estimates of expenditure elasticities of health care expenditures by income quartile and type of health care expenditures based on the 1985 Family Income and Expenditure Survey (FIES).[5] This information tells us that changes in the incomes of the low income households are likely to result in proportionately larger expenditures for medical, dental, and hospital services than changes in the incomes of higher income groups. One could use this information to infer that macroeconomic adjustment policies that adversely (favorably) affect the incomes of low income groups are likely to result in significant adverse (favorable) effects on the health status of the population through a reduction (increase) in health care expenditures.

Figure 3 shows estimates of predicted probabilities of using health facilities by income quartile based on the 1987 National Health Survey. The data suggest that lower income groups tend to use more public health facilities than higher income groups which prefer to use private health facilities. Thus, the pattern of health facility use is likely to change with the pattern of income change generated by macroeconomic adjustment policies. A decrease in real incomes due to adjustment policies could lead to greater use of public health facilities and more pressure on the government to provide such health facilities. This could also possibly increase waiting time for service and reduce the quality of health service in public facilities, especially if the public budgets for health are not increased to deal with such increased levels of utilization.

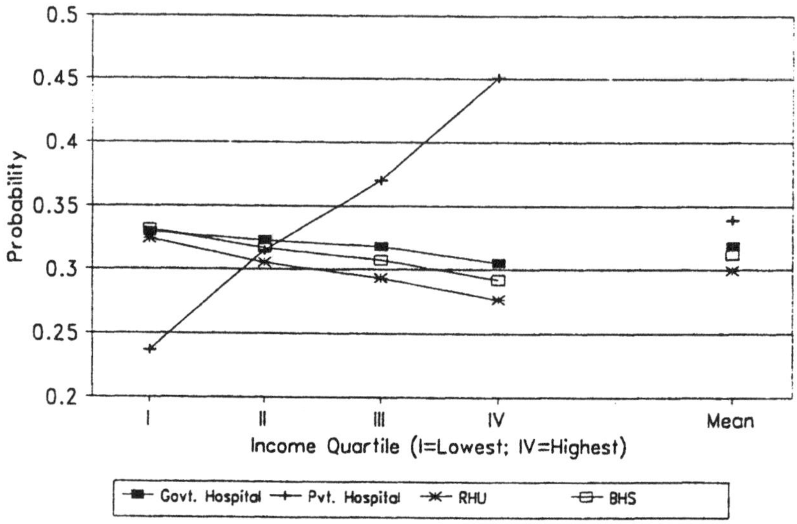

Source: Russo, G. and A.N. Herrin (forthcoming); data from 1987 National Health Survey.

Figure 3. Predicted Probabilities of Using Health Facilities: Philippines, 1985

Data on enrollment rates by age of child and household incomes in both rural and urban areas obtained from the Household and School Matching Survey of the Department of Education, Culture and Sports shown in *Figure 4* and *Figure 5* revealed that enrollment rates are lower among poorer households than higher income households despite the availability of free public elementary education.[6] This is true for each age group of children in both urban and rural areas. Enrollment rates in rural areas, however, are lower than in urban areas in each income decile particularly for older children aged 11-16 years. This information suggests that the impact of macroeconomic adjustment policies on educational performance would depend in part on the type of household (classified by income class) that is being affected by those policies. Obviously, lower income households suffer more from cuts in public expenditure in education.

The Role of the Interaction Among Social Sector Outcomes

It is well known that better nutrition and health status results in better performance in school (e.g., Selowsky and Taylor 1973). Thus, a policy that promotes better nutrition will improve educational outcomes. Likewise, better educational outcomes generate better nutrition and health outcomes. Conversely, policies that will adversely affect any of these social sector outcomes will result into adverse impacts on the others.

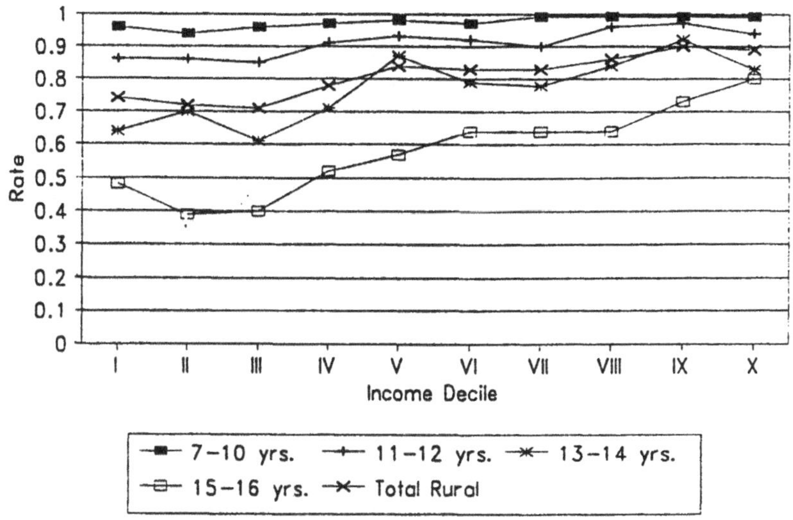

Source: HSMS as reported in World Bank (1988).

Figure 4. Enrollment Rates by Age and Income Decile: Rural Philippines, 1982-1983

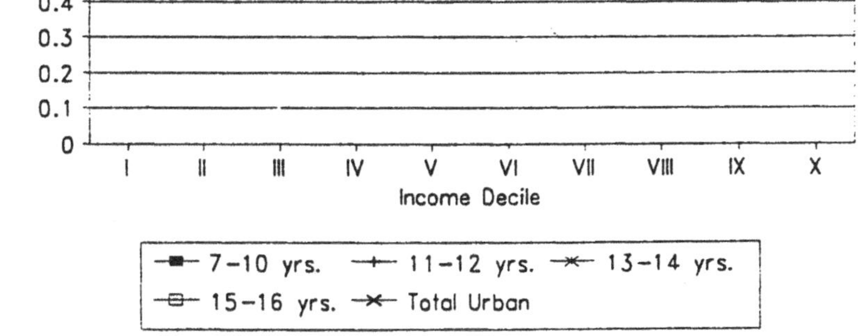

Source: HSMS as reported in World Bank (1988).

Figure 5. Enrollment Rates by Age and Income Decile: Urban Philippines, 1982-1983

B. Some Major Research Issues

Several studies tried to understand the determinants of socioeconomic outcomes (Herrin and Bautista 1989 for health; Herrin 1990 for nutrition; and Paqueo 1985 for education). Although most of the studies were not done in the context of analyzing the impacts of macroeconomic adjustment policies, they can provide some basis for identifying and firming up knowledge on the likely impact of adjustment policies. What follows are the major issues attendant to the analysis of the impact of macroeconomic adjustment policies on social sector outcomes that require empirical validation.

Income, Prices, Contextual Variables and Health Outcomes

Incomes and prices affect health status through their impact on health care utilization and exposure to environmental contamination, among others, and these are compounded by nutritional status and initial demographic and social characteristics of households (such as family size and education of mothers).

Income and Health Expenditures Elasticities

Given the proportionately larger expenditure elasticities of health care expenditures by low income households, one can infer that macroeconomic adjustment policies that adversely (favorably) affect the incomes of low income groups are likely to result in significant adverse (favorable) effects on the health status of the population through reductions in health care expenditures.

Income and Public Health Facilities Utilization

Given that lower income groups tend to use public health facilities while higher income groups tend to use private health facilities, a decrease in real incomes due to macroeconomic adjustment policies could lead to greater use of public health facilities. This could possibly lead to an increase in waiting time for service and reduce the quality of health service in public facilities, especially if public budgets for health are not increased to deal with such increased levels of utilization.

Price Effects on Service Utilization

There is the continuing concern for robust estimates of price elasticities of service utilization. Previous studies show that outpatient, delivery and other primary care are not very sensitive to income, money prices or time prices (Akin et al., 1984; Schwartz, et al., 1988). The 1981 National Health Survey, however, revealed sustained price elasticities of outpatient care for children, and that the price elasticities are higher at lower income levels than at higher income levels (Ching 1991).

Income Effect on Nutritional Status: The Role of Various Filters

A review of determinants of nutritional status suggests that while poverty is often considered as the "major root cause" of malnutrition, increases in income among the malnourished group alone to close the nutrition gap is not sufficient. The reason behind this finding is the fact that the relationship between income and nutritional status has several intervening links. Bouis and Haddad (1990) estimates implied that the doubling of income improves preschooler's nutritional status by only 5 percent. This conclusion was derived from the following estimated elasticities representing the strength of relationship of each link:

1. income and food expenditures, 0.65
2. food expenditures and household calorie intake, 0.17
3. household calorie intake and preschooler's calorie intake, 1.18; and
4. preschooler's calorie intake and preschoolers nutritional status, 0.39.

The net nutritional status elasticity with respect to income is estimated by multiplying the individual elasticities for each link: (0.65) (0.17) (1.18) (0.39) = (0.05). There is then a strong case for direct nutrition interventions that serve to strengthen various links. Such interventions will invariably include nutrition education, focused health interventions, and family planning.

Price Effect on Nutritional Status

Studies reviewed by Behrman and Doelalikar (1988) provide evidence of positive income-compensated food price effects on nutrient intake, reflecting a strong substitution among foods with different nutrient contents. In studies conducted in the Philippines, Bouis and Haddad (1990) find no significant effect of price of rice or corn on household calorie intake; while Garcia and Pinstrup-Andersen (1987) find household calorie consumption with respect to price of rice to be only −0.02. This latter finding implies that a doubling of the price of rice results in a reduction in household calorie consumption of only 2 percent.

Income and School Participation

Data from the Household School and Matching Survey reveal that enrollment rates are lower among poorer households than higher income households. This is true for each age group of children in both urban and rural areas. Enrollment in rural areas, however, are lower than in urban areas in each income decile particularly for older children aged 11 to 16 years. Small area sample survey results suggest that part of the relationship between household income and school participation of children is due to the greater participation of these children in both paid and unpaid work in order to supplement household income. Such a household survival strategy, of courlse, has the Unintended effect of reducing school participation and eventual schooling attainment of children in these households relative to other children (Herrin, 1992).

IV. CONCLUSION

The determination of the micro impacts of macro adjustment policies is a complex undertaking given "difficulty of distinguishing the impact of adjustment policies from those of the structual and policy problems that the adjustment policies seek to address" (Ribe et al., 1990); the number and complexity of channels through which the poor are affected (Heller et al., 1988); the state of estimation methodology and data availability.[7] In the Philippines empirical evidence and documentation showing the impact of Philippine adjustment policies on households are non-existent or at best fragmentary. What we observe are the objective conditions of households that may have been caused by structural and institutional factors, the development strategy and policies earlier adopted by the economy, the adjustment policies themselves or an interplay of a host of these and other causative factors. Indeed the absence of empirical studies on the micro impacts of macroeconomic adjustment policies is manifested in the lack of consensus on how to proceed with the adjustment policies adopted by the economy. Government bureaucrats who prepare the adjustment program with multilateral agencies confine themselves to macro aggregates as targets and indicators of program performance while politicians, nongovernmental organizations and the working class talk in terms of the number of health workers, teachers and agricultural extension workers to be laid off; and the amount and size of infrastructure spending to be postponed (Lamberte, Llanto, Lapar and Orbeta 1991).

However, it can not be denied that there is a need to minimize the welfare loss arising from the implementation of adjustment programs. The little indirect evidence from Philippine social sector data seems to indicate that during periods of adjustment the social costs can be high, especially towards the vulnerable groups. This, however, is not an argument to abandon policy reforms but to package an adjustment program that minimizes the welfare loss especially of the vulnerable groups. In this respect better targeting of public expenditures as well as employment opportunities in favor of the vulnerable groups are just some of the strategies to address the adverse impact of adjustment policies. But higher in the agenda of policymakers should be the formulation of adjustment policies that will *simultaneously* address the growth and equity objectives of the economy. Measures that merely mitigate the social costs of adjustments are at best palliatives and may prove to be unsustainable during the period of adjustment. What is imperative, therefore, is to craft policies which will not only correct the fundamental distortions and flaws of the economy but will restructure it towards more equity and social justice.

But intelligent policies draw from the wellspring of research.

NOTES

1. For an extended discussion please refer to Lamberte, Llanto and Orbeta (1992).
2. The vulnerable groups are mostly those who depend on agriculture, natural resources and the informal sector for their livelihood. In the Philippines they are the coconut and corn farmers, upland farmers, the landless urban and rural poor.
3. I report in this paper the part of the integrative report of the Research Project *Micro Impacts of Macroeconomic Adjustment Policies* which deals with the impacts on the social services sector. See Lamberte, Llanto and Orbeta (1992).
4. See Lamberte, Llanto and Orbeta (1992) for a more detailed discussion.
5. Figures 2 and 3 were supplied by Prof. A. Herrin of the School of Economics, University of the Philippines.
6. The government also established recently free public high schools (secondary level).
7. Even in the World Bank, Kakwani et al. (1990) noted that there has been an expansion of sector and analytical work in the area of poverty and adjustment; but a methodology to measure the impact of adjustment on the poor does not yet exist.

REFERENCES

Akin, John et al. (1984). *The Demand for Primary Health Care in the Third World.* New Jersey: Rowman and Allanheld.

Bouis, H. and Haddad, L. (1990). "Effect of Agricultural Commercialization on Land Tenure, Household Resource Allocation and Nutrition in the Philippines," *Research Report 79,* International Food Policy Research Institute.

Behrman, Jere R. and Deolalikar, Anil B. (1988). "Health and Nutrition" in H. Chenery and T. Srinivasan (Eds.), *Handbook in Development Economics,* New York: McGraw-Hill.

Ching, Panfila. (1991). "Charging Health Care User Fees in the Philippines: Implications on Access Across Income Groups," unpublished manuscript.

Garcia, M. and Pinstrup-Andersen, P. (1987). *The Pilot Food Price Subsidy Scheme in the Philippines: Its Impact on Income, Food Consumption and Nutritional Status,* Research Report 61, International Food Policy Research Institute.

Heller, Peter et al. (1988). "The Implications of Fund-supported Adjustment Programs for Poverty: Experiences in Selected Countries." *Occasional Paper No. 548.* Washington, D.C.: International Monetary Fund.

Herrin, A. (1992). "Consequences of Population Change in the Philippines," Paper prepared for the United Nations Economic and Social Commission for Asia and the Pacific.

Herrin, A. (1990). "Nutrition: Consequences, Determinants and Policy Interventions," Paper prepared for the National Nutrition Council.

Herrin, A. and Bautista, M. (1989). "Health and Development: Determinants and Consequences," *Survey of Philippine Development Research*, Philippine Institute for Development Studies.

Kakwani, N. et al. (1990). "Structural Adjustment and Living Conditions in Developing Countries," *Working Paper Series 467*, Population and Human Resources Department, The World Bank, August.

Lamberte, M., Llanto, G., and Orbeta, A. Jr. (1992). "Micro Impacts of Macroeconomic Adjustment Policies: An Integrative Report." unpublished paper. Philippine Institute for Development Studies, July.

Lamberte, M., Llanto, G., Lapar, L., and Orbeta, A. Jr. (1991). "Micro Impacts of Macroeconomic Adjustment Policies: A Framework Paper and Review of Literature." *Working Paper Series No. 91-02*. Philippine Institute for Development Studies, February.

Paqueo, V. (1985). "An Economic Analysis of Educational Attainment among Elementary School Age Children: Preliminary Analysis," in *Transactions of the National Academy of Science and Technology*, Republic of the Philippines, Vol. VII, Metro Manila.

Ribe, G. et al. (1990). "How Adjustment Programs Can Help the Poor: The World Bank's Experience," *Discussion Paper No. 71*, Washington, D.C.: The World Bank.

Selowsky, M. (1973). "The Economics of Malnourished Children: An Example of Disinvestment in Human Capital." *Economic Development and Cultural Change*.

Schwartz, et al. (1988). "Price and Income Elasticities of Demand for Modern Health Care: The Case of Infant Delivery in the Philippines," *The World Bank Economic Review*.

COOPERATION IN FINANCE OF ASIA: THE CASE STUDY OF CAPITAL FLOW BETWEEN JAPAN AND THAILAND

Masumi Kishi

I. INTRODUCTION

At present the world economy lacks funds, but it seems rational to ease the fund shortage by enhancing saving rather than restricting investment. By this reasoning, how to utilize the savings of Japan is becoming more important as a subject than criticizing her balance of payments surpluses. Japanese foreign securities investment in developed countries such as the United States has declined, and so her foreign direct investment in Asian countries seems to have increased.

In fact, the share of her direct investment sharply increased in the total private sector capital flow of 1990. So far the long-term capital accounts deficits have matched the balance of trade surpluses. For instance, overseas securities investment accounted for the highest share of long-term capital accounts by 1989. But in 1990 it suddenly decreased from $113.2 billion to $39.7 billion compared with loans, which steadily increased to $22.2 billion. Also, foreign direct investment has rapidly increased to $48.0 billion since the mid-1980s.[1]

Research in Asian Economic Studies, Volume 6, pages 181-192.

ISBN: 1-55938-918-4

The role of Japanese foreign direct investment in Asian countries is expected to increase further. In order for this to occur, higher earnings rates will have to be obtained by direct investment rather than securities investment in the United States. It seems to be a necessary condition for smooth fund flow that the Asian countries' financial and capital markets are consolidated.

This paper will consider the need for consolidation on the part of capital recipient countries in order to make capital flow efficient in the situation of world fund shortage. The discussion will focus mainly on the capital flow between Japan and Thailand in this context.

For this purpose, first, I will analyze Thai financial assets and liabilities accounts and Japanese enterprises' financing mode by outlining Japanese capital flows into the ASEAN countries, in order to address the issue of foreign capital flow into the Thai financial market. Second, I will consider the characteristics of Thai financial and capital markets which enable her to implement her economic development plan through her interest rate and money supply policy. Third, I will also discuss the above subjects from the point of view of funds supply.

I. FOREIGN CAPITAL AND THAI FINANCIAL INSTITUTIONS

Active capital flow to Asian countries reflects a high level of economic growth. According to *Asian Development Outlook 1991*, the average economic growth rate of Asian developing countries is 5.8 percent in 1990. This figure greatly exceeds both the average growth rate of 1.7 percent of the world economy and the average growth rate of 2.4 percent of the developing world in 1990. Particularly the ASEAN countries are at the top of the list in terms of the level of growth rate, as indicated by the Thai growth rate of 10 percent in 1990.[2]

Reflecting the fact that Thailand has the highest economic growth rate, the amount of private resource flows to her is the greatest among ASEAN countries in 1989. Also, Thailand is second only to Indonesia in total flows of private and official capital in the same year.[3]

Here, first, I will point out the characteristics of the Thai financial institutions which have accepted foreign capital up to 1990, by examining their assets and liabilities accounts. Second, I will discuss the fact the Japanese enterprises are getting a considerable amount of their financial resources for their overseas direct investment from the invested countries' financial institutions. And I will refer to the consolidation issue of financial institutions, which is indispensable also for the overseas business activity of Japan.

A. Capital Flow to Thai Financial Institution

By analyzing the liabilities[4] of recipient institutions such as the Industrial Finance Corporation of Thailand (IFCT), Bank for Agriculture and Agricultural Co-operatives (BAAC), commercial banks and finance and securities companies, I will highlight the features of capital flow to Thailand. These are the representative financial institutions which undertake the economic development of Thailand. Among them, commercial banks and the IFCT, attracting the long-term funds, are the core institutions. BAAC is responsible for the arrangements in rural financial markets. Finance and securities companies supply short-term funds.

The total liabilities (assets) of commercial banks increased from 305.4 billion baht in 1980 to 1,806.6 billion baht in 1990, or, by about six times, but increase rates of both foreign assets and liabilities overseas were less than 4 percent during this period. Overseas foreign liabilities, except deposits and borrowings, increased by some eight times, while overseas deposits and borrowings respectively increased by only four times.

Total assets (liabilities) or finance and securities companies increased from 65.4 billion baht in 1980 to 371.2 billion baht in 1990 or six times. Moreover it is noteworthy that overseas liabilities sharply increased, by eight times.

The overseas capital flows to commercial banks, and finance and securities companies, especially to the latter, are increasing. The proportion of foreign capital in the total liabilities is not high: only 3 percent in commercial banks and 5 percent in the finance and security companies in 1990. Compared with this, the share of foreign capital is relatively high: 26 percent in the IFCT and 13 percent in the BAAC.

The above capital flow through four financial institutions suggests the restrictive Thai policy on the introduction of foreign capital. That is, official capital mostly flows in through the IFCT and the BAAC in the form of loans, while private capital flows in through finance and securities companies and commercial banks mainly for foreign direct investment.

In fact, Thailand has effectively used the overseas financial resources of both the ODA (Official Development Assistance) and foreign direct investment. This mode of foreign capital inflow is reflected in the stance of the Thai government. In terms of implementing economic development plans, the Thai government has responsibility only for forming infrastructure, leaving the private sector to enforce economic activity for industrialization. The Thai government is deliberately introducing ODA loans, known as setting the guidelines for external debt.[5] On the other hand, the Japanese foreign direct investment mainly directed to manufacturing increased during the 1960s and the first half of the 1970s. After a sluggish period after that, it again began to increase in the mid-1980s.

B. Financing for Foreign Direct Investment

Does the possibility of financing inside of the Thai financial and capital markets promote the foreign direct investment of Japanese firms' Foreign direct investment needs long-term fund for equipment investment and short-term funds as working capital for production and sales.[6] Although the financing mode decides the cost of funds, it seems to differ according to the country in which it is invested. Therefore I will consider the features of financing by Japanese enterprises which have invested in ASEAN Countries including Thailand in comparison with enterprises which have invested in the NIES and the United States.

First, Table 1 shows the characteristics of short-term funds of the manufacturing sector (average of all industries).

1. The share of the investor in total financial resources is relatively low in all regions. Even in the highest case, investment towards the United States, the rate is only 6.4 percent.
2. Therefore firms seem to finance from the financial institutions in the country in which they invest.
3. But the proportion of the Japanese banks is not very high, except for the rate of 62.5 percent in the case of the United States.
4. Hence the firms investing in the NIEs and ASEAN countries are financing most of their short-term funds from the local financial institutions, or about 66.2 percent in the case of the NIEs and 58.9 percent in ASEAN.

Table 1. Financing Structure for Short-term Funds of Japanese Manufacturing Direct Investment, by Resources and Region, 1984 (Percent).

	United States	*Asia (NIEs)*	*ASEAN*
Short-term money borrowed from investor	6.4	4.5	3.4
Japanese investor	5.8	2.4	3.2
Other investors	0.6	2.1	0.2
Financial institutions in the invested countries	93.6	95.5	96.6
Japanese banks	62.5	29.3	37.7
Local financial institutions	3.1	66.2	58.9
Total	100.0	100.0	100.0

Source: Ministry of International Trade & Industry Industrial Policy Bureau, Second General Survey of Overseas Business Activity.

Table 2. Financing Structure for Long-term Funds of Japanese Manufacturing Direct Investment, by Resources and Region, 1990 (Percent).

	United States	*Asia (NIEs)*	*ASEAN*
Corporate bond issues	7.5	16.2	1.1
Long-term money borrowed from banks	92.5	83.8	98.9
Investor	26.1	12.1	39.2
Japanese investor	19.7	8.3	36.8
Other investor	6.4	3.8	2.4
Financial institutions in the invested countries	45.5	64.0	30.7
Japanese banks	20.0	19.3	9.2
Local financial institutions	25.5	44.7	21.5
Other financial institutions	20.9	7.7	29.0
Total	100.0	100.0	100.0

Source: Ministry of International Trade & Industry Industrial Policy Bureau, Second General Survey of Overseas Business Activity.

Second, Table 2 shows the characteristics of long-term funds.

1. In the case of ASEAN, firms do not get their resources so much by issuing bonds. The highest ration is only 16.2 percent in the case of firms investing in the NIEs.
2. In the ratio relative to the investor, the highest is 39.2 percent for ASEAN, followed by 26.1 percent for the United States and 12.1 percent for the NIEs. Also, the ratio financed from Japanese investors is highest in ASEAN: 36.8 percent.
3. The highest ratio is shown in the NIEs, followed by the United States and ASEAN countries in financing from the financial institutions of the countries in which the investment is made.
4. But the ratio of financing from Japanese banks is the lowest in ASEAN or only 9 percent, while it is about 20 percent both in the United States and the NIEs.
5. Therefore the financing ratio from the local and/or other financial institutions is 20 percent or more in all regions.

From the above, we can confirm that financing from local financial institutions accounts for a significant proportion both of short and long-term funds. Particularly in the case of short-term funds, the enterprises investing in the NIEs and ASEAN are commonly obtaining most of their finance from the local financial institutions. Therefore it seems to be significant for foreign investment whether the enterprises investing in Thailand or Korea can raise the necessary funds in domestic financial institutions.

II. MONETARY POLICY OF THAILAND

A. Money Supply and Demand for Money

It is wellknown that the economic and financial development of Thailand has stimulated Japanese capital flow. In this section, by separating the performance of the Thai economy and its characteristics from monetary aspects, I will discuss how financial diversification and the monetary policy of Thailand have affected the Japanese capital inflow.

Of the various indexes of monetary aspects, first, I will examine the M_2/Y ratio or ratio of the money supply (M_2) to gross national product. I will also outline the financial deepening in comparison with the cases of Japan, Korea and Indonesia. Here M_2 denotes interest-and non-interest bearing deposits in the banking system.

For instance, the M_2/Y ratio in Japan has reached a level of over 1.0 since 1985, which was 0.74 in 1970. The ratio in Korea rose to a level of 0.41 in 1990 from 0.33 of 1970. In Indonesia the ratio remained at a level of 0.2 up to 1983, but after that, it rose sharply to a level of 0.37 in 1989. The ratio of Thailand rose steeply to a level of 0.6 in 1985 from 0.28 of 1970 and reached to 0.75 in 1990. From these ratios, it will be seen that the financial deepenings of both Thailand and Indonesia are occuring quickly. That of Thailand is particularly remarkable. The rate of increase of M_2 ratio suggests that public deposits in the form of time deposits was encouraged by the development of the banking system.

Second, I will use a money-demand function (L) in order to analyze the interrelationships between real and monetary sectors of these four countries. Let M_2 denote money supply, P denote price level, Y denote national products, and I denote investment. As Ronald I. Mckinnon[7] has showed, the function is expressed as follows.

$$M/P = L(Y, I/Y, r - \dot{p}/P$$

Here r is the real return and $\dot{p}/P$ is increase rate of price level, and $r\text{-}\dot{p}/P$ is the real return on holding money.

As for the three factors of national product (Y), investment/national product ration (I/Y) and increase rate of price level ($\dot{p}/P$), which decide the amount of demand for money, I will compare the cases of Thailand, Korea, Japan and Indonesia. First, I will examine the first factor, or national product. The absolute size of national product (converted into U.S. dollars by market rate) is $3,190.0 billion for Japan, $235.1 billion for Korea, $80.3 billion for Thailand in relation to the GNP of 1990, and $89.4 billion for Indonesia in 1989. Also, real economic growth rate is 4.4 percent in Japan, 13.3 percent in Korea, 7.7 percent in Thailand on average (comparison averaged with the previous year) for the twenty years from 1970 to 1990, and Indonesia is 10.5 percent on the average for nineteen years from 1970 to 1989.

The second factor, or rate of investment (I/Y) is 32.7 percent in Japan, 29.9 percent in Korea, 26.5 percent in Indonesia, and 26.3 percent in Thailand on average (comparison with the previous year) for the twenty years from 1970 to 1990. But as for the increase in rate of investment (i/I), Indonesia is 32.6 percent, which is the top level among these countries, followed 27.4 percent for Korea. Compared with this, 17.7 percent for Thailand and 10.0 percent for Japan during the same period are relatively low.

The average rate of increase of price level ($\dot{p}/P$) is highest in Indonesia: 13.7 percent on the average (comparison with consumer price of the previous year) from 1970 to 1990. The affect of this rate is to reduce the amount of money-demand. After Indonesia, the highest rates are 12.2 percent for Korea, 7.2 percent for Thailand and 6.0 percent for Japan during the same period.

From these three factors, we can summarize the characteristics by country in the following way.

1. Looking of the money supply (M_2) of 1990, $3190.0 billion for Japan, which is followed by $95.9 billion for Korea, $60.5 billion for Thailand and $47.8 billion for Indonesia, coincides with the high level of national product (Y), ratio of Investment (I/Y), and the stable increase of price level ($\dot{p}/P$). However, the rate of increase of real money supply $(\dot{M_2/p})/(M_2/p)$ is 6.7 percent on average for the twenty years from 1970 to 1990, which is relatively restrained, because of the slow rate of increase of national product and investment.

2. In Korea and Indonesia, the rate of increase of real money supply is at a high level: 13.9 percent and 20.8 percent respectively. It is clear that these high increase rates are supported by the rapid rise of national product and investment, which makes up for the high rate of increase of price level.

3. The case of Thailand is closest to Japan. Thailand's 13.3 percent rate of increase of real money supply is higher than that of Japan, but lower than those of Korea and Indonesia. This indicates that a lower level of national product and investment forces the demand for money down, notwithstanding the low rate of increase of price level. Thus it will be possible to classify the pattern of economic development into two types: the Korea/Indonesia-type, where demand and supply of money are enlarged by a high economic growth

rate and sharp rate of investment, and the Thailand/Japan type, in which a stable relationship is formed between demand and supply of money, symbolized by the low rate of increase of price level. This means that a symmetrical interrelation between the real and monetary sectors and differences in the stages of financial deepening are found in the process of economic development, which is reflected in the economic development policy of these countries.

B. Structure of Interest Rates

The characteristics of the Thai financial market will be made clear through an examination of her structure of interest rates: the ones of commercial banks and finance and securities companies of Thailand, and deposit money banks (commercial banks) and mutual and finance companies of Korea.[8] The policy of management of foreign capital in Thailand will become clear through a comparison with that of Korea. Although the economic development policy of Thailand is enforced through commercial banks and the IFCT, strategic financing, which provides a preferential credit with low interest rate to key industries, has not been adopted so strongly as in Korea. But it is widespread in the sense that the industrial policies of governments are executed by commercial banks and industrial banks. Therefore it seems worthwhile to compare the interest rates of commercial banks which are liable to regulation by each government with the interest rate of finance and securities companies and mutual and finance companies which are not so regulated because they deal with short-term funds.

The sharp increase of inflow of foreign capital into finance and securities companies suggests the very free management of foreign capital. In addition to this, the interest differentials of deposits and loans are relatively small between commercial banks and finance and securities companies. For example, in 1985, the loan rate (with a term of six months and more, and less than one year) of commercial banks ranged from 17.5 percent to 19.0 percent, while that of finance and securities companies was 17.1 percent. Similarly, while the deposit rate (with a term of six months and more, and less than one year) of the former ranged from 10.5 percent to 13.0 percent, that of the latter was 12.9 percent.

The financial institutions in Korea corresponding to Thai finance and securities companies are mutual and finance companies.[9] Their interest on deposits and loans is higher than that of commercial banks. Moreover, interest differentials with commercial banks are more greatly spread than the cases of Thailand. For instance, in 1985, while the loan rate (with a term of six months and more, and less than one year) of commercial banks ranged from 10.0 percent to 11.5 percent, that of mutual and finance companies was 18.0 percent. Similarly, while the deposit rate (with a term of six months and more, and less than one year) of the former was 6.0 percent, the latter was 12.5 percent. Also, mutual and finance companies do not deal with foreign capital. The monetary policy of Korea is considered to be strengthened by this management policy of specifying the trader of foreign capital. However, even in Korea, a market-mechanism based policy is being on December 5, 1988. The sharp increase in deposits in foreign currency is due to this change.

The more the amount of market-based trade is enlarged by liberalizing the financial and monetary markets of the recipient countries, the harder becomes the competition between financial institutions. Correspondingly, an urgent question arises with respect to raising efficiency: namely, how to join private and public sector funds, and how to arrange various financial intermediaries. The improvement of efficiency within the public sector and cooperation with the private sector will be an indispensable issue in order to make the flow of private capital more efficient.

III. DISTRIBUTION PROBLEMS ON THE CAPITAL SUPPLY SIDE

International financial institutions are main dealers of capital flow. The Asian Development Bank (ADB) is one of them. In this section, I will consider various problems left on the capital supply side by discussing the role of the ADB.

The financial resources for the ADB's activities consist of the Ordinary Capital Resource (OCR) and the Asian Development Fund (ADF). First, the OCR is the fund with a market-based interest rate of 6-7 percent, for which the term of payment if 20-25 years. Its resources are financed in capital markets in places such as Japan. Germany and Switzerland. This financing mode is strongly affected by the economic situation of the international financial market. Second, the ADF what are know as ADF "soft loan" is lent on a preferential term of payment of 40 years and a commission of less than 1 percent. Financial resources are lent from a special fund set in the ADF account.

Of a total outstanding loans of $32.6 billion in 1990, loans by a form of the OCR and the ADF respectively account for $21.6 billion and $11.1 billion. The countries with a great quantity of outstanding OCR are Korea, Indonesia, the Philippines, India and Pakistan. On the other hand, most of the ADF funds are directed to South Asia countries such as Bangladesh and Pakistan.[10]

In order to strengthen a market-mechanism based activity, the ADB will emphasise loans based on the OCR. But the fact that demand for the ADB's funds is repressed in the NIES and ASEAN is becoming a serious problem To resolve this situation, the ADB is implementing a market-mechanism loan policy as follows.[11]

1. The ADB has made its investment behavior active by dealing with private enterprise stocks since 1983 and has attached importance to private sector forces by lending to enterprises even without a guarantee from the home country since 1986.
2. The ADB reduced interest rates and commission. For example, judging that higher loan rates produced a sluggish economy, the ADB adopted a floating interest rate system in which the interest rate is re-examined on the basis of the original rate, every six months. Also, the ADB has so far reduced commission from 0.5 percent to 0.4 percent.
3. In order to respond quickly to the change in borrowing countries' needs, the ADB implemented a review of programs by country in order to manage flexibly. For example, it might enlarge a programmed loan permitting the import of raw materials to offer opportunity to use local currency.
4. The ADB decided to proceed with joint-financing with private financial institutions. In fact, the total of joint-financing up to 1988 amounts to $7.1 billion, or close to $9.8 billion of the ADB's loans.

Thus for ADB activities based on both official and private resources, it has become a prior condition to make arrangement with other financial institutions. Up to now, there have been arrangement problems with respect to allocation-efficiency with international institutions such as the World Bank, and Japanese institutions like the Export-Import Bank of Japan (EXIMB) and the Japanese Overseas Economic Cooperation Fund (OECF).[12] When the ADB converts to market-based loans, a new conflict will arise between private financial institutions. Because of this problem involving the ADB, it is likely that problems will arise concerning the whole arrangement policy with respect to the efficiency of capital inflow.

My proposal for relieving the conflicts between funds consists of the following two points. First, distinguishing the separate roles of private and official capital, although all roles which private capital can perform should be left to the private sector, the public sector should be retained to guide private capital. In addition, assigning the work should be done in the public sector, based on the efficiency criteria, also, for official capital. Although the concept of efficiency is required even for grants, efficiency should be particularly pursued in the light of interest rates and terms of redemption.

Projects classed as two-step-loans which have been successful in ASEAN countries provide some hints on the above issue. To proceed with this type of project, for instance, a factor which must be considered is cooperation among the recipient country's financial institutions which have the ability to judge the worth of a project, Japanese financial institutions such as the OECF and the EXIMB, which have knowledge, and the ADB, which has financing ability.

Second, positive cooperation is required between private and official capital. In fact, direct foreign investors sometimes share in the benefits produced by the creation of infrastructure by official capital. Usually it is rational for a beneficiary to bear that cost. But the exact calculation of expenses is difficult. Therefore it will be desirable that the enterprises invested in overseas join open investment funds. For example, the ADB is setting up funds with the object of investment to convertible debenture issued by Asian enterprises. This fund is thought to strengthen a capital market of Asian countries. Subscription by the enterprises invested in overseas seems to be a condition necessary to make capital flow active.

CONCLUSION

The economic development of Asian countries has depended on more consolidated financial and capital markets that that of other regions. It is known that long-term credit banks and commercial banks play an important role as financial intermediaries, not only for domestic but also for foreign funds But notwithstanding the low rates of economic growth of the world economy, the inter-flows of capital between countries seem to have increased. In order to respond to this situation, the ultimate issue will be how financial institutions can support individuals effort as the true leading agent of economic development, and how to raise economic efficiency as a result.

This way of thinking will promote the introduction of foreign capital. From the point of view of an increase not only for the private capital, but also in official capital, as a first step, the question of how to directly absorb the needs of recipient countries' enterprises and households should be considered. And in order to give this trial practical significance, joint-loans with local financial institutions should be examined as a second step.

NOTES

1. Ministry of Finance, *Zaisei kinyu Tokei Gepo* [*Monthly Finance Review*] No. 472 (August 1991), Tokyo, p.1. In detail, see Supachai Panitchpakdi, "*Japan, ASEAN and Thailand: Future Financial Relations*" In Attacharn Pattanajidvilai (ed.), *International Dimensions of Japanese Financial Development: Implications for Asean and Thailand* (1991), Faculty of Economics Chulalongkorn University, Bangkok, pp. 143-177.
2. The Asian Development Bank, *Asian Development Outlook 1991*, Manila, pp. 1-18.
3. The Japenese Overseas Economic Cooperation Fund, *Kaigai Keizai Kyoryoku Binran 1992* (*Manual for Overseas Economic Cooperation 1992*) Tokyo: p. 276 and p. 314.
4. The Bank of Thailand, *Quarterly Bulletin*, various years, Bangkok.
5. This policy is reflected in the debt-service-ratio. For instance, the maximum amount of loans has been defined within 10 percent of fiscal budget since 1976. See Masumi Kishi, *Keizai Hatten to Kinyu Seisaku* (*Economic Development and Monetary Policy*) (1990), Toyo Keizai Shinposha, Tokyo, pp. 147-148.

6. For financing of short-term funds, see Ministry of International Trade and Industry Industrial Policy Bureau, *Kaigai Toshi Tokey Soran* (*Second General Survey of Overseas Business Activity*) (1986), Tokyo, pp. 232-235. Also, for long-term funds, see MITI, *Fourth General Survey of Overseas Business Activity* (1992), Tokyo, pp. 186-188.

7. Ronald I. Mckinnon, *Money and Capital in Economic Development* (1973), The Brookings Institution, Washington, D.C., Ch. 5.

8. For the comparison of monetary policy and financial institutions between Korea and Thailand, see Masumi Kishi, "*The Role of Financial Institutions in Internationalizing Market for small-and-medium-scale Industries: Korea and Thailand.*" In Research in Asian Economic Studies, Vol 4A, Asian Economic Regimes: An Adaptive Innovation Studies, edited by M. Dutta (1992), JAI Press, Greenwich, CT, pp. 101-122.

9. The Bank of Korea, *Monthly Statistical Bulletin*, various years, Seoul.

10. The ADB, *Key Indicators of Developing Asian and Facilities Countries* (1991), Manila, Table 60.

11. Masao Fujioka, *Ajia Taiheiyo Jidai no Kinyu to Keizai* (*Finance and the Economies in the Asian and Pacific Era*) (1990), Toyo Keizai Shinposha, Tokyo, pp. 32-33, pp. 119-121 and p. 134.

12. Derek Healey, *Japanese Capital Exports and Asian Economic Development*, The Organization for Economic Co-operation and Development (1991), Paris, Ch. 5.

REFERENCES

Fujioka, Masao. (1990). *Ajia Taiheiyo Jidai no Kinyu to Keizai* [*Finance and the Economies in the Asian and Pacific Era*], *Tokyo: Toyo Keizai Shinposha.*

Healey, Derek. (1990). *Japanese Capital Exports and Asian Economic Development.* The Organization for Economic Co-operation and Development, Paris.

International Monetary Fund, *International Financial Statistics Yearbook 1991.*

Kishi, Masumi. (1990). *Kaizai Hatten to Kinyu Seisaku* (*Economic Development and Monetary Policy*). Toyo Keizai Shinposha, Tokyo.

________. (1992). "*The Role of Financial Institutions in Internationalizing Market for small-and-medium-scale Industries: Korea and Thailand,*" In *Research in Asian Economic Studies, Vol. 4A, Asian Economic Regimes: An Adaptive Innovation Studies*, edited by M. Dutta. Greenwich, CT: JAI Press.

Ministry of Finance. (1991). *Zaisei Kinyu Tokey Gepo* (*Monthly Finance Review*) No. 472(August), Tokyo.

________. (1992). *Fourth General Survey of Overseas Business Activity*, Tokyo.

Ministry of International Trade and Industry Industrial Policy Bureau. (1986). *Kaigai Toshi Tokei Soran* (*Second General Survey of Overseas Business Activity*), Tokyo.

Mckinnon, I. Ronald. (1973). *Money and Capital in Economic Development*, The Brookings Institution, Washington.

Pattanajidvilai, Attacharn (ed.), (1991). *International Dimensions of Japanese Financial Development: Implications for ASEAN and Thailand* Faculty of Economics Chulalongkorn University, Bangkok.

The Asian Development Bank. (1991). *Asian Development Outlook 1991*, Manila.

________. (1991). *Key Indicators of Developing Asian and Pacific Countries*, Manila.

The Bank of Korea, *Monthly Statistics Bulletin*, various years, Seoul.

The Bank of Thailans, *Quarterly Bulletin*, various years, Bangkok.

The Japanese Overseas Economic Cooperation Fund. (1992). *Kaigai Keizai Kyoryoku Binran 1992* (*Manual for Overseas Economic Cooperation 1992*), Tokyo.

INVESTMENT-LED REGIONALISM AND TRADE LIBERALIZATION: THE ASIAN PERSPECTIVE

Linda Low

I. INTRODUCTION

The world has seen so much economic pluralism that "a return to the idealized paradigm of international trade with '*n*' countries engage in trade producing '*m*' final goods and services with currencies linked to the pure gold standard, is hardly an option" (Dutta 1992, p. 67). The United States has declined in political and economic hegemony with the emergence of a multipolar global system. Neither the gatekeepers of international trade (General Agreement for Tariffs and Trade, GATT) nor of the international financial system (International Monetary Fund, IMF) have been as effective as they had been in the 1950s and 1960s. Regionalism has grown, coexisting with rising globalism. Whether in response to regionalization in Western Europe and North America or out of its own accord, the Asia Pacific region is also experimenting on various concepts and configurations of an economic community, however defined.

Research in Asian Economic Studies, Volume 6, pages 193-209.

ISBN: 1-55938-918-4

II. REGIONALISM IN ASIA IN A GLOBAL SYSTEM

Since World War II, a diverse typography of economies classified as developed, developing, newly industrialising, oil and non-oil economies and centrally planned systems in transition to market economies has evolved.[1] Factor flows in capital, labour and technology, trade in goods and services and other forms of exchanges including cultural, political and diplomatic, have made most economies more open and interrelated. Traditional groups formed under different economic and political regimes are straddled with new globalism or globalization as corporations strive for better competitiveness. International public goods and externalities as in efforts to protect the environment and tackle greenhouse have generated more interlocking interdependence.

While powerful economies still reside in North America and Europe, the axis of dynamism has shifted to Asia Pacific which has acquired a distinct identity. Since the late 1960s, academic-led concepts of regionalism were initiated under the Organization for Pacific Trade and Development (OPTAD) and the Pacific Trade and Development (PAFTAD) (Kojima 1968 and Drysdale 1988). The agenda in the first PAFTAD conference in 1968 was to explore the possibility of a Pacific free trade area given the formation of the EC and the fear that Japan was left out in the cold. The participants comprising Japan, Canada, Australia, New Zealand and the United States vetoed the idea as each country had its own perspective. The United States was adverse to it as its global vision was for an open world trading system. But the 1968 conference was fruitful forging cooperation as economists from both the developed and developing economies had a lot to learn about each other.

In 1980, a tripartite effort involving the academia, government and business was formed under the Pacific Economic Cooperation Council (PECC) which now has 20 members.[2] This was followed by a governmental group called the Asian Pacific Economic Cooperation (APEC) in 1989 which currently has 15 members. Both the PECC and APEC are committed to the principle that cooperation should be outward-looking, building on a consensus of economic issues with regional trade liberalization promoted based on GATT consistent principles (Elek 1992).[3] On the business side, there is the Pacific Business Economic Council (PBEC) which has observer status in the PECC.

Undoubtedly, the most successful economic group in Asia or among developing countries to date is the Association of Southeast Asian Nations (ASEAN), founded more on a political than economic platform in 1967. As political goodwill and networking brought some cohesion, economic cooperation was energized since 1976. More innovative ideas have emerged as the global and regional environment changed including an East Asian Economic Caucus (EAEC). The current thinking is for the EAEC encompassing the ASEAN states, Japan, South Korea, Taiwan, Hong Kong, China and even the Indochinese states to operate under APEC.

A more viable, small and informal economic group is the growth triangle with Singapore as the prime mover involving Johor in Malaysia and the Riau Province in Indonesia in complementary manufacturing-cum-tourism activities (Lee 1991 and Wong and Ng 1992). Officially kicked off in 1991 with ASEAN's blessing, it drew investment from Japan, the United States and Taiwan among some non-ASEAN countries. It has stimulated ideas of other ASEAN growth triangles (Toh and Low 1993).

The third ASEAN proposal which was not new but was successfully revived was the ASEAN Free Trade Area (AFTA) which together with the EAEC, the growth triangle and the Common Effective Preferential Tariff (CEPT) were endorsed as economic framework agreements at the fourth ASEAN Ministers' Summit Meeting in Singapore in 1992. A vision of a Southeast Asian community is considered for both economic and geopolitical reasons. An expanded ASEAN with states in Indochina or Vietnam as a start, is possible with the resolution of the Cambodian conflict and ongoing economic reform there.

III. THE NEW PARADIGM

The new paradigm in international trade is attributed to a number of factors which will be elaborated in this section under various subheadings. In a nutshell, the new paradigm is in economic regionalism driven by direct foreign investment (DFI) and market forces in response to external stimuli. Economic reforms in China, Indochina and Eastern Europe and the Commonwealth of Independent States (CIS) following the collapse of the Berlin Wall and the end of Cold War, mean liberalization and the resurgence of market forces. An integrated and competitive global system seems more viable and fashionable. The limits of export-led growth, provoking a re-examination to generate new sources of growth further needs a new paradigm. The diversity with respect to their stage of development in Asia offers tremendous scope for economic regionalism and regional trade groupings (Adams 1992).

A. GATT and Trade Blocs

The GATT Uruguay Round is past its scheduled date of completion, clouded by the formation of the North American Free Trade Agreement (NAFTA) and the European Economic Area (EEA). Economists (Bhagwati 1992) see little economic logic in free trade areas in their own right or as expressways for trade liberalization. But they have caused anxiety and retaliation in Asia though pure arithmetics of their market size and level of development would show their folly of being inward-looking.

As trade blocs emerge even as a second best option, one worry is the fate of nations which fall in between like the rest of Latin America, Africa, other southern hemisphere nations. Asian countries in ASEAN and Japan may be in some quandary. Japan appears reluctant to lead any Asian response to the NAFTA or the EEA. Other Asian countries boarding the global trading system include China, the Indochina states and South India. But there is little dialogue between South Asian countries and the rest of Asia though the South Asia Association of Regional Cooperation (SAARC) comprising India, Bangladesh, Pakistan, Sri Lanka, Nepal, Bhutan and Maldives was formed in 1985.

B. DFI and MNCs

Undoubtedly, DFI and multinational corporations (MNCs) are the main agents fashioning the new paradigm in international trade (Toh and Low 1994). The benefits and costs of DFI can be balanced with the right policies. The destination of DFI flows has also shifted, from the United States and other developed countries to the developing countries. The shares of DFI have increased in the ANIEs (Hong Kong, Singapore, South Korea and Taiwan) and ASEAN (Indonesia, Malaysia, the Philippines and Thailand). Significant reductions in tariff barriers in the developed countries have encouraged MNCs to adopt internationally oriented strategies often involving highly integrated transnational operations.

C. Economic Restructuring

These DFI trends correspond to structural changes occurring in Asia Pacific countries (Riedel 1991). The structural changes include the shift from agriculture to manufacturing and services, changing cost structures and in demand patterns. In Asia, three groups of economies involving Japan, the ANIEs and ASEAN, replicate the "wild flying geese" pattern of growth observed in the 1960s among the triad of the United States, and Japan and Southeast Asia (Kojima 1962 and Akamatsu 1962). Noting the caveats of comparing investment across countries, Table 1 shows this increasing presence of ANIE investment in ASEAN countries. The negative growth rates reflect constraints in absorbing DFI like infrastructure, rather than other adverse factors.

D. Technology and Borderless World

Technology affects both demand and supply and pushes the spread and pace of MNCs, globalization and borderless production (Kahler 1991 and Ohmae 1991). New technologies, information technology, telecommunications, microelectronics and other processes may have replaced the traditional Vernon

Table 1. Intra-Asian investment, 1992 US$m/%

Fr/To	Thailand		Philippines		Malaysia		Indonesia	
	Amt	% chg	Amt	% chg	Amt	% chg	Amt	% chg
Asia	307	-27	147	-52	623	-63	3951	-34
Japan	210	-5	72	-66	214	-60	1401	51
NIEs	49	-72	69	2	343	-66	2428	23
HK	11	-80	13	52	19	-83	906	226
SKorea	8	-17	43	-5	18	-89	581	93
Spore	5	-65	5	54	78	-47	381	10
Taiwan	26	-74	9	-24	228	-61	560	-47
Europe	112	-18	48	-86	992	429	1141	-3
US	118	8	62	-26	221	34	917	252
World	731	1	284	-64	2185	-3	8074	-8

Notes: Thailand-registered foreign capital of investment projects approved by Board of Investment with promotional privileges. Philippines-Foreign equity investment approved by Board of Investment. Malaysia-Foreign equity in manufacturing approved by malaysian Industrial Development Authority.

Indonesia-Total foreign capital in projects approved by BKPM excluding investment in oil, financial sectors.

Figures from different countries are strictly not comparable with different definitions used.

Source: Merrill Lynch, Asian Economic Commentary, April 1993.

product cycle with computer-aided design and manufacturing (CAD/CAM), computer-integrated manufacturing (CIM), flexible manufacturing system (FMS), just-in-time (JIT) inventory system and others. Time-based competition requiring speed and efficiency are facilitated by satellite and fiber optics telecommunication systems and link-ups practically happen in nanoseconds. Merging technologies as in telecomputing, have also integrated manufacturing and services activities with the growth of "servicization" in modern economies as part of the structural changes. Indeed, MNCs have created a kind of a "spider's web" linking and networking across many countries and industries (Bhagwati 1988).

With the trend toward heterogenous, integrated and service-oriented products, maintaining long term, faithful business relationships override short term cost advantages. This makes networking among suppliers of hardware and software, financial services and distributive systems crucial. In operational terms, "strategic corporate family planning" is the competitive answer to ensure "closeness to market" or "time to market."

E. Limits of Export-led Growth

While regionalism is increasingly propelled by investment and market forces, the formula of quality manufacturing and export-led growth in quality manufacturing as adopted by Japan and the ANIEs may have less validity for succeeding generations of NIEs (Klein 1990). On the demand side, the openness and absorption of exports by Japan and the ANIEs is lagging behind the United States economy which can no longer be the world's locomitive (Gray 1991). The economic rationale and impetus for absorption of exports from the ANIEs is also contrary to political sentiments in the United States. But there are more and more producers on the export-oriented track on the supply side.

The export-led economies of Japan and the ANIEs have succeeded by capitalizing on their availability of intelligent, conscientious, trainable, well disciplined and relatively cheaper labor. Whether the ASEAN and other developing economies can sustain the same conditions would ultimately determine their success of adopting the export-led strategy, assuming simultaneously, some fossilization in the developed countries and the ANIEs. But new technologies may also work against export-led economies if the labor component in value added and cost of manufactures drop and proximity to market to save transportation costs and supplant other impediments.

IV. CHARACTERISTICS OF REGIONALISM IN ASIA

In this section, ASEAN, both its AFTA and growth triangles is used to illustrate the characteristics of the new paradigm in economic regionalism which is investment-led and based on trade liberalization rather than in formal trade blocs. First, a discussion of open regionalism which suits open economies in Asia best, is germane. The concept of open regionalism in Asia Pacific is radically different from the discriminatory of the EC (Elek 1991 and Drysdale 1991). Its essential features include a commitment to non-discrimination in trade and international economic policy approach, cooperation in diplomacy to support the multilateral trading system. Also cooperation in the provision of international public goods among neighboring countries as in environmental protection and energy security are matters requiring collective action and are the spillovers of industrialisation and diplomacy (Drysdale, 1991).

A. AFTA as a Regional Response

The lethargy of ASEAN economic cooperation in the 1960s and 1970s has been attributed to many factors, from institutional structure and machinery to the faulty framework.[5] Programs like the ASEAN industrial project (AIP), the ASEAN complementation scheme (AIC) and the ASEAN industrial joint venture scheme (AIJV) were crafted by bureaucrats rather than by the market. These were based on an inward-looking industrialization strategy which were politically desirable but difficult to attain based principles of equal gains and costs (Tan et al., 1992).

Even what appears the most concrete and enduring in the ASEAN Preferential Trading Arrangement (PTA), suffered initially from the slow product-by-product method. The PTA is to encourage intra-ASEAN trade through the use of long term quantity contracts, preferential terms for financing imports by government agencies, preferential tariff rates and liberalisation of non-tariff barriers (NTBs). Despite the increasing list of items included under the PTA, it was fogged with cosmetic "padding" of items as the philosophy seems based on cooperation to exclude competition rather than to enhance competition.[6] It was only in 1980 that across-the-board tariff reductions were adopted by all ASEAN countries. But "sensitive lists" and suspension of preferential tariffs were provided for where domestic industries might be threatened by "serious injury."

All empirical studies on the likely impact of the PTA on intra-regional trade confirm that the effects of the tariff cuts have been minimal (Tan et al., 1992). The reasons for the dismal record include relatively small tariff cuts, the small number of products included in the PTA in comparison to the total number of items traded among ASEAN countries despite padding and the low price eleasticities of the product groups concerned.

While tangible results are certainly lacking, the intangible human web of linkages and communication networking cannot be underscored. Over the years, the ASEAN spirit and solidarity have evolved to produce sufficient trust and goodwill among politicians, bureacrats and businessmen. This environment and ambience become extremely important and meaningful to condition and stimulate more tangible efforts in economic cooperation. Thus, when a new "glue" is needed in the 1990s to bind the ASEAN countries, ideas and projects found greater reception and expediency than a cold start as in the late 1970s.

As alluded above, a number of new economic and political stimuli from within and outside ASEAN have also accounted for renewed interest in the AFTA proposal. First, there is the external pressure for ASEAN to maintain market shares in the face of other trade blocs like the Single European Market (SEM) (Low 1992), extended to the EEA and the NAFTA. The floundering Uruguay Round under GATT with rising protectionism have shaken the confidence in a free trade system. Even as ASEAN does not believe that retaliatory measures are necessarily the best line of defence, ideas like AFTA and the Malaysian EAEC proposal are at best insurances for East Asian and ASEAN cohesion (Low 1991).

By 1992, ASEAN has a large domestic market of 330 million people with a combined US$300 billion in GNP or US$1,100 per capita. If an enlarged ASEAN is contemplated as suggested by Malaysia, there is another 80 million people in the Indochinese states. Third, ASEAN economies have evolved more complementary industrial bases Singapore and Thailand for instance have specialized in different niches and products and not merely on low-cost labor.

Table 2. Possible winners and losers with AFTA*

	Problem areas	*Areas of probable comparative advantage*
Indonesia		Wood/rattan furniture, Chemicals, Plastics, Cement,
Malaysia	Cement, Textiles, Gems/jewellery	Fertiliser, Pulp, Wood and Rubber products
Philippines	Cement, Textiles, Vegetable oil, Rubber products, Wood/rattan	Fertiliser, Pulp
Thailand	Pulp, Plastic raisins, Glass, mirror, Electrical, Rubber, Leather	Textiles, Gems/jewellery, Plastics, Cement, Chemical products, Ceremics

* Singapore and Brunei are free trading nations with virtually no industries which will suffer from withdrawal of tariff protection

Source: Crosby Research, Quarterly Economic Review, No 1/1992 and Sawamiphakdi, et al., 1992.

Malaysia and Thailand are closely converging to Singapore's in terms of industrial strategies (Low et al., 1993, forthcoming). While Singapore, Malaysia and Thailand are more competitive at the upper end of the industrial ladder, they are complementary with Indonesia and the Philippines at the lower end. Fourth, ASEAN has vastly improved its competitiveness with deregulatory measures over and above the frequent and growing reductions in import tariffs and NTBs. The Common External Preferential Tariff (CEPT) as an incentive to harmonize internal tariffs for selected ASEAN products will represent maximum internal tariff. When this is gradually reduced to zero, there will be a free trade area.[7]

The list of goods under 15 product categories due for deep tariff cuts in 1993 include cement, fertiliser, textiles, pulp, jewellery and gems, electronics, plastics, vegetable oils, rubber products, copper cathodes, pharmaceuticals, leather products, wooden and rattan furniture and ceramic and glass products. These possible winners and loser with AFTA are projected in Table 2.

While AFTA has been endorsed as "do-able" in 15 years, possible obstacles in the form of the "six minus X" formula where member countries are given more time to reduce tariffs on "sensitive products" or allowed to suspend concessions if they perceive "serious injury" to domestic industries remain. More fundamental is that the economic impact of AFTA trade liberalization has been estimated to be minimal.

In earlier elasticity approach studies, the effects of trade creation with economic integration were found to be small (Tan et al., 1992). More recent studies by researchers from the ASEAN countries on the impact of trade

Table 3. Increase in export with 1990 as base year

Tariff reduction	*US$mil*			*As % of Total Export*		
	50%	*80%*	*100%*	*50%*	*80%*	*100%*
Indonesia	411	658	822	1.5	2.3	2.9
Malaysia	574	919	1149	2.0	3.2	4.0
Phillipines	110	176	220	1.4	2.3	2.8
Singapore	554	887	1108	1.0	1.6	2.0
Thailand	380	608	761	1.8	2.9	3.6
ASEAN	2030	3248	4060	1.4	2.3	2.9

Source: Toh and Low (1993).

liberalization come to the same conclusion. In Toh and Low (1993), with complete trade liberalization, it would result in 14.7 percent increase in intra-ASEAN trade and GDP of ASEAN would increase by 3.1 percent (with 1990 as the reference year). Total intra-ASEAN export would increase by about 3 percent of ASEAN's total exports (Table 3).

For effects on individual ASEAN countries, the highest percentage increase in income as the result of AFTA will be Singapore (5.5%) followed by Malaysia (5.1%) as shown in Table 4. However, even the smallest increase in the Philippines is almost 2 percent. Given the wide consensus on the minimal economic impact of trade liberalization under AFTA, it seems fair to conclude that the AFTA will not be discriminatory against outside countries. This substantiates the view that AFTA will not pose a threat as an arrangement for "internationalization of protection" (Johnson 1967, p. 28) as like in the EC, NAFTA and the Closer Economic Relations (CER) Agreement between Australia and New Zealand. ASEAN countries are too dependent on the triad of U.S., EC and Japan to disengage themselves from the global system. Another notable difference in ASEAN and AFTA is the desire for economic integration without political integration.

B. Growth Triangles

While noting that the various waves of direct foreign investment in the Asia Pacific region are still due to both pull and push factors, there was an important phenomenon of "global regionalism" superimposed. This was a simultaneous orientation outwards to the world and inwards within the region of the Asia Pacific countries. Investment-driven and export-oriented economic zones like those in Hong Kong-Guangdong and the southern ASEAN growth triangle are such examples in contrast to regionalism as evident in the EC, the EEA and the NAFTA.

The development of the subregional ASEAN growth triangle involving three ASEAN member countries is an interesting scenario. While bilateral and

Table 4. Tariff reduction and income generated with 1990 as base year

Tariff reduction	*50% Income US$m*	*50% % of base income*	*80% Income US$m*	*80% % of base income*	*100% Income US$m*	*100% % of base income*
Indonesia	1258	1.2	2013	1.9	2517	2.3
Malaysia	1087	2.6	1739	4.1	2174	5.1
Philippines	397	0.9	635	1.4	793	1.8
Singapore	946	2.7	1514	4.4	1892	5.5
Thailand	1069	1.3	1711	2.1	2139	2.7
ASEAN	4757	1.5	7612	2.5	9515	3.1

Source: As in Table 3.

regional economic cooperation among these three ASEAN countries have been on for many decades, the accelerated pace of economic cooperation development on a tripartite basis is a relatively new phenomenon. The growth triangle could also enhance exchanges in human resource development programs.

Economic complementarity propelled by the market was the rationale for the existence of the southern ASEAN growth triangle as for the Hong Kong-Guangdong experiment. But the Singapore Government as the facilator and prime mover in the ASEAN case is noted. The reality is the ASEAN growth triangle reconciles the tension between statism and market forces. It is also important that it is well accepted by the external community, especially the MNCs. The promise of AFTA could further pull in the same direction as the growth triangle.

While a loose alliance under the growth triangle allows flexibility and imagination, the legal aspects with respect to investment laws, protection of property rights and other aspects can prove inhibiting. The experience with the legal provisions under the Canada-USA Free Trade Area may be useful guidelines for the ASEAN growth triangle. The model of a bilateral investment treaty may for instance be studies by the ASEAN states. While international laws and regulations to protect trade, investment and economic cooperation are paramount, a more dynamic frameworld which allows changes and evolving conditions to have their influence must prevail.

The issues of unequal costs and benefits, the related failure to take into consideration short term long versus term negative and positive aspects are reflected by the usual sentiments of Indonesians toward Singapore's apparent gains. With the growth triangle involving a province, a state and a nation, the usual politics of bargaining for balanced growth remain. The distribution and equity issues require a political economy approach in analysis. These involve four areas namely those between locals and foreigners, among the participating countries, and intra-regional or intra-provincial ones. However, the realist would recognize that any inequity suffered by one partner may be attributed to the lack of effective coordination and lack of synchronization of plans rather than blatant exploitation. The opportunities and potential from the growth triangle must be more carefully harnessed by a strong political will to drive the institutions and policy makers harder. Policy-makers in ASEAN must start thinking in terms of the sustainable development concept, that is how an expansion of economic activities can be done with minimum negative social externalities. This would be the only way to prevent the turning of "compensation for the losses" to "losses for the compensation."

The other ASEAN growth triangle in the north has been less concrete as even the mapping of the northern ASEAN growth triangle has no consensus. While Malaysia may be keen in all the 14 Muslim southern states in Thailand to join its four in northern Peninsular Malaysia, the Thai government is more wary of a split along religious lines. Thailand is also more preoccupied with its Southern Seaboard project and the Baht area which involve Bangkok, Laos and Vietnam and has evolved based on market forces. While the potential for ASEAN growth triangles is high, not all of success factors required as in the southern growth triangle may be readily available. These included catalyst, complementarity, cooperation and competition binded by political will and commitment (Toh and Low 1993).

C. Other Regional Responses

It is further suggested that apart from the AFTA and growth triangles, there are other possible responses which fit the characteristics of the new paradigm of economic regionalism driven by investment, technology and market forces. Like most ASEAN schemes, AFTA seems to be urged upon and premised on non-economic, specifically political events. Intensive bureaucratic bargaining to work out the mechanism of both the PTA and the CEPT may be fraught with difficulties under the "six minus X" formula and list of "sensitive products" to avoid "serious injury" to domestic industries.

Thus, other policies to engender the new paradigm include further deregulation and privatization, promotion of local entrepreneurs in small, medium enterprises and generally promoting a market friendly environment. It is perhaps too premature to think of a macroeconomic core of harmonized fiscal and monetary policies. The ideal is the concurrent pursuit of AFTA and effective, conducive economic policies.

Another Asian response lies in the Chinese diaspora where Overseas Chinese found in all ASEAN and many Asian countries as a source of entrepreneurship, business linkages and cross-country investment may be tapped (Mackie 1992). There is an estimated 21 million ethnic Chinese in five ASEAN countries and while they may be minorities in many ASEAN countries, they have astonishing shares of the economic activities (Economist July 18, 1992). As prodigious savers, Chinese capital accumulated have been deployed though a distinctive form of social and business organisation based on personal acquaintance, trust and obligation.

Further, economic regionalism based on market intiatives can be meaningfully harnessed in human resource-led development strategy (Behrman 1990). A related concept is social absorption capacity or the system of organization and utilization of human resources to be enhanced from the demand side (Wong and Ng 1992). Added to traditional market failures as induced by market-distorting policies measures such as minimum wages, import tariffs, ethnic quotas for jobs or inefficient capital market for educational loans and others, are newer ones confronting social absorption capacity. These include institutional and social factors affecting the public and private resource allocation mechanisms to match technological learning capacity, supply and utilization. Governments may well unilaterally, bilaterally and regionally combine resources to tackle these market failures.

V. CONCLUSIONS AND POLICY IMPLICATIONS

The NAFTA proposal is a clear example where the United States appears to have departed from its multilateral principles on which it has based its postwar trade policy (Bonser 1991 and Krueger 1992). It must be appreciated that bilateral and exclusive trading blocs rather than multilateral arrangements as also in bilateral negotiations of voluntary restraints (VERs), telecommunications and intellectual property concerns or threats of "super 301" penalties, reflect the ascendancy of politics and foreign policy concerns more than economic self-interest. If this political economy interpretation of NAFTA is correct, its apparent "GATT-plus" arrangement which is supposed to make it open to otehrs wishing access would be invalidated. This leaves the economists with the job of documentating the economic costs of bilateral policies vis-a-vis more intangible and psychic political gains. Similarly, the "United States of Europe" is another hegemon that potentially challenges the global economy.

The international trading environment has changed both in institutional and structural terms. The global system has become more multipolar as conditions for free trade and exchange have deteriorated over time. Regionalism and trade blocs have emerged as market forces have been reasserted, driven by technology and competition. The positive signs are that many economic systems have become more deregulated and marketized and technological and human resource alliances have emerged. The emergence of regional groups under the trade bloc hybrid may be counterproductive. Retaliatory bloc formations is certainly not the answer.

Be it as it may, an environmental scan shows that trading blocs and regionalism have certainly come to stay. They may be touted as second best solutions to liberalize trade first within the group as in a laboratory, before the relationships and trading patterns are extended to a broader global system. This requires open regionalism to be practiced and be complmentary and supplementary to the ailing GATT framework to the extent possible. But certainly, no trade bloc or alliance should be the centrepiece of any commercial diplomacy and greater sensitivity of others should be noted. Economists are appealing to policy-makers to be sensible about marrying globalism with regionalism. Concepts like open regionalism or global regionalism are just two hybrids asking for the same pragmatism.

As the most successful grouping, the timing for ASEAN economic cooperation and integration as in AFTA is now more opportune. The major economies, Indonesia, Thailand and Malaysia are now more outward oriented and liberalized compared to the early 1980s. The ASEAN has also embarked rapidly on the industrialization path, away from the production of raw materials and agricultural products. The existing and future potential on complementary relationship in the manufacturing sector, has far expanded beyond the competitive relationship in raw materials and primary commodities production of the earlier days. A very important criterion to guide future ASEAN economic cooperation was enunciated by the Prime Minister Mr Goh Chok Tong.[8] As all ASEAN countries are convinced of, and are moving toward more outward orientation in trade, investment and industralization, the old style zero sum cooperation has passed to the new one of "competitive cooperation." By this is meant the stronger and more visible role of the private sector and market forces to render a more efficient and satisfactory allocation of resources and comparative advantages around the region.

A number of policy suggestions and implications can be drawn from the above. One is that despite prima facie attempts since the late 1960s under PAFTAD to the more recent AFTA, trade liberalization under such formal arrangements is fraught with inhibiting procedures. Strong political will and commitment are more important than economic framework agreements.

Second is that apart from traditional concepts like free trade areas, Asian groups can achieve equal if not more success in more practical and innovative schemes such as human resource development programs, intensified deregulation and privatization, harmonized and coordinated fiscal incentives and legal procedures for investment and property rights and other market-based responses. Collaborative, coordinated and growth-oriented policies which speed up economic transformation or restructuring could be extremely helpful. In this regard, both MNCs, Asian Chinese and indigenous factors should be explored.

Third, like most small open economy models, all Asian groups have to practice principles of open regionalism to better integrate with the world system (Elek 1992 and Drysdale 1988 and 1991). Asian regional groups can be both small and broad to achieve their own objectives so long as they remain open and integrated to the global system so as not to be cut out. Otherwise, they cannot sustain their DFI flows, export markets and other dynamic cross fertilization in technology and non-economic exchanges which still contribute to overall welfare.

Fourth, a political economy perspective would serve Asian regionalism better than a pure economic or security based approach. Though the cold war has ended, the region still has minefields of potential conflict in the two-China issue (China and Taiwan), not forgetting the 1997 status of Hong Kong, the two-Korea question, the growing tension in Indochina and even small but frequent squabbles among ASEAN states over territorial boundaries. The role of Japan caught between its Asian constituents and bigger United States trading partner across the Pacific Ocean, is ambivalent as much as it resists stepping into the United States' shoes in the Asian Pacific in both the economic and military senses. Asia has to acquire greater prowness and profile in international relations and diplomacy to assert its role and voice both as a player and gatekeeper of global economics and politics. The political economy frame would also enable a better understanding of the apparent inconsistent trade policy of the United States in NAFTA as political and foreign relations may have higher priorities than economic self-interest in bilateralism.

Finally, the question remaining is should Asia have its own regional grouping or trade bloc? The above survey of developments offers evidence that the inclination is certainly there. However, unlike in North America and Europe, the political impetus and more importantly, the prime mover is absent in Asia at the moment. Asia is both too big and too small at the same time. While it has the largest land mass and population and is richly endowed in resources, apart from Japan and the NIEs, the level of development and wealth accumulation is behind those of North America and Europe. Asia is dependent on extra-Asian trade and capital though with efforts and time, complementarity can be increased to promote greater intra-Asian trade and exchanges.

Given the historical and patterns of development in the Asian countries, responding to rising regionalism and trade bloc formation should not be in another formal pact. Presently, there are sufficient groups and fora for Asian interests to be brought across. Loose alliances driven by market forces and based on investment criteria may be more sustainable and nimble in responses. The private sector as the invisible hand could lessen or override the political imperatives of trade blocs. This strength should not be mistaken as a weakness as the Asian response may appear passive when it is actually proactive.

Asia has to work harder and take a higher profile in revitalizing GATT and ensuring that the Uruguay Round does not fail. In this respect, the stronger constituents in Asia including Japan, Asian NIEs and ASEAN must see their role more clearly rather than be purely preoccupied in their domestic matters or only with near neigbors. There is much more opportunity and potential if large economies like China and India can be helped along the right track for a greater Asia. It is too unwieldly to consider formal regional groups involving both China and countries in South Asia. For a start, ASEAN should develop dialogues with these countries as soon as possible.

NOTES

1. Four tiers of newly industrializing economies (NIEs) may be suggested: first-tier comprising Hong Kong, Singapore, South Korea and Taiwan; second-tier comprising Malaysia, Thailand and the Philippines; third-tier comprising Brazil, Mexico and Argentina; and fourth-tier comprising China and India.
2. The original name was the Pacific Economic Cooperation Conference (PECC) until 1991. See Tan et al., 1992 for a brief discussion of these Asia Pacific groups and for APEC, see Elek 1991 and 1992 and Hughes 1991.
3. The PECC comprises the six ASEAN countries (see footnote 7), Australia, Canada, Chile, China, Chinese Taipei, Hong Kong, Japan, Mexico, New Zealand, Pacific Islands, Peru, South Korea, the United Sstates and the former Soviet Union. The five PECC members which do not belong to APEC are the three Latin American countries, Pacific Islands and the former Soviet Union.
4. Malaysia unilaterally proposed the idea of an East Asia Economic Grouping (EAEG) in 1990 which was later lobbied as an ASEAN package in 1991 but not without changing its label to the EAEC at Indonesia's suggestion; see Low 1991.
5. The original members of ASEAN are Indonesia, Malaysia, the Philippines, Singapore and Thailand. Brunei joined in 1984.
6. Currently, there are 15,752 items on the PTA with a minimum margin of preference of 25 percent. More than 5,000 of these enjoy a deeper margin up to a maximum of 50 percent. But while the list is impressive, it has not increased PTA trade in ASEAN which remained at 1 percent of total intra-ASEAN trade. The items of greater interest to traders are no accorded preferential tariffs whereas the inclusion of snow plows in the PTA list is a classic example of irrelevancy in window-dressing. For instance, of the 15,752 items on the PTA, Singapore only exports 241 or 1.5 percent of them and imports another 289 or 1.8 percent.
7. For a more detailed discussiom of the concept and mechanics of the CEPT and AFTA, see Toh and Low, 1993.
8. The term "cooperative competition" was coined by Singapore's Prime Minister, Mr Goh Chok Tong in his keynote address on 4 March, 1991 at the Centre for Strategic and International Studies-Asia Society Conference on "The ASEAN Countries and the World Economy: Challenge of Change", in Bali, 3-5 March 1991.

REFERENCES

Adams, F.G. (1992). "Complementarity and Competition among the Economies of East Asia: Implications for Formation of Regional Groupings", *East Asian Economic Perspectives,* Kitakyushu: International Centre for the Study of East Asian Development, June, 3(2).

Akamatsu, Kaname. (1962). "A Historical Pattern of Economic Growth in Developing Economies", *The Developing Economies,* Tokyo: The Institute of Asian Affairs, Mar-Aug, (1).

Ariff, Mohamed and Tan Joseph, L.H. (1992). "ASEAN and the Pacific", *ASEAN Economic Bulletin,* special focus in commemoration of ASEAN 25th Anniversary, March, 8(3).

Behrman, J.R. (1990). *Human Resource Led Development. Review of Issues and Evidence*. New Delhi: ILO-ARTEP.

Bhagwati, Jagdish (1988). *Protectionsim*. Cambridge: Harvard University Press.

Bhagwati, Jagdish (1992). "Regionalism and Multilateralism: An Overview", Cambridge University Discussion Paper, No 603, Department of Economics, Columbia University, New York.

Bonser, Charles, F., ed, (1991). *Toward a North American Common Market: Problems and Prospects for a New Economic Community*. Boulder: Westview Press.

Dutta, M. (1992) "Economic Regionalization in Western Europe: Asia- Pacific Economies (Macroeconomic Core: Microeconomic Optimization), *American Economic Review*, May, 82(2), pp. 67-73.

Drysdale, Peter (1988). *International Economic Pluralism: Economic Policy in East Asia and the Pacific*. New York: Columbia University Press.

Drysdale, Peter. (1991). "Open Regionalism: A Key to East Asia's Economic Future", Pacific Economic Papers No 197, Australian-Japan Research Centre, Australian National University, Canberra.

Elek, Andrew. (1991). "Asia Pacific Economic Cooperation (APEC)", in *Southeast Asian Affairs*, Singapore: Institute of Southeast Asian Studies, pp. 33-48.

Elek, Andrew (1992). "Trade Policy Options for the Asia-Pacific Region in the 1990s: The Potential Open Regionalism", *American Economic Review*, 82(2), pp. 74-78.

Gray, Peter H. (1991). "Symposium: Can Export-led Growth Succeed Indefinitely? *Journal of Asian Economics*, 2(1), pp. 145-152.

Hughes, Helen. (1991). "Does APEC Make Sense?", *ASEAN Economic Bulletin*, November 8(2), pp. 125-136.

Johnson, H.G. (1967). *Economic Policies Towards Less Developed Countries*. Washington DC: Brookings Institution.

Kahler, Miles. (1991). "Economics Without Border", *Dialogue*, 2(92), pp. 7-13.

Klein, Lawrence, R. (1990). "Can Export-led Growth Continue Indefinitely? An Asia-Pacific Perspective", *Journal of Asian Economics*, 1(1), pp. 1-12.

Kojima, Kiyoshi, ed. (1968). *Pacific Trade and Development*. Tokyo: Japan Economic Research Center.

Kojima, Kiyoshi. (1962). "The Pattern of Triangular Trade Among the USA, Japan and Southeast Asia", *The Developing Economies*, Preliminary Issues No 1, Mar-Aug, Tokyo: The Institute of Asian Affairs.

Krueger, Anne. O. (1982). "Government, Trade and Economic Integration", *American Economic Review*, May, 82(2), pp. 109-114.

Lee Tsao Yuan., ed,, (1991). *Growth Triangle: The Johor-Singapore-Riau Experience*. Singapore: Institute of Southeast Asian Studies and Institute of Policy Studies.

Low Linda. (1991). "The East Asian Economic Grouping", *Pacific Review*, Oxford University Press, 4(4), pp. 375-382.

Low, Linda. (1992). "ASEAN-EC Economic Relations: Views from ASEAN", paper for conference on "ASEAN and the European Community in the 1990s", jointly organized by the Singapore Institute of International Affairs and the Friedrich Ebert Stiftung Foundation, Singapore, 19-21 May.

Low Linda, Toh Mun Heng, Tan Kong Yam, Soon Teck Wong and Hughes Helen. (1993). *Challenge and Response: Thirty Years of the Economic Development Board*. Singapore: Times Academic Press.

Mackie, J.A.C. (1992). "Overseas Chinese Entrepreneurship", *Asian-Pacific Economic Literature*, May, 6(1), pp. 41-64.

Ng Chee Yuen and Wong Poh Kam. (1991). "The Growth Triangle—A Market Driven Response", *Asia Club Papers 2*, Tokyo: Asia Club, pp. 123-152.

Ohmae, Kenichi. (1991). "The Borderlesss World: Managing in the Global Marketplace", Singapore Institute of Management Inaugural Distinguished Business Lecture, 14 October, Singapore.

Riedel, James. (1991). "Intra-Asian Trade and Foreign Investment:, *Asian Development Review,* 9 (1), pp. 111-146.

Sawamiphakdi, D., Thanomsri, F., Kiatchapipat, P., Srikulwong, M. and Somjit, N. (1992). "AFTA: The Case of Thailand", paper presented at the ICSEAD Model Comparison Seminar on "Trade, Development and Regional Groupings in East and South East Asia" organized by the International Centre for the Study of East Asian Development (ICSEAD), Kitakyushu City, 30-31 July.

Tan Kong Yam, Toh Mun Heng and Low Linda. (1992). "ASEAN and Pacific Economic Cooperation", *ASEAN and the Pacific*, Special Issue, *ASEAN Economic Bulletin,* March, 8(3), pp. 309-332.

Toh Mun Heng and Low Linda. (1993). "Is the ASEAN Free Trade Area a Second Best Option?" *Asian Economic Journal,* 7(3), forthcoming.

Toh Mun, Heng and Low, Linda, eds., (1993). *Regional Cooperation and Growth Triangles in ASEAN.* Singapore: Times Academic Press.

Toh Mun Heng and Linda Low. "The State of Play in Direct Foreign Investment in Asia Pacific", *Journal of Asian Economics,* 5(1), Mar-Apr, forthcoming.

Won Bae, Kim., (1991). "Report on Regional Development in the Yellow Sea Rim", submitted to the Korea Research Institute for Human Settlements and Asia-Pacific Institute of China, Honolulu: East-West Center, Population Institute, September.

Wong Poh Kam and Ng Chee Yuen. eds., (1992). *Human Resource Development and Utilization in the Asia-Pacific: A Social Absorptive Capacity Approach.* Singapore: Institute of Southeast Asian Studies.

JAPANESE SERVICE ENTERPRISES AND ASIAN[1] ECONOMIC INTERDEPENDENCE

Yoko Sazanami

I. INTRODUCTION

How the regional integrations in Europe and in North America will affect Asian economic growth have generated great concerns and inspired the emergence of Asian regional cooperation schemes. The formation of the Asia Pacific Economic Cooperation, ASEAN Free Trade Area and the proposition for the formation of East Asian Economic Caucus are examples. These regional schemes have strong appeal to Asian countries because they will not only strengthen Asian negotiating position in the GATT but also assure the access to Asian markets in case anything goes wrong with GATT's multilateral trading system. In addition to such provision, growing economic interdependence among Asian countries networked by activities of multilateral firms are creating common consensus that "if Asia can get together, the region can continue rapid economic growth."

Research in Asian Economic Studies, Volume 6, pages 211-224.

ISBN: 1-55938-918-4

The purpose of this paper is to assess the role of Japanese service enterprises in promoting Asian economic interdependence in 1986-1990. The reasons for analyzing Japanese service enterprises' activities in 1986-1990 are as follows. Firstly, Japanese FDI to the world showed a phenomenal rate of increase after the appreciation of yen in 1985. Secondly, Japanese FDI in services led this expansion. In 1986-1990, the share of services in total Japanese FDI was as high as 76 percent in Europe, 68.7 percent in North America and 55.1 percent in Asia (see Table 1). Thirdly, in spite of such a high share of services in total Japanese FDI, studies that focus on how deregulation and liberalization in services, namely finance, transportation and distribution, have promoted Japanese service enterprises' activities in the Asia-Pacific[2] are rather limited.[3]

The plan of the paper is as follows. Section II provides an overview of the factors that contributed to the increased share of services in total Japanese FDI to the Asia-Pacific in 1986-1990. Also, comparisons of regional patterns of Japanese FDI in services in the Asia-Pacific. Europe and North America are made in order to illustrate the facilitating function of Japanese service enterprises in networking Asian economic interdependence. In Section III, locational pull factors of the Asia-Pacific countries in attracting Japanese FDI in services are examined.[4] Section IV assesses the role of Japanese service enterprises in promoting Asian economic interdependence in three service fields: financial services, distributive services and commercial services. Section V provides some concluding remarks.

II. JAPANESE FDI IN SERVICES PROMOTING ASIAN ECONOMIC INTERDEPENDENCE—AN OVERVIEW

A part of the upsurge of Japanese FDI in services after 1985 currency appreciation reflected the so-called "bubble phenomenon" in Japan. The Japanese government took expansionary macropolicy in fear of the deflationary impact of sudden rise in yen. An effort to stimulate domestic demand by expansionary monetary policy was helpful for the recovery. However, excessive liquidity boosted the domestic security and real estate prices. The buying spree was soon extended to foreign markets pushing Japanese financial institutions to invest more. Japanese firms found ample investment opportunities in building hotels abroad to fulfill Japanese demand for tourism.

The increase in the share of services in total Japanese FDI between 1951 to 1985 and 1986 to 1990 was the largest in the Asia-Pacific (24.9% to 55.1%) among major regions that hosted Japanese FDI (see Table 1).

Such increase in Asia Pacific was affected by the above mentioned "bubble phenomenon" to a lesser extent than in Europe and North America. For example, in 1986-1990, 60.4 percent of Japanese FDI in services to Europe

Table 1. **Japanese FDI to Asia-Pacific, Europe and North America (Accumulated total for 1951-90 and 1986-90, Million U.S. $.%)**

	Asia-Pacific						*Europe*						*North America*					
	1951-85			*1986-90*			*1951-85*			*1986-90*			*1951-85*			*1986-90*		
	Amount	*Share*		*Amount*	*Share*		*Amount*	*Share*		*Amount*	*Share*		*Amount*	*Share*		*Amount*	*Share*	
Primary	6421	[33.7]		1258	[5.2]		854	[8.1]		740	[1.6]		1507	[5.7]		1216	[1.1]	
Manufacturing	7907	[41.4]		9640	[39.7]		2088	[19.8]		10452	[22.4]		7706	[29.1]		32617	[30.2]	
Services	4743	[24.9]	(100)	13380	[55.1]	(100)	7591	[72.1]	(100)	35503	[76.0]	(100)	17281	[65.2]	(100)	74286	[68.7]	(100)
Construction	218		(4.6)	503		(3.8)	45		(0.6)	72		(0.2)	254		(1.5)	922		(1.2)
Commerce	1044		(22.0)	2686		(20.0)	2486		(32.7)	4216		(11.9)	7420		(42.9)	9563		(12.9)
Finance	775		(16.3)	3433		(25.7)	3695		(48.7)	21434		(60.4)	4558		(26.4)	14835		(20.0)
Other services	1667		(35.1)	3222		(24.1)	252		(3.3)	3012		(8.6)	1087		(6.3)	19654		(26.5)
Transport	241		(5.1)	829		(6.2)	29		(0.4)	200		(0.6)	70		(0.4)	440		(0.6)
Real Estate	196		(4.1)	2689		(20.1)	57		(0.8)	6540		(18.2)	2075		(12.0)	28474		(38.3)
Other non-manual	19071	[100]		24278	[100]		10533	[100]		46695	[100]		26494	[100]		108119	[100]	

Notes: 1. Fiscal year; April/March, % share in total [ ]. % share in services ( ).

2. Asia-Pacific includes Hong Kong, Singapore, South Korea, Taiwan, Indonesia, Malaysia, the Philippines and Thailand.

North America includes the U.S. and Canada.

Europe includes U.K., France, Germany, Belgium, Ireland, Switzerland, Portugal, the Netherlands, Italy, Luxemburg, Spain, Greece, Malta, Australia, Norway, Yugoslavia, Denmark, Iceland, Sweden, Turkey, Poland, Hungary, Romania, Finland, Cyprus, and USSR.

Source: Ministry of Finance.

was in finance. In the same period, 38 percent of Japanese FDI in services to North America was in real estate. In case of the Asia-Pacific, Japanese FDI in services in 1986 to 1990 was relatively equally distributed between sectors: finance (25.7%), other services (24.1%) commerce (20.0%) and real estate (20.1%).

A close link between Japanese FDI in manufacturing and services can be pointed out as one of the most important characteristics of Japanese FDI in services to the Asia-Pacific. In manufacturing fields, the appreciation of yen in 1985, accentuated the trend in producing less skill intensive products in affiliates located in the Asia-Pacific. These Japanese affiliates evidently had a higher ratio of shipment to Japan and to third countries in total sales. Sazanami (1992) found that the share of exports in total sales of Japanese affiliates located in Asia was 32.5 percent in 1986 and 24.9 percent in 1989. Similar ratios were much lower in Japanese affiliates located in Europe and North America. The shipment to other regions required commercial services. According to the 1990 Census of Manufacturing, 14.3 percent of the total affiliates of Japanese manufacturing firms in Asia were in commerce. They accounted for as much as more than two thirds of non-manufacturing affiliates set up by the Japanese manufacturing firms in Asia.

Japanese small and medium sized enterprises participated more actively in FDI in Asia than in other regions. FDI by Japanese small and medium-sized enterprises increased proportionately to the increase in total FDI after 1985. The share of Asia in the world total was much higher in the case of small and medium-sized enterprises (40.3%), than in the case of all sizes (less than 30%). The fields of FDI by small and medium sized enterprises in Asia show a higher concentration in manufacturing.[5] These affiliates in manufacturing needed supporting services from Japanese banks and trading companies. Branches and representative offices of Japanese banks helped them to raise funds at local financial market and also to get various information about the local market. Big trading companies who had accumulated the personal network in the local market also supplied such services. In other words, Japanese service enterprises, banks and trading companies alike, carried out the facilitating function for manufacturing operation carried out by small and medium-sized enterprises.

The appreciation of the currency boosted Japanese tourist demand. There were more hotels needed in Asian cities and resorts to accommodate these tourists. Japanese department stores and supermarkets first opened their affiliated shops to attract these tourists. They soon learned that rapid economic growth of the countries in the Asia-Pacific was expanding the local demand for various consumer goods as well as services. They invested more in hotels, supermarkets, restaurants, and amusement centers, not only for the Japanese tourists but also for the local consumers. Here, the role of Japanese banks included the supply of financial services in raising funds necessary to develop new products that meet Japanese and local demand. Indeed, Japanese service enterprises were linking demand and supply between different countries and also between different industrial fields in Asia. Evidently their networking skills were necessary to promote Asian economic interdependence.

III. LOCATIONAL ADVANTAGE OF ASIA-PACIFIC COUNTRIES IN ATTRACTING JAPANESE SERVICE ENTERPRISES

The share of services in total FDI to developing regions increased in the 1980s. There were notable differences in the factors that contributed to such increases in the Asia-Pacific and other regions. The increase in other regions largely reflected the FDI aimed to enjoy the benefit of tax heavens and flag-of-convenience.[6] In the Asia-Pacific region, the high rate of economic growth and subsequent expansion of Asian regional market attracted FDI in services. As finance and tourism require local presence in order to provide services, Japanese service enterprises rushed to open branches and representative offices in Asia. The export promotion policies followed in the Asia-Pacific countries provided the investment opportunity to Japanese trading companies to use their ownership advantages in distributing the goods produced in Asia to other regions as well as in relocating such goods within the region.

The Asia-Pacific embraces a variety of countries with different per capita income, labor/capital ratio, natural resource endowment and others.[7] Yet, Hong Kong and Singapore, two countries which are the commercial centers of the region and have the most deregulated financial markets hosted the largest amount of Japanese FDI in services in 1986 to 1990. (see Table 2). Sazanami (1994) pointed out three basic conditions that attracted Japanese service enterprises to Hong Kong and Singapore. Those were (1) relaxed restrictions on capital and profit repatriation, (2) locational advantage in logistics and (3) availability of manpower to carry out business operation (preferably in English). Indeed, the leading role of Hong Kong as afinancial center in the Asia-Pacific was the primary factor that attracted Japanese banks and insurance companies to open their branches and representative offices. Locational importance of Hong Kong as a foothold for trading with China attracted Japanese FDI in commerce.

In the late 1980s Japanese multinational enterprises (MNEs) were trying to strengthen integrated management systems encompassing production, sales, distribution, afterservice and finance in three regions—Asia, Europe and North America. They chose Hong Kong or Singapore as the Asian sites for operational headquarters (OHQs), to carry out global procurements of parts and products, financial operations and fund managements, and recruiting personnels for R&D. These MNEs' interests matched with the government policy of Singapore to make her economic structure more global by supporting

Table 2. Japanese FDI in Asia-Pacific Countries (Accumulated total for 1986-90, Million U.S.$, %)

	Hong Kong	*Singapore*	*South Korea*	*Taiwan*	*Indonesia*	*Malaysia*	*Philippines*	*Thailand*	*China*
Primary	7.5	7.0	0.2	0.3	1051.6	69.2	65.6	56.5	75.3
	[0.1]	[0.2]	[0.0]	[0.0]	[33.7]	[4.5]	[9.6]	[1.6]	[3.0]
Manufacturing	475.0	1498.1	1041.2	1367.8	1320.9	1035.3	479.1	2425.9	662.8
	[7.0]	[35.2]	[42.9]	[72.1]	[42.4]	[67.7]	[69.9]	[68.6]	[26.8]
Services	6350.9	2751.1	1385.3	528.1	744.1	423.7	141.0	1055.3	1738.8
	[92.9]	[64.6]	[57.1]	[27.9]	[23.9]	[27.8]	[20.5]	[29.8]	[70.2]
Construction	137.9	140.1	1.9	16.9	13.6	81.5	11.5	99.3	11.5
	(2.2)	(5.1)	(0.1)	(3.2)	(1.8)	(19.2)	(8.2)	(9.4)	(0.7)
Commerce	1675.9	430.9	15.5	298.0	23.7	79.0	12.3	150.3	44.2
	(26.4)	(15.7)	(1.1)	(56.4)	(3.2)	(18.7)	(8.8)	(14.2)	(2.5)
Finance	2036.0	774.1	74.8	11.1	325.3	96.8	35.1	79.4	14.1
	(32.1)	(28.1)	(5.5)	(2.1)	(43.7)	(22.9)	(24.9)	(7.5)	(0.8)
Other services	916.5	302.2	1147.0	82.8	328.1	66.0	39.1	340.5	557.5
	(14.4)	(11.0)	(82.8)	(15.7)	(44.1)	(15.6)	(27.8)	(32.9)	(32.1)
Transport	225.5	512.4	1.2	12.9	2.0	9.5	0.9	63.6	16.7
	(3.6)	(18.6)	(0.1)	(2.4)	(0.3)	(2.3)	(0.6)	(6.1)	(0.9)
Real Estate	1355.4	590.0	144.7	106.8	44.0	84.5	41.9	321.1	94.4
	(21.3)	(21.4)	(10.4)	(20.2)	(5.9)	(19.9)	(29.7)	(30.4)	(5.4)
Other non-	3.4	1.1	—	—	7.3	6.0	—	0.8	1001.8
manufacturing	(0.0)	(0.1)	—	—	(1.0)	(1.4)	—	(0.1)	(57.6)
Total	6833.4	4256.2	2426.7	1896.2	3116.6	1528.2	685.7	3537.7	2476.9
	[100]	[100]	[100]	[100]	[100]	[100]	[100]	[100]	[100]

Source and notes: Table 1., % share in total [ ]. % share in services ( ).

total business activities mainly in services. Since 1988, the government of Singapore started to provide favorable tax treatments for ten years to the firms who received OHQ status. Sony International Singapore enjoys such OHQ status in managing the activities of other Asian affiliates.[8]

More than half of Japanese FDI to Taiwan in 1986-1990 was in commerce. Within commerce, Japanese enterprises' participation was most active in foreign trade related services, reflecting the importance of Taiwan as an offshore production base for Japanese electronics and electric products. A swift delivery to assembly makers located in Japan and in third countries was very important to keep their competitiveness. Thus setting up affiliates in commerce in Taiwan was as important as establishing manufacturing affiliates.

Expansion of local demand for hotels, restaurants and fast food shops as a result of westernization of consumers' tastes in both Taiwan and Korea provided business opportunities to Japanese service enterprises who already had experienced such changes in lifestyle and in business practices at home. Japanese FDI in hotels and restaurants in Taiwan increased in the late 1980s. Also in Korea, Japanese FDI in other services marked rapid growth. The share of other services in total inflow of service FDI to Korea from Japan was as high as 82.8 percent in 1986-1990.

The share of service in Japanese FDI inflow to the other four ASEAN countries in the Asia-Pacific ranged between the highest in Thailand, 29.8 percent to the lowest in the Philippines, 20.5 percent. The share of commerce within service differed between countries reflecting the diverse locational pull factors that attracted Japanese service FDI. A growing importance of Malaysia and Thailand as an offshore manufacturing base for Japanese electronics and electric industries promoted FDI in services.

Similar to the experience in Taiwan as explained before, Japanese FDI in services to establish the network for swift delivery went hand in hand with FDI in manufacturing. A close link between Japanese FDI in services and manufacturing can be pointed out in the case of apparel and food. For example, the Japanese department stores and supermarkets tried to develop and produce apparel and foods of their own brand names in Thailand to sell in Japan. The drive by the Japanese government to increase manufactured imports in order to reduce trade surplus in the late 1980s backed-up such trends.

Tourism traditionally has been the important service industry that attracts FDI to the developing countries. The Japanese started to travel more in the late 1980s for both tourism and business purposes. The number of Japanese travelers increased from 4.9 million in 1985 to 11.0 million in 1990. Asia accommodated about half of such Japanese travelers.[9] High shares of other services in Japanese service FDI to Indonesia (44.1%), Thailand (32.3%) and the Philippines (27.8%) were caused in part by more investment in hotels, restaurants and other related services to accommodate tourists. Locational attractiveness in having beautiful natural landscapes, quiet surroundings and historical sites attracted FDI by Japanese services enterprises.

IV. THE ROLE OF JAPANESE SERVICE ENTERPRISES IN PROMOTING ASIAN ECONOMIC INTERDEPENDENCE

A. Financial Services

The deregulation and liberalization in the world financial market expanded the business opportunities of banks and security companies. As noted earlier, Japanese banks and security companies invested most actively in Hong Kong and Singapore. Both countries started to adopt deregulation policy from the early 1970s and became the financial centers in the Asia-Pacific. In 1989, more than 70 percent of branches and affiliates of Japanese banks in the Asia-Pacific were located in Hong Kong and Singapore.[10] They played a very important role in raising funds from local financial markets for Japanese affiliates located in the Asia-Pacific.

According to the EXIM Bank survey in 1989, foreign affiliates of Japanese firms preferred to raise money through local financial institutions in developed, as well as in developing countries. In the Asia-Pacific, more than three-fourths of the sources of Japanese funds for FDI was raised by local affiliates themselves. The ratio of money borrowed from local financial institutions in the total funds raised by such affiliates was 56.7 percent in NIEs and 64.7 percent in ASEAN.[11]

Tokunaga (1993b) pointed out the following factors which made Japanese affiliates in the Asia-Pacific prefer funds raised in local financial markets. They tried, (1) to avoid risk of yen appreciation, (2) to take advantage of near inter-bank rates applied to affiliates guaranteed by Japanese banks or parent companies, (3) to use low interest rates for export-oriented subsidiaries under export promotion policy and (4) to overcome regulation on borrowing from off-shore funds.[12]

A close linkage between main bank and parent companies in Japan, enabled branch offices of Japanese banks located in Singapore or Hong Kong to issue the guarantee for direct lending by local banks to affiliates located in other Asian countries as illustrated in Figure 1. Also, guarantee by parent companies helped the direct lending by local banks. Such guarantee saved the time and cost needed for further credit inquiry. These branches and representative offices of Japanese banks not only provided the services in international financial operations but also extending their services as investment consultancies. Their services included identification of joint venture partners, assessment of project feasibility and assistance to project implementation.

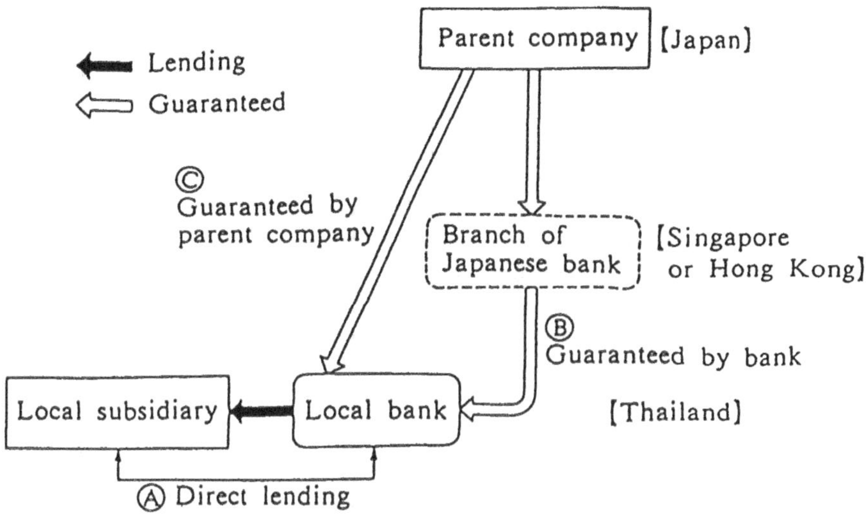

Source: Tokunaga (1992b, Fig. 2, p. 165).

Figure 1. Financial Linkages in Asia

Between 1986 and 1989, the number of branches and representative offices of Japanese banks located in the Asia-Pacific countries increased from 58 to 73 and 67 to 83 respectively. They not only played a crucial role in promoting financial linkages between Japanese FDI and local financial market, but also as low interest rates were applied to promote exports, local lending to Japanese export-oriented subsidiaries contributed to make Asian countries more interdependent in trade within the region as well as with other regions.

B. Distributive Services (Department Stores and Supermarkets)

Japanese distributive service enterprises actively participated in taking advantage of the strong yen. The large department stores and supermarkets started to engage directly in import business, bypassing wholesalers or trading companies. In particular, Japanese distributive service enterprises started "Kaihatsu Yunu" (development of imports) from the Asia Pacific countries. They imported products developed according to their own designs, quality, processing or material specifications and produced by Asian manufacturers. Japanese supermarkets are more active in participating in "Kaihatsu Yunu" than the department stores. The amount of "Kaihatsu Yunu" by supermarkets (11 companies) was more than ten times larger than the amount by department stores (12 companies) in 1987/88.[13]

As for the commodity composition, the share of apparel was the highest in both supermarkets and department stores. But the share of food and beverages was much higher in the former than in the latter. Indeed, Japanese supermarkets were more active in exploiting the comparative advantages of the Asia-Pacific countries in having not only lower labor costs, but also more abundant natural resources by importing foodstuffs. Improvement of inspection facilities and warehouses with freezing facilities together with technological progress in vacuum packing and refrigeration enabled supermarkets to import food and beverages, provided that they could teach Japanese tastes to the local producers.

Japanese department stores at first opened affiliated stores in Europe to supply retail services to Japanese tourists. In the case of the Asia-Pacific countries, their motives in setting up affiliated stores were diverse. Hong Kong and Singapore provided attractive locations to open stores mainly for Japanese tourist shoppers who were interested in buying European duty free consumer goods. In Bangkok and Kuala Lumpur, affiliated stores sold Japanese and local products mainly to the Japanese business community in these countries and also to the Japanese tourists. The high rate of economic growth and subsequent emergence of middle-income class consumers in the Asia-Pacific added momentum to the opening of foreign affiliated stores by Japanese distributive service enterprises in the late 1980s. Now, the clients of Asian stores were not limited to the Japanese or wealthy local consumers but included ordinary local working people as well. They tried to expand the sales of mass consumption type products to the local consumers. The setting up of large supermarkets required new procurement networking.

C. Commercial Services (Wholesaler and General Trading Companies)

The prime motive of Japanese wholesaler's FDI in the Asia-Pacific was to supply wholesale services to Japanese retailers, for instance supermarkets, department store and convenience stores. The emergence of middle-income consumers and the rapid westernization of tastes in the Asia-Pacific expanded the business opportunities of Japanese retailers as supermarkets. But when they tried to expand their operation, they found that local small wholesalers could not provide modern supply services. Also, local firms who opened western-style convenience stores frequently found it difficult to manage the numerous daily commodity supply swiftly, especially when the number of stores increased. They turned to Japanese wholesalers who had the management skills to cope with the situation.

The International Merchandise Market (IMM) Pte. set up in Singapore by Yaohan group is a very interesting example which tried to network the Asia-Pacific wholesale activities. When Yaohan started to open stores in the Asian countries, they had to face the same problem that other retailers faced. They had to negotiate with agents of local producers who were frequently small shops. In order to purchase the merchandise in large quantities from various points of Asia, they found it more advantageous to concentrate the location of wholesale stores. Singapore was picked as the ideal location to establish a wholesale center. With the strong support from the government of Singapore, the wholesale center by IMM opened in 1990. The tenants of the center are Japanese producers (33%), Japanese wholesalers (4%), Asian producers (45%) and others (18%). The products handled by the center were not limited to products from Japan or from Asia. They came from all other regions. Namely, the primary role of such wholesaler center was to provide commercial services which link Japanese and local retailers in the Asia-Pacific to manufacturers in the region and in the world.

Japanese general trading companies (Sogo Shosha) have traditionally played a very important role in providing commercial services, particularly in international trade. However, when the shift in Japanese comparative advantage from traditional textiles to electric/electronics products and autos in the late 1960s started to erode their business opportunities in trade, they responded to such changes by using a number of important ownership advantages that they had accumulated. They used their networking skills in promoting trade between third countries. They participated in large energy related and construction projects abroad by carrying out the coordinating function. Here, their accumulated knowledge in foreign political and economic conditions enabled them to pursue the role of organizer in foreign projects. They also entered into new growing fields such as information, communication and leasing, using their networking skills and financial resources. Their importance as service providers became apparent in various industrial areas ranging from traditional textile to finance, lease, telecommunication and others.

The share of commerce accounted for 44 percent of total FDI by the nine major general trading companies to the world (as of March 1988). In Asia the share of manufacturing was as high as 41.4 percent while the share of commerce was 23.2 percent (see Table 3). The high share of manufacturing as such reflected the importance of Asian offshore production bases for textiles. The general trading companies traditionally had the strength in distributing Japanese textile products to the world market. They frequently carried out FDI with Japanese manufacturing firms and provided management know-how in carrying out international business operations. There were more business needs in Asia because Japanese small and medium-sized textile firms who faced the high wages at home wanted to shift their production locations to Asia. Also the rapid expansion of local markets in Asia for various new products other than textiles necessitated the commercial services provided by general trading company.

Table 3. FDI of Nine General Trading Companies by Industry

(%, billion yen)

Industry	*World total*	*North America*	*Europe*	*Asia*
World total	1,818.0 (100.0)	663.9 (100.0)	473.9 (100.0)	201.7 (100.0)
Primary	(12.3)	(11.6)	(—)	(17.1)
Manufacturing	(15.0)	(11.6)	(4.2)	(41.4)
Commerce	(44.0)	(66.8)	(36.7)	(23.2)
Finance-Insurance	(18.6)	(0.3)	(56.1)	(1.2)
Others	(10.1)	(9.7)	(3.0)	(17.1)

Notes. 1. affiliates include sub-afficiates as of March, 1988.
2. total amount of investment and long term loans from parent company and foreign affiliates to above (1). In billion yen as of end of March, 1988.
3. share in total ( ).
4. others include, construction, real estate, transportation communication and others.

Source. Nihon Boeki Kai "Sogo Shosha no Taigai Chokusetsu Toshi" 1990.

V. CONCLUDING REMARKS

It is well known that the rapid growth of FDI inflows to the Asia-Pacific contributed to strengthen the international competitiveness of manufactured goods produced in the region. Offshore production in Asia by American and Japanese MNEs enhanced the technological capabilities of local firms. Japanese service enterprises played a very important role in this process by providing supportive services in raising funds, providing market information and networking different industries.

The branches and representative offices of Japanese banks in Hong Kong and Singapore assisted Japanese manufacturing affiliates located in the other Asian countries to get loans from local banks. The low interest rates applied to investment in export-oriented industries promoted Japanese FDI. The Japanese affiliates shipped their products to the United States and Japan. They also carried out trade within the Asia-Pacific region.

The dynamic interrelationship between trade and domestic markets were networked by Japanese distributive services enterprises. When Japanese department stores opened affiliated stores in the early 1970s, their clients were limited to the Japanese or wealthy local consumers. But in the late 1980s, Japanese supermarkets started to target their sales to the local new middle-income urban consumers. It is frequently said that good quality apparel can only be processed in countries where workers can actually see the good quality clothing and appreciate the comfort. Higherincome and a rise in living standards of urban consumers in the Asia-Pacific provided the basic condition for further upgrading of apparel and other consumer goods produced in these countries. In other words, expansion of the domestic market for better quality products helped Asian countries to improve their quality of exports and thus to strengthen their international competitiveness in manufacturing.

There was a remarkable growth in Asian economic interdependence in the 1980s. The share of mutual trade in East and Southeast Asia (ASEAN, NIEs, Japan and China) in their total exports increased from 35 percent in 1980 to 41.9 percent in 1991.[14] Increase in such share reflected high rate of economic growth, export-oriented policies, and liberalization of trade in service fields. Japanese service enterprises helped to promote such economic interdependence by networking Asian financial markets, by providing commercial skills to export and by transmitting distributive know-how in linking the emergence of new Asian demand for convenience stores, fast food chains and others to local suppliers.

ACKNOWLEDGMENT

An earlier version of this paper was presented at the conference "Economic Regionalism: Macroeconomic Core and Microeconomic Optimization" sponsored by the American Committee on Asian Economic Studies (ACAES) jointly with Chulalongkorn University, December 16-18, 1992 Bangkok.

NOTES

1. Asia in the present paper includes, NIEs (Korea, Taiwan, Hong Kong, Singapore) ASEAN (Malaysia, Thailand, Indonesia and the Philippines), and Japan unless noted otherwise.
2. Excluding Japan from Asia in 1.
3. See Tokunaga (1992), and Sazanami (1994).
4. As for the discussion on ownership specific advantage, locational pull and push factors, see Dunning (1985), Chapter 13.
5. See Chusho Kigyo Kinyu Koko Geppo (1991), 8-9 pp. 17-20 for details.
6. See Takeuchi (1990) for details on the relationship between government policies and FDI to developing countries.
7. Riedel (1991) illustrated that the relative resource endowment of the Asian economies vary enormously, perhaps more than in any other regions.
8. Besides, Sony, Fujikura Densen, Omron Matsushita Electric and Hitachi received OHQ status between 1988 and 1990, see Tokunaga (1992a) for details.
9. 5,055,000 Japanese traveled to Asia out of the total 10,594,000 in 1991.
10. See Sazanami (1994). Table 5-1.
11. Tokunaga (1992b) Table 1.
12. Tokunaga (1992b) pp. 166.
13. See Sazanami (1994) for details.
14. See Okamoto (1993) Table 1-3.

REFERENCES

Chusho Kigyo Kinyu Koko Geppo (1991). "Tokushyu/Kokusaika no Shinten to Chusho Kigyo" (Special issue/*Development of Internationalization and Small and Medium Sized Enterprises*).

Dunning, J. H. ed., (1985). "Multilateral Enterprises, Economic Structure and International Competitiveness". New York: John Wiley and Sons.

Mukaiyama, M. (1991). "Oroshiuri Kigyo no Kaigai Shinshutsu" (Foreign Operation of Wholesale Firms), *Shoko Kinyu*, June, pp. 4-39.

Nihon Boeki Kai (1990). "Sogo Shosha no Taigai Chokusetsu Toshi" (FDI of Trading Companies).

Okamoto, Y (1993). "Historical Consideration of Economic Cooperation Schemes in the Asia-Pacific Region and their Prospects in the Future" paper presented at *Conference on Regional Integration and its Impact on Developing Countries,* Institute of Developing Economies, Feb. 3-4, Tokyo.

Riedel, James (1991). "Intra-Asian Trade and Foreign Direct Investment", *Asian Development Review,* vol. 9, pp. 111-146.

Sazanami, Yoko (1992). "Globalization Strategy of Japanese Manufacturing Firms and Its Impact on Trade Flows between Europe, Asia and North America" paper presented at Colloque "Europe et Japon, Concurrents or Partenaires?" Feb., Universite De Paris I Pantheon-Sorbonne.

Sazanami, Yoko (1994). "Japanese Service Enterprises in the Asia Pacific." In Sletmo, G.K. and Gavin Boyd, eds., *Pacific Service Enterprises and Pacific Cooperation,* Westview Press.

Tokunaga, Shojiro ed., (1992). "Japan's Foreign Investment and Asian Economic Interdependence", University of Tokyo Press.

Tokunaga, Shojiro (1992). "Japan's FDI—Promoting Systems and Intra-Asia Networks: Investment and Trade Systems Created by the Borderless Economy", in Tokunaga ed. Chapter 1, p. 5-48.

Tokunaga, Shojiro (1992b). "Moneyless Direct Investment and Development of Asian Financial Markets: Financial Linkages Between Local Markets and Offshore Centers" in Tokunaga ed., Chapter 6, pp. 153-189.

Takeuchi, Kenji (1990). "Does Japanese Direct Foreign Investment Promote Japanese Imports from Developing Countries?" *The World Bank, WPS 458,* June.

TECHNOLOGY AND TRADE FRICTION IN ECONOMIC DEVELOPMENT: CASES OF JAPANESE INDUSTRIES

Michiko Ikeda

I. INTRODUCTION

Living in an age of increasing trade conflicts among advanced and developing nations—a great many of these conflicts involve Japan—and facing the present surge of protectionism, we worry about the direction of the world economy. Protectionist trends have increased worldwide despite recent warnings by economists. On the other hand, governments of advanced and developing nations have responded with much lip-service to halt protectionist practices.

Today, the world economy is becoming increasingly segmented: "blocks" of nations have formed to represent not only economical, but also political and social motivations.

Under this trend, we economists wonder how the world economic course should be oriented to achieve a higher level of happiness of humankind. We

Research in Asian Economic Studies, Volume 6, pages 225-238.

ISBN: 1-55938-918-4

do not know how much burden today's protectionism imposes on the world economy. Nor do we know whether the development of protectionism inevitably parallels the development of the world economy."[1] Two questions are relevant to this position.

1. How and why trade friction could easily occur in the growing process of developing countries which inevitably contributes to the world development?
2. These trade frictions occur more as an interdependency increases in the dynamism of the developing world economy. What will happen when the protectionist trend all over the world with restrictions on imported products and retaliatory measures that would evoke other repercussions?

When import restrictions are applied on exports of a developing country, the latter's overall trade networks, trade patterns, and trading commodity compositions will change by required adjustments for restructuring the domestic economy. In that case, trading partners of advanced countries impose further countervailing measures against the developing country's retaliations, the trade and economy of both sides consequently will be distorted and their sizes will shrink. This brought on a need for further changes in trade policies to overcome the difficulties confronted in the both economies.

A. The Angle of Approach

One theme of this investigation is to try addressing a belief that trade friction will inevitably occur as long as backwards countries attempt to catch up with advanced countries. This belief is because, first, the development of the world economy essentially embraces the industrialization of developing countries. Second, once a backwards country succeeds in its industrial upsurge, the growth rate of such an economy is high-in particular, in certain manufacturing sectors-surpassing the rate of growth of other economies and grows even amid a depression of the world economy.[2]

II. WHEN A BACKWARD COUNTRY CATCHES UP

B. Textiles

In the inter-war period, between World War I and World War II, Japan was one of the developing countries and a newcomer trying to catch-up with Western industrialized nations.

In 1926, Japan had high hopes in the new Showa era, that it would be equally treated with the Western nations. With this hope, Japan lifted the gold ban to establish the gold standard system in 1930. Could that hope have been realized if socioeconomic attitudes of world powers had been much closer, as they are today?

In 1928, when a domestic financial crisis ended, Japan embarked on a deflationary policy to re-establish the gold standard at the prewar parity. Her large companies in leading industries, notably the cotton textile industry, made full efforts to achieve efficiency; its members purchased the most advanced technology, cut wages, and reduced the number of workers. They had to prepare for the coming of two international issues. First, they had to stop nightwork by the year of 1929 on advice of the International Labor Organization. Second, they had to acquire international competitiveness to be ready for the expected re-establishment of the gold standard at the old parity that would highly appreciate the value of the Japanese currency.

Domestic prices were falling by the deflationary policy and deepened the widespread agrarian crisis.[3] The foreign exchange rate appreciated 21 percent from 1925 to 1930 as a result of the deflationary policy and government overseas purchases of yen.[4]

By 1930, the cotton industry strongly stood for international competition, surpassing the British in output and exports in the ensuing years due mostly to a higher productivity.

In January 1930, Japan re-established the gold standard, but the effect of the Great Depression soon began to be felt and further aggravated the hardship which the Japanese had been experiencing under the deflationary policy. The compound effects of the deflation and the Depression pushed the Japanese economy into a depressionary spiral in 1930 and 1931. Complaints and outcries filled the cities and countryside.

Japan broke with the gold standard at the end of 1931, following Great Britain, which had broken earlier that year, in September.

Japan then embarked on an expansionary economic policy; it lowered the interest rate and increased public expenditures to save millions of poverty stricken-peasants. Subsidies for enhanced military expenditures for the Manchurian Incident and to the Agriculture Sector were made possible by expanding the budget for 1932 by 33.6 percent over its 1931 level.[5] The Japanese expansionary monetary and fiscal policy realized its desired effect, which was to increase industrial output in the second half of 1932.[6]

The Japanese economy then entered a fourth, a new stage of industrial upsurge while the economies of other nations were still in the throes of the Depression. New products and new industries appeared and grew: with "light" industries gradually being supplanted by "heavy" industries. Industrial output reached a prewar peak in the 1936-1937 period.

After severing all ties with gold, the value of the yen dropped. Exports then picked up in the latter half of 1932 and surged. Many countries condemned

Japan for "dumping." Among all, the most damning point was a high rate of devaluation of the yen, 66 percent from the 1929 level that was stated in the statistics of the League of Nations.[7]

However, if one carefully observes the overvaluation of the yen in 1929 by 21 percent above the 1925 level due to an effort of the government to restore the gold standard.[8] If one takes the base year as 1925 instead of 1929, the rate of devaluation was not 66 percent but 30.9 percent.

In Japan's steady recovery in world exports, there were two different trends; one still sharply deteriorating and the other bouncing back and growing. Severe falls in exports were mainly registered in markets of the United States, China proper, the British Empire, and some colonies and other possessions of Western countries due to many types of imposed import restrictions discriminating Japan.

C. Japanese Textiles in the U.K. Market

Cotton textiles became the Japanese prime export commodity after the deterioration of raw silk exports in the end of 1920s. But soon Japanese textile products faced prohibitive import restrictions in the first half of the 1930s.

The cotton textile was an age-old industry, which was precisely why Japan was able to catch up with the advanced countries. The industry had a low degree of technological development, a small technological gap for a catch-up nation like Japan which was the borrower of modern technology. (This small technological gap also allowed developing countries, such as China, India, and Chile, to catch up with Japan.)

Great Britain imposed a heavy strain on world trade by concluding the Imperial Preference Agreements with her Commonwealth Dominions and colonies at the Ottawa Conference in 1932. Often-revised British Imperial preferential tariffs of 5 to 20 percent failed to check effectively the Japanese competitiveness in cotton and rayon textiles in Japan's principal markets in the British Commonwealth markets.

After the defeat of silk by rayon in the United States market, the Japanese cotton textile industry had tried to learn quickly the technology of rayon production and exported synthetic textiles to markets in British colonies. Large Japanese synthetic textile firms were also large cotton textile products. Japan utilized the technology and know-how in the cotton textiles industry to produce synthetic textiles. Japan acquired little diversification in manufactured exports to rely heavily on products besides textiles in the 1930s.[9]

After Japan passed through a series of import restrictions, discriminations, prolonged and mostly ineffective negotiations, and finally trade wars against Canada and Australia and by resultant new agreements in Japan's principal markets in the British Empire her trading position deteriorated progressively from the implementation of the British Indian trade link system, to the

Canadian customs valuation system, to quotas and the import-licensing system in Australia.

There was a great shrinkage in Japan's trade in the British markets. Besides, the quality of Japanese cotton textiles became downgraded because of the obligation of Indian raw cotton purchases.

Japan was vulnerable with scarce resources and heavy dependence on trade, but she was eager to export both to feed its population and to catch-up with advanced countries. No other developing country was efficiently following Japan at that period: Japan was alone and in this aspect was also vulnerable.

This section is concluded with a survey on the British cotton textile industry. Before Japanese competition started in the second half of 1920s, the Lancashire area had long suffered from a serious, prolonged depression and high unemployment. The Lancashire problems were aggravated because of losing overseas markets, especially in the East because of the growth of Japanese exports. There were at least five reasons to explain for loosing competitiveness of the Lancashire textile industry:

1. Britain's re-adoption of the gold standard at the old parity in 1925 which overvalued the British currency. The strong appreciation of the pound sterling aggravated Lancashire's difficulty.
2. Most British organizations were small in scale in comparison with Japan's large cotton textile industry.
3. The Japanese cotton textile industry was integrated vertically from purchases of raw cotton through spinning, weaving, and marketing.
4. The productivity of Japanese workers was higher because of scale merits based on modern technology.
5. Japan's relatively low and downward flexible real wages contributed to Japan's competitiveness of that time while the British economy was experiencing downward wage rigidity.

D. Japan's Manufactured Exports to the U.S. Market

The United States share registered 43 percent of Japan's exports to the world in 1929, but it fell to 20 percent in 1937. From 1930 onward, Japan's balance of trade with the United States also swung from a sizable yearly surplus to a grave annual deficit. The swing was mostly attributable to a dramatic fall in the value of exports of raw silk.

Non-raw silk exports accounted for 17 to 18 percent of the total of Japanese exports to the United States, which did not grow enough to make-up even partially for the fall in silk earnings over the period of 1926-37. The following summary highlights causal factors for the retarded growth in Japanese nonsilk exports.

1. U.S. tariffs on many Japanese manufactured goods were raised after 1932, adding to those already increased by the 1930 Tariff Act.
2. Japan was excluded from the United States general tariff concession program in the New Deal. The United States kept the *conditional* most-favored-nation (MFN) clause with Japan. Due to the retention of this clause, the benefits of bilateral, concessional tariff agreements between the United States and third nations and the extension of benefits to terminate the "cost-equalization" scheme were not applied to Japanese products. In 1933, under the "flexible" cost equalization clause of the 1930 Tariff Act, duties were raised on Japanese seafood products. The "voluntary export restrictions" (VERs) for Japanese cotton textiles were initiated by the U.S. market after 1932, in spite of Japan's large purchases of U.S. raw cotton. The United States government exercised quotas on Japanese cotton products after 1937 also, despite Japan's minimal share of the products in the U.S. market. Fees were mounted for Japanese cotton products under the National Recovery Act of the New Deal. The maximum amount of shipments of cotton rugs and certain kinds of pencils were specified by the agreement with Japan, which were similar to voluntary export restraints (VERs) today.[10]
3. Antidumping duties were rarely levied except for specific cases involving Japanese products, as seen in U.S. Customs documents, during the period 1934 through 1937.
4. The effective ad valorem incidence of specific duties were unfavorable for Japan when they applied to many cheap Japanese manufactured exports, although nominal rates of tariffs were nondiscriminatory applicable to all countries.

In the Philippine market, quotas and VERs were applied also for Japanese cotton textiles between Japanese and U.S. manufacturers under the authority of the United States government.

E. Japanese Textiles in Markets of Developing Regions

As a result of the discrimination in the *Netherlands East Indies market,* Japan was forced to diversify exports. This was an inescapable course for Japan to develop international competitiveness in a variety of manufactured goods, which was realized in the postwar period.

Latin America's low income level created an increasing demand for competitively priced Japanese products. But these countries easily applied strict policies to limit imports by means of foreign exchange control, the trade-balancing system, and any other restrictions because they had always balance-of-payments problems, common in the developing countries.

The Japanese faced two dimensions of trade friction in the Latin American market: (a) competition against American, British and other Western industrialists' vested interests and (b) competition against local producers' interests because of a small margin of technological levels between Japanese and some local industries in Latin American countries. Japan was in this sense doomed to be discriminated against in Peruvian and Chilean markets because local governments protected their own infant cotton textile industry. Around 1933, Japan, in trading provoked some unfavorable feelings of the United States and of other Westerners in Latin America. There were two reasons for this: i) Japanese export growth was so rapid that it came under careful observation even if the total value of Japanese exports itself was a small portion of that of the United States. ii) Japan tried to increase imports from Latin American countries to fulfill two objectives: to increase manufactured exports to Latin America for its growing manufactured products in many small sectors.[11] At the same time, Japan wanted to reduce imports from the United States with which Japan's trade balance incurred a large deficit after 1930.

Thus, when Japanese trade activity increased in the Latin American market, it induced double-sided losses to the United States; loss of exports to the Latin American market because of substitution by Japanese products and loss of exports of materials to Japan.

On the Japanese side, as long as Japanese manufactured exports were unable to expand in the U.S. market after 1930 and Japan had to purchase from the United States the best materials (of raw cotton for its most competitive cotton textile industry), modern industrial equipment, and more munitions, Japan had no other alternatives for reducing the trade deficit with the United States except via Latin American trade.

F. Dumping and Discrimination

Concerning the term 'discrimination,' one may refer to the nondiscriminatory principle of the General Agreement on Tariffs and Trade. It is well known, however, that in the 1950s when the United States proposed to grant a GATT membership to Japan, some European countries strongly opposed the proposal. The opposing countries were often quoted that they were scared by the memory of Japan's unfair trade practice with an emphasis on its dumping problems in the 1930s. After Japan became a member, tough attitudes of some EC countries remained for long time as described in Dr. G. Patterson's book.[12]

In many of the original documents of the 1930s, dumping was used as a synonym for 'unfair' to explain the cause of increasing Japanese competitiveness in Japan's major overseas markets in the 1930s. Finally, they used dumping to reproach Japan because the Japanese were offering goods at ridiculously low prices. There are three factors for offering a lower price in the international market: 1) lower production costs essentially stemming from an increase in productivity, 2) a fall in foreign exchange rates, and 3) sales temporarily at a price lower than the cost of production to increase market share and to monopolize the market. Most of the documents relevant to the subject understood the competitive power of the Japanese in price margin, the second and the third factors only and ignored the first factor. Only the British Embassy in Tokyo recognized and warned the British government about Japanese competitive ability in cotton textiles and some other manufacturings in the 1930s as stemming from improved production efficiency.

Another strong point of the Japanese economy relevant to foreign trade lay in the advantages of being backwards in Gerschenkron's notion-borrowed technology and learning from the advanced countries' discreetly chosen paths for development. Furthermore, Japan turned its disadvantages into advantages via foreign trade. For example, resource-scarce Japan already had acquired by 1926 one of the most selective positions for supplying materials for its industries. Instead of relying on its small amount of domestic production, Japan purchased in a lump sum varieties of good-quality raw cotton around the world and blended them. Some of Japan's industries became beneficiaries of scale merits due to the adoption of high standard of technology on a large scale.

The Japanese cotton textile industry still kept a competitive edge in quality cum price in the finer-count, bleached, dyed, and printed cloth vis-à-vis Chinese and British ones in the first half of 1930s.

G. The Steel Industry in the Post-War Period

A close country survey on technological standard of the iron and steel industry was published by OECD economists before the implementation of "the trigger price' of the United States on Japanese products. There existed on average a ten-year advance of the Japanese technology over the United States. Another few-year advance of U.S. technology existed over European ones. The standard of the British industry was the most behind among the European advanced countries.

We comprehended by this report in 1978 that the United States auto industry would have international disadvantages in costs of production because a higher price of steel as one of basic input for the industry would adversely affect the cost of U.S. auto production. The trigger price was a device to take out the margin of import price. We comprehended that U.S. domestic prices would increase, because autos were shoes for the Americans and an increase in transportation costs would affect the whole economy. The higher price of steel would result a higher cost of production in considerable fields of American industries and a higher cost of living for the Americans.

Before the trigger price was levied, Japanese iron and steel were produced by purchasing materials from Australia. The materials were shipped to Japan, fabricated, and shipped to the U.S. market. The average price of Japanese iron and steel products in the U.S. market was still cheaper than that of U.S. products.[13] The technology of the U.S. iron and steel industry as getting obsolescent internationally but it kept an allright status. International competition from outside of the country only spurred the decline of the industry.

The steel makers in the United States at first could reject Japanese competition. Then EC products soon and the United States applied the trigger price as well. Soon after Korean products followed the suit into the same field so that the United States had to implement the trigger price on Korean ones.

H. Japanese Car-Makers

In 1955, a Toyota car was landed in a port in the United States for an exhibition purpose (The size of the Japanese economy in 1955 just recovered to the prewar highest 1936-37 level). The Toyota car failed to climb up and ordinary slope en route for the car exhibition hall. The Japanese desperately pushed, but the car didn't climb up the road. Finally they had to ship it back too Japan. Two decades later a large number of Japanese cars were exported to the U.S. market. "Time flies quickly. It's like yesterday when we were teared by the brand new troubled Toyota car" said one of executives of the firm in Washington D.C. in 1986.

The case of the Japanese car shows one aspect of the technological catching-up processes. The process by means of borrowed technology became much speedier in the post war period compared with the interwar period and is speeding-up more now. Korean auto-makers caught up with the Japanese in recent years in markets of the United States and of developing countries. Korea caught up with Japan in ship-building and steel-making years ago. In some fields of business machines and household electric appliances, Korea caught up with the Japanese products in a large extent now. Taiwan has caught up with Japan in various fields, Malaysia has also, and other NIES and ASEAN are following. Once developing countries succeed in their initial industrialization their catching-up time becomes shortened relative to the case of Japan which started to produce the above products in the late 1920s and again after the 1950s.

The Multi Fiber Agreements

Many developing countries caught up in the field of cotton textiles then, caught-up in the synthetic textile industry, such as the Japanese historical case.

Why is it the textile industry that starts the industrialization of latecomers and why even today to the developing countries one after another enter into international competition in this field? Causal factors are not confined to only technological and financial aspects. Any country has a secured domestic demand at a certain scale for textile products, even if the industry can't become the beneficiary of scale economies. Local people need some cloth, clothes, and other textiles even if they are making them like the Bedouins who make special tents, carpets and clothes mostly for their own use. In many developing countries, the textile industry is set up for an import substitution scheme and to initiate their industrialization. Once they succeeded in substituting foreign products, they soon appear as international suppliers in the world market. Because, first, they try to expand the industry to become a beneficiary of the scale economies but the size of domestic market won't allow it except for enlarging the market via exports. Second, those catching-up countries have classic comparative advantages in the cost of production as the industry is in general labor-intensive. Many developing countries have an abundant labor force at a low wage rate.

Today some newly industrialized developing economies have caught-up with industrialized countries in the synthetic textile industry such as in the cases of Korea, Taiwan, and Hong Kong exporting products to the United States by importing fine chemical fibers from Japan.

The number of the developing countries, which are asked by the advanced countries individually to mitigate export surge in some textile products, has been increasing in the post Second World War trade history. Thus they, increasingly in numbers, have joined the entangled Multi Fiber Agreements (MFAs). The MFA is nothing but the application of the quota system or imports restrictions in the form of voluntary exports restraints (VERs).

The MFAs have been negotiated outside of the GATT framework in bilateral bases between only two importing and exporting countries: not on multilateral bases of the GATT principle. The MFA has disguised import quantity restrictions. The MFA problem is now taken up as one of subjects to be solved in the GATT Uruguay Round. The MFA should be terminated because it is requested by the advanced country for its trading partner, a developing country, to restrain the amount of textile exports. By the way, Japan is only one industrialized country that has not implemented the MFA.

III. TECHNOLOGY AND TRADE FRICTION IN ECONOMIC DEVELOPMENT

In trade friction of advanced countries versus developing countries, there are three technological aspects relevant to our approach. First, once a backwards country succeeds in its industrial upsurge by borrowing technology from advanced countries, its growth rate is high, surpassing those of advanced (in relative terms) economies, and may grow even amid a depression of the world economy. By adapting borrowed technology, the developing country could save a historical long time of research and development in production. When its economic growth rate becomes higher than those of advanced countries, it will be conspicuous in contrast to the trend if the world economy is declining. Trade friction will occur at this point because advanced countries will try to defend their markets. When the size of the world economy is not growing or even shrinking, producers in advanced countries feel uneasy because their sales may fall due to imports from foreign countries. They ask to step-up on protectionist measures politically. This is one of the explanatory reasons that trade friction is deeply related to the development of the world economy, developing countries' industrialization, and the world recession.

One of other causal factors to explain for the increased sales of products from developing countries in the world market in the depression period is that the people of advanced countries will substitute products from developing countries for domestic products due to their declining income level.

This wold be the case if import restrictions are not applied to products of developing countries, producers of advanced countries feel a threat to their profits and their market shares.

The second technological aspect is that the developing countries are able to catch-up, at the initial stage of its industrialization, only in an industrial field where technological frontiers are narrowly limited. Technological frontiers become narrow when the industries of advanced countries because old with almost no innovation. They failed to bring about a new wave in their industrial sector by defusing new technologies. Some big firms in the industries of advanced countries had often enjoyed profits in the past due to their status of the top in the leading industry. Because in most cases they had monopolistic or oligopolistic power for a long time, their entrepreneurial spirit disappeared without competition.

The third, economic growth occurs together with shifts in the emphasis of industries in an economy: there are some rising industries, some young ones, some maturing ones, and some dying ones. For the old industry being in the state of technological retardation, its growth rate and profit are declining in comparison to its own past and to those of rising industries. Thus, the industry had been losing its weight of emphasis in the country's economy. The relative importance of the industry has shifted away to other rising industries.

Why do developing countries catch-up only in the technologically retarded industrial sector? Because a technological gap exists. The developing countries in general have an abundant unskilled labor force, but scarce skilled labor. A low level of nourishment, degree of literacy, educational standard, the lack of opportunity for professional training and the social welfare system—all contribute to make a technological gap and low per worker productivity. Those, in turn, will be the sources to repeat the vicious circle.

The fourth, we know technological indivisibility and complementarity. The most advanced industrial production processes require certain technological combinations in terms of quantity to produce such as combinations in numbers of parts. For example, to produce a car it requires a combination of one car body, one engine, four wheels, four or five wheel tires, a certain number of car seats and windows, and so on. Complementarity requires not only in the numbers of parts produced but also in terms of technological stages: for example, the shape of the car body and the type of the engine must be suitable to each other (to speed, etc.)

Besides, financial limitation is the other discouraging factor related to technological indivisibility because the banking systems for developing countries are not often set-up well. A huge amount of financing for establishing large combinations of production capacity such as integrated production processes for developing countries is usually not possible. If the industry is a beneficiary of scale merits, the demand for capital is huge to set up the new industry.

Also, the size of the domestic market for a developing country is very limited to think of building any such large combinations in the production process for successful operation.

This creates difficulty for developing countries to catch-up with advanced countries in technology and financing. A developing country tends to start its industrialization in an industrial field where technological divisibility is easier relative to large, modern, high-tech industries. Thus, many developing countries cluster in similar fields such as the textile industry to start with their industrialization.

Because of the existence of technological indivisibility and complementarity, of a technological gap between advanced and developing countries and financial difficulty confine their catching-up fields to certain industries. The phenomenon continues today.

A newcomers' competition to the producers in advanced countries is a threat. The threat will repeat because the entry will be followed by another new catching-up country, and then, the latter is followed by other developing countries.

One can argue protectionism of the Japanese domestic market, particularly, during the catching-up period, but by protective measures one country is able to protect its domestic market only. The industry can survive or even flourish only domestically: it is unable to compete in foreign markets where it can't have fortifying barriers.

One can also argue that today the high-tech industries in advanced countries are able to order their parts from developing countries in the borderless world economy. We will quote an airplane made in the United States, though some parts could be made in Japan, Korea, or other countries. But still, its production is bound to be under the influence of existing indivisibility and complementarity in production technology.

IV. CONCLUSION

Protectionist trend develops when the world economy is in recession or depression. There are some similarities in the development of protectionism in the 1930s and recently. When the British hegemony over the world became weaker and the United States was rising in the 1920s and 1930s: the United Kingdom made efforts to defend and protect the power of the Empire for the sake of the mother country, and the latter was not aware to take up the world leadership.

In the post-war period, the United States became the best, strongest world leader. Once it had two-thirds of the world GNP. Its power relatively declined as economies of other countries headed by EC and Japan, followed by NIEs, and so forth, have grown from the mid 1970s.

After the ending of the two polar system, the world is in a great transition stage and we are concerned of the future world in recession and developing protectionism.

What are the implications of our findings for the current world economy? The world economic development embraces the catching-up process of developing economies by borrowing technology. The speed of the catching-up today becomes more rapid than in the inter-war period and much speedier than in the historical European industrialization period. The extent of borrowing technology today is limited by a widening technological gap between industrialized and developing countries and even among developing countries generating wide gaps in per capita income among themselves. Those are also attributable to the existence of technological indivisibility cum complementarity. Thus, there is a clustering phenomenon of developing countries to a catch-up in relatively limited industrial fields. All these lead us to the continuing occurrence and inconclusive trade friction between relatively advanced, the developing economies, and among developing nations.

As long as we are aware of these, we may objectively look at trade friction and how to deal with it. Understanding this, we may reconsider the problems in transfer of technology, and financial aids for the sake of both donors and recipients of aid from a different angle, a broader and longer historical perspective to improve the worldwide situation.

NOTES

1. The inferred idea seems exemplified also today by the emergence of the NIEs with speedy growth rates and strong competitiveness.

2. Alexander Gerschenkron's "Relative Backwardness" notion seems especially applicable when the world economy turns from an upward secular trend to a downward direction or to a plateau stage of growth, as it did both in the 1930s and today. *Economic Backwardness in Historical Perspective,* The Harvard University Press, Cambridge, 1957. He claims that the latecomers in

economic development enjoy faster growth because of borrowed technology and learning from development paths experienced by the advanced (in relative terms) countries.

3. Japanese price index for all commodities fell from the 1925 level to 83 percent in 1929 and to 61.3 percent in 1930 due to this deflationary policy. The Bank of Japan, *Honpo Shuyo Keizai Tokei* (Hundred-Year Statistics of the Japanese Economy) Tokyo, 1966, p. 80 and p. 76.

4. Ippey Yamazawa and Yuzo Yamamoto, *Boeki Tokei* (Statistics of Foreign Trade). In Kazushi Ohkawa et al., ed., *Choki Keizai Tokei* (Estimate of Long-term Economic statistics of Japan since 1868) Vol. 14, (Tokyo, 1965), p. 257.

5. The Bank of Japan, *Ibid.* p. 132.

6. Finance Minister, Korekiyo Takahashi exercised Keynesian fiscal and monetary policies in Japan in 1932 without knowing the Keynesian model. Takahashi, acting on intuition, significantly limited his expansionary policy so that inflation would not overheat the Japanese economy. Denounced for limiting expansion, he was assassinated at age of 83 by members of a radical young military officers group on February 26, 1936.

7. League of Nations, *Remarks on the Present Phase of International Economic Relations* (Geneva, 1936) p. 17, Table 36. The Bank of Japan, *Ibid.,* Foreign exchange rates. p. 320.

8. Before the government purchase of yen abroad, 100 yen was equivalent to 40.75 U.S. dollars in 1925. In 1929, it equaled 46.5 dollars, up 12.4 percent. When Japan went back to the gold standard, 100 yen was appreciated to 49.368 U.S. dollars in 1930, up 17.5 percent. It dropped to an equivalent of 28.120 dollars in the end of 1932.

9. There were newly budding other manufactures in Japan: chemical fertilizers, weaving machines (Toyota), bicycles, and a few other products, such as electric bulbs and miscellaneous mechanical goods including telescopes. Their growth rates were rapid, but amounts were small.

10. This United States tightening of its trade policy with Japan was a partial expression of conflicting provisions in the New Deal. The policy had two objectives: the recovery of the U.S. domestic economy by protecting domestic industries and the desire to remove quantitative restrictions and reduce tariffs.

11. Except for textiles, they mostly belonged to miscellaneous export items.

12. Patterson, Gardner, *Discrimination in International Trade* (New Jersey, 1966). GATT Article VI deals with dumping cases, but the definition is still vague today.

13. For protective tariffs, there were series of historical antecedents. One similar case was in French tariff policy. Before the Cobden-Chevalier Treaty of 1860 was concluded between Britain and France, the French government protected the stagnating coal and iron production by high tariff walls. Since those products were industrial raw materials, the results were a hike in costs of production in the French engineering industry and entailed a general retardation of the French economy. In historical perspective, the French government should have protected its new engineering industry instead of the monopoly of coal and iron industries. The latter were large but old industries; their technology was obsolescent and inefficient. France at that time protected an old industry at the cost of the new rising industry. This protective tariff policy adversely contributed to the development of the French economy at that time.

SAVING IN SOUTHEAST ASIA: SOURCES, RATE AND CONTRIBUTION TO GROWTH

Richard Hooley

In the study of economic growth few variables have received more attention than saving. Leading theorists from Adam Smith to the present have focused attention on saving. Researchers and policy-makers have likewise exhibited special concern for the twin activities of saving and capital formation. This paper analyzes saving behavior in the major countries of Southeast Asia, with special attention to determinants of the rate of saving, the major sources of national saving, and is contribution to growth in the region.

The role of saving in the process of economic growth has been viewed with a certain ambiguity from the start. Although the name of Adam Smith is closely associated in the popular mind with his theory of equilibrium pricing, his main concern in the *Wealth of Nations* was with the accumulation of capital. In his view the main source of saving was profits, so he limited the analysis of saving sources to motives for reinvestment (Smith 1776; Ch. 1 BkII). The reaonsing was not circular however, because in his view profits depend not only on the volume of capital employed but also on market size. In fact, he

Research in Asian Economic Studies, Volume 6, pages 239-254.

ISBN: 1-55938-918-4

was particularly taken with the interaction between technical change (or productivity), reinvestment and capital formation.

In contrast to Smith's eclecticism, Ricardo found it theoretically convenient to make capital formation an appendage to the labor theory of value. A first blush this appears to do no violence to Smith's approach since they both held a similar theory of value. In fact however, there was a fundamental change. For Ricardo, profits became the *exclusive* source of saving, and the rate of capital formation (under the assumption of reinvestment of all profits) became nothing more than the mirror image of the rate of profit (Ricardo 1817; Ch. 6). Ricardo's formulation radically altered the framework of the saving-investment mechanism by eliminating technical change as a significant independent variable in the total process. The emphasis on the volume of saving as the principal determinant of capital formation remained a hallmark of classical and neoclassical economics long after the identification of saving with profits had disappeared.

Marx's influence on this issue is essentially ambivalent. On the one hand, his complete acceptance of the labor theory of value reinforced the Ricardian profits-reinvestment-capital formation thesis. However, Marx's obsession with private property rights as a vehicle of exploitation led him to reemphasize capital formation as the engine of growth and exploitation. At the same time he introduced an additional variable—productivity—to assist in explaining the rate of capital formation and exploitation (Marx 1867; Chs. 7 and 15). The rate of capital accumulation now is mainly influenced by the rate of profit, the size of the capital stock and the level of labor productivity. In the Marxian variant of classicism the theory of saving and investment remained hostage to the theory of exploitation. But by reintroducing the role of productivity—which had really been shelved since the time of Smith-Marx left the door ajar to further consideration of the impact of technical change on the volume of saving and investment.

Empirical work on the role of productivity in the growth process began only in the 1940s with the studies of Colin Clark (Clark 1951) which pointed to international patterns of labor productivity differences by sector, and emphasized the significance of systematic shifts of activities from low to high productivity sectors as a part of the growth process. The same thesis of an interplay between capital formation and productivity change is evident in the early NBER studies (Fabricant 1940) which focused on the role of productivity and capital formation in the growth of American manufacturing. But all of these studies were based on partial productivity measures which constrained the quality of inferences that could be made with respect to the impact of productivity change on macroeconomic growth.

The contribution of Stigler (Stigler 1947) was to provide an empirical basis for distinguishing between partial and total measures of productivity change which opened the door to empirical studies of the role of capital formation and productivity change over long periods and culminated in a series of studies (Abramovitz 1956, Kuznets 1966) outlining in detail the contribution of capital accumulation and productivity change for industrialized countries. The theoretical capstone to these studies was the path-breaking article of Solow (Solow 1957) formulating the theory of the aggregate production function. In addition, Solow provided estimates of the contribution of capital formation and technical change which showed that for the United States, technical change contributed considerably more to long-run growth than the accumulation of capital. Denison's work (1962; 1967) confirmed this inference for a number of developed countries. In addition, Denison emphasized the role of education in raising the quality of labor inputs, helping to explain a significant part of Solow's "residual." This gave additional impetus to a broadening of the definition of capital to include human capital—a development which had been initiated earlier by Becker (Becker 1964).

While the contribution of capital formation was undergoing these changes, saving was also being redefined. The work of Keynes is widely regarded as marking the fundamental linking of saving with income. His treatment of saving (Keynes 1936) emphasized the role of households in the saving process, and shifted the central locus of saving decisions from reinvested profits to households. This shift was essential to the development of modern macroequilibrium models, but it also changed completely the analytical framework for the analysis of the role of saving in long-term growth.

The net impact of Keynes' approach was to shift the long-term focus on capital formation to saving behavior. The implication for development economics was the significance it assigned to increases as in the *rate* of saving that might occur during the growth process. As Arthur Lewis put it "No nation is so poor that it could not save 12 percent of its national income if it wanted to..." (Lewis 1955). What Lewis was arguing against is the notion that the saving *rate* is a function of the *level* of income. Today the consumption function used in most macro models is some variant of a permanent or relative income hypothesis. In such a function, consumption is a function of one or more *lagged* consumption and/or income variables, the household saving rate positively responsive to increasing rates of output growth. The entire family of these functions produce saving functions in which the saving-income ratio is *not* a constant, although it usually displays an element of 'stickiness' in its behavior. The saving function becomes more complex if it incorporates intergenerational income transfers along the line suggested by Barro and others (Kotlikoff 1989).

In addition to developments in the theory of consumption which helped recast our approach to saving behavior in developing countries, pioneering work by empiricists like Raymond Goldsmith (Goldsmith 1955) made it abundantly clear that while the government sector and business (in the form of retained profits) were significant contributors to national saving, the lion's share still came from households. This finding, documented for a variety of developed and less developed countries, pointed up the need to explain household saving behavior with greater precision, while at the same time giving appropriate attention to the non-household sectors.

II

The primary questions to which this paper is addressed can be simply stated as Who saves, In what Form and at what Rate, in the Southeast Asian (SEA) economies? An additional question with respect to how effectively savings are used is also addressed. These questions are considered by reviewing data for the five major Southeast Asian countries for which reliable information is available, viz. Malaysia, Indonesia, the Philippines, Singapore and Thailand. Data for two other East Asian countries are also shown—Korea and Taiwan—used essentially as a foil in making comparisons. The reader should keep in mind that most of the data are shown as rates of saving, that is saving in various forms as a fraction of GNP.

The rate of gross national saving to GNP is shown in Table 1. The average for all SEA countries has risen from about 24 percent in 1977 to 31 percent in 1989. This increase is close to the approximately 9 percentage point increase in the gross saving ratio for Korea over the same period. The SEA countries' rate is now slightly above that of Taiwan. The largest increases of 14 percentage points were registered by Indonesia and Singapore. The Thailand and Malaysia rates increased by 9 and 5 percentage points respectively while the Philippines declined by six percentage points. Virtually all of the countries showed declines in the gross national saving rate from 1981-1982, a reflection of the cyclical downturn in worldwide economic activity in those years. The overall saving rate of the region returned to the upward long-term trend by 1983.

Table 1. National Gross Saving-Income Ratios

	Kor	*Tai*	*Mal*	*PI*	*Sng*	*Thai*	*Indo*	*Avg. SEA*
1977	25.94%	32.58%	24.50%	23.68%	30.70%	22.01%	20.69%	24.31%
1978	27.86%	34.39%	29.05%	23.73%	31..90%	24.00%	18.45%	25.43%
1979	27.03%	33.38%	34.89%	24.40%	35.05%	22.42%	23.88%	28.13%
1980	21.17%	32.28%	30.42%	24.65%	36.50%	21.10%	25.89%	27.71%
1981	20.60%	31.34%	26.23%	26.68%	39.28%	20.90%	20.64%	26.15%
1982	21.80%	30.06%	25.15%	21.38%	40.67%	20.02%	15.90%	24.62%
1983	26.15%	32.15%	28.11%	21.42%	44.76%	21.35%	25.88%	28.30%
1984	28.00%	33.80%	30.80%	16.76%	46.34%	20.88%	26.27%	28.21%
1985	28.27%	33.57%	27.56%	14.15%	42.72%	19.78%	26.82%	26.21%
1986	31.91%	38.46%	27.22%	14.85%	40.76%	21.34%	24.17%	25.67%
1987	35.21%	38.46%	22.15%	16.89%	40.86%	24.13%	29.50%	28.90%
1988	37.45%	34.45%	32.55%	17.80%	42.38%	29.09%	30.57%	30.58%
1989	35.06%	30.82%	29.77%	17.76%	44.18%	30.72%	33.96%	31.28%

Source: ADB, KEY INDICATORS OF ASIAN AND PACIFIC COUNTRIES, Various Years.

The contribution of the government sector to national saving is about the same in Southeast Asia as in East Asia, averaging between 5 and 7 percent for the region as a whole. However, the SEA average masks great variation. It includes the towering 15-17 percent rate of Singapore as well as the impressive 8-10 percent rate of Indonesia. These are juxtaposed against rates of roughly 2-4 percent for Thailand and the Philippines, and a rate of not more than one percent for Malaysia. The performance of the region as a whole is still impressive even if Singapore is eliminated. So while government intervention apparently plays a major role in the high saving rates of Singapore and Indonesia, it plays a much smaller—but still a positive—role in the economies of Malaysia, the Philippines and Thailand. These wide differences in government sector saving contribution reflect differences in fiscal expenditure patterns (e.g. differing educational expenditure ratios), and differences in the structure and operation of government savings institutions. They also contain implications regarding the productiveness of government projects.

The average private sector saving rate for SEA rose from about 20 percent in 1977 to 28 percent in 1989. This rise of 8 percentage points also conceals wide variations among countries. The Indonesian rate increased by 16 percentage points while Malaysia, Singapore and Thailand each increased by about 10 percentage points. In contrast, the Philippine rate fell by about 3 points. Most of the Philippine decline took place over a period of only three years (1984-87) and is obviously connected with events surrounding the fall of the Marcos regime. However, it is worth noting that there is as yet only a slow recovery of the Philippine private sector saving rate, suggesting that the decline may have been the result of systemic damage inflicted on the

Table 2. General Government Gross Saving-Income Ratios

	Kor	*Tai*	*Mal*	*PI*	*Sng*	*Thai*	*Indo*	*Avg. SEA*
1977	5.62%	7.00%	1.17%	3.21%	11.60%	2.46%	9.65%	5.62%
1978	6.48%	7.86%	2.21%	4.06%	9.97%	1.87%	9.53%	5.53%
1979	7.36%	8.62%	1.05%	5.09%	12.57%	1.87%	11.59%	6.43%
1980	6.39%	7.16%	0.60%	4.98%	14.29%	1.61%	11.93%	6.68%
1981	6.63%	5.98%	0.22%	3.79%	18.00%	1.23%	14.27%	7.50%
1982	6.94%	4.44%	0.03%	3.20%	17.49%	-0.40%	12.07%	6.48%
1983	7.40%	4.97%	0.35%	4.38%	18.15%	1.20%	10.48%	6.91%
1984	7.49%	5.12%	1.35%	3.88%	14.03%	0.64%	11.95%	6.37%
1985	7.17%	4.58%	1.47%	3.44%	9.83%	-0.31%	11.21%	5.13%
1986	6.98%	3.75%	-0.83%	2.00%	12.63%	0.46%	9.20%	4.69%
1987	7.36%	5.70%	-2.73%	1.72%	17.36%	2.26%	10.40%	5.80%
1988	7.98%	6.65%	0.18%	-0.77%	15.52%	5.31%	7.96%	5.64%
1989	4.77%	7.24%	-1.01%	0.05%	13.09	5.60%	8.26%	5.20%

Source: UN, YEARBOOK OF NATIONAL ACCOUNTS and IMF, GOVERNMENT FINANCE STATISTICS YEARBOOK, various years.

Table 3. Private Sector Gross Saving-Income Ratios

	Kor	*Tai*	*Mal*	*PI*	*Sng*	*Thai*	*Indo*	*Avg. SEA*
1977	21.82%	26.20%	27.44%	20.80%	20.28%	19.87%	14.59%	20.60%
1978	22.74%	26.76%	31.54%	19.44%	22.16%	22.88%	12.73%	21.75%
1979	21.36%	24.72%	38.50%	19.35%	22.87%	21.67%	16.93%	23.86%
1980	18.29%	25.25%	33.55%	20.19%	25.95%	20.32%	18.38%	23.68%
1981	18.26%	25.91%	29.63%	21.44%	25.36%	21.29%	9.93%	21.53%
1982	19.19%	25.66%	29.97%	19.60%	25.99%	22.02%	7.12%	20.94%
1983	22.18%	27.01%	34.43%	19.51%	27.07%	20.89%	19.63%	24.31%
1984	24.16%	27.60%	36.69%	15.37%	30.43%	21.43%	18.97%	24.58%
1985	24.63%	27.35%	33.75%	12.73%	29.41%	21.85%	19.68%	23.48%
1986	28.06%	32.30%	35.21%	13.56%	25.73%	22.97%	19.05%	23.30%
1987	30.12%	30.75%	42.51%	15.54%	22.15%	23.69%	23.92%	25.56%
1988	30.85%	25.34%	38.30%	18.84%	26.36%	25.46%	27.48%	27.29%
1989	311.14%	21.30%.	36.96%	17.47%	30.90%	26.44%	30.61%	28.48%

Source: Table 1 and Table 2.

financial system during the chaotic period accompanying the transition of political power. If the SEA average is computed excluding the Philippines the increase between 1977 and 1989 is nearly 11 percentage points, larger than either the Korean or Taiwan increases.

The private sector consists of two behaviorally distinct sub-sectors: households and business enterprises. To get a good grasp on private sector saving behavior it is necessary to analyze the performance of each of the two subsectors—households and business enterprises. At the moment data on household saving are available for only two SEA countries—the Philippines and Thailand—and these data along with estimates for Korea and Taiwan are shown in Table 4. Thai households exhibit a net saving rate of between 9 and 10 percent. On a gross basis (i.e., before deducting depreciation) this suggests a rate of 12 percent or so. Since gross private sector saving is in the order of 20 percent, the implied corporate sector rate is then about 8 percent. The Thai household saving rate, though it appears high by international standards, is still considerably below that of Korean and Taiwanese households—which display rates of net household saving in the 15-20 percent range.

The Philippine household rate is still lower. Even before the Marcos regime began to totter, the net rate was about 6 percent, implying a gross rate of no more than 9 percent at most. With a gross private sector rate of 20 percent, this would imply a contribution of corporate business of 11 percent. The implied relative contribution for Philippine households is substantially less than that for Thai households, and about one-half that of Korean and Taiwanese households. The relative contribution of Philippine corporate sector is probably greater than in Thailand. Note also that the economic chaos accompanying the change of political power (1983-85) brought about a

Table 4. Household Net Saving-Income Ratio [*]

	Kor	*Tai*	*Mal*	*PI*	*Sng*	*Thai*	*Indo*	*Avg. SEA*
1976								
1977	15.69%	13.26%	na	na	na	na	na	
1978	15.03%	13.44%	na	na	na	na	na	
1979	15.51%	12.91%	na	6.54%	na	10.78%	na	
1980	16.47%	11.48%	na	5.87%	na	10.59%	na	
1981	16.75%	13.62%	na	6.47%	na	10.62%	na	
1982	15.75%	13.78%	na	3.20%	na	11.20%	na	
1983	20.27%	14.44%	na	0.92%	na	10.34%	na	
1984	22.76%	15.39%	na	0.91%	na	9.68%	na	
1985		16.29%	na	1.15%	na	8.86%	na	
1986		19.39%	na	2.41%	na	8.41%	na	
1987		19.45%	na	0.08%	na	8.54%	na	
1988		16.29%	na		na	9.04%	na	
1989		12.48%	na		na		na	

[*] Only net saving data available for households. Ratio is (Net S) / GNP
Source: UN, YEARBOOK OF NATIONAL ACCOUNTS, Various years.

cataclysmic decline in the Philippine household saving rate—a decline which has still to be reversed. The decline in corporate saving was even steeper because the private sector rate was negative for several years. A major reason for these declines is undoubtedly the wholesale pilferage of the banking system during the latter part of the Marcos era. The Philippine banking system (even after 'reconstruction') remains saddled with large amounts of non-earning loans and investments. It is recuperating by feeding off of a scandalously wide interest rate spread—roughly 18 percent on loan funds in contrast to 4-5 percent on deposits. When compared to inflation rates of 15 percent the real deposit rate has been substantially negative for a number of years. Naturally savers look for alternative outlets, which results in financial shallowing and low saving rates.

One reasonable hypothesis to explain the differences between household saving rates in SEA and East Asia is that in early stages of development business relies more on reinvested earnings (a la Adam Smith) partly because the financial system is underdeveloped, partly because family owned and operated business is more widespread in early stages of development, or because the number of truly urbanized households is small, or possibly for all three reasons. Whatever the cause(s), it appears that on the basis of the limited data available, there is a fundamental difference in household and business saving rates in East and Southeast Asia.

Net income from abroad has averaged approximately −2 percent each year for the SEA countries.[1] Malaysia and Indonesia represent the upper end of the range, 4 to 6 percent a year outflow, while the Philippines and Thailand are at the lower end at 1 to 2 percent per year outflow (Table 5). The largest

Table 5. Net Foreign Income from Abroad

	Kor	*Tai*	*Mal*	*PI*	*Sng*	*Thai*	*Indo*	*Avg. SEA*
1977	-1.50%	-0.62%	-4.11%	-0.34%	-1.18%	-0.32%	-3.56%	1.90%
1978	-1.36%	-0.23%	-4.70%	0.23%	-0.24%	-0.75%	-3.81%	-1.85%
1979	-1.69%	0.03%	-4.67%	-0.04%	-0.39%	-1.13%	-4.64%	-2.17%
1980	-3.51%	0.14%	-3.73%	-0.53%	-3.73%	-0.83%	-4.42%	-2.65%
1981	-4.29%	-0.55%	-3.62%	-1.55%	-4.07%	-1.61%	-3.56%	-2.88%
1982	-4.33%	-0.04%	-4.86%	-1.43%	-2.81%	-1.60%	-3.28%	-2.80%
1983	-3.42%	0.16%	-6.68%	-2.58%	-0.47%	-0.74%	-4.33%	-2.92%
1984	-3.65%	1.07%	-7.24%	-2.49%	1.88%	-1.19%	4.65%	-2.74%
1985	-3.53%	1.64%	-7.65%	-2.02%	3.49%	-1.77%	-4.06%	-2.40%
1986	03.12%	2.41%	-7.15%	-9,71%	2.40%	-2.09%	-4.08%	-2.33%
1987	-2.27%	2.01%	-6.62%	-0.36%	1.35%	-1.82%	-4.82%	-2.46%
1988	-1.37%	2.46%	-5.93%	-0.27%	0.49%	-1.67%	-4.87%	-2.45%
1989	-0.85%	2.28%	-6.18%	0.23%	0.19%	-1.32%	-4.91%	-2.40%
1990	-0.75%	2.45%	-4.52%		-1.87%	-1.02%		-0.73%

Source: ADB, KEY INDICATORS OF DEVELOPING ASIAN AND PACIFIC COUNTRIES

item in this category is the remittance of profits earned by foreign investors which has grown along with increased foreign investment from abroad. In the past decade interest payments on foreign debt have also become a significant factor affecting the outflow of savings abroad, and this is another reason for the tendency of this ratio to rise over the period. That rise has been damped however, because some countries such as the Philippines and Thailand, have substantial inflows from workers employed abroad (especially in the Middle East) which has acted as an offset to the remittances on foreign investments and foreign borrowings..

Foreign saving—in the form of direct investment and borrowing from abroad—has made a contribution to the saving rate of the region. On average, it has contributed from 2 to 3 percent of total saving requirements for SEA countries. (Table 6). But there are wide variations by country and by subperiod. The inflow of foreign saving which had been 2 to 3 percent during the period 1977-80 rose to a high of over 7 percent during the worldwide recession of 1981-83. Foreign saving then dropped off sharply and after 1987 became an outflow. The contribution of foreign saving has also been country-specific. Malaysia and Singapore registered large inflows for much of the period up to the mid-eighties. After that the foreign component became an outflow. Indonesia and Thailand have registered the most consistent pattern of foreign saving inflows, although here too the foreign component has diminished in recent years. The Philippines has absorbed less foreign saving than the other countries, primarily because political events there have not been favorable toward the invitation of foreign capital. In recent years there has been a significant net outflow reflecting the sizeable service charges on the country's large foreign debt.

What were the sources of foreign capital for SEA? Clearly one of these was Taiwan which exhibits a huge outflow—in many years equal to 10 to 15 percent of national gross saving—throughout the decade of the 1980s. This outflow peaked at 21 percent of national savings in 1986. Another source of foreign capital for SEA countries was the private banking systems of Japan and the United States, along with multilateral agencies like the World Bank and Asian Development Bank. The tightening of overseas lending by Japanese and American commercial banks, the decline in the outflow of private capital from Taiwan and a more sober assessment of needs by multilateral agencies have all been instrumental in the declining contribution of foreign sources to SEA saving.

A decline in foreign sources implies a decline in the rate of capital formation unless it is offset by an increase in domestic sources. The foreign sector provided a steady though modest flow of funds to SEA countries during the decade of the 1970s. It reached a peak of 7-1/2 percent of gross national saving in 1982. (Table 6). Thereafter it decreased, becoming negative (i.e. an outflow) from 1987-89. How did SEA countries deal with this development? On the whole they substituted increased domestic saving for the shortfall in foreign saving. If we take the period 1981-89, the shift in sectoral sources of savings was as follows:

Decrease in foreign sector saving rate	−.0757
Less: Decrease in domestic Cap. formation rate	−.0252
Equals: Decrease in foreign sector saving to be offset by increase in domestic saving rate	−.0505
Change in domestic sector saving rate:	
Increase in private sector saving	+.0663
Increase in net foreign income from abroad	+.0039
Decrease in government saving	−.0197 +.0505

Of the total decline in external resources of 7-1/2 percent, only 2-1/2 percent was translated into a decline in domestic capital formation. The remainder of the shortfall was taken up by an increase in the domestic saving rate. And within the domestic economy it was the private, not the government sector, which took up the slack. Again however, the Philippines proves the exception. A decline of nearly 6 percent in foreign sector capital inflows (1981-89) was fully registered as a reduction in domestic capital formation. Indeed, instead of offsetting this decline, private sector saving registered a further, equiproportional decline of its own, bringing on a devastating decline in the rate of capital formation in that country of approximately 10 percentage points during that period.

Output growth is dependent not only on high saving and investment rates but also on investment efficiency. Indeed, quite a few studies have concluded

Table 6. Foreign Saving (+ = inflow; — = outflow)

	Kor	Tai	Mal	PI	Sng	Thai	Indo	Avg. SEA
1977	3.04%	-4.30%	0.33%	1.41%	5.88%	4.96%	0.16%	2.55%
1978	5.64%	-6.12%	-1.13%	-0.20%	7.22%	4.37%	2.90%	2.63%
1979	9.58%	-0.49%	-4.62%	1.19%	8.48%	5.10%	-1.93%	1.64%
1980	11.68%	1.56%	1.14%	2.10%	11.57%	5.55%	-4.05%	3,26%
1981	10.13%	-1.31%	10.02%	4.14%	8.92%	5.79%	1.53%	6.08%
1982	8.03%	-4.83%	13.97%	4.10%	8.61%	3.47%	7.45%	7.52%
1983	3.59%	-8.70%	11.97%	-1.98%	3.37%	4.79%	4.10%	4.45%
1984	-9.92%	-11.87%	5.19%	-1.37%	1.24%	4.33%	1.20%	2.12%
1985	2.04%	-14.82%	2.13%	-0.26%	-1.68%	4.70%	2.41%	1.46%
1986	-2.68%	-21.34%	0.62%	-3.32%	-3.14%	0.90%	5.30%	0.07%
1987	-5.08%	-18.40%	-8.44%	-3.08%	-2.39%	0.23%	3.45%	-2.04%
1988	-6.39%	-11.69%	-5.06%	-2.91%	-6.07%	0.23%	2.54%	-2.25%
1989	-1.42%	-8.51%	0.84%	-1.89%	-9.72%	0.76%	2.56%	-1.49%

Source: Tables 1 and 7.

Table 7. Rate of Gross Capital Formation (GCF/GNP - curr prs)

	Kor	Tai	Mal	PI	Sng	Thai	Indo	Avg. SEA
1976	25.45%	31.06%	22.73%	26.81%	40.31%	23.32%		28.29%
1977	28.98%	28.28%	24.83%	25.08%	36.58%	26.97%	20.85%	26.86%
1978	33.50%	28.27%	27.92%	23.53%	39.11%	28.37%	21.35%	28.06%
1979	36.61%	32.88%	30.26%	25.60%	43.53%	27.51%	21.95%	29.77%
1980	32.85%	33.84%	31.56%	26.75%	48.07%	26.65%	21.84%	30.97%
1981	30.74%	30.03%	36.25%	27.82%	48.20%	26.70%	22.17%	32.23%
1982	29.82%	25.23%	39.12%	25.48%	49.28%	23.49%	23.35%	32.14%
1983	29.75%	23.43%	40.08%	19.43%	48.13%	26.13%	29.98%	32.75%
1984	29.27%	21.93%	35.99%	15.39%	47.57%	25.21%	27.47%	30.33%
1985	30.32%	18.74%	29.69%	13.89%	41.04%	24.47%	29.23%	27.67%
1986	29.23%	17.11%	27.84%	11.53%	37.61%	22.24%	29.47%	25.74%
1987	30.13%	20.06%	24.71%	13.80%	38.47%	24.36%	32.95%	26.86%
1988	31.06%	11.76%	27.49%	14.90%	36.31%	29.32%	33.11%	28.23%
1989	33.64%	22.30%	30.62%	15.87%	34.45%	31.48%	36.53%	29.79%

Source: ADB. KEY INDICATORS OF DEVELOPING ASIAN AND PACIFIC COUNTRIES

that the productivity of investment and not the rate of capital formation is of paramount importance for long-term growth. In an effort to introduce evidence regarding investment efficiency into the discussion, we now turn to a consideration of incremental capital output ratios (ICOR) in the region.

While ICORs have often been used as a measure of investment efficiency, the concept has a variety of known defects which must be kept in mind. The gestation period for new investment may differ among industries and create lags between new investment and output growth which are not well reflected in the usual one year-lag model used for measuring the ICOR. In addition,

ICORs differ significantly by industry so that change in the national average may reflect primarily changes in the distribution of industries rather than intraindustry investment efficiency. Again, changes in output (especially over short periods) often reflect the interplay of a variety of factors, some exogenous to the economic system under study, resulting in considerable instability of the ICOR. For all these reasons the data on ICORs which will now be considered should be treated with considerable discretion.

The ICOR based on gross investment averaged between 3 and 3-1/2 for the SEA countries in 1977-78 and moved up to a little over 4 by 1989 (Table 8). This is somewhat higher than the corresponding ICORs for Korea and Taiwan which, during the same period, averaged between 2 and 3-1/2. During the period 1980-85 the SEA ICOR rose markedly and then declined, in contrast to the East Asian ratio which displayed an essentially level trend. The main reason for this difference appears to be the severe contraction in primary goods markets in the early eighties which stultified SEA output growth while having little or no impact on East Asian growth.

On a country basis, the ICORs for Malaysia and Thailand are about the same as the SEA average. Singapore is somewhat below the average while Indonesia is above it. The Philippine ICOR is somewhat higher than the SEA average at the beginning of the period, rose steadily to 1983, then turned negative at about the time of the collapse of the Marcos regime before settling down to the 2-1/2 to 3 range during the period 1987-89. This suggests either gross overstatement of capital values or gross inefficiency in the use of capital, or both, during the closing years of the Marcos regime.

Table 8. ICOR-Total Investment [GCF(t)/GNP (-1)/(dGNP (t)/GNP (-1))]

	Kor	*Tai*	*Mal*	*PI*	*Sng*	*Thai*	*Indo*	*Avg. SEA*
1977	2.88	2.78	3.20	4.03	4.71	2.73	2.34	3.4
1978	3.45	2.08	2.45	4.30	4.55	2.72	2.77	3.36
1979	4.82	4.02	-12.33	4.08	4.68	5.18	3.51	1.02
1980	-15.20	4.63	58.61	5.12	4.96	5.57	2.21	15.29
1981	4.58	4.87	6.16	7.16	5.02	4.21	2.80	5.07
1982	4.09	7.11	11.87	8.75	7.18	5.78	10.39	8.80
1983	2.53	2.77	38.56	21.38	5.88	3.60	1.30	14.14
1984	1.92	2.07	17.53	-2.56	5.73	3.54	4.08	5.66
1985	4.37	3.79	58.43	-3.26	-25.02	6.97	11.83	9.79
1986	2.36	1.47	2.58	7.97	20.39	4.95	4.95	8.17
1987	2.50	1.63	-146.56	2.93	4.07	2.90	6.92	-25.95
1988	2.71	3.10	7.19	2.41	3.26	2.67	5.79	4.26
1989	5.47	2.90	6.96	2.64	3.73	2.66	4.65	4.13
Avg.	2.04	3.32	4.20	4.99	3.78	4.11	4.89	4.40

Although there are some reasons to expect higher ICORs for SEA than East Asia, the persistent differences observed between SEA and East Asia appear to reflect other factor(s) as well. A reasonable inference from the consistently higher ICOR in SEA is that investment efficiency in SEA is below that in East Asia. The degree of difference suggested by these data is certainly not overwhelming, but it does appear to be significant. This point deserves additional attention, particularly with respect to more refined comparisons of basically similar sectors and industry groups, adjustment for differences in purchasing power parities among countries, and use of a more comprehensive measure of efficiency which takes into consideration other productive factors, particularly labor.[2]

Indexes of output per worker are shown for Korea and five SEA countries in table 9. In the first place notice that the index of output per worker for Korea stood at 174 in 1989 compared to 126 for the SEA countries as a group. The Singapore and Thailand indexes at approximately 150 were substantially higher than the SEA average. Indonesia and Malaysia are much lower, and the Philippines actually showed a decline, although there was a modest rise after 1986.

Investment efficiency is apparently significantly higher in Korea than in SEA, because modest increases in the Korean ICOR have been accompanied by improvements in output per worker, and impliedly in output per unit of additional investment in all (i.e., combined) inputs. This is somewhat less true in the SEA countries, although the record is still strong for some countries in the region. However, in Indonesia and particularly the Philippines, the ICORs are not low, and at the same time additional investment has apparently

Table 9. Indexes of Output Per Worker

	Kor	*Mal*	*PI*	*Sng*	*Thai*	*Indo*	*Avg. SEA*
1978							
1979							
1980	100.00	100.00	100.00	100.00	100.00	100.00	100.00
1981							
1982	108.90	111.40	98.50	109.80	115.30	94.50	105.90
1983							
1984	120.70	121.70	89.80	124.80	120.30	104.70	112.26
1985							
1986	148.50	115.10	80.80	127.90	123.30	104.70	110.36
1987	157.80	117.40	85.40	134.80	130.10	106.10	114.76
1988	170.50	123.60	87.40	144.50	130.00	108.20	118.74
1989	174.30	128.50	91.10	152.90	147.10	112.20	126.36
1990							

Source: F. Alburo, R. Bobel, P. Intal, R. Hooley, E. Medalla and D. Tayl, Philippine Trade and Investment Regimes: A Comparison with Asian Neighbors DAI, Washington D.C. 1991, p. 77.

boosted output per worker little if at all. The implication is that real returns to investment are not so high in some SEA cases. These inferences are fragile in the sense that they depend on factor costs remaining roughly the same. In particular, a decline in real wages could offset a decline in the (physical) efficiency of investment. However, such a situation would hold out that little hope as a long-term solution, since a decline in real wages must reach a point of no return sooner or later, carrying implications for social and political turbulence which can only have negative implications for the volume of investment.

At the outset of this paper a question was posed regarding the determinants of the rate of saving. There is a commonly expressed view in development economics that relates the *rate* of saving to the *level* of income. It was also pointed out at an earlier point that any specification of the saving function has to be consistent with an acceptable form of the consumption function. The only consumption function which portrays the rate of saving as positively associated with the level of income is of the form $C(t) = a + bY(\mathrm{t})$. Accordingly, the rate of saving is given as $S/Y(t) = -a/Y(t) + (1\text{-}b)$. Even in this form however, S/Y will vary with Y only at very low levels of Y. After that low level of income is passed, the saving rate is indicated by the constant (1-b).

A consumption function which makes today's consumption a function of consumption lagged by one or more periods is consistent with the permanent income theory as well as relative income theories of consumption. For example, the alternative consumption function $C(t) = a + bC(t\text{-}1) + c[dY(t)$ portrays today's saving rate as positively associated with yesterday's rate and the rate of change of income. Accordingly the above, after rearranging terms, defines the rate of saving as $S/Y(t) = -a + bS(t\text{-}1) + c[dY/Y(t)]$. The essential difference between the rate of saving function based on the permanent or relative income consumption hypothesis and that based on the absolute income consumption hypothesis is a question of the significance of the $dY/Y(t\text{-}1)$ term. If the current period saving rate is simply a function of the previous period rate, then the inference is that the saving rate is a function of the level of income and is correspondingly small at low levels of income. If however, the second term (rate of growth of income) proves to be statistically significant, then the inference is that the saving rate is not dependent on the level of income but rather on past period saving rate *and* the rate of growth of income.

A regression was calculated for each SEA country in addition to Korea and Taiwan for the period 1977-1989. The regression equation relates the current period national saving rate to the previous period rate and the rate of growth of income. The results are shown in table 10. In the first place, all the fits are good except that for Malaysia. The poor fit for Malaysia seems to be largely the result of extreme variability in the estimates of national income. It is not clear at this point whether this variability is mainly due to the collapse of primary export markets during the 1980s or statistical problems with the national income estimates. The latter are now undergoing a major revision.

Table 10. S/Y(t) = a + b (S/Y (-1) + c (dY (t)

	Korea	*Taiwan*	*Malaysia*	*Phil.*	*S'pore*	*Thai*	*Indon*
Const	0.04	0.14	0.26	0.03	-0.02	0.02	-0.01
Coef 1	0.82	0.46	0.17	0.80	0.98	0.74	0.94
SE	0.18	0.19	0.27	0.06	0.08	0.17	0.28
Coef 2	0.25	0.53	-0.36	0.39	0.46	0.63	0.48
SE	0.25	0.16	0.20	0.06	0.12	0.15	0.24
R2	0.79	0.67	0.32	0.96	0.94	0.89	0.54

Source: Basic data from Table 1 and U.N. Yearbook of National Accounts.

In general, the regression results are quite good. The constants are not large (except for Malaysia), and the estimates of the coefficient b are generally between .5 and 1.0, all (except Malaysia) statistically significant at the .01 probability level. The coefficient *c* is also significant in most cases (except for Korea). This implies that the national saving rate is indeed a function of income change as well as past saving (and consumption) patterns.

SUMMARY AND CONCLUSION

The main questions addressed in this paper deal with the rate of saving for SEA countries, differences over time and among countries, and the relevant explanatory variables of the rate of saving for the region. The countries studied were the five major economies of Southeast Asia. The sources of saving were analyzed for each country and evidence was presented on trends in the efficiency of investment. Data was also presented for two East Asian countries—Korea and Taiwan—which were used as a foil for purposes of comparison.

National saving rates are generally high in the SEA region and appear comparable to those in East Asia. An additional similarity with East Asia is that while the lion's share of saving takes place in the private sector, a substantial contribution to national saving is also made by the government sector. The foreign sector contributed significantly to total saving for the SEA group up to the mid-1980s, but in recent years this has changed and there is now a small outflow of saving to the rest of the world. The change in trend is associated with a slowdown in foreign direct investment (and hence increase in net capital repatriation), as well as the heavy foreign debt amortization burden of some countries in the region. The diminished role of foreign saving has had little impact on the rate of capital formation however, because much of the shortfall in foreign sources has been offset by increases in private domestic saving.

Private sector saving rates are high in SEA and comparable to those in East Asia. However the structure of saving sources differs markedly between the two regions. On the basis of data for two SEA countries, it appears that business enterprises make a relatively larger contribution to domestic saving compared to households. While there may exist some difference in household saving propensities between East Asia and SEA, this fact probably reflects underdevelopment of the financial system in SEA economies. As a result, business enterprises in SEA are required to generate a larger share of investment funds from internal sources.

A saving function was fit to data on domestic savings for each country. The implications of those fits is that the saving rate is a function of past saving (and consumption) patterns as well as the current period rate of growth of output. Experimentation with functions introducing the level of income as an explanatory variable produced inferior results. Further improvements may be obtained by experimenting with functions appropriately designed and fit to sectoral data.

There has been a rise in SEA country ICORs which goes beyond what has occurred in the East Asian countries. This implies a lower efficiency of investment in SEA. Additional data on changes in output per worker seem to corroborate this inference, though for reasons explained in the text, the implications on this point are extremely fragile. In any case, the SEA countries do seem to be making significant progress on the issue of efficiency, as there appears to be some decline in the regional ICOR while at the same time output per worker has been increasing significantly. The only exception to this is the Philippines. This argues well for continued high rates of saving of most countries in the region and steady macroeconomic growth.

ACKNOWLEDGMENT

The author acknowledges the assistance of Donald Steel in preparing the data base and of Anita Tilford in editing and typing of the paper. Any remaining errors are the author's alone.

NOTES

1. This is net factor income from abroad and includes net receipts from the rest of the world on income from investments abroad such as interest, dividends and branch profits. It also includes earnings of residents working abroad along with any other factor incomes of normal residents.
2. Aside from measurement problems, the higher ICOR in SEA does not necessarily imply that production efficiency is lower. If the higher ICOR is accompanied by an equiproportionate increase in output per unit of non-capital inputs, the higher ICOR would not imply a lower level of efficiency in the use of capital. However, if the reverse is the case, then the higher ICOR would imply a lower level of efficiency.

REFERENCES

Abramovitz, Moses. (1956). *Resource and Output Trends in the United States Since 1870,* New York. Occasional papers 52: National Bureau of Economic Research.

A.D.B. *Key Indicators of Developing Asian and Pacific Countries.* Manila. Asian Development Bank. (various issues).

Albaro, F., Bobal, R., Intal, P., Hooley, R., Mendalla, E. and Taylor, D. (1991). *Philippine Trade and Investment Regimes: A Comparison with Asian Neighbors.* Washington DC: DAI for VSAID.

Arndt, H.W. (1991). "Saving, Investment and Growth: Recent Asian Experience," *Banca Nazionale del Lavoro Quarterly Review.* June.

Becker, Gary S. (1964). *Human Capital,* New York: Columbia University Press for NBER.

Clark, Colin. (1951). *The Conditions of Economics Progress,* London: MacMillan.

Denison, Edward F. (1962). *The Sources of Economic Growth and the Alternatives Before Us,* New York: The Committee for Review Development.

———. (1967). *Why Growth Rates Differ,* Washington, DC. The Brookings Institution.

Fabricant, Solomon. (1940). *The Output of Manufacturing Industries, 1899-1937,* New York: National Bureau of Economic Research, Inc.

Goldsmith, Raymond. (1955). *A Study of Saving in the U.S.,* Princeton: Princeton University Press.

Keynes, John M. (1936). *The General Theory of Employment, Interest and Money,* London: MacMillan.

Kotlikoff, Lawrence J. (1989). *What Determines Savings?* Cambridge, MA: MIT Press.

Kuznets, Simon. (1966). *Modern Economic Growth,* New Haven: Yale University Press.

Lewis, W. Arthur. (1955). *The Theory of Economic Growth,* London: Allen & Unwin.

Ricardo, David. (1817). *Principles of Political Economy and Taxation,* New York: E.P. Dutton (Everyman Edition).

Smith, Adam. (1776). *The Wealth of Nations,* London: P.F. Collier.

Solow, Robert. (1957). "Technical Change and the Aggregate Consumption Function," *The Review of Economics and Statistics,* August.

Stigler, George. (1947). *Trends in Output and Employment,* New York: National Bureau of Economic Research.

U.N. *Yearbook of National Account Statistics,* New York: United Nations (various issues).

FOREIGN TRADE LIBERALIZATION IN SOUTH KOREA: LESSONS FOR CHINA

Xiaoxuan Liu

Experience with foreign trade liberalization in South Korea may hold valuable lessons for China as China seeks to further open its trade and accede to GATT. There are many similarities between South Korea and China that suggest relevant lessons may be found in the Korean experience. These similarities include common cultural traditions and mores, autocratic political systems, and comparable levels of development at the outset of liberalization.

The first part of this paper will describe the process of trade liberalization in South Korea. The second part will analyze problems in China's foreign trade and suggest reforms based on the experiences of Korea. A final section offers brief conclusions.

Research in Asian Economic Studies, Volume 6, pages 255-265.

ISBN: 1-55938-918-4

I. FOREIGN TRADE LIBERALIZATION IN SOUTH KOREA

A. Import Liberalization

Progress in liberalizing imports in South Korea was achieved through tariff reforms and reductions in quantitative restrictions (QRs).

In 1955, the Korean government adopted a semi-annual trade program to control imports. Initially, the list of commodities that could be imported comprised 207 items, with this number steadily increasing to 3082 in 1967. Of these, the number of items granted automatic import approval rose from 185 to 2950 (Kim 1991). The year 1967 marked an important turning point for South Korea's trading system. The "positive list" of items that *could* be imported was replaced with a "negative list" of items that *could not* be imported. In effect, all items not explicitly prohibited from coming in could thereby be imported. Some of them were put under area diversification control or other regulations. Twice a year the government announced the number of import-restricted items. The quantitative restrictions were applied to import competing items and imports of unessential or luxury goods (Das 1992). Generally speaking, every six months the import-plan was determined on the basis of balance-of-payments and import demands.

The reform in 1967 constituted a significant trade stride forward in import liberalization. From 1967 through the following decade the pace of reform slowed. It picked up again in 1978-79, and has since been steady.

In 1952, South Korea imposed tariffs on 1695 imported commodities. The average tariff rate in 1952 was 25.4 percent, but this average increased markedly to nearly 40 percent in 1962. In more recent years, efforts to liberalize trade have brought a reversal in the trend with the average tariff rate falling to 21.9 percent by 1984. The disparity in tariff rates across goods has also shown a decline over time, the coefficient of variation dropping from 0.77 in 1962 (when tariffs ranged from 0% to 250%) to 0.61 in 1984 (See Table 1).

Table 1. The Changes of Tariffs (Regular) in South Korea

	52	*57*	*62*	*68*	*73*	*77*	*79*	*84*
A	1695	1269	2013	3150	3971	2495	2185	2283
B	25.4	30.3	39.9	39.1	31.5	29.7	24.8	21.9
C	0.7	0.7	0.77	0.71	0.7	0.61	0.69	0.61

A: The number of items by tariff rate.
B: Simple average tariff rates (%).
C: Coeffient of variation in tariff rates.
Source: ***Kim, Kwang Suk, 1991***

Table 1 represents such course of tariff changes in South Korea. It shows the trend that tariffs were getting higher and then lower. Actually this course was parallel to the liberalization from QRs.

Although the average legal tariff rate was high when South Korean began its trade liberalization program, the actual tariff rate—obtained by dividing actual tariffs remitted by the total value of imports—was much lower. The difference between nominal and actual tariffs was due to the prevalence of exemptions to and reductions in prescribed tariffs. Special treatment was given in particular to the import of raw materials to be used in export production and to selected capital goods imports. The actual tariff rate increased in the late 1950s, up to 54.5 percent (1959) but dropped sharply to 12.4 percent in 1962. After 1965, the average actual tariff rate has been less than 10 percent (see Table 2).

From Table 2, it can be seen that the actual tariff rates were also getting higher and then lower. It seems that the trend in actual tariff rates had something to do with the trend in legal rates, but the actual tariff rates changed earlier than the legal tariff rates did.

B. Export Liberalization

During the post-war reconstruction period, South Korea's currency, the won, was chronically overvalued due to Korea's high rate of domestic price inflation. In order to offset the resulting unfavorable impact on exports, the Korean government adopted a variety of export incentives. Those incentives covered preferential access to credit, tariff exemptions on raw material imports or intermediate inputs—because Korean exports were higherly dependent on intermediate imports, the income tax rate on foreign exchange earning concessions, and tariff and indirect tax exemptions for domestic suppliers of intermediate goods used in export production. Potential exporters were thus ensured access to inputs at prices that would not inhibit their competitiveness on output markets.

The subsidies could be considered as the value of such preferetial supports. The won value of export subsidies (including import tariff exemptions, tax reductions, preferential credit, and so forth), for each US$ of exports is shown

Table 2. Estimation of Actual Tariff Rates (58-83)

	58	*59*	*60*	*61*	*62*	*63*	*64*	*65*	*66*		*83*
R	23.2	54.5	45.7	13.5	12.4	8.7	8.0	10.0	9.1	.....	7.0

R: Actual tariff rates(%).
Source: Kim, Kwang Suk, 1991.

for selected years in Table 3. Subsidy values are higher in earlier years indicating a greater need for artificial incentives to overcome the export impediment created by exchange rate distortions. As exchange rate adjustments succeeded in more closely aligning the official exchange rate with the market value of the won, export subsidies diminished and were finally eliminated in 1983.

South Korea began attempts to reform its multiple exchange rate system in 1961 with an increase in the official won-to-dollar exchange rate that devalued the won by 100 percent. This drastic devaluation contributed to absorbing the import premiums caused by quantitative controls (Kwon, 1991). This progress was undermined, however, as macroeconomic policy remained expansionary and inflation persisted. Exports were not stimulated as had been expected.

During 1964-1965, the government made its second attempt to unify exchange rates by again raising the official won-to-dollar rate sharply. The rate was from 130 won to 256 won per US$, which reduced inflation pressure. By March 1965, the government had implemented a floating, unified exchange rate policy to maintain real exchange rate stability. Since then, a policy of continual devaluations has been followed with the objective of moving from a fixed to a unified floating exchange rate system.

In 1971, the won devalued by 20 percent in consideration of the weighted percentage difference in inflation rates between Korea and her major trading partners. In January 1980, Korea devalued her currency by 20 percent again. A new exchange rate regime was adopted in February 1980. Under the new

Table 3. Estimates of Ratio of Net Subsidies for Per Dollar Export to Exchange Rate 58-83 (Annual Averages)

Year	*(B) Official Exchange Rate (Won Per US$)*	*(A) Net Export Subsidies (Won) (Export Per US$)*	*Ratio (%) (A/B)*
58	50.0	65.2	130.4
60	62.5	85.1	136.2
61	127.5	23.1	18.1
63	130.0	47.6	36.6
65	265.4	9.9	3.7
67	270.0	20.0	7.4
69	288.2	18.4	6.4
71	347.7	22.8	6.6
73	398.3	8.7	2.2
75	484.0	12.9	2.7
77	484.0	12.3	1.9
79	484.0	11.0	2.3
81	686.0	15.0	2.2
83	781.2	0.0	0.0

Source: Kim, Kwang Suk, 1991

system, the dollar exchange rates were mainly determined by movements of the exchange rates of major trading partners. This system has allowed for more flexible management of the exchange rate to maintain external competitiveness (Kwon, 1991). As a result of those reforms, the exchange rate system facilitated greatly the growth of export.

C. Trade Liberalization Progress

There were three principle stages in South Korea's trade liberalization program. The first was marked by the devaluation of the Won and associated export liberalization in 1961. The second, in 1965-1967, began with a further devaluation accompanied by a shift from quantitative restrictions on imports to tariffs. The third, in 1978-79, again involved import liberalization from QRs and reduction in tariffs.

The devaluation of the won was the cornerstone of the liberalization program of 1961. The official exchange rate was raised from 62.5 won per US$ to 127.5 won per US$. The devaluation permitted the government to abolish its foreign exchange tax and to reduce the average rate of import tariffs actually paid. On the export side, subsidies were reduced greatly.

The reforms of 1965-1967 were more comprehensive. The won was again devalued to offset the inflation that had occurred since 1961. More systematically than in 1961, a conversion was made from quantitative restrictions on imports to tariffs. Relatedly, the former list of commodities that could be imported was replaced by a list of commodities that could not be imported.

The two liberalization efforts of the 1960s, while of some effectiveness in promoting trade, did not achieve sustainable results. Subsequent problems with international payments imbalances, domestic inflation, and recession prompted the government to retrogress in its liberalization policies. Finally in 1978-79, a trade liberalization program was implemented and successfully sustained (Kim 1991).

The third efforts have some difference from first two. Besides the relaxing QRs again, the main efforts devoted in reducing tariffs and promoting liberalization as a long-run policy. The advanced notice system was adopted for those. It usually announced some intentions, for example, loosening QRs or reducing tariffs, one to four years prior to taking action in order to give domestic firms adequate time to adjust. According to Kim (1991), this may be the reason for success.

The liberalization progress must make many efforts. The third effort is an inevitable outcome of first two. It is important for taking every step liberalization as a part of a strategy of promoting economic development in long-run.

II. LIBERALIZING TRADE IN CHINA: LESSONS FROM SOUTH KOREA

An understanding of the existing system of Chinese foreign trade is necessary to infer any lessons from South Korea. China had a centrally planned economy prior to the recent economic reforms. Under central planning, foreign trade was strictly controlled by the government. According to the World Bank, the degree of trade liberalization achieved by China in the mid-1980s was similar to that characterizing South Korea prior to 1962. In this stage, high tariffs, heavy protection, and administrative restrictions on trade prevail.

To reach the next stage of liberalization will require exchange rate adjustment, incentives to promote exports, more selectivity in import protection, and a reduction in administrative controls on trade. China's transition is more difficult than that of South Korea because China's domestic economy must undergo greater change to become more reliant on markets that can in turn be integrated with the rest of the world. Since the initiation of reforms in 1978, the market-oriented component of China's economy has expanded through the growth of private and collective enterprises, foreign joint ventures, and state enterprises operating under the contract responsibility system. Foreign trade liberalization can proceed in concert with the development of domestic markets. Each can benefit from the other.

A. China's Foreign Trade Regime

As the traditional planned economy is gradually replaced by the market economy, administrative controls over foreign trade must also be relaxed. Strict and broad administrative controls are the principal manner in which China's international trade flows have been managed.

China's foreign trade is conducted by state-owned monopolies that block direct contact between Chinese enterprises and the international marketplace. Under this system, Chinese firms are denied access to market information, new technologies, and new products. Moreover, many inefficient enterprises are protected from competitive pressure. The full potential benefits of foreign trade are therefore not transmitted to the domestic economy.

Although the South Korean Government intervened in foreign trade to great extent, it did not exert monopoly power over exports and imports as the Chinese Government has. The South Koreans also have some big trading companies. The top ten companies handled 13.6 percent of Korea's exports (1975) and by 1983 the share of that had increased to 51.3 percent. The Korean government regularly raised the minimum export value requirement for them. So, if some of them had poor performance and could not get those levels, they will lose their positions and also lose their benefits, such as subsidies linked with their exports and favorable credits from government (Song 1990). In this way, the trading companies compete with each other to provide good services in assisting with transactions and communications. Therefore, the intervention with regard to export virtually was stimulative and through the competition.

The first step in China's trade liberalization should be a change from monopoly trading companies to competitive entry into international markets. Enterprises should have a choice not only among trading companies, but to engage directly in business with foreign firms. This step will contribute to greater productive efficiency within enterprises and to the growth of the economy as a whole.

B. Quantitative Restrictions on Imports

The import is controlled by the central planner in China. The program of import is adopted to regulate most imports from abroad. This system correspond to the administrative control over foreign trade.

The import applications should be examined in detail by government. If they can get the approval, they automatically get the foreign exchange for imports. About 30-40 percent of imports are provided with local governments' or the firm's own foreign exchange. So they are not directly controlled by central planners' program, but regulated by the import license (World Bank 1986).

Due to such imports not belonging to the central import plan, they are restricted specially. In order to import such restricted items, the firms who want to import must apply for import licenses in advance. Officially, there are now about 45 items that can be imported under license. It is difficult to get the license for those import items, because the licenses are issued as the quota and the limitation is strict. So, unlike South Korea, nothing falls into the automatic approval category, with the limited exception of some items imported under compensation trade or material processing arrangements.

One of the aims of China's quantitative restrictions is to prevent trade imbalances. The domestic demand for some imported goods exceeds the supply at current domestic prices even though domestic prices are inflated by high tariffs. While import licensing reduces the foreign exchange outflow that would otherwise follow from this disequilibrium, the shortage situation results in unproductive rent-seeking activity. The rents at present go to monopoly suppliers of scarce imported goods. A change from quantitative restrictions to tariffs would have the combined advantages of reducing rent-seeking behavior and increasing government revenues.

In South Korea, imports receiving automatic approval reached 60.4 percent of total imports in 1967, and 95.2 percent in 1988 (Kim 1991). The general trend has been toward a reliance on tariffs rather than quantitative restrictions to regulate imports.

If China is to become a member of GATT, quantitative restrictions will need to be eliminated. Korea began its liberalization by emphasizing:

1. domestic products already competitive on international markets;
2. items whose liberalization might contribute to domestic price stabilization;
3. items that could contribute to greater energy efficiency;
4. basic raw materials;
5. items on which basic tariffs exceeded 50%;
6. items with a ratio of domestic wholesale price to import price exceeding 500 won to the US dollar, given an official exchange rate of 270:1 (Kim 1991).

With the elimination of quantitative restrictions begun in 1978, the Korean government adopted a policy of advanced notice. The key concern is to avoid exposing infant industries to overly destructive competition to quickly. The Korean government played an active role in assisting domestic firms to achieve economies of scale by concentrating financial resources in large companies. Korea's success in this area may be useful for China.

C. Tariffs

Tariff rates in China range from 0 percent to a relatively high 200 percent. Tariffs are generally higher on luxury items than on necessities. The World Bank (1986) estimated China's average legal tariff rate (unweighted) at 38.4 percent in 1986. The actual tariff rate is significantly less than this at 16.3 percent due to the widespread use of exemptions. The coefficient of variation in tariffs across goods is about 0.73. These numbers are similar to those observed in South Korea in 1962.

In Korea's trade liberalization, the average legal tariff rate declined very slowly over time, as did the variation among tariff rates. The slow decline was due to the increase relative reliance on tariffs as opposed to quotas and to the deliberate decision to protect infant industries as they gradually gained in competitiveness.

High tariffs must be cut in order to stimulate less efficient enterprises to improve productivity, but reducing protection too quickly could be unnecessarily destructive to industries with long-run potential for viability. The advanced notice system is also useful for tariff cutting in China. The timing of tariff reductions is important. If tariffs are lowered gradually, domestic prices can be brought into line with world prices at a pace that will encourage cost-cutting and innovation while yet not forcing existing enterprises out of business.

D. Exports and the Exchange Rate

Under the current trade system in China, the revenues of export producers are determined by domestic rather than world prices. The result is similar to that in South Korea, where the multiple exchange rate system was adopted from the late 1950's to early 1960's and the exchange rate varied according to the different pattern of export and import (World Bank 1986).

In Korea, it took about five years to complete the transition from a multiple exchange rate system to a unified floating exchange rate system. From then, because the exchange rate was allowed to float, the won depreciated during the period of continuing domestic inflation, the government could gradually reduce the subsidies for export and exports were maintained.

In China, before the liberalization of domestic market, the exchange rate is often distorted, even though there is not the multiple exchange rate as South Korea had. It can be said that the exchange rate, as a tool of adjustment for balance of payment, has not fully exerted its role yet. But as a stimulative tool for export it can play a part of promoting export.

China has adopted a dual exchange rate system as part of its reform program. The official exchange rate is pegged to the U.S. dollar. A second exchange rate is determined in foreign exchange transaction centers in response to market forces.

China has afforded a role in the transition to supplementary foreign exchange markets on which exchange rates float freely but to which access is limited. Enterprises or other agents that receive the necessary permission may exchange export earnings to domestic currency at a more favorable rate in these "swap" centers. Although the rate is determined by demand and supply, it does not truly reflect the scarcity value of foreign exchange given the limits on access to the swap centers. Nevertheless, the swap center rate serves as a useful reference for guiding adjustments in the official exchange rate.

The principal incentive used in China to encourage exports is to allow exporting enterprises to retain a portion of their foreign exchange earnings. The retention rate is set generally at 12.5 percent (Yang 1989). Retained foreign exchange can be converted to Renminbi in the swap centers. This is advantageous to the exporting enterprises. Raising the retention rate would not only stimulate growth of exports in existing product categories but expand the range of exports to products that do not yield profits in Rmb terms at the official exchange rate. Raising the retention rate should therefore be given high priority in future reforms.

III. CONCLUSIONS

Theory suggests and experience confirms that a trade system based on administratively controlled exports and imports is less efficient than one relying on tariffs to guide decentralized decision-making, and that this system in turn is less efficient than one in which the exchange rate alone guides trade decisions. During a transition from the first type of system to the second to the third, quantity restrictions are gradually eliminated, the tariffs will be substituted for QRs at first and then gradually reduced, and the exchange rate will play more and more roles. South Korea has just such experience. China is going along with such progress of liberalization, so following this transition step-by-step, is very important.

It is valuable to study the process of trade liberalization in South Korea. From that we can see how to liberalize the foreign trade, including how to take main steps and how long every reform will take to be effected and continued. Although there are some common things between China and South Korea, the schedule of liberalization in South Korea would not be suitable well for China. The key is whether the effects and disturbances brought by liberalization could be receptive in Chinese economy. If it can not bear that, the progress of liberalization would be slowed down, otherwise the progress would be sped up.

Trade liberalization must seek to combine more efficient microeconomic choices with a stable macroeconomic environment. Inevitably however, liberalization programs aimed at achieving greater microeconomic efficiency pose risks to macroeconomic stability. Macroeconomic policy instruments must be developed to maintain stability. South Korea similarly had problems with instability following from liberalization, such as inflation, imbalance of payment and so on. To minimize such disturbances in China, policy-makers must be careful to choose the appropriate degree of liberalization and to time new reforms judiciously. In this way, a stable environment can be maintained, and the reform program can be continued.

With respect to trade liberalization, it is important to adjust the trade environment at a pace commensurate with the capacity of Chinese enterprises to respond to more competitive circumstances. Tariffs and other protective barriers should be relaxed according to the competitive capacity of domestic infant industries.

ACKNOWLEDGMENT

I would like to thank Professor Calla Wiemer, University of Hawaii. She was especially helpful to me.

REFERENCES

Das, Dilip K. (1992). *Korean Economic Dynamism*, pp. 69-73, 154. London: Macmillan.

Kim, Kwang Suk. (1991). Korea. In Michael Michaely eds., *Liberalizing Foreign Trade: The Experience of Korea, the Philippines, and Singapore*, pp. 31-50. Cambridge, MA: Basil Blackwell.

Kwon, Jane K. ed. (1991). *Korean Economic Development*, pp. 79-85. New York: Greenwood Press.

Song, Byung-Nak. (1990). *The Rise of the Korean Economy*. Pp. 98-100 Oxford University Press.

World Bank. (1986). *China: External Trade and Capital*, p. 15, 60, 92-94, 108-112, 119-120. Beijing: Zhongguo Caizheng Jingji Chubanshe. (Chinese version).

Yang, Liping, eds. (1989). *Encyclopedia of Foreign Trade*. p. 326. Shanghai: Fudan University Press (In Chinese).

BRUNEI DARUSSALAM:
THE STATE OF THE ECONOMY

Hajjah Rosni Haji Tungkat

I. INTRODUCTION

Brunei Darussalam is a Malay Islamic Monarchy situated on the north-west coast of the Island of Borneo, between east longitudes 114 23' and 115 23' and between north latitudes 4 and 5, 5' covering a total area of 2,226 square miles (5,765 sq. km) and a coastline running for 100 miles (161 km). It is covered mainly by primary and secondary tropical rain forests with only a narrow coastal strip being cultivated. It has a common border with Sarawak, one of the two states of East Malaysia, which also divides Brunei Darussalam into two parts.

Administratively Brunei Darussalam is divided into four districts namely Brunei/Muara District, Belait District, Tutong District and Temburong, the last being the district cut-off from the rest of the country by Sarawak and is only accessible by boat.

Brunei Darussalam has a tropical climate, characterized by high temperature, high humidity and high rainfall. The temperature normally ranges

Research in Asian Economic Studies, Volume 6, pages 267-273.

ISBN: 1-55938-918-4

between 73 F (23 C) and 89 F (31 C) and annual rainfall between 110 inches in the lowland areas to 150 inches in many parts of the interior.

Brunei Darussalam resumed full independence from Great Britain on January 1, 1984. Prior to that, the country was known only as BRUNEI and was a British Protectorate with the Sultan as Head of State and a British Commissioner to advise on external affairs.

On resumption of its status as a fully independent sovereign state on January 1, 1984, BRUNEI DARUSSALAM became more active in international affairs. The new nation became the 49th member of the COMMONWEALTH on the same date. She joined the Association of South East Asian Nation (ASEAN) on January 7, 1984 as its 6th Member, the Organization of Islamic Conference (OIC) on January 15, 1984 as its 45th Member and the United Nations Organization (UN) on September 21, 1984 as its 159th Member.

Since its independence on January 1, 1984, Brunei Darussalam has adopted the Ministerial System of Government. As well as being the Head of State, His Majesty the Sultan is also the Prime Minister and the Defense Minister.

II. ECONOMY

Brunei Darussalam's economy is highly dominated by the oil and gas sector and is highly susceptible to the changes in the current world oil situation. In the seventies, when prices of oil kept increasing, Brunei Darussalam benefitted and recorded growth around 12.0 percent per annum. However with the recent drop in oil prices and the worsening world economic condition, Brunei Darussalam's economy suffered a setback.

In 1991, the economy grew at 3.6 percent while in 1992 it declined slightly and grew at a negative rate of 1.1 percent. However in 1993, the economy picked up a bit and grew at 0.5 percent while in 1994, the economy grew by 1.8 percent and predicted to grow by 2.0 percent in 1995. In 1991, oil and gas accounted for 63 percent of the Gross Domestic Product, about 90 percent of the Government Revenue and virtually all the exports of the country. In 1992 the Gross Domestic Product at constant prices was estimated to be B$3698 million of which contribution from oil and gas was estimated to be B$2201 million. Agriculture, forestry and fishery accounted for only about 1.7 percent of the total whilst manufacturing only contributed about 1.8 percent. Construction, which used to be the second largest industry after oil and gas contributed 2.8 percent.

The current Sixth National Development Plan 1991-1995 now enters its fifth and final year. During the formulation of the Plan, it was forecast that the price of oil would remain unfavorable. This unfavorable condition and other challenges, typically faced by a developing country, have set the tone for the objectives and policy direction of the current Plan which are basically to diversify and maximize the economic utilization of the country's natural resources, widen the economic base and create a favorable climate for industries, improve facilities for industrial development and to accelerate the development of human resources.

III. POPULATION

The population of Brunei Darussalam in 1991 (Census), is around 260,482 persons of which 137,534 or 52.8 percent are male and 122.948 or 47.2 percent are female, with an annual increase of 3.0 percent over the previous year. About 170,107 persons or 65.3 percent of the population live in the Brunei/Muara District, 20.3 percent in Belait, 11.4 percent in Tutong and 3 percent live in Temburong.

The population of Brunei Darussalam is a young population with the median age at 21.5 years. 89,757 or 35 percent of the population are below 15 years old, 55,648 or about 21 percent of which aged between 5-14.

The literacy rate of total population aged 9 years and over is 89.2 percent. Out of the total literate population, 55.5 percent are male and female 44.5 percent.

About 67 percent of the population is made up of the Malay race, other indigenous population accounts for 6 percent, Chinese 15.5 percent and other races which include the Indians, Europeans, Japanese, Koreans, Australians, Philippines, Thais, Americans, and so forth, make up the remaining 11.5 percent of the population.

Malay is the official language, but English is widely spoken. The official religion is Islam, but other religions are allowed to be practiced in Brunei Darussalam.

IV. LABOR FORCE & UNEMPLOYMENT

In general, although the economy does not grow as fast as we have expected, the labor market could be considered as heated, with excess demand for all categories of labor (Table 1). The private sector, in particular, suffers from a persistent shortage of local skilled and unskilled labor and consequently depends on immigrants workers. This is supported by the high growth in the services industry and, to a lesser extent, by the growth in the construction industry and in other sectors. The result of the 1991 Population Census showed that the labor force of that year was heavily made up of immigrant workers coming principally from ASEAN, in particular Thailand, Philippines and Malaysia. Of the total 106,746 thousand employed in 1991, 44.0 thousand

Table 1. Labor Force

(Thousand)

	1981 Census	*1991 Census*
1. Local Labour Force	45.9	61.9
a) Male	32.7	39.8
b) Female	13.2	22.1
1.1 Citizen	37.8	54.6
a) Male	26.9	34.7
b) Female	10.9	19.9
1.2 Permanent Residents	8.1	7.3
a) Male	5.8	5.1
b) Female	2.3	2.2
2. Temporary Residents	24.8	44.0
a) Male	21.1	32.0
b) Female	3.6	12.0
Total	70.7	106.7

persons or 41.2 percent were guest workers. This represents an increase of 23.0 percent from the last Population Census conducted in 1981. The rate of female participation was 38.7 percent in 1991 as compared to 31.3 percent in 1981, representing an increase of 7.4 percent. This reflects government policy to promote equal job opportunities for females. The rate of male participation, on the other hand, was lower in 1991 than in 1981, declining from 83.1 percent to 80.0 percent. This was mainly due to the slowing down in the construction activities which engage a large number of foreign male workers. To some extent, this is due to the large share of the labor force absorbed by the public sector and the size of which had expanded rapidly due to the creation of new ministries and departments since independence in 1984.

Consequently, one would assume that under this condition, the country would be free from unemployment. This is not so. On the contrary, the unemployment situation had worsened and the figures had doubled that of the Population Census conducted in 1981. The 1991 Population Census recorded a total of 5,209 unemployed or 4.7 percent as compared to the 2,566 or 3.6 percent in 1981 (Table 2). 73.3 percent of those unemployed were in the age group of 15-24. Coherent policies to overcome further youth unemployment are therefore of great urgency, in particular, the necessity to instill the right attitude towards job seeking and nation-building as it is ironic to have a large level of unemployment in a country such as Brunei Darussalam. In addition, producing the right manpower to ease the shortage of technicians, skilled and semi-skilled labor should be of top priority. Perhaps to implement the National Training Scheme could be the first step towards solving the problem of labor shortage in the country.

Table 2. Unemployment by Residential Status and Sex, 1981 & 1991

		Economically Active			*Unemployed*		
		Population		*Number*			*Percentage*
Category		*1981*	*1991*	*1981*	*1991*	*1981*	*1991*
Citizens	M	26,882	36,849	759	2,131	2.8	5.8
	F	10,934	21,887	1,188	2,010	10.9	9.3
	T	37,816	58,736	1,947	4,141	5.1	7.1
Permanent	M	5,791	5,402	143	315	2.5	5.8
	F	2,327	2,484	111	207	4.8	8.4
	T	8,118	7,866	254	548	3.1	6.6
Temporary	M	21,200	32,832	220	299	1.0	0.9
Residents	F	3,619	12,521	145	247	4.0	2.0
& Others	T	24,819	45,353	365	546	1.5	1.2
Total	M	53,873	75,083	1,122	2,745	2.1	3.7
	F	16,880	36,872	1,444	2,464	8.6	6.7
	T	70,753	111,955	2,566	5,209	3.6	4.7

Source: 1981 & 1991 Population Census.

V. INFLATION

Since virtually all of Brunei Darussalam's needs, including 80 percent of food requirements, are imported, an increase in domestic prices is largely due to imported inflation. The inflation rate for the year 1991 to 1994 was 1.6 percent 1.3, 4.3 percent and 2.4 percent respectively. Low prices of world commodities and stiff competition among retailing outlets are the main reasons for the low rate of inflation enjoyed by Brunei Darussalam. However, as world prices of commodities start to recover, its impact will be felt in the near future and the rate of inflation is expected to be higher.

VI. GOVERNMENT REVENUE AND EXPENDITURE

The government spending in 1991 was approximately $2,750 million, which was 1.1 percent lower than the previous year spending of $2791 million. However in 1992 and 1993 the government spending increased significantly by to $3057 million and $3230 million respectively.

The major portion of the government income is derived from dividends, royalties, taxes on oil and gas industry. Income tax from other sectors and imports duties are small in terms of total annual revenue. However, due to the weak price of oil, the government revenue continues to decline further from

Table 3. Imports, Total Exports and Balance of Trade

Year	*Total Exports(1)*	*Imports*	*Total External Trade*	*Balance of Trade*
1982	8,153,258,051	1,571,652,308	9,724,910,362	6,581,605,746
1983	7,170,675,666	1,542,170,903	8,712,846,569	5,628,504,763
1984	6,813,939,833	1,331,397,723	8,145,437,556	5,482,442,110
1985	6,532,888,162	1,348,387,618	7,881,275,780	5,184,500,544
1986	3,990,101,420	1,456,960,944	5,447,062,364	2,533,140,475
1987	4,005,605,692	1,350,183,131	5,355,788,823	2,655,422,561
1988	3,436,446,637	1,497,301,689	4,933,748,326	1,939,144,948
1989	3,672,610,393	1,675,006,102	5,347,616,495	1,997,604,291
1990	4,010,146,988	1,813,161,523	5,823,308,511	2,196,985,465
1991	4,266,965,616	1,922, 383,495	6,189,349,111	2,344,582,121
1992*	3,863,200,000	1,916,800,000	5,780,000,000	1,946,400,000
1993*	3,684,500,000	2,012,500,000	5,697,100,000	1,671,900,000
1994*	3,383,200,000	2,497,000,000	5,880,200,000	886,200,000

Notes: *Preliminary Estimates.
1. Total exports = exports + re-exports

$2706 million in 1990 to $2686 million, $2730 million, in 1991, and $3416 million 1992 and 1993 respectively.

VII. EXTERNAL TRADE

After a sharp decline in the external trade in 1988, it has improved since then. The total value of exports of $3463.4 million in 1988 has increased by 6.6 percent to $3693.5 million in 1989 and further increased by 16.9 percent to $4316.5 million in 1990, but in 1991 it declined slightly by 0.5 percent to $4266.9 million. It declined further to $3863.2 million and $3684.5 million in 1992 and 1993 respectively.

The total value of imports remained almost stagnant for the period of 1989 to 1993. Due to the appreciation of the yen, value of imports for the year 1991 were estimated to be $1922.4 million or 6.0 percent higher than that of the previous year, while that of and 1992 1993 were $1916.8 million and $2012.6 million respectively.

With the decrease in the estimated value of exports in 1989 and increase in the value of imports, the balance of trade, although still favorable, shows a decline of 2.1 percent from $2012.12 million in 1988 to $1970.74 million in 1989. However, in 1990, the balance of trade increased due to the increase in the value of the exports to $4010.1 million and increased further by 6.4 percent to $4267 million in 1991 but decreased slightly by 9.5 percent to $3863.2 million in 1992.

The key commodities imported into Brunei Darussalam during the year 1991 and 1992 are not much different in order of magnitude, there were: Machinery and Transport equipment (36.3%), Manufactured goods (29.3%), Food (12.6%) and Chemicals (6.3%).

As mentioned earlier, exports during the year 1991 fell by 0.6 percent, which is still dominated by 'Mineral Fuels', the value of exports of crude oil, petroleum products, liquefied natural gas. They constituted 98.8 percent of all commodities exported. The contribution of other commodities exported were almost negligible. However, at present there are four garment manufacturing companies, which make garments a new export commodity for Brunei Darussalam. The scope for increase in the export from Brunei Darussalam is plentiful in spite of textile quotas being levied on traditional textile exporters by EEC and the United States.

THAILAND'S TRADE IN SERVICES WITH THE ASIA-PACIFIC REGION

Suthiphand Chirathivat

I. GENERAL FRAMEWORK OF THAILAND'S TRADE IN SERVICES

The service sector is recognized as playing an important role in Thailand's recent economic experiences. The growth of this sector is closely related to a number of macroeconomic aspects in the national economy such as overall growth, income distribution, and employment. If the services are related to the global economy, they can contribute to improve Thailand's trade performance. In international trade although Thailand's trade in services is less apparent in the external economy as compared to trade in goods, its importance has been observed with the trend of an overall change of the external economy of Thailand.

Looking from this prospective, Thailand's international trade in services constitutes around one-fourth of the country's international trade in goods. And the prospects are considered bright as several factors are responsible for the increasing amount of international activities of Thailand's service sector with the word economy. The overall growth of the national economy,

Research in Asian Economic Studies, Volume 6, pages 275-304.

ISBN: 1-55938-918-4

its inter-linkage with the Asian-Pacific region, the rise of technological developments in data processing and telecommunication activities, are among several important factors contributing to this change.[1]

As far as to support the above mentioned statement, the expansion of the services trade of Thailand is almost as fast as the one of merchandise trade. It ranks second in ASEAN in terms of exports after Singapore. About half of these receipts are generated by travel, especially tourist inflow into Thailand. A strong dependence on revenue from tourists is not necessarily bad for Thailand, as in fact, a number of Asian countries have also similar dependencies upon a particular sector of services: South Korea for construction, the Philippines for labor, Singapore for the infrastructural development and technology in telecommunications and transportations. Thailand, as many other countries, has of course, the possibility to develop the particular sector in which she is in the position to offer her best comparative advantage. However she can not solely be dependent on this particular sector along during her future course of development.

In fact, a number of different sectors of services of Thailand have now become well connected and developed with the present trend of the world economy. Some firms are concerned with the services offered at the international level and have invited foreign participation in the development of various sub-sectors such as, finance, transportation, telecommunications, travel, construction, wholesale and retail trade.[2] Other national firms are more preoccupied with their own building up of strength to compete more fiercely with joint venture firms.

With this present trend, the macroeconomic core of government policies has varied much in different sub-sectors, Thus allowing microeconomic adaptation to optimize each operation differently. For instance, the tourist sector had greatly opened, allowing the private sector to operate quite freely, while telecommunications, transportations, banking and insurance for example which used to be tightly regulated, have started to become more liberalized. Policy directions, in connection with the development of different sub-sectors, in relation to the global economy, will be important in these regards, especially the service discussion within the GATT Uruguay Round. The global trend seems to suggest that Thailand has to prepare well to liberalize most of these sub-sectors in the longer run. The improvement of competitiveness strength is also the key for the successful development upon which both the government and business community should work together.

Apart from addressing different issues, related to trade in services, this paper seeks to address, in particular, Thailand's trade in services with the Asian-Pacific region. Because of the nature and the low tradibility that services seems to suggest when compared to goods,[3] cross-border services are confined very much within the special condition. Thus, regional proximities seem to be an important criteria for the future growth of trade in services. And for this reason,

Table 1. Service Production in Gross Domestic Products at 1972 Prices (million baht)

Year	*GDP*	*Agriculture*	*Manufacturing*	*Service*	*Service/GDP*
1970	155,694	42,064	29,345	84,285	54,14
1975	204,428	50,700	44,972	108,756	53.2
1980	299,472	61,700	72,901	164,801	53.03
1985	394,113	78,539	91,364	224,210	56.89
1989	574,155	92,386	152,362	329,447	57.37
1990	631,610	90,711	174,181	366,718	58.06

Source: National Accounts Division, National Economic and Social Development Board.

demand for trade in services is generally characterized by regionalization rather than globalization, especially for those non-factor services such as tourism, transportation, and telecommunications which will be shown in this paper. This study is limited in such a way that it will not cover trade in services to capital investment in services which would cover also human and infrastructural investment, although the links between the two areas can not be denied in terms of their importance.

II. RECENT PATTERN OF THAILAND'S TRADE IN SERVICES

The importance of the service sector is generally know through the macroeconomic data conceptualized by the U.N. statistics.[4] With this concept, Thailand's service share in gross domestic products has increased from about 54 percent in 1970 to about 58 percent in 1990 (see Table 1). Over these two decades, the service sector as well as the manufacturing sector (including mining and quarrying) has increased around 5 times while GDP in agriculture has increased only about two times. There is not doubt that the share of the agricultural sector has decreased its importance in GDP's contribution.[5]

On the other hand, international trade in services of an economy is generally done through the coverage of international service proposed by IMF. It is mainly today that most countries' trade in services are classified by this method. However, official links between the domestic and international classification has been established up to date. This is why the analysis of trade in services is generally more complex when one would like to extend its impact on the rest of the economy. The scope of Thailand's trade in services overall, in this analysis, is then done mainly through the balance of payments recorded by the Bank of Thailand.

In general, one can say that the service account of Thailand has continuously helped to contribute to lessen the overall current account deficit of the country. In 1987, this positive contribution represents a figure of almost 29 billion baht.

Table 2. Services and the Balance of Trade 1987-1991 (billion baht)

	1987	*1988*	*1989*	*1990*	*1991*
Merchandise:					
1. Exports (f.o.b).	298.10	399.17	509.92	583.21	720.54
2. Imports (c.i.f).	341.68	449.24	647.80	832.60	963.80
3. Non-monetary gold import	0.55	1.18	2.30	5.74	4.29
4. Merchandise Deficit	44.13	101.25	140.18	2555.14	247.54
Service:					
1. Total Services Receipts	107.19	150.34	180.97	216.72	243.06
1.1 Freight and insurance of merchandise	10.05	11.60	11.56	11.89	15.21
1.2 Other transportation	8.44	13.58	16.12	22.25	22.97
1.3 Travel	50.02	78.86	96.39	110.57	115.70
1.4 Investment income	6.65	9.36	16.60	27.76	32.42
1.5 Government, n.i.e.	3.19	3.28	3.58	3.26	3.57
1.6 Other Services of which:	28.84	33.66	36.72	41.00	53.19
Workers, remittance	21.60	23.44	24.24	24.91	25.70
2. Total Service Payments	78.51	96.06	112.08	153.20	195.72
2.1 Freight and insurance on merchandise	5.13	7.26	9.40	9.33	12.49
2.2 Other transportation	3.78	4.72	6.07	8.21	9.78
2.3 Travel	9.90	15.25	19.20	36.53	48.50
2.4 Investment income	48.09	53.15	57.78	69.19	83.95
2.5 Government, n.i.e.	2.69	2.66	3.12	3.81	4.74
2.6 Other Services	8.92	13.02	16.50	26.12	36.26
3. Net Services	28.68	54.28	68.90	63.53	47.34
Net goods and services deficit	15.45	46.97	71.28	191.61	200.20

Source: Bank of Thailand.

And its size has increased to 47 billion baht in 1990. (see Table 2). Such an amount of service surplus is not enough to offset the overall figure of Thailand's trade deficit during the same period which has increased rapidly from 44 billion Baht in 1987 to 248 billion baht in 1991.[6] (see Table 2).

When considering the receipts of Thailand's trade in services, three of the most important sub-sectors are travel, investment income and workers' remittance. Travel, especially tourism, has now contributed almost 5 billion US dollars or almost half of the total receipt. The investment income, on the other hand, has also become more important especially between 1987 and 1991. The workers' remittance, which used to be important in the past, has remained quite constant during this period. Also, it is noticeable that sub-sectors' categories such as other transportation and other services have become more important for Thailand resulting from the income from the national airline that is, Thai International and telecommunications.

The payments of Thailand's trade in services; on the other hand, have centered around three sub-sectors: investment income, travel and other services. The investment income, the most important category, has increased rapidly from 48 billion baht in 1987 to 84 billion baht in 1991. The payments of travel and other services have also increased significantly from around 10 and 9 billion baht in 1987 to around 49 and 36 billion baht, respectively, in 1991. The payment increases of various sub-sectors are mainly due the rapid growth of the Thai economy that requires the demand for foreign trade in services which in itself is derived mainly from the rapid income expansion.

Against this background, the role of trade in services will continue to be related to the various economic activities within Thailand, with the degree of foreign participation varying from one sub-sector to another. However, overall, these sub-sectors will be more and more liberalized and better connected through the world economy. Travel is one of the sub-sectors that will increase by fluctuation due to difficulties at home and abroad. On the other hand, some of the other sub-sectors related to infrastructural development like, transportation, telecommunications, construction and insurance would be telecommunication come relatively larger with higher degrees of foreign involvement.[7]

From these perspectives, various sub-sectors of trade in services would contribute to Thailand's future economic development in different ways. For example, telecommunications are tremendously important for the flow of information. Telecommunications are, from this sense, not only an important trade issue, such as the demand for and the supply of telecommunications, but also an important infrastructural issue due to its importance as to facilitate the economic growth. Transportation, on the other hand, is, in general, helping the flows of people and goods. Its future depends very much on the development and expansion of infrastructure to support its growth. And finally, travel mainly in terms of tourism will most likely continue to produce substantial earnings to the country, especially if major problems related to this sub-sector will be better unregulated and guided with control.

III. LINKAGES OF THAILAND'S TRADE IN SERVICES WITH THE ASIAN-PACIFIC REGION

This section focuses on the increasing importance of the Asian-Pacific region in Thailand's trade in services. In terms of share of trade in services among Asian-Pacific countries, Thailand now has had 1.4 percent for the exports and 1.2 percent for the imports between 1987-89. The combined figure would be around half of Singapore's figure, similar to Malaysia and Indonesia,[8] and more important than the Philippines.

It is clear, in the case of Thailand that her service exports have greatly improved their share among the Asian-Pacific countries during 1980's. Its share has increased from 1 percent during 1980-1982 to 1.4 percent during 1987-1989 as mentioned earlier-Her annual growth rates, for her trade in services, are among the highest in the Asian-Pacific region and stood at 19.5 percent for

Table 3. Share of Thailand's Trade in Services

(Percentage)

	World			*APEC*			*Non-APEC*		
	1980-82	*1983-86*	*1987-89*	*1980-82*	*1983-86*	*1987-89*	*1980-82*	*1983-86*	*1987-89*
Receipts	2,307.2	3,043.9	5,738.5	1,110.0	1,554.9	3,388.5	1,197.2	1,189.0	2,350.0
1. Freight & Insurance	205.1	302.8	435.3	124.8	167.8	274.0	80.3	135.1	160.4
2. Other Transportation	126.5	141.8	499.0	66.1	97.3	166.4	60.2	44.6	332.5
3. Travel	944.1	1,178.9	2,946.6	460.2	632.6	1,632.3	483.0	546.3	1,314.3
4. Investment Income	251.4	226.6	426.0	137.7	63.2	366.9	443.7	53.7	59.1
5. Government, n.i.e.	107.5	116.7	131.8	45.7	152.2	95.1	61.8	53.5	36.7
6. Other Services	681.7	1,081.0	1,299.8	275.2	29.1	853.0	406.5	628.8	445.9
Payment	2,880.0	3,377.2	5,675.3	1,608.6	1,847.7	3,266.1	1,191.4	1,529.5	2,409.2
1. Freight & Insurance	1,026.6	1,088.6	2,123.2	596.4	547.7	1,087.5	430.2	540.8	1,035.7
2. Other Transportation	98.2	123.5	190.8	65.3	82.8	128.4	32.9	40.7	62.4
3. Travel	257.1	299.1	580.2	194.5	230.3	517.8	62.6	68.8	62.4
4. Investment Income	1,102.7	1,513.9	2,083.6	559.1	740.5	1,052.8	543.6	773.4	580.8
5. Government, n.i.e.	57.9	62.0	111.0	36.7	38.5	70.0	21.2	23.5	41.0
6. Other Services	257.5	290.2	499.4	186.0	202.8	367.6	71.5	87.4	131.8

Note: 1. exclude data of People's Republic of China.
2. include data of People's Republic of China.

Source: Bank of Thailand

Table 4. Share of Thailand's Trade in Services

	World			*APEC 1*			*Non-APE 2*		
	1980-82	*1983-86*	*1987-89*	*1980-82*	*1983-86*	*1987-89*	*1980-82*	*1983-86*	*1987-89*
Receipts	100.0	100.0	100.0	48.1	51.1	59.0	51.9	48.9	41.0
1. Freight & Insurance	100.0	100.0	100.0	60.8	55.4	63.2	39.2	44.6	36.0
2. Other Transportation	100.0	100.0	100.0	84.3	110.8	73.8	15.7	(10.8)	26.0
3. Travel	100.0	100.0	100.0	48.7	53.7	55.4	51.3	46.3	44.0
4. Investment Income	100.0	100.0	100.0	54.8	76.3	36.1	15.2	23.7	13.0
5. Government, n.i.e.	100.0	100.0	100.0	42.5	54.2	72.2	57.5	45.8	27.8
6. Other Services	100.0	100.0	100.0	40.4	41.8	65.6	59.6	58.2	34.0
Payment	100.0	100.0	100.0	57.5	54.7	57.5	42.5	45.3	42.5
1. Freight & Insurance	100.0	100.0	100.0	58.1	50.3	62.0	44.9	49.7	38.0
2. Other Transportation	100.0	100.0	100.0	66.5	57.1	67.3	33.5	32.9	32.7
3. Travel	100.0	100.0	100.0	75.6	77.0	89.2	24.4	23.0	10.8
4. Investment Income	100.0	100.0	100.0	50.7	48.9	72.1	49.3	51.1	27.9
5. Government, n.i.e.	100.0	100.0	100.0	63.4	62.1	63.1	36.6	37.9	36.9
6. Other Services	100.0	100.0	100.0	72.2	69.9	73.6	27.8	30.1	26.4

Note: 1. exclude data of People's Republic of China.
2. include data of People's Republic of China.

Source: Bank of Thailand

exports and 16.5 percent for imports between 1987-1989. As a matter of fact, Thailand's total exports of services now reaches about half the amount that Asian NIEs and could become the highest among ASEAN countries with the exception of Singapore.

By the end of the 1980's, Thailand's trade in services represented one-fourth of the country's trade in goods. The average annual receipt of Thailand's trade in services with the world stood at 5.7 billion U.S. dollars between 1987-1989 while the figure with the Asian-Pacific countries was valued at 3.4 billion U.S. dollars (see Table 3). During the 1980's, it is clear that Thailand had much increased her receipt of trade in services from Asian-Pacific countries, changing from an annual average share of 48.1 percent between 1980-1982 to 59.0 percent between 1987-1989 (see Table 4). The payments of trade in services to the Asian-Pacific region; on the other hand, has not changed much and is the same figure of her share with the Asian-Pacific region of 57.5 percent for both periods, 1980-1982 and 1987-1989.

The important finding here is that the receipt structure of Thailand's trade in services has become closer to that of the rest of the Asian-Pacific region while the payment structure has remained mostly unchanged. This observation would lead to an important message: Thailand's trade in services is growing stronger in relation to the region than to the world. Both receipt and payment of her trade in services with the region shows a strong growth of 21.3 percent and 18.5 percent respectively between 1987-1989. Thus, the stronger growth of trade in services is very much related to the interdependence of economic activities with the region.

In general, when categorized into sub-sectors, it is found that the receipt structure of Thailand's trade in services with the Asian-Pacific is quite similar to that of Thailand with the world with travel taking the share of 48.2 percent between 1987-1989, followed by other services (25.2 percent), freight insurance and other transportation (19.0 percent) (see Table 5). Somehow, the payment structure of Thailand's trade in services with the region is different from that of Thailand with the world: investment income with the region standing at 46 percent,[9] probably due to the role played by the regional financial centers such as Hong Kong and Singapore.

In terms of regional and sub-regional groupings, Thailand's share of receipt in services from ASEAN, EAEC and APEC between 1987-1989 represents 10.7 percent, 35.1 percent and 59.0 percent respectively. While the same share of payment in services to ASEAN, EAEC and APEC between 1987-89 represents 5.0 percent, 30.7 percent and 57.5 percent respectively (see Table 6 and Table 7). This would bring one to the conclusion that Thailand's receipt in services has been much increased, especially due to the Asian NIEs and Japan, and not ASEAN, which is probably due to the currency appreciation resulting in an income increase in those economies making them available with the incremental income to spend more on services with Thailand and other

Table 5. Share of Thailand's Trade in Services

(Percentage)

	World			APEC			Non-APEC		
	1980-82	*1983-86*	*1987-89*	*1980-82*	*1983-86*	*1987-89*	*1980-82*	*1983-86*	*1987-89*
Receipts	100.0	100.0	100.0	100.0	100.0	100.0	100.0	100.0	100.0
1. Freight & Insurance	8.9	9.9	7.6	11.2	10.8	8.1	6.7	9.1	6.0
2. Other Transportation	5.5	4.7	8.7	6.0	6.3	1.9	5.0	3.0	14.0
3. Travel	40.9	38.7	51.3	41.5	10.7	48.2	40.4	36.7	55.0
4. Investment Income	10.9	7.4	7.4	12.4	11.1	10.8	9.5	3.6	2.0
5. Government, n.i.e.	4.7	3.8	2.3	4.1	4.1	2.8	5.2	3.6	4.6
6. Other Services	29.5	35.5	22.7	24.8	29.1	25.2	34.0	42.2	19.0
Payment	100.0	100.0	100.0	100.0	100.0	100.0	100.0	100.0	100.0
1. Freight & Insurance	36.7	32.2	37.4	37.1	29.6	33.3	36.1	35.4	43.0
2. Other Transportation	3.5	3.7	3.4	4.1	4.5	3.9	2.8	2.7	2.6
3. Travel	9.2	8.9	10.2	12.1	12.5	15.9	2.3	4.5	2.6
4. Investment Income	39.4	44.8	36.7	34.8	40.1	32.2	45.6	50.6	24.1
5. Government, n.i.e.	2.1	1.8	2.0	2.3	2.1	2.1	4.8	1.5	1.7
6. Other Services	9.2	8.6	8.8	11.6	11.0	11.3	6.0	5.7	5.5

Note: 1. exclude data of People's Republic of China.
2. include data of People's Republic of China.

Source: Bank of Thailand

Table 6. Thailand's Trade in Services in Relation to APEC Countries

(million US dollars)

	Export			*Import*			*Net*		
	1980-82	*1983-86*	*1987-89*	*1980-82*	*1983-86*	*1987-89*	*1980-82*	*1983-86*	*1987-89*
Total	2,307.2	3,043.9	5,738.5	2,800.0	3,377.2	5,675.3	(492.8)	(333.3)	63.3
APEC-members	1,110.0	1,554.9	3,388.5	1,608.6	1,847.7	3,266.1	(498.6)	(292.9)	56.4
North America	400.9	599.8	1,202.7	923.4	935.2	1,488.9	(522.5)	(235.1)	(286.2)
USA	381.0	573.5	1,139.4	918.8	925.0	1,472.1	(537.8)	(351.5)	(332.7)
Canada	19.9	26.3	63.4	4.6	10.2	16.9	15.3	16.1	46.5
Japan	231.0	310.6	732.3	326.8	471.4	1,108.6	(95.8)	(190.8)	(376.4)
Asian NIEs-3	188.2	223.5	669.1	186.6	221.9	349.6	1.6	1.8	253.5
Hong Kong	113.6	147.0	343.1	170.7	200.2	294.9	(57.0)	(53.1)	48.1
Taiwan	61.5	53.4	276.2	10.8	11.1	29.9	50.7	42.3	180.3
Korea	13.1	23.1	49.8	5.1	10.6	24.8	7.9	12.5	25.0
Asean	238.8	345.9	615.5	159.5	205.7	282.3	79.2	140.1	333.2
Malaysia	102.7	149.9	266.9	12.5	16.3	30.8	90.2	133.6	0.0
Brunai	0.7	2.6	7.9	0.0	0.6	3.9	0.7	2.1	4.0
Singapore	89.8	160.2	288.7	133.7	172.0	232.2	(43.9)	(11.8)	56.5
Phillipines	17.2	11.4	24.8	8.7	8.8	8.8	8.6	2.6	15.9
Indonesia	28.4	21.7	27.2	4.6	4.3	6.5	23.7	17.4	20.7
Oceania	51.2	75.1	168.9	12.3	13.6	36.6	38.9	61.5	132.3
Australia	46.0	68.3	150.5	11.4	12.3	34.6	34.6	55.9	115.9
New Zealand	5.2	6.8	18.4	0.9	1.3	2.0	4.3	5.6	16.3
China									
EAEC1	657.9	880.0	2,016.9	672.9	899.0	1,740.5	(15.0)	(19.0)	210.4
Non-APEC2	1,197.2	1,489.0	2,350.0	1,191.4	1,529.5	2,409.2	5.8	(40.4)	6.8
EC	494.3	442.4	972.3	363.8	385.6	692.2	130.4	56.8	280.1
Others	703.0	1,046.7	1,377.7	827.6	1,143.9	1,717.0	(124.6)	(97.3)	(273.3)

Notes. 1. EEC = ASEAN + Asian NIEs-3 + Japan.
2. Include data of People's Republic of China.

Source. Bank of Thailand

countries of the region. This was in conjunction with the promotion "Visit Thailand Year" in 1987 in which the Tourist Authority of Thailand had led the campaign all throughout the year with its representatives and agents around the world. As a result, these combining factors had helped to push the numbers of travelers to Thailand up to an unprecedented level by the end of the 1980's. Also, visitors from the Asian NIEs have since then started to discover Thailand and to come in greater number.

Finally, for the inflow of foreign direct investment in services, in Thailand, the total value has not been substantial in Thailand until the end of 1987 when this figure started to go up to 472 million U.S. dollars in 1990. Investment

Table 7. Share of Thailand's Trade in Services in Relation to APEC Countries

(Percentage)

	Export			*Import*			*Export*			*Import*		
	1980-82	*1983-86*	*1987-89*	*1980-82*	*1983-86*	*1987-89*	*1980-82*	*1983-86*	*1987-89*	*1980-82*	*1983-86*	*1987-89*
Total	100	100	100	100	100	100						
APEC-members	48.1	51.1	59	57.4	54.7	57.5	100	100	100	100	100	100
North America	17.4	19.7	21	33	27.7	26.2	36.1	38.6	35.5	57.4	59.8	45.6
USA	16.5	18.8	19.9	32.9	27.4	25.9	34.3	36.9	33.6	57.1	59.1	45.1
Canada	0.1	0.1	0.1	0.2	0.3	0.3	1.8	1.7	1.9	0.3	0.6	0.5
Japan	10	10.52	12.8	11.7	14	19.5	20.8	20	21.6	20.3	25.5	33.9
Asian NIEs-3	8.2	7.3	11.7	6.7	6.6	6.2	17	14.4	19.7	11.6	12	10.7
Hong Kong	4.9	4.8	6	6.1	5.9	5.2	10.2	9.5	10.1	10.6	10.8	9
Taiwan	2.7	1.8	4.8	0.4	0.3	0.5	5.5	3.4	8.2	0.7	0.6	0.9
Korea	0.6	0.8	0.9	0.2	0.3	0.4	1.2	1.5	1.5	0.8	0.6	0.9
Asean	10.3	11.4	10.7	5.7	6.1	5	21.5	22.2	18.2	9.9	14.1	6.6
Malaysia	4.4	4.9	4.7	0.4	0.5	0.5	9.2	9.6	7.9	0.8	0.9	0.9
Brunai	0	0.1	0.1	0	0	0.1	0.1	0.2	0.2	0	0	0.1
Singapore	3.9	5.3	5	4.8	5.1	4.1	8.1	10.3	8.5	9.3	9.3	7.1
Phillipines	0.7	0.4	0.4	0.3	0.3	0.2	1.6	0.7	0.7	0.5	0.5	0.3
Indonesia	1.2	0.7	0.5	0.2	0.1	0.1	2.6	1.4	0.8	0.3	0.2	0.2
Oceania	2.2	2.5	2.9	0.4	0.4	0.6	4.6	4.8	5	0.8	0.7	1.1
Australia	2	22	2.6	0.4	0.4	0.6	4.1	4.4	4.4	0.7	0.7	1.1
New Zealand	0.2	0.2	0.3	0	0	0	0.5	0.4	0.5	0.1	0.1	0.1
China												
EAEC[1]	28.5	28.9	35.1	24	26.6	30.7	59.3	56.6	59.5	41.8	48.7	53.3
Non-APEC[2]	51.9	48.9	41	42.6	45.3	42.5						
EC	21.4	14.5	16.9	13	11.4	12.2						
Others	30.5	34.4	24	29.6	33.9	30.3						

Notes: 1. EAEC = ASEAN + Asian NIEs-3 + Japan.
2. Include data of People's Republic of China.

Source: Bank of Thailand

in services are concentrated in three main areas: housing and real estate (270 million U.S. dollars), hotel and restaurant (120.8 million U.S.dollars), transportation and travel (41.8 million U.S. dollars). These figures coincide with the figures obtained from the Board of Investment (BOI) of Thailand where joint-venture projects are mainly originated from the APEC countries, especially from those of Asian NIEs and Japan.

IV. THREE CASES OF SERVICES AND THEIR LINKAGE TO THE ASIAN-PACIFIC REGION

As shown in the case of Thailand, service exports have increased as fast as merchandise exports. The linkage of service exports is also getting stronger with the Asia Pacific region, especially since the 1980's. This can be related to the relationship of the overall growth of the Thai economy and the size of international transactions of services that the country has gone through. The importance of the service sector in output and employment increased with GDP per capita. Of course, Thailand's industrialization in the 1980's means very much for the service sector in terms of capital investment per capita and human capital improvement per sector.

It is, however, that analysis on international transactions on services can only he done mainly through the balance of payments data published by the IMF and these data do not provide a sufficient basis for the estimation of international transactions on services which take place via foreign investments.[10] This has caused this analysis to confine the scope of study within such limits. and to illustrate Thailand's linkage to the Asian-Pacific region, travel, telecommunications and transportation will be the three sub-sectors of non-factor trade in services which will be the subject to the analysis (see Table 8). Their direct contribution to GDP and employment is important for travel to the economic development, in general, for transportation and telecommunications. These sub-sectors of services are, in fact, the backbone of the economic activity and, indeed, its infrastructure.

For telecommunications, for example, it is an important service for the flow the information. Telecommunications are generally considered, not only as an important trade issue, but also as an important infarstructural issue due to its importance as to facilitate the economic growth. Transportation, on the other hand, is, in general, helping the flows of goods and people. Air transportation services have become a good source of foreign exchange earnings from travelers and air freight. Maritime transportation is closely related to the flows of goods between home country and abroad and Thailand is a net, payer for a substantial amount of foreign exchanges. The future of both kinds of transport depends very much on the development and expansion of infrastructure related to them. And finally, travel, as a sector has produced

Table 8. Major Services Sector Revenue and Expenditure of Thailand

	(Million Baht)					Share (%)				
Revenue	*1986*	*1987*	*1988*	*1989*	*1990*	*1986*	*1987*	*1988*	*1989*	*1990*
Telephone[1]	9,757	12,156	15,423	19,230	24,420	0.89	0.97	1.02	1.08	1.19
(TOT and CAT)										
- international Phone	1,929	2,749	4,385	8,009	10,017	0.18	0.22	0.29	0.45	0.49
Tourism	37,321	50,024	78,859	96,386	110,572	3.41	3.99	5.23	5.43	5.39
Labor Remittance	20,900	21,596	23,436	24,213	24,799	1.91	1.72	1.56	1.36	1.21
Air Transport[2]	28,165	35,918	43,108	43,615	51,943	2.57	2.87	2.86	2.74	2.53
(Thai Airways)										
Total Revenue	96,143	119,694	160,825	188,443	211,734	8.78	9.55	10.67	10.61	10.32
GDP Current	1,095,368	1,253,147	1,506,977	1,775,978	2,051,208	100.00	1100.00	100.00	100.00	100.00
Expenditure										
Sea Transport	28,326.00	38,112.60	56,695.90	67,458.70	92,307.60	2.59	3.04	3.76	3.30	4.50

Notes: 1. Domestic and International Revenue. 2. Domestic and International Revenue.

Source: TOT. "Annual Report". (Various issue) CAT. "Annual Report". (Various issue) TAT. "Thailand Tourism Statistical Report". (Various issue). Bank of Thailand.

Table 9. Share of International Tourist Arrivals to Thailand 1980-1990

Countries	*1980*	*1981*	*1982*	*1983*	*1984*	*1985*	*1986*	*1987*	*1988*	*1989*	*1990*
Total	100.00	100.00	100.00	100.00	100.00	100.00	100.00	100.00	100.00	100.00	100.00
Pacific Members	61.29	61.69	N.A.	62.84	64.86	64.78	66.02	67.01	66.56	66.89	67.44
North America	6.50	6.70	6.28	6.70	6.96	7.41	7.22	7.18	6.81	6.83	6.69
USA	5.63	5.79	5.13	5.71	5.86	6.18	6.12	6.10	5.61	5.55	5.39
Canada	0.87	0.91	0.84	0.98	1.10	1.23	1.10	1.07	1.20	1.28	1.30
Japan	13.19	12.19	11.30	10.71	9.73	9.29	9.28	10.04	10.69	11.55	12.31
Asian NIEs-3	10.71	11.38	11.16	10.01	9.15	9.36	11.29	14.03	15.99	18.86	19.51
Hong Kong	7.00	7.72	6.77	5.88	5.41	5.41	5.84	7.22	8.98	8.23	7.22
Korea, Replublic	1.00	1.20	1.29	1.15	1.15	1.13	0.93	0.97	1.51	2.32	2.79
Taiwan	2.70	2.46	3.09	2.97	2.59	2.83	4.51	5.84	5.50	8.31	9.50
Asian	26.62	26.75	N.A.	34.87	34.47	33.18	33.09	31.21	28.30	23.34	22.42
Brunei	N.A.	N.A.	N.A.	N.A.	N.A.	N.A.	N.A.	N.A.	N.A.	N.A.	N.A.
Indonesia	1.81	2.12	N.A.	1.37	1.35	1.36	1.10	0.90	0.84	0.89	0.97
Malaysia	18.26	16.84	23.18	24.89	24.40	22.71	23.17	21.32	19.93	15.30	14.18
Phillipines	1.65	2.39	N.A.	1.63	1.30	1.31	0.99	1.03	1.00	1.11	0.94
Singapore	4.91	5.39	6.36	6.99	7.42	7.79	7.83	7.96	6.53	6.04	6.33
Aceania	4.10	4.24	N.A.	0.00	3.91	4.41	4.04	3.94	3.98	5.22	5.37
Australia	3.64	3.82	3.48	3.40	3.47	4.05	3.67	3.54	3.42	4.55	4.76
New Zealand	0.46	0.42	0.00	0.00	0.44	0.36	0.38	0.40	0.56	0.67	0.61
Hina	0.18	0.43	N.A.	0.56	0.65	1.13	1.10	0.62	0.79	1.09	1.15
EAEC	50.70	50.76	N.A.	56.14	53.99	52.96	54.75	55.89	55.76	54.84	55.39
	38.71	38.31	N.A.	37.16	35.15	35.22	33.98	32.99	33.44	33.11	32.56
Europe	23.61	22.02	N.A.	17.37	17.51	18.67	19.59	20.67	21.41	23.03	23.21

Source: Tourism Authority of Thailand. Thailand Tourism Statistical Report (Various Issues).

substantial earnings to the country with strong prospects. Cooperation and competitiveness in tourism services are becoming vital and are key elements which help to bring about the success of such an industry.

At present, in the Asian-Pacific region, there is a belief,[11] that, in addition to the individual impact of each T (telecommunication, tourism and transportation), one must develop a clear understanding and awareness of the integration of these three subsectors altogether of .both the national and regional level. Although, this section aims at showing each individual T, still the study has kept in mind in what way each T should become integrated together, in the final analysis.

A. Travel and Tourism

This sub-sector is characterized by the traded services in which the consumer moves. With the kind of worldwide development, nowadays, travel has extended easily to visitors from far-away lands who move from place to place. Thailand seems to have a relative advantage in this part of the world in terms of its location, and historical, archeological and cultural aspects. There are also other attractions such as food and sightseeing as well as gift and souvenirs, and day and night life activities. There seem to be various factors contributing to the success of tourism in Thailand.

In fact, Thailand has bėen one of the most rapid tourism developments in Asia. The decade of the 1980's has been considered a period of great success in attracting the international tourist arrivals to Thailand. The number of total tourist arrivals has been tripled from the level of 1.86 million in 1980 to the one of 5.30 million in 1990. The tourist sector has become the largest foreign exchange earner when compared to other ASEAN countries contributing more than an annual income of 4 billion U.S. dollars since 1990.[12] In fact, tourist related industries such as hotel accommodation and restaurants, tour activities, and wholesale and retail trade have actually enjoyed a rather too fast paced growth which has caused the industry to suffer from increasing concerns of "image" problems stemming from the environmental, social and other ramifications related to the quick paced economic growth.[13]

It is, however, today that Thailand has become an active participant of international tourism in the Asian-Pacific region and the world. When considered by a group of countries, the revenue share from the ASEAN region has shown Thailand's total tourist receipts have somehow slowed down from 16.5 percent from 1980-1982 to 14.9 percent from 1987-89. If the ASEAN region is included with in the EAEC region, this same share is evidently increasing over time from 36.7 percent between 1980-1982 to 42.3 percent between 1987-1989. And of course, for all of the APEC countries, the revenue share of tourism is shifting from 48.7 percent between 1980-1982 to 55.4 percent between 1987-1989. The number of international tourist arrivals to Thailand from APEC countries has also substantially increased. Its share has changed from 61.3 percent in 1980 to 67.4 percent in 1990. At this point, one can say that more than two thirds of tourist arrivals in Thailand are now from the Asian-Pacific region.

When compared to the world, the share of ASEAN receipts in tourism as a whole was 4.1 percent in 1988 and Thailand takes the highest share of 1.6 percent followed by Singapore, Indonesia, Malaysia and the Philippines, in that order. The world share of tourist arrivals in the Asia-Pacific countries is 22.5 percent or 93.3 million persons compared to the world tourist arrivals of 414.2 million persons of which Europe and North America takes a share of 62.9 percent. With this fact, one can understand that the tourist arrivals in the Asian-Pacific region are more limited, mainly by air transport, while in Europe and North America, there are other kinds of transportation that can be combined for tourism and travel. It is then, within the Western Pacific countries, especially Japan, Asian NIEs, ASEAN, and Australia that air transport has become closely linked to the future expansion of tourist arrivals.

As noted earlier, trade in tourism will be regarded as encompassing both the purchases by individual tourists and the activities of tourism enterprises. While a number of developing countries are major participants in international tourism, it is the more developed countries with high incomes that account for the bulk of tourism arrivals. International hotel industry unlike, for example, the situation in manufacturing, foreign direct investments is not a main method of multinational involvement in hotel companies—management contracts and franchise agreements assume greater importance. This fact can be observed among the countries in the Asian-Pacific region including Thailand, and the larger the absolute size of the hotel sector in any particular industry, the lower the foreign participation rate in the provision of accommodation is likely to be.

B. Telecommunications

Telecommunications are services ranging from basic telecommunications (via telephone and telegraph) to more sophisticated or enhanced services. Two important distinguishing aspects of telecommunications should be stressed here. First, there are those closely related to the provision of telecommunication infrastructure and equipment which are considered of particular importance for many countries around the Asian-Pacific region including Thailand where such facilities may be insufficient or deficient. Second, telecommunication services, in general, are highly regulated, due to a rise in particular sensitivities in a context of trade expansion. The obstacles to competing in the market for telecommunication services stem largely from the monopoly enjoyed by a single state authority, Post, Telegraph and Telephone (PTT).

Table 10. International Telecommunication Services

	1986	*1987*	*1988*	*1989*	*1990*
Telegraph (million)	0.21	0.19	0.17	0.15	0.14
Telex (Outside Calls: million minutes)	7.65	7.63	7.41	6.37	5.46
Telephone (Outside Calls: million minutes)	19.44	27.71	42.45	64.70	89.96

Source: Communications Authority of Thailand. "Annual Report 1990."

Thailand's situation of telecommunication services can be described as above. More importantly, the economic growth of the country, in recent years, has pushed an increasing demand for telecommunication services. In terms of GDP, the share of telecommunication services has doubled its value during the 1980's from a share of 0.55 percent of GDP in 1980 to 1.14 percent of GDP in 1990. In terms of international telecommunication services, telegraph and telex have been much reduced in use during the second half of 1980's while international telephone has very much increased its importance to more than 4 times for example taken the short time span of 1986 to 1990 (see Table 10).

The total revenue of telecommunication services of Thailand has greatly increased, and has fallen under the two state enterprises, the Communication Authority of Thailand (CAT) and Telephone Organization of Thailand (TOT). The revenue of domestic telephone has changed from 9.4 billion baht in 1978 to 16.4 billion baht in 1990. The revenue of international telephone has increased even more rapidly from 2.7 billion baht in 1987 to 8.0 billion baht in 1990 and 10.0 billion baht in 1991. This is not including other kinds of services which also provide substantial revenue such as mobile phones, radio communications, telex, data transmission, and so forth. (Table 11). For the data related to international communication services, it is believed that this would likely follow the pattern of economic linkages with the Asia-Pacific region.

With regard to such an increase in demand for telecommunication services, it is actually a fact that a state of telecommunication structure is underdeveloped in Thailand. For example, the total telephone lines in usage in Thailand now total 1.3 million[14] or the average of 2.4 lines per 100 people in 1989.[15] Only the Philippines and Indonesia have a lower telephone density than Thailand: the Philippines, 0.9 line per 100 people in 1987 and Indonesia, 0.4 line per 100 people in 1989. If taking the potential demand from a waiting list of 1 million telephone numbers, the increasing demand for telephone lines is of 0.4 to 0.5 million per year while the public sector can only satisfy the demand of 0.25 to 0.3 million per year. In overall terms, the general states of telecommunication infrastructure can be very much improved considering the future growth of Thailand compared to that of neighboring countries such as Malaysia and Singapore,—and other countries in APEC. This is why the

Table 11. Telecommunication Revenue of CAT and TOT

	Value (Million Baht)					*Share (%)*					*Growth (%)*			
	1987	*1988*	*1989*	*1990*	*1991*	*1987*	*1988*	*1989*	*1990*	*1991*	*1988*	*1989*	*1990*	*1991*
TELECOM, REVNUE OF CAT														
International Telephone	2,749.54	4,384.82	6,023,59	8,009.88	10,017.49	62.68	53.24	74.32	77.16	78.43	59.47	37.37	32.98	25.06
Telex	960.31	3,015.13	902.94	736.39	612.31	21.89	36.61	11.14	7.09	4.79	213.97	(70.05)	(18.45)	(16.85)
Telegraph	171.55	168.77	177.49	168.30	162.01	3.91	2.05	2.19	1.62	1.27	(1.62)	5.17	(5.18)	(3.74)
Radio Communication	263.19	365.86	640.61	1,056.55	1,473.81	6.00	4.44	7.90	10.18	11.54	39.01	75.10	64.93	39.49
Leased Circuits	80.78	68.60	50.20	43.74	4.17	1.84	0.83	0.62	0.42	0.3	(15.08)	(26.82)	(12.87)	(90.47)
Data Transmission	126.43	177.90	179.20	209.58	267.58	2.88	2.16	2.21	2.01	2.09	40.71	0.73	16.73	27.92
Other	34.70	54.76	131.43	157.38	235.65	0.79	0.66	1.62	1.52	1.84	57.81	140.01	19.74	49.73
TOTAL	4,386.50	8,235.84	8,105.46	10,381.42	12,773.02	100.00	100.00	100.00	100.00	100.00	87.75	(1.58)	28.08	23.04
TELECOM. REVENUE OF TOT														
Ordinary Phone	9,406.50	11,038.60	13,206.60	16,410.20	N.A.	99.50	98.44	97.40	N.A.	N.A.	17.35	19.64	24.26	N.A.
Mobile Phone	47.06	175.45	352.79	N.A.	N.A.	0.50	1.56	2.60	N.A.	N.A.	272.82	101.08	N.A.	N.A.
TOTAL	9,453.56	11,214.05	13,558.99	N.A.	N.A.	100.00	100.00	100.00	N.A.	N.A.	18.62	20.91	N.A.	N.A.

Source: Communication Authority of Thailand

3 million telephone lines forecast to be contracted out to the private sector for installations[16] proves to have shown a major willingness of the government to improve the state of services in the coming years.

It is at this particular juncture, that Thailand has recognized that the potential and the efficiency of the country does depend to some extent on a strong and efficient telecommunications network. Such a network is important for both domestic and international transactions. This is why apart from a major telephone project, there are various new services that have now fallen under enchanced or value-added services. One can observe that a number of new services have been offered during the last 4-5 years pushing the telecommunications scene to a new era. The government has imposed deregulations of many enhanced and value-added services by requesting participation from the private sector into the telecommunication services: mobile phones paging, data transmission satellite, optical fiber communications, and so forth, At the same time, governmental agencies have also tried to keep up with changes of the new concepts of telecommunications such as electronic data interchange (EDI), teleports, and data processing zones (DPZ) and also they have tried to deregulate new services in cooperation with the private sector both from home and abroad.

C. Transportation

Only two major modes of transportation services have been taken into account here : air transport services and sea transport and shipping services. Due to the nature of their difference, the analysis will be done separately here.

1. *Air Transport Services*

Trade in air transport services is well known to be regulated by a system of bilateral agreements between countries which establish, on each route, a basis of country-specific import quotas.[17] This system is somehow threatened because of changes in air transport services. Findlay[18] outlines these changes as rapid growth in traffic volume and hence the density of the market, new technologies in aircraft and information processing, and a recognition of scale economies from efficient networks.

The traffic of air transport in Thailand has constantly increased during the 1980s. This air transport has consisted of passenger and freight services operated by both regular and charter flights. Bangkok is mainly the gateway for international air transport services between Thailand and abroad. For departure passengers at Bangkok International Airport, 67.9 percent of them are from APEC countries in 1990, particularly from Asian NIEs (29.2 percent), ASEAN (19.8 percent) and Japan (11.7 percent). In general, EAEC as a group represents already 59.7 percent of the total passengers. The similar pattern can

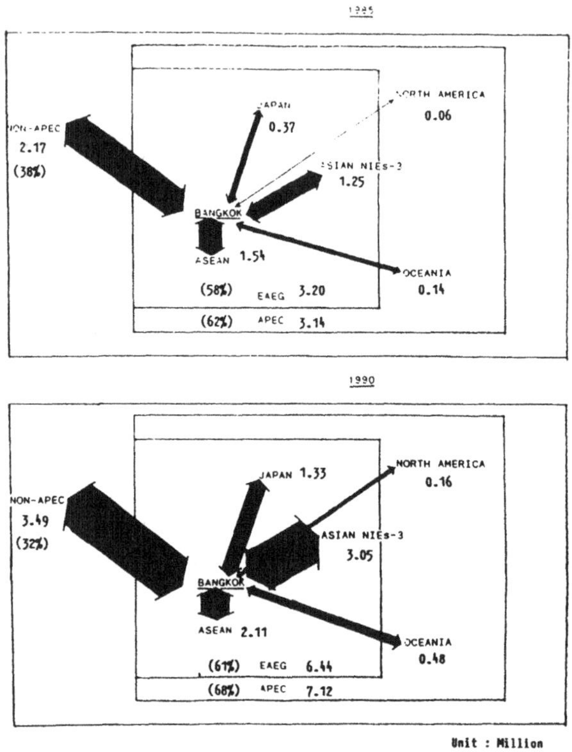

Figure 1. International Passengers at Bangkok International Airport Classified by Origins and Destinations

be found when looking into arrival passengers at Bangkok International Airport. Also for freight services to and from Bangkok International Airport, APEC region seems, in general, to weigh up to more than 60 percent of the total air freight service (see Figure 1 and Figure 2).

The number of international scheduled airlines at Bangkok International Airport are 59 in 1990 with the movement of 36,342 flights in 1990 or an annual increase of almost 15 percent with the first 10 airlines' movement. Although, Thai Airway International Company Ltd., has expanded quickly, since its beginning with 3 aircrafts in 1959 for 9 cities, to gain now with 60 aircrafts in 1992 serving 71 destinations.[19] Its capacity still apparently has not been enough since, in fact one can notice the reduction of its share from 42.7 percent in 1985 to 37.5 percent in 1990 for passenger departure at Bangkok International Airport and from 42.7 percent in 1985 to 37.3 percent in 1990 for passenger arrival at Bangkok International Airport. The freight loaded and unloaded with Thai Airways International has been reduced as well to 35.0 percent for freight loaded and 50.1 percent for freight unloaded in 1990.

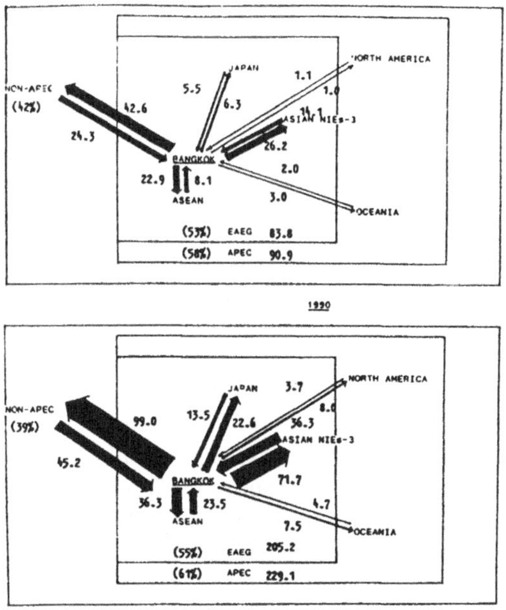

Unit : 1,000 Tons

Figure 2. International Freight at Bangkok International Airport Classified by Origins and Destinations

In terms of financial operations of major airlines of the region, it was shown that Thai Airways International has performed well in terms of operating profit and net income when compared to other carriers in the Asian-Pacific region. And in terms of the traffic volume of the Western Pacific Countries, Thailand ranks number six after Tokyo, Hong Kong, Singapore, Seoul and Taipei and from the forecast of McDonal Douglas, the future growth of air traffic will be highest in the Asian-Pacific region both in the short and long term, especially in Mid and North Pacific and Intra-Far East zones. Due to such increases Thailand has already financed[20] the extension of existing Bangkok International Airport increasing the capacity from 16 million passengers per year to 25 million passengers per year in the years between 1998-2001.[21] At the same time, air freight capacity has to increase from 0.5 million tons per year to around 0.9 million tons per year by the mid of 1990s and to 1.4 million tons year when the Bangkok International Airport's extension would be completed. In addition, the government has decided to finish the project of the second international airport around Bangkok by the year 2000 with the capacity of 21 million passengers per year.

As Thailand will be a key part of this growth with the Asia-Pacific region, the traffic growth to and from Northeast Asia is expected to be strong and to total about 7.9 million passengers in 1995 and nearly 21 million passengers by 2000.[22] The most important country pair is Thailand-Hong Kong with over 2 million passengers in 1990.[23] By 1995, total passenger traffic on this route is expected to be at 3 million. And the other important country pair is Thailand—Singapore with 1.5 million passengers in 1990 which is also expected to grow fast in the 1990's.

2. *Sea Transport and Shipping Services*

The sea transport and shipping services are difficult to characterize in general terms. It is an area of activities containing elements of both extensive regulation such as liner shipping) and relative freedom from government intervention (such as the bulk trades). Due to technological and structural changes as technologies become widely diffused, these services have then experienced parallel development of both the areas of intense competition and of growing government intervention. The Thai case can well illustrate this point.

In fact, Thailand's maritime transport has grown quickly since 1987: its increase has been registered 1.6 times between 1987-89 much higher than the world average. This increase has been forecasted annually at a rate of 9 percent during the seventh national economic and social development plan (1992-1996). Also, it is shown that traditional general cargo ships have declined its importance while rapid expansion has been registered in large oil tankers, dry bulk carriers and container ships. This is problably the direct reflection of the need to economize high labor and handling costs and of the importance of oil in the economy.

Bangkok is up to present a major seaport for maritime transport. But due to its congestions and various limitations, Laem Chabang seaport has become an important extention to alleviate the traffic at Bangkok seaport. In both places, inland services are normally controlled by the Port Authoriting of Thailand (PAT) with the participation from the private sector in some specific areas of services where PAT has deregulated and given more participation to the private sector. Major structural changes have also taken place in shipping markets in Thailand as in many parts of the world: the growth of containerized vessels has prompted shipping services to adapt them selves close within the industry in order to deep the contribution of the trade expansion.

For the maritime transport between Thailand and the world, the APEC countries' share of arrival vessels at Bangkok Port was 70.4 percent in 1989, especially from ASEAN, Asian NIEs and Japan. The APEC's share of departure vessels from Bangkok Port was somehow standing at 63.8 percent in 1989 of which ASEAN is the most important region, followed by Asian NIEs and Japan (See Figure 3). Most operation is foreign (236 number in 1990) and only the Thai operation is in small number (29 in 1990). The Thai market share of freight value has not much varied (from 5.5 percent in 1981 to 7.0 percent in 1989). The cargo tonnage for both departure and arrival vessels are

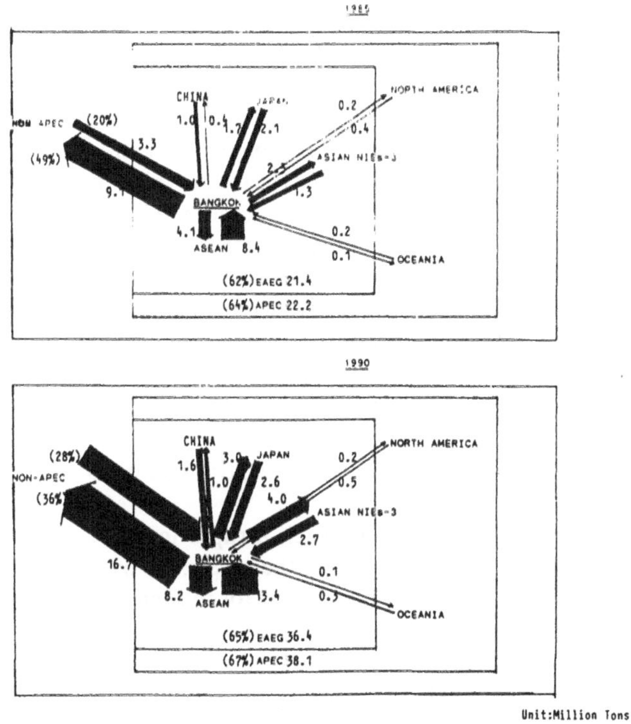

Figure 3. International Freight at Bangkok Port Classified by Previous and Next Port of Call

small, as, in fact, the major of cargo tonnage are in the hands of open registered companies (Panama, Liberia, for example) which make it sometimes difficult to identify its flag's nationality, especially the United States and Japan.

Apart from the infrastructural aspects, Thai maritime transport is not competitive compared to other APEC countries. The Thai vessel fleet is small: 13th position from 15 countries of APEC. Small size, old conditions, fleet too small, no modernize technologies in containerization are major weak points contributing to other major obstacles. The strong point for Thai vessels is its specialization in short distance transportation between Bangkok and other seaports in Southeast Asia, especially Singapore and Hong Kong where feeders become major types of transport.

V. PROSPECTS OF INCREASED SERVICE TRANSACTIONS WITH THE ASIAN-PACIFIC REGION

As shown in previous sections of this chapter, Thailand had been increasingly linking her trade in services with the Asian-Pacific region in the 1980s both, in terms of her overall travel in services and the three chosen sub-sectors: travel and tourism, telecommunications and transportation. Looking into the future, as the Thai economy is continuing to expand with such a dynamic tendency, it is expected that the continuity of trade in services' development will press forward. It means that the benefit of expansion in those sub-sectors is not aiming at themselves only, but also should involve how to support the uninterruption of those other sectors like manufacturing and agriculture.

This section aims at continuing further other important aspects of growth that are related to the overall trade in services and especially those three sub-sectors. These other aspects are factors explaining the changes, problems arising from the changes and barriers remaining as major obstacles for future development, and finally policy orientation with regard to the prospects of those subsequent sub-sectors.

A. Factors Explaining the Changes

There are various factors behind such a rapid increase of Thailand's trade in services. These factors include among the others: the overall economic growth of the Thai economy, the flexible adaptation for the demand for trade in services, the relative endowment and potential of each sub-sector of services, the increasing internationalization of Thailand's trade in services, the relative advantageous location of Thailand among the countries around the Pacific rim.

It is, firstly an overall economic growth of the Thai economy that has caused the rapid expansion of the service sector. This is clear especially in the areas of telecommunications and transportation where those services are playing a supportive role in economic development. Travel and tourism; on the other hand, are also related to the increasing disposible income of people wishing to make their trips to Thailand and the regions. The overall growth of Thailand in connection with the Asian-Pacific had amplified the growth of these sub-sectors and the overall trade in services.

The relative adaptation of the Thai economy is also a key factor to capturing the demand for trade in services. In fact, Thailand is relatively open in service activities allowing both national and foreign entrepreneurs to participate in service transactions. This kind of adaptation is doing well given the relative endowment of Thailand which permits those sub-sectors of services to each show their own potential for development and their increasing competitiveness comparative to the other countries. Although the results indicating relative endowment in those subsectors are not shown here,[24] still the future observations for these sub-sectors are especially interesting as academic exercises, in order to determine the relative strengths and weaknesses of Thailand's trade in services.

The process of internationalization of the service sector, on the other hand, is an evident phenomenon related to international transactions. The advancement of new technologies have opened up new frontiers in international trade in services. It has also encouraged significant change for technical and managerial management as concerns domestic service activities related to transactions abroad. Travel and tourism, telecommunications and transportation have also started to feel the pressure to keep pace with foreign competitors in these changes. It is important, for the future, to guarantee the successful development of any sub-sector of services by combing together the advantageous indigenous conditions and new technological advancement. This is to better respond to the constant changes in the world demand for services.

Finally, one cannot deny the centrally located position that Thailand has in this part of the world. Between at least two busy hubs such as Hong Kong and Singapore, the country has, of course, been able to enjoy many advantages for those sub-sectors under the study. The relatively easy access of the transportation to Thailand has also created the travel and tourism related very much with the overall region. Telecommunications which have grown faster than the economy have also linked up not only between Thailand and Western Pacific economies, but across the Pacific Coasts as well. Inter-personnel and business communications are flowing well with the relative position of Thailand among the Asian-Pacific region.

B. Problems and Barriers Relative to Growth and Development

As Thailand has moved along with the fast growth of her economy, many sub-sectors of services have been able to adapt less well to these changes. As a matter of fact, many problems have been arising as well from such a growth. The downward turn of Thai tourism, for example, in the last two years, should be examined with more seriousness. Many international tourist arrivals in Thailand are sensitive to problems such as: overly high accommodation prices in relation to neighboring countries, security and public health especially related to AIDS and prostitution, tourist rip-offs in various forms, environmental deterioration in various tourist spots, inadequate infrastructures to suit tourist needs, and so forth. These problems would need to be improved quickly and cannot be put aside if the competitiveness of the industry is to be kept alive and well and hopefully the above mentioned problems will be able to be alliviated.

Telecommunications and transportation, on the other hand, have also shared the burden from such an economic growth of Thailand, but in a different dimension when compared to travel and tourism. These sub-sectors are not able to capture the rising trend of demand for such services when economic growth does occur. This is related to the creation of new services of these two sub-sectors which has to depend on the supply of a lump of capacity to service customer demand. The nature and the supply of such conditions of these sub-sectors involve a greater degree of infrastructural provision. And generally, these sub-sectors are more or less regulated with a greater degree of governmental involvement. In the case of Thailand which is not much different from other countries of the region, the government is continuing to play a vital role in providing such services and infrastructural development. In the case that the government cannot cope with the overall new investment in services to support the economic development, there will be a transition to a deregulated structure allowing the private sector to join in such provisions of services, thus generally leading to a greater foreign participation in the industry.

As already seen from the problems arising from growth both in terms of both trade and infrastructure, one needs to see also the barriers existing in the countries as well, as these can, also, represent obstacles to the future development of such services. In the case of Thailand, a reduction in domestic barriers to trade in services is likely to give rise to development opportunities in the sub-sectors such as telecommunications, and transportation. The reason is that gains in efficiency are realized as the price and quality of services could become better, as the costs of protection are lowered, and resource allocation is improved. In the long run, there are likely to be dynamic growth opportunities from the transfer of skills, frequently as a consequence of the operations of multinational service providers.

As most restrictions to services are essentially nontariff barriers,[25] Thailand is no exception and also exercises these kinds of restrictions. There are barriers which limit the right to establish foreign affiliates in terms of the foreign participation in the industry and also other barriers which limit the domestic provision of any type of foreign services.[26] For telecommunications, these services were traditionally provided by government-owned and-operated Public Telecommunications Organizations (PTOs), thus a natural monopoly. The technological changes somehow removed much of this national background and several countries, including Thailand, have introduced competition in the provision of such services, especially valued-added services as mentioned earlier. Somehow, the most important barriers for telecommunications in Thailand are contained in its telecommunication law BE 2477: it gives the whole authority to those governmental agencies concerned which have not yet at all harmonized to meet the future needs of services in an efficient manner. Transport services, on the other hand, are regulated by bilateral country quotas. Each route is constrained by a set of country-specific quotas. As the framework is set, the national airlines are operated within these limits of the Air Services Agreement (ASA) set between the governments involved.

C. Policy Issues

As for the general framework of trade in services, Thailand has never conducted a harmonized policy related to the overall trade in services. In general, each sub-sector will operate within its own framework, reflecting the nature and the type of services offered to the demanders. The varieties and the complexities of services have recently become more complex with the technological and economic changes with the world in which Thailand is increasingly evolving. The existing structure and organizations related to these services have then to improve accordingly. There are different areas that need policy support, these areas are quality and competitiveness improvement, liberalization measures, infrastructural improvement and cooperative efforts with other countries.

It is for sure, at the macro level that Thailand's trade in services has linked up more and more with the changing pattern of the world economy and more sporadically with the Asian-Pacific region. The market forces, in the area of travel and tourism, for example, have to be understood in order to be set according to the market plans. Quality and competitiveness improvements, in all major sub-sectors of services, need to represent policy targets in the long run. All other efforts which would help to improve the overall conditions are important elements as policy support needs as well.

It is, of course, with the GATT Uruguay Round, that the government has also come to be closer to the liberalization policy related to different areas of services. As liberalization will gain ground in the world economy in the long run, The government has, in these regards, started to realize the importance of such a trend. In fact, the government has proposed more possibilities to the private sector in order that it would cooperate and participate in such efforts in helping to create greater efficiency and accessibility to the market demands, especially in telecommunications and transportation. As the protective barriers are lessening, it is expected that competition will grow stronger among domestic and international service providers especially in the sub-sectors depending on the advance of technology from abroad.

For the infrastructural improvement, the government will continue to play an important role in the development of public utilities such as telephone, roads, water and electricity supply. These public utilities investments in both human and physical infrastructure have to be considered with great importance because these improvements are highly related to various services that Thailand shares linkages with in the other parts of the world. Good telecommunication services for example, do depend on the provision of good infrastructural availability and the infrastructural issue becomes important in developing one nation's need in relation to the former. These issues are important for other services as well, as already considered above. And finally, cooperative efforts among other countries should be closely examined. In travel and tourism, for example, there already exists a platform through the ASEAN Committee on Travel and Tourism (COTT), to discuss and study tourist-related issues for mutual benefits. There also exists others for which Thailand participates at present. In other areas such as sub-marine cablecommunication systems and use of the Indonesian satellite, PALAPA, Thailand with other ASEAN countries should make better progress in improvement of the networks as to remain as a driving force for further economic development. This is in line with the globalization trend wittnessed in all ASEAN countries. Thailand, also should not underestimate the role that APEC can play at the infrastructural level, in related services, in the long run.

ACKNOWLEDGMENT

A part of this paper is derived from my previous paper "Thailand's Trade linkages with the Pacific Rim: Trade in Services", presented at the TDRI/EEC Joint Workshop of the Asia-Pacific Project, held at Thailand Development Research Institute (TDRI) in February 1992. I am grateful to TDRI and ECC for permission to present some of the research findings in this paper.

NOTES

1. Sapir, in this regard, has listed these various factors. In Andrea Sapir, "North-South Issues in Trade in Services". *The World Economy* (8), 1985, p.27

2. This would include the familiar names like Citibank, Burger King, Kentucky Fried Chicken, Regent, Club Med, down to the unfamiliar ones belonging to Japanese and Korean construction firms. Somchai Ratanakomut, "Industrializing the Services Sector", Paper presented at the Conference on "The Making of a Fifth Tiger? : Thailand's Industrialization and Its Consequences", held at the ANU, 7-9 December 1992.

3. Nicolaides, Phedon, "Services in a Growing Economies and Global Markets", A Paper presented at the OECD Informal Workshop with ADEs on "Trade, Investment and Technology: New Patterns and Interactions and Associated Policy Issues in a Global Economy", Paris 9-10 April 1990 (unpublished).

4. Services are commonly defined as a residue, that is, GDP less agriculture and industry.

5. Nevertheless, one should not overlook the future role of the agricultural sector as its major part now has transformed into the agro-business industry which is now a part of the manufacturing sector.

6. Finally, in order to offset the current account deficit, Thailand has generally encouraged the inflows of capital to adjust the figure of the overall balance of payments.

7. Somchai Ratanakomut, "Industrializing the Service Sector", op.cit.

8. Except that these two countries suffer very much from the deficit of their trade services.

9. 36.7 percent with the world

10. As Arndt, (1989) thinks it necessary to distinguish between factor and non-factor services transactions. In Arndt's view, if firms move, then it is a case of DFI and should not be treated as a trade in non-factor services.

11. "The Triple-T Revolution and New Pacific Cooperation" (March 1991) and "Economic Development of the Pacific Region and Triple-T Networking" (July 1992), Prepared by the Japan National Committee for Pacific Economic Cooperation Conference for the PECC Triple-T Task Force.

12. With almost half of one million employment involved in the sector.

13. This question to be further addressed whether this situation is sustainable in the future and causes alarm to improve with more harmonious development of the industry.

14. Of which 0.9 million in metropolitan areas and 0.4 million in provinces.

15. With the average of 6.1 lines per 100 people in Bangkok and 0.5 line per 100 people in provinces.

16. 2 million lines for Bangkok and 1 million lines for provinces which are equivalent to the total investment of 100 billion baht or almost 40 billion U.S. dollars involved, which would be to cover the increasing demand up to, between 1995-1996.

17. Findlay, Christopher and Peter Forsyth "Trade on Air Transport and Tourism Services" in Castle, Leslie and Christopher Findlay, *Pacific trade in Services*, Allen & Unwin, Australia Pty Ltd., 1988, pp. 99-123.

18. Ibid.

19. Thai Airways International will need another 15 aircrafts on top of the 23 already approved for purchase by the government, in bid to further its leadership position in the Asia-Pacific region. *Bangkok Post*, February 20, 1992, p.13.

20. Around 270 million U.S. dollars

21. According to IATA forecast, the total passengers at Bangkok International Airport will be 27 million in the year 2000 that works out to an average annual growth of 9.8 percent in 1990-95, overtaken by China (14.7 percent growth forecast) and Malaysia (11.6 percent).

22. Around 270 million U.S. dollars

23. According to IATA forecast, the total passengers at Bangkok International Airport will be 27 million in the year 2000. That works out to an average annual growth of 9.8 percent in 1990-95, overtaken by China (14.7 percent growth forecast) and Malaysia (11.6 percent)

24. Attempts of this kind have especially been done by Sapir, Andre (1985).

25. Quibria (1990): 30-35.

26. Such as local content requirements licensing, exchange restrictions, limitations on sales, and so forth.

REFERENCES

Arndt, H.W. (1989). "Trade in Services," *ASEAN Economic Bulletin*, Vol. 6, No. 1., July, pp. 1-7.

Baumol, W.J. (1967). "Macroeconomics of Unbalanced Growth: The Autonomy of Urvan Crisis," *American Economic Review*, 57, pp.415-26.

________. (1984a). "Why are Services Cheaper in Poorer Countries?," *Economic Journal*, 94, 374 (June), pp.276-86.

Bhagwatl, J.N. (1984b). "Splintering and Disembodiment of Services and Developing Nations," *The World Economy*, June, pp.133-44.

________. (1987). "Trade in Services and the Multilateral Trade Negotiations," *The World Bank Economic Review*, Vol, 1, No 4 (September).

Castle, L.V. and Findlay, C. (1987). "Issues in Services Trade in the Pacific," Pacific Economic Papers No. 154, Australia-Japan Research Institute, Research School of Pacific Studies, Australian National University, Canberra, Australia.

Clark, C. (1940). *The Conditions of Economic Progress*, London: Macmillan.

Findlay, C. (1990). "Trade in Services in the Asia-Pacific Region," *Asian Pacific Economic Literature*, Vol 4, No. 2, September, pp.3-20.

Fuchs, V. (1968). *The Service Economy*, New York: Columbia University Press.

Giarini, O. (ed.), (1987). *The Emerging Service Economy*, Oxford, Pergamon Press.

Grubel, H.G. (1989). *Liberalization of Trade in Services*, Institute of Southeast Asian Studies, Singapore.

Hill, T.P. (1977). "On Goods and Services," *Review of Income and Wealth* 23, 4 (December), pp.315-38.

Hindley, B., and A. Smith. (1984). "Comparative Advantage and Trade in Services," *World Economy*, 7, December, pp.369-89.

Inman, R.P. (ed.), (1985). *Managing the Service Economy: Prespects and Problems*, New York: Cambridge University Press.

Japan National Committee for Pacific Economic Cooperation. Conference (1992). *Economic Development of the Pacific Region and Triple-T Networking*. Unpublished.

———. (1991). *Tripple-T Revolution and New Pacific Cooperation*. Unpublished.

Kravis, I.B., A. Heston, and R. Summers. (1978). *International Comparisons of Real Product and Purchasing Power*, Baltimore, Maryland: The Johns Hopkins University Press.

———. (1982). *World Product and Income: International Comparisons of Real Gross Product*, Baltimore, Maryland: The John Hopkins University Press.

Langhammer, R.J. (1991). *Trade in Services Between ASEAN and EC Member States*, Institute of Southeast Asian Studies, Singapore.

Leveson, I. (1985). "Services in the U.S. Economy," in Inman, Robert (ed.), *Managing the Services Economy: Prospects and Problems*. New York: Cambridge University Press.

Melvin, J.R. (1989). "Trade in Producer Services: A Heckscher-Ohlin Approach," *Journal of Political Economy*, Vol. 97 No. 5, October, pp.1180-1196.

Messerlin, P., K. Saurant. (1990). *The Uruguay Round: Services in the World Econmy*. The World Bank and the United Nations Centre on Transnational Corporations.

Nicolaides, P. (1990). *Services in Growing Economies and Global Markets*. Informal Workshop With DAES, Organized by OECD, Paris, 4th July 1989, (unpublished).

Pongsrikul, T., and S. Ratanakomut. (1989). "Trade in Services," Background Paper No. 5 The 1989 TDRI Year-End conference "Thailand in the International Economy" Ambassador City Jomtien, Chonburi, December 16-17.

Porter, M. (1990). *The Competitive Advantage of Nations*, London: Mcmillan.

Quibria, M.G. (1990). "Trade in Services and Asian Developing Economies," *Asian Development Review*, Vol. 8, No. 2, pp. 116-143.

Ratanakomut, S. (1992). "Industrializing the Service Sector," Paper presented at the Conference on "The Making of Fight Tiger: Thailand's Industrialization and It Consequences," held at the ANU, 7-9 December 1992.

Sampson, G.P., and R.H. Snape. (1985). "Identifying the Issues in Trade in Services," *World Economy*, 8, 2 (June), pp.171-81.

Sapir, A. (1985). "North-South Issues in Trade in Services," *World Economy* (8), pp. 27-42.

TRADE IN MANUFACTURED GOODS:
PROSPECTIVE GAINS FOR THAILAND IN ASIA-PACIFIC ECONOMIC COOPERATION

Dr. Paitoon Wiboonchutikula

Since Thailand's industrialization policy shifted from import substitution to export promotion in the early 1970s, both imports and exports of manufactured goods have expanded rapidly. Their spectacular growth rates of over 20 percent a year were found in the late 1980s when the world economy changed to the advantage of Thailand's exports and investment climate. In addition, Thailand's macroeconomic and outward-oriented trade policies throughout the 1980s also contributed to rapid growth. These policies provided a stable macroeconomic environment and at the same time reduced biases against exports. As a result of these policies, Thailand's industrial performance has become increasingly dependent upon trade expansion as a source of the sector's export demand growth as well as the source of imported inputs.

Nevertheless, Thailand has tried to diversify its markets by trading with an increasing number of countries in order to minimize its export fluctuations. In the 1970s Thailand's trade of manufactured goods was mainly with Western countries such as the United States, the United Kingdom, Germany, and the

Research in Asian Economic Studies, Volume 6, pages 305-342.

ISBN: 1-55938-918-4

Netherlands. Over time, as Thailand's manufacturing sector grew and the production structure changed, Thailand's export destinations and import supply sources slowly diversified to more countries in the Asia-Pacific region. On the whole, it seems that Thailand's trade and industrialization policies have evolved to benefit industrial growth as long as world economic conditions are favorable and the international trading system remains open to all.

Unfortunately recent world economic conditions, though still optimistic, are very uncertain especially as problems of structural adjustments and various macroeconomic imbalances many of Thailand's trading partners have persisted. These conditions have been accompanied by slow world economic growth and increased protectionist sentiments in the industrialized countries. Indeed, trade negotiations at the multilateral level took a long time to reach an incomplete conclusion. Thus, it seems that the world trading system has developed in such a way that it is becoming increasingly difficult for a small open economy such as Thailand's, to reap maximum gains from opening to trade.

As a matter of fact, all other countries in the Asia-Pacific region have lately shared similar concerns of whether their industrial growth based on trade-oriented policy can be sustained under the uncertain future world trading environment. It is evident to these countries that, although most industrial countries' tariffs have been reduced, their trade policies have become increasingly complicated and less transparent with nontariff barriers and bilateral trading arrangements proliferating. In addition, the formation of trade blocs is in progress or under negotiation in almost all parts of the world.[1] There is no doubt that protectionist measures are mounting in various industrialized countries despite the recent conclusion of the GATT negotiation. As a response to these protectionist concerns, Thailand finds it necessary to cooperate with countries whose common interest is to assert joint efforts to strive for a more open world trading system.

This chapter will examine Thailand's trade patterns with individual countries in the Pacific Rim region and explores prospective gains from economic cooperation. Such economic cooperation is expected to help expand trade in manufactured goods among member countries and at the same time, to generate a collective position for freer trade at the global level. The first section will provide an overview of Thailand's trade in manufactured goods with individual Pacific Rim countries. Section II will seek an explanation for Thailand's trade with different groups of countries. Section III will assess the prospects for trade expansion in the region and draw implications on potential gains from the expansion. The last section will identify areas for cooperation so as to expand trade in the region and hopefully to all other countries under the existing world trading environment.

I. THAILAND'S TRADE WITH ASIA PACIFIC COUNTRIES

Although Thailand trades manufactured goods with most countries in the world, trade has been most intense with countries in the Pacific Rim area. Table 1 shows that during the past two decades, Thailand's manufactured exports to Pacific Rim countries accounted for over 60 percent of all manufactured exports. In addition, almost 70 percent of Thailand's manufactured imports came from the Pacific-Rim region.

Table 2 illustrates that Thailand's share of exports to Japan remained lower than 10 percent and exhibited some declines. However, the share to the North American market increased steadily to over 25 percent of the total manufactured exports during the past decade. In fact, since the mid-1980s the United States has become Thailand's largest importer. Thailand's exports to the ASEAN countries increased slowly, albeit steadily, from 14 percent in 1980

Table 1. Pacific Rim Countries' Trade in Manufactures Within the Region as a Percentage of their Trade with the World

		1970	*1975*	*1980*	*1985*	*1987*
Thailand	Import	70.02	66.78	69.78	67.19	65.30
	Export	59.29	76.68	56.08	64.57	60.55
USA	Import	58.05	54.20	54.78	47.29	81.99
	Export	38.13	38.32	40.39	45.83	76.18
Canada	Import	83.29	77.64	85.27	85.54	80.47
	Export	56.40	79.60	77.78	89.58	88.67
Japan	Import	69.26	54.31	53.26	55.60	58.62
	Export	60.85	47.30	46.16	62.25	66.23
NICs	Import	71.83	71.36	71.47	70.82	63.45
	Export	66.86	60.17	54.99	63.98	69.99
ASEAN	Import	69.86	67.15	71.81	70.57	70.15
	Export	57.87	65.89	63.96	74.63	72.05
Australia	Import	50.33	54.84	60.15	63.65	63.12
	Export	47.77	51.44	42.06	60.07	71.96
New Zealand	Import	50.76	56.62	62.99	68.47	n.a.
	Export	72.59	80.41	70.48	74.03	n.a.

Source: Table 1 to 15 are computed from United Nations' trade statisties recompiled by the Economic Council of Canada's Database Section.

Table 2. **Shares of Individual Countries in Thailand's Trade in Manufactured Goods in the 1980s**

	1980		*1985*		*1987*	
	Import	*Export*	*Import*	*Export*	*Import*	*Export*
SITC 5-8						
USA-Canada	24.76	21.45	14.52	29.83	15.09	26.14
Japan	33.79	9.47	38.88	8.32	33.72	8.51
NICs	4.05	7.86	4.55	5.86	4.75	6.15
ASEAN	2.28	14.32	5.16	15.07	6.91	16.51
Australia-NZ	2.36	1.69	1.88	2.55	1.47	2.37
China	2.11	1.59	1.22	1.97	2.81	0.92
APEC	69.35	56.39	66.21	63.59	64.75	60.60
EC	18.45	26.45	20.07	19.33	18.72	21.21
Total	87.68	82.84	86.28	82.92	83.47	81.81
SITC 5						
USA-Canada	21.89	2.16	14.95	2.53	14.59	3.79
Japan	28.31	22.93	24.93	10.90	22.86	15.04
NICs	1.81	18.03	5.29	20.30	3.69	23.14
ASEAN	2.04	22.19	7.65	22.48	8.09	18.49
Australia-NZ	1.65	0.45	1.44	3.60	1.13	2.83
China	2.72	0.00	2.01	6.47	2.89	5.93
APEC	58.41	65.76	56.28	66.27	53.25	69.22
EC	26.70	11.36	26.66	3.49	25.96	3.52
Total	85.11	77.12	82.94	69.76	79.21	72.74
SITC 6						
USA-Canada	9.97	21.19	7.89	23.47	6.25	20.79
Japan	42.94	12.51	42.31	11.17	31.10	12.02
NICs	10.83	7.17	7.40	8.30	8.80	10.49
ASEAN	3.76	5.82	2.50	8.38	3.87	10.77
Australia-NZ	6.28	20.1	4.76	4.04	3.55	4.64
China	3.07	2.86	2.04	4.08	6.11	1.98
APEC	76.84	51.55	66.92	59.45	59.68	60.74
EC	7.79	33.20	12.78	24.43	12.53	22.79
Total	84.63	84.75	79.50	83.88	72.21	83.53
SITC 7						
USA-Canada	28.23	21.61	13.22	29.28	19.50	28.01
Japan	39.19	0.73	48.87	10.64	44.07	8.04
NICs	0.98	10.48	2.35	2.84	2.58	4.22
ASEAN	1.41	58.24	5.55	41.35	0.37	46.32
Australia-NZ	0.70	0.35	0.31	0.67	0.34	0.79
China	1.58	0.04	0.46	0.37	1.17	0.33
APEC	72.14	91.46	70.77	85.16	76.01	27.70
EC	17.80	3.02	21.33	8.01	16.29	8.14
Total	89.94	94.48	92.10	93.17	92.30	95.84

(continued)

Table 2. Continued

	1980		1985		1987	
	Import	*Export*	*Import*	*Export*	*Import*	*Export*
SITC 8						
USA-Canada	20.97	25.32	16.06	41.55	17.44	30.97
Japan	27.72	5.18	32.18	2.96	27.42	5.34
NICs	12.06	6.12	6.14	2.99	7.99	2.80
ASEAN	2.01	3.66	4.26	5.53	6.98	4.91
Australia-NZ	4.25	2.11	3.82	1.82	2.30	1.52
China	3.16	0.00	1.48	0.02	2.27	0.10
APEC	71.15	42.39	64.13	56.88	64.40	45.62
EC	18.74	32.83	20.84	22.21	17.97	27.97
Total	89.89	75.22	84.97	79.09	82.37	73.59

to 17 percent in 1987. Meanwhile, the exports to the NICs fluctuated in the range of 6 to 8 percent throughout the past decade. There is thus still much room for expanding trade between Thailand and all of the Pacific Rim countries.

Japan's share of Thailand's manufactured exports was only about a quarter of Japan's share of Thailand's manufactured imports. Table 3 also shows that until recently Thailand's exports to Japan concentrated on a few categories namely, food processing and precious stones. After the mid-1980s the exports diversified into garments and electrical and nonelectrical machinery parts. Exports to the United States have long been more diversified. They include canned fruits and seafoods, all types of garments, footwear, jewelry, and electronic products. The major importing countries in the ASEAN and the Asian NICs groups were Singapore, Malaysia, Hong Kong, and more recently, Taiwan. Traditional export items to these countries were processed food and textile fabrics. After 1985 the high growth items were electrical machinery and electronic goods' exports (see Table 2).

On the import side, Japan and the United States have always been Thailand's major import suppliers. Total imports from these countries were almost 50 percent in Thailand's late 1980s. In recent years imports from Japan have grown rapidly making it the largest import supplying country. About 20 percent of all imports from Japan were automobiles and parts, and the balance consisting mostly of industrial machinery and equipment, electrical and electronic appliances and parts, and iron and steel sheets. The second largest source of imports was the United States. Of all the United States imports, about 25 percent were electrical and electronic goods such as office machines, computers and peripherals, and telecommunications equipment. Roughly 10 percent were aircraft and parts and the rest were nonelectrical machinery and equipment, and chemical products.

Table 3. Thailand's Commodity Composition of Manufactured Trade with Individual Countries in the 1980s

Destination of Export/ Origin of Import	*1980*		*1985*		*1987*	
	Import	*Export*	*Import*	*Export*	*Import*	*Export*
USA						
SITC 5	22.64	0.21	27.19	0.25	19.96	0.44
SITC 6	8.87	60.87	17.02	32.96	8.65	24.66
SITC 7	63.50	17.24	51.83	22.04	64.15	25.12
SITC 8	4.99	21.68	8.96	44.75	7.24	49.78
Japan						
SITC 5	16.27	5.16	13.39	4.18	13.42	5.68
SITC 6	31.00	82.71	27.59	56.38	24.51	42.12
SITC 7	48.87	1.34	53.98	27.59	57.57	21.82
SITC 8	3.86	10.79	5.04	11.85	4.50	27.38
NICs						
SITC 5	8.87	4.87	25.36	11.27	15.71	12.09
SITC 6	66.77	56.93	43.01	60.72	50.35	54.37
SITC 7	10.48	22.89	23.13	10.66	24.43	15.82
SITC 8	13.88	15.31	8.50	17.35	9.51	17.72
ASEAN						
SITC 5	19.62	3.17	32.79	4.76	23.89	3.52
SITC 6	45.35	24.57	13.00	24.15	15.34	20.39
SITC 7	30.49	67.32	48.93	59.54	55.00	63.40
SITC 8	4.54	4.94	5.28	11.55	5.77	12.96
APEC						
SITC 5	17.80	2.42	18.67	3.32	16.61	3.60
SITC 6	29.42	55.86	26.93	39.34	25.00	31.39
SITC 7	47.70	27.24	48.25	28.86	52.77	32.78
SITC 8	5.08	14.48	6.15	28.48	5.62	32.23
EC						
SITC 5	33.59	0.85	28.97	0.57	30.87	0.53
SITC 6	12.31	74.19	16.84	52.63	20.02	33.89
SITC 7	48.58	1.86	47.64	8.86	43.14	8.75
SITC 8	5.52	23.10	6.55	37.94	5.97	56.83

Imports from ASEAN and the NICs have been increasing in the recent years. ASEAN imports concentrated on petroleum and petroleum products (mostly from Singapore) and electronic parts and components. On the other hand, the imports from NICs included mostly computers and peripherals, telecommunications equipment, electrical appliances and parts, iron and steel sheets, textiles, yarn, fabrics, and jewelry. It is expected that intermediate and capital goods imports from these countries will continue to outgrow imports from elsewhere.

II. EXPLANATION OF COMMODITY TRADE BETWEEN THAILAND AND PACIFIC RIM COUNTRIES AND FUTURE PROSPECTS

Thailand's trade of manufactured goods with individual country groups in Asia Pacific can be explained by various theories from Heckscher-Ohlin to intra-industry trade, including those linked with foreign investment or the internationalization of production hypothesis.

The trade of Thailand with most industrialized countries is expected to comprise more of the Heckscher-Ohlin-type goods because Thailand and these countries have greater differences in per capita income and resource endowment than any other country groups. Thailand, which is abundant in unskilled labor should have a comparative advantage in the export of low-technology, unskilled, labor-intensive goods. At the same time, Thailand should import capital and technology-intensive goods from capital abundant countries such as the United States and Japan.

On the other hand, it can be hypothesized that Thailand's trade with the Asian NICs and ASEAN countries should satisfy such theories as intra-industry trade or those that connect trade with foreign investment. In fact, it is usually found that the explanation for trade among the developed countries or within the developing countries, each group of which is similar in terms of per capita income and resource endowment, deviates somewhat from the Heckscher-Ohlin theorem. A large proportion of trade among these countries involves the simultaneous export and import of similar goods which is called intra-industry trade. The goods traded under this hypothesis are based on similarity rather than difference of income levels between countries.

Although Thailand's manufactured exports are still predominantly labor-intensive goods, in recent years a number of exports have also shifted to more skilled and technology-intensive goods. Many of these are produced by export-oriented, foreign-invested firms in Thailand. Most of these firms came from Japan and the Asian NICs. The explanation for this type of traded good is expected to be related to the direct foreign investment from countries which formerly had a comparative advantage in the production of these goods, but later on, due to changes in the domestic and world economic environment, they needed to relocate their production to a lower cost country in order to maximize global profits. Production from recipient countries could be finished goods for exports to third countries, or intermediate products for export to the home countries for further fabrication.

Thus, we expect that the explanation for Thailand's manufactured trade pattern varies among different groups of countries. In the next section, evidence will be gathered and prospects for future comparative advantage in each country group will be determined in order to seek room for further trade expansion under freer trade in the Pacific Rim region.

A. The Factor Proportion Explanation

The 2X2X2 Heckscher-Ohlin's factor proportions theorem hypothesizes that Thailand, as a relatively more labor abundant country compared to the rest of the world, should export labor-intensive goods and import capital-intensive goods. When many goods and many countries are included in the model, and allowing for the goods to be ranked in a chain according to factor intensity, the theorem can be extended to postulate that Thailand, which is more labor-abundant than the developed countries (DCs), should export above-average labor-intensive goods to the DCs and import above-average capital-intensive goods from them. On the other hand, as Thailand is relatively more capital-abundant than countries at lower levels of development (e.g. the least developed countries), Thailand should export capital-intensive goods to these countries and import labor intensive goods from them.[2] In fact, the above extended version of the theorem further implies that the greater the difference in per capita income and resource endowment between Thailand and another country, the greater the volume of trade between them can be expected.

Many methods can be used to test the factor proportions hypothesis on determinants of trade patterns between Thailand and individual Pacific-Rim countries.[3] All these methodologies can however, be grouped into two categories : the Leontief-type analysis of the factor content of trade, and the regression analysis of the commodity composition of trade. The factor content analysis requires an input-output table to measure the capital and labor embodied in Thailand's trade with each trading partner to test, for example, whether Thailand's exports to the United States have a greater labor-capital ratio than its imports from the United States.

In this study, we have chosen regression analysis as Thailand's input-output table for the years after 1985 has not been published. Besides, by using regression we can do our testing by using more up-to-date data. In addition, while the factor-content version requires a cardinal ranking of factor intensities in the analysis, the commodity or regression version only needs an ordinal ranking of factor intensities.[4] Based on regression analysis we postulate the determinants of trade between Thailand and each Pacific Rim country in the following general form:

$$T = f(X)$$

where T is the trade performance variable and X the vector of gross factor intensities.

Furthermore, since we simply want to determine the direction of the relationship between the trade performance variable and its determinants, we follow Harkness and Kyle (1975) and Hellvin and Torstensson (1985), among others, to define the trade performance variable as a binary instead of a continuous variable. To be specific, we used the probit technique to find determinants of Thailand's comparative advantages in trading with different Pacific Rim countries, where the determinants are related to Thailand's factor endowments: physical capital, human capital, and labor. The various methods of estimation are available in the Appendix.

The regression results showing determinants of Thailand's trade pattern with each Pacific Rim country during the past two decades are presented in Tables 4 and 5. For Thailand's trade with the United States, the probit coefficients between net exports and the combined capital intensity were negative and significant for all years. This means that Thailand's net exports to the United States were labor-intensive.

Table 4. Estimated Probit Coefficients of the Factor Proportions Model, 1980 (Using Balassa's Factor Proporation Data)

Trade between Thailand and	*Total Capital per worker*	*Human Capital per worker*	*Physical Capital per worker*
U.S.A.	-2.3631*		
	(-4.6510)		
		-2.1481*	-0.5405
		(-3.70.8)	(-1.225)
Japan	-1.8122*		
	(-3.6053)		
		-1.2879*	-0.7184
		(-2.2865)	(-1.5495)
NICs	-1.0472**		
	(-2.4080)		
		-1.7125*	-0.3057
		(-3.2165)	(-0.8074)
ASEAN-4	0.4050		
	(0.8752)		
		0.2892	-0.0356
		(0.5164)	(-0.0917)
Australia-New Zealand	-1.1065*		
	(-2.9829)		
		-0.8109	-0.4471
		(-1.5653)	(-1.1179)
China			

Note: Figures in parentheses below regressions coefficients are t-statistics where * denotes the coefficients are significent at the 1 percent level and ** significant at the 5 percent level.

Table 5. Estimated Probit Coefficients of the Factor Proportions Model, 1989

Trade between Tailand and	*Total Capital per worker*	*Human Capital per worker*	*Physical Capital per worker*
U.S.A.	-2.3586*		
	(-4.8046)		
		-1.3695**	-1.1685**
		(-2.5967)	(-2.7740)
Japan	-2.1529*		
	(-4.4639)		
		-1.5801**	-0.7638
		(-2.8982)	(-1.8614)
NICs	-1.2392**		
	(-2.8982)		
		-1.3783**	-0.1518
		(-2.7038)	(-0.4107)
ASEAN-4	-0.2965		
	(-0.7094)		
		-0.2697	-0.0752
		(0.5366)	(-0.2088)
Australia-New Zealand	-1.0089**		
	(-2.4678)		
		(-1.2114**	-0.1391
		(-2.7112)	(-0.3989)
China			

When the total capital intensity is separated into physical and human capital intensities, the results show that Thailand's net exports had a significantly negative relationship with human capital intensity. However, the relationship with physical intensity was positive, albeit insignificant. Thus, while we can conclude that Thailand was a net importer of human capital-intensive goods from the United States, we still cannot conclude that Thailand was a net exporter of physical capital intensive goods to the United States.

Thailand's net exports to Japan also correlated negatively with total capital intensity, and the relationship was significant. The correlation with human capital intensity was both negative and significant. That with physical capital intensity was positive, but insignificant. Thus, similar to trade with the United States, Thailand had a significant tendency to export labor-intensive goods to Japan. Furthermore, as the differences in human capital endowment were more pronounced between the two countries, it is significantly indicated that Thailand's net imports from either the United States. or Japan were human-capital intensive goods.

Thailand's net exports to the Asian NICs were negatively related to total capital intensity (either in flow or stock)[5], but because the significance levels were rather high, it cannot be concluded that the net exports were labor intensive, as in the case of Thailand's trade with the United States or Japan. When breaking down the total capital intensity into physical and human capital components, the signs of the regression coefficients for human capital intensity were negative, but those with physical intensity were positive for all years. Thus, although the trade patterns between Thailand and the NICs were again similar to trade with the United States or Japan, the relationship was, regrettably, not significant.

The relationship between Thailand's net exports with the ASEAN countries and the factor intensities of commodities shows even poorer statistical results compared to the testing with the NICs. That is, the signs in the tests between Thailand's net exports and total capital intensity or separated capital intensities show varying results and are insignificant. However, Thailand's net exports to China were positively related to total capital intensity and significant, which means that Thailand was a net exporter of capital-intensive goods to China. When the capital intensity is divided into the stated two components, the regression coefficients show that Thailand's net exports to China were physical-capital intensive, but not human-capital intensive.

There are certain conclusions we can draw from all of the above findings. In the two-factor model, Thailand's trade with the United States and Japan followed the Heckscher-Ohlin explanation of trade patterns. That is, Thailand was a net exporter of labor-intensive goods. When total capital intensity was separated into physical-and human-capital intensities in the three-factor model, Thailand tended to be a net importer of human-capital-intensive goods. However, the findings that Thailand was a net exporter of physical-intensive goods to the United States or Japan, though contrary to the Heckscher-Ohlin prediction, were not statistically significant, and therefore still inconclusive.

In trading with China, Thailand was a net exporter of capital-intensive goods under the two-factor model. Under the three-factor model, Thailand had a comparative advantage in physical-capital-intensive goods, but not in human-capital-intensive goods. These findings seem to correspond to the Heckscher-Ohlin theorem since the factor endowment of Thailand and China was relatively more diverse than that of Thailand's endowment differences with any other less developed countries in the Pacific Rim.

It should also be noted that Thailand's factor endowment gap with the NICs was less than that with the developed countries, such as the United States and Japan. On the other hand, Thailand's factor endowment gap with the ASEAN countries was less than that with China. Therefore, the factor proportions theorem gives a better explanation of Thailand's trade patterns with the DCs and China than for any other Pacific Rim country. In fact, Thailand's trade pattern determinants with the NICs or ASEAN were not clear at all. To explain trade between Thailand and its neighboring countries with a relatively more similar factor endowment, we must then examine other models.

Table 6. Index of Thailand's Intra-Industry Trade with Pacific Rim Countries, 1973-1989

Year	*Canada*	*U.S.A.*	*Japan*	*NICs*	*ASEAN*	*Aust-NZ*
1973	7.6	1.0	7.2	15.1	7.4	6.9
1975	5.9	2.2	5.1	28.4	8.5	8.9
1976	13.5	2.8	3.6	29.6	3.3	5.1
1980	6.7	2.0	4.6	13.6	6.1	6.3
1981	8.1	2.2	4.9	12.5	6.5	6.7
1982	11.4	2.4	6.3	14.0	6.8	6.5
1983	12.0	2.9	4.3	13.4	10.0	6.5
1984	n.a.	n.a.	n.a.	n.a.	n.a.	n.a.
1985	12.1	2.7	9.8	23.4	7.6	6.7
1986	16.7	3.4	10.6	21.3	8.3	6.7
1987	n.a.	n.a.	n.a.	n.a.	n.a.	n.a.
1988	32.6	5.8	12.3	19.2	15.1	3.4
1989	28.8	6.2	15.1	21.9	6.7	8.5

B. Intra-Industry Trade

Following Grubel and Lloyd (1975)'s method, we computed Thailand's intra-industry trade with different groups of Pacific Rim countries based on the 3-digit-SITC level of aggregation. The computation results are shown in Table 6.

For almost two decades in the 1970s and the 1980s Thailand's intra-industry trade indices with the NICs were the highest, followed by Thailand's intra-industry trade with ASEAN and natural resource rich countries such as Canada, Australia, and New Zealand (see Table 6.) The indices showing the intra-industry trade between Thailand and the United States or Japan were always lower than those of other countries.

With the NICs, the intra-industry trade was high in the categories of textiles and textile products, electronic goods, and jewelry. Although the intra-industry trade index between Thailand and ASEAN was larger than the index between Thailand the United States or Japan, it was much smaller than that between Thailand and the NICs because trade was mainly in a few electronic goods such as parts and components, and computer peripherals. The intra-industry trade between Thailand and Canada and Australia was mostly in imports and exports of natural-resource-based products such as agro-based and mineral-resource-based goods.

Tables 7 and 8 show Thailand's industries with high and low intra-industry trade indices in the late 1980s. The industries with high intra-industry trade indices were mostly exportable products with high net export indices. Almost 50 percent were industries that began having high export growth after 1985. They were such as electronic parts and computer peripherals, office machines

Table 7. Thailand's Industries with High Intra-Industry Trade Index in the Late 1980s

SITC	Industry	ITT	High Net Export Ratios Before 1985	After 1985
611-2	Leather and Leather Products	0.88	X	
621	Rubber sheets	0.82	X	
628	Rubber Products	0.92		X
642	Paper board	0.96		
652-6	Woven Fabrics	0.85	X	
665	Glassware	0.93		
667	Precious Stones	0.91	X	
678	Iron Tubes and Pipes	0.89		X
691-9	Metal Tools and Cutlery	0.78		X
716	Electric Parts	0.71		
749	Nonelectric Parts	0.71		
751+759	Office Machines and Parts	0.78		X
761-764	Radio and Telecomms	0.84		X
733	Electronic Parts	0.78	X	
776	Computers and Peripherals	0.78		X
871	Optical Goods	0.99		X
885	Watches and Clocks	0.86		X
895	Plastic Products	0.83		X

Table 8. Thailand's Industries with Low Intra-Industry Trade Index in the Late 1980's

SITC	Industry	ITT	High Net Trade Ratio Import	Export
022-24	Dairy Products	0.045	X	
037	Preserved Fish	0.026		X
042	Rice	0.000		X
056+058	Preserved Veg. & Fruits	0.058		X
061-2	Sugar	0.141		X
071-3	Coffee and Chocolates	0.140	X	
081	Animal feeds	0.312		X
51	Organic Chemicals	0.088	X	
52	Inorganic Chemicals	0.061	X	
53	Dyeing extracts & Paints	0.159	X	
541	Pharmaceutical Products	0.137	X	
562	Fertilizers	0.001	X	
582-3	Polymer	0.254	X	
591-2	Insecticides, etc.	0.253	X	
671-7	Iron & Steel	0.128	X	
71-4	Heating & Cooling Equipment	0.109	X	
78-9	Transport Equipment	0.178	X	
821	Furniture Parts	0.093		X
831	Travel Goods	0.058		X
842	Clothing	0.101		X
851	Footwear	0.019		X
822-3	Photographic Equipment	0.316	X	

and telecommunications equipment, watches and clocks, plastic products, iron tubes and pipes, and rubber products. The industries with high intra-industry trade indices that have longer history of high export growth were leather and leather products, rubber sheets, woven fabrics, and precious stones. Apparently, many of these industries with high intra-industry indices were nontraditional export-oriented industries with high direct foreign investment content. In the late 1980s direct foreign invested firms divided their activities among countries including Thailand, to maximize their global profits. Goods produced in Thailand were finished products for export to third countries or products for export to the home countries for further fabrication. (A discussion on direct foreign-investment-related trade follows in the next section).

Thailand's industries with low intra-industry trade indices include industries with either very high net import indices or those with very high net export indices. The importables with low intra-industry trade indices due to Thailand's low domestic production or exports were items such as dairy products, chemicals, pharmaceutical products, fertilizer, polymers, iron and steel, and transportation equipment. The exportables with low intra-industry trade indices were agro-based industrial goods such as rice, preserved foods, and animal feed ; and labor-intensive exports in the categories of clothing, travel goods, and footwear. These industries all had very high net export ratios.

C. Direct Foreign Investment Related Trade

As suggested earlier, Thailand's exports have recently shifted from natural-resource-based and labor-intensive to more skilled and technology-intensive goods, mostly produced by export-oriented, foreign-invested firms. Table 9 provides further evidence of changes in the composition of exports between Thailand and individual Pacific Rim countries, where exports are classified into four groups namely, natural-resource-based goods, unskilled labor-intensive goods. technology-intensive goods, and human-capital-intensive goods[6] The table shows that significant changes in the export patterns between Thailand and most Pacific Rim countries were found after 1985 when Thailand experienced exceptionally high growth in both direct foreign investment inflows and real income of the whole economy. Thus, the discussion below will emphasize the changes in export structures in two comparable periods namely, before and after 1985.

Prior to 1985, Thailand's exports to most Pacific Rim countries consisted mostly of natural-resource-based and labor-intensive goods. Over 60 percent of Thailand's exports to North America and Japan were natural-resource based goods. Labor-intensive goods accounted for 20-30 percent of total manufactured exports, and only less than 10 percent of exports were either technology-intensive or human-capital-intensive goods. However, there was a trend starting in the early 1980s towards a decline in the percentage of

Table 9. Structural Change of Thailand's Manufactured Exports to Pacific Rim Countries by Major Industry Group, 1976-1989

Major Industry Group	*1976*	*1980*	*1983*	*1985*	*1986*	*1988*	*1989*
(A) To the United States							
Natural-resource-based	61.6	64.2	50.1	41.6	36.2	24.2	22.4
Unskilled-labor-intensive	27.2	19.4	31.9	34.6	30.0	29.4	32.6
Technology-intensive	6.9	13.8	14.4	15.9	20.9	32.8	32.7
Human-capital intensive	4.4	2.6	3.6	7.9	13.2	13.6	12.3
(B) To Canada							
Natural-resource-based	33.4	51.6	51.3	51.9	54.7	35.1	31.5
Unskilled-labor-intensive	51.5	41.5	46.0	45.1	39.3	27.2	29.9
Technology-intensive	10.5	0.1	0.3	3.0	1.7	9.7	13.1
Human-capital intensive	4.6	6.8	2.4	2.7	4.3	28.0	25.5
(C) To Japan							
Natural-resource-based	89.2	76.3	80.0	63.2	64.0	47.9	37.6
Unskilled-labor-intensive	7.1	16.0	12.2	12.2	13.0	22.7	26.4
Technology-intensive	2.4	4.	5.0	19.7	17.7	19.7	24.5
Human-capital intensive	1.2	3.4	2.8	4.9	5.2	9.7	11.6
(D) NICs							
Natural-resource-based	62.0	43.8	46.8	36.2	35.7	30.9	27.2
Unskilled-labor-intensive	16.3	14.1	17.8	17.2	16.7	16.5	15.8
Technology-intensive	15.0	32.9	27.4	38.2	37.7	41.4	44.1
Human-capital intensive	6.6	9.2	8.0	8.3	9.6	11.2	13.0
(E) To ASEAN-5							
Natural-resource-based	89.6	75.9	75.5	65.3	50.3	47.9	76.1
Unskilled-labor-intensive	3.7	4.7	6.0	6.9	9.5	9.5	4.3
Technology-intensive	4.0	15.9	12.9	22.0	31.7	33.3	10.4
Human-capital intensive	2.6	3.5	5.7	5.8	8.6	9.3	9.2

Thailand's exports of natural-resource-based goods while the exports of technology-intensive goods grew significantly. Nevertheless, the export base of technology-intensive goods was still small, and the share of exports in both technology-intensive goods and human-capital-intensive goods remained minor from 1970 to 1985.

Before 1985, Thailand's exports to the NICs, which are poorly endowed with natural resources consisted mainly of natural-resource-based goods. A distant second and third largest exports to these countries were unskilled-labor and technology-intensive goods. Exports of human-capital intensive goods were still minor.

Despite a much smaller natural resource endowment gap between Thailand and ASEAN compared to Thailand and the NICs, over 70 percent of Thailand's exports to ASEAN countries before 1985 was still natural-resource-based goods, whereas imports of natural-resource-based goods from the ASEAN countries accounted for less than 30 percent of Thailand's total imports. Despite Thailand's rapid growth in the export of technology-intensive goods to ASEAN in the early 1980s, Thailand remained a net importer in this trade group. Furthermore, Thailand's export of human-capital-intensive goods to ASEAN were still quite small.

After 1985 however, Thailand's proportion of exports of natural-resource-based goods to total exports in each of the Pacific Rim countries was considerably reduced while the proportions of the exports of technology-intensive as well as skilled labor-intensive good increased substantially. The proportion of Thailand's exports of labor-intensive goods to total exports to North America and Japan increased at a moderate rate, whereas the fraction Thailand's export of these goods to the NIC and ASEAN declined.

Table 10. Net Direct Foreign Investment Inflows of Thailand by Sector

	1980	*1985*	*1986*	*1987*	*1988*	*1989*	*1990e*
1. Financial Institution	(4.5)	(27.9)	7.4	4.9	9.6	7.9	6.2
2. Trade	19.4	24.4	25.8	9.4	13.9	15.5	22.2
3. Construction	20.2	35.7	17.9	14.9	6.9	8.7	5.6
4. Mining & Quarrying	15.4	11.6	3.5	2.1	1.7	1.3	1.8
4.1 Oil exploration	11.4	9.7	3.4	2.8	1.4	0.7	1.4
4.2 Others	4.0	1.9	0.1	(0.7)	0.3	0.1	0.4
5. Agriculture	5.4	1.7	2.9	3.2	1.1	1.3	1.3
6. Industry	26.2	30.6	30.7	52.5	57.9	45.6	44.0
6.1 Food	2.4	8.9	4.2	4.8	4.4	4.4	1.3
6.2 Textile	(0.0)	1.3	1.2	1.0	4.0	1.5	3.0
6.3 Metal based and Non-metallic	1.2	(2.8)	(0.3)	4.0	6.9	5.6	4.5
6.4 Electrical appliances	11.6	6.3	8.9	2.6	22.3	19.0	15.3
6.5 Machinery & Transport Equipment	2.4	0.7	(0.2)	1.8	2.6	1.6	4.2
6.6 Chemical	5.5	11.0	7.0	9.6	6.9	5.6	7.7
6.7 Petroleum products	0.1	0.0	0.1	(0.2)	3.0	(2.7)	1.5
6.8 Construction Materials	0.0	0.9	0.1	0.1	0.1	0.2	-0.1
6.9 Others	3.1	4.3	9.8	8.8	7.8	10.3	6.3
7. Services	18.0	23.9	11.8	13.0	8.9	19.1	18.0
7.1 Transportation & travel	5.5	4.5	3.7	2.4	1.4	1.2	1.5
7.2 Housing & real estate	3.9	6.9	0.6	3.6	3.2	8.7	9.6
7.3 Hotel & Restaurant	2.3	5.0	1.5	1.0	2.0	6.9	4.9
7.4 Others	6.3	7.9	6.0	6.8	2.4	2.4	1.7
8. Others	—					0.6	0.5
Total	100.0	100.0	100.0	100.0	100.0	100.0	100.0
(mil. Baht)	38,878.2	4,441.8	6,908.1	9,043.7	28,243.8	44,742.3	57,962.8

Source: Bank of Thailand

Table 11. Source of Direct Foreign Investment in Major Industrial Groups in Thailand, 1980-1990

Investing Country	*1980*				*1983*			
	1	*2*	*3*	*4*	*1*	*2*	*3*	*4*
U.S.	34.9	38.5	3.4	74.4	37.1	10.2	1.2	65.2
Japan	23.3	11.7	50.0	10.7	16.8	9.1	67.0	7.5
NICs	5.2	39.5	20.2	10.5	17.4	38.2	14.3	13.4
ASEAN-5	2.0	1.1	0.0	1.4	0.2	0.2	0.0	0.0
Others	34.6	9.2	26.4	20.0	28.5	42.3	17.5	13.9
Total	100.0	100.0	100.0	100.0	100.0	100.0	100.0	100.0

Investing Country	*1987*				*1988*			
	1	*2*	*3*	*4*	*1*	*2*	*3*	*4*
U.S.	18.5	25.0	10.0	9.9	7.3	11.7	3.0	5.0
Japan	10.3	22.7	57.9	72.6	75.4	28.4	59.4	74.0
NICs	21.9	22.1	16.3	16.3	6.9	32.3	23.6	20.2
ASEAN-5	0.1	0.0	0.1	0.0	0.0	0.3	0.9	0.0
Others	49.0	30.2	15..7	12.0	10.4	27.3	13.1	0.8
Total	100.0	100.0	100.0	100.0	100.0	100.0	100.0	100.0

Investing Country	*1989*				*1990*			
	1	*2*	*3*	*4*	*1*	*2*	*3*	*4*
U.S.	30.1	13.2	7.7	13.6	4.4	7.9	13.2	14.3
Japan	13.3	32.8	58.2	65.5	43.6	27.8	53.2	54.2
NICs	13.2	50.4	20.0	18.5	11.8	56.3	10.6	15.2
ASEAN-5	0.4	0.3	0.1	0.0	0.2	0.1	0.0	2.9
Others	43.0	3.3	14.0	24.0	40.0	7.9	23.0	13.4
Total	100.0	100.0	100.0	100.0	100.0	100.0	100.0	100.0

Note: The Headings 1, 2, 3, and 4 denote natural-resourced based, unskilled-labor-intensive, technology-intensive, and human-capital-intensive industries respectively.

A major explanation for the rapid growth of Thailand's exports of technology-intensive and skilled-labor intensive goods, which were mostly electronics, electrical machinery and equipment, automobile parts and components, is associated with large increases in direct foreign investment inflows into these industries since the mid-1980s (see Table 10). In fact, the share of direct foreign investment to total investment in Thailand increased from a few percent in the 1970s to an all time high of about 15 percent in 1988. Foreign investment, particularly in the technology and skill-intensive industries, increased from 14 percent in 1980 to a peak of 25 percent in 1988, then declined to 20 percent in 1990 (see Table 10). This direct foreign investment came from various sources, but mainly from Japan, the United States, and the NICs (see Table 11).

This direct foreign investment had a significant impact on the change in both the production and export structures in industries which foreign firms invested. While the proportion of direct foreign investment in these industries increased, the export-output ratios also increased. In the electronics industry, for example, there was a particularly high growth in the late 1970s when large amounts of foreign capital were invested. With the help of this direct foreign investment the structure of production changed from home-market-oriented consumer electronics to export-oriented parts and components, and finally to computer peripherals and telephones.

Firms in the electronics industry also traded more among themselves than firms in other industries.[7] The internationalization of production in this industry and division of labor among countries in the East Asian region, that is, Japan, Asian NICs, and ASEAN were also much greater than in any other industry. This is because this particular industry's production technology generally changes very rapidly and each product has a very short life span. As technology becomes increasingly advanced, the prices of standard products decline rapidly, and this phenomenon forces each country to specialize in the production of only that segment of products which offers comparative advantages.

As the industry develops along with the rapidly changing technology firms in the industry usually inevitably face two options in order to sustain their expansion rate. The first option is to continue changing their output composition to include larger proportion of more capital and technology-intensive production items. At the same time they might have to import some of labor-intensive intermediate imports that they used to produce before the rise in real wages that led to the structural change within the industry. The second option of these firms is to relocate that segment of production where they are losing cost competitiveness to another country where factor costs are still favorable so as to maintain the market share of their existing products and exports.

In the late 1980s, foreign (East-Asian) firms relocated the part of production which needed labor-intensive processes to Thailand for additional reasons which were related to changing global and domestic economic conditions. First there were a number of world currency realignments which resulted in the appreciation of currencies of many major exporters such as Japan and the Asian NICs. When combined with rising production costs (mainly from increasing wage rates) in these countries, their price competitiveness in the world export market declined. Second, protectionist pressures increased in major world import markets, mainly in the United States and the EC. It became increasingly difficult to get access to or penetrate these markets, particularly for the exports from the major exporting countries. To avoid these problems, multinational electronics firms from the United States, which had operated assembly plants in most Asian NICs, relocated their plants in countries whose wage rates were lower and whose export volume was still below the protectionist threshold. Japanese and Asian NIC firms responded similarly by increasing their investment in lower-cost countries in order to maintain their competitiveness and to use the host countries as an export base. In fact, the aggregate foreign investment outflows of the latter countries also helped slow down the appreciation of their currencies and their eroding price competitiveness.

The lower wage countries which obtained large direct investment inflows from the United States, Japan, and the Asian NICs in the mid-1980s were mostly in the Asian region. Thailand is one of these foreign investment recipient countries where economic conditions are goods, labor remains relatively inexpensive, and the country's exports are still a small percentage of the world export share and not yet severely affected by all trade barriers. Finally, the country is providing incentives and improving its infrastructure to attract even more direct foreign investment.

D. Prospects for Thailand's Future Trade Patterns

The competitiveness of an export from a country can be compared to other countries at a given point in time, or with itself over a period of time. A measurement which is widely used for such an assessment is the "revealed comparative advantage (RCA) index", developed by Balassa (1965). It assumes that relative costs as well as non-price factors are reflected in the pattern of commodity trade. The index is defined as the ratio of the share of a commodity in total exports of a country to the commodity's share in total world exports (see the Appendix). It indicates the extent of commodity specialization in a country's exports relative to that of other exporting countries.

Table 12 shows the changing revealed comparative advantage of Thai exports. The top ten exports with the highest revealed comparative advantage indexes in the 1980s were rice, sugar, frozen and canned foods and fruits, nonferrous metal products, wood and wood products, and textile fibers. They are all products intensive in using agricultural, forestry, and mining products as intermediate inputs. The exports with the highest revealed comparative advantage over the period were thus the ones that benefited from the low prices of relatively abundant natural resources in Thailand. Further, these exports were produced with a combination of unskilled labor, and little capital, and they used simple technology to process the raw materials.

In the 1980s, however, the number of exports with revealed comparative indexes greater than one or steadily rising have increased. The new export items with revealed comparative advantage indices greater than one by the late 1980s were various kinds of garments, textile yarn, footwear, electronic goods, leather products, ceramic goods, travel goods, plastic products, toys, and jewelry. Those exports whose indices rose particularly rapidly were leather goods,

Table 12. Change in Revealed Comparative Advantage of Individual APEC Countries, 1980-1989

	1980		1989	
Ranking	*SITC*	*RCA*	*SITC*	*RCA*
1. Thailand				
1	042	65.5	042	64.2
2	689	33.6	037	25.9
3	061	10.5	061	11.6
4	037	9.5	612	8.6
5	772	7.2	897	8.1
6	056	6.6	689	8.0
7	121	6.0	844	7.2
8	844	5.4	843	6.3
9	047	5.3	056	6.1
10	653	3.4	842	5.3
11	635	3.3	047	5.1
12	658	2.9	667	5.0
13	667	2.5	846	3.8
14	652	2.6	635	3.4
15	842	2.4	845	3.3
16	843	2.4	776	3.2
17	081	2.3	831	3.0
18	846	2.0	653	2.8
19	848	2.0	121	2.6
20	628	2.0	851	2.3
2. United States				
1	896	3.31	792	3.81
2	792	2.98	042	3.40
3	121	2.85	122	3.35
4	269	2.84	714	3.08
5	714	2.82	121	2.88
6	752	2.68	872	2.43
7	723	2.49	524	2.38
8	751	2.36	896	2.14
9	598	2.26	562	2.07
10	874	2.18	516	1.69
11	872	2.14	269	2.01
12	042	2.10	723	2.06
13	081	2.06	751	1.92
14	883	1.91	752	1.82
15	882	1.81	081	1.77
16	591	1.78	516	1.69
17	516	1.73	046	1.54
18	562	1.66	784	1.53
19	784	1.64	591	1.51
20	524	1.49	882	1.37

(continued)

Table 12. Continued

	1980		1989	
Ranking	*SITC*	*RCA*	*SITC*	*RCA*
3. Canada				
1	251	10.40	251	8.32
2	686	7.29	686	5.49
3	641	5.89	791	5.32
4	254	3.28	683	4.96
5	562	3.29	641	4.40
6	676	3.20	679	4.09
7	047	3.08	782	4.09
8	684	2.92	783	3.14
9	721	2.92	562	3.02
10	784	2.92	784	2.82
11	782	2.47	684	2.71
12	791	2.42	254	2.70
13	037	2.08	685	2.44
14	635	2.06	883	2.16
15	233	2.03	721	2.00
16	685	2.02	711	1.98
17	682	1.91	712	1.84
18	714	1.86	635	1.79
19	511	1.71	522	1.59
20	783	1.70	714	1.56
4. Japan				
1	762	4.59	881	3.43
2	881	3.20	764	2.93
3	884	3.07	759	2.88
4	782	3.02	781	2.27
5	678	2.92	782	2.20
6	761	2.84	871	2.18
7	785	2.83	884	2.03
8	764	2.66	776	2.02
9	793	2.57	785	1.94
10	781	2.56	736	1.83
11	674	2.35	778	1.79
12	898	2.29	713	1.77
13	783	2.25	724	1.75
14	653	2.22	674	1.72
15	885	2.14	678	0.91
16	666	2.07	898	1.68
17	711	2.06	882	1.62
18	696	1.89	783	1.62
19	673	1.83	625	1.55
20	337	1.65	772	1.51

(*continued*)

Table 12. Continued

	1980		1989	
Ranking	*SITC*	*RCA*	*SITC*	*RCA*
5. South Korea				
1	844	2.31	848	9.18
2	848	9.36	786	7.74
3	831	6.77	871	2.60
4	847	5.93	653	5.40
5	261	5.87	831	4.71
6	653	5.68	847	4.50
7	871	5.48	761	4.27
8	696	5.47	762	4.09
9	634	5.48	844	3.96
10	672	5.44	451	3.20
11	761	5.38	776	3.04
12	656	5.20	693	2.92
13	842	4.84	846	2.81
14	843	4.55	793	2.69
15	661	4.27	661	2.67
16	625	4.27	898	2.60
17	846	4.21	697	2.57
18	451	4.15	842	2.56
19	654	3.76	657	2.50
20	693	3.65	656	2.25
6. Taiwan				
1	261	104.67	785	9.41
2	65X	16.14	894	7.57
3	658	12.97	831	7.20
4	89X	11.95	655	6.01
5	652	11.18	899	5.92
6	613	9.50	851	5.62
7	847	8.95	635	5.49
8	899	8.67	762	4.64
9	042	7.03	893	3.92
10	654	6.92	761	3.91
11	848	6.54	598	3.76
12	666	6.31	845	3.62
13	659	5.83	697	3.56
14	842	4.05	666	3.53
15	014	3.86	689	3.35
16	846	3.73	842	3.14
17	785	3.49	821	3.13
18	55	3.42	657	3.11
19	895	3.24	812	2.99
20	653	3.13	846	2.85

(continued)

Table 12. Continued

Ranking	1980 SITC	1980 RCA	1989 SITC	1989 RCA
7. Hong Kong				
1	844	16.79	884	8.15
2	884	14.15	261	7.27
3	846	9.39	844	6.80
4	894	9.33	831	6.01
5	842	9.15	655	6.01
6	762	8.87	894	5.73
7	845	7.81	845	5.54
8	831	7.78	846	5.01
9	848	6.02	652	4.59
10	652	4.93	843	4.48
11	843	4.80	842	4.44
12	847	4.57	762	4.29
13	883	4.17	899	4.04
14	897	3.26	848	3.63
15	697	3.25	696	3.28
16	658	3.21	654	2.95
17	775	3.11	656	2.89
18	751	2.86	122	2.73
19	655	2.76	897	2.72
20	812	2.65	771	2.72
8. Singapore				
1	762	13.79	431	10.67
2	431	11.79	762	7.91
3	776	11.19	091	6.01
4	091	7.97	761	5.46
5	689	692	752	5.13
6	634	6.90	689	4.37
7	761	6.28	776	3.69
8	046	3.87	111	3.20
9	111	3.78	751	2.98
10	793	3.39	764	2.73
11	844	2.79	743	2.53
12	846	2.33	073	2.27
13	764	2.31	634	2.10
14	653	2.26	716	1.87
15	048	2.24	895	1.75
16	723	2.10	845	1.60
17	898	1.94	846	1.40
18	772	1.88	046	1.15
19	743	1.73		
20	751	1.68		

(continued)

Table 12. Continued

	1980		1989	
Ranking	*SITC*	*RCA*	*SITC*	*RCA*
9. Malaysia				
1	689	64.74	431	27.75
2	776	23.18	689	14.28
3	091	14.20	762	14.06
4	431	11.28	776	10.18
5	634	10.61	073	7.54
6	635	4.96	634	5.98
7	037	4.90	848	5.02
8	073	4.61	771	4.62
9	621	3.72	621	3.98
10	847	3.41	844	3.64
11	844	2.87	864	2.93
12	266	2.70	091	2.86
13	058	2.41	845	2.76
14	762	2.35	037	2.66
15	653	2.32	635	1.91
16	848	2.21	741	1.79
17	111	2.06	628	1.44
18	652	1.82	666	1.29
19	628	1.75	058	1.24
20	771	1.70	598	1.23
10. Philippines				
1	061	27.24	058	13.66
2	634	19.40	846	8.44
3	683	18.69	061	8.08
4	058	14.92	842	7.42
5	846	11.51	899	6.92
6	899	7.94	776	6.74
7	841	5.18	037	6.63
8	037	492	847	5.55
9	121	4.30	845	5.30
10	661	4.2	635	456
11	081	4.10	843	4.43
12	635	3.87	848	4.26
13	842	3.79	821	4.15
14	821	3.67	773	4.09
15	657	3.17	844	3.77
16	512	3.00	834	3.38
17	848	2.93	885	3.03
18	843	2.64	512	2.68
19	845	2.41	831	2.34
20	655	2.38	666	2.14

(*continued*)

Table 12. Continued

	1980		1989	
Ranking	*SITC*	*RCA*	*SITC*	*RCA*
11. Indonesia				
1	698	57.03	634	83.21
2	844	16.51	656	7.24
3	842	15.20	431	6.44
4	634	12.36	661	6.38
5	845	11.83	653	5.11
6	121	11.54	635	4.94
7	551	9.43	844	4.85
8	846	9.50	684	4.65
9	883	8.49	846	4.58
10	081	7.17	652	4.13
11	847	4.92	562	4.11
12	776	4.47	842	4.01
13	661	4.20	845	3.79
14	658	3.49	073	3.52
15	073	2.88	121	3.33
16	431	2.68	551	2.89
17	889	2.49	843	2.60
18	671	1.71	851	2.44
19	562	2.41	689	1.74
20	843	2.38	657	2.30
12. China				
1	261	92.54	261	24.36
2	89X	13.65	831	10.32
3	84X	13.37	894	8.54
4	648	13.00	056	7.17
5	056	10.79	762	6.63
6	652	10.63	658	647
7	847	9.59	844	6.36
8	65X	8.90	654	6.04
9	844	8.73	652	5.98
10	899	841	842	5.97
11	55X	7.81	845	592
12	848	7.80	846	5.72
13	654	7.78	899	5.63
14	613	7.44	848	5.20
15	666	6.66	843	4.93
16	656	5.80	666	4.44
17	846	5.28	847	4.34
18	842	5.02	851	3.66
19	042	4.74	689	3.65
20	66X	4.33	659	3.26

woven textiles, clothing, footwear, electronic goods, toys, and jewelry. However, in that period, several industries also experienced declines in revealed comparative advantage; they were animal feed, textile wastes and fibers, nonferrous metals, and wood and wood products. This pattern of change of comparative advantage supports the earlier findings that, while natural resource-based manufacture goods such as rice and canned foods, were still among the top-ranking exports, other exports had expanded into skilled-labor-intensive manufactured goods.

Apparently, Thailand's comparative advantage changed substantially in the 1980s from specializing mostly in processed agricultural and natural resource based products to include a large variety of higher value-added manufactured goods. In fact, the export concentration index also showed a decline from 0.38 in 1975 to 0.30 in 1980 and 0.17 in 1989[8]. The expansion and diversification of these exports was made possible by benefits from both the comparative labor-cost advantage and the opening up of marketing opportunities in some importing countries in the early 1980s. For example, most of the light, labor-intensive products used to be extensively exported by the NICs, but as they became more industrialized and labor became increasingly expensive, exports had to shift to higher valued-added items to sustain growth. As a result, marketing opportunities for these labor-intensive products became more available for Thai exports (or those of other LDCs).

Below we examine the changing revealed comparative advantage of Pacific Rim countries and the implications of the changes on Thailand's exports. We first examine the changes in revealed comparative advantage of the neighboring ASEAN countries whose endowments are similar to Thailand's and ask how the direction of their changed comparative advantage will either affect Thailand's competitive position or provide areas for cooperation. Second, we discuss the revealed comparative advantage of the Asian NICs, noting that these countries not only compete with Thailand's labor-intensive exports, but that they are also the countries whose traditional exports might be taken over by countries such as Thailand. Third, we examine the revealed comparative advantage of a few major developed countries such as the United States, Japan, Australia, and Canada. How does their comparative advantage contrast with Thailand's, and how will their changes have an impact on Thailand through their effect on the changing competitiveness of exports from the NICs? Last, we study the revealed comparative advantage of China which has been or will become Thailand's potential world market competitor in the export of unskilled labor-intensive products.

ASEAN

In the early 1980s most exports with high revealed comparative advantage indexes in ASEAN were natural resource-based goods such as nonferrous metal products, vegetable oil, wood products, rubber products, rubber products, sugar, and preserved goods. The diversification to labor-intensive manufactured goods was relatively slow because of ASEAN countries' relatively high per capita natural resource endowment. However, in the late 1980s the change in comparative indices was in clothing, textiles, woven man-made fabric, footwear, and electrical machinery. These industries are labor-intensive and obtain their advantage from lower wages and the availability of more quotas in the DC markets than in the Asian NICs.

NICs

The NICs are natural resource-poor countries whose comparative advantage changes most rapidly. The standard deviations of revealed comparative advantage of these countries were higher than ASEAN countries in the 1970s, but decreased over time. This shows the rapid export diversification of these natural recource-poor countries. The direction of the change in export composition with top ranking revealed comparative advantage indices went from labor-intensive to capital-intensive or to high-technology-intensive, higher value-added products. The countries with faster increases in real wages and per capita stocks of physical and human capital had the most rapid changes in revealed comparative advantage. The exports whose revealed comparative advantage declined in all NICs included cotton fabrics, clothing, yarn, footwear, travel goods, toys, jewelry, and miscellaneous goods. The declines were mostly due to rising real wages, restricted markets in the DCs, or both. Those whose revealed comparative advantage indices increased were skilled-labor and technology-intensive goods such as manmade woven fabric, knitted clothing, electronic goods, telecommunications equipment, and transportation vehicles. The changes in the export competitive position of the NICs allowed low-wage countries (such as ASEAN countries) to benefit from the opening up of markets for labor-intensive exports such as electronic goods, textile products, clothing, and miscellaneous goods.

Industrial Countries

It is interesting to compare the changes in the comparative advantage of Japan, which is a natural-resource-scarce DC, with the resource-abundant countries such as the United States, Canada, Australia, and New Zealand. Evidence shows that, while the latter countries relied firmly on the exports of resource-based goods, the principal exports of Japan (mainly physical capital-intensive and technology-intensive goods) were more diversified and their composition changed much more rapidly than that of the other countries. The natural resource-rich DCs tended to retain a comparative advantage in resource-based production despite high levels of capital accumulation and competition from the resource-rich LDCs. This is due to their high per capita endowment or their trade barriers. If the productivity of their production of natural resources were not accelerated too rapidly or the resource-based sector were not under protection, the structure of their principal exports would have changed more rapidly and the opportunities for resource-rich LDCs to specialize in exporting of resource-based products would have also been extended. At the same time, if both Japan and other DCs were to continue diversifying their exports to become specialized in the areas of high-technology products, the NICs would be able to supplant their human and physical capital-intensive exports more rapidly. In fact, the more rapid the structural changes in production and trade in the DCs are, the more rapid the effects of the changes are on the changes in the comparative advantages in the rest of the world.

China

China's exports with top and stable rankings of revealed comparative advantage indexes throughout the 1980s were silk and preserved vegetable. Exports with and increasing revealed comparative advantage in the 1980s were travel goods, toys, radios and televisions, cotton fabrics, and all types of clothing. It seems as if China has been catching up with the ASEAN countries in the production of the various labor-intensive goods in the recent years when China's wage rate has still been lower and rising slower than that of the ASEAN countries.

Conclusion

Similar to other resource rich ASEAN countries, Thailand's comparative advantage is shifting from natural resource-based products to various kinds of higher valued-added products. The revealed comparative advantage for many human-capital and technology-intensive products was still less than unity but increased rapidly after 1985.

Nevertheless, compared with the NICs, the speed of change of revealed comparative advantage indices of Thailand or other ASEAN countries was still less rapid. In the NICs, where natural resource are limited, real wages were steadily rising, while human and physical capital was rapidly accumulating. There has been a shift from the initial specialization of labor intensive products to higher skilled labor and more capital and technology-intensive products. They seemed to move in stages, following a similar path of changing comparative advantage to a natural resource-poor developed country, namely Japan. This should provide opportunities for the expansion of unskilled and skilled labor intensive exports of countries at a lower level of development where unskilled labor is still abundantly available.

Comparing the real wages between ASEAN and countries at a lower level of development such as China whose wages were also lower, we found that there is the possibility of the competition of ASEAN labor-intensive exports from countries such as China. As their per capita income and productivity rises, China with even cheaper labor, will have the comparative advantage that the ASEAN countries presently possess. Thus, the changes in the trade patterns of Asia-Pacific countries seemed to move in harmonious stages, and there is ample room for trade among each other.

III. POTENTIAL GAINS FROM REGIONAL TRADE COOPERATION

In order to evaluate actual and potential trade expansion between Thailand and groups of Pacific Rim countries namely, North America, Japan, the NICs, ASEAN, Australia, New Zealand, and China, we computed various trade indices, namely trade intensity index, trade complementarity index, and trade bias index.[9] The overall computation results show that trade in the region grew less than its potential, most likely due to existing protectionist measures of individual countries in the area.

The trade intensity index which measures the extent to which a Pacific Rim country's share of Thailand's total manufactured exports is larger or smaller compared to the country's share in total world exports show that the Pacific Rim countries were Thailand's relatively large trading partners. From 1976 to 1989, the trade intensity between Thailand and most Pacific Rim countries was relatively high, implying that Thailand traded more with countries in the region than countries outside the region (see Table 13). In fact, the trade intensity was the highest between Thailand and most of the ASEAN countries (except for the Philippines), followed by Hong Kong and Japan. The trade intensity between Thailand and the United States and South Korea was about average in the index values of all Pacific Rim countries, whereas the trade intensity between Thailand and Canada, Australia, and New Zealand was the lowest. Interestingly, Canada and Taiwan were the only countries with increasing trade intensity with Thailand in the late 1980s although their index values were still lower than those of other countries.

Since the trade intensity index can further be broken into two indices namely, trade complementary and trade bias, we additionally computed the latter two indices so as to assess relative contributions of each of the components to Thailand's trade intensity with the different Pacific Rim countries. The trade complementarity index measures the actual degree to which Thailand's export pattern matches a Pacific Rim country's import pattern relative to the import pattern of all countries combined. The computation results in Table 14 show that the actual trade complementarity was not high. In other words, the high intensity of trade between Thailand and other Pacific Rim countries was not explained by strong complementary in actual trade patterns. Furthermore, the

Table 13. Index of Thailand's Trade Intensity With Individual Trading Partners in the Pacific

Year	*Canada*	*USA*	*Japan*	*Korea*	*Taiwan*	*Hong Kong*	*Singapore*
1976	0.10	1.08	8.86	1.63	0.97	5.33	8.18
1979	0.18	1.15	4.80	1.22	0.96	3.62	8.45
1980	0.14	1.39	3.15	1.30	0.87	3.73	7.32
1981	0.15	1.30	2.83	2.77	0.94	3.23	5.93
1982	0.16	1.28	2.96	1.41	0.65	2.96	5.71
1983	0.28	1.19	3.37	1.06	0.95	3.10	5.93
1985	0.32	1.20	2.66	0.77	1.13	2.35	6.81
1986	0.42	1.12	2.56	1.19	1.09	2.52	8.55
1988	0.68	1.63	2.72	1.40	n.a.	2.48	7.04
1989	0.68	1.93	3.35	1.30	n.a.	2.15	5.50

Year	*Malasia*	*Indonesia*	*Philippine*	*Brunei*	*Australia*	*New Zealand*
1976	9.88	11.69	2.47	n.a.	0.77	0.16
1976	9.88	11.69	2.47	n.a.	0.77	0.16
1979	6.07	10.41	0.57	5.19	0.94	0.50
1980	5.23	8.60	0.75	4.31	1.01	0.43
1981	6.99	2.97	0.44	5.39	0.88	0.40
1982	7.38	2.75	0.61	4.14	0.87	0.70
1983	5.08	3.62	1.49	3.66	1.28	0.96
1985	6.25	1.46	3.18	6.04	1.20	0.49
1986	7.33	1.55	1.70	3.98	1.38	0.69
1988	6.00	1.50	1.39	n.a.	0.19	1.08
1989	n.a.	2.89	n.a.	n.a.	1.66	1.14

indices did not seem to rise throughout the study period. These results do not seem to support the findings in Section 2 which imply that the "potential" for trade complementarity between Thailand and most Pacific Rim countries should be high.

From Table 14, although among Thailand's major trading partners the trade complementarity indices between Thailand and Japan, Hong Kong and Singapore were the highest, their index value showed little changes over time. The indices between Thailand and the United States and Canada were low although their production and trade structures were quite different and thus potentially complementary. Again, the trade complementarity of Thailand, Canada, and Taiwan, albeit low, showed a rising trend.

The low trade complementarity between Thailand and the United States and the rather constant trade complementarity between Thailand and some other countries such as Japan and South Korea can be postulated to be due to tariff and nontariff barriers existing in these importing countries.

Finally, we computed the trade bias index which measures the extent to which Thailand's exports have been more or less favorably accessible to the

Table 14. Index of Thailand's Trade Complementarity With Individual Trading Partners in the Pacific Rim

Year	*Canada*	*USA*	*Japan*	*Korea*	*Taiwan*	*Hong Kong*	*Singapore*
1976	0.54	0.88	2.27	2.33	0.47	1.53	0.35
1979	0.53	0.91	1.83	1.29	0.53	1.75	1.54
1980	0.60	0.91	1.56	2.93	0.52	1.61	1.36
1981	0.56	0.86	1.47	1.59	0.51	1.66	1.27
1982	0.62	0.83	1.60	1.31	0.54	1.70	1.09
1983	0.60	0.87	1.53	0.90	0.53	1.80	1.15
1985	0.61	0.87	1.42	0.58	0.60	1.64	1.06
1986	0.63	0.87	1.43	0.68	0.65	1.70	1.22
1988	0.74	0.96	1.46	0.88	0.88	1.62	1.33
1989	0.77	1.07	1.41	0.73	0.81	1.61	1.08

Year	*Malasia*	*Indonesia*	*Philippine*	*Brunei*	*Australia*	*New Zealand*
1976	0.75	1.53	1.62	2.36	0.67	0.74
1979	1.66	1.17	0.54	1.23	0.55	0.78
1980	1.07	1.36	0.51	1.25	0.58	0.66
1981	1.59	1.76	0.55	1.54	0.51	0.59
1982	1.76	1.20	0.69	1.22	0.56	0.80
1983	1.33	2.22	0.67	1.32	0.64	0.76
1985	1.45	0.70	0.67	1.75	0.70	0.76
1986	1.18	0.66	0.73	2.20	0.75	0.77
1988	1.64	0.56	1.25	3.25	0.73	0.88
1989	0.93	0.83	0.88	3.85	0.88	0.85

trading partner's import markets than exports from other countries. This bias can be explained by proximity, cultural, or institutional conditions. As expected, the group of countries with which Thailand had the highest trade bias from 1976 to 1989 was the ASEAN countries (see Table 15).

Since the trade intensity index is the multiplication of trade complementarity and trade bias indices, we can interpret that Thailand's higher trade intensity with one country compared to others may be due to the following factors. First, they have matching trade and production structures (trade complementarity). Second, they are close in terms of distance, cultural and institutional environment (trade bias). If Thailand's potential trade complementarity and trade bias with another country is great, but the actual measurement of the trade intensity is low, we should suspect that there are some trade barriers in existence and the barriers reduce or slow down the free flow of goods between the two countries.

Therefore, from the above discussion of all the trade indices between Thailand and individual Pacific Rim countries we can conclude the following. First, Thailand's high trade intensity with Japan and Hong Kong came mostly from the high trade complementarity between them. However, since the actual

Table 15. Index of Thailand's Trade Bias
With Individual Trading Partners in the Pacific Rim

Year	*Canada*	*USA*	*Japan*	*Korea*	*Taiwan*	*Hong Kong*	*Singapore*
1976	0.19	1.23	3.90	0.70	2.06	3.48	23.37
1979	0.31	1.26	2.62	0.95	1.81	2.07	5.49
1980	0.23	1.53	2.02	0.44	1.67	2.32	5.38
1981	0.27	1.51	1.93	1.74	1.84	1.95	4.67
1982	0.26	1.54	1.85	1.08	1.20	1.74	5.24
1983	0.47	1.37	0.84	1.13	1.79	1.72	5.16
1985	0.52	1.38	1.87	1.33	1.88	1.43	6.42
1986	0.67	1.29	1.79	1.75	1.68	1.48	7.01
1988	0.92	1.70	1.86	1.59	0.00	1.53	5.29
1989	0.88	1.80	2.38	1.78	0.00	1.34	4.68

Year	*Malasia*	*Indonesia*	*Philippine*	*Brunei*	*Australia*	*New Zealand*
1976	13.17	7.64	1.52	n.a.	1.15	0.22
1979	3.66	8.90	1.06	4.22	1.71	0.64
1980	4.89	6.32	1.47	3.45	1.74	0.65
1981	4.40	1.69	0.80	3.50	1.73	0.68
1982	4.19	2.29	0.88	3.39	1.55	0.88
1983	3.82	1.63	2.22	2.77	2.00	1.26
1985	4.31	2.09	4.75	3.45	1.71	0.64
1986	6.21	2.35	2.33	1.81	1.84	0.90
1988	3.66	2.68	1.11	0.00	0.26	1.23
1989	0.00	3.48	0.00	0.00	1.89	1.34

trade complementarity between Thailand and Japan did not change for the entire period of 1976 to 1989 one should suspect that some forms of trade barriers still exist in Japan.

Second, Thailand's low and increasing trade intensity with Canada and Taiwan was from the increases of trade complementarity. The increased trade between them in the late 1980s is observed to be from increased intra-industry trade in the machinery and equipment category.

Third, Thailand's trade intensity with the United States was not high (although the two countries had the greatest trade potential owing to different factor endowments) due to the low measurement of trade complementarity indices. We can also argue that tariff or nontariff barriers have not been reduced in the United States.

Finally, Thailand's high trade intensity with the ASEAN countries most likely came from being in the same region and having similar noneconomic conditions. Further increases in trade can be expected if the countries become more unified by having more open trade and investment, and more coordinated policies and institutional framework.

IV. CONCLUDING REMARKS

Thailand traded the most with countries in the Pacific Rim region, particularly with the more developed countries in the area. However, intensifying protectionist sentiments and rising nontariff barriers in many of the above countries tended to restrict Thailand's trade with them to less than potential. In addition, since the growth and structural change of manufactured production and exports of all countries in the region seem to indicate that their trade structures will continue to complement each other, it follows that potential gains from liberalizing trade in the region are very great.

First of all, reduced nontariff barriers in the developed countries should lead to the highest growth in both Thailand and the Pacific Rim countries' trade volumes, and thus provide the greatest potential gains from trade. Second, while reduced trade barriers among countries in NICs and ASEAN can certainly increase their trade volumes, the proportion of trade increment is likely to be smaller. This is simply because the differences in factor endowment between Thailand and ASEAN, or even the NICs, are smaller than the endowment differences between Thailand and countries with larger gaps in development levels. Therefore, Thailand's trade with the NICs or ASEAN, should be increased by stimulating factors determining intra-industry trade, some of which are related to increased direct foreign investment among themselves or from third countries.

On the whole, however, economic cooperation in the region which strives for free trade at the multilateral level still is the first best policy because it is based upon the nondiscriminatory treatment principle. However, given that current multilateral trade negotiations have taken an increasingly longer time to conclude and bilateral trade arrangements are becoming major industrialized countries' trade policies, Thailand's effort to form economic cooperation with countries in the Pacific Rim area is both timely and useful. This is because many industrialized countries in the Pacific Rim are still Thailand's major traditional markets and import sources. Thus, trade liberalization among countries in this group certainly promotes large gains from trade.

If the developed countries should continue to suffer from slow growth and difficulties in eradicating various imbalances and improving productivity, the expectation for freer trade in these countries could also be unrealistic. In which case Thailand, should, in the meantime, not rule out the possibility of forming economic cooperation with a smaller number of neighboring Asia-Pacific countries. In fact, such economic cooperation is also consistent with the country's attempt to diversify its export markets and products for sustaining trade expansion.

APPENDIX

Methods used in the Analysis

1. *Testing the Factor Proportions Explanation*

We apply Harkness and Kyle (1975) and Hellvin and Torstensson (1985)'s methods of using logit and probit analyses to test Thailand's commodity trade pattern and the direction of trade with different Pacific Rim countries. The model for analyzing Thailand's trade patterns is written as follows:

$$T_{ij} = \alpha + \beta X_i + \epsilon_{ij}$$

where T_{ij} measures Thailand's net exports of commodity i to country j, X_i measures the factor intensity of commodity i, and ϵ_{ij} the random error term. T_{ij} is 1 if Thailand has a corrected net export in commodity i in trade with country j. The corrected net export of commodity i to country j is defined as:

$$CNE_{ij} = \frac{X_{ij}/\Sigma_j X_{ij}}{M_{ij}/\Sigma_j M_{ij}}$$

where X_{ij} and M_{ij} are Thailand's exports and imports of commodity i to or from country j. The numerator of CNE_{ij} is Thailand's exports of commodity i per the total exports to country j, and the denominator is Thailand's imports of the corresponding commodity i per the total imports from country j. Thus, CNE_{ij} in fact measures Thailand's net export of commodity i to country j. If $CNE_{ij} > 1$, then $T_{ij} = 1$; if $CNE_{ij} < 1$, then $TI_j = 0$. Note that net, rather than gross, exports are used to represent trade performance because the net variable eliminates the problem of intra-industry trade, for which the HOS model has little to explain.

If we assume that factors of production are capital and labor, the above model can be written as:

$$T_{ij} = \alpha + \beta \left(\frac{K}{L}\right)_i + \epsilon_{ij}$$

where $(K/L)_i$: is the total capital-labor ratio of commodity i.

Assuming further that capital input can be separated into physical capital and human capital, the model becomes:

$$T_{ij} = \gamma_i + \gamma_2 \left(\frac{PK}{L}\right)_i + \gamma_3 \left(\frac{HK}{L}\right)_i + \epsilon_{ij}$$

where $(PK/L)_i$ and $(HK/L)_i$ are physical and human capital-labor ratios of commodity i, respectively.

In our study, the factor intensity variables are defined in terms of both flows (value-added per employee) and stocks (the value of capital stock, measured by the perpetual inventory method, divided by the number of workers). When separating the total capital input into physical and human capital inputs, wage value-added per man was used to represent human capital intensity, and non-wage value-added per man to represent physical capital intensity (See more details in Balassa 1979).

It should be noted that, although the data for computing CNE_{ij} are available in SITC at the 3-digit level of disaggregation, the data on factor intensities, either measured by the flow or the stock concept, are available only at the 3-digit ISIC level, which is much more aggregated than the 3-digit SITC grouping. We thus have to regroup the 3-digit SITC trade data to correspond to the 3-digit ISIC factor intensity data before estimating all the above equations.

However, since Balassa (1979)'s factor intensity data of the US industries are available at the 3-digit-SITC level, we also run regressions of Thailand's net exports against independent variables based on Balassa's factor intensity data, assuming that Thailand and the United States had similar production functions. By using Balassa's data we additionally benefit from having a larger sample size or observations, and it reduced estimation errors.

2. *Intra-industry Trade*

We follow Grubel and Lloyd (1975) in defining intra-industry trade of Thailand's trade. (exports plus imports) in a product group i with a country group j as

$$B_{ij} = 1 - \frac{\left| X_{ij} - M_{ij} \right|}{X_{ij} + M_{ij}}, \qquad \begin{array}{l} i = 1, 2, \ldots\ldots, n, \\ j = 1, 2, \ldots\ldots, k, \\ 0 \leq B_{ij} \leq 1 \end{array}$$

If $X_{ij} = M_{ij}$, there is no net trade and $B_{ij} = 1$, that is, all trade is intra-industry trade.

If $X_{ij} = 0$ or $M_{ij} = o$, all trade is net trade and $B_{ij} = 0$

A measure of the share of intra-industry trade of total trade in all products with a country group j can be obtained by averaging Bij's for the product group, that is,

$$B_{ij} = 1 - \frac{\sum_{i=1}^{n} \left| X_{ij} - M_{ij} \right|}{\sum_{i=1}^{n} X_{ij} + \sum_{i=1}^{n} M_{ij}} , \quad 0 \leq B_{ij} \leq 1$$

Thailand's intra-industry trade with different groups of Pacific Rim countries is computed on the 3-digit-SITC level of aggregation for 1973 to 1989.

3. *Trade Indices*

Following Balassa (1965, 1979), Kojima (1965), Drysdale (1969), and Andersen (1983) the various trade indices for measuring trade performance and trade interdependence between Thailand and the Pacific Rim Countries are defined as follows.

1) *Revealed Comparative advantage Index (RCA)*

RCA is defined as the share of Commodity k in total manufactured exports of Country i relative to the share of total exports of Commodity k in total world exports, namely,

$$RCA_i^k = \frac{X_i^k}{X_i} \Big/ \frac{X_w^k}{X_w}$$

2) *Trade Intensity Index (TII)*

The trade intensity index of Thailand's export to country j is defined as the share of Country j's imports from Thailand relative to the share of Country j's imports from the rest of the world namely,

$$TII = \frac{X_{Tj}}{X_T} \Big/ \frac{M_{Tj}}{M_W - M_T}$$

3) *Trade Complementarity Index (TCI)*

The trade complementarity index measures the degrees to which Thailand's export pattern matches Country j's import pattern relative to the import pattern of all other countries combined, namely

$$TCI_{Tj} = \sum_k \left(\frac{X_T^k}{X_T} , \frac{M_w - M_T}{M_w^k - M_T^k} , \frac{M_j^k}{M_j} \right)$$

4) Trade Bias Index (TBI)

The trade bias index measures the extent to which Thailand's exports have more or less favorable access to Country j's markets than Thailand's exports to other countries, namely.

$$\text{TBI}_{Tj} = X_{Tj} \sum_k \left(\frac{M_w^k - M_T^k}{X_T^k - M_j^k} \right)$$

5) Notations

X_i^k = exports of good k in Country i
X_i = exports of all manufactured goods of Country i
X_{Tj} = exports of Thailand to Country j
X_T = Thailand's total exports of manufactured goods
X_T^k = Thailand's exports of good k
M_w = Total manufactured imports of the world
M_T = Thailand's total manufactured imports
M_j = Country j's total manufactured imports
M_w^k = Total imports of good k in the world
M_T^k = Thailand's imports of good k
M_j^k = Country j's imports of good k

NOTES

1. See for example, Schott (1989).
2. See detailed model in Krueger (1977).
3. A good survey of various methodologies can be found in Deardorff (1984).
4. See Harkness and Kyle (1975) and Hellvin and Torstensson (1985).
5. See definitions and measurement of capital intensity in the Appendix.
6. The classification of industries into the four groups follows Krause (1986).
7. See details in Wiboonchutikula (1993) and recent studies of relationships between trade and direct foreign investment in Southeast Asia, see for example, Naya (1990).
8. We use the Gini-Hirschman coefficient for computing the export concentration index (ECI). The formula is

$$\text{ECI}_i = \left[\sum_k \left(\frac{X_i^k}{X_i} \right) \right]^{1/2} , \quad k = 1, 2, \ldots\ldots\ldots, n$$

where X_i^k = export of Country i of good k
and X_i = export of Country i of all goods.

9. Methods of various trade indices computation can be found in the Appendix.

REFERENCES

Anderdon, K. (1983). "Prospects of Trade Growth among Pacific Basin Countries, "*Developing Economies*, Vol. 21, No. 4.

Balassa, B. (1965). "Trade Liberalization and Revealed Comparative Advantage, "*Manchester School of Economic and Social Studies*, Vol. 33, No. 2, June.

Balassa, B. (1979). "The Changing Pattern of Comparative Advantage in Manufactured Goods, "*Review of Economics and Statistics*, Vol. 61.

Deardorff, A.V., (1984). "Testing Trade Theories and Predicting Trade Flows," in R.W. Jones and P.B. Kenen, (eds.), *Handbook of International Economics*, Vol.1. Amsterdam.

Drysdale, P. (1969). "Japan, Australia and New Zealand: The Prospects for Western Pacific Economic Integration," *Economic Record*, Vol. 45, No. 111, September.

Grubel, H.G. and P.J. Lloyd. (1975). *Intra-Industry Trade: The Theory and Measurement of International Trade in Differentiated Products*. London.

Harkness, J. and J.F. Kyle, (1975). "Factors Influencing United States Comparative Advantage, "*Journal of International Economics*, Vol. 5.

Hellvin, L. and J. Torstensson, (1985). "Factor Proportions in East-West Trade : The Case of Finland and Sweden," *Weltwirtschaftliches Archiv*.

Kojima, K. (1965). "The Pattern of International Trade Among Advanced Countries, "*Hitotsubashi Journal of Economics*, Vol. 5. No.1, June.

Krause, L. (1986). "The Structure of Trade in Manufactured Goods in East and Southeast Asian Region," in C.I. Bradford, Jr., and W.H. Branson, Eds. *Trade and Structural Change in Pacific Asia*. Chicago: University of Chicago Press.

Krueger, A.O. (1977). *Growth, Distortions and Patterns of Trade Among Many Countries*, Princeton Studies in International Finance, No. 40, Princeton University.

Naya, S., (1990). "Direct Foreign Investment and Trade in East and Southeast Asia," in R.W. Jones and A.O. Krueger, Eds., *The Political Economy of International Trade, Essays in Honor of Robert E. Baldwin*, Basil Blackwell.

Schott, J. Ed. (1989). *Free Trade Areas and U.S. Trade Policy*, Institute of International Economics, Washington D.C.

Wiboonchutikula, P. (1993). "Developing a Technology—Intensive Industry in Thailand: Computers and Their Periphelas." *Chulalongkorn Economic Journal*, May.

PART III.

REGIONALIZATION IN SOUTH ASIA

THE PROSPECT OF A TRADING BLOCK IN SOUTH ASIA?

ADV de S Indraratna

INTRODUCTION

South Asia comprises Afghanistan, Bangladesh, Bhutan, India, Maldives, Myanmar (formerly Burma), Nepal, Pakistan and Sri Lanka, to take them in their alphabetical order. Of these, the seven countries of Bangladesh, Bhutan, India, Maldives, Nepal, Pakistan and Sri Lanka, comprising the Indian subcontinent formed themselves into the South Asian Association for Regional Cooperation (SAARC) in 1985.[1] These seven countries, though contiguous, bound by the Himalayas in the North and the Indian Ocean in the South, are so diverse, in extent of their geographical area, size, growth and density of their populations, ethnicity and religion of their peoples and the level of their economic development, apart from several burning bilateral issues of contention,[2] one may be even surprised that they have come so far together even in a loose partnership like the SAARC. Be that as it may, SAARC has made some progress, though slow, in both cultural and economic cooperation during the last seven years.[3]

Research in Asian Economic Studies, Volume 6, pages 345-367.

ISBN: 1-55938-918-4

The object of this chapter is neither to evaluate those achievements nor even to question the original objectives of the SAARC. The aim of this chapter is to ascertain whether SAARC countries can go far enough to form a free trade area, or what may be termed a *trading block* in South Asia. In the absence of detailed country and regional studies, it would be difficult to pass *unequivocal* judgement whether SAARC countries can converge towards greater trade expansion both within their region and between them and the other regions to the net advantage of the members, fulfilling at least the second best condition of Pareto optimality.[4] Therefore the scope of this paper is limited, and its limited purpose would be achieved even if it is possible to indicate the extent of possibility or potential, in this direction.

The chapter will contain six sections. The first section will be the backdrop and the need for regionalism in South Asia. The second section will deal with the scope for greater cooperation in trade expansion. The third will highlight the existing constraints. The fourth will refer to the Macro-economic core or the package of measures necessary for trade expansion. The fifth will highlight the links with others. The sixth and the last will be the summary and conclusion.

The analysis will be presented throughout in respect of all SAARC countries, except when certain statistical indicators are not available as in the case of Maldives and Bhutan. However, their exclusion will not distort the analysis in any way as Maldives is a small island economy accounting for only .02 percent each of the region's population and the GNP and Bhutan only 0.13 percent and 0.9 percent of the region's population and GNP respectively.

I. THE BACKDROP AND THE NEED FOR REGIONALISM IN SOUTH ASIA

Although free trade has been advocated for the most efficient allocation of world resources, global free trade is now in complete disarray and in its place has emerged free trade within groups or *regional trading blocks*. The pattern of the world economy is also changing fast with the end of the cold war and the disintegration of the Soviet Union followed by the birth of the Commonwealth of Independent States (CIS), the unification of Eastern with Western Germany and the integration of the formerly centrally planned East European countries with Western Europe.

The world financial system is under strain due to volatile exchange and interest rates as well as the increasing claims on the global savings for reconstruction of the newly liberated economies, not only of Eastern Europe, but also of South East Asia (i.e., Laos, Vietnam and Cambodia) and Sub-Saharan Africa. Despite the GATT negotiations, there has been increasing protectionism mainly through NTBS and VERS in the traditional export markets of the developing countries of Asia as clearly demonstrated by the marked decline of developed country imports from South Asia.

It is in the above backdrop that the need for regionalism in South Asia is examined here. Within the scope of this paper, however, no attempt is made to define regionalism. Regionalism with its various vertical stages of free trade area, customs union/common market, economic union and total integration (Viner, 1950 and Meade, 1955) is accepted here as generally known. The underlying rationale for regionalism in its least integrated form of free trade within groups/regions of countries, or trading blocks as synonymously used here, is that it is better than no liberalization of trade at all.

At present, there are several major trading blocks such as the EC (in Europe), the NAFTA (in North America), the ASEAN (in Asia), the LAFTA[5] (in Latin America) and AFTA (in Africa). Of these EC is the only one which has gone beyond free trade towards even Economic Union. NAFTA, ASEAN and others are still in the stage of free trade. The EC today comprises 12 countries.[6] With the possible entry of the three Nordic Countries and Austria before the end of the year,[7] the EC with only 7 percent of the world population, will account for 30 percent of the world GDP with a per capita GDP of $18000.[8] NAFTA comprising the United States, Canada and Mexico, though of much more recent origin, would also be equally powerful with a population (6.9%), and GDP (27.8%), of almost equal size and a per capita GDP of $17000.[9] These two are by far the largest and most powerful trading blocks, together enjoying more than half of the world income (57.5%) with a per capita income of more than $17000. These two blocks together with Australia, New Zealand and Japan, but excluding Mexico comprise the group of *Industrial Countries.* As shown in Table 1, all SAARC Countries hitherto have the bulk of their export

Table 1. SAARC
The Share of Trade with Industrial Countries
(Percentage of the total)

	Exports			*Imports*		
Country	*1989*	*1990*	*1991*	*1989*	*1990*	*1991*
Bangladesh	65.0	71.3	75.8	39.6	42.9	37.2
Bhutan	—	—	—	—	—	—
India	52.6	55.2	54.4	58.8	55.8	57.0
Maldives	49.9	61.4	62.6	21.5	16.2	15.7
Nepal	87.1	86.6	88.6	47.2	45.4	48.3
Pakistan	58.7	60.8	56.0	57.6	55.2	58.4
Sri Lanka	62.0	61.5	69.4	41.7	40.2	36.7
Total	58.7	58.0	57.3	55.0	53.1	53.5

Note: — Not available
Source: Direction of Trade Statistics Year Book 1992. IMF, Washington, D.C.

trade with these industrial countries who also supply them, excluding Maldives, 40 percent-60 percent of the latter's imports.

The leaders of South Asian (SAARC) countries have raised their eyebrows about the possible adverse impact of the developments referred to above on their international trade. As precautionary measures, they have been contemplating upon ways and means of enhancing their export competitiveness and diversifying their markets. Regional trading blocks are one such measure. "It has been argued that within a trading block inexperienced producers can learn to compete, become more efficient through learning by doing, and benefit from economies of scale and the sharing of experience" (Asian Development Outlook, 1992).[10] It has also been argued that such a trading block may also considerably cut down on defense expenditure which has considerably militated against the economic progress of SAARC countries. In the SAARC region, in particular, military expenditure has increased far out of proportion to other expenditures (see below) owing to bilateral contentious issues and terrorism. Their containment and resolution is considered a prelude to any serious economic cooperation.

Another compelling reason for regionalism among SAARC Countries in the context of the other regional blocks is the crucial importance of international trade to their economies. As shown in Table 2, as a percentage of GDP, their exports constitute 7 percent (i.e., in the case of India which has by far the largest domestic market) to 28 percent (the highest in the case of Sri Lanka), leaving aside Maldives for which 1990 data are not available, while their imports constitute 10 percent to 37 percent, (the lowest in the case of India and the highest for Sri Lanka) with total trade working out to 16 percent to 65 percent. The expansion of these economies will significantly depend upon the expansion of their trade. These countries will, therefore, have to look for greater economic cooperation among themselves in addition to counteract any possible threat from other trading blocks. What is the scope for greater economic cooperation in the form of a free trade area or a regional trading block, among SAARC countries?

II. Scope for Economic Cooperation

Excluding China and Mongolia of North Asia, Cambodia, Lao and Vietnam of South East Asia, and the petroleum exporting countries of West Asia, for which it is also difficult to obtain statistical data, five sets of countries of Asia can be identified at different levels of development. First, there is Japan with a per capita GNP (1990) of more than $25,000 falling into the most highly industrialized "*Group of Seven*"; second is the four newly industrialized countries of East Asia with per capita GNP ranging from $5,400 to $12,300; the third is South East Asia comprising ASEAN with GNP per capita varying

Table 2. SAARC
Share of Trade as % of GDP

	Imports		*Exports*		*Total*	
Country	*1988*	*1990*	*1988*	*1990*	*1988*	*1990*
Bangladesh	15.46	15.93	6.37	7.32	21.83	23.25
Bhutan	—	42.02	—	12.06	—	52.08
India	9.45	9.31	6.14	7.06	15.59	16.37
Maldives	62.74	—	27.42	—	90.16	—
Nepal	21.95	18.79	6.50	5.61	28.45	24.39
Pakistan	22.09	20.78	12.81	15.75	34.90	36.53
Sri Lanka	35.01	37.09	23.00	27.37	58.01	64.46

Source: Calculated on the basis of data obtained from World Development Report 1992.

between $550 in Indonesia to $2,320 in Malaysia; the fourth is the Pacific Island Economies with $580-$1,770 GNP per capita, and the fifth and the last is the group of least developed countries of South Asia.

Except for the exclusion of the two newly liberated countries of Myanmar (formerly Burma) and Afghanistan, South Asia is synonymous with SAARC Countries. SAARC Countries with only 3.37 percent of the land area of the world contains the bulk of its population of 20.83 percent but with only 1.55 percent of the world income (1990 GDP). She contains nearly half of the world poor of around 500 million people.

Within the SAARC region itself there is also marked disparity and diversity. This is not only in regard to the ethnicity and religion of its peoples, which is generally known, but also in regard to the level of socio-economic development of its members. As seen from Table 3, the land area ranges from 47,000 in Bhutan (if one leaves Maldives out) to 3,288,000 square kilometers in India which has nearly 3/4 of the total area of the region. The size of population also varies from 1.4 million to 849.5 million between the same two countries, India again containing more than 3/4 of the population of the region. With regard to the GDP the position is similar with Bhutan having only 0.09 percent, in comparison with India's 78.85 percent, of the region's total. The per capita income as at 1990 varies between $170 in Nepal to $470 in Sri Lanka with the three countries of Nepal, Bhutan and Bangladesh remaining least developed with less than $200. They also have been growing in the last decade at different rates with Sri Lanka, Bangladesh and Nepal at less than 5 percent, India and Pakistan between 5 percent and 7 percent and Bhutan at more than 7 percent. The enormity of India relative to the other six small countries of SAARC has also cast some fear among the latter.

Because of the present disparity and diversity of the seven SAARC Countries, as briefly explained above, they would not be able to form themselves into a free trade area in the classical sense (Viner, 1950) in the

Table 3. Diversity of SAARC Countries

	Land Area		*Population Mid 1990*		*GDP 1990*		*GDP Growth Rate*		*GNP per Capital 1990*
	Extent '000 sq.k.	*%*	*(Millions)*	*%*	*US$ Millions*	*%*	*1981-90*	*1991*	*US$*
Bangladesh	1444	3.21	106.7	9.65	22280	6.90	4.1	3.3	200**
Bhutan	47	1.04	1.4	0.13	280	0.09	7.3	3.5	190
India	3288	73.36	849.5	76.80	254540	78.85	5.5	2.0	350
Maldives	<0.5	—	0.2	0.02	87f	0.02f	n.a.	n.a.	450
Nepal	141	3.15	18.9	1.71	2890	0.90	4.7	4.0	170
Pakistan	796	17.76	112.4	10.16	35500	11.00	6.3	6.5	380
Sri Lanka	66	1.47	17.0	1.54	7250	2.25	3.9	5.0	470
SAARC	4482	100.00	1106.1	100.00	322827	100.00	5.3++	2.7++	330+

Notes: [f]GNP (and not GDP) for 1989

**Asian Development Outlook gives it 210

+Average for SAARC Countries excluding Maldives.

++Average for South Asia including Myanmar but excluding Maldives & Afghanistan

Sources: World Bank-World Development Report 1992.

Asian Development Bank-Asian Development Outlook 1992.

World Bank Atlas 1990 only for Maldives data of 1989.

foreseeable future. These countries, therefore, have to look for other measures short of free trade in order to expand their international trade which is crucial to the growth of their economies and the alleviation of poverty of their peoples.

Taken as a whole, the international trade of this region today is in a parlous state. SAARC Countries which contain 1/5 of the world population have a very small share of the total world trade. As shown in Table 4, the countries of the SAARC region (excluding Bhutan because of the lack of data) have around 1.2 percent of the total world exports, even less than their share of the world GDP (Table 3). Even of this small share of the world trade, the bulk is with the industrial countries as has been already seen in Table 1. The intra-SAARC trade is relatively very small. As shown in Table 5, the intra-regional exports is less than 4% and the intra-regional imports about 2 percent, of the total exports and imports of this region respectively with the total intra-SAARC trade being in between at 2.6 percent-2.7 percent.

Table 4. SAARC Share of World Exports (Percentages)

Country	*1988*	*1989*	*1990*
Bangladesh	0.10	0.11	0.09
Bhutan	—	—	—
India	0.81	0.77	0.67
Maldives	0.004	0.004	0.00
Nepal	0.02	0.016	0.01
Pakistan	0.27	0.25	0.23
Sri Lanka	0.08	0.08	0.09
Total	1.284	1.230	1.102

Note: No data available for Bhutan
Source: Direction of Trade Statistics Year Book 1992

Table 5. SAARC Intra-Regional Trade

	Exports		*Imports*		*Total*	
Country	*1986-88*	*1989-90*	*1986-88*	*1989-90*	*1986-88*	*1989-90*
Bangladesh	5.00	4.09	4.43	6.23	4.59	5.58
Bhutan	—	—	—	—	—	—
India	2.88	3.38	0.49	0.42	1.43	1.76
Maldives	14.55	15.65	10.58	11.92	11.54	12.85
Nepal	25.87	6.20	21.36	12.54	22.64	10.44
Pakistan	4.15	3.61	1.75	1.60	2.72	2.45
Sri Lanka	5.18	3.78	7.54	6.84	6.62	5.57
Total	3.72	3.54	2.01	1.91	2.66	2.61

Source: Direction of Trade Statistics Year Book 1992.

Several factors have been responsible for these limits to trade expansion both intraregionally and globally in the past. One was their inward-looking policies of import substitution and the lack of incentives for export promotion. Numerous instances could be cited of the relatively high levies on exports including even primary exports for which they have enjoyed a comparative advantage. Another was the protectionist tariffs and NTBS against each other which had been raised with the abandonment of the system of Imperial or Commonwealth Preferences. This, in particular, had militated against the expansion of intraregional trade.

Another limit was set to their trade expansion by the slowing-down of demand since 1983 for their labor-intensive manufactures in DC markets which had been used to absorb the bulk of them. Still another was the increasing competition from the richer Asian neighbors of Newly Industrialized Economies of East Asia and the New Exporting Countries of South East Asia (Indraratna, 1992).[11]

The enhancement of the export competitiveness of SAARC countries through greater productive efficiency, economies of scale through harmonization of industries and removal of export levies and charges is crucial for any trade expansion intraregionally as well as interregionally. To this end, greater economic cooperation through a *South Asian Preferential Trading Arrangement* (SAPTA)[12] for industrial cooperation has already been signed (on April 11, 1993).

SAPTA seeks to establish a framework under which specific measures for trade liberalization among SAARC members could be furthered. The aim of the SAPTA agreement itself is to promote and sustain mutual trade and economic cooperation among the members before their trade can be fully liberalized. It is based and applied on overall reciprocity and to the mutual advantage of members, to ensure equitable trade expansion taking into account their different levels of economic and industrial development and also having due regard to the special needs of the least developed countries in the region. Negotiations shall be conducted step by step and in stages and on the basis of product by product. Among many others, provision for special treatment is provided to the LLDCs of the Region. There is also provision for taking appropriate steps for developing infrastructure facilities for accelerating the growth of trade.[13] All in all, it has been agreed upon only as a first step towards free trade or a trading block, in the region, in the future.

Why should SAARC countries look towards free trade? Obviously, free trade is expected to promote more trade creation than trade diversion, and achieve thereby greater efficiency of resource utilization and increased economic welfare thereby fulfilling at least the second best condition of Pareto optimality. For this, complementarity of economies of member countries is generally considered a prerequisite. Let us examine the prospect of SAARC countries in this regard.

Tables 6, 7 and 8 respectively give the structure of production, structure of manufacturing within it and the structure of exports of the SAARC Countries. Looking at these broad sectoral classifications of production, manufacturing and exports, one may come to the conclusion that SAARC economies are competitive. However, one must not forget that these structures have been built over the years within high tariff walls and other non-tariff barriers rather than under free trade. The present low-degree of complementarity in the production and trade structures could be, therefore, at least partly attributed to trade and other barriers put up by member countries on themselves (Reza, 1992).[14] With opening up of these economies (see below) comparative cost advantages would alter and structural changes in composition of production would follow.

In any case, comparative cost structures do not remain permanent. They may change not only with trade liberalization but also with changes in domestic economic policies or changes in the *"Macro Economic Core"* (see Section 4) of the countries concerned. This is quite evident from the experience of members of both the EC and the NAFTA. The relative importance of their

Table 6. Structure of Production (Percentages)

Country	*Agriculture*		*Industry other than Manufacturing*		*Manufacturing*		*Services*	
	1965	*1990*	*1965*	*1990*	*1965*	*1990*	*1965*	*1990*
Bangladesh	53	38	6	6	5	9	36	46
Bhutan	—	43	—	17	—	10	—	29
India	44	31	6	10	16	19	34	40
Nepal	65	60	8	9	3	5	23	26
Pakistan	40	26	6	8	14	17	40	49
Sri Lanka	28	26	4	11	17	15	51	48

Source: World Development Report 1992

Table 7. Structure of Manufacturing (1989) (Percentages)

Country	*Food/Beverages & Tobacco*	*Textiles & Clothing*	*Machinery & Transport Equipment*	*Chemicals*	*Other*
Bangladesh	23	36	5	18	18
Bhutan	—	—	—	—	—
India	1	12	26	17	33
Nepal	35	25	2	8	30
Pakistan	30	19	8	16	27
Sri Lanka	52	20	2	3	23

Source: World Development Report 1992

Table 8. Export Structure (1990)
(Percentages)

Country	*Fuel, Minerals & Metals*	*Food & Agriculture Raw Materials*	*Machinery & Transport Equipment*	*Textiles & Clothing*	*Other Manufactures*
Bangladesh	01	25	01	60	12
Bhutan	na	na	na	na	na
India	08	19	07	23	43
Nepal	00	25	00	57	17
Pakistan	01	29	00	58	12
Sri Lanka	06	47	01	34	13

Source: World Development Report 1992.

industrial sectors has declined during the last 3 decades and that of the service sectors has correspondingly risen. The service sectors of most of these countries today contribute more than 60 percent of the GDP, unlike in the sixties when they accounted for less than 50 percent (WDR, 1992).[15] It was privatization and deregulation which were primary responsible for this change (Economist, 1993).[16] "The faster growing part of all rich economies is neither manufacturing nor traditional services but the "*Knowledge Sector*" (Economist, 1993).[17]

Gains from international trade, by way of increasing production and welfare, accrue to countries on the basis of comparative costs only when barriers to trade are removed. The SAARC *Study on Trade, Manufactures and Services*[18] identified country-wide lists of intraregional exports and imports. These lists indicate a large number of identical or closely substitutable commodities produced simultaneously by several countries of the region. Without detailed study of the cost data of these individual products one cannot say which of these products are being produced on the basis of comparative costs and international specialization of labor. My reasonable hunch is that many of these products are being produced under protection as part of import substituting policies or autarkical conditions, and their production might not have been undertaken on the basis of comparative costs under free trade. It is clearly demonstrated in international trade theory that in a two-country two product model, the domestic production equilibrium, before barriers to trade are removed, is different from that after the two countries are open to trade. Therefore my conclusion is that within different sectors of the economies of these countries (which I would refer to henceforth as "*intra-sectoral complementarity*"), there would be ample scope for complementarity which would work in favor of trade creation for these countries.

This intrasectoral complementarity should not be considered something peculiar in South Asia. It seems to be the case with the trading blocks of the EC and the NAFTA as well. The entire membership of the EC and the NAFTA, except Mexico of the latter, belongs to the World Bank category of industrial countries. Their overall structures of production are very similar and seem highly competitive but the structures of their manufacturing and agricultural sectors (World Bank, 1992)[19] reveal intra-sectoral complementarity which has enabled them to come together in free trade.

Intra-sectoral complementarity may even be more operative in the SAARC because of the different sizes and the different stages of economic growth of its members as indicated in Table 3. When economies are at more or less the same level of development, it may be difficult for them to complement each other in different sectors of the economy. Their disparity, on the other hand, rather than being an obstacle as considered by some, may actually work in favor of creation of trade. A case in point is the labor-intensive textile and clothing industry and capital-intensive industry of machinery and transport equipment within the same sector of manufacturing. As shown in table 7, all

SAARC Countries, at present, compete with each other in their labor-intensive industries of textile and clothing, while India alone has a complementary edge over others in her machinery and transport equipment. As shown in Table 8, machinery and transport equipment comprise 7 percent of the export structure of India in comparison with zero or 1 percent in the case of the other countries of the Region. Similarly, in the structure of manufacturing of India, this subsector occupies 26 percent whereas in the other countries it ranges between 8 percent in Pakistan and 2 percent in Nepal and Sri Lanka. Trade liberalization in the SAARC region may promote the expansion of capital-intensive industries of India and labor-intensive industries such as textiles and clothing in the other countries.

The opposite side of the coin is, that even in the case of competitive economies, liberalization would make them allocatively more efficient, if inefficient industries had been earlier protected by high tariffs. The removal of tariffs would lead to expansion of the low-cost industries and to the contraction of high-cost industries within the region. Industries which were not efficient on a national scale earlier would become efficient on a regional scale. The argument may equally apply to the case of nascent or infant industries in these countries.

It has already been mentioned that textile and clothing occupy a very important place in the structure of manufacturing and exports in the SAARC countries. Pakistan and India today have maximum tariffs of over 100 percent whereas Sri Lanka has brought them down to 50 percent with its four-band tariff structure (Indraratna, 1992).[20] If tariffs are abolished or brought down to a uniform level among SAARC countries, Sri Lanka would be able to achieve further economies of scale and be more competitive with India and Pakistan in this industry.

It is not only within the manufacturing sector but also within the primary sector that there may be intrasectoral complementarity and scope for inter-country specialization. As shown in the SAARC Study, Bangladesh can specialize in primary products such as raw jute and tea, Pakistan in rice, cotton and dried fish, Sri Lanka in tea and rubber and coconut, Nepal in live animals, oil seeds and vegetable oils and Bhutan in vegetables and fruits.

There is yet another reason why the low degree of country complementarity should not cause fear among the SAARC members. By keeping external tariffs low, trade liberalization among them would be able to avoid much trade diversion which is economically inefficient and welfare-reducing. SAARC Countries, as stated earlier, have been having the bulk of their trade with industrial countries and their intra-regional trade has been minimal. This was attributed largely to the relatively high tariffs on each others' goods. If these were removed and trade were diverted from *Industrial countries* to the region, it is likely to be beneficial because of the low transport costs. Several possibilities in this direction have been highlighted in the SAARC Study (SAARC, 1991).[21]

The foregoing analysis shows that the apparent lack of complementarity of the South Asian Economies should not stand in the way of these countries moving towards free trade in a regional trading block. There are already some positive developments in these countries which favor the creation of the environment necessary for it. The increasing adoption of open market policies by them is one of these developments. Since inward-looking strategies such as of import substitution in agriculture as well as in industry have so far defied solution of their economic ills, these countries are now opening up their economies and adopting strategies of export led industrialization (ELI). Sri Lanka has gone a long way in this direction by reducing its tariff structure to 4 bands with 50 percent duty as the highest. It has also been implementing a package of measures for decontrol of foreign exchange and other financial deregulation (Indraratna, 1992)[22] and for privatization of the public sector enterprises. It is also contemplating upon a convertible Rupee. India and Pakistan are following suit though they still retain higher tariffs than Sri Lanka, but are likely to come down nearer to Sri Lanka's level with increasing liberalization of their economies. Notwithstanding this, India has taken a step even farther than Sri Lanka by announcing in its current year's budget the convertibility of the Indian Rupee and terminating its hitherto existing dual exchange rate. Nepal has also very recently opened its door to India and commenced reducing tariffs on a number of commodities (Meena Acharya, 1992).[23]

Another development is the creation of a better climate for investment coupled with the encouragement of FDI by establishing Free Investment Zones. Sri Lanka once again takes the lead in this direction by declaring the whole country as a "Free Investment Zone."

There are also several external developments which may help. The NICS are moving away from labor-intensive to capital intensive goods and relocating some of their industries in low-labor-cost countries in South East and South Asia. Even NECS of Malaysia and Thailand are moving away from labor-intensive to capital-intensive industries such as electrical goods and electronics.[24] Interest rate cuts in the industrial countries, particularly in the United States and the United Kingdom, will also help. The replacement of the United States by Japan as the key foreign investor in Asia may augur well for SAARC Countries too.

III. MACRO-ECONOMIC CORE

The positive internal and external developments which have been briefly described above, no doubt, augur well for the countries of South Asia in their

Table 9. Budget Deficits, Trade Balance and Current Account Deficits

Country	*Budget deficit as % of GDP*				*Balance of Trade ($ million)*				*Balance of Payments on Current Account ($ million)*				*Balance of Payments on Current Account (As % of GDP)*			
	1988	*1989*	*1990*	*1991*	*1988*	*1989*	*1990*	*1991*	*1988*	*1989*	*1990*	*1991*	*1988*	*1989*	*1990*	*1991*
Bangladesh	6.0	6.8	7.1	7.2	-1444	-1986	-2144	-2122	-286	-1103	-1232	-1175	-1.5	-5.4	-5.4	-4.9
Bhutan	9.7	9.7	2.8	0.6	na	na	na	na	na	na	na	na	na	na	na	na
India	7.8	7.9	8.4	6.5	-6596	-7023	-7848	-7828	-6189	-6936	-8029	-8795	-2.3	-2.6	-2.9	-3.1
Nepal	9.8	13.1	11.1	12.8	-477	-415	-405	-450	-280	-243	-267	-344	-9.4	-8.5	-9.2	-9.3
Pakistan	8.5	7.4	6.7	5.8	-2557	-2573	-2264	-2241	-1682	-1934	-1652	-1900	-4.4	-4.8	-4.1	-4.4
Sri Lanka	15.7	11.2	9.9	9.6	-763	-667	-673	-669	-389	-310	-333	-330	-5.7	-4.5	-4.4	-3.9

Note: na - not available

Source: Asian Development Outlook 1991 & 1992.

move towards a free trade area or a trading block among them. However, they still have a long way to go in converging towards an appropriate macro-economic core for micro-economic optimization, which is necessary for the successful operation of such a regional block.

Most of SAARC countries have not yet been able to avoid the pursuit of expansionary fiscal policies. They have run into persistent budget deficits as shown in Table 9. These deficits have been largely due to the increasing defense expenditure of these countries occasioned by their ethnic problems and insurgency and bilateral contentions. As shown in Table 10, as a percentage of the total government expenditure, the defense expenditure was as high as 6.0 percent (in Nepal) to 30.9 percent (in Pakistan) and it varied between 1.5 percent (in Bangladesh) to 7.1 percent (Pakistan) of GDP. On average, around 1/3 of the deficit was directly due to the military expenditure which was highly expansionary. Deficits were met by increasing both domestic as well as external borrowing and money supply. As shown in Table 11, money supply of these countries has been increasing significantly and this has led to double digit inflation in these countries. External debt and debt service ratios have been also very large (Table 12). The relative high inflation in these countries has also prevented the real effective exchange rate from falling despite the significant fall in the nominal exchange rate of their currencies as shown in Table 13.

The balance of trade has therefore not improved as would be indicated by a J-curve effect. The deficit in the balance of trade and the large external debt with a significantly high debt service ratio have led to persistent current account deficits, as shown in Table 9, maintaining the twin deficit relationship between the budget and the current account of the balance of payments. Thus all in all, despite the opening up of their economies, many of the SAARC Countries have been suffering from both internal and external imbalances (Indraratna, 1992).[25] The external imbalance is also vividly manifested in considerable resource gap, gross domestic savings falling far short of gross domestic investment (see also Reza, 1992).[26]

These countries are also constrained by high population growth of more than 2 percent, except Sri Lanka which has been able to bring it down to less than 1.5 percent. Slackening in the net flow of resources from DCS, and the increasing difficulty of access to world capital markets owing to changes in the global economy referred to earlier may be mentioned as other constraints, on top of the inadequate infrastructure development within the region.

Before these countries can go in for full liberalization of trade, or form a trading block, among themselves, the above mentioned constraints must be eliminated, and they should implement a full package of socio-economic policies. Such a package should include the following:

1. Financial deregulation and privatization.
2. A realistic (floating) exchange rate.

Table 10. Defence Expenditure 1990

	(1)	(2)
	As % Government Expenditure	*as % of GDP*
Bangladesh	10.1	1.5
Bhutan	na	na
India	17.0	2.9
Maldives	na	na
Nepal	6.0	1.8
Pakistan	30.9	7.1
Sri Lanka	7.1	2.3

Source: *Col. (1)*-WDR 1992.
Col. (2)-ADB Outlook 1992.

3. Containment of inflation.
4. Prevention of undue rise in labor costs.
5. Further arrest of population growth.
6. Fiscal and monetary reforms for demand management.
7. Free Investment Zones and other investment incentives.
8. Congenial political environment with stable governments.

The countries of the SAARC, as stated earlier, have already commenced financial deregulation and privatization by removal of controls and restrictions of foreign exchange and abolition of dual exchange rates. They are also going in increasingly for privatization of public sector enterprises. Still, however, there is much to be done. Countries of Nepal and Bhutan will have to maintain an open door policy with India. Following India's example, all other countries of this region will have to accept free convertibility of their currencies. This will prevent the overvaluation of currencies which is almost characteristic of these countries now.

Containment of inflation with a floating currency will prevent the appreciation of the real effective exchange rate. This, with the prevention of undue rise in labor costs, would ensure the export competitiveness. Further arrest of population growth will enable per capita incomes to rise. This, together with the necessary fiscal and monetary reform for demand management, would prevent import inducement. These, coupled with the containment of inflation, in turn, would increase domestic savings. The increase in domestic savings would reduce the resource gap and the burden of external debt.

Free Investment Zones, congenial political environments with stable governments and the absence of terrorism will attract foreign direct investment. Incentives to MNEs would attract them with transfer of technology. Stable governments and the absence of terrorism will also help these countries to

Table 11. Money Supply and Inflation

Country	% Changes in CPI					Average Annual Rate of Inflation (%)		Annual (%) Changes in Money Supply (M_2)			
	1988	*1989*	*1990*	*1991*	*1992 (Projected)*	*1971-80*	*1981-90*	*1988*	*1989*	*1990*	*1991*
Bangladesh	9.4	10.0	8.1	7.4	9.1	20.6	10.7	9.0	16.3	16.9	12.1
Bhutan	10.1	8.8	10.2	11.5	10.5	n.a	9.2	31.0	34.9	10.5	10.3
India	9.4	6.2	9.0	14.4	7.5	8.2	8.9	18.3	16.4	7.3	17.6
Nepal	9.0	8.8	8.2	15.4	16.0	7.8	10.2	22.1	21.1	18.5	20.7
Pakistan	8.8	7.9	9.0	12.2	8.0	12.4	7.0	7.7	7.4	11.6	17.9
Sri Lanka	14.0	11.5	21.5	12.0	11.0	8.9	12.4	16.5	12.5	19.1	19.0

Note: CPI = Consumer Price Index
Source: Asian Development Outlook-1992

Table 12. External Debt and Debt Service Ratios (as % of GDP)

	External Debt			Debt Service Ratios			
	88	89	90	88	89	90	91
Bangladesh	53.8	52.9	53.5	21.2	19.9	25.4	21.0
Bhutan	22.0	n.a.	29.6	n.a.	n.a	n.a	n.a
India	24.6	27.4	27.5	29.8	26.5	26.8	26.9
Maldives	n.a.	n.a	n.a	n.a	n.a	n.a	n.a
Nepal	41.0	48.4	56.1	12.4	15.8	18.3	19.0
Pakistan	49.8	51.1	58.3	24.6	23.0	23.7	23.7
Sri Lanka	81.22	81.4	80.7	21.7	18.6	13.8	17.2

Source: World Development Reports 1990, 1991, 1992.
Asian Development Outlook 1992.

reduce their military expenditure which, as shown earlier, take a heavy toll on their government budgets.

The increase in domestic savings and the reduction of the public sector borrowing requirements would also enable the containment of domestic interest rates. These outcomes together will reduce the budget deficits which in turn would help to contain inflation. The reduction of budget deficit along with the prevention of import inducement and realistic real effective exchange rates would help to eliminate current account deficits. The twin deficit relationship would thus hold on the positive side with contained budget deficits and sustainable current account deficits.

The package of measures discussed above include the macro-economic core necessary for micro economic optimization in industries in these countries. Some of these variables referred to in this package such as inflation rate, interest rates, budget deficit, the public debt and exchange rates have also been identified elsewhere (Green, 1992)[27] as measures of "economic convergence for individual countries." A macro-economic core for micro-economic optimization in domestic industries is a necessary condition for trade expansion through free trade with Pareto optimality[28] for the SAARC Region.

Until such time the SAARC countries are successful in implementing a "convergent macro economic core" in them, they may have to be satisfied with preferential trading arrangements among them as from 1997, as set out by SAPTA. Details of possibilities in this direction have been discussed in the *SAARC Study on Trade, Manufactures and Services* (SAARC, 1991).[29] This study highlighted several areas of possible industrial cooperation. One of them is the prospect for joint industrial ventures in a wide range of products.[30]

Table 13. Nominal and Real Effective Exchange Rates (REER)

	1988		*1989*		*1990*		*1991*	
Country	*NOM.*	*REER*	*NOM.*	*REER*	*NOM.*	*REER*	*NOM.*	*REER*
Bangladesh	31.733	83.938	32.270	91.741	34.569	86.718	35.720	85.236
Bhutan	13.917	. . .	16.225	. . .	17.504	. . .	26.000	. . .
India	14.480	76.958	16.650	72.056	17.943	66.239	24.583	57.182
Nepal	23.289	85.138	27.189	75.147	29.369	71.931	32.438	65.697
Pakistan	17.599	91.901	19.180	68.558	21.390	66.322	22.370	66.194
Sri Lanka	31.807	83.818	36.047	81.115	40.063	86.846	41.500	91.960

Notes: Nominal (NOM.) Exchange rates given in the respective currency of the country.
REER : 1985 = 100

Source: Asian Development Outlook 1992.

IV. LINKS WITH OTHERS

It has been already stated that despite its large population, the SAARC region has only 1.5 percent of the world income with about $330 per capita GNP, the lowest category. At present their share of the export trade is also around 1 percent of the total export trade of the world. Liberalization of trade among these countries would increase their intraregional trade. However, even if it doubles, without any increase in their share to other regions and in the total exports of the whole world it would increase their share of world trade only marginally. Therefore they have to enhance their share of trade with the other regions as well as in order to make a substantial impact on their economies and significantly alleviate their poverty. For if this trade doubles as well, the SAARC share of world trade would also nearly double. If the total world exports also increase as would be the case, the effort of the SAARC group must be correspondingly even greater. It is, therefore, of paramount importance that they have to not only maintain but even improve their links with the richer neighbors of ASIA, namely ASEAN, NICS and Japan and Oceania, as well as the countries of the EC and the NAFTA of the West.

NICS and Japan, in particular, are more resilient to deteriorating global economy because of the positive armoury which they possess unlike the SAARC countries, such as of:

1. contained inflation,
2. arrested population growth,
3. positive current account balances,
4. declining foreign debt burden
5. little or no unemployment and
6. increasing domestic savings. Therefore, their domestic markets are likely to further expand. The SAARC countries must convert this to their advantage.[31]

SAARC countries also must remain export competitive with NICS and ASEAN. This, they can do by not allowing their real effective exchange rates and domestic labor costs to rise. At present, because of their low labor costs, some NICS as well as some ASEAN countries such as Singapore and Thailand have been relocating some of their labor-intensive industries in South Asian countries like Sri Lanka.

The SAARC countries have not been able in the past to penetrate into industrialized countries as much as the NICS. They have to penetrate more into markets of the industrialized countries as well, to have sustained growth of their economies through ELI. This can be done only by enhancing their export competitiveness vis-à-vis the countries of ASEAN and NICS.

There are quotas imposed by the United States and the EC on certain manufactured goods from the NICS, such as garments. No such quotas may be operative on similar goods from the SAARC Countries for quite some time. For example, no quotas are so far operative on Sri Lanka's garment exports. The garment industry of Sri Lanka will have very much expanded after the establishment of the total number of 200 garment factories under a proposal of Mr. R. Premadasa, the late President of Sri Lanka. The EC has at present relaxed quota restrictions on Sri Lanka's garment manufactures except four items. Even on these four items the EC has decided to increase the quota by 7 percent-8 percent annually. In order to make use of these concessions Sri Lanka must be competitive with East Asia. The same argument would apply to other exports as well as other countries of SAARC. There must be a convergent macro-economic core in these countries as discussed in the preceding section to ensure the micro-economic optimization in industries necessary to maintain this export competitiveness.

V. SUMMARY AND CONCLUSION

In place of global free trade, there has emerged several trading blocks in different parts of the world. The underlying rationale for this is that free trade within groups is better than no free trade at all. The seven countries of South Asia, Bangladesh, Bhutan, India, Maldives, Nepal, Pakistan and Sri Lanka have formed themselves into a loose partnership called the South Asian Association for Regional Cooperation (SAARC) in 1985. In view of the changing developments in the world economy and the threat posed by other trading blocks of the EC, NAFTA and ASEAN, these seven countries are now contemplating upon greater economic cooperation among them.

These seven countries though contiguous are very diverse. All of them belong to the category of low income countries. Their economies appear more competitive than complementary. However, within sectors there is enough complementarity to exploit for trade creation for their mutual advantage and attain the second best Pareto optimality.

The expansion of their trade is of crucial importance to the SAARC countries. Their export income and import expenditure respectively constitute a sizeable proportion of their GDP. The expansion of their economies and the alleviation of their characteristic poverty largely depend upon the expansion of their export trade. At present their share of the world exports is only about 1.2 percent, and of this also, the bulk is with the industrial countries. The intra-regional trade is very little.

The inappropriate domestic policies of these countries themselves and the protectionist tendencies of the developed country markets along with the slowing down of their demand for the former's products and the increasing competitiveness of their richer Asian neighbors have been mainly responsible for their small share of the world trade.

To increase this share, their export competitiveness must be substantially enhanced. This requires the removal of the existing constraints and the establishment of a Macro-economic core for Micro-economic optimization of their industries.

Once this is done, existing intra-sector complementarities can be exploited in free trade for the mutual benefit of the members. Until then, these countries may have to be satisfied with preferential trading arrangements, short of complete free trade, as set out in SAPTA and indicated in the SAARC Study.

Free trade among members themselves, however, will not be enough. They must maintain and even improve their links with other trading blocks and industrial countries, as well as their richer Asian neighbors. It is the expansion of the export trade with these groups that will make a substantial impact on their economies.

NOTES

1. For the history and evaluation of SAARC see Bhargava, KK. "Regionalism: The SAARC Experience" presented at the First Special Conference on APEC: SAARC/ASEAN on the theme Regionalism: Macroeconomic Core and Microeconomic Optimization, held in Bangkok in December 16-18, 1992.
2. See Meena Acharya "Trading Arrangements and Policy Options: The Case of Nepal". First Special Conference on APEC: ASEAN/SAARC. December 16-18, 1992, Bangkok.
3. Bhargava op.cit.-for SAARC's achievements.
4. M. Dutta-"Economic Regionalisation in Western Europe: Asian Pacific Economies, Macroeconomic Core: Microeconomic Optimization", in American Economic Review, papers and proceedings 1992.
5. Now renamed as Latin American Integration Association (LAIA).
6. Belgium, Denmark, France, Germany, Greece, Ireland, Italy, Luxembourg, Netherlands, Portugal, Spain and United Kingdom (in alphabetical order).
7. See "European Community: A Strange New Pattern of Stars" in Economist, February 6-12, 1993, p. 52.
8. Computed from the Data given in Tables 1 and 3 of the World Development Report 1992.
9. World Development Report 1992.
10. P. 22.
11. Indraratna, ADV de S-"Essays in Asian Economics". SLISES, Colombo, 1992. Paper 5 and 6 respectively.
12. Draft Agreement on SAARC Preferential Trading Arrangement (SAPTA). This will be placed for ratification before the Seventh Summit to be held at Dhaka in April 1993. This is expected to come into force in 1997.
13. Trade in this region is constrained by the inadequacy of regional transport and communication systems. SAPTA mentions several possibilities of cooperation to alleviate this inadequacy.
14. Reza, Sadrel-"Issues in Trade Cooperation in South Asia: A Bangladesh Perspective"-in this series op.cit.
15. See WDR Tables 3, 4 and 6.

16. Feb. 20-26, 1993-"Wealth in Services," pp. 13-14.
17. Ibid. p. 14
18. SAARC Secretariat, 1991. Kathmandu. See Table 24 therein.
19. See WDR Tables 3, 4 and 6.
20. Essays in Asian Economics. op.cit.-Paper on "The Impact of Liberalization of Trade in a Small Island Economy: Sri Lankan Experience 1978-1989".
21. op.cit.
22. op.cit. Note 20 above.
23. See note 2 above.
24. Note 20 above and Economist, Feb. 20-26, 1993-"Welcome Mr. Nice Guy" p. 14.
25. This has been discussed in relation to Sri Lanka in my Paper. op.cit. Note 20.
26. Reza. op.cit.
27. Green, David J. "Convergence and Cohesion Within the ASEAN-4" in this series. op.cit.
28. Dutta, op.cit.
29. Page 53 of SAARC Study.
30. See Chapter 7 of SAARC Study as well as Reza Sadrel, op.cit.
31. See Indraratna. op.cit.

REFERENCES

Acharya, Meena. (1992). "Trading Arrangements and Policy Options: The Case of Nepal," First Special Conference on APEC: ASEAN/SAARC. December 16-18, Bangkok.

Asian Development Bank. (1991-92). *Asian Development Outlook.*

Bhargava, K.K. (1992). Regionalism: The SAARC Experience. Special Conference, op.cit.

Dutta, M. (1992). Economic Regionalism: Macroeconomic Core and Microeconomic Optimization. First Special Conference op.cit.

________. (1992a). "Economic Regionalisation in Western Europe: Asia Pacific Economies (Macroeconomic Core: Microeconomic Optimization)" American Economic Review, Papers and Proceedings.

The Economist (1993). The Economist Newspaper Ltd. London.

Fernando, S.N. (1985). "Regional Import Substitution - Strategy for Regional Cooperation in Industry in South Asia": Occasional Paper No. 12, Central Bank of Ceylon.

Government of Sri Lanka (1992). Draft Agreement on Preferential Trading Arrangement (SAPTA).

Green, David J. (1992). Convergence and Cohesion within the ASEAN - 4. Special Conference, op.cit.

Indraratna, ADV de S. (1992). *Essays in Asian Economics,* Sri Lanka Institute of Social & Economic Studies, Colombo.

IMF. (1992). Direction of Trade Statistics Year Book.

Meade, James. (1955). *The Theory of Customs Unions,* Amsterdam: North Holland Publications.

Reza, Sadrel. (1992). "Issues in Trade Cooperation in South Asia: A Bangladesh Perspective." Special Conference, op.cit.

SAARC. (1991). Regional Study on Trade, Manufactures and Services.

________. (1991a). Sixth SAARC Summit & Sixth Meeting of the Heads of State or Government - Colombo Declaration, Colombo. 21 December.

________. (1992). Agreement on South Asian Preferential Trading Arrangement.

UNCTAD. (1990). *Handbook of International Trade & Development Statistics.*

Viner, Jacob. (1950). *The Customs Union Issue.* New York: Carnagie Endowment for International Peace.

World Bank. World Development Reports.

ISSUES IN TRADE COOPERATION IN SOUTH ASIA:
A BANGLADESH PERSPECTIVE

Sadrel Reza

I. INTRODUCTION

The South Asian Association for Regional Cooperation (SAARC) comprising Bangladesh, Bhutan, India, Maldives, Nepal, Pakistan and Sri Lanka was launched in 1985 after some intensive political activities following the first-ever meeting of Foreign Secretaries of the region in April 1981. Aware of the long legacy of conflict and mutual suspicions in South Asia—in spite/because of a shared history, a common ecology and a common past—the SAARC architects adopted, from the very beginning, a somewhat cautious, step-by-step approach towards regional cooperation. As a result, no dramatic results of immediate import could be expected out of this organization. However, the extremely slow progress, relating particularly to substantive issues as well as procedural problems and other handicaps have already evoked some sharp criticisms about its current role and future prospects (Halim, 1992).

Research in Asian Economic Studies, Volume 6, pages 369-395.

ISBN: 1-55938-918-4

All the same, the very fact that a diverse group of countries could gather under some institutional umbrella for cooperative promotion of their economic development should in itself be considered a significant achievement for the region (Mukherji 1987, Kappagoda 1987). Note that it took South Asia only four years from the beginning of its journey to hold the first summit and that the second-cycle seventh summit is also already over. This contrasts very well with the relatively more successful, dynamic and vibrant Association of South East Asian Nations (ASEAN), which took ten years to hold a summit after its establishment in 1967.

The objectives of SAARC, as laid down in its Charter, have been set keeping the priorities of the region in view. They include the following: improving the standard of living of the people of South Asia; economic development of the region, social progress and hastening of cultural development; affording each citizen within SAARC countries the right to live a life of dignity and facilitating to the utmost the expression of his or her talents; promoting and strengthening collective self-reliance in South Asia; extending the hand of cooperation in solving each others' problems in a climate of mutual understanding and trust; accelerating regional exchange in the socio-economic, cultural, scientific and technical spheres; and strengthening of mutual cooperation in international forums in pursuit of shared interests.

So far the areas which have been identified for cooperation in SAARC and included in its Integrated Programme of Action (IPA) are: Agriculture and Rural Development; Meteorology; Telecommunications; Scientific and Technical Cooperation; Health and Population Activities; Transport; Postal Services; Sports, Arts and Culture; Prevention of Drug Trafficking and Drug Abuse; Women in Development; Audio-Visual Exchange; SAARC Chairs, Fellowships and Scholarships; Youth Volunteer Exchange; Prevention of Terrorism; Tourism, and so forth. Clearly, these are all based on mutual commonality of interests with significant functional relevance. But many other areas of critical importance, such as trade, industry and finance, which bear significantly on the long-term development of the region have still been left out of the SAARC agenda. Some forms of economic integration and trade cooperation are, however, deemed essential if a regional grouping of this nature is to achieve a greater efficiency of resource utilization and fulfill the second best condition for Pareto optimality (Dutta 1992). This is the reason why the issue of trade expansion features prominently in most such schemes of regional cooperation. For example, the basic aims of ASEAN, as defined in the Declaration of ASEAN Concord (1967) and the Preferential Tariff Arrangement (PTA) concluded in 1977, are the promotion of intra-regional trade by such means as reduction of tariff and non-tariff barriers, short-and long-term bilateral and multilateral trade agreements within and outside the region and creation of industrial complementarity, particularly through joint ventures involving two or more countries.

Unfortunately, SAARC suffers from certain abiding constraints in choosing the areas of cooperation and the modalities for achieving the objectives of cooperative endeavor. For example, Article X(2) of its Charter provides that all bilateral and contentious issues shall be excluded from the deliberations. Moreover, all decisions of the Association have to be made on the basis of unanimity and in a spirit of friendship, trust and mutual understanding. This means that even the smallest member can exercise a veto power which, however, is understandable since the first precondition for economic cooperation is to create an environment of peace and mutual support in an otherwise strife-torn area (Singh 1987). But there is also a dawning realization in the region that concrete results can be achieved within the SAARC framework only by gradually extending the IPA from the purely innocuous ones to such more fundamental areas as trade, finance and industry. Detailed studies have already been carried out in this regard and there is a hope that a draft treaty could be signed in the 1992 summit to establish a South Asian Preferential Trading Agreement (SAPTA) by 1997 or even earlier.[1] As stated by the current SAARC Chairman, "This would be the first major step towards an eventual economic community in South Asia... We need to look closer also at the feasibility of a payments unit for regional trade and commercial exchanges."[2]

The basic object of this chapter is to highlight the issues which need careful consideration for the success of the proposed trading arrangement and for the possible graduation of SAARC into an economically well integrated group at some point in time in the near future. However, it would be appropriate at this stage to briefly examine the nature of the SAARC economies, the structure of their products and trading relations in order that the major relevant problems can be judged in their proper perspective.

II. SOUTH ASIAN ECONOMIES: BASIC INDICATORS

South Asia is one of the most densely populated areas, with high rates of population growth projected to continue over the nineties.[3] Occupying a land mass of only 3.3 percent South Asian population exceeds one-fifth of the world total. On the other hand, per capita income shows that all of the seven countries are in the 'low-income' category.[4] The contrast against the developed countries as shown in Table 1, clearly demonstrates the extent and severity of poverty in the region. Over time, there has occurred some significant sectoral shifts in the production structure, away from agriculture towards industry and services but the variations in the magnitude of change amongst countries can be easily discerned from Table 2. On the whole, however, the industries sector in all these countries have still remained underdeveloped. Relatively speaking, India has the most diversified industrial structure in the area and its dominance over all others is striking: its GDP is more than three-fourths of the regional

Table 1. Basic Economic Indicators of South Asian Countries: Population, Land area and GDP

Country	Population						per capita		GNP	
	(Billion) mid-1990	*Percentage Share in The Region*	*Area '000 sq. km.*	*Population Density*	*Average Annual Growth Rate Population (percent) 1980-1990*	*Projections for (1989-2000)*	*US dollars 1970*	*Average Annual Growth Rate (%) 1965-90*	*Millions of Dollars 1990*	*Percentage Share in The Region*
1. Bangladesh	106.7	9.65	144	741	7.3	1.8	210	0.7	22,830	7.07
2. Bhutan	1.4	0.13	47	30	2.1	2.4	190	—	230	0.09
3. India	849.5	76.80	3,288	258	2.1	1.7	350	1.9	254,540	78.70
4. Maldives	0.21	0.02	0.3	713	3.2	—	450	2.8	96	0.03
5. Nepal	18.9	1.71	141	134	2.6	2.5	170	0.5	2,890	0.89
6. Pakistan	112.4	10.16	796	141	3.1	2.7	380	2.5	35,500	10.98
7. Sri Lanka	17.0	1.54	66	258	1.4	1.1	470	2.9	7,250	2.24
Total South Asia	1106.11	100.00	4,482.3	247	2.4	2.0	338	1.9	323,436	100.0
High-income Economies	816.4		31,790	26	0.6	0.5	19,590	2.4	163,16,290	

Note: —Not available
Figures in parentheses are percentage of World total.
Source: World Bank. *World Development Report*, 1992.

Table 2. Structure of Production in South Asian Countries: Distribution of GDP (Percent) by Sectors

	Agriculture		*Industry*		*(Manufacturing)*[a]		*Services*	
Country	*1965*	*1990*	*1965*	*1990*	*1965*	*1990*	*1965*	*1990*
Bangladesh	53	38	11	15	5	9	36	46
Bhutan	—	43	—	27	—	10	—	29
India	44	31	22	29	16	19	34	40
Nepal	54	60	11	14	3	5	23	26
Pakistan	40	26	20	25	14	17	40	49
Sri Lanka	28	26	21	26	17	15	51	48

Note: [a]Share of Manufacturing in GDP shown separately from industry which includes, apart from manufacturing, mining, construction, electricity, water and gas.

Source: Same as Table 1, Data on Maldives are not available.

Table 3. Structure of Manufacturing in South Asian Countries

	Value Added in Manufacturing (millions of current dollars)		Distribution of Manufacturing Value Added Percent: Currect Prices									
			Food, Beverage and Tobacco		*Textiles and Clothing*		*Machinery and Tr. Equipment*		*Chemicals*		*Others*[a]	
Country	*1970*	*1989*	*1970*	*1989*	*1970*	*1989*	*1970*	*1989*	*1970*	*1989*	*1970*	*1989*
1. Bangladesh	527	1,730	30	23	47	36	3	5	11	18	10	18
2. Nepal	32	151	—	35	—	25	—	2	—	8	—	30
3. India	7,928	44,445	13	11	21	12	20	26	14	17	32	33
4. Pakistan	1,462	5,923	24	30	38	19	6	8	9	16	23	27
5. Sri Lanka	369	969	26	52	19	20	10	2	11	3	33	23

Notes: [a]Unallocated items.
—not available.

Source: Same as Table 1. Data for Bhutan and Maldives not available.

Table 4. Structure of Merchandise Exports of South Asian Countries (Percentage share in total)

Country	*Fuels, Minerals and Metals*		*Other Primary Commodities*		*Machinery and Tr. Equipment*		*Other Manufactures*		*Textiles and Clothing*[a]	
	1965	*1990*	*1965*	*1990*	*1965*	*1990*	*1965*	*1990*	*1965*	*1990*
1. Bangladesh	—	1	—	25	—	1	—	72	—	60
2. India	10	8	41	19	1	7	48	66	36	23
3. Nepal	—	—	—	25	—	—	—	74	—	57
4. Pakistan	2	1	62	29	1	—	35	70	29	58
5. Sri Lanka	—	6	99	47	—	1	1	47	—	34

Source: Same as Table 1. Data for Bhutan and Maldives not available.

Table 5. Structure of Merchandise Imports of South Asian Countries
(Percentage share in total)

	Food		*Fuels*		*Other Primary Commodities*		*Machinery and Tr. Equipment*		*Other Manufactures*	
Country	*1965*	*1990*	*1965*	*1990*	*1965*	*1990*	*1965*	*1990*	*1965*	*1990*
1. Bangladesh	—	30	—	14	—	6	—	17	—	33
2. India	22	8	5	17	14	12	37	18	22	45
3. Nepal	—	9	—	9	—	10	—	26	—	46
4. Pakistan	20	19	3	17	5	8	38	7	34	29
5. Sri Lanka	41	16	8	15	4	4	12	22	34	44

Source and Notes: Same as Table 4.

Table 6. Direction of Trade of South Asian Countries by Country Groups
(in %)

Country	*Industrial Market Economies* 1984	1987	1990	*Countries of Eastern Europe* 1984	1987	1990	*Developing Market Economies* 1984	1987	1990	*Of which: South Asia* 1984	1987	1990
Export												
1. Bangladesh	50.9	66.1	71.3	4.0	5.9	4.7	45.1	28.1	24.0	11.4	4.1	3.6
2. India	53.4	61.1	60.3	19.2	14.1	13.8	27.4	24.8	25.8	3.8	2.8	2.7
3. Maldives	13.9	15.1	50.2	—	—	—	86.1	84.9	49.8	22.2	22.2	8.1
4. Nepal	44.1	68.7	72.7	—	—	—	55.9	31.3	27.3	48.5	27.8	20.6
5. Pakistan	46.9	60.2	60.8	3.2	3.4	2.3	49.9	36.4	36.8	3.3	3.9	4.0
6. Sri Lanka	44.1	58.6	61.5	12.1	6.7	6.2	43.8	34.7	32.3	4.5	4.1	3.7
South Asia Total	50.9	61.0	61.3	14.1	10.4	10.3	35.0	28.6	28.4	4.6	3.5	3.2
Import												
1. Bangladesh	44.0	44.9	42.9	18.3	19.9	15.0	37.7	35.2	42.1	3.1	4.3	6.8
2. India	49.1	59.7	60.6	11.1	7.9	7.6	39.8	32.3	31.7	0.7	0.5	0.6
3. Maldives	23.5	25.9	23.1	—	—	—	76.5	74.1	76.9	11.1	10.2	7.7
4. Nepal	38.4	53.6	39.1	—	—	—	61.6	46.4	60.9	45.3	18.8	26.7
5. Pakistan	51.7	58.4	55.2	1.0	0.9	1.0	47.3	40.7	43.8	2.1	1.6	1.0
6. Sri Lanka	46.2	43.4	40.1	0.4	0.8	0.2	53.4	55.3	59.7	7.3	6.7	7.0
South Asia Total	48.8	56.6	55.9	8.7	6.9	6.4	42.6	3.5	37.7	2.2	1.9	2.2

Source: *IMF, Direction of Trade Statistics Yearbook, 1991.*
— Indicates nil or negligible.

Table 7. Bilateral Trade of SAARC Member Countries, 1984 and 1990
(Millions of dollars)

Exports to	*Bangladesh*		*India*		*Maldives*		*Nepal*	
Imports to	*1984*	*1990*	*1984*	*1990*	*1984*	*1990*	*1984*	*1990*
Bangladesh:								
Exports	—	—	28.3	21.7	—	—	14.6	7.4
Imports	—	—	60.1	170.3	—	—	—	1.5
India:								
Exports	90.0	201.0	—	—	2.0	4.0	95.5	123.0
Imports	27.0	16.0	—	—	—	—	44.0	56.0
Maldives:								
Exports	—	—	0.06	0.02	—	—	—	—
Imports	0.3	—	1.74	4.24	—	—	—	—
Nepal:								
Exports	—	1.40	39.83	51.07	—	—	—	—
Imports	16.09	8.09	104.47	135.76	—	—	—	—
Pakistan:								
Exports	38.2	102.8	25.3	49.0	1.6	0.5	0.1	1.1
Imports	72.5	38.2	12.7	45.7	1.3	—	0.6	0.4
Sri Lanka:								
Exports	14.1	9.8	12.5	20.2	3.9	7.4	—	0.1
Imports	0.2	8.9	115.5	118.0	1.8	6.2	—	—

Bangladesh:								
Exports	63.3	23.2	0.3	8.2	106.5	60.5	931.3 (11.4)	1671.8 (3.6)
Imports	18.6	70.1	4.1	8.0	82.8	249.9	2692.8 (3.1)	3656.1 (6.8)
India:								
Exports	11.0	30.0	117.0	128.0	315.0	486.0	8231.0 (3.8)	18183.0 (2.7)
Imports	20.0	48.0	14.0	14.0	105.0	134.0	15115.0 (0.7)	23321.0 (0.6)
Exports	1.19	—	1.65	5.67	2.91	5.69	13.11 (22.2)	69.94 (8.1)
Maldives								
Imports	1.79	0.61	4.34	8.14	7.89	12.99	70.84 (45.3)	168.84 (26.7)
Exports	0.52	0.40	—	0.01	40.35	52.88	83.26 (48.5)	256.61 (20.6)
Nepal								
Imports	0.09	1.26	0.02	0.09	120.67	145.2	266.64 (11.1)	542.87 (26.7)
Pakistan:								
Exports	—	—	20.1	68.9	8.53	222.4	2558.7 (0.3)	5587.2 (3.9)
Imports	—	—	36.0	37.0	123.1	121.3	5852.2 (2.1)	7383.0 (1.6)
Sri Lanka:								
Exports	34.2	32.5	—	—	64.7	70.0	1435.6 (4.5)	1895.3 (3.7)
Imports	17.1	50.3	—	—	134.6	183.9	1845.6 (7.3)	26.33.5 (7.0)

Notes: 1)Ideally, figures in rows and columns of corresponding inter-country transactions should match since one country's exports are the other country's imports. But for well-known reasons, wide deviations may occur.

2)Figures in parentheses are the respective country's share in South Asia as percent of world total.

total and its manufacturing value added was more than five times the combined figure for the rest of the region in 1989, as can be seen in Tables 1 and 3.

By and large, the South Asian economies are predominantly exporters of primary products and traditional manufactures, such as textiles and clothing, as Table 4 demonstrates. Imports of the region, on the other hand, chiefly consist of capital goods, 'other manufactures', food and fuel as brought out by Table 5. Over the recent years, the dependence of the region upon the industrial countries has increased both for exports and imports which is shown in Table 6. Intra-regional trade, in contrast, is low and declining in relative terms, and with the exception of Nepal, such trade accounted for less than 10 percent of their total trade as demonstrated in Table 7.

Moreover, all the South Asian countries suffer, as is shown in Table 8, from significant trade and current account deficits which have been increasing over time. There is also considerable resource gap—gross domestic saving falling far short of gross domestic investment—and as a percentage of GDP, the gap has been widening over the years, which can be seen from Table 9.

To sum up, South Asia is a densely populated region, primarily agricultural with a low level of per capita income, low savings and significant external deficits. Intra-regional trade is small and declining while trade and aid dependence on industrialized countries substantial and growing. Naturally, therefore, these countries are highly susceptible to the prevailing external economic development. Such factors as global recession, rising protectionism, depressed commodity prices, lower export earnings, decline in concessional aid, and so on, can very adversely affect the development prospects of the region. Against such backgrounds, the importance of economic cooperation amongst SAARC members for alleviation of poverty and for promoting national and collective self-reliance through an optimum utilization of their human and material resources can hardly be overemphasized.

In any regional integration schemes, trade cooperation, of course, receives top priority for the multifarious gains which are expected to arise out of specialization, economies of scale, possible improvements in the terms of trade, increased competition and greater allocative efficiency and increased capital flows and technological advances. In South Asia, besides commercial policy barriers to expansion of intra-SAARC trade, there are a number of other well-known impediments such as: supply constraints, dependence on aid-giving industrial countries for import finance, domestic priorities for protection of infant industries, overlapping production structures and lack of complementarity, weak infra-structural links, lack of information and political sensitivity (Bhuyan 1989). However, even if there occurs a substantial expansion of intra-regional trade which is policy induced, this will not make any real dent in the overall trade pattern within SAARC because of the structural and other constraints. The scope for gainful trade can be widened and economic cooperation can be meaningfully sustained in the long run only if such efforts

Table 8. Balance of Payments, Reserves and External Debt Position of South Asian Countries

Country	*Current Account Balance (Million dollars)*		*Gross International*			*Total Long-term Outstanding Debts 1990*		*Debt Service as Percent of*	
			Million Dollars		*In Months of Import Coverage*				
Country	*1970*	*1990*	*1970*	*1990*	*1990*	*Million dollars*	*As % of GNP*	*GNP 1990*	*Export of goods and services 1990*
1. Bangladesh	-234	-1,541	—	660	1.8	12,245	53.8	1.5	25.4
2. Bhutan	—	-38	—	86	7.4	83	32.3	—	6.8
3. India	-591	-9,828	1,023	5,637	1.9	70,115	25.0	2.0	28.8
4. Nepal	-25	-316	94	354	5.4	1,621	53.0	1.0	18.2
5. Pakistan	-705	-1,902	195	1,046	1.2	20,683	52.1	3.6	22.8
6. Sri Lanka	-71	-474	53	447	1.7	5,851	73.2	3.8	13.8

Source: Same as Table 1. Data not available for Maldives.
—not available.

Table 9. Structure of Demand: Distribution of GDP (percent)

	Government Consumption[a]		*Private Consumption*		*Gross Domestic Investment*		*Gross Domestic Savings*		*Export of Goods and Non-factory Services*		*Resource GDP*[ab]	
Country	*1965*	*1990*	*1965*	*1990*	*1965*	*1990*	*1965*	*1990*	*1965*	*1990*	*1965*	*1990*
1. Bangladesh	9	9	83	89	11	12	8	2	10	8	-4	-10
2. Bhutan	—	20	—	58	—	36	—	22	—	29	—	-14
3. India	9	12	76	68	17	23	15	20	4	8	-2	-3
4. Nepal	a	12	100	80	6	18	—	8	8	12	-6	-10
5. Pakistan	11	15	76	73	21	19	13	12	8	16	-8	-7
6. Sri Lanka	13	9	74	76	12	22	13	15	38	30	1	-8

Notes: a) Government consumption figures are not available separately: they are included in private consumption.
b) Resource gap is the difference between export of goods and non-factor services and imports of goods and non-factor services.
—not available.

Source: Same as Table 1. Data on Maldives Not available.

Table 10. Composition of Intra-Regional Exports and Imports for SAARC Member Countries by Commodity Category and Their Share in Regional Exports and Imprts by Commodity Category, 1985

	Food Items (SITC 0+1+22+4)		*Agricultural Raw Materials, etc. (SITC 2-22+67+68)*		*Fuels (SITC 3)*	
	Composition	*% Share in Intra-regional Trade*	*Composition*	*% Share in Intra-regional trade*	*Composition*	*% Share in Intra-regional Trade*
Bangladesh:						
Exports	31.09	11.99	38.35	21.42	0.00	0.00
Imports	9.56	8.04	24.65	29.08	4.35	12.17
India:						
Exports	18.40	31.83	10.19	25.54	2.65	36.77
Imports	32.24	13.91	30.66	18.55	0.00	0.00
Nepal:						
Exports	61.82	26.48	10.70	6.64	0.00	0.00
Imports	19.13	26.69	5.90	11.54	18.92	87.83
Pakistan:						
Exports	14.85	13.72	27.41	36.67	2.89	21.47
Imports	53.24	26.70	42.03	29.57	0.00	0.00
Sri Lanka:						
Exports	52.96	15.98	22.16	9.37	17.15	41.76
Imports	40.98	24.66	13.33	11.25	0.00	0.00
Intra-region-1980						
Exports	23.62	—	17.59	—	17.31	—
Imports	31.59	—	16.68	—	1.15	—
Intra-region-1985						
Exports	26.52	—	18.31	—	3.30	—
Imports	26.53	—	18.91	—	7.97	—

	Commercial Products (SITC 5)		*Machinery and Equipment (SITC 7)*		*Other Manufactures (SITC (6+-(67+68)*	
	Composition	*% Share in Intra-regional Trade*	*Composition*	*% Share in Intra-regional trade*	*Composition*	*% Share in Intra-regional Trade*
Bangladesh:						
Exports	1.29	1.26	0.41	0.26	28.85	11.64
Imports	12.31	26.53	27.35	45.12	21.70	21.30
India:						
Exports	7.79	33.96	30.81	88.28	30.16	54.60
Imports	9.59	20.61	1.34	1.11	26.17	13.18

(continued)

Table 10. (Continued)

Nepal:						
Exports	6.57	7.09	0.00	0.00	20.90	9.37
Imports	12.53	44.79	13.04	35.63	30.18	19.62
Pakistan:						
Exports	24.48	57.02	7.39	11.31	22.97	22.21
Imports	0.99	1.28	1.12	1.11	2.62	1.57
Sri Lanka:						
Exports	0.88	0.67	0.27	0.14	6.84	2.17
Imports	10.87	16.79	14.37	16.96	20.45	14.36
Intra-region-1980						
Exports	4.51	—	15.58	—	21.39	—
Imports	6.25	—	18.40	—	25.93	—
Intra-region-1985						
Exports	10.52	—	16.01	—	25.34	—
Imports	10.35	—	13.52	—	22.72	—

Source: M.R. Aggarwal and P.R. Pandey, *op. cit.*

are backed up simultaneously on other fronts by means of industrial cooperation, financial cooperation, development of physical infrastructure, cooperation in the services including trade information and also standardization of product specification and trade procedures. These are all issues which need careful attention and towards which the Association should now immediately turn if its avowed ideals have to be translated in concrete reality.

III. PROSPECTS OF ECONOMIC COOPERATION IN SAARC

This section deals with all the relevant issues in the realms of trade, industry, financial and monetary matters, infrastructure, harmonization of documentation and so forth, and cooperation in the service sector which need careful consideration by the Association for inclusion in its IPA. The issues may be elaborated as follows:

A. Trade Cooperation

Table 10 indicates the product structure of intra-SAARC trade by broad commodity groups. While the composition of intra-regional product trade is not symmetrical, the dominance of "food items", "other manufactures" and "agricultural raw-materials" is clear as they accounted for around 70 percent of intra-regional trade in 1985. Within the region, India's shares in the export of "food terms", "machinery and equipment" and "others manufactures" are the highest. Pakistan is the highest exporter of "agricultural raw-materials" and "chemical products", and ranks second in case of "machinery and equipment" and "other manufactures." On the other hand, Pakistan is the highest importer of "food items" and "agricultural raw-materials"; Bangladesh in "machinery and equipment."

In order to evaluate the future prospects of trade expansion in the region, a number of indices can be calculated to assess the degree of "existing" and "potential" complementarities. Some attempts have been made recently to estimate such relevant indicators as "trade intensity", "complementarity", "country bias" and "revealed comparative advantage" (Asher and Wadhva 1985, Reza 1982, 1983 and Aggarwal and Pandey 1992). The trade-intensity index measures the extent to which one country's share in another country's exports (imports) is larger or smaller in relation to the former country's share in world trade. If the index value is more than unity it will indicate that a country is exporting more (or less) to another country than might be expected from the country's share in world trade. The trade-intensity index can be decomposed into two indices of, "complementarity" and "country bias." The former measures the extent to which one country's export pattern matches another country's import pattern more closely than it matches the country's import pattern for world imports. The latter index measures the extent to which one country's exports have more or less favorable access to another country's market than might be expected from both country's share in world trade. The revealed comparative advantage (RCA) index shows the comparative advantage in terms of the share of a particular industry in a country's total exports relative to the industry's share in total world exports. If the value of RCA, calculated separately for exports and imports is greater (less) than unity, it indicates a strong comparative advantage (disadvantage) for the economy in the export/import of a given country.

On the whole, the results obtained so far by the various studies on the above indices indicate that the existing low level of intra-regional trade in South Asia follows from the low degree of complementarity in the production and trade structures of the countries in the region. The low complementarity has been caused significantly by trade and other barriers put by the member countries on their intra-regional trade (Aggarwal & Pandey 1992). Recently, however, there has been a marked trend towards trade and industrial policy liberalization in most of the SAARC countries, and the economies are increasingly being characterized by privatization and deregulation where market forces are being allowed a more dominant role to play than in the past.

Nevertheless, the conventional methods of trade cooperation, like free trade area, customs union or common markets where internal trade barriers are completely dismantled are unlikely to find favor in the region in the near future. There is apprehension that such methods will benefit the larger countries at the expense of the smaller ones. However, drawing on the experience of other existing integration schemes such as Latin American Integration Association (LAI) which replaced Latin American Free Trade Association (LAFTA) and ASEAN, it may be quite possible for South Asia to design a mechanism of trade expansion acceptable to all partner countries. For example, there is a continuing effort within ASEAN to improve its PTA scheme which is soon expected to graduate into the ASEAN Free Trade Area (AFTA). LAIA envisages an economic preference area made up of regional tariff preferences and partial agreements on bilateral tariff reductions. These partial agreements could be multilateralized through a negotiated process.

Within SAARC, bilateral agreements exist between India on the one hand and Bangladesh, Nepal, Pakistan and Sri Lanka on the other on a variety of products such as coal, minerals, cotton and silk textiles for mutual trade. Trade within the region could start on such mutually agreed products which could indicate the process of building collective self-reliance in South Asia (Adiseshiah 1987). Expansion of trade on mutually agreed lines should prove beneficial to both stronger and weaker countries as opposed to an "across the board" approach which may favor countries with diversified exports.

However, note that all the SAARC countries are essentially resource-based competitive economies, producing by and large, a similar range of primary products and simple manufactures which has hindered the growth of intra-regional trade. Appropriate supply-side measures are needed to expand and diversify the production structure of the individual countries which can create useful complementarities in the region. Industrial cooperation can play a significant role in this respect.

B. Industrial Cooperation

Concerted efforts are needed from both the governments as well as from the private sectors of the member countries for greater industrial cooperation. At the government level, there is a need to identify industries which are best suited to the respective countries from the regional viewpoint. At the private levels, as a result of the enlarged market, there is greater prospect for profitable joint ventures on a wide range of manufactured items. However, since all the SAARC countries are relatively capital poor, it would not be realistic to expect any significant intra-regional inflow of direct foreign investment although the prospects of exploiting the larger market may encourage transnational corporations from the industrialized countries to look for suitable investment opportunities in the region.

Although the necessity for industrial collaboration is recognized, it is obviously a difficult task to identify the potential areas as well as the mode of cooperation. Thorough studies will be needed in this regard keeping particularly in view of the existing resource endowment, skill, technology, physical infrastructure and institutional facilities of the collaborating countries. Some preliminary investigations have already indicated bright prospects for joint industrial ventures in a wide range of areas such as:[5]

i. resource based industries like paper, rubber, fertilizer, cement, fisheries, and agro-based industries like forest products, processed and packaged foods, fruits and vegetables;
ii. intermediate products like chemicals, pesticides, refractories, solvent extractions, auto-parts, other transport equipment and components, agricultural pumps and motors, foundries, machine and hand tools, and so on, and
iii. consumer goods like electricals, edible oils, leather goods, handloom and handicrafts, bicycles, film-making, and so forth.

However, the creation of a regional industrial structure must be accompanied by appropriate precautionary measures to prevent unequal distribution of gains amongst the partner countries. Polarization of benefits has created serious dissatisfactions within many of the existing integration schemes. Past experience will suggest the adoption of a policy of balanced regional industrialization through agreed specialization. For example, the "joint industrial programming" of the Andean Group seeks to allocate industries to particular countries based on their actual or potential comparative advantage as determined by respective resource endowments, location and availability of physical and infrastructural facilities. The allocation of such industries may be exclusive or shared between two or more members.

Similarly, the ASEAN Industrial Project (AIP) assigned priority industries to each member country in accordance with comparative advantage to reap the benefits of economies of scale and to avoid wasteful parallelism. Although some projects in the first AIP package had to be scrapped because of some technical and administrative problems due to lack of necessary preparatory work, there is sound logic in the principle adopted for ensuring a fair inter-country distribution of industrial projects. Again, the ASEAN Industrial Complementation (AIC) Scheme, which aims at simple horizontal specialization in production, where member countries produce complementary products also provide some lessons for SAARC.

In any case, it must be noted that successful industrial cooperation will call for some degree of plan harmonization among countries in order that wastes of duplication can be avoided.[6] Joint ventures should also be encouraged in the private sector to pool resources in the region so that, besides establishment of new industries, there can also occur cooperation in R & D efforts for product development and improvement in technology.

C. Financial and Monetary Cooperation

South Asia as a region suffers from serious resource constraints which has made the countries heavily dependent on external assistance for their essential development imports. This has limited intra-SAARC trade and circumscribed the region's access to adequate international liquidity. In order, therefore, to achieve the objectives of trade expansion and industrial growth in South Asia, it is necessary for the SAARC countries also to cooperate in financial and monetary spheres. Thus, the growth of a regional financial system through the establishment of a regional development bank, a regional import export bank and a regional finance corporation as joint venture of all member countries could, by drawing on the region's resources, not only help ease the region's resource constraints but also reduce its dependence on the global financial system and thereby facilitate trade and investment in the region.[7] Note that already a SAARC Fund for Identifying and Developing Projects has been set up by the Fifth SAARC Summit in 1990 and that there is also an on-going study for establishing a South Asian Development Fund (SADF).

Cooperation amongst commercial banks in South Asia is also expected to play an important role by exchanging information and experience on credit policy for devising appropriate methods for effective utilization of bank credits. Similarly, for regional joint ventures, commercial banks can mobilize funds by undertaking joint project financing. They can also facilitate expansion of intra-regional trade through provision of credits to the export sector.

Since trade imbalances pose a serious constraint to trade expansion in South Asia it is necessary that a clearing arrangement be made to settle payments among member countries for clearing their current transactions. Like the Asian Clearing Union (ACU), a mechanism can be so devised as to allow the central banks to periodically settle the net outstanding balances of all transactions of member countries which are recorded multilaterally by commercial banks of each country.[8] Such an arrangement helps economies in the use of foreign exchange—since it is needed only to settle the net imbalances at the end of the specified periods—and also save transaction costs. While a South Asian Clearing Union may be set up, it may also alternatively be possible to expand the present ACU by admitting Maldives and Bhutan—two of the SAARC members currently outside the Union. In case South Asia is not prepared as yet for a centrally operated multilateral network of credit lines, they may even consider, at a minimum, agreeing on a swap arrangement of bilaterally determined credit lines as a complement of the clearing agreement.[9]

The clearing arrangement, however, provides only interim finance—ranging from two months to one year as evidenced from experiences of the existing Unions—and the credit margin available also differs greatly between various schemes. Persistent trade imbalances, therefore, may make the settlement of net debt balances burdensome particularly to the weaker members. This warrants that clearing arrangements are supplemented by provisions of short to medium-term credit arrangements. That is, a payments union may render valuable services by providing an insurance against adverse intra-trade balances and this should be of interest for adoption by SAARC.[10] Funds for Payments Union which will be necessary for handling possible lags or delays in convertible currency payments and receipts may come from the surplus member countries' contributions, though it must be noted that given the overall balance of payments situations in the region, some financial support from external sources including developed countries and financial institutions would probably need to play a critical role in this regard. Alternatively the proposed widened ACU's scope of activity may also be expanded in order for it to function as a Payment Union as well.

Another important factor for ensuring liberalization and expansion of trade is cooperation in respect of exchange arrangements. Although not widely dissimilar, the SAARC members currently follow different exchange rate system such as pegging to a particular currency or a basket of currencies and limited flexibility and "managed floating." The basic distinction is thus in the extent of flexibility of the exchange rate but the variation in such rates of individual countries over the past years has been, by and large, in the same direction. The central banks of the member countries could easily cooperate to stabilize the exchange rate, which is found to be a favorable factor for mutual trade expansion as indicated by the experiences of existing integration schemes.

D. Infrastructural Development

Although the South Asian markets have the advantage of physical proximity to each other, trade is constrained by inadequacies of regional transport and communication systems. It is important to extend cooperation to these sectors for development and expansion of intra-regional trade and industry. Attempts have already been made to promote functional cooperation in some of these areas in SAARC. However, considerable scope yet remains for cooperation by (i) establishing a regional transportation network such as the Asian Highway Project and the Trans-Asian Railway Project, (ii) developing inland water-ways with special provision for transit facilities for land-locked Nepal and Bhutan, (iii) establishing a regional shipping line with multi-modal transport including containerisation, regional shipbuilding and repairing facilities and (iv) developing air linkages by pooling together resources of different national airlines. Simultaneously, there is considerable scope for cooperation in the communication side covering postal, telephone, telegraph, telex, fax and also radio and television. Particularly, a telecommunication network is vital not only for promoting greater South Asian cohesion but also for developing a fast growing research-intensive sector which has recently been found to be at the forefront of promoting global trade and industry.

Side by side with physical infrastructure, it is also necessary to strengthen the institutional infrastructure of the region for facilitating and consciously promoting economic cooperation amongst the SAARC countries. A SAARC Chamber of Commerce and Industries, on which there is already an agreement in principle, may be set up for dissemination of information of business environment, potential tradeable goods and possibility of joint ventures. They may also work together in identifying and resolving various trade bottlenecks viz., tariff and non-tariff barriers, inadequate production capacity, lack of information, absence of standardization, poor quality control, and so forth.

Networking of trade and technology information centers, of experts and institutions engaged in studies and research on trade and investment matters, networking among State Trade Organization and other relevant public sector organizations are all necessary for profitable exchange of information on trade, technology and consultancy matters.

The SAARC countries should also have frequent exchange of trade delegations and hold trade fairs on rotation basis. Organization of buyers-sellers meets and technology expositions in the region can contribute over time to significant trade expansion.

E. Harmonization of Documentation, Customs, Procedures, Standardization and So Forth

Measures to promote trade and economic cooperation have to be accompanied by trade facilitation measures using uniform standards of trade classification, procedural formalities and documentation. Documents that need standardization are: (i) offer, acceptance, contract and proforma invoice, (ii) bank documents, (iii) handling documents, (iv) transport and insurance documents, (v) forwarding instructions, and (vi) certificates relating to customs valuation and customs control.

Export promotion Centers, Chambers of Commerce and Industries, and official pre-shipment inspection agencies of the SAARC countries should work out appropriate mechanisms to ensure quality control, delivery schedules and after-sales services, and for expeditions disposal of traders' compliants.[11] Similarly, national arbitration laws and procedures should be harmonized so as to generate confidence among exporters and investors in joint venture projects. In this regard, consideration may be given to evolving of common code of conduct for importers, exporters and investors.

Finally, there is need to relax curbs on travel, particularly with respect to bonafide businessmen. The SAARC countries may consider allowing measures such as visa-free travel/multi-journey visas as well as exemption from police reporting to commercial travellers within the region.[12]

F. Cooperation in the Service Sector

The service sector has a strategic role in the development process. So far cooperation and trade in services within SAARC has been negligible. Moreover, with the exception of Nepal, all other South Asian countries have been facing serious problems with trade in services (Reza 1989). Some areas which have been recently identified by the SAARC Secretariat for cooperation in the service sector include:[13]

a. Institutional promotion of tourism and hotel industry;
b. Consultancy and design;
c. Services for small-scale industry development;
d. Banking and development finance;
e. Insurance, including re-insurance;
f. Joint investment for R & D;
g. Transport network, telecommunication and postal services;
h. Information technology and related software development;
i. Construction industry; and
j. International trade matters.

Unless these services are developed, which may be helped by cooperative endeavors, only measures to promote growth and trade within the region will attain but limited success.

IV. A BANGLADESH PERSPECTIVE

Judged by its ratio to GDP, foreign trade is found to play an important role in the economy of Bangladesh.[14] However, the country has been suffering from a serious export-import gap and therefore, is heavily dependent upon external financial resources for her essential imports. The debt service of Bangladesh as a percentage of her exports of goods and services exceeds 25. Export expansion is necessarily of critical importance to the country in the existing context and, hence, there is a compelling need for inclusion of 'trade' in the SAARC IPA from the Bangladesh point of view.

Presently, however, the magnitude of Bangladesh's exports to South Asia is very small. Moreover, the share of South Asia has declined from pre-SAARC 11.4 percent to 3.6 percent in 1990 in the country's total world exports. There has been an increase in imports from intra-regional sources, particularly from India and Pakistan signifying significant trade imbalances for the country even within the SAARC framework.

Looking at the commodity structure of Bangladesh's intra-SAARC trade relationship in Table 10, one can find it to be dominated by food items and agricultural raw-materials, besides 'other manufactures'. The prospects for export expansion to South Asia with the country's present commodity structure—mostly competitive with other partners—is not really very bright. Even then it is possible to identify some items which account for a significant portion of Bangladesh's exports to the region and which deserve greater attention from the relevant quarters.

Queries received by the Bangladesh Export Promotion Bureau and consultations with representatives of Chambers of Commerce and Industry indicate that depending on availability of sufficient exportable surplus, the country's exports have considerable prospects within SAARC in such items as, fruits and vegetables, potato, pulses, wheat bran, tortoise and turtles, crabs, lizard skin, agar wood, duck chest feather, sunhemp, footwear, pharmaceuticals, soaps and detergents, cosmetics, P.V.C. pipe, particle board, safety machines, handicrafts, insulators, electric wires and cables, G.I. pipes, ceiling fans, gas generators, handloom products, bees wax, feature films, earthen pottery, coir and coir products, glass sheets, stationery articles, and so forth.

It should be evident that a significant increase in exports will entail considerable product diversification and industrial growth in the country. Intra-SAARC trade is inhibited at present by domestic narrow markets and supply side constraints. Currently, the manufacturing sector in Bangladesh is quite small and accounts for no more than 10 percent of GDP. In recent times, there has been some marked growth in the country's garment sector, shrimp processing and natural gas-based fertilizer production. Regional industrial collaboration can obviously play a significant role in product diversification and manufactured growth through joint ventures and a degree of plan harmonization based on the country's comparative advantage. A recent exercise to determine Bangladesh's comparative advantage on the basis of effective rates of protection indicate that she has good investment prospects in the following broad industrial categories:[15]

i. Some categories of textiles and garments;
ii. Some agro industries;
iii. Leather and products; and
iv. Some engineering items besides some miscellaneous goods.

A good number of these products are exportable and some may also be developed primarily for sale in the domestic market. Clearly these will get a boost if deliberate measures are taken within the South Asian framework to promote joint ventures and trade in these product lines.

Trade and Industrial collaboration also calls for strengthening existing transportation and communication linkages of Bangladesh with her SAARC partners. There should also be cooperative efforts in other service related areas, including financial collaboration.

For example, Bangladesh holds out significant prospects of improving its air and road links with Nepal and Bhutan which could provide important alternative outlets to these land-locked countries. Rail links to move freight in particular can easily be developed with India. Similarly, in the field of waterways, the formulation of river conservancy measures jointly by India and Bangladesh is urgently needed over the entire river route from Calcutta onwards into Neamati. Hydrographic and hydrological surveys and planning conservancy works will have to be jointly worked out by both the countries. There are also considerable prospects for cooperation in road transport between Bangladesh and India which, in turn, with some transit facilities, will imply improved trade regulations with both Nepal and Bhutan as most of Bangladesh's trade with these countries have to move through India. Note that improved road, rail, water and air transport will not only provide a boost for intra-SAARC trade but will also facilitate the growth of tourism with concomitant implications for hotel and restaurant as well as recreational and personal services. Similarly, in the energy sector, Bangladesh can gainfully cooperate with Nepal and India to tap the huge Himalayan resources. Without collective and coordinated possibilities vast potentials will be wasted in all these areas which a poor region like SAARC can hardly afford.

V. CONCLUSIONS

The creation of SAARC has been an important event in South Asian regional history. But confining it only to non-contentious issues cannot fulfill the objectives of national development and attainment of collective self-reliance. The Association has to address itself to the more fundamental issues of economic cooperation in the realm of trade and industry if it is to thrive as a vibrant organization. For furthering intra-regional trade, not only trade policies need to the liberalized but positive measures are needed to promote industrial joint ventures and adopt some harmonization plans. Besides, cooperation in such areas as infrastructural development, communication, services, and standardization of products and trade procedures are all considered matters of vital importance. Also, significant potential exists for cooperation in agriculture and rural development, water resources, energy, science and technology, education, health and population control, and so forth. Moreover, South Asia can expect to benefit significantly by taking a common stand on external economic relations and by projecting a unified viewpoint on such issues as trade, aid and development in various international forums namely, the World Bank, the IMF, UNCTAD and GATT.[16] The governments in the SAARC countries appear to be aware of the urgency of the issues and some progress has already been made under the agencies of SAARC Secretariat in this regard. Concerted and determined efforts are now needed to further consolidate, strengthen and diversify the areas of cooperation.

ACKNOWLEDGMENT

The author would like to express his gratitude to the participants of the First Special APEC: ASEAN/SAARC Conference on "Economic Regionalism: Macroeconomic Core and Microeconomic Optimization" held in Bangkok during December 16-18, 1992 for providing valuable comments. Special thanks are due to M. Dutta and K. K.. Bhargava for inspiration and also clarification of various issues.

NOTES

1. See *The Daily Star,* Dhaka, Monday, October 5, 1992. The 1992 Summit, already postponed twice because of some internal problems in India, was rescheduled for April 1993.
2. *Ibid.*
3. However, population density varies widely amongst the SAARC participants.
4. For example, with a GNP per capita of $610 or less in 1990. Note that four members of SAARC—Bangladesh, Bhutan, Maldives and Nepal—belong to the category of 'least developed countries, (LDCs).
5. See Arif A. Waqif (ed.), *op.cit.*
6. For political and psychological reasons, harmonization of plans may be difficult, but if the potential advantages of coordinated development are recognized, a consensus on intra-regional specialization should not be difficult to achieve.
7. See A.R. Bhuyan, *op.cit.*
8. The Asian Clearing Union was established in 1974 with Bangladesh, Burma, Iran, Nepal, Pakistan and Sri Lanka as members. ACU started operation in 1976.
9. Under swap arrangement, national currencies can be swapped for convertible currencies on a short-term but unconditional basis. Cf. Madan, B.K. (1985). *Payments Arrangements and Monetary Cooperation in South Asia,* CSCD, Colombo.
10. Under payments union the participatory countries agree to provide medium term balance of payments credit to each other. There may be variations in the actual form of payments, the key issues being determination of shares of participating countries, the denomination of the currency of subscription, the credit limits, the repayment period, whether credit will be automatic or discretionary, etc.

A number of payments unions are now in operation in different developing regions, such as the Central American Stabilization Fund, the Santo-Domingo Agreement, the Andean Reserve Fund, the Arab Monetary Fund and the ASEAN Swap Arrangement.

11. SAARC Secretariat (1991), *SAARC Regional Study on Trade, Manufacturing and Services,* SAARC/Sc/14/17, Kathmandu.
12. *Ibid.*
13. SAARC Secretariate, *op.cit.*
14. The export-GDP ratio is estimated at about 8 percent and the import-GDP ratio at about 16 percent for the early 1990s.
15. See, Bangladesh Planning Commission (TIP Reform Programme), Overview of Industrial Assistance Policy in Bangladesh and Recommendations for Reform, Doc. TIP-EPSO/MU-H-Part I, March 1987.

16. It is noteworthy that the South Asian States presented a joint position on environmental issues at the recently held UN conference on environment and development.

REFERENCES

Adiseshiah, Malcolm S. (1987). "The Economic Relationale of SAARC", *South Asia Journal*, Vol. 1, No. 1.

Aggarwal, M.R. and Pandey, P.R. (1992). "Prospects of Trade Expansion in the SAARC Region", *The Developing Economies*.

Asher, Mukul and Wadhva, Charan eds., (1985). *ASEAN-South Asia Economic Relations*, Singapore: ISEAS.

Bhuyan, A.R. (1989). "Trade Cooperation in South Asia: A Case Study of Bangladesh", Bangladesh Planning Commission, Dhaka, Mimeo.

Dutta, M. (1992). "Economic Regionalization in Western Europe: Asia Pacific Economies—Macroeconomic Core: Microeconomic Optimization", *American Economic Review*, Papers and Proceedings.

Halim, Md. Abdul. (1992). "Wither Away the White Elephant Called SAARC?" *Perspective in Social Science*, Vol. 4, Dhaka.

Kappagoda, Nihal. (1987). "Current Policy Issues", in *Towards Regional Cooperation in South Asia*, Manila: ADB/EWC Symposium.

Mukherji, I.N. (1987). "India's Trade and Investment Opportunities in South Asian Manufactures", in Arif A. Waqif ed., *South Asian Cooperation in Industry, Energy and Technology*, New Delhi: Sage Publication.

Reza, Sadrel. (1982). "Trade Intensities of Bangladesh with South Asia and Asean: Some Estimates", *The Bangladesh Development Studies*, Vol. X, No. 4.

Reza, Sadrel. (1983). "Revealed Comparative Advantage in the South Asian Manufacturing Sector: Some Estimates", *Indian Economic Journal*.

Reza, Sadrel. (1989). *South Asian Cooperation in the Service Sector: A Bangladesh Perspective*, Bangladesh Planning Commission, mimeo.

Singh, Tarlok (1987). "Economic Cooperation in South Asia: An Overview", in Arif A. Waqif ed., *op.cit.*

TRADING ARRANGEMENTS AND POLICY OPTIONS:

THE CASE OF NEPAL

Meena Acharya

South Asia as a region is still to emerge as a major trading block in the world scenario. Inspite of its geographical contiguity and socio-cultural commonalities, the history of intra-regional relations have been marked more by conflicts than cooperation. Countries in the region differ widely in their political philosophy and models of development followed by them. Evolution of a trading block or a common market presupposes some uniformity in the approach to development and management of the national economies. Today, when the issues of cooperation in trade and commerce are being negotiated within the South Asian Association for Regional Cooperation,[1] the history of the Nepal-India relationship are presented below in some detail so as to highlight the problems involved. It is argued that despite a series of policies and measures undertaken by Nepal to accelerate the growth of exports and to diversify her trade, Nepal's achievements have been modest. Among various causes retarding the growth of Nepal's external sector, her landlocked situation

Research in Asian Economic Studies, Volume 6, pages 397-426.

ISBN: 1-55938-918-4

and open border relationship with India have played a major role. A unique feature of Nepal-India Cooperation in contrast to other regional groupings is the free movement of both goods and factors of productions. While theoretically this may benefit Nepal by opening up the Indian market, Nepal so far has benefitted little from this arrangement. As such caution is advised in the choice of policies and pattern of development Nepal adopts.

The paper is divided into four parts. The first section presents background information and setting against which Nepal's trade and exchange rate policies have to be viewed. The second long section summarizes Nepal-India trade and transit relationships during the last forty years. Policies followed by Nepal and their achievements and failures are presented in the third section. The final section highlights the current situation and the policy options open to Nepal.

I. HISTORY AND THE SETTING

The role of the external sector in Nepal's economy has been increasing steadily in the last few decades. Entrepot trade between India and China has always been an important economic activity throughout Nepal's history, but her external sector has expanded fast, and acquired much greater importance in the national economy in the last three decades (Table 2). Her imports have increased from about 11 percent in 1974/75 (Nepal's Fiscal Year (FY) runs Mid-July to Mid-July (AI)) to more than 25 percent of GDP in 1991/92. Growth of exports, however, has been slower and erratic. Exports were only slightly more than 14 percent of GDP in 1991/92. Consequently, the trade deficit has gone up to more than 10 percent of GDP.

Nepal's structure of trade has also undergone substantial changes. Primary goods as percent of total exports have declined from an overwhelming 87 percent in 1975/76 to just about 19 percent in the FY 1991/92. This, however, must be attributed to both expansion in the exports of non-primary goods and decline in the volume of exports of primary goods, particularly to India. The structure of imports has also changed in favor of primary products.

Country-wide direction of trade has also changed dramatically. Third country share (i.e., countries other than India) in total exports increased from 16 percent in the FY 1974/75 to just about 89 percent in the FY 1991/92. Similarly third country share in total imports has crossed 60 percent. Although during India-Nepal trade crisis it had reached 74 percent, it is coming down and may be expected to stabilize at around 50 percent with normalization of relationship with India (Table 1).

Services have consistently played a positive role in Nepal's balance of payments (Table 2). Tourism is a major income earner under services. Net private transfers have also been positive over the years. Miscellaneous capital inflows have also turned positive in recent years. This item, however has been very erratic primarily because of the unrecorded transactions on Nepal-India account.

Table 1. Selected Indicators on Trade and Balance of Payments

	GDP Real Growth	Exports/GDP	Imports/GDP	Trade Deficit/GDP	Share of Primary Goods in Total Exports	Third Country Share	
						Exports	Imports
1974/75	—	5.4	11.0	5.6	82.6	16.0	19.0
1975/76	4.4	6.8	11.4	4.6	87.5	25.0	38.0
1976/77	3.0	6.7	11.6	4.9	85.5	33.0	33.0
1977/78	4.4	5.3	12.5	7.2	82.6	52.0	38.0
1978/79	2.4	5.8	13.0	7.1	78.0	50.0	45.0
1979-80	-2.3	4.9	14.9	10.0	69.5	55.0	49.0
1980/81	8.3	5.9	16.2	10.2	74.8	38.0	51.0
1981/82	3.8	4.6	15.9	11.1	80.2	33.0	54.0
1982/83	-3.0	3.4	18.7	15.3	63.6	26.0	60.0
1983/84	9.7	4.5	17.1	12.6	60.6	32.0	53.0
1984/85	6.2	6.6	18.5	12.0	55.8	42.0	50.0
1985/86	4.3	6.2	18.9	12.7	41.9	60.0	58.0
1986/87	3.9	5.2	18.9	13.7	44.0	57.0	61.0
1987/88	7.3	6.1	20.4	14.4	36.0	62.0	67.0
1988/89	4.2	5.4	21.0	15.6	22.2	75.0	74.0
1989/90*	6.1	5.7	20.2	14.5	17.0	88.0	75.0
1990/91**	5.6	7.0	22.1	15.1	20.4	79.0	69.0
1991/92***	3.1	10.7	25.2	14.6	19.3	89.0	64.0

Source: 1) Ministry of Finance: Economic Survey, Various Issues.
2) Nepal Rastra Bank: Quarterly Economic Bulletin, Various Issues.
3) Own Computations.
*Revised Preliminary Estimates.
**Preliminary Estimates.
***Tentative Estimates.

Table 2. Balance of Payments Summary

(In Rs. million)

Year	Trade Balance	Services Net	Transfer Net	Current Account Balance	Official Capital Net	Official Capital Foreign Loans	Official Capital Amortization	Miscellaneous Capital	Change in Reserves Net
1974/75	-925	281	524	-80	87	104	-17	-389	422
1975/76	-813	284	589	60	146	164	-18	152	358
1976/77	-856	493	518	255	215	233	-19	-159	311
1977/78	-1,451	572	588	-292	291	311	-19	10	11
1978/79	-1,509	779	870	39	429	448	-19	116	583
1979/80	2,403	873	1,188	-342	577	598	-21	-209	26
1980/81	-2,830	1,117	1,417	-296	634	665	-31	-144	194
1981/82	-3,452	1,378	1,682	-392	744	807	-32	-120	502
1982/83	-5,197	1,635	1,891	-1,671	924	964	-40	72	-675
1983/84	-4,824	1,407	2,073	-1,343	1,204	1,274	-71	14	-126
1984/85	-5,022	1,080	2,094	-1,849	1,270	1,363	-92	-287	-866
1985/86	-6,266	1,575	2,241	-2,471	1,812	2,005	-194	1,220	561
1986/87	-7,924	2,327	2,692	-2,904	1,888	2,098	-210	1,393	377
1987/88	-9,755	2,212	2,931	-4,622	4,368	4,675	-307	2,528	2,273
1988/89	-12,086	3,048	2,718	-6,320	5,922	6,302	-380	474	76
1989/90	-13186	2,613	2,819	-7,751	4,978	5,706	-729	5,420	2,650
1990/91	-16,608	2,692	3,661	-10,255	6,300	7,154	-854	8,736	4,132
1991/92	-19,040	3,893	4,294	-10,852	7,326	8,710	-1,384	7,860	4,333

Source: Nepal Rastra Bank, Quarterly Economic Bulletin, Vol. XXVI, No 3 & 4.

Nepal's external economic relationships and related policies have been shaped throughout by her landlocked geography and historical and cultural ties with India. Specific features of this relationship are characterized by the predominating role India plays in both trade and flow of services. Nepal borders India on the south, east and west while the Himalayan heights and the Tibetean plateau form her northern borders. The border with India is 500 miles long and virtually open. The northern borders are mostly snow capped and negotiable only through a few passes.

Although Nepal was never incorporated formally in the British Empire, in practice it was a semi-colony, whose relationship with the outside world was controlled by the British rulers in India. Internal affairs, if it did not impinge on British interests, were left to the Nepalese rulers. The Treaty of Sugauli (1816) between Nepal and British India by which the British Indian Army was allowed to recruit Gorkha soldiers from Nepal[2] and the 1923 Treaty of Trade and Commerce which secured the Nepalese market for British goods[3] were twin pillars of the semi-colonial status of Nepal vis-à-vis British India.

The 1950 Treaty of Peace and Friendship between India and Nepal was a natural corollary of this relationship after India gained independence in 1947. Article six in this treaty binds the two countries "to give to the nationals of the other, in its territory, national treatment with regard to participation in industrial and economic development of such territory and to the grant of concessions and contracts relating to such development." Article 7 specifies further that they will grant "on a reciprocal basis, to the nationals of one country in the territories of the other same privileges in the matter of residence, ownership of property, participation in trade and commerce, movement and privileges of a similar nature." Letters exchanged with the Treaty, however, allow Nepal to protect Nepalese nationals "from unrestricted competition" for some time and with mutual agreement. Thus, independent India was able to get concessions from Nepal, which the British colonial rulers had not been able to obtain, inspite of their persistent attempts in the past.[4]

In addition there are other restrictions on Nepal's military activities. Article 5 combined with the second point in the Letter Exchanged allows Nepal to import arms and ammunition only with assistance of and agreement with India. The Letter further states that "Neither Government shall tolerate any threat to the security of the other by a foreign aggressor. To deal with any such threat, the two Governments shall consult with each other and advise effective counter measures." It also binds Nepal to give Government or nationals of India first preference in seeking foreign assistance in regard to the development of the natural resources. This Treaty is supposed to be everlasting unless terminated by one year's notice by either of the parties.

Thus, the Nepal-India relationship is multidimensional and the economic context of these relationships are very much conditioned by India's underlying

Table 3. Trade Dependency Ration, 1990

Country	*Exports*	*Imports*	*Total Trade*	*GDP*	*% of total trade to GDP*
Nepal (Rs in millions)	6,160.000	20,157.000	26,157.000	84,911.000	31
India (U.S. $ in billions)	17.967	23.692	41.384	254.540	16
Pakistan (Rs in billions)	121.345	160.134	281.479	862.451	33
China (Yuan in billions)	293.060	251.230	544.290	1,768.600	31
Thailand (Bhat in billions)	589.813	844.447	1,434.260	2,051.200	70
Sri Lanka (Rs in billion)	79.481	107.729	187.210	321.057	58
S. Korea (Won in billion)	46.016	49.433	95.449	169.701	58
Singapore (S. $ in billions)	95.245	110.033	205.279	62.711	327
Taiwan					84
Hongkong (U.S. $ in billions)	29.002	82.495	111.497	59.670	187

Source: ISD, 1992.

security concerns and Nepal's persistent efforts to establish her own independent national identity. Attempts to free the Nepalese economy from the predominating effect of the Indian economy has been one very important facet of these efforts. Nepal is a small country with a limited national resource base, and the degree of its openness to external factors naturally will be much more than that of India, which has a vast domestic market, large natural resource base and developed industrial infrastructure (Table 3). Conflicts in economic relations have occurred fundamentally because Nepal has attempted to open up her economy to the world beyond India and followed more liberal trade and exchange rate policies than those of India, while maintaining a 500 mile open border with her.

Neither India nor Nepal seem to be willing to consider regulation of the open border. Indians do not want to regulate the Nepal-India border because of the costs involved and also because with a regulated border, India's free access to Nepalese northern borders may be restricted. Nepal wanted to keep the border open, because the rudimentary nature of her internal transport network and her landlocked situation made her dependent on Indian transport network even for Nepal to Nepal movement. Moreover, the age-old tradition of free movement across the border makes it a culturally unpalatable idea for the people to have the border regulated. Finally, it is beyond the capacity of Nepal to police such a long border without the Government of India's cooperation. Nepal's trade and exchange rate regimes, its achievement and failures need to be viewed in the context of this open border and a series of trade and transit treaties with India.

II. REVIEW OF TRADE COMMERCE AND TRANSIT TREATIES WITH INDIA

A. 1950 Treaty of Trade & Commerce

The Treaty of Trade and Commerce concluded concurrently with the Treaty of Peace and Friendship, while providing transit facilities for Nepal's trade with third countries, it ensured conformity in Nepal's tariff policies with that of India, entrusted management of Nepal's foreign exchange earnings to the Reserve Bank of India and collection of duties on third country imports to Indian customs. The Government of Nepal also agreed to levy export duties on Nepalese manufactures which were exported to India on par with the excise duties payable for corresponding Indian goods.[5]

Thus, although the 1950 Treaty of Trade and Commerce carried elements of a custom's union, it was unequal and reinforced India's pre-dominance in Nepal's economy. Management of Nepalese foreign exchange by the Reserve Bank of India according to its own rules and regulations caused much inconvenience to Nepalese citizens. Establishment of the Nepal Rastra Bank, regularization of IC-NC (Indian Currency-Nepalese Currency) transactions and control over her own foreign exchange reserves undertaken by Nepal in 1957, were the first tentative steps towards independent economic management in Nepal. In 1957, Nepal also obtained the right to levy duties on her own exports. Import duties were still levied and collected by India.[6] All available statistics indicate overwhelming dominance of India in Nepal's external economic relations in this period.[7]

B. 1960 Treaty of Trade and Transit

The 1960 Treaty of Trade and Transit envisaged development of a "common market" between the two countries. Its objectives were to "expand the exchange of goods" between the two countries, "encourage collaboration in economic development and facilitate trade with third countries." This treaty was more elaborate on provisions of transit to Nepal and her trade with third countries. A specific provision for avoiding "diversion of commercial traffic or deflection of trade" was also included. Article II exempted "goods originating in either country and intended for consumption in the territory of the other," from all duties and "quantitative restrictions." However, both sides could "maintain or introduce such restrictions on such goods as were necessary for the purpose of protecting public morals and safeguarding national treasures." Nepal was allowed to impose duties on Indian imports to protect her infant industries.

Trade with third countries was to be regulated by their respective laws, rules and regulations. Article VI secured for Nepal complete independence of and control over her foreign exchange account. However, both sides were obliged "to prevent infringement and circumvention" of the foreign exchange rules, regulations and laws of the other country. The Treaty was for five years from the date of signature and extendable for another five years with mutual consent and necessary modifications. Periodic consultations were envisaged for sorting out differences.

Implementation of the Treaty encountered several problems arising out of the developing nature of both the economies and Nepal's attempts to follow an independent external trade and payments policy from that followed by India. The questions of adequate storage facilities in Calcutta, delays in movement of goods to and from third countries and general bureaucratic intervention in smooth transit facilities were the main complaints voiced by Nepal. India, on the other hand, was dissatisfied with the policies undertaken by Nepal to promote third country trade. Nepal's policies of Bonus Voucher Scheme (1962) and a Gift Parcel Scheme initiated in 1967 were perceived as the main instruments of trade deflection by India. Further, the phrase "goods originating in each other" were interpreted differently by Nepal and India. India interpreted this clause to mean goods containing 100 percent Nepalese raw materials while Nepal maintained that goods imported by Nepal from India contained unspecified amounts of third country raw materials.

Exporters' Exchange Entitlement Scheme (EEE) introduced by Nepal in 1962 to encourage her exports to third countries became a bone of contention between Nepal and India. This system continued until August 1978, in varying forms. Under this scheme entrepreneurs exporting goods to third countries were entitled to obtain certain proportions of foreign exchange earnings for import of goods of their own choice, within a specified list. Originally the system was simple and the proportion of entitlement was fixed at 90 percent of the earnings for all goods. The system grew progressively complex. Towards the end in 1978 when it was replaced by the dual exchange rate system, the export items were classified into two groups. One group of commodities was entitled to 45 percent bonus from their export earnings and another group to 60 percent.[8]

Nepal had to introduce the scheme to divert her exports to countries other than India because: (a) all Nepalese exports had so far been destined to India and some times reexported from India, for example, medicinal herbs, raw skin and hides and so on (b) Nepal had neither an export infrastructure of its own, nor a class of entrepreneurs linked to the international market and to foster such a class Nepal had to offer special facilities, (c) Nepal had no resources to subsidize her exports as India did, (d) India had a quota system on most of the development good such as cement, iron and steel and necessary consumer goods such as sugar and milk powder, because of which, Nepal had to face shortages in these commodities. Nepal's reserve of Indian currency grew continuously during the early sixties (Table 4) which could not be used to import development and basic consumer goods needed by her, and Nepal had to generate her own convertible currency reserves for such imports, and (e)

Table 4. Foreign Exchange Reserve Position

Mid July	*In Thousand US Dollars* Foreign Exchange	Convertible	Incovertible*	Import Coverage (months)
1957	3,993	1,232	2,761	—
1958	5,629	1,505	4,124	—
1959	9,869	2,425	7,444	—
1960	16,297	5,489	10,808	—
1961	22,553	6,866	15,687	—
1962	26,485	10,048	16,437	—
1963	28,549	13,569	14,980	—
1964	44,546	19,098	25,448	—
1965	53,438	23,450	29,988	—
1966	43,613	30,437	13,176	—
1967	46,101	37,808	8,293	—
1968	51,670	39,885	11,785	—
1969	69,124	51,897	17,227	—
1970	80,923	59,625	21,298	—
1971	94,495	71,198	23,297	—
1972	100,175	82,495	17,680	—
1973	111,656	99,204	12,452	—
1974	119,225	110,972	8,253	—
1975	100,655	88,690	11,965	8.6
1976	112,311	101,073	11,238	10.7
1977	137,370	128,737	8,633	12.8
1978	132,748	118,219	14,529	9.9
1979	167,798	142,262	25,536	11.1
1980	172,866	156,437	16,429	9.1
1981	182,148	127,242	54,906	8.0
1982	219,489	149,771	69,718	9.1
1983	149,951	67,840	82,111	5.8
1984	110,804	68,331	42,473	5.6
1985	64,182	52,318	11,864	3.7
1986	87,611	71,123	16,488	4.4
1987	114,440	88,844	25,596	4.7
1988	223,979	204,604	19,375	6.1
1989	235,653	226,547	9,106	6.1
1990	293,983	244,076	49,907	7.6
1991	346,057	312,155	33,902	9.6
1992	448,282	438,279	9,993	8.7

Notes: *Mostly Indian Currency.
Source: Nepal Bank Quarterly Economic Bulletin. Vol. XXVII No. 1.

most consumer and developmental goods were cheaper in the international market than in India.

A "Gift Parcel" scheme was introduced in Nepal in 1967 to facilitate the flow of goods from third countries and to encourage Nepal's new entrepreneurs. Under this scheme all types of goods up to the value of NR one thousand could be imported from third countries without obtaining an import license. This facility was soon mis-utilized by the business interests to import large amounts of luxury goods from third countries with the objective of re-exporting them to India.[9] India lodged strong protests against the scheme, and it was withdrawn in 1969.

C. 1971 Treaty of Trade and Transit

In the 1971 Treaty of Trade and Transit, the concept of "common market" between the two countries was abandoned. The provision of free entry of Nepalese manufactured goods into India was greatly diluted. Now such entry was to be restricted only to those goods, which contained not less than 90 percent of Nepalese or Nepalese and Indian materials. In the case of other manufactured goods in which the value of Nepalese materials and labor added in Nepal was at least 50 percent of the ex-factory price, the access to the Indian market was to be decided case by case by the Government of India. Pending mutual agreement sixteen agro-industrial products such as matches, strawboard and handicrafts were exempt from basic custom duties and quantitative restrictions.

Concessions in excise duty available to small units in India were also to be granted to products imported from similar units in Nepal. As earlier, the excise and other duties collected by the Government of India on goods exported to Nepal was to be refunded to the government of Nepal to the extent of the import duties levied by Nepal on similar imports from other countries. The Treaty permitted the government of Nepal to impose duties on Indian products on Most Favored Nation basis.

Transit facilities and procedures were elaborated in some more detail. While the Government of India agreed to lease facilities at the Calcutta port, procedural details laid down greatly restricted freedom of transit for Nepal.[10]

Transit routes were specified from Calcutta to 22 railway heads in India across the Nepal border. Provisions were also made for the transport of goods between Calcutta and Nepal by road. Additional space was provided to Nepal at the Calcutta port and customs procedures were simplified. Freedom of transit, however, was conditioned on taking all indispensable measures to ensure that such freedom in any way did not infringe on India's legitimate interests of any kind. Elaborate procedures were prescribed for clearing goods in transit. Several restrictions were accepted by Nepal for preventing the deflection of trade. Nepal agreed not to issue licenses for third country imports on the basis of the foreign exchange to be arranged by importer himself. Evidence of foreign exchange authorization from the Nepal Rastra Bank was required by Indian customs for the release of goods at transit points. Varied interpretations of these various restrictive clauses subsequently resulted in unnecessary delays making the transit system more restrictive and costly for Nepal.

During the seventies Nepal's third country trade expanded rapidly and EEE became a persistent irritant in Nepal-India relations. EEE had also created distortions in the Nepalese investment patterns by encouraging smuggling to and from India and introducing multiple exchange rates on account of the varying rates of profit on items of exports and imports. But, this system was as much a response of Nepal to ease the supply shortages created by the strictly regulated nature of the Indian economy and the overvalued Indian currency as an attempt to take advantage of the huge market for foreign goods in India. A natural response for India would have been to seal her borders with Nepal. Given the huge cost of such endeavor, and India's perception of the Himalayas as her northern border for security purposes, India applied consistent pressure on Nepal to get rid of this system. Because of the distortions introduced in the investment patterns and reasonable cushion of convertible exchange reserves built by Nepal by that time (Table 4), the system was replaced by a dual exchange rate system in 1978.

D. 1978 Treaties of Trade, Transit and Control of Unauthorized Trade

Separate treaties on Trade and Transit were signed in 1978 after a long stalemate on account of Nepal's demand for separate treaties on Trade and Transit and India's allegations of trade deflection. An Agreement on Cooperation in Controlling Unauthorized Trade on the border was also signed. The requirement imposed by the 1971 Treaty that the Nepalese manufactured goods had to contain 90 percent Nepalese or Nepalese plus Indian raw material for "customs duty and quantitative restriction free" entry into India was now reduced to 80 percent. Other manufactured goods in which the value of Nepalese and Indian materials and labor added was at least 50 percent of the ex-factory price were to be considered by Government of India on a case by case basis for preferential treatment in the Indian market. Separate applications had to be made for each commodity for getting this preferential treatment as earlier.

The treaty of Transit and the annexed protocol laid down the procedures to be followed for Nepal's traffic in transit through India. The Treaty was to be effective for seven years that is, until 1985. Storage space at Calcutta was expanded. Containerized movement of goods by road was also allowed. But, transit routes from Calcutta to the Nepalese border areas were now reduced to 13. Provisions of duty insurance, import licensing, documentation requirements and so on, were specified in further details. Duty insurance[11] premiums on Nepalese transit goods were reduced, but the insurance premiums on Nepalese exports and imports still amounted to up to 30 percent of the import or export costs.[12]

The Treaty of Trade and Commerce and Memorandum on Unauthorized Trade were renewed for a period of another five year in March 1983. Ten more

Nepali products, in addition to 26 products, specified earlier, were added to the list of goods entitled to unrestricted entry into India. Nepal agreed to adopt vigilance and promote contacts between the border authorities of the two countries to stop smuggling and unauthorized trade.

E. 1983-1989

The Treaty of Trade and Commerce was extended to 1988 by mutual agreement. The Treaty of Transit expired in March 1985, Nepal requested a seven year extension while India proposed an ad-hoc extension to December 31, 1985.[13] The arrangement for trade and transit was left undisturbed until march 1989 by the Government of India, although no agreement on transit seems to have been signed in that period.

F. 1989-1990 Crisis

The Treaty of Trade expired in 1988 and a new Treaty of Trade and an Agreement on Checking Unauthorized Trade were finalized and initialled by two sides in October, 1988 awaiting final signatures. The Government of India issued a letter to the Commerce Secretary of the government of Nepal stating that the Treaty of Trade and the Agreement on Checking Unauthorized Trade "would have deemed to expire in March 1989" as the Treaty of Transit was also due to expire on that date. India wanted to negotiate a new unified Treaty on Trade and Transit and a new Agreement of Cooperation to control unauthorized trade. The reasons for this kind of stand-off were mainly political and a discussion of details is beyond the scope of this paper.[14]

India stopped all entry points except four (two on India-Nepal border and one each for Nepal's trade with Bhutan and Bangladesh) on its borders for transit of goods to and from Nepal. India-Nepal trade was virtually stopped. Even the supply of essential commodities such as petrol, kerosene, coal and dry milk were stopped. According to Muni[15] the Indian side maintained that Nepal should (a) not discriminate against Indian goods in matters of levying duties; (b) it should renegotiate a single treaty of Trade and Transit with India; and (c) it should comply with the letter and spirit of the 1950 Treaty of Peace and Friendship and other arrangements governing bilateral relations. Particularly India contended that Nepal should grant equal treatment to Indian nationals on par with Nepalese nationals on matters of employment, trade, industry and commerce, and that Nepal had no right to import arms from China without consulting India, and that Nepal should give preference to Indians even in international commercial bids.

Nepal, on the other hand, maintained that (1) India was imposing an economic blockade on Nepal; (b) that it would not negotiate a unified Trade and Transit Treaty, and would trade with India on the principles of "most favored nation", and (c) that it did not want any "special relationship" with India as imposed by the 1950 Treaty of Peace and Friendship.

In spite of the series of high-level meetings, the stand-off continued. Nepal expected a more friendly Government in India after the forthcoming general elections, while India was hopeful that the snow-balling democratic movement in Nepal would bring a more India-friendly regime in Nepal. Both these assumptions proved right. The Congress Government in India was voted out of power in November, 1989, bringing the Janata Dal Government to power with V.P. Singh as Prime Minister. The Bhartiya Janata Party, with special political sympathies for the Nepalese King, was part of the ruling coalition and the Government of India negotiated new treaties of Trade and Transit with Nepal. However, due to the growing strength of the democratic movement in Nepal which also had strong supporters in the Janata Dal, the new Indian Government did not take prompt action to restore normalcy in India-Nepal trade relations.

The Panchayat System[16] in Nepal collapsed in April 1990, and a more India-friendly coalition of Nepali-Congress and the United Left Front of the communist parties (UML) came to power. The *status-quo-ante* of April 1, 1987 was restored in all aspects of bilateral relations by a Joint Communique of the Nepalese and Indian Prim-ministers in June 1990. "Mutual respect for each other's security concerns" was agreed upon between the two countries. Nepal also agreed to withdraw the registration requirements imposed on foreigners, including Indian nationals, working in the Kathmandu valley. India had persisted in calling this a "work permit system" imposed by Nepal on the people of Indian origin which was clearly not the case.

The 1989-90 crisis clearly proved that Nepal-India trade and transit relations are conditioned by India's overwhelming security concerns and an attempt to maintain free entry and employment of Indian nationals in Nepal. Nepalese people, on the other hand, are concerned about being overwhelmed by the inflow of foreigners into Nepal and India's intervention in Nepal's internal affairs. Moreover Nepal has wanted to follow more liberal external policies than those followed by India. This has created constraints in Nepal - India relations. It is true that during the last 30 years, preservation of a non-democratic Panchayat System and the King's political power have been additional factors in Nepal's attempts to assert her independence from India. However, a wish for establishing an independent identity and an independent policy framework for Nepal is common to all Nepalese.

G. 1991 Treaties of Trade, Transit and Control of Unauthorized Trade

With the installation of a democratically elected Nepali Congress government in Nepal, which is more sensitive to India's security concerns, the environment of India-Nepal dialogue improved significantly at the

Government to Government level. Separate treaties on Trade and Transit and an Agreement for the control of Unauthorized Trade were concluded in December 1991. The preferential treatment to trade in primary products originating in the two countries was restored on a reciprocal basis. India agreed to grant on the "basis of non-reciprocity" preferential treatment to certain categories of industrial products manufactured in Nepal in matters of quantitative restrictions and customs duty. The protocol to the Treaty of Trade specified mutually agreed routes through which Nepal-India trade was to move. Fourteen primary products were specified for preferential treatment to enter each other's territory. The concessions with respect to basic and auxiliary customs duty and quantitative restrictions granted to Nepalese manufactured articles which contained not less than eighty percent of Nepalese and Indian materials and excise rebate granted on par with products of similar "small" units in India, were restored. Concessions on import duties on other manufactures which contained not less than 40 percent Nepalese and Indian materials and labor were also restored. Except for already identified products, the eligibility for concessions was to be decided by the Government of India case by case on the basis of proforma submission by Nepalese exporters, as specified under the 1978 Indo-Nepal Treaty of Trade.

The Transit Treaty with 7 years validity, once again specified 15 transit routes allowed for Nepal's third country trade. Procedural details were laid down as in the 1978 Treaty of Transit.

The Agreement of Cooperation on Unauthorized Trade lays down that each contracting party shall prohibit and cooperate with the other to prevent:

a. re-exports from its territory to third countries both goods imported from the other and products which contain materials imported from the other exceeding 50 percent of ex-factory value of such products;
b. re-exports of third country goods or goods containing more than 50 percent third country imports to the territory of the other.

Other clauses bind the contracting parties to take prohibitive actions for preventing such deflection of trade, to compile and exchange information on such movement of goods, to cooperate in the prevention of unauthorized trade, and to maintain smooth and uninterrupted movement of goods across their territories.

Some of the clauses of the Trade Treaty have been modified by a Joint communique of the two Prime Ministers in October 1992. Particularly,

1. The proforma clearance system by which Government of India was to decide for preferential treatment case by case was replaced by a system of certificate of origin to be issued by His Majesty's Government of Nepal.

2. In order to determine the eligibility of a Nepalese product's access to the Indian market, free of custom's duty and quantitative restrictions, Nepalese labor content will be included, and
3. Nepalese products with more than 50 percent Nepalese and Indian material content and labor will be eligible for duty and quota free access to the Indian market.

The concessions granted to Nepalese primary products in respect of entry to the Indian market are reciprocal and to manufactures non-reciprocal. Nepal is to exempt Indian imports from duties to the maximum extent and "will waive additional customs duty on all Indian exports" during the validity of the Treaty. Both parties shall accord unconditionally to each other treatment "no less favorable" than accorded to any third country with respect to (a) customs duties and any other charges on exports and imports, and (b) import regulations including quantitative restrictions.

III. POLICY INITIATIVES, ACHIEVEMENT AND FAILURES

Since 1957 when Nepal established her own Central Bank, regularized the exchange rate transactions between Nepalese Currency and the Indian Currency, gained control over her foreign exchange earnings and holdings, and initiated her own trade and tariff policy distinct from that of India-Nepal's trade and exchange policies have been directed to achieving growth of exports and country and commodity-wise diversification of trade.[17] However, until about the late sixties, the gains were moderate. In 1969/70 Nepal's trade was still overwhelmingly India-oriented. Between 1956/57 and 1959/60 third country share in the total exports averaged 2 percent and in imports 4 percent. Imports from both India and overseas grew steadily during the sixties while growth of exports to overseas was negligible. However, between 1960/61 and 1969/70 the average share of third countries in Nepalese exports remained around one percent and in imports about 5-6 percent.[18]

As noted above Nepal, introduced the Export Entitlement Scheme in 1962 and the Gift Parcel Scheme in 1967. Third country share in exports and imports started to increase. Nevertheless in 1974/75, Nepal sent only 16 percent of her exports to third countries and imported 19 percent of her requirements from countries other than India. These figures jumped to 52 percent and 38 percent respectively for exports and imports in 1977/78. By that time Nepal had built a convertible foreign exchange reserve to finance 9.9 months of her import needs (Table 4). In spite of the predominance of Indian capital in trade, Nepal had promoted its own exporter class and established access to major world markets in developed countries such as Japan, the United States, and EEC.

She had also been able to divert her own exports such as jute and jute goods, medicinal herbs and handicrafts away from India, from where they had often been re-exported to overseas destinations as Indian products. Structure of her overseas exports, however, was changing only slowly, and raw-materials and unprocessed goods continued to predominate exports (Table 1).

Nevertheless, a high margin of profit on trading under EEE led to the distortions in resource allocation and private investment in industrial and agricultural sectors lagged far behind. The pattern of trade did not reflect Nepal's comparative advantage, rather it reflected the premium rates commanded by various goods in the curb market in India. The incentives to exporters fluctuated widely depending on the opportunities for deflection of trade to India. The magnitude of trade deflection was perceived to be growing to India's great consternation and the EEE became a major irritant in Nepal-India relations. The multiplier effect in Nepal of such trading activities was also claimed to be zero by several Nepalese intellectuals.[19]

In March 1978, the EEE was abolished and a Dual Exchange Rate System was introduced. Under this system, the basic exchange rate of Nepalese currency vis-âvis US$ was fixed at Rs. 12. Only imports of certain developmental goods and petroleum products, chemicals, fertilizer, certain raw materials and machineries were entitled to receive foreign exchange at this rate. Payments for other imports and receipts from exports were to be converted at Rs. 16 per US dollar. Quantitative restrictions on imports were abolished. But this system could not be sustained as it encouraged heavy imports both from overseas and from India while exports to third countries could not grow concurrently. Growth of exports to third countries between 1979/80 and 1982/83 was negative throughout (Table 5). Imports both from India and overseas grew rapidly. Exports to India fluctuated widely with positive and negative swings. It was clear that under the dual exchange rate system the premium on overseas imports were much higher than on exports.

The dual exchange rate system was replaced by a single exchange rate at Rs. 13.20 per US dollar in September 1981. A small subsidy of 10 percent of FOB value for exportable items on other than leather and leather goods was introduced. On December 1982 the Nepalese Rupees was devalued by 7.7 percent vis-âvis US dollar. In spite of the devaluation, the Nepalese rupee continued to be overvalued and overseas exports continued to decline. Even exports to India declined (Table 5) in 1982/83.

Exports to India were very erratic. Between 1975/76 and 1977/78. Nepal was facing a shortage in Indian currency and she had to exchange Rs. 12.9 million of her subsidized dollar with India to pay for Indian imports. The shortage continued during the subsequent years and between 1978/79 and 1979/80 Nepal had to exchange additional dollars worth NRs. 1496 million for Indian currency.[20] In June 1983 the fixed exchange rate system was replaced

Table 5. Growth of Imports and Exports

(In Percent)

	Imports				*Exports*			
	India		*Overseas*		*India*		*Overseas*	
Year	*(A)*	*(B)*	*(A)*	*(B)*	*(A)*	*(B)*	*(A)*	*(B)*
1975/76	-16.9	-16.9	122.7	97.0	19.7	20.2	104.2	80.6
1976/77	9.5	9.5	-12.1	-12.1	-12.8	-12.8	31.8	32.1
1977/78	14.1	10.2	41.0	45.5	-36.2	-38.5	42.3	46.8
1978/79	3.1	2.4	39.2	40.6	30.5	29.7	18.1	19.2
1979/80	12.9	12.9	30.0	30.0	-19.8	-19.8	-2.6	-2.6
1980/81	22.0	22.0	32.8	29.1	90.4	90.4	-2.2	-4.9
1981/82	4.7	4.7	17.8	9.8	0.2	0.2	-19.3	-24.9
1982/83	9.6	9.6	44.0	31.1	-15.2	-15.2	-41.9	-46.9
1983/84	22.3	22.3	-9.4	-19.9	37.7	37.7	87.9	65.7
1984/85	27.4	25.7	11.3	0.4	38.0	36.1	109.8	89.1
1985/86	1.9	-10.8	39.6	20.0	-22.5	-32.2	61.3	38.6
1986/87	7.3	7.4	23.7	20.4	5.0	5.0	-8.1	-10.5
1987/88	17.2	17.2	39.6	30.8	20.3	20.3	50.8	41.2
1988/89	-15.2	-15.1	29.7	11.1	-34.0	-34.0	24.1	6.3
1989/90	10.3	10.3	13.5	5.1	-41.7	-41.8	44.1	33.4
1990/91	56.6	56.6	16.5	-12.0	157.4	157.5	28.1	-3.3
1991/92	61.4	61.4	32.9	-2.4	1.1	1.1	112.0	55.7

Source: Reejal, 1982 for 1956/57-1969/70
NRB Bulletin Different Year Compiled from Table 29, 31, 32 and 34
A = At current exchange rate
B = At 1980 exchange rate

by a system based on a trade weighted basket with the US dollar as the intervention currency.

However, imports from overseas continued to grow and the trade balance continued to deteriorate. Although annual accrual to convertible foreign exchange reserves continued to be positive, the overall balance of payment started to deteriorate. Nepal faced balance of payments deficits in FY 1983/84 to 1984/85 despite substantial growth in exports and heavy inflow of official capital. Consequently, the Nepalese currency was devalued by 14.7 percent both against US dollar and the Indian rupee in November 1985 (Table 6).

Quantitative restrictions on imports were sought to be eased through an auction system since FY 1985/86. Import licenses for items to be imported under this system were grouped into three categories: (q) industrial raw materials and construction materials, (b) semi luxury items, and (c) luxury items. The list of goods underwent several changes between 1986 and 1992. According to the final change in FY 1990/91, the goods importable under the auction system were classified in two categories: (a) industrial raw materials, medicine, baby food and other essential commodities, and (b) other consumption goods.

Table 6. Exchange Rates: Nepalese Rupees per Currency Unit

	US Dollar		Indian Rupees	
Mid July	*Buying*	*Selling*	*Buying*	*Selling*
1960[1]	7.60	7.68	1.5975	1.6000
1961	7.60	7.68	1.5975	1.6000
1962	7.60	7.68	1.5975	1.6000
1963	7.60	7.68	1.5975	1.6000
1964	7.60	7.68	1.5975	1.6000
1965	7.60	7.68	1.5975	1.6000
1966[2]	7.60	7.68	1.0125	1.0160
1967	7.60	7.68	1.0125	1.0160
1968[3]	10.10	10.20	1.3500	1.3515
1969	10.10	10.20	1.3500	1.3515
1970	10.10	10.20	1.3500	1.3515
1971	10.10	10.20	1.3500	1.3515
1972[4]	10.10	10.20	1.3900	1.3915
1973[5]	10.50	10.60	1.3900	1.3915
1974	10.50	10.60	1.3900	1.3915
1975	10.50	10.60	1.3900	1.3915
1976[6]	12.45	12.55	1.3900	1.3915
1977	12.45	12.55	1.3900	1.3915
1978[7]	11.90	12.10	1.4500	1.4515
1979	11.90	12.10	1.4500	1.4515
1980	11.90	12.10	1.4500	1.4515
1981	11.90	12.10	1.4500	1.4515
1982	13.10	13.30	1.4500	1.4515
1983[8]	14.40	14.60	1.4500	1.4515
1984	16.30	16.50	1.4500	1.4515
1985	17.60	17.80	1.4500	1.4515
1986[9]	21.10	21.30	1.6800	1.6815
1987	21.80	22.00	1.6800	1.6815
1988	23.50	23.70	1.6800	1.6815
1989	27.40	27.60	1.6800	1.6815
1990	29.10	29.30	1.6800	1.6815
1991[10]	42.70	42.90	1.6500	1.6515
1992	42.60	42.80	1.6500	1.6515

Notes:

1. Effective April 13, 1960 the exchange rate of the rupee vis-a-vis the Indian rupee was fixed at Rs. 1.5975 buying and Rs. 1,6000 selling per Indian ruppe.
2. On June 6, 1966 following the devaluation of the Indian rupee the exchange rate of the rupee vis-a-vis the Indian rupee was appreciated by 57.5 percent.
3. On December 8, 1967 the rupee was devalued by 24.8 percent.
4. Following the realignment of currency on December 17, 1991, the exchange rates of the rupee vis-a-vis Pound sterling, Deutche mark, Japanese yen and Indian rupee were revised effective December 22, 1971. The exchange rate of the Pount sterling was floated from July 3, 1972.
5. After the devaluation of the US dollar, the exchange rate of the rupee vis-a-vis the US dollar was changed effective February 9, 1973. The exchange rates of Deutsche mark, Swiss france and Japanese yen were floated since February 20, 1973.
6. Effective October 9, 1975, the exchange rate of the ruppe vis-a-vis the US dollar was revised. The exchange rates of other convertible currencies were quoted daily with reference to the US dollar rate in the international currency market.

7. On March 22, 1978, the rupee was devalued by 4.0 percent vis-a-vis the US dollar.
8. On December 17, 1982, the rupee was devalued by 7.7 percent vis-a-vis the US dollar. On June 1, 1983, the existing exchange rate system was pegged to US dollar.
9. On November 30, 1985, the Nepalese rupee was devalued by 14.7 percent against foreign currencies. Nepalese rupees was pegged to a basket of currencies inclusive of Indian rupee in May 1986.
10. On July 1, 1991 the Nepalese Rupee was revalued against Indian currency by 1.79 percent, and on July 1 and 3, 1991, was devalued against US Dollar with cumulative effect of 20.9 percent. However, the system of exchange rate fixation was not changed.

Source: Nepal Rastra Bank, Quarterly Economic Bulletin.

The break-down in trade and transit arrangements between Nepal and India in March 1989, put Nepal's foreign trade and economy in turmoil. India's unilateral abrogation of treaties, which was mainly due to political causes, pushed Nepal to initiate emergency measures to fulfill her import needs and to encourage exports to overseas. Incentives in the form of reduction of export duties to 0.5 percent of the f.o.b. value of exports and subsidies at various rates were announced. Open General Licensing (OGL) was introduced to facilitate the import of raw materials and essential commodities. Some consumer goods were also incorporated in this arrangement.

With the change of government in Nepal in April 1990, the trade and transit relationship between India and Nepal were normalized as discussed above. Trading patterns reverted to pre-crisis years. Preferential treatment accorded to Nepal's exports of primary goods and specified manufactures to India were restored. Nepal has, on her part, revised all customs duties and surcharges to conform to the treaty requirements of preferential treatment to Indian imports (see Table 9 for selected items).

IV. CURRENT SCENARIO AND THE POLICY OPTIONS

Thus, Nepal's policy options are limited by her landlocked situation and her prior commitments to India. With the new policy of liberalization in India, Nepal can perhaps follow a more open door policy. However, what is in India's best interest may not be in the best interest of Nepal. For example, His Majesty's Government chose to devalue the NRS by almost 21 percent because of the devaluation of Indian currency by 21.3 percent in July 1991.

Nepalese Rupees rate against Indian Rupees was slightly adjusted upwards from NR 1.68 per IRS to NR 1.65. Because India moved to partial convertibility in March 1992, Nepal also moved to partial convertibility. Further, in anticipation of moving to a unified rate Nepal also moved to unified exchange rate system for convertible currencies in February, 1993. IR—NR exchange rate, however, is fixed and the Indian Rupee is still freely convertible within Nepal. To eliminate the discrepancy in cross exchange rates the Nepalese currency was revalued against Indian currency by 3 percent.

Table 7. Balance of Payments (India)

(In million Rs)

Year	*Trade Balance*	*Services Net*	*Transfer Net*	*Current Account Balance*	*Official Capital Net*	*Misc. Capital*	*Change in Reserve Net (Increase -)*
1975/76	-356	110	300	54	2.6	64	-120
1976/77	-580	207	395	22	2.6	-60	35
1977/78	-1,063	198	280	-584	0.1	-109	693
1978/79	-952	319	388	-246	0.0	-50	296
1979/80	-1,339	258	458	-623	0.0	-511	1,134
1980/81	-1,200	604	577	-20	0.0	-49	69
1981/82	-1,300	735	564	-1	-0.9	364	-362
1982/83	-1,671	750	446	-476	109.0	573	-206
1983/84	-1,911	660	656	-594	0.0	241	354
1984/85	-2,315	319	630	-1,366	0.0	148	1,218
1985/86	-2,753	901	666	-1,187	-1.1	1,488	-300
1986/87	-2,970	1,024	911	1,035	-1.2	1,297	-261
1987/88	-3,039	1,237	997	-805	0.0	733	73
1988/89	-3,221	1,548	976	-697	0.0	478	219
1989/90*	-4,090	1,279	1,030	-1,781	0.0	3,125	-1,344
1990/91*	-6,085	1,556	1,277	-3,251	0.0	3,385	-134
1991/92*	-10,275	998	1,782	-7,495	0.0	6,348	1,147

Note: *Provisional
Source: NRB Files

Table 8. Balance of Payments (Overseas)

(In million Rs)

Year	*Trade Balance*	*Services Net*	*Transfer Net*	*Current Account Balance*	*Official Capital Net*	*Misc. Capital*	*Change in Reserve Net (Increase -)*
1975/76	-456	174	289	6	143	88	-238
1976/77	-277	286	223	233	212	-99	-346
1977/78	-388	374	307	293	292	120	-704
1978/79	-656	460	482	285	429	166	-879
1979/80	-1,064	616	730	282	577	302	-1,161
1980/81	-1,630	514	841	-276	622	-84	-263
1981/82	-2,152	643	1,118	-392	775	-245	-139
1982/83	-3,526	885	1,445	-1,195	819	-505	-881
1983/84	-2,913	747	1,417	-749	1,204	-227	-228
1984/85	-2,707	761	1,464	-483	1,270	-436	-352
1985/86	-3,533	674	1,575	-1,284	1,813	-265	-263
1986/87	-4,954	1,303	1,782	-1,870	1,890	96	-116
1987/88	-6,727	827	2,130	-3,770	4,413	1,702	-2,346
1988/89	-8,865	1,441	1,785	-5,638	6,045	-112	-295
1989/90*	-9,097	1,335	1,789	-5,973	5,889	1,390	-1,305
1990/91*	-10,523	1,135	2,384	-7,004	6,300	4,702	-3,998
1991/92*	-8,765	2,895	2,512	-3,358	7,326	1,512	-3,187

Note: *Provisional
Source: NRB Files

Table 9. Exise and Total[1] Customs Duties on Selected Items (Effective Feb. 3, 1992)

(In Percent Advalorem)

Goods	Domestic Production	Import (India)	Import (Overseas)
1. Vegetable Ghee[1]	8.2	23.9	29.2
2. Soyabin Oil[2]	8.2	18.7	23.9
3 Piparment/Chocolates	13.3	38.0	55.3
4. Noodles	7.6	32.0	43.0
5. Biscuits	13.3	41.5	58.7
6. Coke & Pepsi	32.3	55.3	72.5
7. Paints	19.6	42.6	59.9
8. Toilet Soap	11.1	56.0	68.0
9. Polythene Pipe	12.8	40.9	58.1
10. Plastics Utensils	12.2	40.3	57.6
11. Tyre & Tubes	11.1	38.6	55.1
12. Synthetic Clothes	26.5	68.0	86.0
13. Synthetic Readymade Garments	38.0	80.0	98.0
14. Sports & Track Shoes	18.5	59.6	77.6
15. Leahter Shoes	—	56.0	74.0
16. Iron Rods	8.2	29.8	40.8
17. G.I. Sheets & Wire	19.6	36.9	48.3
18. Radio & Transister	23.2	63.3	80.5
19. Television (color)	32.3	89.8	112.8
20. Watch	13.3	59.6	77.6
21. Bulb per Pec.	5.0	38.0	55.2
22. Electric Wire	13.2	41.6	58.7
23. Steel Furniture	17.7	34.2	45.2
24. Foam & Sponz	27.2	63.2	81.2
25. Zeep Fastner	38.0	98.0	122.0
26. Tooth Paste & Powder	5.0	26.5	37.1
27. Umbrella	10.0	26.5	37.5
28. Stainless Steel Utensils	5.0	37.5	54.0
29. Nails	10.0	26.5	37.5

Notes: [1]Includes basic additional duties and surcharges if any.
[2]50% discount in Sales Tax on Domestic Production.

Source: Nepal Rastra Bank, Unpublished documents.

Except for the categories of goods (currently six) which are restricted for imports in India, no license is required for imports. Foreign exchange for imports of the restricted category of goods are allocated by auction. The imports of petroleum products, fertilizers and essential medicines were allowed at official rate of exchange prior to February 1993. Currently all exchange transactions are at open market rates.

Current changes, thus had to be totally tailored to changes in India. Each depreciation or a devaluation involves reduction in purchasing power of the Nepalese population. Nepal had to undertake such a heavy dose of devaluation just to comply with Indian policies.

Partial convertibility was a backward step for Nepal imposed by her geo-political situation. It is only another form of a dual currency exchange system with slight variations from what Nepal had experimented with between 1978 and 1981. Further, the auction system operational for twelve categories of restricted commodities because their entry in India restricted also introduced multiple exchange rates in the system. There was a high difference between buying and selling rates of convertible currencies as the buying rate was the weighted average of the market and official rates in 75:25 proportion, while the selling rate was 100 percent market rate under the partial convertibility system. This introduced incentives to curb market operations in foreign exchange dealings and anti-export bias in the system.[21] Currently list of restricted goods have been reduced to six in accordance with the list of restricted goods in India.

After 40 years of efforts to chart out an independent external economic policy from that followed by India, the Nepalese economy seems to have moved only inches away from India. The efforts to diversify trade from India have apparently been successful, as India's share in Nepal's exports and imports are much lower than what used to be in 1969/70. But a more indepth analysis would reveal that even her overseas exports and imports were dependent on India. Exports seem to have a remote relationship with GDP or exchange rates.[22] Rather, Indian currency reserves are positively correlated with volume of overseas imports.

Currently Nepal is facing persistent balance of trade (BOT) and balance of payments (BOP) deficit with India. Both these deficits have been widening rapidly in the last three years (Table 7). One major cause of this increasing gap between imports and exports from India is the favorable treatment accorded to Indian imports vis-à-vis imports from third countries. Effective exchange rate of Nepalese Rupees vis-à-vis Indian currency has appreciated by 14.5 percent between 1980 and 1991 (Table 10), while NRS exchange rate vis-à-vis US$ depreciated by 118 percent. With last two appreciations of Nepalese rupee vis-à-vis Indian rupee amounting cumulatively to 4.8 percent (from NC 168 = IC 100 to NC 160 = IC 100) the situation has deteriorated further. In addition, the distinct concessions granted to Indian imports with respect to customs duty has further aggravated the problem (see Table 9).

Exports to third countries have also been increasing. However, the growth has been concentrated in carpets and garments. An analysis of the cost structure of both these industries reveal that they have a large foreign material content. Particularly the garment industry is largely based on Indian textile imports and operated in Nepal just to take advantage of the import quota granted to Nepal by the United States and EEC countries. Any increase in textile import quota to India by these countries might cause a collapse of this industry in Nepal. Nepal had free access to EEC and the United States for garment exports until 1986. Because this facility was misutilized by unscrupulous elements to

Table 10. Nominal and Real Exchange Rates Indices (with respect to US $ and Indian Rupees)

	Nominal[a] *Exchanges Rate Levels*		*Index*		*Real Exchange*[3b] *Rate Index*		*Equivalent*[c] *Real Exchange Rate Level*	
	IC	*US $*	*IC*	*US $*	*IC*	*US $*	*IC*	*US $*
1975	1.39	11.00	95.80	92.00	87.50	77.10	1.27	9.25
1980	1.45	12.00	100.00	100.00	100.00	100.00	1.45	12.00
1985	1.47	18.25	101.40	152.10	91.40	130.40	1.33	15.65
1990	1.68	29.35	115.80	244.70	82.80	173.40	1.20	20.81
1991	1.68	38.90	115.80	324.20	85.50	218.30	1.24	26.20

Notes: a. Napalese rupees per unit of foreign currency, average rate of calender year based on monthly rates.

b. Real average rate is computed as follows:-
= Nominal Exchange Rate Index * Foreign Price Index/Domestic Price Index.
The domestic price index used here is the Consumer Price Index for Nepal.
The foreign price index is the Indian Wheelesale Price Index for India, and the CPI for industrialized countries for US $ rate calculations.

c. The amount of Nepalese Rupees in 1980 constant value required to purchase what US $ 1 purchased in 1980 or what one IC Rupee purchased in 1980.

Table 11. Thread and Textile Imports from India (Rs in million)

Years	*Thread*	*Textile*[1]	*Readymade Garments*
1985/86	111.4	633.0	57.0
1986/87	100.0	604.0	54.0
1987/88	101.3	407.0	72.2
1988/89	131.0	505.0	69.0
1989/90	153.1	505.0	69.0
1990/91	220.7	680.7	82.3
1991/92	288.8	1068.6	148.7

Notes: [1]Readymade garments not included.
Source: Nepa; Rastra Bank: Nepal's Foreign Trade Statistics, Various issues.

export Indian garment manufactures as Nepalese product, a quota was introduced for Nepal as well. Moreover, an increase in overseas exports of garments automatically causes an increase in textile imports from India (Table 11).

In addition, in the garment industry the labor content is 70 percent Indian. Thus, Indian capital, labor and materials are used to manufacture garments in Nepal for exports to advanced industrial countries with quota arrangements. Any attempt by Nepal to increase Nepalese labor content in these industries or other employment invites strong protest from India. Income and employment multiplier effect of this industry is largely exported to India.

Table 12. Estimated Cost Structure of Garment Industry

	NRS per piece of shirt
Textile	60.0
Other Materials[1]	16.5
Total Materials	76.5
Tailor Rate	10.0
	86.5
Overhead + Profit (20% of direct cost)	17.0
Total Cost	103.5

Note: [1]Includes button, label, thread, paper box, poly bag, poly sheet and strapping.
Source: Estimates of a manufacturer.

The arrangement for a free flow of labor between India and Nepal embodied in the 1950 Treaty of Peace and Friendship which impinges on the right of Nepalese nationals to preferential treatment in employment, trade and commerce, has a direct relationship to increasing trade and balance of payments deficit with India. While the two way flow of people between India and Nepal has been a historical tradition, the issue of which country has benefitted more or disproportionately from this free flow has been controversial.[23] Even today, there are no statistics to evaluate mutual benefits from this kind of open border.

Free flow of labor is felt to be depressing the Nepalese labor market, at least in the Terai areas and large cities. It is often contended that the efficiency of imported labor in the industrial field is much higher because of better training and work attitudes of the workers (e.g., they are willing to work long hours). If the national goal is to improve the living standard of the Nepalese population, how far this can be achieved by allowing labor market to be depressed by free flow of cheap labor, is a question which needs to be explored in detail.

Composition wise also, Nepal's trade with India has not changed much in the last 2 decades. While Nepal's import of textile and other manufactured items from India is expanding rapidly, Nepal's exports of manufactured goods to India have been erratic and reached just about 16 percent of total exports. In contrast, proportion of manufactured articles in Nepal's exports to overseas has gone up to 88 percent in 1991/92 from 30 percent in 1974/75.

The net inflow of goods and labor and payments on accounts of invisible is felt to be increasing. This is not reflected well in service and transfer categories in the balance of payments statistics. Transfers net in BOP statistics reflect mostly transactions undertaken through banking channels. Border transactions are allocated to different headings on the basis of a 20 year old survey, and therefore are not realistic. Miscellaneous capital inflow may be assumed to reflect such border transactions and unauthorized trade to a large extent.

In spite of the huge inflow of capital under miscellaneous and exchange of dollars worth Rs. 3 billion for Indian currency in last two years (1990/91 - 1991/92). Indian currency reserves declined by more than 24 million dollars (Table 4).

Trade deficit with third countries declined by more than NRS 1.7 billion in FY 1991/92 compared to the preceding year. This was most probably the effect of devaluation of the Nepalese Rupee vis-à-vis convertible currencies, as well as the liberalization of trade and exchange regime in India. Alignment of Nepalese and Indian rules on third country imports, have also helped to reduce the premium on import for deflection to India.

A major policy option for Nepal is to unify the exchange rate system and to float NRs vis-à-vis the Indian Rupees (ISD, 1992b). As discussed above, compared to 1980 the Nepalese currency has effectively appreciated against the Indian currency and depreciated against the US$. However, all arguments on currency rates start with the assumption that at zero period the rate of exchange was at equilibrium. In the case of exchange rates between Indian currency and US dollar on the one hand and Nepalese Rupees and Indian Rupees on the other may not have been equilibrium rates to start with. As long as convertibility of Indian currency remains restricted, the free float of Nepalese currency against Indian currency may tend to encourage deflection of trade in restricted and other items with different Indian and Nepalese customs duty rates and cause depreciation of IRS rather than increase its value against NRS. When Indian currency becomes freely convertible, there may not be a need for Nepal to maintain separate exchange rate system for Indian and other convertible currencies. With liberalization of trade and exchange regime in India, many of the irritants in Nepal-India trade and transit relationships may disappear.

Moreover, given Nepal borders India's most depressed areas of U.P. and Bihar, that the proportion of landless laborers in U.P. and Bihar are much larger than in Nepal, that Nepal's industrial labor class is largely unskilled, that Nepal has very rudimentary physical infrastructure and financial markets, that Nepalese capital is too weak to compete with large Indian conglomerates, it is not clear how Nepal can take benefit of the large Indian market presumably opened by the Trade Treaty. The processes involved in micro-economic optimization with macro-economic liberalization are not clear at all.[24]

Moreover, unless Nepal completely follows the Indian policies in relation to her trade, tariff and exchange rate policies with the third countries, the possibility of trade deflection will remain.

Given free flow of labor between the two countries, the income and employment multiplier effect of industrial investment, infrastructure building and development of service industries is likely to flow largely to India as in the past.

Table 13. Structure of Export and Import

	To India						To Overseas					
Categories	*1970/71*	*1977/78*	*1980/81*	*1982/83*	*1987/88*	*1991/92*	*1970/71*	*1977/78*	*1980/81*	*1982/83*	*1987/88*	*1991/92*
A. *Export*												
Primary Goods*	90.3	97.0	97.4	76.9	83.5	81.0	69.0	70.1	38.3	28.7	7.5	11.6
Manufactured Goods**	9.7	2.9	2.5	23.0	16.3	18.8	30.9	29.9	61.4	71.2	82.4	88.5
Not Classified	0.1	0.0	0.1	0.0	0.1	0.0	0.0	0.0	0.2	0.0	0.0	0.0
Total	100.1	99.9	100.0	99.9	99.9	99.9	99.9	100.0	99.9	99.9	99.9	100.1
B. *Imports*												
Primary Goods*	38.4	31.0	29.6	31.7	34.9	33.2	5.0	24.3	34.5	30.4	27.2	38.4
Manufactured Goods**	61.4	68.9	70.1	68.2	65.0	66.8	94.6	75.5	65.3	69.5	72.7	60.7
Not Classified	0.2	0.1	0.4	0.0	0.0	0.0	0.4	0.0	0.2	0.0	0.1	0.8
Total	100.0	100.0	100.1	99.9	99.9	100.0	100.0	99.8	100.0	99.9	100.0	99.9

Note: Totals may not tally due to rounding.
*Includes SITC categories 0-5
**Includes SITC categories 6-8

Source: NRB Bulletin (Different Years)

For the Nepalese to benefit substantially from this relationship, preferential treatment for Nepalese nationals in matters of employment, investment, trade and commerce is a must. It is estimated that there are 100 thousand garment workers in the Kathmandu capital area alone, of which 70,000 are Indians. Even the small scale industries in the Terai area employ a large number of Indian nationals, while the Terai settlers have started going to Indian market as agricultural laborers.

Nepal, therefore, must invest primarily in agricultural development, develop a physical infrastructure and concentrate on education and skill training for the rural population, so as to receive the maximum benefit from the multiplier effect generated by developmental activities and exports. Island's of joint venture establishments based on Indian or other foreign capital, labor and goods will only push the economy towards a more dualistic structure with no benefit for the mass of the Nepalese population. It might also push the Nepalese economy towards more dependency on India. However, there is a difference between Indian capital investment or aid in Nepal and other foreign flow of capital. Other foreign investment use and train Nepalese labor while Indian capital and aid tends to import labor as well.[25] Any negotiation on Nepal's part with India on joint ventures or cooperation in Nepal within or outside the SAARC, must include conditionalities of preferences to Nepalese nationals. Nepal should also negotiate with India for regulation of the border movement in a planned manner.

ACKNOWLEDGMENT

Paper presented at the first conference under the initiative of APEC/ASEAN/SARC on "Economic Regionalism: Macro-economic Core and Micro-economic Optimization" sponsored by the American Committee on Asian Economic Studies (ACAES) and the Chulalongkrn University, Bangkok, December 16-18, 1992.

NOTES

1. South Asian Preferential Trading Arrangements (SAPTA) has been signed at the Seventh SAARC Summit held in Dacca in April 1993. For detailed discussions of the forms of cooperation see Banskota (1990) and Shrestha (1988). Also see K.P. Nayar (1993), I.N. Mukherji (1993) and SAARC (1993).
2. Hussain, 1970.
3. Chaturvedi, 1990, pp. 30-33.
4. See Chaturvedi, 1990.
5. Lama, 1985, p. 6.
6. Ibid. p. 9.
7. Reejal, 1982, pp. 28-29.
8. See Poudyal, 1988; pp. 107-125, for details on the systems.
9. *Ibid.* pp. 13-14.

10. Pradhan, 1990; pp. 160-175.

11. Under the duty insurance policy Nepalese importers and exporters had to buy an insurance policy for amounts equal to Indian customs duty to be assigned to the collector of customs. Alternatively, a guarantee by an established Indian undertaking, usually the banks, could be submitted to the collector of customs and this also involved the premium cost. For a detailed discussion on transit problems see Pradhan ((bid).

12. Pradhan 1990, pp. 198-199.

13. For a event by event description see Upadhya, 1991.

14. For both sides of the story see Muni, 1992 and Upadhya, 1992.

15. *Ibid*, p. 130.

16. The system of Government prevailing in Nepal between 1960-1990 in which the king ruled as the absolute monarch with advisory cabinet and parliament, was known by this name.

17. See Pant, 1991, Pant and Pant, 1990 for a summary.

18. Reejal, 1982; pp. 28-29.

19. Acharya, 1969; P.S. Rana, 1971.

20. Poudyal, 1993.

21. See ISD, 1992a.

22. ISD, 1992a.

23. HMG, 1983.

24. See Klitgaard, 1991 for a detailed theoretical discussion of these issues.

25. See Lama, 1985.

REFERENCES

Almeen, Ali. (1989). *Landlocked States and International Law.* New Delhi: South Asian Publishers.

Acharya, Meena. (1969). Foreign Trade and Its Impact on Economic Development of Nepal in *Nepal Industrial Digest,* Kathmandu: NIDC.

Banskota, N. (1990). *Regional Economic Cooperation in South Asia* (Nepalese Perspective): Delhi: Daya Publishing House.

Chaturvedi, S.K. (1990). *Indo-Nepal Relations in Linkage Perspective,* Delhi: B.R. Publication Corporation.

Nepal, HMG. (1983). *Internal & International Migration in Nepal. Summary and Recommendations,* National Commission on Population, Kathmandu.

Husain, Asad. (1970). *British India's Relations with the Kingdom of Nepal, 1957-1947,* London: Gorge Allen and Unwin Ltd.

ISD (1992a). "A Study of Implementation of The Full Convertibility of Nepal Currency", Institute for Sustainable Development, Kathmandu, (Mimeograph).

ISD (1992b). "Balance of Payment (BOP) situation with India-A Medium Term Proposal for its Correction, 1992" ISD, Kathmandu, Mimeograph.

Klitgaard, Robert. (1991). Adjusting to Reality: Beyond State versus Market in Economic Development: International Centre for Economic Growth, USA.

Lama, Mahendra P. (1985). The Economics of Indo-Nepalese Cooperation, New Delhi: M.N. Publishers Distributors.

Mukherji, I.N. (1993). "SAPTA, a slow beginning", in *The Economic Times,* New Delhi, April 17.

Nayar, K.P. (1993). "Indian business will benefit most from SAPTA". *The Economic Times,* New Delhi, April 25.

Pant, Bhubanesh. (1991). "Trade Strategy of Nepal During 1980s" in *Nepalese Economic Review* 5(1), Jan.-June.

Pant, Girish and Pant, Bhubanesh. (1990). "Trade Policy of Nepal: Review and Repercussions" in *The Economic Journal of Nepal 13*(3), July-September.

Poudyal, Sriram. (1983). *Planned Development in Nepal, A Study:* Educational Enterprise, Kathmandu.

Poudyal, Sriram. (1988). *Foreign Trade, Aid and Development in Nepal,* New Delhi: Commonwealth Publishers.

Pradhan, Gajendra Mani. (1990). *Transit of Landlocked Countries and Nepal.* New Delhi: Nirala, Publication.

Pashupati J.B. Rana. (1971). Indo-Nepal Trade and its Policy Implications for Nepal. *CEDA Occasional Paper,* Kathmandu.

Reejal, Pushkar, R. (1982). "Nepal's Foreign Trade and Economic Development, 1956/57 to 1979/80", CEDA, Tribhuban University, Kathmandu.

S.D. Muni. (1992). *India and Nepal: A Changing Relationship,* New Delhi: Konark Publishers Pvt. Ltd.

SAARC Secretariet. (1993). Draft Agreement on SAARC preferential Trading Arrangements (SAPTA).

Shrestha, B. P. (1988). "Prospects of Economic Coperation in South Asia", *The Economic Journal of Nepal, 1*(1) Jan.-March.

Upadhyaya, S.K. (1991). *Tryst with Diplomacy,* New Delhi: Vikas Publishers Pvt. Ltd.

REGIONALISM:
THE SAARC EXPERIENCE

K.K. Bhargava

I. INTRODUCTION

The 1950s witnessed the coming into being of nation building structures in South Asia and subsequent creation and perfection of processes of State. As newly independent nations, the countries of the region were keen to uphold and project their distinct identities. The 1960s were marked by regional turmoil, serious mistrusts and apprehension about one another which continued in the 1970s. This resulted in the birth of Bangladesh as well as the unfortunate armed conflicts between India and Pakistan. The 1980s will be remembered for the germination and shaping of the concept of South Asian regional cooperation (SAARC), leading to the institutionalization of it in the form of South Asian Association for Regional Cooperation (SAARC) by the historic Dhaka Summit in 1985.

Research in Asian Economic Studies, Volume 6, pages 427-447.

ISBN: 1-55938-918-4

II. THE EVOLUTION OF SAARC AND ITS RATIONALE

The seven countries comprising SAARC, Bangladesh, Bhutan, India, Maldives, Nepal, Pakistan and Sri Lanka are all situated in the geographical region in South Asia, between the Himalayas in the North and Waters of the Indian Ocean in the South. Their people have close cultural affinities, ethnic bonds and face similar developmental problems. They all belong to the Group of 77 of the developing countries. The G-77 has all along perceived South-South Cooperation, as an end in itself and also for fostering their unity and solidarity for negotiating better with the developed countries. This explains why, even though the South Asian countries had differing foreign policy perceptions and unresolved bilateral problems, all of them realized that the development of cooperation between themselves as neighbors and in the spirit of South-South Cooperation could be beneficial to all of them, particularly in the economic, technical, social, cultural and scientific fields. They reckoned that there were many more issues which united them than those which divided them and shared the view that regional cooperation could help them considerably in tackling the common issues better.

The first concrete step was, however, taken only in 1980 by the late President of Bangladesh Mr. Zia-ur-Rehman who made to his colleagues a specific proposal for the establishment of regional co-operation. This was followed by an active period of diplomacy by Bangladesh for over a year. This led to the first meeting of Foreign Secretaries on Regional Cooperation in Colombo in 1981 which considered the Bangladesh working paper as well as the paper prepared by the host Government of Sri Lanka and the Indian note regarding possible areas of cooperation. It identified for co-operation five important areas for example, Agriculture, Rural Development, Telecommunications, Meteorology, Health and Population Activities and set up study groups for making in-depth studies and concrete recommendations. It needs to be stressed that the beginning was modest, cautious and hesitant. The enthusiasm of Bangladesh was not shared initially by India and Pakistan. There was a school of thought in India which felt that if any regional grouping got established in South Asia, then India may become isolated and the rest of the Members may "gang-up" against it. There was also the apprehension that bilateral and contentious issues may be injected for discussions in such a Forum thereby vitiating the atmosphere.

The next two years witnessed intensive work at the technical level which was periodically taken stock of in the subsequent meetings of foreign secretaries held in Kathmandu, Islamabad and Dhaka in 1981, 1982 and 1983 respectively. Later on, four more areas, Postal Services, Science and Technology, Sports, Arts and Culture, and Transport were also identified. It became apparent that mutually beneficial cooperation was possible in all the nine areas. The need was felt to institutionalize the process of cooperation and raise it to a political level. Accordingly the Foreign Ministers met for the first time in Delhi in August 1983 when an integrated Programme of Action (IPA) was adopted. This was followed by their second meeting in Male in July, 1984 when they agreed to recommend to their Heads of State/Government the convening of the first Summit Meeting of South Asian countries in Dhaka in the last quarter of 1985. In their third meeting held in May, 1985 in Thimphu, the Ministers, inter-alia, agreed that South Asian countries should consult closely and concert on the economic issues in the relevant international, inter-governmental and regional fora.

Transformation from South Asian Regional Cooperation on an ad-hoc basis to its institutionalization through South Asian Association for Regional Cooperation (SAARC) was effected when the first SAARC Summit met in Dhaka in 1985 and adopted the Charter. It was clear from the way the charter laid down the terms of reference of Technical Committees and defined the functions of the Standing Committee of Foreign Secretaries and of the Council of Ministers that a step by step approach was preferred and the evolutionary process was considered as the best methodology.

III. OBJECTIVES OF SAARC

The objectives of SAARC as enshrined in its Charter are to promote the welfare of the peoples of South Asia and to improve their quality of life; to accelerate economic growth, social progress and cultural development in the region and to provide all individuals the opportunity to live in dignity and to realize their full potentials, to promote and strengthen collective self-reliance among the countries of South Asia; to contribute to mutual trust, understanding and appreciation of one another's problems; to improve active collaboration and mutual assistance in the economic, social, cultural, technical and scientific fields; to strengthen cooperation with other developing countries; to strengthen cooperation among themselves in international forums on matters of common interests; and to cooperate with international and regional organizations with similar aims and purposes.

IV. PRINCIPLES OF SAARC

The SAARC Charter spells out the cardinal principles on which cooperation within the SAARC framework is to be based. These include, respect for the principles of sovereign equality, territorial integrity, political independence, non-interference in the internal affairs of other States and mutual benefit. Further, the Charter stipulates that regional cooperation shall not be a substitute for bilateral and multilateral co-operation. Interestingly, the Charter permits setting up by the Standing Committee of Action Committees comprising Member States concerned with the implementation of projects involving more than two but not all Member States.

V. GENERAL PROVISIONS IN THE SAARC CHARTER

The Charter contains general provisions that decisions at all levels shall be taken on the basis of unanimity and that bilateral and contentious issues shall be excluded from the deliberations.

VI. SAARC MACHINERY

The Charter provides for (a) a Secretariat of the Association; (b) the Technical Committees (which normally meets once a year) responsible for determining the potential and the scope of regional co-operation in agreed areas, formulating programs and preparing projects, determining financial implications of sectoral programs, formulating recommendations regarding apportionment of costs, implementing and co-ordinating sectoral programs and monitoring of progress in implementation; (c) the Standing Committee comprising of Foreign Secretaries which approves projects and programs and the modalities of their functioning; mobilizes regional and external resources and identifies new areas of cooperation based on appropriate studies. It may meet as often as necessary; (d) the Council of Ministers consisting of Foreign Ministers of the Member States which formulates policies of SAARC, reviews progress of cooperation, decides on new areas of cooperation and establishes additional mechanisms under the Association as deemed necessary. It meets twice during a year; and (e) the Summit meetings which take place once a year, or more often as, and when considered necessary by the Member States and which act as the supreme authority for approving regional cooperation programs, give new ideas and lay down guidelines.

It needs to be noted that though the SAARC Charter specifically refers acceleration of economic growth and improvement of active collaboration and mutual assistance in the economic field as objectives of SAARC, the core areas of economic cooperation were included in the SAARC program only in July 1991 when the Committee on Economic Co-operation was set up by the Council of Ministers.

The Sixth SAARC Summit held in Colombo in December, 1991 decided to establish an Adhoc Committee on environment to examine the recommendations contained in the SAARC Study on "Causes and Consequences of Natural Disaster and Protection and Preservation of Environment" and also to identify measures for immediate action and to decide modalities for their implementation. This Committee met in Dhaka in February, 1992 and recommended certain measures, the modalities of implementation which were discussed at the subsequent meeting held in Islamabad.

VI. IPA

Since its establishment in 1985, SAARC has worked out programs and devised projects on the basis of decisions taken with scrupulous compliance of Charter provisions. One set of these owe their origin to the IPA referred to earlier and which now covers thirteen subjects, Agriculture; Education; Health and Population Activities; Meteorology; Postal Services; Prevention of Drug Abuse and Drug Trafficking; Rural Development; Science & Technology; Sports, Arts and Culture; Telecommunication; Transport; Tourism; and Women in Development. Activities in the framework of the IPA include holding of seminars, workshops, short-term training courses, exchange of information and data, preparation of State of Art Reports, networking of institutions, meeting of counterpart scientists, and so on. These activities are conceived, identified and selected by the Technical Committees concerned and thereafter approved by the Standing Committee of Foreign Secretaries. There is also the provision to involve the non-Governmental organizations also in activities in these areas. Approximately 500 SAARC activities have taken place so far. As a result, there now exists a wide gamut of socio-economic co-operation in above mentioned areas.[1]

The second set relates to strengthening of people to people level contacts on the basis of the decision taken by the second SAARC Summit in 1986 at Banglore (India) and subsequent initiatives.

The third set concerns establishment of SAARC Regional Institutions where a step by step approach has been followed in each case.

The fourth set is about cooperation in subjects suggested at the Annual Meeting of representatives of planners of Member countries of SAARC.

The fifth set concerns those areas where general directives were first issued at Summits level and followed by careful preparatory work at the technical level and specific recommendations leading to decisions that were later on taken or endorsed on a political level by the Council of Ministers.

The sixth set relates to decisions taken at the Summit level regarding observance of SAARC years on specific themes with a view to focussing attention of the entire region on common problems.

Finally, of late some progress has been made in regard to SAARC establishing Co-operation with other regional and international organizations.

VII. STRENGTHENING OF PEOPLE TO PEOPLE LEVEL CONTACTS

The following five programs were initiated at the Second SAARC Summit (Bangalore, 1986):

i. SAARC Audio-Visual Exchange (SAVE) programme;
ii. SAARC Documentation Centre;
iii. Organized Tourism within SAARC countries;
iv. SAARC Chairs, Fellowships and Scholarships; and
v. SAARC Youth Volunteers Programme.

These were aimed at promoting people-to-people contact and to reflect the importance that SAARC leaders attached to increased interaction among different sections of people in South Asia. SAVE is already operational since November 1987 and this Programme has been singularly successful. Under this programme, on every first day of the month one program about a SAARC Country is shown at the same time on TV network of all SAARC countries. Also, co-production of films on socio economic and technical themes apart from the popular cultural themes have added new dimensions to SAVE. The setting up of a Documentation Centre which will provide reliable and up to-date information on technical, scientific and developmental matters is now at an advanced stage of consideration. The Member States are on the verge of finalizing a travel voucher scheme which will help in the promotion of intra-SAARC tourism without outflow of foreign exchange. The scheme on instituting Chairs and the granting of Fellowships and Scholarships is now operational, and is being monitored by the Technical Committee on Education. The Youth Volunteers Programme now constitutes an integral part of the working of the Technical Committee on Rural Development.

Of late, some important developments at the political level have taken place which are aimed at improving people-to-people contacts. The "Association of SAARC Speakers and Parliamentarians" is now functional. A meeting of the leaders of opposition parties took place in Karachi in September, 1992. A decision has been taken according to which the Members of Parliaments and the Judges of the Supreme Courts will be able to undertake travel within the region without visas. Views have been exchanged about the possibility of setting up a South Asian Parliament. A series of meetings of representatives of professional organizations in different areas were organized in Colombo in 1992. Already a number of regional NGOs have sprung up in fields such as management development, accountancy, ophthalmology, media, and so forth. The SAARC Chamber of Commerce and Industry has been formed and granted official recognition. The Chamber is expected to contribute positively to enhancing co-operation in the crucial areas of trade relations.

VIII. REGIONAL INSTITUTIONS

The SAARC Agricultural Information Centre (SAIC) is already functional in Dhaka. The SAARC Tuberculosis Centre is being set up in Kathmandu. The proposal relating to the SAARC Meteorological Research Centre which has the approval in principle of the Council of Ministers is now being processed. The cost effective modality of networking of national institutions is also being actively pursued in different areas.

IX. CO-OPERATION IN AREAS SUGGESTED BY PLANNERS

A workshop on Plan modelling techniques was held in New Delhi in 1990.

Energy was identified as one of the important areas for possible cooperation by the Planners. A meeting of experts in the field of Energy Model Techniques took place in 1989 which recommended an effective networking arrangement among institutions and agencies working in the field of energy in the SAARC region for ensuring regular exchange of information and expertise.

An expert group on Statistics met in Islamabad in 1990 and finalized the format for a database on socio-economic indicators of the Member States.

Pursuant to the decision of the Third Summit (1987), the Secretary General of SAARC prepared a Study in consultation with the national coordinators on cooperation in the areas of trade, manufactures and services. The study contains a large number of policy recommendations covering practically all possible aspects of economic cooperation in the regime.[2] They deal with production and exchange of goods and services as well as the requisite institutional measures. The most important among them concern liberalization of trade policies to encourage intra-regional trade and to this end "negotiation of tariff structures and preferential trading within a mutually acceptable time frame." Other noteworthy recommendations relate to measures for disseminating trade information; infrastructural development; harmonizing of documentation, customs procedures, standardization, and so forth; clearing and payment arrangements and trade financing, co-operation in the service sector; institutional measures, and special measures that may be undertaken by the larger and more developed economies in the region to promote trade and industrialization of least developed and smaller economies.

The Study, together with its recommendations was endorsed by the SAARC Council of Ministers in July 1991. The Council set up a high-level Committee on Economic Co-operation (CEC) with the mandate to examine the specific recommendations, identify measures for immediate action and oversee their implementation.

A few months later, the Sixth Summit (Colombo, December 1991) directed the CEC to work out an agreement on an institutional framework under which specific measures, for trade liberalization among SAARC Member States could be undertaken. The Committee was also asked by the SAARC leaders to examine the proposal to establish a South Asian Preferential Trade Arrangement (SAPTA) by 1997. By November 1992, the CEC was successful in reaching a draft agreement on SAPTA.

The agreement was signed by the Foreign Ministers of Seven SAARC countries on 11th April, 1993 in the presence of the leaders at the Seventh Summit (Dhaka, April 1993).[3] What more, the leaders have stressed that all necessary steps should be taken to begin the first round of trade negotiations to exchange trade preferences among Member States under the arrangement. 'The Summit' further underlined the critical importance of urgently promoting intra-regional co-operation, particularly in the area of manufactures in order to enhance the productive capacity of the member countries, and to promote sustained growth and development to prevent the marginalization of South Asia's trade interest in the larger global context.[4] At the Summit, Bangladesh Prime Minister Begum Khalida Zia observed "Meaningful co-operation in hard core economic areas lies at the very heart of what we need at the moment."[5] On the same occasion, Indian Prime Minister Narasimha Rao stated forcefully the Indian view when he said "We must make a renewed effort to break down the trade barriers between our countries and jettison the irrational past which created and sustained these barriers. A renewal must also mean building upon old and discovering new complimentarities, opportunities and avenues for economic collaboration among 7 countries. In this, our interdependent world, let us begin by recognizing, reinforcing and capitalizing our own regional interdependence. Let not our modest beginnings as a regional co-operation movement belie the great potential there is for co-operation. If we believe this, the difficulties we face should not deter us from moving purposively towards the exponential benefits for our peoples that genuine regional co-operation would bring."[6] The nuanced position of Pakistan was underlined in the speech of Prime Minister Nawaz Sharif, when after observing that "Trade and Economic Co-operation forms the bedrock for any organization for regional co-operation. SAARC has taken the first and important steps towards achieving this goal through SAPTA. I greatly welcome and endorse the objectives of SAPTA", he went on to say "I firmly believe that our hopes for an even more active role by SAARC in contributing to socio-economic development and cultural renewal can best be fulfilled if we—the Member countries—resolve all outstanding issues through negotiations and other peaceful methods stipulated in the U.N. Charter. A tension free and politically conducive environment is essential for promoting effective and harmonious regional co-operation."[7] A somewhat different view of regional economic co-operation was taken by Sri Lankan Prime Minister Prema Dasa when he said "we should also strive to achieve closer economic collaboration in South Asia. Joint ventures, investment inflows, technology exchanges, common marketing arrangements, buy back arrangements, should also be vigorously promoted. It is also time that we look ahead. In the years to come we should work towards the establishment of an Asian Community. This could include our neighbors as well" and at the same time added "I am of the view that bilateral questions should not inhibit regional co-operation. Our growing regional co-operation should facilitate and further friendly bilateral relations. Such co-operation will help dispel suspicions which may still linger. Such co-operation will build confidence and trust where there was misunderstanding."[8]

In the succeeding section that deals with 'Prospects for SAARC', some conclusions have been drawn on the basis of the above developments.

The Third SAARC Summit (Kathmandu, 1987) had expressed deep concern at the fast and persistent degradation of environment in the region and had noted that frequent natural disasters such as floods, droughts, earthquakes, cyclones and so forth, affected the region. These disasters and the environmental degradation gravely undermined the development process and prospects of South Asian Countries. The leaders mandated the Secretary-General to prepare a regional study on "Causes and Consequences of Natural Disasters and the Protection and Preservation of the Environment." This study was finalized in October, 1991 and it contains several important recommendations.[9] Subsequently, the Council of Ministers decided in December 1991 to establish a Committee on Environment to (a) examine the recommendations of this study; (b) identify measures for immediate action, and (c) decide modalities of their implementations. The Committee on Environment has already formulated some important recommendations.

The Regional Study on the "Greenhouse effect and its impact on the Region" was completed and submitted to the Seventh Summit. The leaders have recognized this development as a significant step forward in promoting regional co-operation in this vital area and have also stressed the importance of continuing the ongoing SAARC activities in the field of environment. They have stressed that international actions in the area of environment should be based on common but differentiated responsibilities, collective endeavours and a balanced perspective and must consider the protection of environment, economic growth and eradication of poverty as mutually reinforcing.

Poverty Alleviation Strategies was the theme of the Fifth Meeting of planners held in Sri Lanka in March 1990. Subsequently, comprehensive exchange of views on the subject took place in a workshop organized by Sri Lanka in 1991. The Sixth Summit (Colombo, December 1991) decided to established an Independent South Asian Commission on Poverty Alleviation to conduct an in-depth study of diverse experiences of the seven countries on poverty alleviation and frame its recommendations. Its report was considered at the Seventh Summit (Dhaka, April 1993) where the SAARC leaders have committed their governments unequivocally to the eradication of poverty in South Asia, preferably by the year 2002 A.D. For this purpose, they have thought of an Agenda of Action that embodies a strategy of social mobilization, a policy of decentralized agricultural development and sharply focussed household level food security, a policy of decentralized small scale labor intensive industrialization, a policy of human development and of support to the aforesaid initiatives with adequate financial resources. A national level pro-poor plan is to be drawn up by each Member State and this is to be harmonized with the open economy and structural adjustment strategies. The leaders have urged all major actors in the world economic scene to create an enabling international atmosphere that is supportive of poverty alleviation program in South Asia and have suggested a new dialogue with donors.

X. DIRECT SUMMIT DECISIONS

The SAARC Regional Convention on Suppression of Terrorism was signed at the Third Summit (Kathmandu, November 1987). The Sixth Summit (Colombo, December 1991) urged Member States to give full effects to their obligations under this Convention and stressed in particular the urgent need for the expeditious enactment of enabling legislation by Member States for the implementation of the Convention. Leaders also stressed the need for a constant dialogue and interaction among the concerned agencies of Member-States, including submission of periodic recommendations to the Council of Ministers. Experts have suggested nomination of specific liaison officers for facilitating the effective exchange of information. The liaison officers would be empowered to rapidly transmit information relevant to the countering of terrorism to their counterparts in the region on "need to know basis." A unit is to be established in Sri Lanka for assisting the work of liaison officers. At the Seventh Summit (Dhaka, April 1993), the leaders have called for expeditious implementation of the above recommendations.

The Fifth SAARC Summit (1990) approved the establishment of a fund for regional projects. Subsequently, modalities for the sources of funds were agreed to and the fund is now operational with initial capital of Five Million US Dollars. The fund is being managed by a Council consisting of representatives of Development Financing Institutions of Member countries of SAARC. Currently it is being coordinated by the Industrial Development Bank of India.

That Summit Meeting also decided that measures for establishing joint ventures in the field of cottage industries and handicrafts should be taken up forthwith. Agreement has been reached on proposals in regard to training and design, and joint promotion and marketing. Immediate attention is expected to be focussed on products such as hand knotted carpets, handloom textile products, leather products including leather garments, wooden handicrafts, bee-keeping and honey production, pottery and ceramic products.

The Fifth SAARC Summits recognized the vital importance of Bio-technology for long term food security of developing countries as well as for medicinal purposes. It decided that cooperation in the framework of SAARC should be extended to this field and, in particular to the exchange of expertise in genetic conservation and maintenance of germplasm bank. An offer of training facilities from India was welcomed and it was agreed that cooperation in the cataloging of genetic resources of different SAARC countries would be mutually beneficial. It was also agreed that the Member States will also participate in the project of G-15 for the establishment of a Gene Bank for developing countries.

At the Sixth Summit (Colombo, December 1991), the leaders had directed the Secretary General to set up a panel of experts for preparing a feasibility study for the establishment of South Asian Development Fund. After considering the report of this panel, the Council of Ministers recommended the establishment of an Inter-Governmental Group (IGG) on South Asian Development Fund (SADF) on an ad-hoc basis. At the Seventh Summit (April 1993), the leaders endorsed this recommendation and directed that the IGG define in clear terms the size, structure, resources and operational modalities of the proposal Fund. They also directed the IGG to examine the complementarities between the SAARC Fund for Regional Projects (SFRP) and SADF, and their relationship, including the possibility of their merger.

At the Seventh Summit, the leaders stressed the need to integrate demographic objectives and population strategies in the formulation of the development strategies of Member Countries. They called for co-operation among Member States through sharing of experiences and urged developed countries as well as all concerned international and regional organizations to strengthen their financial and technical support in the areas of health and education as part of their strategy of assistance to developing countries in their development efforts.

XI. OBSERVANCE OF SAARC YEARS

The successive SAARC Summits have taken decisions in regard to the observance of 1989 as the SAARC year for Prevention of Drug Abuse, 1990 as the SAARC year for the Girl Child, 1991 as the SAARC year of Shelter, 1992 as the SAARC year of Environment and 1993 as SAARC year for Disabled Persons and 1994 as SAARC year of the Youth. The decade of the 1990s is being observed as the SAARC decade for the Girl Child. Proper programs have been worked out for observing these years and the decade for the Girl Child.

XII. COOPERATION WITH OTHER REGIONAL AND INTERNATIONAL ORGANIZATIONS

A significant step in forgoing cooperation with other regional and international organizations was taken by the SAARC Council of Ministers held in July 1972 which authorized its Chairman to explore possibilities of mutually beneficial cooperation with organizations such as ASEAN, European Community and Asian Development Bank. Contacts have been established and specific areas of possible co-operation are now being explored. It has also been agreed to encourage consultations among representatives of member States of SAARC at international fora and to promote articulation by them of collective positions. A Ministerial Meeting on International Economic Issues was held in Islamabad in 1987. A meeting of the Environment Ministers of the SAARC countries was held in Delhi in April 1992. It issued a joint communique outlining common positions on issues before the June 1992 United Nations Conference on Environment and Development (UNCED). This is the first successful experience in intra SAARC consultations and coordination at an international conference. At the Seventh Summit (Dhaka, April 1993), the leaders supported the convening of a World Summit for Social Development. They stressed the need to develop a common South Asian perspective on the issues to be discussed at this Conference as well as in the forthcoming Second World Conference on Human Rights in 1993, the World Population Conference in 1994 and the 1995 World Conference on Women.

XIII. PROBLEMS AND CONSTRAINTS

SAARC has made some commendable progress during the last seven years. The fact, however, remains that the authentic dawn of meaningful regional cooperation has yet to begin. Significant results have not flowed so far from SAARC activities. Concrete and result-oriented programs and projects are lacking. In the words of the Indian Prime Minister "the content and range of co-operation within the SAARC region has been slower than what we wished for."[10]

One of the reasons why SAARC has not made greater strides is the fact that bilateral differences continue to cast very long shadows on prospects of regional cooperation. Even though the Charter specifically states that bilateral and contentious issues are to be excluded from the deliberations, the fact remains that a symbiotic relationship exists between tension-free ties among the Member States and healthy regional cooperation. Other constraints in the development of regional cooperation in South Asia are slowness in the process of decision-making, absence of a regional fund which can finance regional cooperation programs, and lack of progress so far in mobilizing assistance from international organizations and donor agencies for implementing regional projects.

An important geographical factor limits the potential of regional cooperation in South Asia. Though all SAARC members share the same space between the Himalayas in the North and the Indian Ocean waters in the South, India is centrally located. It occupies a very large area and has borders with all other Member States of SAARC. On the other hand, none of the other Members of SAARC are geographically contiguous. The overall lack of geographical propinquity among Member States other than India leads to a system subsuming a collection of bilateral relationships between India and its neighbors and not so much between India's neighbors themselves. There is also the factor that South Asia represents the most complex web of inter-ethnic interactions in the world involving multiplicity of religions and languages and that in the region one State, that is, India has practically all groups represented inside it while other Member States are relatively homogeneous and have within their confines much fewer in number of different kinds of ethnic groups.

The South Asian region faces overlapping dilemmas such as economic backwardness, national and territorial conflicts, demands on the part of a segment or segments of population for different degrees of autonomy which at times amount to secession, difficulties that Governments have to overcome for having politically stable regimes or for strengthening stable democracy which all Member States wish to seek.

Another negative factor in regional cooperation attaining its optimal potential is poor communication policy in the region. Media has shown a low level of interest in SAARC and instead of projecting the good side of its members, the media highlights the problems and the conflicts. Education policies followed by Member States are not geared to generation of consciousness and proper knowledge about the potential and prospects of regional cooperation in South Asia.

XIV. THE SAARC EXPERIENCE

The SAARC experience so far leads us to some important conclusions. Healthy regional cooperation among developing countries is dictated by geography, and by needs of functional cooperation. In many cases, it is in line with what history has bequeathed. Regional cooperation can help in diffusing bilateral tensions, in bringing out the potential in each one of the SAARC Member States to do good to others, and in highlighting the value of collective self-reliance. In fact, substantial progress in regional cooperation could even be an integral part of the process of problem-solving in South Asia and can contribute to confidence building. When countries are having common developmental objectives, regional cooperation can facilitate better and faster achievement of those objectives. Regional cooperation needs to be insulated from the stresses and strains of bilateral problems. It can not be a panacea for all ills. On the other hand, it should not wait for an ideal conducive atmosphere to emerge or be held hostage to existing bilateral problems. Even though the requirement of decision making on the basis of the principle of unanimity has resulted in slow progress, it is important that this principle should not be modified as all Member States should develop a stake in the future of SAARC and a durable and viable cooperation program should emerge.

XV. PROSPECTS FOR SAARC

SAARC is a process. Therefore, it is more relevant to evaluate its progress in terms of ground realities and in a longer term context. Is SAARC a reaction to the international environment? To some extent, "Yes." But essentially, it should rather be seen as based on felt regional needs. Given the political realities of the day, SAARC cannot be a conflict-resolving mechanism through misplaced cooperation, but a cooperation-promoting device in feasible areas. In view of the central and crucial role of India, it is important that the Indian society should be seen by other South Asian societies as an asset and not a source of fear and threat. On the one hand, the climate for regional cooperation is not too hospitable because of intra-regional differences and disputes, and conflicting responses to political changes of the times, divergences in pursuit of foreign policies and incongruous economic interests. On the other hand, there are challenges and opportunities for SAARC in a world characterized by sweeping political changes and universal realization of the importance of ecological and environmental matters, and so on. The need to address systematically and methodologically challenges and opportunities is now. It is wrong to confuse the sober option of negotiations with catapulting. In earlier times, compromise used to be equated with treason. In modern times the edifices of meaningful regional and international co-operation are built on carefully worked out compromises through painstaking negotiations. It is in the individual and collective interest of SAARC countries to initiate at least a dialogue on negotiations on all core political and economic issues. It is of paramount importance that decision makers in SAARC Member States realize that the inexorable socio-economic trends in today's world will create a more integrated society that will increasingly withstand better the pulls and strains of ethnic and religious unrest. These trends will promote regional cooperation and will, in turn, get accentuated by it.

On the economic front, it may be safely concluded that there is now the trend to view the SAARC in the context of the shared realization by its Member States that the core issue which they have to face is the paradigm of "Economic Regionalization." In concrete terms not much has been done so far. But an important beginning has been made at Dhaka at the Seventh Summit. The pace of progress will depend upon a variety of economic and political factors such as (a) the ability of concerned officials, to decide on a rapidly convergent series of steps, that will be necessary to secure implementation of agreed policy recommendations in the short term, medium term and long term for achieving common goals, (b) the rapidity with which negotiations are completed under SAPTA, (c) the efficiency and effectiveness with which the SAARC Chamber of Commerce and Industry set up recently can function and (d) the availability of supportive external economic environment.

XVI. SAARC: THE WAY AHEAD

Now, as economic cooperation in the framework of SAARC has made some progress, it will be timely to devise instrumentalities that would impart dynamism to and promote cooperation among economies of Member States of SAARC. The theme of the first Conference of APEC; ASEAN/SAARC sponsored by the American Committee on Asian Economic Studies and Chulalongkorn University, Bangkok, Thailand that is, "Economic Regionalism: Macro Economic Core and Micro Economic Optimization" suggests some possible instrumentalities. In brief, they will encompass policy ideas and analyses in regard to the creation of a supportive economic environment in these countries, measures in regard to regional cooperation in the framework of SAARC, and external support that may be extended to this region particularly by the resurgent economies in the Asia Pacific region. Some very deep seated thinking needs to be done in order to clarify ideas in regard to the essential ingredients which can stimulate economic regionalization and dynamize economies in South Asia in a world of increasing complimentarities and growing inter-dependence. SAARC Member countries should use the instrumentality of regional cooperation for providing themselves with macro economic space for micro economic optimization. The SAARC countries are today ready for greater and more intensive action within the SAARC framework as well as with other economies in the rest of the Asia Pacific region. An important facet of their dynamism is the current simultaneous pursuit of three approaches that is, intra-SAARC regional or sub-regional cooperation, cooperation with other countries, and regional groupings; and forging of links as deemed necessary with a view to facilitate discussions on issues of common interest.

In this context, it would be opportune to reflect on a possible Agenda for SAARC for the future. What is the way ahead for it? There is a need for creation of appropriate politico-economic environment. The full potential of bilateral and regional cooperation needs to be harnessed.

In the SAARC region, bilateral and regional co-operation have been hindered because of political problems between India and Pakistan. India and Bangladesh, India and Sri Lanka, Pakistan and Bangladesh and so on. Even though, in many cases the instrumentalities of joint commissions for furthering bilateral co-operation exist, progress has been tardy and inadequate. Because of the Indo-centric nature of the SAARC region, bilateral co-operation between Indian and its neighbors will always retain its crucial importance and primacy. The dictum that one can choose his friends but not neighbors applies equally as well to nations. The geographical compulsions, and the requirements of functional co-operation in different fields of human endeavour dictate the necessity for bilateral co-operation in South Asia based on mutual advantages. At best, regional co-operation can only supplement bilateral co-operation which should be developed fully by countries concerned so that it results in optimal benefits.

Of late, a great deal of time and attention has been devoted to examination of many common interests and possibilities of meaningful cooperation in the SAARC region, thereby making SAARC a vibrant institution. The growing interest among the peoples of the region in demanding regional solutions for many problems that are besetting it should be channeled towards productive purposes so that regional cooperation plays an increasingly important role in dynamizing South Asian economies. The masses should be made aware of the symbiotic relationship between tension free bilateral ties and healthy regional cooperation so that their support will be forthcoming for efforts for economic cooperation to continue despite the existence of bilateral problems. At the same time the South Asian nations must engage themselves in serious dialogues both governmental as well as non-governmental with a view to substantially improve the chances of their economic growth by bringing about improvements in the political climate of the region.

The improvement of transport and communication infrastructure in the SAARC region is a crucial requirement for facilitating intra-regional and inter-regional economic cooperation. Specific programs should be formulated in these fields and implemented expeditiously.

Private sectors in South Asia must be energized so that it leads to a more efficient and rapid growth of the economies. In line with the present trend of privatization and marketization, South Asian countries should reorient the process of regional cooperation. So far it has progressed mainly in the inter-governmental framework. Henceforth, regional cooperation should be increasingly market driven and led by the private sector. The Chambers of Commerce and Industries in SAARC countries must be encouraged to take keen interest in promoting bilateral and regional trade and investment. There is a need for establishing a regional center for business information that will help in the promotion of cooperation between private sectors of SAARC countries.

Bilateral cooperation suitably supplemented by sub-regional, and regional cooperation when found necessary, needs to be established in the field of water resources as early as possible.

South Asian countries need to effect considerable reduction in their defence budgets. They must seriously tackle all problems that cause friction bilaterally and regionally. All such problems should be viewed and examined in the context of the totality of their foreign policy objectives and not in terms of narrow domestic political considerations. Such a course of action would result in a reduction of tensions in the region and induce increased flows of foreign investment which would promote rapid growth in their trade including intra-regional trade.

The recommendations of the Independent Commission on Poverty Alleviation in South Asia were considered carefully at the Seventh SAARC Summit (Dhaka, April 1993). A medium-term poverty alleviation program should be drawn up and arrangements made for monitoring its implementation.

In the ultimate analysis, beneficial regionalism and benign bilateralism in South Asia should reinforce each other. Whenever necessary, sub-regional cooperation programs should also be worked out. Governments of Member States of SAARC have to improve the perspectives of regional economic cooperation and, at the same time take measures for confidence building, and problem solving that will ensure political stability in the region. Only parallel and simultaneous action on these broad fronts will succeed in creating a friendly climate and propitious environment for economic growth. Whenever SAARC leaders meet, they must accord top priority to these macro issues in their deliberations.

SAARC countries need to expand their relationship with Japan, ASEAN and newly industrializing economies of the Asia-Pacific region. Appropriate roles for ESCAP and ADB in the changed context should also be devised. South Asian Countries must negotiate supportive measures by the international community. They need to energize and encourage their private sectors, non-governmental organizations and professional organizations so that they establish cooperation among themselves and between them and their counter-parts in the rest of Asia-Pacific region. With full realization of the complimentary of trade, investment opportunities and transfer of technology, such co-operation between private sectors can contribute to more rapid and efficient growth by making trade liberalization and investment decisions more meaningful. Thus, they may succeed in providing themselves a macro economic core for micro-economic optimization in the form of most productive utilization of their national and human resources by attracting large foreign investment. They may also be able to increase their capabilities to cope with the challenges of change resulting from new macro-level management of economies and to exploit the opportunities for development that are arising in the increasingly interdependent multipolar world.

XVII. CONCLUSIONS

Regional cooperation will help Member States in achieving their policy objectives better in the current setting which is characterized by rapid pluralization of their societies and multi-polarity in an inter-dependent world. The recent changes in the North, and particularly the end of East-West cold war, seriously challenge some aspects of the political and economic basis of the Group of 77 of the developing countries. The Group of 77, in spite of shared interests of its Members, will now find it increasingly difficult to translate these into coordinated strategies in its dealings with the North. On the other hand, the developed countries and international organizations may find it more practicable to deal with developing countries through their regional groupings. The member countries of SAARC must, therefore, take due note of all these factors and accordingly chalk-out their strategies to address the present challenges and emerging problems. In fact, in his recent speech at Dhaka, Indian Prime Minister observed perceptively "we are witness to an international situation subject to contradictory trends of centripetal and centrifugal forces at work. While established political entities and plural societies have disintegrated, there are emerging patterns of socio-economic integration between Nation States underpinned by a unilinear structuring of the global economy.

Our Association must therefore evolve meaningful policy approaches to deal with the world-wide trends in regional co-operation, economic groupings and trading blocs as witnessed in Western Europe, North and South America, ASEAN, and the Asia-pacific region. For economies like ours, particularly at a time when we have liberalized and adopted outward-oriented policies, these trends have important implications. They may well present new trading and economic opportunities for us. Our collective economic strength and weight as a mega-market of over 1 billion consumers and the pooling together of our abundant and manifold talents, skills and resources will alone enable us to be a serious player in the global economy."[11]

Developments in the framework of SAARC are encouraging, though the pace of progress is painfully slow. Even on bilateral planes, it is noticed that though there are occasional spurts of crises nursing and crises escalating, the unmistakable trend is towards crises control and search for crisis resolution. For SAARC to be able to make rapid progress, a strategic vision with several components is required.

All member states must develop the political will to forge ahead by taking into account the realities of the region and not allowing deceleration in any regional cooperation activities.

Media in the member states should make disciplined and conscious efforts to ensure balanced reporting of developments in the region in their totality and to highlight positive aspects.

Non-governmental organizations need to involve themselves more and more in SAARC activities and their efforts in this regard merit encouragement by member states. This will enable SAARC to be turned into a "people's movement."

The peoples of South Asia need to draw lessons from the new thinking sweeping the globe and develop the capacity to imbibe the right messages and signals, which are being sent. A well thought out regional communication and education policy should be developed.

Member states should make determined efforts for improving their bilateral relations.

Such co-operation, given the geographical and economic realities of the region, will mainly be of a bilateral nature between India and the neighbors though sub-regional and regional co-operation can usefully complement and supplement it. The potential for the latter has not been fully explored. India would like that whatever threat perceptions exist in the minds of its neighbors should be replaced by friendly perceptions. In this context, there is considerable interest in South Asia in the evolution of regional groupings involving big countries. Limitations to sovereignty should apply to all constituent states-big and small. A stable structure needs to be built brick by brick by mutual consent. As regards the persistence of bilateral problems, which no doubt prove detrimental to a faster pace of regional cooperation, there is growing realization that progress in economic cooperation will inevitably contribute to improvement in political relations which in turn will assist in the containment of these problems and their eventual resolution. Regional Co-operation in the framework of SAARC is not to be confused with the sum total of India's bilateral co-operation with its neighbors. But there is an obvious synergy between the two. Thus, it is vitally important for SAARC nations to ensure that the present trend continues and adequate momentum of regional co-operation gets generated.

In the meantime, serious efforts must continue for analyzing correctly the causes and consequences of the totality of internal conflicts and bilateral problems that exist within, and between South Asian countries and for cultivating the habit of looking jointly into the problems which arise from common concerns and whose solutions need to be contrived patiently through dialogue, cooperation and compromise.

Regionalism and regional cooperation presupposes that those practicing it must possess certain common characteristics in terms of economy, cultural background, political structure, geography and so forth. The viability of regionalism is certainly a function of such common characteristics. In South Asia, while there are similarities, many disparities also exist. The Member countries of SAARC are unequal in size, population, military strength and economic progress. The economies are also not complementary and in many cases they are competitive. Foreign policy orientation and strategic perceptions are diverse.

At the same time, the experience of SAARC for the last seven years amply demonstrates that bilateralism and regionalism in this part of the world can be mutually reinforcing. The potential for mutually profitable socio-cultural interaction and economic cooperation is considerable. The ground realities in the SAARC region are such that at present the economic forces do not have such a dominant position in the society that they can make the narrow national attitudes of the political elites in these countries subservient to its dictates. With deliberate efforts economic forces can and should be strengthened significantly. Another important emerging factor is that in the future there would be a close relationship between regional cooperation in the framework of SAARC and inter-regional cooperation between SAARC and its neighbors and their groupings. Can one hope that the fruits of economic cooperation will override the politico-strategic discord that is currently prevailing in South Asia?

The answer to this question will depend on whether the statesmen and politicians in the region can rise to the occasion and guide their peoples. There has to be widespread acceptance of the hard fact that the search of solutions for problem areas is best undertaken in terms of well thought-out foreign policy objectives that is not hindered by considerations of domestic politics which are unfortunately still dominated by the unhappy memories of the past. It is important for the SAARC countries to remember that while history is important, what counts is future.

In terms of economic regionalism, SAARC has a long way to go. At present, intra SAARC trade is even less than the trade of the SAARC countries with ASEAN countries. In terms of existing economic realities, economic regionalism in SAARC will have to be rooted in the relentless search by its members for macro economic space where they can operate with a view to achieve micro economic optimization. For this, while intra-SAARC co-operation is important, inter-regional co-operation between SAARC and ASEAN and indeed in the inter-APEC setting is crucial. In turn, the external inputs for the development of the SAARC region will depend upon the political stability of the region and absorptive capacity and financial economic and technological attractiveness of the countries. The present picture does not warrant pessimism. The Member countries of SAARC seem to be following steadfastly the road of economic reforms and liberalization. An impetus has been given to trade liberalization with the signing of SAPTA. Implementation of several suggestions made above and in the preceding section is certainly not beyond the capabilities of the South Asian countries. It can, together with trade liberalization, stimulate economic growth and progress and accelerate economic regionalism. The conclusions of the first special Conference on

"APEC: ASEAN SAARC Economic Regionalism: Macroeconomic core and Microeconomic optimisation" ought to be studied closely by policy makers in SAARC with a view to draw right kinds of lessons and formulate proper approaches to Economic Regionalism.

NOTES

1. For a detailed account of progress achieved in the thirteen areas which comprise the Integrated Programme of Action, reference may be made to the SAARC Secretariat (Kathmandu) Publication. June 1991 entitled to "The SAARC Record."

2. The Study has been published by the SAARC Secretariat in 1991 under the title "SAARC Study on TRADE, MANUFACTURES AND SERVICES".

3. The agreement on SAARC Preferential Trading Arrangement (SAPTA) includes: interalia, arrangements relating to tariffs: para-tariffs, non-tariff measures: and direct trade measures. It permits the Member States to conduct their negotiations for trade liberalization in accordance with any or a combination of the following approaches and procedures:

a. Product by product basis;
b. Across-the-board tariff reductions;
c. Sectoral basis;
d. Direct trade measures. Initially the negotiations will be conducted on a product-by-product basis.

SAPTA shall be based and applied on the principles of overall reciprocity and mutuality of advantages in such a way as to benefit equitably all Member States taking into account their respective levels of economic and industrial development, the pattern of their external trade, trade and tariff policies and systems. In SAPTA, the special needs of the least developed countries are clearly recognized and concrete preferential measures in their favor are to be agreed upon. Member States have agreed under SAPTA to undertake appropriate steps and measures for developing and improving communication system transport infrastructure, and transit-facilities for accelerating the growth of trade within the region.

4. Declaration of the Seventh SAARC Summit (Dhaka, 10-11 April 1993).

5. Speech delivered at the inaugural session of the Seventh Summit.

6. *Ibid.*

7. *Ibid.*

8. *Ibid.*

9. The study has been published by the SAARC Secretariat in 1992 under the title "Regional Study on the Causes and Consequences of Natural Disasters and the Protection and Preservation of the Environment."

10. *Ibid. 5.*

11. *Ibid.*

Printed and bound by CPI Group (UK) Ltd, Croydon, CR0 4YY

15/09/2026

14962364-0006

Printed and bound by CPI Group (UK) Ltd, Croydon, CR0 4YY
15/09/2026
14962364-0006